HOLOCAUST HIGH PRIEST

ELIE WIESEL, *NIGHT*, THE MEMORY CULT, AND THE RISE OF REVISIONISM

To the memory
of Pope Pius XII

Holocaust High Priest

Elie Wiesel, *Night*, the Memory Cult, and the Rise of Revisionism

By Warren B. Routledge

Castle Hill Publishers
P.O. Box 243, Uckfield, TN22 9AW, UK
March 2017

HOLOCAUST HANDBOOKS, Volume 30:
Warren B. Routledge:
Holocaust High Priest:
Elie Wiesel, "Night," the Memory Cult, and the Rise of Revisionism
Uckfield, East Sussex: CASTLE HILL PUBLISHERS
PO Box 243, Uckfield, TN22 9AW, UK
2nd, slightly corrected edition, March 2017

ISBN10: 1-59148-180-5 (print edition)
ISBN13: 978-1-59148-180-5 (print edition)
ISSN 1529-7748

Published by CASTLE HILL PUBLISHERS
Manufactured worldwide

Distribution:
Castle Hill Publishers, PO Box 243
Uckfield, TN22 9AW, UK
shop.codoh.com

Set in Times New Roman

www.HolocaustHandbooks.com

Cover Illustrations: front center: Elie Wiesel addressing the UN General Assembly; surrounded by the official portraits of the six U.S. Presidents who have been or are serving under Wiesel; bottom: various images of Elie Wiesel; most notably, from right to left: with U.S. President Bill Clinton; with U.S. President Barack Obama talking at the U.S. Congress; with U.S. President Ronald Reagan and his wife in the White House; with U.S. President Obama and German Chancellor Angela Merkel at the Buchenwald Memorial.

Table of Contents

Page

Foreword

"What are you writing?" the Rebbe asked. "Stories," I said. He wanted to know what kind of stories: true stories. "About people you knew?" Yes, about people I might have known. "About things that happened?" Yes, about things that happened or could have happened. "But they did not?" No, not all of them did. In fact, some were invented from almost the beginning to almost the end. The Rebbe leaned forward as if to measure me up and said with more sorrow than anger: "That means that you are writing lies!" I did not answer immediately. The scolded child within me had nothing to say in his defense. Yet, I had to justify myself. "Things are not that simple, Rebbe. Some events do take place but are not true; other are—although they never occurred."

—Elie Wiesel in *Legends of Our Time*, Schocken Books, New York, 1982, p. viii (Introduction), about an exchange he had in Tel Aviv with the Hasidic teacher of his childhood, twenty years after he had last seen him in Hungary during the war.

In October 1944, the victorious Red Army crossed the German border for the first time by penetrating briefly into East Prussia. When the German army managed to throw back the Soviet forces for a short while, they discovered with horror that many German civilians as well as French and Belgian PoWs had been raped, tortured and slaughtered in the most bestial ways imaginable.

When the Red Army advanced again during the following winter, more massacres were reported. Hence the German High Command ordered the evacuation of the entire German civilian population from East Prussia via the Baltic Sea, code-named "Operation Hannibal" – the biggest naval rescue effort ever undertaken.

In early 1945, the Red Army was approaching another German border area in the southeast: Silesia. Auschwitz was right in its path. Although this time the German civilian population was not to be evacuated, the inmates of the regional labor camps were slated to be deported west.

In history's best-selling Holocaust book *Night*, Elie Wiesel, who at that time was incarcerated at the Monowitz labor camp near Auschwitz, wrote about this:[1]

> *A doctor came into the room and announced:*
> *"Tomorrow, immediately after nightfall, the camp will set out. Block after Block. Patients will stay in the infirmary. They will not be evacuated."* [...]

At that time Wiesel was in the camp's infirmary, where he was recovering from minor foot surgery. He had the option to stay and be liberated by the Soviets, or to leave with the Germans. Here is what he decided to do (p. 78):

> *"What shall we do, father?"*
> *He was lost in thought. The choice was in our hands. For once we could decide our fate for ourselves. We could both stay in the hospital, where I could, thanks to my doctor, get him entered as a patient or a nurse. Or else we could follow the others.*
> *"Well, what shall we do, father?"*
> *He was silent.*
> *"Let's be evacuated with the others," I said to him.*
> *He did not answer. He looked at my foot.*
> *"Do you think you can walk?"*
> *"Yes, I think so."*
> *"Let's hope that we shan't regret it, Eliezer."*

We need to realize what this means: According to his book, Elie Wiesel and his father had been living for three-quarters of a year in a camp system where Jews had been burned alive *en mass* by their German tormentors. The living inmates had been abused and mistreated by every method one can think of. Then in early 1945 there was a chance to escape the clutches of these mass murderers and to be liberated by the advancing Soviets.

How would you have decided?

Elie decided to flee *from* their liberators *with* their diabolic tormentors. They decided to remain slave workers in the hell allegedly created by the evil Germans.

Arguing in my book *Lectures on the Holocaust* along these lines, I came to the conclusion that these lines prove that Wiesel never really felt threatened by the Germans, that the atrocity stories he tells in his book must therefore be untrue.[2]

---

1 New York: Bantam, 1982, p. 77.
2 G. Rudolf, *Lectures on the Holcoaust* (2nd ed., Washington D.C.: The Barnes Review, 2010), 403.

But it's not that easy. When retired German judge Günter Bertram, who opposes the prosecution of peaceful historical dissidents in Germany,[3] read my book, he criticized me for having omitted a crucial passage from Wiesel's text which he claimed refutes me hypothesis. I checked it and found that Bertram was correct, superficially speaking, because Wiesel, after having been told by a doctor that they will be evacuated, writes (pp. 77f.):

> *This news made us think. Were the SS going to leave hundreds of prisoners to strut about in the hospital blocks, waiting for their liberators? Were they going to let the Jews hear the twelfth stroke sound? Obviously not.*
> *"All invalids will be summarily killed," said the faceless one. "And sent to the crematory in a final batch."*
> *"The camp is certain to be mined," said another. "The moment the evacuation's over, it'll blow up."*

So maybe he was afraid that he'd be executed when staying behind. Wiesel confirms himself, though, that these were only false rumors (p. 78):

> *I learned after the war the fate of those who had stayed behind in the hospital. They were quite simply liberated by the Russians two days after the evacuation.*

Even if he thought the Germans might kill anyone staying behind, it still would have made more sense to stay behind, because at that point in time it was clear to everyone that Germany was about to lose the war. Wiesel even says so in his book, which is full of references to the inmates' understandable longing for Germany's impending defeat and thus the end of their ordeal. Therefore Wiesel's captors would have to leave him behind eventually anyway. It was merely a matter of when this would happen. Hence, if Wiesel really thought that the SS would kill inmates rather than leave them behind, it would have made sense to try and get away from the Germans as early as possible, because the more desperate the Germans' situation was getting, the more likely excesses of violence would become.

There are other facts indicating that Wiesel could not have taken those rumors seriously, if they even circulated in the first place. First of all, the Monowitz camp, where Wiesel was housed, had no crematory. Next, the nearest crematories at the Birkenau camp had been taken out of service in late 1944 and dismantled in December 1944. Furthermore, Wiesel himself had experienced that thousands of inmates had been successfully cured of various ailments in the camp hospital where he was recovering at that time. Hence, Wiesel knew that sick inmates were *not* killed by the SS at Auschwitz, but that the German authorities went to great lengths to restore their slave laborers' health. Finally, it was most certainly clear that the few

---

3 See Günter Bertram, "Panischer Schnellschuss: Die Volksverhetzungs-Novelle 2005," in: *Mitteilungen des Hamburger Richtervereins*, no. 2, 2005, 24-28; www.richterverein.de/mhr/mhr052/m05213.htm.

members of the SS camp staff who would stay behind – the vast majority of them was about to leave the camp with the inmates – could not have carried out a major operation like killing and disposing of hundreds of sick inmates within a day or two before the Soviets' arrival.

Cross-checking with another famous inmate at the Monowitz camp, the Italian Jew Primo Levi, can clarify the matter. In his entry of January 17, 1945, Levi writes in his book *Survival in Auschwitz* how he would have followed common instincts and would have joined the other inmates that fled with the SS, if only he had not been so sick and had to stay behind in the same hospital where Wiesel claims to have been at the same time:[4]

> *It was not a question of reasoning: I would probably also have followed the instinct of the flock* [and fled with the Germans] *if I had not felt so weak: fear* [of the invading Red Army] *is supremely contagious, and its immediate reaction is to make one try to run away.*

The atrocities committed by the conquering Red Army induced fear and panic everywhere in Central and Eastern Europe, including the camps the Red Army was supposedly liberating. It turned out that such fears were indeed justified to some degree, for many a female inmate was raped by these "liberators,"[5] and many detainees conquered by the Soviets ended up in Soviet labor camps rather than being liberated.[6] Wiesel was therefore right to run with the Germans, whatever his subjective reasons were at the time. The Red Army, after all, did not come as a liberator, but as an army of conquest, occupation and oppression.[7]

I therefore maintain that the choice Wiesel made is truly revealing. Fritz Berg once wrote fittingly about it:[8]

> *The choices that were made here in January 1945 are enormously important. In the entire history of Jewish suffering at the hands of gentiles, what moment in time could possibly be more dramatic than this precious moment when Jews could choose between, on the one hand, liberation by the Soviets with the*

---

4 Primo Levi, *Survival in Auschwitz* (New York: Summit Books, 1986), 154.

5 Laurence Rees, "Raped by their saviours: How the survivors of Auschwitz escaped one nightmare only to face another unimaginable ordeal," *Daily Mail*, Febr. 2, 2010; www.dailymail.co.uk/news/article-1247157; similar: Tom Hundley, "Struggle to mark horror of Auschwitz," *Chicago Tribune*, January 27, 2005; http://articles.chicagotribune.com/2005-01-27/news/0501270319:

> *Although the Soviets were welcomed as liberators, it was only a matter of weeks before they began plundering and raping those they liberated. Women who survived the Nazis were raped to death by Soviet soldiers, according to survivor testimonies.*

6 Jennifer Mascia, "Surviving the Camps but Struggling in Brooklyn," *New York Times*, January 21, 2010; www.nytimes.com/2010/01/21/nyregion/21neediest.html.

7 On the Red Army's atrocious style of warfare see Joachim Hoffmann, *Stalin's War of Extermination, 1941-1945: Planning, Realization and Documentation* (Capshaw: Alab.: Theses & Dissertations Press, 2001).

8 Friedrich Paul Berg, "Poison Gas 'Über Alles'," *The Revisionist*, vol. 1, no. 1, 2003, 37-47; here 39; www.codoh.com/library/document/1417.

> *chances to tell the whole world about the evil 'Nazis' and to help bring about their defeat – and the other choice of going with the 'Nazi' mass murderers and to continue working for them and to help preserve their evil regime. In the vast majority of cases, they chose to go with the 'Nazis.'*
> *The momentous choice brings Shakespeare's Hamlet to mind:*
> *"To remain, or not to remain; that is the question:" to remain and be liberated by Soviet troops and risk their slings and rifles in order to tell the whole world about the outrageous 'Nazis' – or, take arms and feet against a sea of cold and darkness in order to collaborate with the very same outrageous 'Nazis.' Oh what heartache – ay there's the rub! Thus conscience does make cowards of us all.*

Considering all this, I contemplated revising my statements about this issue in a new edition of my book *Lectures*. However, since even just this one choice by Elie Wiesel is such a complex topic, and because the *Lectures* are designed to give a brief, encyclopedic overview of many facets of "the Holocaust," there was simply no way to give this topic the room it deserved. Hence, in order to keep the *Lectures* at a reasonable size, I don't plan on elaborating in it more on Wiesel or on other similar "survivors" (who should more accurately be called "camp veterans," just like soldiers returning from a war are not called "survivors" but war veterans). Still, something needed to be done to address this and other problematic statements by Wiesel.

The solution to this dilemma was a thorough, critical analysis of Elie Wiesel, his activities and his various published statements in a stand-alone monograph, to which I could then refer the reader in my *Lectures*. But who would undertake this effort?

* * *

In the spring of 2014, I was editing the English edition of yet another book by the prolific Italian revisionist Carlo Mattogno. I had edited the German edition in 2011, but the publishers of the English edition did not like its German title *Schiffbruch: Vom Untergang der Holocaust-Orthodoxie*,[9] which translates to *Shipwreck: On the Sinking of Holocaust Orthodoxy*. They came up with a radically different yet catchy title, which describes the fact that the book addresses and debunks basically all the Nazi-gas-chamber claims ever made: *Inside the Gas Chambers: The Extermination of Mainstream Holocaust Historiography*.[10]

A few days after I had listed the book with Amazon, I checked its availability there by searching their website for that title. This is when I ran into Shlomo Venezia's book *Inside the Gas Chamber: Eight Months in the Sonderkommando of Auschwitz*, which had been published in 2009.[11] It's

9 Uckfield: Castle Hill Publishers, 2011.
10 Washington, D.C.: The Barnes Review, 2014.
11 Cambridge, UK: Polity.

the story of a person who in 1992 suddenly decided to claim that he had been a former Auschwitz inmate who had worked in and around the gas chambers of Auschwitz.[12] On Amazon.com, Carlo's book debunking the gas chamber myth was listed right next to Venezia's alleged eyewitness account. A more jarring contrast was impossible.

First I was dismayed that we had picked a title which had already been taken. But then I realized that this accident was giving Carlo's book a fortuitous placement it would otherwise never have received.

That is when the idea crossed my mind that a thorough, scholarly critique of each of the more popular eyewitness accounts – rated by Amazon sales statistics – should be published, starting with the bestseller and then working down the ranks, one by one. We would give each of these monographs a title which includes the keywords people would search on when looking for the original, and – bingo! – next to the camp veteran's testimony, the interested reader would also find a critical study of it.

There can be no doubt that Elie Wiesel's *Night* is *the* best-selling book among all the "eyewitness" literature, just as Wiesel has for decades been the politically and socially most influential of all the camp veterans. Wiesel with his book *Night* was therefore the number one on my list, followed by Rudolf Höss, the former commandant of Auschwitz, and then the lesser so-called eyewitnesses like Miklos Nyiszli, Filip Müller, Rudolf Vrba and so on.

In early 2015, when I reached out to the usual revisionist suspects who would be interested in taking on such a project, I quickly found takers for Höss and Nyiszli, two narrowly defined and rather limited subjects. But for the omnipresent Elie Wiesel I did not find anyone. The challenge seemed too big.

A few weeks later I got contacted by Prof. Dr. Warren B. Routledge, who was completely unknown to me at the time. He mentioned that he was looking for a publisher of his revisionist book project on Wiesel and his novel *Night*. As a last-ditch resort he had thought of Castle Hill Publishers, since no established publisher would dare touch this debunking of a modern-day saint. Needless to say I was more than delighted to hear that what I had merely spelled out as a future project might already have been accomplished.

As it turns out, the book you are holding in your hands is much more ambitious in scope than what I had originally envisioned, which was basically limited to a critique of Wiesel's various statements about the so-called Holocaust. Routledge's study is in fact the first-ever critical biography of

---

[12] For a critique of this book see Carlo Mattogno "'The Truth about the Gas Chambers?' Historical Considerations relating to Shlomo Venezia's 'Unique Testimony'," *Inconvenient History*, vol. 2, no. 1, 2010; www.inconvenienthistory.com/archive/2010/volume_2/number_1

Elie Wiesel. Interwoven with this critical review of Wiesel's writings and activities is an overview of the development of Holocaust revisionism, which is a resistance movement formed in reaction to what Elie Wiesel, the "Living Symbol of the Holocaust," personifies: the perpetuation of war-time propaganda for insidious political, social and monetary ends.

Another strength of the present study is that it deals with the festering subject of the betrayal of Pope Pius XII by his own Church. The author contends that Pius XII can actually be considered as a forerunner of the revisionists, since he clearly never believed that Nazi Germany was carrying out an extermination program against Europe's Jews.

Finally, Routledge points out the toxic effect which the orthodox Holocaust narrative has on ordinary Jews. It makes them paranoid and has driven them to the exits through intermarriage with non-Jews, which assures that most of their children will probably not be raised in the Jewish traditions. The author also reveals that there are Jewish revisionists who have come to understand the menace which the falsity and venality of the Holocaust cult pose for Jewry in general. Granted, this issue is not explored in depth here, but it may serve as a call to action for others to investigate and develop it more thoroughly.

For me as the editor of the series *Holocaust Handbooks*, of which this present study is the 30th volume, working with the author on this ambitious project was a pleasure not only because of its interesting and multifaceted contents, but also due to the many improvements we managed to put in place during our many exchanges. Hence I can wholeheartedly endorse the book's message. I hope the reader will find it just as edifying as I did.

Ultimately there was only one point on which Dr. Routledge and I agreed to disagree. The author refers repeatedly to the detrimental brainwashing effect today's omnipresent Holocaust propaganda has on young people. But when he runs into one concrete example of such an effect, he seems to side with Elie Wiesel. I am referring here to the case of Eric Hunt (see p. 335 of this book). Hunt was in his early twenties when he suddenly discovered that what he had been taught about the Holocaust might be profoundly wrong. At school he had been forced to read Elie Wiesel's *Night*, but now he came to understand that he had been duped. He became angry, understandably so. When he heard that Elie Wiesel would attend a conference near his home, he took matters into his own hands. He grabbed his copy of *Night* and a video camera and sought to confront Wiesel. He wanted to do "ambush journalism," that is to say, suddenly showing up in front of an unsuspecting individual with a running camera, asking some tough, provocative questions. But Hunt was too angry, too excited, and too disorganized. What unfolded when the two men met is unclear. Wiesel claims that Hunt became violent, whereas Hunt insists that he merely grabbed Wiesel by his sleeve trying to get him to stand still and answer his questions. The court believed Wiesel, so Hunt ended up in prison for 18 months.

After reading the present study, readers should be well-equipped to judge for themselves whether they would believe at face value anything Wiesel claims. I am convinced that Hunt would not have ended up in court, let alone in prison, had the person he confronted been Joe Shmoe rather than the world's Holocaust High Priest. Hunt's fate merely shows how Wiesel handles opponents.

With all this said, the book's stance is clear: It shows unambiguously that Wiesel's confession with which I started this Foreword has to be taken more seriously than any mainstream critic has ever dared.[13] Put bluntly, Wiesel's business is writing down lies. Exposing this shocking fact ineluctably required that the author, while writing the present study, had to defy the Holocaust taboo, or else he could not have gotten to the core of the many untruths spread by Wiesel in his various writings and public statements.

By revealing the unvarnished truth about Wiesel, his novel *Night*, and the Holocaust cult which Wiesel helped establish, this book has the potential to enlighten and therefore liberate readers from the conditioning they have received in schools and through the media.

But beware: when reading this book, you have a right to become upset, but your emotions *must* be harnessed to serve constructive and productive objectives. Violence is never an option.

Germar Rudolf
March 21, 2015

---

13 See for instance how Gary Weissman beats around the bush after having quoted this very passage in his book *Fantasies of Witnessing: Postwar Efforts to Experience the Holocaust* (Ithaca, New York: Cornell University Press, 2004), 67ff. (http://books.google.com/books?id=kXO9wXvYuAQC&pg=PA67); Ruth Franklin takes a similar approach in her *A Thousand Darknesses: Lies and Truth in Holocaust Fiction* (New York: Oxford University Press, 2011), 69ff. (https://books.google.com/books?id=4jdOJO-XxQUC&pg=PA69)

Introduction

The present study seeks to accomplish several goals simultaneously. Written both for non-revisionists interested in learning more about Holocaust revisionism and its relationship to the Jewish Holocaust Story of World War II, as well as revisionists of various information levels, the work does not presume any prior knowledge. Its first objective is to provide the reader with a general, introductory overview of the revisionist movement, including its main arguments, key players, and historiographical achievements. The study covers the period from the 1960s to the year 2010, and its purpose is not only to bring forth new revisionist arguments and information, but also to summarize and contextualize the accomplishments of the leading revisionist scholars. The terminus date of 2010 was selected because the close of the first decade of the twenty-first century corresponds roughly to a half-century of revisionist activity.

The book's second goal is to tell the story of the emergence and blossoming of Holocaust revisionism within the context of Elie Wiesel's life and career. His name has become synonymous with the Holocaust, and not a few people have called him the "Holocaust High Priest." Indeed, the vast majority of Holocaust devotees (both Jews and non-Jews) look upon him as a holy man of sorts, in part because of his supposedly miraculous survival at Auschwitz and Buchenwald, but also because of the key role he played in the founding of the U.S. Holocaust Memorial Museum in Washington, DC.

An additional benefit of this approach is that, by telling the revisionist story in the context of Wiesel's career, I have been able to add the theme of "Catholic-Jewish Dialogue" to the mix. This is so because Wiesel's greatest benefactor from the very beginning of his career was the French Catholic novelist, man of letters, and Nobel Prize winner François Mauriac (1885-1970). Mauriac "discovered" Wiesel, helped him to get his first book, the supposedly autobiographical *La Nuit* (1958), published in Paris, and wrote a flattering review of it when no one else seemed interested in it. He also had a very close personal attachment to Wiesel until his death in 1970.Their relationship is connected to another of the present study's themes: the problematic and at times abusive relationship that has existed between the various international Jewish organizations and media outlets on the one hand, and the men who served as Pope of the Catholic Church from Pius XII to Benedict XVI. In exploring this latter theme, I document and analyze the subversive role played by various Catholic "Holocaustians." Such men and women, nominally Catholics, often advance their careers in Zionist media or academic environments by claiming, without proof and to various degrees, that Pius XII and the Catholic Church as a whole somehow bear "guilt" for the Holocaust. It is a very cynical and mendacious game, but it pays quite well. The discussion of their activities, coupled with the surrender of the popes to the Zionist agenda, adds further insight into the reasons for the incredible and unprecedented decline of the Catholic Church over the past half century in every imaginable way.

While Holocaust revisionism is a truly international movement in which citizens of many nations are involved to varying degrees, the special focus here is on revisionism in France and the United States. In France, Professor Robert Faurisson has been the unquestioned leader in the effort for the past four decades. In the U.S., however, there has been a succession of actors over the years. From the emergence of Professor Arthur Butz in the 1970s, to the Institute of Historical Review in the 1980s and beyond, to the work of Bradley Smith and his Committee for Open Debate on the Holocaust (CODOH) for the past thirty years, many hands have lent themselves to this work. With regard to Elie Wiesel, Carolyn Yeager's blog site, "Elie Wiesel Cons the World," has played an enormous role in recent years by bringing to light a great deal of valuable information about Wiesel. I hope that her work, and that of other revisionists, will continue to flourish.

This study is divided into three main sections. The first contains four chapters dealing with the Mauriac–Wiesel relationship and the genesis of his novel *Night*, while the second section's two chapters offer a close critical reading of Wiesel's novel. In the third section, I seek to combine my unauthorized biography of Wiesel with an overview of the development of historical revisionism in the U.S. (and to a lesser degree in Europe), from the appearance of *Night* in English in 1960 to 2010. These themes are presented chronically in order to give the reader a sense of how far revisionist arguments have advanced in a mere half-century of activity, as well as to document the inability of the Holocaustians to rebut them. I have also woven into this narrative the related issues of the abandonment of Pius XII by the post-Conciliar Catholic Church, and the negative reaction among many Jews to both Wiesel and the Holocaust narrative in general. While this ambitious, but focused, narrative might seem disjointed at times to some readers, it does adhere to this general outline and seeks as much as possible to avoid repetitions.

Chapter I
François Mauriac:
Waiting for the Modern-Day Messiah

François Mauriac, Catholic Novelist and Man of Letters

François Mauriac (1885-1970) emerged in France in the 1920s as a "Catholic novelist" who used the traditions, symbolic world and belief system of Catholicism in his work. Although he rejected the term "Catholic novelist," preferring instead to be known as a "Catholic who writes novels," the term did nonetheless point up that his fiction portrayed a hidden and mystical world of divine grace active within every living person. In France, Mauriac was probably read by non-Catholics as much as by Catholics, for anticlerical readers enjoyed Mauriac's fictional portrayal of the hypocrisy of upper-class Catholic families. In his novels of the interwar years, Mauriac mercilessly skewered and pitilessly laid bare the obsession with money and property that characterized the Catholicism of many members of his social class.

The theme of repressed sexual desire also figured prominently in his novels, with the result that fellow Catholics were often among his most hostile reviewers. For example, the Assumptionists, the religious order that owned and published the nationally distributed Catholic daily newspaper *La Croix,* often found fault with Mauriac's novels on moral rather than esthetic grounds. Other opposition came from an influential Catholic priest with the improbable name of Louis Bethléem, who, during the interwar years, compiled a series of guidebooks on moral reading for Catholics. Of course, he warned them against reading Mauriac's novels. One of the supreme rebuffs from this Catholic milieu came from a highly respected and widely read priest and literary critic, the abbé Jean Calvet. In his book *Le renouveau catholique dans la littérature contemporaine* (Paris: Lanore,

1927), he refused even to classify Mauriac as a Catholic novelist. In his assessment of Mauriac's work, Calvet reflected the widely held belief among French Catholics that Mauriac was obsessed by sexual desire and its repression. They were repelled by his exploitation of Catholic signs and symbols to covertly sell sex to his readers. Yet, for better or for worse, in the Catholicism of many members of what we can call "mainstream" French culture, during the interwar years Mauriac was as "official" a Catholic intellectual as any man in France. In somewhat altered form, the same could be said of the twenty-five years from the end of the war until his death in 1970, during which he remained active as a novelist, political journalist and man of letters.

Illustration 1: François Mauriac postage stamp on the 100th anniversary of his birth (fifteen years after his death)

Mauriac, the youngest of four boys, grew up in a very wealthy family. The Mauriacs' wealth was largely based on property that included pine forests, which were lucrative for the manufacture of turpentine and related products in the naval stores industry. His mother was a staunch Catholic, while his father, who died when Mauriac was a boy, was an unbeliever. Mauriac had the feeling of being "different" as a boy growing up in Bordeaux. He never felt at home playing with the other boys and showed little interest in their games. He was subjected to terrible teasing by his older brothers (he was the youngest of five children) as well as by his schoolmates. Mauriac scholars have known for the last twenty-five years that Mauriac led a secret homosexual life, despite being married and fathering four children. In part to avoid embarrassing his children and grandchildren, this hidden aspect of his life was sometimes alluded to, but never directly discussed.

However, this situation has changed following the publication of Jean-Luc Barré's new two-volume biography of Mauriac.[1] In it, Barré candidly addresses an aspect of Mauriac's life that had been hidden until now. Thus, we know today that Mauriac began to feel homosexual tendencies as a boy. During adolescence and in early adulthood, he had a close relationship with the openly homosexual François le Grix. In fact, Mauriac's engagement to Marianne Chausson, the daughter of a well-known composer, was broken off by her family in 1911 because of his relationships with other "out" homosexuals, including Lucien Daudet and Jean Cocteau. Homosex-

1 Jean-Luc Barré, *François Mauriac, biographie intime I, 1885 – 1940*, vol. 1 (Paris: Arthème Fayard, 2009), and *François Mauriac, biographie intime II, 1940 – 1970*, vol. 2 (Paris: Arthème Fayard, 2010).

ual urges would trouble Mauriac throughout his life. It will be argued in the pages which follow that these proclivities probably played a role of some kind, never before discussed, in his bizarre "amitié," or "friendship," with the ambitious young Jew Elie Wiesel. In fact, it is inconceivable that Wiesel could have been unaware of Mauriac's homosexuality when he burst into Mauriac's life, completely unannounced and unexpected, in 1955. Wiesel's main reason for trying to establish contact with Mauriac was because he was perceived by fellow Jews in Paris as a loyal friend of the Jewish people. At the same time, his Jewish informants almost certainly told him of the rumors that circulated in Parisian literary circles at the time with regard to Mauriac's ongoing attraction to young men.

Mauriac Abandons the French Right and Supports the Jewish People

When Mauriac was elected to membership in the ultraconservative Académie Française, that is, as one of the forty "living immortals" of French culture, in 1933, he was still politically a man of the French Right. He belonged to the right-wing nationalist strain in French politics led by Charles Maurras, and depended on support from key conservative members of the Academy for election to that body. For Maurras, French Jews were dangerous not only because they were a culturally alien element in the French body politic; even worse, they also tended to be pro-German. In 1933, Mauriac implicitly shared such views.

By 1936, however, he began to move leftward and to support Jewish political causes. After criticizing Mussolini in 1936 for his invasion of Ethiopia, in 1937 Mauriac joined with the Catholic novelist Georges Bernanos and the neo-Thomist philosopher Jacques Maritain in denouncing General Franco's revolt against the Spanish Republic. To Mauriac, who had supported Franco during the first few months of rebellion, Catholics could not make common cause with Fascists. Most European Catholics, including of course the Vatican, rightly recognized Franco as an authentic anti-Communist, and supported him for this reason, but Mauriac could not be persuaded. To him, the execution of fourteen Basque priests by forces under Franco's control for having supported the Republican government could not be excused.[2] While Mauriac had a valid point, at the same time

2 Jean-Jacques Bozonnet, "Des évêques basques défient leur hiérarchie en honorant la mémoire de prêtres tués par des soldats de Franco," *Le Monde*, July 14, 2009. www.lemonde.fr/europe/article/2009/07/13/des-eveques-basques-defient-leur-hierarchie-en-honorant-la-memoire-de-pretres-tues-par-des-soldats-de-franco _1218241_3214.html. These deaths are still an issue in Spain. In July 2009, Basque bishops apologized for having kept silent about these deaths over the years. Yet, these same bishops have never questioned the myth of the angelic nature of those who fought for the Spanish Republic, and have never demanded an apology from those who slaughtered thousands of non-combatant and defenseless priests and nuns.

he turned a blind eye to the deaths of the thousands of priests and nuns who had been slaughtered by the Spanish Republicans and their Communist allies. The death toll of 6,832 victims included 13 bishops, 4,172 diocesan priests and seminarians, 2,364 monks and friars, and 283 nuns.[3] He also discounted the vast inventory of Church property that was confiscated and destroyed by the Republicans. The Catholic Mauriac's position on Franco was thus closer to that of most of the pro-Stalinist intellectuals of the day.

Luckily for the Spanish people and for Western Europe, the Communists did not win the Spanish Civil War. Franco's victory meant that Spaniards were not forced into Marxist servitude, as were over a hundred million innocent people in Eastern Europe (most of them Catholics) after World War II. For many years, it was fashionable for Western leftist intellectuals to denounce certain repressive aspects of Franco's regime as it continued into the 1970s. But Franco's rule over Spain, in comparison to the Communist regimes that persecuted the peoples of Eastern Europe after the war, was relatively benign. It also had the virtue of being homegrown, rather than imposed and enforced from without, as were the governments of the Soviet satellites.

By 1938, Mauriac was a fully-committed and fervent supporter of Jews and Jewish causes, and had begun to denounce the German government's policy of pressuring Jews to emigrate from the Reich. When many French intellectuals, fearful that Jews were trying to get France involved in another war with Germany, were urging caution and moderation regarding events within the borders of another sovereign nation, Mauriac called for direct involvement. By this time, he had come to reject the Maurrasian idea that Jews were foreigners on French soil. In February 1938, he wrote:[4]

> *If there is an issue that requires our intervention, it's the one that engulfs Israel* [Jewry] *with such a wave of hatred. The question is not to know what we think of the Jews as Jews any more than what we think of Auvergnats as Auvergnats. Before examining the problems created by this exodus of the persecuted* [Jews], *we must begin by means of a public act of opposition to anti-Semitism.*

---

3 Julio de la Cueva, "Religious Persecution, Anticlerical Tradition and Revolution: On Atrocities against the Clergy during the Spanish Civil War," *Journal of Contemporary History,* 33 (1998), 355. See also: Arnaud Imatz, *La Guerre d'Espagne revisitée* (Paris: Economica, 1993) [2nd edition, revised and expanded], pp. 47-50; Vicente Orti, *La Persecución religiosa en España durante la segunda república (1931-1939)* (Madrid: Rialp, 1990).

4 François Mauriac, *Mémoires politiques* (Paris: Grasset, 1967), 73f.: "S'il est un drame qui exige notre intervention, c'est bien celui qui dresse Israël contre une telle vague de haine. La question n'est pas de savoir ce que nous pensons des Juifs en tant que Juifs, pas plus que des Auvergnats en tant qu'Auvergnats. Avant d'examiner les problèmes que soulève déjà l'exode des persécutés, nous devons commencer par un acte public d'opposition à l'antisémitisme."

Taking aim at the Maurrasian beliefs that revolved around the doctrines of integral nationalism and anti-Semitism, and that had played a major role in his life as a youth, he wrote:[5]

> *So let us be even more watchful against anti-Semitism, even unconscious, especially since all of us – yes all of us, without exception – are the heirs to this age-old hatred. If it's not actually hatred, it is at least a form of hostility that has been kept alive within us, we must admit in our defense, by the faults and missteps of the Jewish people as well as by the fearsome flame that persecution keeps alive within their breast.*

Mauriac then concludes his essay with his own advice about overcoming feelings of anti-Jewish hatred:[6]

> *To this element of hatred I have always contrasted the admiration that I feel for certain Jews, deceased or living, and the affection that more than one of them has inspired in me. There is no better antidote against racial hatred than to center our thoughts on certain people who are dear to us. There is no better response to anti-Semitic doctrines than to recall what both French and German culture owe to its Jewish ingredient – and what, in return, the Jewish genius owes to Western civilizations.*

This kind of statement exposed Mauriac to criticism from some of his former friends on the Right. But it also showed his deep commitment to justice for his Jewish friends and for the Jewish people as a whole.

Mauriac Supports the Allied War Effort

Mauriac completed his move to the Left during the war years. As early as 1940, de Gaulle's follower, Robert Schumann, in his BBC broadcasts from London, identified Mauriac by name as a writer and intellectual who had remained in France and who incarnated the virtues of traditional Republican France. Unlike so many other writers who quietly went into exile abroad, Mauriac remained sequestered at his home in the southwest of France. There, under terms of the 1940 armistice, he could be required to provide lodging for German military personnel. Thus, an SS officer, Major Westman, who commanded the German garrison in the nearby town of

---

5 *Ibid.*: "Gardons-nous d'autant plus de l'antisémitisme, même larvé, que nous sommes tous – oui, tous et sans exception – les héritiers de cette haine séculaire; sinon de cette haine, du moins de cette hostilité entretenue en nous, il faut le dire à notre décharge par les fautes, par les maladresses d'Israël; et par cette flamme redoutable que la persécution attise en lui."

6 *Ibid.*: "A ce ferment de haine, j'ai toujours opposé l'admiration que je ressens pour quelques Juifs, morts ou vivants, et l'affection que plus d'un m'inspire. Il n'est pas de meilleur antidote à la haine de race que d'arrêter sa pensée sur certains êtres qui nous sont chers. Il n'est pas de meilleure réponse aux doctrines antisémites que de constater ce que la culture française et la culture allemande doivent au ferment juif – et ce que doit en retour, le génie d'Israël aux civilisations occidentales."

Langon, presented Mauriac with a requisition order a few days after Christmas 1940. The next day he moved in, occupying an upstairs bedroom, while his orderly slept on a cot in the dining room. The demarcation line between the free (Vichy-ruled) and occupied zones ran right through the grape vines surrounding his home.

Mauriac watched and waited, while also spending the dark days between the fall of France in the summer of 1940 and Christmas of that year writing the novel *La pharisienne* (*Woman of the Pharisees*). Despite a shortage of paper, which limited the number of copies that could be printed, and the refusal of the pro-Vichy press to review his book, since they considered Mauriac to be a Jewish puppet, *La pharisienne* sold thirty thousand copies in the first two months, and went through several editions. It was widely read by the French people, who looked upon it as the quintessential "roman de l'Occupation" (novel of the Occupation). Amazingly, even though Mauriac had intended to write a "roman catholique," or Catholic novel, about his dominating and smothering mother and those whose lives she affected, his readers, for reasons that lack of space does not permit exploring here, saw the book as an allegory of their own condition under German occupation.

The pro-German Vichy intellectuals despised Mauriac, and portrayed him as a traitor to his nation, his class and his religion. They mocked his obsession with sex in his novels, and hinted, correctly as we now know, that he was a closet homosexual. In other words, certain vices that these same intellectuals routinely associated with the Jews were attributed to Mauriac.

Mauriac Is "Silent" about the Jews in *Le Cahier Noir*

Mauriac's most significant achievement on behalf of the Allies during the war was the publication of his pro-Allied propaganda pamphlet *Le cahier noir* in 1943. Smuggled out of France and rapidly translated in Britain as *The Black Notebook* by the Catholic intellectual (and future biographer of Mauriac) Robert Speaight, it became a success overnight. Mauriac's little book expressed the ideals espoused by the Allies in a way that no one in the United States or Great Britain had yet been able to achieve.[7]

Le cahier noir, and Mauriac's strategy in writing it, tells us much about the context in which we must understand the alleged World War II "silence" about the supposed extermination of the Jews that Mauriac, and many others, imputed to Pope Pius XII after the war. Mauriac, writing under the pseudonym of "Forez," had as one of his many goals in the book

---

7 Robert Speaight, *François Mauriac: A Study of the Man and the Writer* (London: Chatto & Windus, 1976).

the arousal of sympathy for Jewry. His problem, as he wrote this piece of pro-Jewish propaganda, was to communicate his message without leaving himself open to the accusation, readily leveled by the pro-Vichy intellectuals and others, that those who championed the Jews were simply political puppets in Jewish hands. To be sure, by publishing *Le cahier noir* he was also risking his life, for the Germans could probably see through his pseudonym. Since the French press, whether in the occupied zone or in the Vichy-controlled area, repeated the principal German propaganda line throughout the war, namely, that the Allies were fighting a self-destructive war for the Jews and that Aryan boys were needlessly dying for Jewry, Mauriac chose to make his case indirectly, by writing of the travails of Jews in France but not referring to them by name.

Faced with the challenge of making a special plea for Jews without mentioning them as such, Mauriac used coded language. The code he followed involved the use of a simple little story in which the reader had to fill in the blanks. He told his readers that he had seen a train carrying a group of children at Austerlitz Station in Paris about a year earlier. This station was one of about a half-dozen major stations in Paris at the time, and provided train service to cities like Toulouse and Bordeaux in the southwest of the country. Since Jews at the time were being deported from Austerlitz Station to the transit camp at Pithiviers, it was likely that the children in question were Jewish.

The key point here is that Mauriac, like Pius XII, did not mention that these children were Jewish. He wrote:[8]

> *To accomplish Machiavelli's plans, groups of people have been shuffled around and deported, and whole races have been condemned to perish. At what other moment in history have jails enclosed so many innocent people? At what other time have children been ripped out of their mothers' arms, and piled into cattle cars, as I saw one sad morning at Austerlitz Station?*

Mauriac did not witness this event; he heard about it from his wife and son. He also gratuitously added the detail about "cattle cars," which his wife and son had not mentioned. Mauriac left it to his readers to fill in the blanks as to the children's being Jewish. This anecdote was very effective, for readers in Britain and the U.S., under the sway of the Allied propaganda that filled the "mainstream" press, were easily able to identify the children as Jewish. Furthermore, they could just as easily pencil in the idea that they were being sent to a concentration camp. Thus, there was no need to

---

[8] François Mauriac, *Le cahier noir*, in: *Œuvres complètes*, vol. 10 (Paris: Arthème Fayard, 1952), 366f.: "Pour accomplir les desseins de Machiavel, les peuples sont brassés et déportés, des races entières sont condamnées à périr. A quel autre moment de l'histoire les bagnes se sont-ils refermés sur plus d'innocents? A quelle autre époque les enfants furent-ils arrachés à leurs mères, entassés dans des wagons à bestiaux, tels que je les ai vus par un sombre matin à la gare d'Austerlitz?"

tell these readers that the children were Jewish, for the Allied public would assume that otherwise the story would not have been told in the first place. Similarly, the propaganda movies that Hollywood studios made to support the war effort generally refrained from mentioning the Jewish dimension of the war. This fact is especially salient in the explicitly propagandistic series *Why We Fight*. Here, the predominantly Jewish producers followed the same script as Mauriac had in *Le cahier noir*, and largely sublimated the Jews, at most equating their sufferings with those of Christians.

It is in the context of this resounding "silence" by both Mauriac and Hollywood, of which the above are only two examples, that we must understand the supposed "silence" of Pope Pius XII. In following the strategy of "silence," these entities behaved much as did the Pope, who also undeniably favored the Allies and world Jewry. They all observed this "silence" for the same reason: because outright and explicit support of the Jews would have lent support to the Axis claim that they were acting as Jewish stooges and puppets.

Even after the war was over, Allied leaders and publicists – many of them Jewish – observed what was for all practical purposes a similar sublimation at the main Nuremberg tribunal. Mention of the Jews was virtually absent from the original indictment. In an edition of his father's letters from Nuremberg, where the latter had been a prosecutor, former Senator Christopher Dodd (D-CT) expressed shock at this, although lead U.S. prosecutor Justice Robert Jackson and the rest of the prosecution team were following a protocol of "silence" analogous to, though different from, that of Pius XII during the war years. After all, the Allies were utterly and unconditionally triumphant at Nuremberg, with Axis propaganda no longer a factor. Yet, as the letters reveal, concern lest the Allied populations see the war as a "Jew's war" was widespread among the Jews and the gentiles who conducted the Nuremberg tribunal. Mauriac's refusal during the occupation to describe child deportees as Jewish, Hollywood's downplaying the Jewish issue to ensure gentile support for the war, and the comparative neglect at Nuremberg of the alleged genocide of the Jews are but three instances of a policy of "silence" that was carried out by various participants on the Allied side. The Allied policy has been largely forgotten, while accusations of a culpable "silence" that has been wrongly attributed to Pius XII have grown louder and more frequent since the war.[9]

---

9 Christopher J. Dodd, Larry Bloom, *Letters from Nuremberg: My Father's Narrative of the Quest for Justice*. (N.Y.: Crown, 2007), 135f. In September 1945, Thomas Dodd wrote to his wife that the prosecution staff was overwhelmingly Jewish, a fact that has been erased from the official history of the event. Is it any wonder that the Germans were denied justice there? Dodd wrote: "The staff continues to grow every day. Col. Kaplan is now here, as a mate, I assume, for Commander Kaplan. Dr. Newman has arrived, and I do not know how many more. It is all a silly business – but 'silly' isn't the right word. One would expect that some of these people would have sense enough to put

This book, which addresses the various silences of, and accusations of silence by, François Mauriac and Elie Wiesel, will examine the chief charge against Pope Pius XII in some detail – that he knowingly failed to speak out against an extermination of the Jews. Here it should also be recalled that the Catholic Church was officially a neutral party between Nazi Germany – whom Pius XII had not hesitated to speak against before the war – and the Communist Soviet Union. Those Jewish leaders in the U.S. who, somewhat hypocritically, requested that Pius XII explicitly "speak out" on behalf of the Jews in his various Christmas messages during the war years knew in advance that he could not. He simply could not speak specifically about the Jews without compromising his credibility as a neutral party. Even worse, with his loss of credibility would have come the charge by the Germans that he was just another Jewish puppet. In reality, as Professor Faurisson has pointed out in his study *Le révisionnisme de Pie XII*,[10] Pius XII was committed to the Allied cause, and his public "neutrality" was a smokescreen intended to hide that fact. Yet the Jewish leaders in the U.S., so selfish, so short-sighted and so self-referential, as if nobody else in Europe was suffering, made their demand, knowing full well that the Pope could not comply with it. They also knew that the Pope, like the Allies – including many influential Jews – and like Mauriac, relied on the perspicacity of the public to recognize that Jews were included in his condemnation of persecution. He could no more do their bidding than he could allow himself to publicly endorse the French Catholics who fought Communism on the eastern front. The volunteers of the *L.V.F.* (*Légion des Volontaires Français*) and later the Frenchmen of Germany's Charlemagne Division, would have appreciated such recognition. Yet the Pope always refused to give his blessing to such Catholic anti-Communist crusades, whether or not he would have liked to support them. When he turned them down, he did so for precisely the same reason he turned down the impossible requests from U.S. Jewish leaders. He had to maintain his public posture of neutrality.

Let us now return to Mauriac's simple little story. He was able to arouse sympathy for Jews indirectly, without mentioning them by name, by recounting in *Le cahier noir* that he had seen the Jewish children on the train. Yet, he himself had not seen them. Mauriac simply repeated his wife and

---

an end to this kind of a parade. You know better than anyone how I hate race or religious prejudice. You know how I have despised anti-Semitism. You know how strongly I feel toward those who preach intolerance of any kind. With that knowledge – you will understand when I tell you that this staff is about seventy-five percent Jewish. Now my point is that the Jews should stay away from this trial – for their own sake. For – mark this well – the charge 'a war for the Jews' is still being made, and in the postwar years it will be made again and again."

10 Robert Faurisson, *Le révisionnisme de Pie XII* (Genoa: Graphos Edizioni, 2002). English translation: *Pope Pius XII's Revisionism* (Uckfield, UK: Historical Review Press, 2006).

son's account, but made two important changes. First, he claimed that *he* had seen the children with his own eyes, which was not true. He no doubt felt that he was prevaricating on behalf of a good cause, the fight against anti-Semitism, but he was in fact bearing false witness. A lie, even a white lie told with the best of intentions, is still a lie. Thus, ironically, Mauriac, a Catholic, became one of the first of the many false witnesses in what would later become the Jewish Holocaust narrative, a genre in which false testimonies proliferate, even dominate. The second change that he made in the story was to delete specific mention that the children were Jews, for reasons mentioned above. Mauriac, like Pius XII, could do this because he knew that, given the power of Allied propaganda during the war, his readers would be able to fill in the gaps and supply the word "Jew."

The publication of *Le cahier noir* won Mauriac many Jewish friends around the world. In addition, during the war years, French Catholics and Jews (primarily under the auspices of the Communist party) worked very closely together. Both groups, despite their many differences, supported de Gaulle and his call for internal "resistance" to the occupier. Judged security risks by the Germans, many resistors, Catholic and Jewish, were deported to work camps in Germany and Poland. Many of them died there, primarily of disease. And, finally, both groups shared the short-lived euphoria that followed the Liberation, with their respective ordeals being read into the record – however inaccurately – at Nuremberg. Mauriac was, in short, a living icon of the Catholic-Jewish alliance that had existed, however briefly and imperfectly, during World War II.

At the liberation of Paris in August 1944, Mauriac was commissioned to write the lead article in the first post-occupation edition of *Le Figaro.* Since that prestigious newspaper, which had been banned during the occupation, wanted a patriotic piece in honor of General de Gaulle, Mauriac penned "Le premier des nôtres" ("The First among Us").[11] Mauriac's selection as author of this article was laden with symbolism, for he was not only a Catholic, but one deeply committed to the Jews. His devotion to Catholicism and to French republicanism mirrored the symbolism of de Gaulle's flag, the French tricolor emblazoned with the Cross of Lorraine. The Catholic Church and the French Republic had been engaged in a cultural and political war since the separation of Church and State in 1905. When de Gaulle decided to include the Cross of Lorraine, invoking the memory of Joan of Arc, who had come to the aid of the nation in a time of crisis centuries earlier, he was imposing a symbol of traditional Catholic France on the ultimate symbol of the anti-clerical Republic. In terms of the political and ideological realities of occupied France, this flag embodied the temporary alliance of the many Catholics in the French Resistance with the Jews and

---

[11] François Mauriac, "Le Premier des nôtres," *Le Figaro*, August 25, 1945, 1.

Communists who played a disproportionate role in its ranks and leadership. The general reluctance to mention the Jewish role even after Allied propaganda was no longer a factor underlines yet again how strong the inclination was to downplay Jewish prominence for gentile eyes. As times changed, the major role that Jews, many from Eastern Europe, especially Poland, had played in the Resistance began to be acknowledged by the influential "Nazi-hunters" Serge and Beate Klarsfeld as well as other Jewish voices.[12]

In a word, Mauriac incarnated de Gaulle's Catholic-Jewish alliance quite well. Of course, once the war was over and the alliance had dissolved, the Cross of Lorraine would disappear from the French flag. But for this brief moment, Mauriac's authoring this first article in liberated France was tangible proof that he had behaved during the war like a true patriot. He was a living symbol, however briefly, of what de Gaulle liked to call *la France éternelle*.

Flash Forward: Seeds Planted for the 1952 Nobel Prize for Literature

Mauriac's support of the Jews during the war, more than his work as a novelist (he had not written a novel since 1940!), would be rewarded in 1952, when, most likely with Jewish support, he received the Nobel Prize for Literature. Due in part to the fact that the wording of the award was rather vague, most observers were astonished at his selection, especially during the heyday of existentialism, when names like Sartre and Camus dominated the headlines. Many had the distinct impression that Mauriac was receiving the prize as much for his political support of de Gaulle and the Allied cause during the war as for his fiction. After all, his best novels, *Thérèse Desqueyroux* (1927) and *Le noeud de vipères* [*Vipers' Tangle*] (1932), belonged to another era, and the literary pulse of France had changed dramatically since then. In fact, as François Durand reminds us, Mauriac's literary fortunes had hit rock bottom in the late 1940s. Not only had his last play, *Passage du malin* (December 1947), been a total flop, he spent a good part of the next two years in "an almost constant battle," in his newspaper columns in *Le Figaro*, "against the Communists and their sympathizers, and their exchanges were often lively. In addition, a new generation of writers and thinkers was reaching the crest of fame – with Sartre and Camus in the lead – for whom Mauriac belonged to the past: Mauriac's failure with *Passage du malin* coincided in time with the success of Sartre's play *Les mains sales*."[13] Thus Mauriac, with his career in a tailspin, and the ob-

---

12 Monique-Lise Cohen, Jean-Louis Dufour, *Les juifs dans la résistance suivi de la présence juive en Europe et l'écriture de l'histoire* (Paris: Tirésias, 2001).

13 François Durand (ed.), *Mauriac: Œuvres autobiographiques* (Paris: Pléiade, 1990), 993: "Il est depuis deux ans en lutte, dans les colonnes du *Figaro*, contre les communistes et

ject of ridicule in the eyes of many of the rising literary stars of the younger generation, would be open by then to friendly gestures coming from young Jews. They admired him for his courageous defense of Jews and Jewish interests during the war years, and were determined to show their gratitude. Mauriac's receipt of the 1952 Nobel Prize for Literature shocked his enemies, but did not inspire them to change their opinion of him as a vestige of a dead past. It did, however, re-ignite his career, for he began writing novels again, and found renewed inspiration and a younger audience as a political commentator.

Another reason for the consternation of many Parisian literati when Mauriac was awarded the 1952 Nobel was their naïve assumption that the Nobel awards are free of politics. They did not understand that there were forces, including influential Jews, behind the scenes who appreciated what Mauriac had done for the Jews during the war years. In addition, Mauriac's literary jousting with France's Communists at a time when Communist influence was a distinct threat to France's role as a U.S. ally in the opening years of the Cold War must have endeared him to the CIA. We now know that the CIA brought its influence to bear on the selection for the 1958 Nobel Prize for Literature when CIA efforts enabled the Russian dissident Boris Pasternak to win out over the Italian Communist Alberto Moravia. They did so to embarrass the Soviet Union. Did they also do the same thing for Mauriac in 1952?[14] In summary, only the naïve would believe that his novels of the 1920s and 1930s secured the 1952 award, and it is not an accident that the inner workings of the Nobel selection process remain hidden from view.

Mauriac, a Bridge between Catholics and Jews

Wiesel has never given a straightforward answer to the question of why he sought out Mauriac. But part of the affinity can be explained by the feeling among French Jews that Mauriac was very sympathetic to them, a feeling Wiesel came to share as a young man living in France. He claims to have been a "voracious reader of Holocaust Literature. […] I still want to understand what happened."[15] In keeping abreast of books being published

---

leurs sympathisants et les échanges sont souvent très vifs; d'autre part, une nouvelle génération d'écrivains et de penseurs arrive au zénith, Sartre et Camus en tête, pour qui l'œuvre de Mauriac appartient au passé: à l'échec de *Passage de Malin* succède la réussite des *Mains sales*."

14 Mark Franchetti, "How the CIA Won *Zhivago* a Nobel," *Sunday Times* (London), January 14, 2007, 6; Anatoly Korolev, "*Doctor Zhivago* and the 1959 Nobel Prize: The CIA's Secret Triumph," *RIA-Novosti*, January 20, 2009. http://en.rian.ru/analysis/20090119/119705315.html

15 Harry James Cargas, *Harry James Cargas in Conversation with Elie Wiesel* (N.Y.: Paulist Press, 1976), 89.

on the camps as they came out in the early 1950s, he must have noticed that Mauriac was widely known for supporting publication of memoirs associated with the war, even writing forewords for such works.

Thus, for example, Mauriac wrote a foreword for a memoir by a Belgian professor of history named Léon-Ernest Halkin. Entitled *À l'ombre de la mort* [*In the Shadow of Death*] (Tournai: Casterman, 1947), the book recounted how Catholics had clandestinely practiced their faith in the German camps. The fact that Mauriac had contributed a moving foreword probably did not hurt the book's fortunes, for it was awarded the *Prix Littéraire de la Résistance* in 1947. Mauriac also wrote an introduction for *Pays de rigueur* [*Land of Hardship*] (Paris: Seuil, 1951) by Boris Bouïeff, a young friend who had been imprisoned by the Germans during the war. Sickly before his arrest, Bouïeff, thanks to his religious faith, was able not only to survive, but to care for others. In Bouïeff's experience Mauriac found yet further evidence not only of man's inhumanity to man, but also of the power to overcome it through union with Christ. He wrote a third foreword for *Un camp très ordinaire* [*A Quite Ordinary Camp*] (Paris: Minuit, 1957), a memoir written by Micheline Maurel. A *lycée* teacher in Lyon in 1941-42, she joined the Resistance in 1943 and was arrested as a security threat shortly thereafter. Her book told of her twenty-month incarceration in Germany. Mauriac's foreword might have helped the book to succeed, for it received the *Prix des Critiques* in 1957. This foreword is of special interest because it was written while Mauriac was helping Wiesel prepare the proofs of *La Nuit* for publication by the same publisher, *Les Éditions de Minuit*.[16]

Mauriac Was the First Major Cultural Figure to Accuse Pius XII of "Silence"

We cannot be sure if Wiesel was familiar with the forewords discussed above. But there was another foreword by Mauriac that he almost certainly read, for it introduced a book that indicted the Nazi regime for what we call today "the Holocaust:" Léon Poliakov's *Bréviaire de la haine* [*Harvest of Hate*] (Paris: Calmann-Lévy, 1951). Mauriac's foreword to this book would prove to be an additional factor in his favor when the Nobel Prize for Literature was awarded to him a year later. That Poliakov asked Mauriac to write the foreword to his book, and that the author agreed to do it,

---

16 Another important foreword that Mauriac wrote in these years introduced *Cinq Années de ma vie* (Paris: Fasquelle, 1962). This book was the "édition définitive" of Captain Alfred Dreyfus's 1901 autobiography. Although published only in 1962, when Wiesel was already established in New York, it showed Mauriac's ongoing commitment to Jewish causes. He seemed to want to make public penance for the anti-Dreyfus opinions held and expressed by his mother and siblings over the years.

testifies once again to the prestige that Mauriac enjoyed within the Jewish community of France.

Bréviaire de la haine is essentially a rehash of the Nuremberg documents as presented in the Blue Set (containing the transcripts of the main trial and documents presented in evidence). What Poliakov did was to rearrange the various atrocity claims found therein and present them by theme and in chronological order. Poliakov gave a great deal of importance to the supposed "confession" of former SS officer Kurt Gerstein. Thus, thanks in no small part to Mauriac's involvement, Poliakov became a historian of repute, while Mauriac earned another stripe on his sleeve as a friend of the Jews, and took a step up on the ladder that would lead to the Nobel Prize a year later. Yet the same nagging question that dogged Mauriac's wartime *Le cahier noir* bedevils his foreword to *Bréviaire de la haine*: was Mauriac a friend of the Jewish organizations, or their puppet?

The title of Poliakov's book was not chosen at random, for the word "breviary" refers to the book of scriptural readings that Catholic priests are enjoined to read each day. The provocative and scornful use of the word "bréviaire" by Poliakov contains a powerful dose of anti-Catholic venom, for it implies that the Catholic Church was the wellspring of Nazi-sponsored, anti-Jewish hatred. Poliakov purports to provide "readings" of his own that supposedly document German plans of extermination during the war. In Poliakov's view, Catholics were heavily responsible for Jewish suffering during the war years because many of the principal Nazis had been baptized as Catholics. Poliakov overlooks the Nazi persecution of the Catholic Church, including the thousands of Catholic priests who died in the camps, for he had no interest in writing a balanced history. His chief concern was to defame the Catholic Church and to help launch the attack on Pope Pius XII as the man responsible for Jewish suffering during the war.

In support of Poliakov's attack on the Pontiff, Mauriac, in his foreword, contrasts Pius's behavior with that of the local clergy who, according to him, were more heroic and charitable. He writes:[17]

---

17 François Mauriac, foreword to Léon Poliakov, *Bréviaire de la haine* (Paris: Calmann-Lévy, 1951), 63: "Mais ce bréviaire a été écrit pour nous aussi Français, dont l'antisémitisme traditionnel a survécu à ces excès d'horreur dans lesquels Vichy a eu sa timide et ignoble par – pour nous surtout, catholiques français, qui devons certes à l'héroïsme et à la charité de tant d'évêques, de prêtres et de religieux à l'égard des Juifs traqués, d'avoir sauvé notre honneur, mais qui n'avons pas eu la consolation d'entendre le successeur du Galiléen, Simon-Pierre, condamner clairement, nettement et non par des allusions diplomatiques, la mise en croix de ces innombrables 'frères du Seigneur.' Au vénérable cardinal Suhard qui a d'ailleurs tant fait dans l'ombre pour eux, je demandai un jour pendant l'occupation: 'Eminence, ordonnez-nous de prier pour les Juifs [...]', il leva les bras au ciel: nul doute que l'occupant n'ait eu des moyens de pression irrésistibles, et que le silence du pape et de la hiérarchie n'ait été un affreux devoir; il s'agissait d'éviter de pires malheurs. Il reste qu'un crime de cette envergure retombe

But this breviary has also been written for us Frenchmen, whose traditional anti-Semitism has survived all the horrors in which the Vichy government played its timid and shameful role. And it has been written especially for us, French Catholics, whose honor was preserved by the heroism and charity of so many bishops, priests and members of religious orders who protected Jews, but who never had the consolation of hearing the successor of the Galilean, Simon Peter, condemn clearly, openly and not by diplomatic allusions the crucifixion of innumerable "brothers of the Lord." One day during the Occupation, I asked the venerable Cardinal Suhard [of Paris], *who did so much behind the scenes for the Jews, "Your Eminence, order us to pray* [publicly] *for the Jews* [...at Notre Dame Cathedral]*." He lifted his arms up to heaven: there can be no doubt the occupiers had irresistible means of bringing pressure to bear, and that the silence of the Pope and the hierarchy was in fact a horrible duty; they wanted to avoid even worse misfortunes. Nonetheless, the guilt for a crime of this size falls to a large extent upon those who did not cry out, whatever might have been the reasons for their silence.*

How ironic it is that Mauriac, who knew enough not to mention the word "Jews" in his 1943 *Le cahier noir* lest his enemies dismiss him as a Jewish apologist, should reveal here that he had asked Cardinal Suhard to break the code of silence that he himself had observed in his book! Here he is also impugning Pius XII, who had followed the same pro-Allied protocol – and for the same reason – during the war years. Pathetically, Mauriac also tries to offer Cardinal Suhard as an example of heroism, yet the latter evaded responding to Mauriac's request to pray publicly for the Jews at Notre Dame. Instead, he raised his hands to heaven. He could not pray publicly for the Jews in his parish church, the seat of the Archbishop of Paris, for the same reason that Pius XII had been "silent" and that Mauriac had been "silent." Overt support of the Jews by a man who was supposedly neutral would have been tantamount to admitting that he too was a Jewish puppet, and Cardinal Suhard could not do that. Furthermore, there were instances when denunciations of German Jewish policy by Catholic clergy had led to reprisals, as when the Germans deported Jewish converts to Catholicism from the Netherlands after condemnation of Jewish deportations from the pulpits.

Elie Wiesel later declared, with characteristic magnanimity:[18]

For many centuries the Christian defined himself by the suffering he imposed on the Jew. [...] *Mauriac was sensitive to the problem. We became so close because of his recognition of Christian responsibility. He understood the part of*

---

pour une part non médiocre sur tous les témoins qui n'ont pas crié et quelles qu'aient été les raisons de leur silence."

When the English translation of Poliakov's book was published by Syracuse University Press in 1954 under the title *Harvest of Hate*, Mauriac's foreword was replaced with a new one by Reinhold Niebuhr.

[18] Cargas, *Conversation,* 35.

> *the Vatican, and he was the first to come out against Pius XII. It wasn't Rolf Hochhuth, it was Mauriac.*

Of course, in this instance Wiesel is correct, and his words clearly indicate familiarity with Mauriac's foreword to Poliakov's *Bréviaire de la haine.*

In writing this foreword in 1951, Mauriac provided cover and legitimacy for those extremists in the French Jewish community who wanted to stigmatize Pope Pius XII. He apparently gave no thought to how his words would be manipulated in the future, nor did he understand that he was entering into conspiracy with the Jewish organizations, the forerunners of today's Holocaust fundamentalists, that backed Poliakov. Yet, in attacking the Pontiff he was acting in a way that could bolster his candidacy for the Nobel Prize a year later. When he cashed his Nobel check in late 1952, he not only secured financial independence for his family, he also established a paradigm for later generations of ambitious Catholic intellectuals. Here the names of three such persons come to mind: the Rev. Robert Drinan, S. J.; Sr. Carol Rittner, RSM; and the former Paulist priest, James Carroll. All of them have advanced their careers by denying their religious heritage in order to cater to powerful Zionist Jewish interests.

Ironically, Mauriac's foreword for Poliakov in 1951 came back to haunt him in 1963. In that year, Mauriac's words about never having the consolation of hearing "the Galilean, Simon Peter, condemn clearly, openly and not by diplomatic allusions, the crucifixion of innumerable 'brothers of the Lord,'" were used to promote an anti-Catholic indictment of Pius, Rolf Hochhuth's play *The Deputy*. Hochhuth and his producers excerpted the line and placed it in a prominent place in the program distributed to theatergoers. When Mauriac, who had not been informed in advance of this use of his words, found out about it, he was thunderstruck and terribly embarrassed. He must have come to a sudden realization that certain of his Jewish "friends" were now using his words in a context that he could not have imagined possible back in 1951. But if he had received help and support from European Jews when he was nominated for the Nobel Prize for Literature in 1952, certain chickens were coming home to roost, and he had nothing to complain about. To add insult to injury, Mauriac's verbal assault on Pius XII still appears in the foreword to printed versions of Hochhuth's theater production.

Mauriac's Four Jewish Messiah Figures Prior to Meeting Wiesel

When Elie Wiesel burst into Mauriac's life in 1955, he fit neatly into Mauriac's philo-Semitic worldview. In fact, Mauriac's obsession over – and abusive relationship with – Wiesel, which would span the years 1955-1967, was not the first attachment he formed to a Jewish figure. At the top of his list was Jesus, whom he revered as a member of the Trinity and Son of God. Then there was Captain Alfred Dreyfus, whose guilt had been taken on faith in his right-wing family during his childhood. (Mauriac's mother, a traditional Catholic, referred to the chamber pot that graced each bedroom as "le zola," in memory of the journalist Emile Zola, who had defended Dreyfus.) Such was the political background from which Mauriac had come: contempt for Dreyfus as a German spy. But, as I have shown above, after his abrupt move to the left and his alliance with Jewish interests after 1936, Dreyfus became a hero to him.

The third Jewish figure to whom he developed a strong personal attachment was the converted Jew and Catholic priest Jean-Pierre Altermann. Of Russian-Jewish heritage, Altermann was seven years Mauriac's junior. He had started out in life as a poet, painter and art critic before converting to Catholicism and studying for the priesthood. He was baptized at the age of 27 and, six years later, ordained a priest in 1925 at age 33. It was in part through Mauriac's friendships with Jacques and Raïssa Maritain and with the lesser-known writer Charles du Bos that Altermann entered Mauriac's life in the late 1920s. Altermann, who had been instrumental in converting du Bos to Catholicism about 1927, became Mauriac's confessor on du Bos's recommendation in 1929. At this time, Mauriac's life was in turmoil. In his forties, married and the father of four children, he had been involved for the past few years in an adulterous homosexual relationship with a young Swiss diplomat whose identity remained a taboo subject for years. Jean Lacouture, for instance, in his highly detailed but conformist 1980 biography of Mauriac, dismisses the question completely:[19]

Details about the personal crisis he had just been through are of little interest.

But thanks to the publication of the new Mauriac biography by Jean-Luc Barré, we know that this lover was Bernard Barbey, an extremely handsome man who was fifteen years Mauriac's junior. A novelist as well as diplomat, he and his wife Andrée would remain closely tied to Mauriac until the latter's death in 1970. Thus, it seems that both wives tolerated their husbands' relationship for many years. In the late 1920s, however, Mauriac seems to have undergone a spiritual crisis over this relationship with Barbey, since it was putting a severe strain on his family life.

---

19 Jean Lacouture, *François Mauriac* (Paris: Seuil, 1980), 231: "Peu importe les détails de l'épreuve affective qu'il vient d'affronter." Mauriac's detractors would later hint that he had been a closet homosexual. Robert Brasillach, the novelist and columnist for the collaborationist newspaper *Je Suis Partout* during the Occupation, made reference to such rumors. Later, Roger Peyrefitte made the same accusation. Writing in a deliberately scandalous and exaggerated manner, he nonetheless encapsulated comments that Mauriac's enemies liked to repeat about him. Peyrefitte's "Lettre ouverte à François Mauriac" appeared in *Arts*, May 6, 1964, 1.

Altermann arrived on the scene just as Mauriac was writing the novel *Ce qui était perdu* [*That Which Was Lost*] (Paris: Grasset, 1930), in which he was trying to bring closure to the experience he had just been through. Incredibly, Altermann, as Mauriac's confessor, read drafts of the book as it progressed and made suggestions for improvement. Thus, he not only combined his two vocations, to literature and to the priesthood, he also had a decisive influence on *Ce qui était perdu*, the only one of Mauriac's novels that gives prominence to a homosexual character. By May 1930, Altermann had been du Bos's confessor for several years, but du Bos was growing tired of the man, and complained to Mauriac about him. Mauriac reminded him that they should not allow Altermann's domineering personality to become an obstacle to spiritual progress, but rather chalk up their problems with Altermann to differences in ethnic origin, education and personality. The period of deepest rapport and understanding between Mauriac and his confessor occurred while Mauriac was writing *Ce qui était perdu*, but from then on it was all downhill. Although the priest was invited to attend Mauriac's inauguration into the French Academy in 1933, he stayed away, for by this time their friendship was over.

Lacouture attributes their breakup to a number of factors, including the fact that religion and literature had been too intimately combined, with Altermann abusing his entree into Mauriac's life to trespass even further into his creative life. He fails to consider the possibility that there might have been a homosexual dimension to the relationship between the two men, and Jean-Luc Barré seems to agree with him. Nonetheless, Mauriac's relationship with Altermann, a Jewish man with a domineering personality, was one-sidedly abusive and self-destructive. This experience prefigures the nature of his later deep attachment to Wiesel. Mauriac would later write that Altermann was a holy man:[20]

> [...] *on the border-line between the two Testaments* [...] *the ideal priest for helping a lost sheep who was worn out and who did not put up a fight, asking only to be carried on strong shoulders, and letting himself be carried along.* [...] *But as he got his strength back, he felt more and more uncomfortable about being led along in this way* [...]

Mauriac would later use the same image to describe Wiesel, stating that, "like John the Baptist, he stands on the border between the two testaments."[21]

---

[20] Mauriac, *Œuvres autobiographiques*, 748: "[...] à la frontière des deux Testaments [...] le prêtre le mieux fait pour secourir une brebis exténuée qui ne se débat plus, qui ne demande plus qu'à être prise sur des épaules robustes et à s'abandonner. A mesure que les forces lui reviendront, elle souffrira plus malaisément d'être portée [...]"

[21] François Mauriac, *Bloc-Notes*, ed. Jean Touzot (Paris: Seuil, 1993), vol. 3 (May 29, 1963), 362: "Elie Wiesel se tient sur les confins des deux testaments: c'est la race de Jean-Baptiste [...]"

Mauriac's Admiration for Pierre Mendès-France

In 1954, Mauriac was still conscious of the debt he owed to those Jewish friends who had presumably helped him win the Nobel Prize in 1952. Thus, in his "*Bloc-Notes*" newspaper columns during 1953 and early 1954, he made much of a young politician named Pierre Mendès-France. His obsession with the man offers an eerie echo of his earlier obsession with Altermann. As Jean Lacouture has written: "It's slowly that Pierre Mendès-France, deputy from the Eure [Department], enters Mauriac's field of vision,"[22] but by the time "PMF" came to power as prime minister in June 1954, Mauriac was beside himself. He wrote in his "*Bloc-Notes*" column as if "PMF" was nothing less than another expression of his long-awaited Jewish messiah. Although he belonged to the anticlerical Radical Party, he was acting in accordance "with our faith and our hope as Christians."[23] Mendès-France, who became prime minister on June 18, 1954, fourteen years to the day after de Gaulle's historic plea to the French people from London to continue the battle against Germany, was in Mauriac's opinion a Jew who brought Catholics and Jews together. When "PMF" was booted out after only eight months in office, Mauriac claimed that his fall was caused by the fact that he was too courageous and too honest, and compared him to Alfred Dreyfus, who had also been, in Mauriac's view, courageous and innocent.

Wiesel would fit neatly into Mauriac's world-view, for whom Jesus, Dreyfus, Altermann and Mendès-France all shared a common trait in their Jewishness. After getting to know Wiesel and hearing him talk, Mauriac would have no difficulty in comparing this foreigner from a mysterious background to Jesus himself. In fact, when he dedicated his book *Le fils de l'homme* (*The Son of Man*, 1958) to Wiesel, he called him a "crucified Jewish child." Unlike Dreyfus and Mendès-France, who were born into prominent Jewish families that were highly acculturated and thoroughly French, Wiesel had been raised as a Hasid in a ghetto atmosphere in Eastern Europe. Although Wiesel spoke French, his speech was accented, and he had no university degree. Nonetheless, Mauriac would embrace him without hesitation.

---

22 Lacouture, *Mauriac*, 542: "C'est lentement que Pierre Mendès-France, député de l'Eure, entre dans le champ de vision de Mauriac."

23 Mauriac, *Bloc-Notes*, vol. 1, 118. "Pierre Mendès-France, tout radical qu'il est, a agi en Indochine, à Tunis et va agir demain au Maroc selon ce qu'exigent notre foi et notre espérance de chrétiens."

Chapter II
Wiesel before Mauriac: Inherited Hatreds and Suspicions

The Myth of Wiesel's Idyllic Childhood

The Zionist media fuel the myth that Elie Wiesel is a moral authority because he survived "the Holocaust."[37] As *Time* put it in 1986, he is special not only because he survived to bear "witness to the century's central catastrophe," but also because his name is virtually synonymous with "the Holocaust," "a term Wiesel brought into currency," according to *Time*.[38] This hymn of praise arose from that influential pro-Zionist weekly as Wiesel's career was at its zenith. He had just been awarded the Nobel Peace Prize. He was now a living saint in a secular society.

This exalted status helps to explain why Jack Kolbert, his English-language authorized biographer, paints an idyllic picture of Wiesel's childhood. If Wiesel is considered to be a saintly man today, the reasoning goes, his early life must have already given signs of his future sanctity. Kolbert, intent on delivering a work bordering on hagiography, wanted to show that the man's sanctity and intelligence dated back to his ghetto childhood in Romania. Thus, he emphasizes Wiesel's violin lessons, but studiously

---

37 I shall argue below that "the Holocaust," with its implications of a sacrificial offering and its generally accepted definition as the attempted extermination of European Jewry, resulting in some six million deaths, is far from describing the historical reality. Due to the prevalence of the term in this book, I have chosen to employ it without quotation marks or the skeptic's "so-called" or "alleged." The reader should bear in mind that my skepticism of the orthodox Holocaust narrative is implicit throughout.

38 Richard Zoglin, Mitch Gelman, "Lives of Spirit and Dedication; The World Pays Tribute to Eleven Who Stirred Emotions and Laid Foundations; Peace: Elie Wiesel," *Time*, October 27, 1986, 66f.

avoids mentioning his subject's childhood mental problems and neurotic fears. He writes:[39]

> *Happy were the days of Wiesel's childhood. Growing up in a tightly knit family of loving parents and siblings was indeed a joyful period.*

While Kolbert systematically omits the dark side of Wiesel's childhood, the great man's other authorized biographer, Philippe-Michel de Saint Cheron, who writes in French, is a bit more forthcoming.

There is very little objective documentation about the early years of Elie Wiesel's life. Most administrative records have either been lost or destroyed. Since Wiesel is still alive, various administrative organizations deny researchers access to what they consider private records. Thus, if we want to know about Wiesel's life before Auschwitz, we must depend in large part on what he has chosen to reveal about himself. The primary sources for reconstructing these years are the two volumes of autobiography, *Tous les fleuves vont à la mer* (Paris: Seuil, 1994), and *…et la mer n'est pas remplie* (Paris: Seuil, 1996).[40] In addition, there are various articles, interviews and nonfiction books that contain autobiographical material. Wiesel also claims that *Night* is an autobiography, and the opening pages of that work deal briefly with his life before being deported to Auschwitz.

As a boy, Wiesel was very frail, both physically and mentally. He was the third of four children, and the only boy. His parents owned a successful grocery store on the ground floor of their home. They had two Jewish employees at the store, and a gentile maid named Maria. Wiesel's father was often absent from the store, but his wife and two older daughters routinely stood in for him. Wiesel himself hardly ever did. Instead, he spent his time away from studying the Talmud or praying in the synagogue in hanging out with the village eccentric, a man called Moshe the Beadle. According to Saint Cheron, Wiesel "preferred by far to spend his time with Moshe the Beadle, also called Moshe the Madman, listening to him tell his weird stories."[41] There is no evidence that Wiesel played with other children or that he had any friends, either boys or girls; he preferred to hear his bizarre adult acquaintance's tall tales. Moshe prefigures other "friendships" with older men in the years ahead, including his Talmud tutor in Sighet in 1943/44, when he was at the threshold of adolescence; the Jewish doctors at the Monowitz SS hospital in January 1945; a man calling himself "Shu-

---

39 Jack Kolbert, *The Worlds of Elie Wiesel* (Selinsgrove, Pa.: Susquehanna University Press, 2001), 23.

40 These works have been translated as Elie Wiesel, *All Rivers Run to the Sea* (N.Y.: Knopf, 1995), and Elie Wiesel, *And the Sea Is Never Full* (N.Y.: Knopf, 1999).

41 Philippe-Michel de Saint Cheron, *Elie Wiesel: Pèlerin de la mémoire* (Paris: Plon, 1994), 21: "Il préférait de loin passer ses rares temps libres avec Moché-le-Bedeau, appelé également Moshé-le-Fou, l'écouter raconter ses histories un peu bizarres."

shani" in Paris after the war, and of course the closet homosexual François Mauriac.

Wiesel had a neurotic attachment to his mother, which helps to explain why he liked to stay in bed all day. He simply wanted to be close to her at all times. He later wrote:[42]

> *Does that make you smile, Dr. Freud? I was attached to my mother. Too attached? All she had to do was leave me to go help my father in the store, and I started to shake under the covers. If I was separated from her, even for a few moments, I felt rejected, exiled.*

His parents could not understand why their son was so strange. According to Saint Cheron, "he was such a skinny kid, and his health caused his parents so much concern that they took him to one doctor after another."[43] Of particular worry to them was another one of his neurotic obsessions, the one about being "buried alive."[44] To their credit, they realized that a fear like this was abnormal. According to Saint Cheron, Wiesel's father, "when he wasn't waiting on customers, was an avid reader, including the works of Freud."[45] One can only speculate that he might have been reading Freud in an attempt to find out what made his son tick. Because of Wiesel's mental problems, his parents took him to a number of psychiatrists for analysis:[46]

> *Childhood, for me, was sickness. I was often sick. My mother used to take me to Hasidic Jewish sages to have them bless me, and to consult eminent professors. That's how I came to visit Budapest; doctors had referred me there to be examined by renowned specialists.*

Clearly, Wiesel's problem was psychological, not physical. As for his physical appearance, we have to imagine him "with his *payess*, the curly sidelocks that hang down in front of the ears of Orthodox Jews, his Hassidic hat, and his *talith qatane*, the little prayer shawl that the most pious of Jews wear daily under their clothes."[47]

---

42 Elie Wiesel, *Tous les fleuves vont à la mer* (Paris: Seuil, 1994), 18f.: "Cela vous fait sourire, docteur Freud? J'étais attaché à ma mère. Trop? Il suffisait qu'elle me quitte, qu'elle aille aider mon père au magasin, pour que je me mette à trembler sous ma couverture. Loin d'elle, ne fût-ce que le temps d'une brève absence, je me sentais rejeté, exilé."

43 Saint Cheron, *Elie Wiesel,* 25: "[…] il était un enfant maigre, qui consultait médecin après médecin, tant sa santé causait d'inquiétude à ses parents. "

44 *Ibid.*, 25: "Enterré vivant."

45 *Ibid.*, 22: "[…] entre deux clients, il lisait beaucoup, jusqu'aux ouvrages de Freud."

46 François Mitterrand, Elie Wiesel, *Mémoire à deux voix* (Paris: Odile Jacob, 1995), 41: "L'enfance, c'est aussi pour moi la maladie. J'étais souvent malade. Ma mère m'emmenait chez les maîtres hassidiques pour leur bénédiction, et consulter des professeurs renommés. Si j'ai pu visiter Budapest, c'est parce que les médecins m'y envoyaient me faire examiner par les grands spécialistes."

47 Saint Cheron, *Elie Wiesel*, 16: "[…] avec ses *payess*, ces mèches de cheveux qui pendent derrière les oreilles des juif orthodoxes, son chapeau hassidique et son *talith qatane*, son petit châle de prière que les plus pieux portent sous leur vêtements en permanence."

As a child, Wiesel admired his father. But since Shlomo Wiesel was devoted to helping others, Wiesel seldom saw him:[48]

> *I used to see him only on the Sabbath. And the rest of the week he would go around taking people out of jail.*

In a word, while Wiesel was zealously studying his religious texts, his father was a community activist. This physical and psychological distance between the two would be a real problem after the Germans deported them to forced labor. Since Wiesel and his father barely knew each other, the chasm between them would widen in the stressful atmosphere of Auschwitz and Buchenwald. Ironically, while Wiesel laments the fact that he hardly knew his father as a boy, later he became, like his father, a Jewish activist. While Elie's own son, Shlomo, was growing up, Wiesel was often absent:

> *As for my son, I can tell you one thing. Since he was born, I have become doubly involved in public affairs. Because I brought a life into the world, it's my duty to make the world better for him.* (Journey, 83)

In any case, Wiesel has tended to present his father as a non-observant Jew who, philosophically, would be called a secular humanist today.

Ellen Fine, who taught courses in French literature at the City University of New York (CUNY) during the approximately seven years when Wiesel also worked there (1969-1976), struck up a friendship with him and became his first biographer. In her study of his literary career, she contrasts the secular humanism of Wiesel's father with his mother's religious beliefs and observance. His mother, she tells us, wanted him "to be both a rabbi and a Ph.D."[49] Fine, a pioneer in creating the Wiesel myth, tells us that, at the age of twelve, he wrote a long commentary on the Bible. His mother was understandably quite proud of this alleged accomplishment. Then, after the war, Wiesel is said to have made an astonishing discovery. According to Fine, who presumably relied on Wiesel for her information, his lengthy commentary, which had been written in 1941, was "found some twenty years later under a pile of discarded volumes in the only synagogue left in Sighet." (*Legacy*, 4) Fine accepts this tale at face value. Kolbert, who rivals Fine for sheer gullibility, also believes the story, and claims that it foreshadows great things to come:[50]

> *Decades following his departure from Sighet, when he returned, he was surprised to find among the hundreds of Jewish books that still remained in an otherwise destroyed community a copy of a book containing the same boyhood*

---

48 John Joseph Cardinal O'Connor and Elie Wiesel, *A Journey of Faith* (N.Y.: Fine, 1991), 48f.

49 Ellen Fine, *Legacy of Night* (Albany: SUNY Press, 1982), 4.

50 Kolbert, *Worlds*, 22.

commentaries. This rediscovery confirmed his decision someday to become a professional writer.

Saint Cheron avoids any reference to the alleged discovery, thus telegraphing his doubts about the "commentary."

Wiesel himself considerably downsized his claim to youthful brilliance in the first volume of his autobiography. Of his discovery at the former synagogue, he wrote:[51]

> *I wanted to see the synagogues again. Most were closed. In one I stumbled upon hundreds of holy books covered with dust. The authorities had taken them from abandoned homes and stored them here. In a frenzy, I began to look through them, and of course I discovered a few that had belonged to me. I kept on searching, and then searched some more. In a book of commentaries on the Bible, I stumbled upon yellowed and withered sheets of paper. I had written them at the age of thirteen or fourteen. It was my commentary on other commentaries. The writing style was clumsy, the thoughts confused.*

Finally, in his interview book with François Mitterrand, *Mémoire à deux voix*, Wiesel seems to express remorse about the fibs he has told about himself over the years:[52]

> *For me, it's a dialogue. A dialogue between the child in me and the adult that he has become. He* [the child] *weighs on my work. Sometimes I feel as though that child is with me, asking me questions, and judging me.*

Wiesel's Divine Election Is Foretold

In addition to the tale of his youthful commentary on the Torah, Wiesel also concocted a tale according to which his divine selection as "a great man in Israel" had been revealed to his mother before her death. This story, repeated by Wiesel over the years, received its definitive form in the opening pages of *Tous les fleuves*. By then, Wiesel had been the High Priest of the "Holocaust," the secular faith of the United States, since 1985, when President Ronald Reagan awarded him the Presidential Medal of Freedom at the White House. This high office would later be confirmed by Presidents Bush I, Clinton, Bush II and Obama. Perhaps his story of his desig-

51 Wiesel, *Tous les fleuves*, 477: "Je tiens à revoir les synagogues. La plupart sont fermées. Dans l'une, je bute sur des centaines d'ouvrages sacrés qui traînent dans la poussière: les autorités les ont ramassés dans les maisons abandonnées et déposés ici. Fiévreusement, je me mets à fouiller et, bien entendu, je découvre quelques livres qui m'appartenaient. Je fouille encore, et encore. Dans un livre de commentaires de la Bible, je tombe sur des pages jaunies, flétries: je les avais écrites à l'âge de treize-quatorze ans. Mon commentaire des commentaires. Ecriture maladroite, pensées confuses [...]."

52 Mitterrand, Wiesel, *Mémoire*, 31f.: "Pour moi, il s'agit d'un dialogue. Un dialogue entre l'enfant en moi et l'adulte qu'il est devenu. Il pèse sur mon œuvre. Parfois je sens que l'enfant m'accompagne, m'interroge, et me juge."

nation as "a great man in Israel" is an effort to justify these undeserved honors.

According to the story, in 1936, when he was eight years old, a famous rabbi, the "Rabbi of Wizhnitz," came to Sighet, and gave his blessing to those of the faithful who sought it. When Wiesel's mother presented little Elie to him, he was able, through his mystical powers, to divine her son's extraordinary calling to be a "great man in Israel." When the rabbi prophesied Wiesel's future greatness to his mother, she began to cry, but little Elie, unaware of the content of the prophecy, did not understand her tears. Thus, for the last years of her life, from 1936 to her untimely death in the summer of 1944, she never told him the reason why she cried. After the war, Wiesel learned the Rabbi of Wizhnitz's secret from his cousin, Reb Anshel Feig, who was gravely ill in New York. Feig allegedly sent for Wiesel in order to have his blessing before he died. When Wiesel went to see him at the hospital, Feig told him the words from the rabbi that had made his mother cry:[53]

> *Sarah, know that your son will become a* gadol b'Israël, *a great man in Israel, but neither you nor I will be there to see it; that's why I'm telling you now* [...]

Feig then went on to explain why he had summoned Wiesel before dying:[54]

> *If the Rabbi of Wizhnitz had so much faith in you, your blessing must count for something in heaven.*

Ironically, by the mid-1990s, Wiesel's claim to be "a great man in Israel" was becoming increasingly less persuasive in that country. For while he could claim with some validity to be a "great man in the pages of the *New York Times*," or a "great man in the Zionist-tilted U.S. media," of all places on the planet it is Israel where Wiesel's self-promotion is the most harshly criticized. In fact, one cannot help but think of the term used by the Israeli philosopher and man of letters, Avishai Margalit, to describe Wiesel: "kitschman of genius."[55] The term seems a lot more precise than "great man in Israel."

The rabbi's alleged prediction of Wiesel's future greatness shares a number of points with the story of the presentation of Jesus to the prophet Simeon in the Gospel of Luke (2: 33-5). There, Simeon, who has been assured by God that he will not die before seeing the Messiah with his own eyes, recognizes Jesus immediately. As he tells Mary and Joseph of their son's future greatness, "the child's father and mother stood there wonder-

---

53 Wiesel, *Tous les fleuves*, 22: "Sarah, sache que ton fils deviendra un *gadol b'Israël*, un grand homme en Israël, mais ni moi ni toi ne serons là pour le voir; c'est pourquoi je te le dis maintenant [...]"

54 *Ibid.*, 23: "Si le Rabbi de Wishnitz avait une telle foi en toi, ta bénédiction doit compter au ciel [...] "

55 Avishai Margalit, "The Kitsch of Israel," *NYRB*, November 24, 1988, 23.

ing at the things that were being said about him." Simeon is explicit about Jesus' calling: "You see this child: he is destined for the fall and for the rising of many in Israel, destined to be a sign that is rejected – and a sword will pierce your own heart too – so that the secret thoughts of many may be laid bare." In Wiesel's telling of his life, the Rabbi of Wizhnitz reminds us of Simeon, his mother plays the role assigned to Mary (and Joseph), while he, of course, is the future "great man in Israel." In his own personal mythology, as well as in the existential and absurdist religion of "the Holocaust," Wiesel takes the place of Jesus.

Wiesel Taught to Hate Catholicism as a Child

Wiesel's family and culture inculcated in him a dislike and distrust of Catholics. He developed these attitudes early in life. The Hasidic Jews among whom he was raised generally avoided contact with gentiles who, according to Wiesel, were about 60 percent of the population in Sighet.[56] Hasidic Jewish people, then and now, have considered non-Jews potential enemies, and this must be taken into consideration when evaluating Wiesel's fierce and determined hatred of Catholicism. This hatred sprang in part from the system of segregation enforced by the town's rabbis. To ensure that their flocks shunned gentiles (the fear of intermarriage was even stronger than it is today), they filled their heads with terrifying ideas. Thus, Wiesel grew up in a Judeocentric world with attitudes to match. Years later, he wrote:[57]

> *My dream back then? To live in a Jewish world, completely Jewish, a world where Christians would have scarcely any access. Before the war, I avoided everyone who came from the other side – that is, from Christianity. Priests frightened me. I avoided them; so as not to pass near them, I would cross the street. I dreaded all contact with them. I feared being kidnapped by them and baptized by force. I had heard so many rumors, so many stories of this type; I had the impression that I was always in danger.*

In addition to his strange obsession about being buried alive, mentioned by Saint Cheron, and his fear of being kidnapped, alluded to here, Wiesel had a neurotic fear of the incense used in some Catholic religious ceremonies. Of course, as an Orthodox Jew he was strictly forbidden by Jewish law from entering a Catholic church, but Wiesel's obsession went a bit beyond what the law required. He later recalled:[58]

---

56 Elie Wiesel, "The Last Return," *Commentary*, March 1965, 44. In this essay, Wiesel estimated Sighet's Jewish population to have been 10,000 out of 25,000, or 40 percent.

57 Elie Wiesel, *From the Kingdom of Memory* (N.Y.: Summit, 1990), 138. This same recollection is also presented in Wiesel's essay "Recalling Swallowed-Up Worlds, "*The Christian Century*, May 27, 1981, 609.

58 Mitterrand, Wiesel, *Mémoire*, 40: "Moi, j'avais peur de cette odeur-là. Chaque fois que

> *I was really afraid of that smell. Every time I walked in front of a church and smelled incense, I crossed the street.*

The rumors and stories with which the rabbis had filled young Wiesel's head worked quite well.

Wiesel has always claimed that his dislike of Catholics was reinforced by experiences at school:[59]

> *At school I sat with Christian boys of my age, but we didn't speak to one another. At recess we played separated by an invisible wall. I never visited a Christian schoolmate in his home. We had nothing in common. Later, as an adolescent, I stayed away from them. I knew them to be capable of anything: of beating me; of humiliating me by pulling my payess or seizing my yarmulka (skull cap) without which I felt naked.*

Wiesel nursed his anti-Catholic fears and feelings, even though he was not required to attend public school every day. According to Saint Cheron, (who calls Wiesel by the diminutive name for Elieser, "Lazar," in this part of his book):[60]

> *Lazar went to school very rarely, as he himself has admitted, because his father bribed his teachers, as was often done in the shtetl. During the last month of the academic year, he went to school only to prepare for his exams, which he passed without difficulty.*

In other words, Wiesel benefited from special consideration as a child and in an environment in which his Jewish family lived above the laws that theoretically covered everybody. According to Saint Cheron, this special treatment was permissible because of the superior training he had received at his yeshiva school: learning how to study and to learn quickly.[61] But in hindsight it clearly would have done this neurotic child good to interact with other youngsters, especially those from diverse backgrounds. Young Elie would have been far better off if he had had playmates. Instead, he spent too much time in the company of an adult, the eccentric Moshe, who would later be transformed into a character in *Night*.

Wiesel's Hatred of the Blessed Virgin

In 1991, Wiesel mentioned the Rabbi of Wizhnitz in *Journey of Faith*. There, however, instead of using the story to remind us of his own divine

---

je passais devant une église et que je sentais l'encens, je changeais de trottoir."

59 Wiesel, *Kingdom*, 138.

60 Saint Cheron, *Elie Wiesel*, 20: "Lazar alla fort peu à l'école, comme il le confie lui-même, car son père 'soudoyait' les maîtres, comme cela se faisait couramment au Shtetl. Au cours du dernier mois de l'année, il y venait pour se préparer aux examens, qu'il réussissait sans difficultés."

61 *Ibid.*, 20: "C'était là l'un des précieux apports de la *yeshiva*, que de savoir travailler et apprendre rapidement."

selection, he used it to impugn Catholic veneration of the Blessed Virgin. Recalling a trip back to Sighet, he described discovering that another family was living in his former home. They were Catholics. He stated:

> *When I was seven or eight, the Rabbi of Wizhnitz, who was a kind, compassionate man, came to my town. He sat me on his knee and examined me. That was the custom. I was the last child to be examined. I loved him with passion and fervor. I remember when he died. I took his picture and put it on the wall over my bed. Now* [...] *the nail was there, but not his picture! There was, I think, a picture of the Virgin Mary. And that hit me with excruciating pain. I left silently, and in a way I'm still there.* (*Journey*, 58)

Wiesel later modified this evidence of anti-Catholic bigotry, with its implication that the picture of the Virgin Mary was at least as offensive as the removal of the rabbi's picture, replacing the picture of the Virgin Mary with a crucifix. In *Tous les fleuves* he wrote:[62]

> *The nail is still there, and a large cross is hanging on it.*

This gratuitous change from the Blessed Virgin to Christ on the cross also suggests that the story is a pure invention to begin with. It is also important to understand that Wiesel's intent in including this incident in *Journey of Faith* was to offend his naïve and gullible "friend" and co-author, Cardinal O'Connor. Such insults are an essential part of the "dialogue" that has been taking place between Catholics and Jews since Vatican II, with the self-hating "interlocutors" on the Catholic side apparently enjoying every minute of the abuse they receive.

In a 1995 piece in the weekly magazine *Parade*, Wiesel put yet another spin on his return visits to his house in Sighet:[63]

> *Dear Maria. If other Christians had acted like her, the trains rolling toward the unknown would have been less crowded. If priests and pastors had raised their voices, if the Vatican had broken its silence, the enemy's hands would not have been so free.*

We have no way of knowing whether this person actually existed or is simply another creation of Wiesel's imagination. I say this because this particular type, the good-hearted Catholic servant in a Jewish household, or the Catholic of humble background who befriends Jews, is a standard feature of the master narrative of the Jewish Holocaust story. This character is thrust forward as a means of criticizing, by innuendo, Pius XII and the various Catholic institutional elites who were "silent" or who reacted to the Holocaust as "bystanders." Maria should thus be seen as a stock character who is used in counterpoint to Pius XII and the institutional Church.

Finally, the bigoted atmosphere in which Wiesel was raised brings to mind the words from the famous Rogers and Hammerstein song about

---

[62] Wiesel, *Tous les fleuves*, 95: "Le clou y est toujours. Une grosse croix y est suspendue."

[63] Elie Wiesel, "The Decision," *Parade*, August 27, 1995, 6.

prejudice from *South Pacific*. In order to hate, "you have to be taught, carefully taught," and that was how the rabbis of Sighet formed the young Wiesel.

Wiesel's Abusive Relationships with Older Men

An interesting and very important subject ignored by the conformist academic critics who comment on Wiesel's life and work is the tendency he exhibited as a young man to gravitate to, and then be abused by, older men. In the opening pages of *La Nuit*, when he talks of Moshe, the local eccentric, he makes it clear that this man had been watching him as he prayed in the local synagogue, and in fact it was there that Moshe initiated contact with Wiesel and began their liaison. As Wiesel sat lamenting the destruction of the Jewish temple in bygone days, the older man kept eyeing him. One evening, he approached and asked: "Why do you cry while you pray?"[64] The two whiled away days and nights together, supposedly in conversation on the Kabbala:[65]

> *We would talk this way almost every evening. We would stay in the synagogue after all the faithful had left, sitting there in the darkness by the light of a few flickering candles.*

In his autobiography, he relates a story of an abusive relationship with a Kabbalist master named Zalmen. He states that two other boys, Yiddele and Sruli, also joined in this relationship with Zalmen, but fell ill, losing the ability to speak. Neither the local rabbis and doctors, nor specialists brought in from as far away as Sweden, could cure them. Despite the consequences of this bizarre and sick relationship, Wiesel continued to see this man, against his father's strong opposition (*Tous les fleuves*, 50-53). He was now completely under his master's control. When, in 1943, his family decided to forgo its annual summer vacation, Elie was unperturbed: his "Kabbala master" needed him:[66]

---

64 Elie Wiesel, *La Nuit* (Paris: Les Éditions de Minuit, 1958), 17: "Pourquoi pleures-tu en priant?"

65 *Ibid.*, 18: "Nous conversions ainsi presque tous les soirs. Nous restions dans la synagogue après que tous les fidèles l'avaient quittée, assis dans l'obscurité où vacillait encore la clarté de quelques bougies à demi consumées."

66 Wiesel, *Tous les fleuves*, 56: "D'autres familles partaient en villégiature mais, moi, j'étais content de rester à la maison [...] Mon Maître avait besoin de moi [...] je m'attardai chez mon Maître et nous veillâmes toute la nuit [...] je sentis qu'une force terrible m'attirait, me faisait tomber dans un précipice, puis dans un autre [...] je me réveillai en sueur, hors d'haleine. Je délirais, je ne savais plus quand je rêvais ou quand j'étais lucide. Je ne savais même plus qui ni où j'étais. Assis par terre, cognant sa tête contre un mur, mon Maître me sembla désespéré: des sanglots secouaient tout son corps. Je sentis alors que la folie nous guettait. Mais j'étais déterminé à poursuivre notre quête, coûte que coûte."

> *Other families left on vacation, but I was content to stay at home. My Master needed me.* [...] *I stayed late at his house, and we stayed up all night.* [...] *I felt a terrible force pulling me, making me fall off one cliff, then another.* [...] *I awoke in a sweat, breathless. I was in a state of delirium and didn't know when I was dreaming or when I was lucid. I had lost touch with who and where I was. Seated on the floor and banging his head against the wall, my Master seemed desperate; his sobbing shook his whole body. I felt as if madness was overtaking the two of us. But I was determined to continue our quest, whatever the cost.*

This relationship with Zalmen foreshadows Wiesel's later strange liaison with a man called "Shushani."

It is unclear when Wiesel's relationship with Shushani actually began, but it seems to have lasted for two or three years, ending in 1948. Much as he had been picked out by Moshe back in Sighet, he was picked up by Shushani. The event occurred on a commuter train returning from Paris to the town where Wiesel lived with other refugee children. Thus began a perverse relationship in which Wiesel would prove to be no match for his abuser. In 1985, as he was becoming our Holocaust High Priest, he put the following spin on this early relationship:[67]

> *For three years, in Paris, I was his disciple. Alongside of him, I learned much concerning the perils of reason and language, concerning the ecstasies of the wise man and madman, concerning the mysterious evolution of a thought through the centuries.*

If, as Wiesel claims, he was later able to "study at the Sorbonne," it was not because of his non-existent secondary school training, but because of Shushani:[68]

> *Also, my teacher after the tempest, in the postwar tears, was Mordecai Shushani.* [...] *he was the man who made me become what I am, who left an imprint on my thought, on my feelings, on my language. I took him as a prototype for many of my messengers, for many of my teachers, in many of my tales.* [...] *he taught me philosophy.* [...] *He prepared me for the Sorbonne. Whatever I knew, I got from him.*

A decade later, while writing his autobiography, Wiesel was more honest about this abusive relationship. He reveals that Shushani would force him to state that he hadn't learned anything yet, while demanding that he beg for further instruction. But what was the real subject being taught? (*Tous les fleuves*, 154) One day, his abuser, as a pleasant surprise after all his previous maltreatment, gave him a special present: he decided to learn the Hungarian language in a mere two weeks, so they could speak in Wiesel's native language from time to time! (*Tous les fleuves*, 155) Wiesel, of

---

67 Irving Abrahamson, *Against Silence: The Voice and Vision of Elie Wiesel* (N.Y.: Holocaust Library, 1985), vol. 1, 27.

68 *Ibid.*, vol. 2, 134.

course, expects his reader to believe this nonsense. Yet, two weeks or not, this is a classic scenario of manipulation, in which the dominating abuser turns suddenly "nice." Wiesel admits the extent to which he was dominated:[69]

> *I couldn't and I didn't want to break with Shushani.*

Shushani constantly played mind games directed at Wiesel, who described the process this way:[70]

> *He would disappear, then come back again. Then there were his mood swings and temper tantrums, whether feigned or real.*

Their relationship ended on a sour note in 1948, when Shushani dumped him and disappeared. They supposedly met again in Boston in the early 1960s. As he, Wiesel, was about to give a lecture there – Shushani magically materialized out of nowhere and would not let him speak. Seizing the microphone, Shushani cried out:[71]

> *But I know who he* [Wiesel] *is. A faker, that's who he is. I read an article he once wrote in a Yiddish newspaper in Paris. And he misquoted the Midrash. Anyone who misquotes the sources has no right to speak in public!*

Needless to say, neither of Wiesel's authorized biographers, Kolbert or Saint Cheron, bothers to inquire into this strange relationship. Both prefer to play dumb, mentioning Shushani only in passing. Their reticence hints that Wiesel's relationship with this man has become a taboo subject too hot to touch.

It should be noted, however, that Wiesel learned, as a victim of abuse at the hands of Shushani, how to apply abuse to others as needed. An excellent example of such behavior occurred when, upon first meeting François Mauriac at his home in one of the swankiest neighborhoods in Paris, he got up and stormed out on his host for no apparent reason, as described below in Chapter III. This theatrical and manipulative gesture, which was a flagrant abuse of the manners practiced and expected in Mauriac's very much upper-bourgeois French social milieu, was abusive in both form and content. Wiesel's deliberate abuse of Mauriac's generous offer of hospitality apparently convinced his host that he had somehow, unintentionally, said or done something of an "anti-Semitic" nature. Since such an act would be

---

69 Wiesel, *Tous les fleuves*, 157: "Mais je ne pouvais ni ne voulais me détacher de Shoushani."

70 *Ibid.*, 159: "Ses disparitions, ses réapparitions, ses changements d'humeur, ses accès de colère, feints ou sincères."

71 Elie Wiesel, *One Generation After* (N.Y.: Random House, 1970), 122. This book is supposedly a "translation" of Wiesel's volume of essays, published a few months earlier, entitled *Entre deux soleils* [Between Two Suns] (Paris: Seuil, 1970). In reality, however, it contains only several chapters from the French book. The chapter in which the present quote is found, entitled "The Death of My Teacher," has no corresponding equivalent in the French volume.

severely frowned upon in Mauriac's social sphere, he followed Wiesel down the hall and begged him to come back into his apartment.

Learning French in Paris

According to Wiesel, the four hundred Jewish children who were sent from Buchenwald to France were divided into two groups: one religious and the other secular. He belonged to the religious group, consisting of about one hundred children. Illustration 2 shown here on p. 52 shows some of these boys; this photo and the accompanying caption come from the website of the U.S. Holocaust Memorial Museum (USHMM). The caption claims that Wiesel is pictured, but does not identify him. Wiesel began his studies in the town of Ambloy (Loir et Cher), and continued them at Taverny (Val d'Oise), a bit closer to Paris. Wiesel had continued to study the Talmud while at Auschwitz and Buchenwald, although the circumstances hardly lent themselves to such work. There exists no evidence to prove that Wiesel ever attended public schools in France or obtained a French *baccalauréat*, the secondary school graduation diploma, which is needed to enter the university system. The mystery surrounding the matter of his education as an adolescent, like that regarding his early sexual experiences, are taboo subjects that he passes over in complete "silence," and that friendly interviewers know is off limits.[72] Thus, it should come as no surprise that "Professor Wiesel," as Cardinal O'Connor obsequiously addressed him in *Journey of Faith*, has not a word to say about his non-existent secondary school studies in his two-volume autobiography.

Yet Wiesel would have us believe that he studied at the Sorbonne:[73]

> *I went on studying French – mainly to absorb the language – and I entered the Sorbonne to study literature, psychology, philosophy, psychiatry – in a very autodidactic manner. All I wanted was to study.*

The trick word here is "autodidactic." Wiesel might have attended a public lecture or two, but he never enrolled in a degree program. Nonetheless, his hagiographer, the irrepressible Jack Kolbert, proclaims naively:[74]

> *So proficient did he become that between 1948 and 1951 he felt comfortable enough with the language that he could enroll and study at the University of Paris's liberal arts program at the celebrated Sorbonne.*

Despite Wiesel's claim that he entered the Sorbonne, and Kolbert's assertion that he enrolled "in the liberal arts program at the celebrated Sor-

---

72 The prolix Wiesel has made a career of denouncing gentiles' "silence," but is himself silent all too often about matters relating to various contradictory aspects of his published work and official biography. Another subject of silence concerns Jewish responsibility for the ongoing injustices committed against the Palestinians.

73 Cargas, *Conversation*, 79.

74 Kolbert, *Worlds*, 26.

Illustration 2: Group portrait of Jewish displaced youth at the OSE (Œuvre de Secours aux Enfants) home for Orthodox Jewish children in Ambloy. Elie Wiesel is said to be among those pictured. Ambloy, France, 1945. (USHMM photo #28147)

bonne," there is no record that Wiesel ever entered a degree program at the Sorbonne, much less received a degree. Yet Kolbert wants us to believe that Wiesel advanced to at least the point where he could write a doctoral dissertation.

Ellen Fine, in her generally uncritical and laudatory book on Wiesel, also misleads her readers about Wiesel's education. She tells us that "a young French philosopher, François Wahl, helped him to learn French by introducing him to the great classical authors, beginning with Racine. Wiesel learned the language by listening in silence" (*Legacy*, x). Pious nonsense, of course, but it gets worse. Fine then claims that Wiesel embarked upon a plan of university study, but she is evasive, indeed totally silent, about dates, courses, programs and professors. Thus, she relates that "he took courses at the Sorbonne in philosophy and literature and, although he never officially completed his studies, he wrote a long dissertation on comparative asceticism" (5f.). In her narrative, Wiesel emerges as a hard-working student enrolled in a degree program at the university, not merely someone who hung out on the fringes in an "autodidactic manner." As for the "long dissertation," Fine identifies neither the subject of the thesis nor its director. One wonders, also in vain, which members of the Sorbonne faculty were on his dissertation committee. Unfortunately, Fine does not produce the name of even one former professor who is able to attest to having worked with the future Nobel laureate. Furthermore, it does not seem to have dawned on Fine that the writing of a thesis is the last obstacle in the academic steeplechase. It comes only after one has passed the preliminary hurdles, *i.e.*, course requirements and general exams. When did Wiesel take these exams, and what results were obtained? Is there any record of Wiesel ever having been a student at the Sorbonne? Has Fine been able to locate former friends, classmates or professors from these years? These questions all beg for answers, but Fine offers none.

With regard to the enigmatic François Wahl, about whom Fine furnished no details other than that he was a "young French philosopher," Wiesel claims in *Tous les fleuves* that the refugee organization in whose care he had been placed assigned the young Wahl to give him "private lessons" ("des cours particuliers," 150), and that they took place at Wahl's mother's apartment ("nos leçons ont eu lieu chez sa mère," 151). Did the other Jewish refugee children receive similar private tutoring services? It was Wahl, says Wiesel, who taught him to speak and read French, but the two broke up when Shushani reappeared in Wiesel's life in 1947 (151). The unreliable Jack Kolbert, wanting to present Wiesel as a full-fledged French intellectual before beginning his career as a writer, completely transforms both Fine's and Wiesel's portrait of Wahl. For Kolbert, Wiesel already speaks French when he meets Wahl at the Sorbonne where he teaches. Thus, Wahl is not Wiesel's language tutor, but his mentor in the field of philosophy. Bizarrely, Kolbert also changes Wahl's first name to Gustave! He writes:[75]

> *Elie Wiesel seems always to have been susceptible to influences by his greatest teachers. Throughout his life, he had* [sic] *generously acknowledged his indebtedness to them. One of these teachers was Gustave Wahl, a philosophy teacher in Paris.*

Later in his book, Kolbert tells us more about their relationship. He writes:[76]

> *Once he had gained sufficient competency in French, the young man moved to Paris, where he could pursue a university degree at the Sorbonne. Selecting mainly courses in philosophy and literature, he fell under the spell of his philosophy teacher, Gustave Wahl, who seems to have exerted much influence on his intellectual formation.*

Despite the attempts by Wiesel and his biographers to blur François Wahl's true identity, we know that he was born in 1925, accepted his homosexuality at the age of fifteen, and was an active homosexual for the rest of his life.[77] He also passed the very competitive civil service "*agrégation*" exam,

---

[75] *Ibid.*, 26-7.

[76] *Ibid.*, 181.

[77] Elizabeth Roudinesco, "François Wahl (éditeur et philosophe), est mort," *Le Monde*, September 14, 2014. www.lemonde.fr/disparitions/article/2014/09/15/mort-de-l-editeur-et-philosophe-francois-wahl_4487663_3382.html

which entitled him to be employed in the state education system as a "*professeur agrégé*," a prestigious title. His father, arrested by the Germans and deported to Auschwitz, died there in 1943, which helps to explain his interest in helping Wiesel. Wahl was a member of the Zionist Stern Gang between 1945 and 1948. Later in life, Wahl lived as a couple with his partner of many years, the Cuban artist and writer Severo Sarduy, until the latter's death in 1993.[78] Could Kolbert, whose book appeared nineteen years after Fine's, have known more about François Wahl's private life than Fine did? In fact, by 2001, Wahl was not only a well-known member of the Parisian intelligentsia, he was also an open and unapologetic homosexual. Did Kolbert change Wahl's name to "Gustave" in order to throw readers off the track of the real François Wahl? Did he do so in order to protect Wiesel from any possible suspicions of homosexuality because of his youthful association with this openly homosexual man who had come out of the closet at the age of fifteen?

In *From the Kingdom of Memory*, Wiesel presents himself as a consummate loner during these years in Paris:

> *I practiced asceticism on my own: in my home, in my little world in Paris, where I cut myself off from the city and from life for weeks on end. I lived in a room much like a prison cell – large enough for only one. The street noises that reached me were muffled. My horizon became smaller and smaller: I looked only at the Seine; I no longer saw the sky mirrored in it. I drew away from people. No relationship, no liaison came to interrupt my solitude. I lived only in books, where my memory tried to rejoin a more immense and ordered memory. And the more I remembered, the more I felt excluded and alone.* (142)

Yet Jack Kolbert presents a completely different and somewhat far-fetched view of the young man:

> *An almost instant convert to the Parisian lifestyle, Wiesel frequented the left-bank cafés, where as his favorite pastime he enjoyed playing chess.* (*Worlds*, 181)

The neurotic loner has also claimed that during his "Sorbonne days" he held a two-year graduate-level internship in psychiatry at a Parisian teaching hospital. He told Brigitte-Fanny Cohen that he did this internship because he had always been interested in the problem of mental illness:[79]

---

[78] Alain Badiou, "François Wahl ou la vie dans la pensée, " *Le Monde*, September 16, 2014. www.lemonde.fr/disparitions/article/2014/09/16/francois-wahl-ou-la-vie-dans-la-pensee-un-temoignage-d-alain-badiou_4488663_3382.html

[79] Brigitte-Fanny Cohen, *Elie Wiesel, qui êtes-vous?* (Lyon: La Manufacture, 1987), 63: "[…] les fous m'ont toujours fasciné. A Sighet, il y avait un asile de fous, et je m'y rendais tous les samedis pour leur porter de la nourriture. Après la guerre, à Paris, j'ai renoué avec eux; j'étudiais la littérature à la Sorbonne et j'avais choisi de préparer un certificat de psychothérapie. Pendant deux ans, tous les matins, je suivais des cours à l'hôpital Sainte-Anne. J'observais les malades."

> [...] *the insane have always fascinated me. In Sighet there was an insane asylum, and I went there every Saturday to bring them food. After the war I reestablished contact with them: I was studying literature at the Sorbonne, and had decided to prepare a minor in psychotherapy. For two years, every morning, I took classes at the Hôpital Sainte-Anne and observed the patients.*

His long-time friend, Jean Halpérin, also assures us that this is why Wiesel is so interested in mental illness:[80]

> *It's important to realize that during his school years in Paris he spent two years studying psychiatry at Saint-Anne Hospital in Paris.*

Nowadays, of course, neither Wiesel, in his autobiography, nor his two official biographers make any mention of these alleged advanced studies in psychiatry; the claim is just another one of Wiesel's many tall tales. The only scenario that makes sense is that Wiesel, lacking any diploma or training in medicine, came in contact with the renowned psychiatric hospital as a patient, not a practitioner. Did the morose and solitary Wiesel, battling doubts about his sexual, ethnic, religious, and linguistic identity, go there for outpatient counseling? Is that the real connection?

Despite his lack of either a secondary school degree or a college diploma, two major U.S. universities later gave Wiesel faculty appointments – appointments for which a Ph.D. degree is usually required. Since the early 1970s, he has taught first at the City University of New York and later at Boston University. At the latter institution, he still occupies his endowed chair, even though he has not been able to teach since June 2011, when he underwent open-heart surgery. It is possible that Wiesel invented the myth of his formal attendance at the Sorbonne and the internship at Saint-Anne Hospital in order to justify his academic appointments, for which he is clearly unqualified.

Wiesel's Trip to India

Wiesel made a trip to India in January 1952, traveling by boat, and seems to have stayed there for several weeks.[81] This journey has now been deleted, more or less, from his life story and except for Downing his commentators generally do not discuss it. Yet at one time he seemed to be pretending that the trip to India was linked to his advanced studies at the Sor-

---

80 Jean Halpérin, "Itinéraire, paysages intérieurs et message," in: David Banon *et al.*, *Présence d'Elie Wiesel* (Geneva: Labor et Fides, 1990), 29: "Il faut noter d'ailleurs, dans son itinéraire, pendant ses études à Paris, les deux années pendant lesquelles il fut étudiant en psychiatrie à l'Hôpital Sainte-Anne."

81 Frederick L. Downing, *Elie Wiesel: A Religious Biography* (Macon, Ga., Mercer University Press, 2008), 89.

bonne, for he claims to have gone there as a student of philosophy, seeking to broaden his philosophical base and to write his "dissertation":[82]

> *Later I went to India, having in mind to write a dissertation on comparative asceticism: Jewish, Christian, Hindu. I had written a huge volume, some six hundred pages or so, which I'm afraid to open – I'm sure it's not good. One day I will and probably will have to rewrite it. I didn't complete my studies. I had to work as a journalist, and it was hard work.*

The impression he gives here is that he had been an "ABD," an "all but dissertation," someone who had finished all the course work and examinations for a doctorate from the Sorbonne, and had simply failed to complete his dissertation. Wiesel's trip to India took place in 1952, and it enabled him to continue to work on learning English.[83] The trip was once touted as one of the major educational experiences of his life. In *From the Kingdom of Memory*, Wiesel expands somewhat on his statement above, which he had made to Harry Cargas some twenty years earlier. He tells us that in these years he was attracted to Eastern philosophy, but provides no dates or specifics:[84]

> *Disgusted with the West, I turned toward the East. I was attracted by Hindu mysticism; I was interested in Sufism; I even began to explore the occult domains of marginal sects here and there in Europe.*

These days, however, the importance of his trip to India has been downsized, and he says very little about it in *Tous les fleuves*.

Zionist Newspaperman

Wiesel started out in life earning his living as a teacher in the Jewish community in Paris. Ellen Fine tells us that "he earned a living as a tutor in Yiddish, Hebrew, and the Bible" (*Legacy*, 5). In *A Jew Today*, Wiesel said:[85]

> *Ten years of waiting, of intense study, of earning my keep as best I could: as choir director, camp counselor, tutor, translator. I obtained a scholarship from OSE, the children's aid organization that brought me to France. I taught the Bible and Talmud in Yiddish to children of the rich who understood only French; after all, I had to pay the rent. There were times when I had only two*

---

82 Cargas, *Conversation*, 79.

83 Fine, *Legacy*, 6.

84 Wiesel, *Kingdom*, 140-1.

85 Wiesel, *Un juif aujourd'hui* (Paris: Seuil, 1977), 26: "Je gagnais ma vie comme je pouvais; chef de chorale, moniteur de colonie de vacances, boursier de l'OSE, précepteur, répétiteur. J'enseignais la Bible et le Talmud, en yiddish, à des gosses de riches qui ne comprenaient que le français. Il me fallait bien payer le loyer. Quant aux repas, il m'arrivait de n'en prendre que deux par semaine. La guerre était finie, mais je continuais à souffrir de la faim. Puis le hasard voulut qu'un journal m'acceptât comme collaborateur."

> *meals in a week. The war was over, but I continued to live with hunger. Then, thanks to a stroke of luck, a newspaper hired me as a contributor.*

Wiesel began working as a journalist as early as 1947, when he was only nineteen years old. He was hired by the Zionist paper *Zion in Kanf*, a mouthpiece of the Irgun Zvai Leumi, which, led by Menachem Begin, carried out numerous terrorist attacks and several massacres in furtherance of its Jewish apartheid policies. He eventually came to be an editor of this Yiddish newspaper and "in the late forties, published articles five, six times a week."[86]

His early association with this group confirms his commitment, from his youth on, to the quite narrow, parochial and ultimately racist worldview in which he had been raised.[87] Ironically, he refers romantically – and approvingly – to this Zionist Jewish terror group as the "Palestinian Resistance movement."[88] Yes, terrorism is deplorable if Palestinians engage in it, but morally uplifting if Jews do so.

The Ten-Year Vow of "Silence"

After the success of *La Nuit* paved the way for Wiesel's gradual ascent to media celebrity, he began claiming that, right after the war, he had decided to write a book about his wartime experiences. At the same time, however, he claimed that, in order to make sure he told the story correctly, he had also imposed a ten-year vow of silence upon himself. With regard to this alleged ten-year vow of "silence," the only one of Wiesel's commentators to have probed the subject with any degree of skepticism has been Brigitte-Fanny Cohen. In her book-length interview of Wiesel in 1987, she asked why he needed ten years, and he answered:[89]

> *I felt that I needed ten years of preparation. Afterwards, it was time to leave the period of silence behind.*

Dissatisfied with this response, she raised the question again, and Wiesel retreated into existentialist jargon to formulate his response:[90]

> [...] *I had to act in such a way that silence would remain in the spoken word; silence and speech were not to be in opposition. And that takes time: I had to*

86 Wiesel, *One Generation*, 122.

87 Wiesel, *Tous les fleuves*, 194-5.

88 *Ibid.*, 194: "mouvement palestinien de Résistance."

89 B.F. Cohen, *Qui êtes-vous*, 41: "Je sentais que j'avais besoin de dix ans de préparation. Ensuite, il a fallu sortir de l'ère du silence."

90 *Ibid.*, 44: "En même temps, il fallait faire en sorte que le silence demeure dans le verbe; la parole et le silence ne devaient pas s'opposer l'une à l'autre. Et cela exige du temps: je devais être sûr que je pourrais dire ce que j'avais à dire, et surtout que je saurais le dire."

> *be sure that I could say what I had to say and especially that I would know how to say it.*

What Wiesel was really saying here was that, before publishing his book, he wanted to be sure that any alleged German atrocities allegedly proven at Nuremberg were still a part of the official history. He also wanted to write something original, and not simply repeat what other survivors had already written on the topic of Auschwitz:[91]

> *As soon as the Other appears*[92]*, he must out of necessity influence our own project. And that frightened me. That's why I gave myself ten years of silence.*

He also claimed that he waited ten years "because the number ten is a biblical number."[93]

---

91 *Ibid.*, 41: "Dès que l'Autre apparaît, il influe nécessairement sur notre projet. Et cela me faisait peur. Voilà pourquoi je me suis accordé dix ans de silence."

92 Probably a reference to Jean-Paul Sartre's famous phrase: "L'enfer, c'est les autres," meaning "Hell, this is other people." Hence, for Wiesel, if someone else (l'autre) were to publish a work dealing with the Holocaust before his work in progress (notre projet) appeared, it would in some way or other influence what he would or could say in his book. Since that possibility frightened him, he let ten years go by before publishing his book.

93 *Ibid.*: "Et aussi parce que le chiffre dix est un chiffre biblique."

Chapter III
Mauriac and Wiesel: The First Meeting

Mauriac's Version of the First Meeting

There are two versions of the first meeting between the two men. In 1958 Mauriac described it in a laudatory column on Wiesel that appeared in his regular space in *Le Figaro littéraire*.[94] The content of the column mirrors the text he had written for the foreword to *La Nuit*. His intention in publishing this foreword as a newspaper article was to promote Wiesel's book. While Mauriac's column did little to boost sales, we are fortunate to have it today. It offers an important touchstone to the self-serving version of their first encounter that Wiesel would publish in 1977, seven years after Mauriac's death.

Mauriac's sense of modesty prompted him to say nothing in the 1958 column about his behind-the-scenes role in convincing *Les Éditions de Minuit* to publish *La Nuit*.[95] Nor did he mention his editorial work on the manuscript, after Jérôme Lindon, the editor at *Les Éditions de Minuit*, had agreed to publish it. Finally he neglected to specify that his first interview with Wiesel had taken place in 1955, three years before the book was published. (I shall return to each of these points later.) Mauriac did, however, write of the emotions he experienced when the young Jewish man first came to his home. He began by stating that he had always been wary of

---

94 François Mauriac, "Un enfant juif," *Le Figaro littéraire*, June 7, 1958, 1, 4.

95 This publishing house, founded clandestinely in February 1941 by Pierre de Lescure and Jean Bruller (*alias* Vercors), had published Mauriac's patriotic pamphlet *Le cahier noir* in 1943. Mauriac wrote under the pseudonym of "Forez," a mountain range in south-eastern France. Starting in 1948, when Jérôme Lindon, scion of a very wealthy Jewish family, became publisher, *Les Éditions de Minuit* gradually became associated with avant-garde writers like Beckett and Robbe-Grillet.

granting interviews to foreigners, who might distort what he said and use it against France:[96]

> *That morning, the young Israeli who interviewed me for a Tel-Aviv newspaper inspired in me right away a sympathetic reaction that I couldn't fight off for very long because our conversation quickly touched on personal matters.*

Mauriac was still remarkably clear-headed at the age of seventy-three, for he seems to remember quite well what it was like to have lived in Paris during the war years, and what most people felt when they saw or heard of Jews being sent off to work in the East.[97] If during the war years he was incapable of imagining what he terms in the article the "Nazi extermination methods," he was certainly not alone. According to even the Jewish Holocaust narrative, scarcely anyone else, including the very well-informed Pope Pius XII, the Allied leaders, and even the various Jewish organizations, had any better information about an alleged "Nazi extermination," and much information that contradicted such claims. After all, Germany, a small country, was at war with the rest of Europe and the United States. It had an insatiable thirst for manpower, especially since Nazi ideology dictated that women remain at home and, as a general rule, be discouraged from working in factories. It was partly for this reason that by 1943 there were already over a million Frenchmen voluntarily working in Germany under the *STO* (*Service du Travail Obligatoire*) program.[98]

Jews drafted to be deported for work at Auschwitz were chosen for relocation to Poland not by the French or the Germans, but by the *Union Générale des Israélites de France* (*UGIF*), the governing body of the Jewish community in France that Marshall Pétain had created in 1941 specifically to look after Jewish interests during the Occupation. These people published their own newspaper, *Les Informations Juives*, and had a nearly complete registration list of all Jews residing in France. It was from these lists that the Jewish elders assembled the groups of people (mostly stateless Jews who had come to France from Eastern Europe) to be sent off to work in German factories in Poland.[99] Letters and packages came and went rou-

---

[96] Mauriac, "Enfant juif," 1: "Ce matin-là, le jeune Israëlien qui m'interrogeait pour le compte d'un journal de Tel-Aviv m'inspira dès l'abord une sympathie dont je ne pus guère me défendre longtemps car nos propos prirent vite un tour personnel."

[97] Mauriac discusses these issues in his *Journal du temps de l'Occupation*, in *Œuvres Complètes*, *op. cit.*, vol. II, 347-351. Other relevant information is found in his book *Le Bâillon dénoué: Après quatre ans de silence* (Paris: Grasset, 1945), 18.

[98] Pierre Arnaud, *Les STO: Histoire des Français requis en Allemagne nazie, 1942-1945* (Paris: Centre National de Recherche Scientifique, 2010.)

[99] Ariel Goldman, "Dannecker," in: Georges Wellers, André Kaspi, Serge Klarsfeld (eds.), *La France et la question juive, 1940-1944: actes du colloque du Centre de documentation juive contemporaine (10 au 12 mars 1979)* (Paris: S. Messinger, 1981), 281. Regarding the UGIF, see the two-volume study by Maurice Rajsfus, *Des Juifs dans la collaboration: L'UGIF, 1941-1944* (Paris: ÉDI, 1980); *Des Juifs dans la collaboration: Une Terre promise?* (Paris: L'Harmattan, 1989). See also: Michel Lafitte, *Un engrenage fa-*

tinely, despite the obvious transportation problems caused by the war. In addition, many French people, that is, non-Jews, also had relatives and friends who were already working in Germany or Poland, called "the General Government" by the Germans at the time. Thus, as the detainee literature has amply demonstrated in retrospect, the many factories located at camps like Auschwitz, for example, contained a veritable hodgepodge of nationalities in their work force, with forced laborers working side by side with "free" workers. Given this context of people routinely departing, voluntarily or not, to support the German war effort in the East, and with Jewish children sometimes left in the care of the Jewish elders of the *UGIF* when their parents were shipped off to concentration camps, we can better understand an astonishing remark that Mauriac now makes to Wiesel.

Mauriac told Wiesel that he reminded him of the Jewish children he claimed to have seen on the train at Austerlitz Station in 1942. As noted in Chapter I, Mauriac was actually telling a white lie here, for he did not actually witness that particular event. In reality, it was his wife and his eldest son who had seen those children. Mauriac later wrote that he thought nothing of it at the time, for it was an everyday event. Mauriac writes: "I was far from thinking that they were going to the gas chamber and the crematorium,"[100] and his skepticism was justified. It was only after the war, when the Allies discovered numerous corpses in certain camps in Germany, that these same Allies were able to impose the myth of "extermination camps." In so doing, they exploited the sufferings of men and women who had for the most part perished of disease, above all typhus, and who had often lacked proper treatment due to the interruption of food and medical supplies by Allied bombing. The newsreels and photos presented to the public became the basis of, and the justification for, the Allied version of what the war had been about. The new explanation was rolled out at Nuremberg, and came to undergird political arrangements in the postwar world. Mauriac, like the rest of those who had lived through the war, discovered only later that what had seemed like so ordinary, if deplorable, an event in 1942 now had to be completely reinterpreted. Some, including Pope Pius XII, never accepted this new interpretation of events. The Pope's disbelief has resulted in decades of defamation at the hands of the Holocaust fundamentalists and the Zionist media.

Most of those who, like Mauriac's wife, saw or heard of the deportations, gave them little thought at the time. Transferring the Jewish population to the East was growing in appeal to the Nazis, especially after a scheme for resettling European Jewry to Madagascar could not be realized.

tal: L'UGIF face aux réalités de la Shoah, 1941-1944 (Paris: L. Levi, 2003).

100 Mauriac, "Enfant juif," 1: "J'étais à mille lieues de penser qu'ils allaient ravitailler la chambre à gaz ou le crématoire."

The pro-German writer and intellectual Pierre Drieu la Rochelle, writing even before the war began, on July 29, 1938, gives a good idea of what kinds of resettlement people were thinking of when they talked about this subject:[101]

> *As for a solution to the Jewish problem, it can only be settled on a worldwide basis. Since Palestine is not large enough, other territories must be found. The Russians have created two Jewish Republics in their huge empire, one in the Crimea and the other in Siberia.*

Thus, when Mauriac wrote in 1958 that nobody, including him, had imagined that trains headed for the East meant extermination for the Jews on them, he was telling the truth. Similarly, his son Claude, who was with his mother on the morning they saw the Jewish children on the train at Austerlitz Station, speaks for both his father and the average Frenchman when he says:[102]

> *I want to state categorically that at that time we had no knowledge of the* [extermination] *camps.*

Here are the two future winners of Nobel prizes talking about the war years. One, the gullible older man, a closet homosexual, father of four, unfaithful husband and "Catholic writer," is physically attracted to this young Jewish man who has suddenly appeared in his life. The other is applying to the utmost the lessons he has learned from his masters. As Mauriac tells his visitor how terrible he feels about the Jewish children on the train, Wiesel brusquely asserts that he was in fact one of those children. Wiesel, of course, is not speaking literally, for he was nowhere near France in 1942. His claim is that he and his family were deported from Sighet, at that time in Hungary, to Auschwitz in 1944. At least three of the six members of his family survived the war. Nonetheless, Mauriac proclaims:[103]

> *He was one of them, he had seen the disappearance of his mother, a beloved little sister and his whole family, except his father, in the furnace fed by living creatures.*

Mauriac was apparently overwhelmed by the atrocity stories – regardless of their veracity – that Wiesel told him that day.

---

[101] Pierre Drieu la Rochelle, "Journal Politique: à Propos du Racisme," in: Philippe Ganier-Raymond (ed.), *Une Certaine France: l'Antisémitisme 1940-1944* (Paris: Balland, 1975), 46: "Pour ce qui est de la solution sioniste, elle ne peut être réglée que par une entente mondiale. Puisque la Palestine est insuffisante, il faut trouver d'autres territoires. Les Russes ont créé dans leur immense empire colonial deux républiques juives: l'une en Crimée, l'autre en Sibérie."

[102] Claude Mauriac, *Le temps immobile X: L'Oncle Marcel* (Paris: Grasset, 1988), 230: "Je précise que nous n'avions alors aucune connaissance des camps."

[103] Mauriac, "Enfant juif," 1: "Il était l'un d'eux; il avait vu disparaître sa mère, une petite sœur adorée et tous les siens, sauf son père, dans le four alimenté par des créatures vivantes."

Wiesel's Version of Their First Meeting

Wiesel wrote nothing about his first meeting with Mauriac during the latter's lifetime. Instead, he waited until 1977, seven years after Mauriac's death, before describing the event. He did so in a collection of essays entitled *Un juif aujourd'hui* (*A Jew Today*). Wiesel's story is that he first saw Mauriac in person at a reception held at the Israeli Embassy in Paris in 1954. This date is a complete invention on Wiesel's part, for he actually did not meet Mauriac until May 1955. With Mauriac dead, however, Wiesel seems to have thought that nobody would notice. Since it will be instructive to track him through this exercise in mendacity, let us play along with him.

First, why did Wiesel move the date of the first meeting forward one year? What role did Pierre Mendès-France play in his deception? Let us try to find out.

It was well known in 1954 that Mauriac's political affections were centered on Pierre Mendès-France, a Jew who had been prime minister since June 18, 1954. To Mauriac, he was France's new savior, replacing de Gaulle, who had gone into retirement in 1947. Mauriac heaped praise on the man in his newspaper columns. According to François Durand:[104]

> *It was Pierre Mendès-France who, in Mauriac's view between 1954 and 1956, incarnated France's highest hopes. At most, both men* [de Gaulle and Mendès-France] *were equally venerated, but he preferred the one who was actually in power at the time.*

When, in 1977, Wiesel claimed that his first meeting with Mauriac had taken place in 1954 rather than in 1955, he was unaware that Mauriac had mentioned, in his "*Bloc-Notes*" newspaper column of May 14, 1955, that he had recently made the acquaintance of a young, unidentified Jewish man. This entry had been generally lost from view until the eminent Mauriac scholar and Sorbonne professor Jean Touzot began publishing a paperback collection of Mauriac's "*Bloc-Notes*" newspaper columns. The article in question appeared in 1993 in the first of what would become Touzot's five-volume collection of reprints of Mauriac's newspaper columns, and when it did, Wiesel's claim to have first met Mauriac in 1954 was exposed as false. Mauriac wrote:[105]

---

104 François Durand, "Mauriac et de Gaulle," in: Jean Serroy (ed.), *de Gaulle et les Ecrivains* (Grenoble: Presses Universitaires de Grenoble, 1991), 42. "C'est Pierre Mendès-France qui, de 1954 à 1956, représente pour Mauriac l'espoir de la France. Tout au plus associe-t-il les deux hommes [de Gaulle et Mendès-France] dans une même vénération, mais avec une préférence pour celui qui est aux affaires."

105 Mauriac, *Bloc-Notes*, vol. 1, 271: "Que d'êtres différents m'ont longuement parlé tous ces jours-ci! Entre plusieurs autres, le professeur d'une université américaine; un Japonais, professeur lui aussi; des étudiants musulmans; un jeune Israélien qui fut un enfant juif dans un camp allemand où il a vu, à treize ans, tous les siens enfournés dans une

> *How many different people have come to see me in recent days! Among others, a professor at an American university, a Japanese professor, several Moslem students, and a young Israeli who as a child was interned in a German camp and, at the age of thirteen, saw his whole family killed in the gas chamber; but there was a revolt in the camp, and it was liberated on the very day when he was to be killed.*

Obviously, that "young Israeli" was Wiesel. Putting aside the exaggerations that Mauriac would later ascribe to his Jewish visitor in his 1958 newspaper column, "L'enfant juif," most notably that he saw "his whole family killed in the gas chamber," a falsehood that Mauriac credulously accepted, and such lesser fibs as Wiesel's claim that his "camp was liberated on the very day he was to be killed," which Mauriac also seems to have believed, this column confirms that Mauriac first met Wiesel in 1955, not 1954.

I now return to Wiesel's version of his first meeting with Mauriac. Wiesel claims in *Un juif aujourd'hui* that his editor in Israel had been urging him to arrange an interview with Mendès-France. He goes on to say that he decided that the best way to meet PMF would be to convince Mauriac, a Catholic, whom he did not know, to make the introduction:[106]

> *Knowing the admiration the Jewish prime minister bore the illustrious Catholic member of the Académie, why not ask the one to introduce me to the other?*

In retrospect, it is not too difficult to see why Wiesel, who was twenty-six years old in 1954, was drawn to Mauriac. The fact that he links Mendès-France to Mauriac also shows that he was well aware not only of Mauriac's high regard for PMF, but also of his sincere sympathy for Jews and Jewish causes. He considered the aging Catholic writer to be what he called an "ayev Yisrael," a friend of the Jewish people, and he was right. Wiesel clearly intended to exploit Mauriac's philo-Semitic views to advance his own career. In order to understand why Wiesel waited until 1977 to float his tale of approaching PMF through Mauriac, it is necessary to situate Wiesel in relation to both PMF and to French culture. PMF came from an established and highly assimilated French Jewish family, and possessed university degrees and political connections. Wiesel was fully aware that he was an outsider in French culture. He spoke French with an accent, had no family connections, and, perhaps worst of all, lacked any evidence of formal education.

As Wiesel tells it, summoning his courage to ask the great writer for an interview, he approached Mauriac and was surprised at the cordial response

---

chambre à gaz, et le camp s'est soulevé et a été délivré le jour même qui avait été marqué pour lui."

[106] Wiesel, *Un juif*, 28: "Sachant l'admiration que le président du Conseil (juif) vouait à l'académicien (catholique), pourquoi ne prierais-je pas celui-ci de me présenter à celui-là?"

he received. The great man actually asked whether he would like to visit him at home:[107]

> *"Would you like to come next Tuesday or Wednesday?" he asked me in his gravelly voice after consulting his appointment book. "Would early afternoon suit you?"*

As Wiesel relates the story, he was so overwhelmed that such a great man had turned out to be so approachable that he could not help but say to himself:[108]

> *Would it suit me? "Yes, thank you." I would have accepted any date, any hour. I felt myself blushing. I admired the great novelist's work, but I had no intention of questioning him about his characters, his technique or his life. Imposter, I thought, I am an imposter.*

Wiesel was indeed an impostor, for he wanted to ingratiate himself with Mauriac in the hope the aging Frenchman would be able to help him to find a publisher for a French version of his Yiddish novel, *Un di velt hot geshvign*, which was scheduled to appear a few months later, in November 1955, in Argentina.

Wiesel's comments on this first visit supplement Mauriac's and, on one key point, contradict them. He tells us that, as he listened to Mauriac, he became irritated at what he was hearing. As a Jew, he was indignant at having to listen to a Catholic intellectual compare the Jewish children on the train at Austerlitz Station to Christ. Forgetting the ostensible purpose of his visit, obtaining Mauriac's introduction to Mendès-France, Wiesel relates that "For the first time in my life I exhibited bad manners."[109] Before getting up to stomp out of Mauriac's flat, Wiesel blustered:[110]

> *"Sir." I said, "you speak of Christ. Christians love to speak of him. The passion of Christ, the agony of Christ, the death of Christ. In your religion, that is all you speak of. Well, I want you to know that ten years ago, not very far from here, I knew Jewish children every one of whom suffered a thousand times more, six million times more, than Christ on the cross. And we don't speak about them. Can you understand that, sir? We don't speak about them."*

---

[107] *Ibid.*, 29: "'Voulez-vous mardi ou mercredi prochain?' m'a-t-il demandé dans sa voix rauque en consultant son agenda, 'En début d'après-midi, est-ce que cela vous va?'"

[108] *Ibid.*: "Si cela m'allait? 'Oui. Merci.' J'aurais accepté n'importe quelle date. Je me sentis rougir. J'aimais l'œuvre du grand romancier, mais je n'avais nullement l'intention de l'interroger sur ses personnages, ni sur sa technique, ni sur sa vie. Imposteur, me dis-je. Je suis un imposteur."

[109] *Ibid.*, 17f.: "Pour la première fois de ma vie, je manquai de manières."

[110] *Ibid.*, 18: "Vous parlez du Christ. Les chrétiens aiment en parler. La passion du Christ, l'agonie du Christ, la mort du Christ. Dans votre religion, il ne s'agit que de cela. Et bien, sachez qu'il y a dix ans, pas trop loin d'ici, j'ai connu des enfants juifs dont chacun avait souffert mille fois plus, six millions de fois plus que le Christ sur la croix. Et nous n'en parlons pas. Pouvez-vous comprendre cela, Maître? Nous n'en parlons pas."

In recounting this outburst, Wiesel displayed the bad manners he would later show with regard to popes and presidents, knowing full well that his "Auschwitz dividend" (*dividende d'Auschwitz*) would provide the necessary cover.[111] At this point, Wiesel arose and walked out on Mauriac without even saying goodbye. As he waited for the elevator in the hallway, Mauriac hastened after him. The guilt-ridden Catholic approached Wiesel and, "with an infinitely humble gesture the aged writer was touching my arm, asking me to come back."[112]

Back inside, Mauriac sat sobbing as Wiesel began to tell his story. Wiesel describes him as follows:[113]

> *Motionless, his hands knotted over his crossed legs, a fixed smile on his lips, wordlessly, never taking his eyes off me, he wept and wept. The tears were streaming down his face, and he did nothing to stop them, to wipe them away.*

Wiesel writes that he also felt uneasy. After all, what was he doing crashing into this man's life and causing all this distress? He too felt guilty:[114]

> *This exemplary man, whose behavior had been irreproachable during the Occupation, this man of heart and conscience, what right had I to come and disturb him?*

Wiesel even felt guilty over alienating Mauriac from his own feelings of love for Christ. He tells us:[115]

> *And then, inexcusable insolence on my part, on whose behalf had I allowed myself to cause him uneasiness and pain by detracting from his love for someone who, for him, represented Love?*

Although these lines are perhaps among the most touching that Wiesel has ever written, they obscure the fact that his very pretext for barging into Mauriac's life – to obtain from him an introduction to Mendès-France – was itself an outrageous lie. After all, Mauriac's 1955 "*Bloc-Notes*" column makes no mention of this issue, and there exists no record that Mauriac ever tried to bring the two men together. In fact, Mauriac's version of

---

[111] Elie Wiesel, *...et la mer n'est pas remplie* (Paris: Seuil, 1996), 167-171. The idea of an "Auschwitz dividend," first articulated by Jean-Marie Domenach, is a very valuable one, for it helps us to understand why some self-designated "survivors," like Wiesel, behave the way they do. In a word, because of their experiences in the camps, they act as if they are entitled both to monetary compensation and the right to behave in an uncivil and rude manner.

[112] Wiesel, *Un juif,* 18: "[…] d'un geste infiniment délicat, le vieil écrivain me toucha le bras et me pria de revenir."

[113] *Ibid.*, 18: "Immobile, les mains nouées sur les genoux croisés, un sourire figé autour des lèvres, sans dire un mot, sans me quitter des yeux, il pleurait et pleurait. Les larmes lui coulaient le long du visage et il ne faisait rien pour les arrêter, pour les essuyer."

[114] *Ibid.*, 18f.: "Cet homme irréprochable pendant l'occupation, cet homme de cœur et de conscience, de quel droit étais-je venu le déranger?"

[115] *Ibid.*, 19: "Et puis, l'insolence inexcusable de ma part, au nom de quoi m'étais-je permis de le troubler, de le peiner en amoindrissant son amour pour celui qui, pour lui, représentait l'amour?"

the event makes it clear that from the very beginning of the interview Wiesel insisted upon discussing the war years, not PMF.

Once his tears stopped, Mauriac wanted to know everything about Wiesel's sufferings. Wiesel has claimed that he refused to tell him, due to a vow he had made after the war to give himself ten years of silence in order to digest his sufferings before speaking and writing about them. (The decade-long vow would have been in force if the first meeting had occurred in 1954, but not for the actual date as recorded in Mauriac's "*Bloc-Notes*" article.) This claim contradicts Mauriac's version of events, given above, in which he speaks of Wiesel having told him he saw all his relatives killed at Auschwitz. In fact, the "ten-year vow of silence" is another one of Wiesel's fabrications, for he had already been working on his book for several years before he met Mauriac. Holocaust theologian Naomi Seidman, citing the Yiddish version of *La Nuit*, puts it this way:[116]

> *Eliezer began to write not ten years after the event of the Holocaust but immediately upon liberation, as the first expression of his mental and physical recovery.*

Thus, Wiesel had completed his Yiddish book well before coming to see Mauriac, who, he hoped, would help him to find a publisher for it. Wiesel writes that, as he got up to leave, Mauriac encouraged him to record his experiences for posterity. On the way to the elevator, Mauriac impressed on him his duty to speak out, chastising Wiesel for his vow of silence:[117]

> *You are wrong not to speak.* [...] *Listen to the old man that I am: you have to speak* [about your experiences], *you also have to speak* [in addition to writing about them].

In other words, according to Wiesel's 1977 version of their first meeting, at that point – because of the alleged "ten-year vow of silence" – he had not yet written anything, even in Yiddish. Thanks to Mauriac's exhortation, Wiesel would have us believe, he began to write furiously and, a year later, was able to show the old man a manuscript. He ends his account by writing:[118]

> *One year later I sent him the manuscript of* Night, *written under the seal of memory and silence.*

---

[116] Naomi Seidman, "Elie Wiesel and the Scandal of Jewish Rage," *Jewish Social Studies,* 3 (Fall, 1996), 7.

[117] Wiesel, *Un juif,* 19: "Vous avez tort de ne pas en parler. [...] Ecoutez donc le vieillard que je suis: il faut parler – il faut parler *aussi* [...]"

[118] *Ibid.*, 19: "Une année après, je lui fis parvenir le manuscrit de *La Nuit*, écrit sous le signe du silence et de la fidélité."

Why the Difference of One Year Matters

One year's difference between meetings might seem trivial, but it is of enormous significance, as I shall explain. In his 1977 *Un juif aujourd'hui,* Wiesel first propagated the myth that he wrote *La Nuit* in Paris between 1954 and 1955, only after Mauriac had encouraged him to put his experiences of the war in writing. This claim is an outright lie. Wiesel had two reasons for telling it. First, he had already written the original version of the book in Yiddish,[119] and submitted it for publication before even meeting Mauriac in May 1955. His second reason for lying was to prop up his claimed "ten-year vow of silence" after the war. Even if, as Seidman assures us, Wiesel had been working on a book in the first days after liberation, it would have been impossible for him to meet Mauriac in mid-1955, decide to write the book, and then have it published in Yiddish in November of that year. Thus, when Wiesel claimed that he first met Mauriac in 1954, representing that he had sought him out as a conduit to Prime Minister Mendès-France, who was out of power by the next year, he was in effect allowing himself an extra year to account for the production of his book. Despite the clear evidence of a first meeting of the two men in Mauriac's "*Bloc-Notes*" column on May 14, 1955, Wiesel's lie went unchallenged for years.

Wiesel was quite explicit in *Un juif aujourd'hui* about his telling Mauriac at their first meeting that he had not yet begun to write:[120]

> *I can't, I can't talk about it. He wanted to know why I hadn't written about all that stuff. I answered that I had forbidden myself to do so. He wanted to know why; so I told him. And, again, he sat there thinking.*

Although Wiesel said nothing in *Un juif aujourd'hui* about the pre-existence of a Yiddish version of his book, he had, a year earlier, revealed for the first time to the gentile world that there was also a Yiddish version of *La Nuit,* telling Harry Cargas: "I wrote *Night* first in Yiddish in 1955."[121] In other words, the existence of the Yiddish version of Wiesel's novel had for all practical purposes been suppressed for some twenty years, from 1955 until 1976. When Wiesel actually wrote the book remains open to conjecture, but it is probable that it had already been accepted for publication in Yiddish before he barged into Mauriac's life in May 1955. The book was then translated, shortened and condensed in French. The identity of the person or persons who helped Wiesel with this initial translation, or what I

---

[119] *New York Times*, December 5, 1985, 17. According to this brief note, the book appeared in Buenos Aires in December 1955. It actually came off the printing presses on November 10, 1955, and appeared shortly thereafter.

[120] Wiesel, *Un juif*, 19: "Je ne peux pas, je ne peux pas en parler. Il voulut savoir pourquoi je n'avais pas écrit *tout cela*. Je lui répondis que je me l'étais interdit. Il voulut savoir pourquoi; je le lui dis. Et il se remit à méditer."

[121] Cargas, *Conversation*, 88.

call below the "bridge text," has never been divulged. "Meanwhile," he tells us, "I met Mauriac and we had many conversations. I couldn't find a publisher for that book in France or for that matter in America; Mauriac took the manuscript, and he brought it personally to one of his publishers. That was the beginning of my adventure in literature."[122]

When the news of the Yiddish version of *La Nuit* emerged after 1976, it was soon evident that Wiesel's story of meeting Mauriac in 1954 – to gain an introduction to PMF – and of Mauriac's exhortation to break his vow of silence was untrue. By way of damage control, he launched a new spin on the story in 1985:[123]

> *Mauriac was not instrumental in making me write. He was instrumental in making me publish my work. I would have written anyway. It was he who prevailed upon me to publish.*

Even here he refused to admit that the book had already been written before he met Mauriac. In his autobiographical *Tous les fleuves*, he made yet another claim: that he wrote the original version in 1954 while traveling on a ship to Brazil:[124]

> *I spent all my time working on my narrative, in Yiddish, of my years in the concentration camps.* [...] *My vow of silence will soon come to an end; next year, it will be the tenth anniversary of my liberation.*

By the time Wiesel began writing his autobiography in the 1990s, Mauriac's 1955 newspaper column had apparently been brought to his attention, and the lie that he had first met Mauriac in 1954 exposed. Within Wiesel's inner circle of admirers, it was P.-M. de Saint Cheron, his authorized biographer in French, who first corrected the record. Of course Saint Cheron was circumspect as to the details of Wiesel's deceit. He writes:[125]

> *Their first meeting took place at a reception at the Israeli Embassy, not in 1954, as Wiesel wrote without providing any further information, but at the beginning of May 1955, a date confirmed by Mauriac.*

Saint Cheron conveniently omits mentioning Wiesel's motives in dating that meeting a year earlier: to justify his claim to Mauriac that he had not begun writing about his wartime experiences. Nor does he explain that Wiesel's intention in falsely dating that first meeting was to deceive his readers. Worse, Saint Cheron, who interviewed Wiesel while writing his authorized biography of the man, admits that he was unable to get the truth

---

122 *Ibid.*, 89.

123 Abrahamson, *Against Silence*, vol. 3, 109.

124 Wiesel, *Tous les fleuves*, 302: "Je passe tout mon temps dans ma cabine à rédiger en yiddish mon récit sur les années concentrationnaires [...] Mon vœu de silence arrivera bientôt à son terme: l'an prochain, ce sera le dixième anniversaire de ma libération."

125 Saint Cheron, *Elie Wiesel*, 148: "Leur première rencontre eut lieu au cours d'une réception offerte à l'ambassade d'Israël, non en 1954 comme Wiesel l'écrit sans autre précision, mais début mai 1955, date attestée par Mauriac."

out of Wiesel about what Mauriac was encouraging him to do: whether "to write the manuscript of *Night* – or to rewrite it from the Yiddish original."[126] Jack Kolbert, Wiesel's other authorized biographer, tells us that the book had already been written in Yiddish when Wiesel met Mauriac, and that he "urged the young Jewish journalist to rewrite his Yiddish opus in French." Then, according to Kolbert, "Wiesel allowed himself to be persuaded by the great French author, reducing the 888 pages of his Yiddish manuscript to 127 pages of gripping French text."[127]

Amazingly, in his interview with the so-called Academy of Achievement, now online and most recently updated on September 28, 2010, the mendacious Wiesel turned his back on the admission made in his autobiography that he had written his novel in 1954, a year before the expiration of his vow of silence. He now seems to have returned, for the most part, to the 1977 version of events. Speaking in his usual broken English, he states:[128]

> *He took me to the elevator and embraced me. And that year, the tenth year, I began writing my narrative. After it was translated from Yiddish into French, I sent it to him. We were very, very close friends until his death. That made me not publish, but write.*

Wiesel has a blank check to contradict at any time the already-established facts of his career without any fear of academic or media criticism. In this respect, he truly incarnates the master narrative of the Jewish Holocaust story which, despite its many internal contradictions, is always considered to be true.

Use of Retroactive Continuity to Explain the Genesis of *La Nuit*

The official line now seems to be that Mauriac talked to Wiesel only about rewriting the Yiddish book in French, not writing *La Nuit* from scratch. But this claim undercuts the legend of Wiesel's "ten-year vow of silence." It is on this point of contradiction that we can see clearly the connection between the Holocaust myth and other forms of lowbrow popular culture like television series, soap operas, comic books, professional wrestling and similar continuous narratives. In each of these genres, the creators employ a narrative tool known as "retroactive continuity." Thanks to it,

---

[126] *Ibid.*, 154: "[…] écrire le manuscrit de *La Nuit* – ou le récrire à partir de l'original yiddish."

[127] Kolbert, *Worlds*, 29. Kolbert insists that Wiesel compressed the original Yiddish version of the novel from 888 to 127 pages! Seidman, however, disputes this page count, claiming that the comparative page count of the two books is 245 in Yiddish to 158 in French. She comments: "What distinguishes the Yiddish from the French is not so much length as attention to detail, an adherence to that principle of comprehensiveness so valued by the editors of the Polish Jewry series." ("Elie Wiesel," 5)

[128] www.achievement.org/autodoc/page/wie0int-3

they are able to create new episodes that contradict earlier ones, usually through the suppression of earlier characters and events from the narrative if they impede further development of the plot line. There is no problem in such a situation, for they disappear as if they had never existed. Since the Jewish Holocaust tale is essentially a work of fiction, it too must have continual recourse to rewriting through the use of "retroactive continuity." Thus, a lesser myth like Wiesel's "ten-year vow of silence" is slowly being deleted from the Holocaust story as if it had never existed. Likewise, numerous more grandiose claims, such as the lampshades made out of human skin, the bars of soap made from Jewish fat, and the four million dead at Auschwitz,[129] are also slowly being phased out of the official narrative of the Holocaust as if they had never existed.

The Mystery of Mauriac's Initial Attachment to Wiesel

After getting to know Wiesel and hearing him talk of his life experiences, Mauriac became very attached to Wiesel. Indeed, he had no difficulty in comparing the foreigner from a mysterious background to Jesus himself. When he later dedicated his book *Le fils de l'homme* (*The Son of Man*) to Wiesel in 1958, he called him a "crucified Jewish child." Unlike Dreyfus, Altermann and Mendès-France, each of whom had been born into highly acculturated Jewish families that were thoroughly integrated into French culture, Wiesel had been raised as a Hasid in a ghetto atmosphere in Eastern Europe. Although he spoke French fluently, his speech was accented, and he had no formal education. Nonetheless, Mauriac embraced him, literally and figuratively, without hesitation. These cultural and class barriers crumbled before the reality of Mauriac's hidden homosexual life.

Mauriac's homosexuality, from its awakening during his student days in Paris in 1906 through the rest of his life, is a theme running through his unpublished *journal intime* or private diary. It is unclear how many of these diary entries Mauriac's son Jean (b. 1925) allowed Jean-Luc Barré to see, but in the end he was only allowed to quote from a limited number of them. As a result of his two-volume biography, however, there can no longer be any doubt about Mauriac's hidden homosexual desires and behaviors. His obsession, throughout his life, with the beauty of the masculine, not the female, body was the cause of his lifelong interest in meeting young men. Barré writes that Mauriac "understood at an early age that he couldn't share his secret with anyone, neither with his mother, for fear of the pain it would cause her, nor his brothers, who would be shocked."[130]

---

129 On the development of claims regarding the Auschwitz death toll, see Robert Faurisson, "How many deaths at Auschwitz?", *The Revisionist*, vol. 1, no. 1, 2003, 17-23; www.codoh.com/library/document/1424.

130 Barré, *François Mauriac*, vol 1, 115: "Il a compris très tôt qu'il ne pourrait partager son

One of Mauriac's lovers was Louis-Gabriel Clayeux, who would later become the part owner and artistic director of the famous Parisian art gallery, la Galerie Maeght. Described by Barré as a *jeune esthète homosexuel* (*François Mauriac*, vol. 1, 459), he was a student in the mid-1930s when he began his affair with the fifty-year-old Mauriac. For the latter, this was his preferred type of relationship. Obsessed as he was with the esthetic beauty of young men's bodies, the thirty-year difference in age between the two remained a key ingredient in his desire. Barré argues that this affair "allowed him to become once again, at about the age of fifty, the 'young man' he had been."[131]

Mauriac's obsession also helps to explain why he was so attracted to Wiesel when the latter introduced himself at the Israeli Embassy in 1955. The seventy-year-old Mauriac was not only accustomed to having young men seek his friendship, he also must have found Wiesel to be the physically attractive type he preferred. In addition, his Jewishness enabled Mauriac to conveniently insert him within his personal, philo-Semitic "Jesus, Dreyfus, Altermann, Mendès-France" pantheon. That is why he immediately invited Wiesel to his home and then volunteered to help him publish his book. He wanted at all costs to remain close to this young man. Their close relationship endured until their 1967 breakup over Israel's treatment of the Palestinians.

Although Mauriac was indeed attracted to Wiesel, there is no evidence that there ever existed a truly sexual dimension to this relationship. Strangely, one key to understanding this attraction can be found in Mauriac's belief, for a short time anyway, as adumbrated in the following chapter, that Wiesel was interested in converting to Catholicism. Since Mauriac ardently hoped that this would happen, he was able to project Wiesel as having been "crucified," and situated him "between the two testaments," like John the Baptist. Also, and more obviously, Mauriac probably thought that, in helping this young Jewish writer, he would be atoning for the French state's violation of the civil rights of many Jews during the war years. Misguided, he also probably wanted to compensate for his family's traditional "anti-Semitism."

---

secret avec personne, ni avec sa mère, par crainte de la faire souffrir, ni avec ses frères pour ne pas les scandaliser."

[131] *Ibid.*, vol. 1, 459: "lui permit de redevenir le 'jeune homme' qu'il avait été."

Chapter IV
Wiesel's Exploitation of Mauriac, 1955 – 1970

Mauriac Helps Wiesel to Prepare *La Nuit* for Publication

After their initial meeting, Mauriac continued to do what he could to help Wiesel, even after he had established permanent residence in New York in 1956. Here is how the deal was made. In late 1956, following Wiesel's departure for New York, Jérôme Lindon, the editor of *Les Éditions de Minuit*, called Mauriac to ask him to write a foreword for *Un camp très ordinaire* by Micheline Maurel, a book about her wartime experiences. In the course of their conversation, Mauriac told his friend about Wiesel's book. Lindon asked that he send it over and, "eighteen months later, it was published."[132]

I now follow the official chronology of events as found on the *Les Éditions de Minuit* website, adding my comments along the way.[133] Lindon wrote to Wiesel on December 19, 1956, telling him of his interest in publishing his book under the title *And the World Was Silent* (*Et le monde se taisait*). This would have been a direct translation of the Yiddish title. Here it is necessary to recall that the text which Lindon read was not the "bridge text" that Wiesel had made for Mauriac from the Yiddish version of his novel, but Mauriac's rewrite on the basis of that bridge text. With regard to the sensitive question of whether or not Wiesel received help in preparing this bridge text for Mauriac to read, Wiesel has provided two different and contradictory answers. In *Tous les fleuves* he omits claiming to have actually written this bridge text himself. He writes of Mauriac:

---

132 Saint Cheron, *Elie Wiesel*, 154: "[…] dix-huit mois plus tard, il était publié."
133 www.leseditionsdeminuit.com/f/index.php?sp=liv&livre_id=2518.

I owe him a lot. He was the first reader of Night *and suggested it, in vain, to his own publisher.*

In *All Rivers*, however, which is supposedly the English "translation" of the French original, he writes something quite different for his American audience, claiming that he himself composed the bridge text for Mauriac to work on:

I owe him a lot. He was the first person to read Night *after I reworked it from the original Yiddish.*

In any case, three days later, Wiesel wrote back, giving Lindon the authority to make "minor corrections" (*corrections de détail*) in the final text. But who was going to make these "minor corrections"? Lindon, one of his staffers, or Mauriac? According to the official story, it was Lindon who made these changes, but that is difficult to believe, as I will explain. Four months later, in April 1957, so the story goes, Lindon had decided on the title of *A Year of My Childhood* (*Un an de mon enfance)*, and it was under that title that the contract was signed in November 1957. During the early months of 1958, however, there ensued a three-way discussion in which Lindon and Mauriac, in Paris, discussed the title with Wiesel, who was still bedridden in New York. On March 13, 1958, Wiesel finished reading the galley proofs. He wrote back to Lindon to suggest that the book be published on April 11, the date of the liberation of Buchenwald. He also told Lindon:[134]

This book expresses you as much as it expresses me. The voice is mine, but you are the sound engineer.

Thus far, this official version of events has completely excluded Mauriac's role in preparing the novel for publication, except for his participation in choosing the title. But the official story is belied by an incident that postponed the original plan for publication on April 11. Mauriac left Paris on a trip, taking with him the sole corrected copy of the page proofs. If Mauriac played no role in adapting *La Nuit* from Yiddish to French, why were the final page proofs in his possession just as the book was to go to press? Also, why was he taking them with him on a trip, if he did not intend to work on them further?

The *Les Éditions de Minuit*'s website provides no answer to these questions and indeed completely avoids them. As for the choice of a title, the website states that the process was not an easy one, for there was "a long list on which both Elie Wiesel and François Mauriac expressed their opinions and made suggestions until everybody agreed on *La Nuit* in May

134 *Ibid.*, "Oui, ce livre vous exprime autant qu'il m'exprime, moi. La voix est la mienne, mais l'ingénieur du son, c'est vous."

1958, but publication was delayed until June 1958." Left out of this discussion is the question of who was responsible for the new title.

Was it Mauriac? This standard version's tendency to blur the facts in order to downplay Mauriac's involvement in the creation of the book, including the selection of a title, degenerates into sheer mendacity when it states that this new publication "was quickly noticed by publishing houses abroad, especially in the United States." In reality, however, the English-language version of *La Nuit* did not appear until 1960, and the German translation was not published until 1962, under the title *Die Nacht zu begraben, Elisha* (*To Bury the Night, Elisha*; Frankfurt am Main-Berlin: Ullstein).

Despite Mauriac's editing, and despite Wiesel's later claim in 1992 that the book had received a "very, very big reception,"[135] *La Nuit* stumbled from the outset. It simply did not sell. In an effort to lend it publicity and momentum, Mauriac published an excerpt from his foreword to *La Nuit* as a stand-alone article in *Le Figaro*.[136] Later in 1958 Mauriac published his life of Christ under the title *Le fils de l'homme* (*The Son of Man*). Still thinking fondly of his relationship with Wiesel, who by then had taken up permanent residence in New York, he dedicated it "To Elie Wiesel, a crucified Jewish child." (*A Elie Wiesel, un enfant juif crucifié*). Mauriac intended nothing but good in making this dedication, for Wiesel had made a strong impression on him, and Mauriac was dearly attached to him. Yet after Mauriac's death, for theatrical effect on his fellow Jews, Wiesel would strongly object to it, thereby continuing the pattern of abuse – abuse of truth, abuse of decorum – established from the beginning. For when Wiesel, upon his first visit to Mauriac's apartment, had stormed out as if Mauriac had offended him, he was simply employing one of the manipulative techniques that he had learned in his abusive relationships with Shushani and other Jewish "masters."

Wiesel's career in France attained its first important peak when, in 1963, he received the Rivarol Prize, awarded annually to a non-French person who writes in French. By this time he had published four books, *La Nuit*; *L'Aube* (1960) [*Dawn*, (1961)]; *Le Jour* (1961) [*The Accident*, (1962)]; and *La Ville de la chance* (1962) [*Town beyond the Wall*, (1963)]. Mauriac was happy for Wiesel, and devoted his "*Bloc-Notes*" column of May 29, 1963, exclusively to him. Writing of "my friend Elie Wiesel," Mauriac reminds his reader of how they met:[137]

---

135 Elizabeth Devereaux, "Elie Wiesel," *Publisher's Weekly*, April 6, 1992, 30.

136 Mauriac, "Un enfant juif," 1.

137 Mauriac, *Bloc-Notes*, vol. 3, May 29, 1963, 361: "Comme je décrivais à ce jeune journaliste d'Israël venu m'interviewer ce train bourré d'enfants juifs que, pendant l'occupation, ma femme avait vu un jour, en gare d'Austerlitz, il me dit: 'J'étais l'un d'eux.' Notre amitié est née de ces quelques mots. Elie Wiesel était revenu des camps,

> *As I was describing to this young Israeli journalist, who had come to interview me, the train full of Jewish children which, during the war, my wife had seen one day at Austerlitz Station, he said to me: "I was one of them." Our friendship was born of these few words. Elie Wiesel had come back from the camps, after having seen every member of his family burned – he, the mystical child, after having lost, or rather after having thought that he had lost his faith in the God of love and consolation.*

Once again we are reminded how powerful this image of the children at Austerlitz Station was for Mauriac. He regarded himself as an eyewitness to this event, even though other eyes – those of his wife and eldest son – had seen it for him. Likewise, Wiesel had "seen every member of his family burned" at Auschwitz. Mauriac then compared Wiesel to Christ, writing about Wiesel's technique:[138]

> [The book's novelistic] *technique is linked to the need that this innocent child, escaped from Herod's massacre, has to cry out to us. In fact, it consists much less of a deposition made about historical facts than of the inner feelings of a soul* [emphasis added] *which was able to believe for a while that even God, eternal innocence itself, had been massacred.* [...] *Elie Wiesel's four books comment upon the return of a child from the depths of horror.*

By 1963, it is clear that Mauriac could see that *La Nuit* had little to do with "the facts of history," and that it was basically concerned with recounting Wiesel's personal feelings. As such, *La Nuit* was, in Mauriac's opinion, a novel, like the three other novels mentioned in the article, and not a memoir. He thus hints here, but does not actually say, that he considered Wiesel to be, in a sense, an unreliable witness to history.

Mauriac refers to Wiesel in Christian terms, likening him to one of "the holy innocents," the infants in the Gospel of Matthew, 2:16-18, who were massacred after King Herod learned from the three wise men that a new king had just been born. Mauriac did not use this terminology to offend Wiesel, but simply because these were the only terms at his disposal. His frame of reference was Christian. Since he believed that there is only one God, the God of the Christians and the Jews alike, he felt justified in the comparison. After Mauriac's death, Wiesel would take rather vigorous exception to such statements. Writing for Jews who shared his views, he would twist and distort Mauriac's intentions, which can be seen here to have been purely beneficent.

---

après avoir vu brûler tous les siens, – lui, l'enfant mystique, après avoir perdu, ou plutôt après avoir cru perdre la foi au Dieu d'amour et de consolation."

[138] *Ibid.*, 361f.: "La technique y est liée à l'exigence de ce qu'a à nous crier cet innocent échappé au massacre d'Hérode. *Au vrai, il s'agit beaucoup moins d'une déposition portant sur des faits d'histoire que de l'aventure intérieure d'une âme* qui a pu croire durant quelque temps que Dieu avait été massacré, lui aussi, lui l'innocent éternel. [...] Les quatre livres d'Elie Wiesel commentent le retour de ce voyage d'un enfant au bout de l'horreur."

In the next paragraph of Mauriac's 1963 article, we get a glimpse of the serious disagreement that would become the major focus of their correspondence during the 1960s, and ultimately tear apart their friendship. Here Mauriac contrasts the "Jewish mystics," whom he loves, with the hawks in the State of Israel, who visit fire and destruction upon their enemies. Four years before the Six Day War, Mauriac was able to analyze the situation lucidly. He wrote:[139]

> *How I love the Jewish mystics, these witnesses of the first love! Maybe there are still quite a few of them, but not in the State of Israel with which we have to deal nowadays, and whose particular genius is oriented toward conquest and domination* [...]

When, in 1963, almost fifty years ago, Mauriac saw Zionists doing to innocent Palestinians what the Germans had done to the Jews during the Occupation, he could not help but make the connection. Mauriac's condemnation of the Jewish "conquest and domination" of Palestine outraged Wiesel's blind sense of Jewish solidarity. But a paragraph at the end of the article would enrage him even more. There Mauriac seems to hint that Wiesel had considered, or perhaps was still considering, becoming a Catholic. He writes:[140]

> *Elie Wiesel will take me to the Holy Land someday. Due to his unique understanding of Christ, he wants* [to take this trip with me] *very, very much. He imagines Christ wearing phylacteries, as Chagall envisioned him, a son of the synagogue, a pious Jew and a servant of the law – and who did not die "because, being man, he made himself into God."* [...] *Elie Wiesel stands upon the boundaries of the two testaments: like John the Baptist* [...]

First, what does Mauriac mean when he says that Wiesel has a "unique understanding" (*connaissance singulière*) of Christ? One explanation might be that Mauriac imagined that Wiesel simply saw Christ as a pious Jew who was a product of Jewish culture, but who was considered by the rabbis to be out of the mainstream. According to this reasoning, Wiesel would have held the traditional rabbinical view that Christ was a Jewish heretic. He might have been sincere, but he was a heretic.

Yet, there is a problem with this interpretation of Mauriac's remarks. If Mauriac thought that Wiesel shared the traditional rabbinical view of Christ, he would have said so. But when he talks of Wiesel's "unique un-

---

[139] *Ibid.*, 363. "Que j'aime les mystiques juifs, ces témoins du premier Amour! Peut-être en existe-t-il beaucoup encore. Mais non parmi l'Israël auquel nous avons affaire et dont le génie est tout tourné à la conquête et à la domination. "

[140] *Ibid.*, 362. "Elie Wiesel m'amènera un jour en terre sainte. Il le désire d'un grand désir, ayant du Christ une connaissance singulière! Il l'imagine sous des phylactères, comme l'a vu Chagall, fils de la synagogue, juif pieux et soumis à la loi – et qui ne serait pas mort 'parce qu'étant homme il s'est fait Dieu [...]' Elie Wiesel se tient sur les confins des deux testaments: c'est la race de Jean-Baptiste [...]"

derstanding" of Christ, he is clearly not referring to the standard view of Orthodox Jews. On the contrary, Mauriac's words can be interpreted to imply, not Wiesel's rejection of Christ, but a very serious interest in him. Could Wiesel at one time have thought about becoming a Catholic? Did Wiesel's desire to become more fully a French writer also include a religious dimension? In light of Wiesel's words and behavior over the past half century, these questions must be answered in the negative.

Or, more perversely, did the cynical and ambitious Wiesel plant such a seed in Mauriac's mind to manipulate and abuse him? Saint Cheron, himself a Catholic who converted to Judaism, asked Wiesel about Mauriac's remark, which obviously raised the touchy issue of Wiesel's possible interest in becoming a Catholic at that time. Wiesel's answer was in keeping with his public persona:[141]

> *That's the way he saw me; that was his view. In reality, I have never been "on the border of the New Testament." I respect Christians who are committed to the New Testament provided they respect my commitment to our Bible.*

One cannot expect Wiesel to have admitted to Saint Cheron that he deliberately gave Mauriac the impression that he was considering the possibility of converting to Catholicism in order to string the old man along. Yet it is clear that Mauriac thought Wiesel might be contemplating conversion, and the only person who could have planted the idea in his mind was Wiesel. When he wrote of Wiesel's "*connaissance singulière du Christ*" in his May 29, 1963, newspaper article, Mauriac was making it clear that Wiesel – in their personal conversations – did not look upon Christ with the eyes of an Orthodox Jew. The conclusion is inescapable. They had obviously discussed the subject.

Claude Mauriac, Mauriac's oldest son, offers more information about his father's belief that Wiesel wanted to convert. He recounts in an entry to his diary dated July 2, 1959, his mother's involvement in a very serious automobile accident. Although her car was almost completely destroyed, she survived without serious injury. His mother and grandmother attributed this outcome to the intervention of Divine Providence. Claude, who by this time had ceased to consider himself a Catholic, discussed the subject with his father. The elder Mauriac, of course, believed in Providence, and brought up Elie Wiesel to make his point:[142]

---

[141] Saint Cheron, *Elie Wiesel*, 155f.: "C'est sa vision de moi, sa perception. Pourtant, je n'ai jamais été 'aux confins du Nouveau Testament.' Je respecte les chrétiens qui sont attachés au Nouveau Testament, s'ils respectent mon attachement à notre Bible."

[142] Claude Mauriac, *Le Temps immobile II: Les Espaces imaginaires* (Paris: Grasset, 1976), 332f.: "Pour moi, je crois, c'est une certitude, à des interventions surnaturelles mais dans le seul domaine de la vie spirituelle. J'en ai eu de nombreuses confirmations dans ma vie. Certes, ces évidences sont personnelles, je ne pourrais les justifier. Mais je sais d'une certitude absolue. […] Tiens, ces jours-ci encore. Tu sais, Wiesel, ce jeune juif qui perdit dans les camps la foi, la foi juive (j'ai préfacé son admirable témoignage), eh

> *As for me, I definitely believe in supernatural interventions, but only in the spiritual realm. I have had this experience a number of times in my life. Of course, these experiences are personal, and I couldn't explain them objectively. But I know with absolute certainty.* [...] *Listen, just in the last few days, Wiesel, you know, this young Jew who lost his faith, his Jewish faith, in the camps (I wrote the foreword for his admirable account of his experiences), well, I didn't want to try to teach him about Christ. I left it in His hands.* [...] *Then, while having dinner, last evening, with the daughter of Ramon Fernandez, I learned that Wiesel has entered into contact with her husband (a converted Jew, and a fervent Catholic) and that, by correspondence (Wiesel is in the United States) he has asked him about Christ, so you see, the very thing that I had ardently desired has begun, that everything is possible* [...]

Finally, when Mauriac mentions, in this 1963 article, the trip to Israel that Wiesel wanted to share with him, he refers to that place as the *terre sainte*, or Holy Land, not Israel. Despite Mauriac's good intentions toward Wiesel personally, by the 1960s he could not accept what Zionism had become – a truly murderous ideology. How could Mauriac, as France's foremost public intellectual, support self-determination for the people of Morocco, Algeria and Tunisia, while denying the validity of the legitimate national aspirations of the Palestinians? There was a point beyond which the two men just could not agree. Wiesel kept silent about this article during Mauriac's lifetime, prudently waiting until after his benefactor's death to discuss it.

When Wiesel finally did get around to discussing Mauriac's complex and suggestive 1963 article in *Tous les fleuves,* he wrote angrily:[143]

> *First,* Night *is not a novel. Secondly, never having been at Austerlitz Station during the Occupation, I could not have told him that I was in the train loaded with children. Thirdly, his criticism of Israel was unjustified. Fourthly, with regard to Jesus Christ, he attributes thoughts to me that have never been in my mind but only in his. And fifthly, he adds, and I don't know why, that "Elie Wiesel, like John the Baptist, is on the borderline between the two Testaments."*

---

bien, je n'ai rien voulu tenter pour lui apprendre le Christ. Je le Lui ai confié. [...] Et en dînant, hier soir, avec la fille de Ramon Fernandez, j'ai appris que Wiesel était entré en rapport avec son mari (un juif converti, chrétien fervent) et que, par lettre (Wiesel est aux Etats-Unis) il l'avait interrogé sur le Christ, justement, que ce quelque chose que j'avais passionnément souhaité avait commencé, que tout devenait possible [...]"

143 Wiesel, *Tous les fleuves*, 342: "Premièrement, *La Nuit* n'est pas un roman. Deuxièmement, n'ayant pas été à la gare d'Austerlitz pendant l'Occupation, je n'ai pas pu dire que je me trouvais dans le train bourré d'enfants. Troisièmement, sa critique d'Israël n'était pas justifiée. Quatrièmement, il m'attribue concernant Jésus-Christ une pensée qui n'était pas la mienne, mais la sienne. Et cinquièmement, il ajoute, je ne sais pourquoi, qu'Elie Wiesel se tient sur les confins des deux testaments: c'est la race de Jean-Baptiste."

Wiesel's response to Mauriac, some thirty-two years after the fact, broadcasts his notional sensitivity about its suggestive elements, discussed above.

With regard to Wiesel's first point, he was upset with Mauriac because he characterized *La Nuit* as a novel. The implications here are huge, for even his greatest benefactor felt the book was a work of fiction. Wiesel's sarcastic second point hints at his underlying scorn and contempt for all those well-meaning but naïve gentiles, like Mauriac, who labor mightily, against the evidence, to convince themselves that events contained in the Jewish Holocaust narrative are all true and really happened. Wiesel's third point merely reiterates his belief that Israel is above the law, a concept abhorrent to Mauriac and to most civilized people. Finally, with regard to Wiesel's fourth and fifth points, which concern Mauriac's belief that he was interested in converting, Wiesel categorically denies this, and in so doing he also denies that the only person who could have planted that idea in Mauriac's mind was Wiesel himself.

The irresistible conclusion is that Wiesel deceived Mauriac about his interest in Christianity, probably to advance his own purposes. Wiesel continues to suppress his correspondence with Mauriac, presumably to keep this deceit intact.

1958: Publication of *La Nuit* Coincides with the Death of Pius XII

The years from 1954 to 1958, during which Wiesel wrote *Un di velt* and later prevailed upon François Mauriac to rewrite it for him in French as *La Nuit*, coincide in time with the last illness, physical decline and death of Pius XII. Ironically, one of that Pontiff's last episcopal appointments was of Karol Wojtyla to the post of auxiliary bishop of Krakow. The latter, thirty-eight years old at the time, thus became Poland's youngest bishop in September 1958. Pacelli (Pius XII) died of heart failure on October 9, 1958, at the papal summer residence in Castel Gandolfo at the age of eighty-two. The funeral procession into Rome that followed his death was unprecedented in its size and depth of feeling. Golda Meir, Israel's minister of foreign affairs at the time, spoke for world Jewry when she sent the following message:[144]

> *We share in the grief of humanity at the passing away of His Holiness, Pope Pius XII. In a generation afflicted by wars and discords, he upheld the highest ideals of peace and compassion. When fearful martyrdom came to our people in the decade of Nazi terror, the voice of the Pope was raised for its victims.*

---

[144] Margherita Marchione, *Crusade of Charity: Pius XII and POWs (1939-1945)* (Mahwah, N.J.: Paulist Press, 2006), 38.

The life of our times was enriched by a voice speaking out about great moral truths above the tumult of daily conflict. We mourn a great servant of peace.

Elie Wiesel, the future High Priest of the Holocaust, was still unknown, and the campaign by the Holocaust fundamentalists to defame the historical Pius XII, to whom Golda Meir had rightly paid homage, had not yet begun. In retrospect, however, it is clear that hidden forces were at work to change completely the world's view of Pius XII and the Catholic Church, and to replace it with a new world religion, the Holocaust, fronted by Elie Wiesel – the world we are now living in.

The Mauriac/Wiesel Correspondence, 1958-1970

As Wiesel's career advanced through the 1960s, he continued to exchange letters with Mauriac. Only four letters from that correspondence were published in 1989 by Mauriac's daughter-in-law, Caroline, in her edition of selected letters from Mauriac's correspondence with many different people. A few years after that publication, I had occasion to visit with Jean, Mauriac's youngest child, born in 1925, and his wife Caroline at their home in Paris. In our discussion, I inquired as to why only four letters from Mauriac to Wiesel had been published in 1989 and why none of the many letters Mauriac had received from Wiesel were included or even referenced in her anthology. In response, Jean Mauriac showed me the large accordion-style folder in which his father had originally filed both the carbons of his own letters and the originals received from Wiesel. Unfortunately, there were only four carbon copies of Mauriac's originals, the ones published by Caroline Mauriac in 1989 and cited in the present study. As for the letters Mauriac received from Wiesel, they were all gone.

Fortunately, these letters that we do have shed more light on the problematical "*Bloc-Notes*" column of May 29, 1963, and provide additional clues about the development of the relationship of their writers between 1958 and 1970. But Wiesel is in possession not only of Mauriac's letters to him, but also of his to Mauriac. Of course, he could have simply made a carbon copy of some or all of the letters he sent to Mauriac, but that does not explain how and why the letters originally sent to Mauriac were no longer in the possession of the Mauriac family in the late 1980s. If Wiesel tried to get those letters back from Mauriac before the latter's death, it might have been because he felt compromised by some things he had written to Mauriac. If that is in fact the case, such a scenario would offer further evidence of the abusive relationship in which Mauriac was trapped with Wiesel.

In any case, shortly before Mauriac's death in 1970, Wiesel disclosed that he was in possession of all the letters, that they cover a variety of topics, that he hoped to publish them someday, and that their contents would reveal the fundamental disagreement that existed between the two men on the subject of Israel. Since the Mauriac family no longer has the letters that Wiesel originally sent to his friend and mentor, if Wiesel ever decides to publish this correspondence, he will be free to manipulate these letters in any way he sees fit without fear of contradiction.

On the disagreement about Israel, Israel Shenker wrote about six months before Mauriac's death, which would take place on September 1, 1970:[145]

> *The two* [Mauriac and Wiesel] *became close friends, and Mr. Wiesel plans to publish a volume of their dialogues – which have had strongly polemical moments, notably on the subject of Israel.*

Seven years later, in 1977, a full decade after the Israeli conquest and occupation of the West Bank, Wiesel put a different spin on the letters' contents:[146]

> *From our conversations* [in the letters], *which I should publish, and that I will publish one day, I've extracted comments, stories and anecdotes about different subjects and people. The exchange of view between the Jew and the Christian often took the form of a "disputation," as in the Middle Ages. But our friendship was able to overcome our disagreements. At the turning points of my life as a writer, he was always there as a protector and an ally, full of generosity and sincerity, just as he had been since the beginning.*

Eight years later, in 1985, Wiesel claimed that he was still determined to publish the letters, and was by then working on the project. He told his friend Irving Abrahamson, for instance, that

> *my story with Mauriac has not been told altogether. What I wrote in* A Jew Today *has only one short chapter. I am preparing a book called* Disputations. *I use the word in the medieval sense – of disputations between Jews and Christians. It will be based on dialogues, conversations, and letters between the two of us for fifteen or eighteen years.*

A little further along in the same interview Wiesel stated:[147]

> *That is when we decided to start our disputations. And when they will be published they will create some stir.*

---

[145] Israel Shenker, "The Concerns of Elie Wiesel," *New York Times*, February 10, 1970, I, 48.

[146] Wiesel, *Un juif*, 28: "De nos conversations, que je devrais publier et que je publierai un jour, j'ai retenu paroles et confidences, histoires et anecdotes sur des sujets et des personnages variés. Souvent l'échange entre juif et chrétien prenait forme de 'disputation,' comme au Moyen Age. Notre amitié résista aux désaccords. Aux tournants de ma vie d'écrivain, il se trouvait là, protecteur et allié, émouvant de sincérité et de générosité, comme avant, au temps des débuts."

[147] Abrahamson, *Against Silence*, vol. 3, 110.

But Wiesel, mindful of their contents, has not only held the letters back from publication, he no longer mentions their existence. Here we see yet another example of his resounding "silence." But why does Wiesel continue to suppress these letters? Could it be in order to hide the role that Mauriac played in the rewriting of *Night* from the Yiddish original? Or could it be to disguise the fact that their definitive breakup in 1967 was caused by their basic disagreement with regard to Israel's imperial ambitions at the expense of the Palestinians?

Luckily, as mentioned earlier, we have copies of four letters that Mauriac wrote to Wiesel between 1958 and 1970. Each one gives a hint of what the preceding letter from Wiesel must have contained. The first letter is dated May 5, 1958, or about a month before the publication of *La Nuit.* Mauriac had already written the book's foreword and sent it to Wiesel in New York for his perusal. He wrote:[148]

> *Dear Lazarus Wiesel: I am happy that this foreword touched you. I believe that I've described* [in it] *the essence of your personal experience. I believe that I'll see you soon and that you'll be in Paris for the release of your book. You can count on me: I'll do everything in my power to make it a success. Yours truly.*

Mauriac's generosity shines through in every word of this letter, the principal goal of which seems to have been to answer Wiesel's thank-you note for the foreword to his book. Not only did Mauriac arrange to have the book published and write a foreword for it, he also reprinted an excerpt from the foreword as a separate article in his "*Bloc-Notes*" column on June 7, 1958. Mauriac had more than earned Wiesel's thanks.

Mauriac's second letter to Wiesel is dated June 22, 1959. By this time, *La Nuit* had been in print for a year, and Wiesel was at work on the draft of his second book, a novel called *Aube* (*Dawn*). Now committed to remaining in New York, he was apparently planning to visit Paris later in the summer. Wiesel had sent a copy of the typescript to Mauriac. In his response to Wiesel's letter, Mauriac touched on several matters, including the possibility of seeing Wiesel over the summer. He wrote:[149]

---

[148] Mauriac, *Nouvelles Lettres d'une vie*, ed. Caroline Mauriac (Paris: Grasset, 1989), 297: "Cher Lazare Wiesel: Je suis heureux que cette préface vous ait touchée. Il me semble que j'y ai marqué l'essentiel de votre drame. Je pense que je vous verrai bientôt et que vous serez à Paris pour le lancement de votre livre. Vous pouvez compter sur moi; je ferai tout ce qui sera possible pour le servir. Bien affectueusement vôtre."

[149] *Ibid.*, 301: "Cher ami, Je ne serai pas à Paris pour le 15 août, je serai sans doute à ce moment-là en montagne et je serai probablement à la fin du mois d'août et les premiers jours de septembre à Vémars (Seine-et-Oise) qui n'est qu'à trente kilomètres de Paris. J'espère donc vous voir à ce moment-là, soit que vous veniez jusqu'à moi, soit que nous nous donnions rendez-vous à Paris. Bien affectueusement vôtre."[P.S.] "Il me semble que les deux interlocuteurs de la dernière scène doivent en venir à *s'aimer* et pour cela se confier l'un à l'autre, ou plutôt le bourreau se confier à sa victime. Reçu lettre de Feuer qui me parle de *son ami* Wiesel. Je suis heureux que vous soyez l'ami de ces admirables chrétiens."

Dear Friend: I won't be in Paris for the 15th of August, I'll probably be in the mountains at that time, and probably, at the end of August and the beginning of September, in Vémars (Seine-et-Oise) [site of the house and property that his wife had inherited, and where Mauriac is buried] *which is only 30 kilometers from Paris. So I hope to see you then, either you come up to our house or we meet in Paris. Very truly yours.*
[P. S.] *It seems to me that the two characters in the last scene have to come to* love each other *and, for that to happen, to confide in one another, or rather the hangman confide in his victim. Received the letter from Feuer who talks to me of* his friend *Wiesel. I'm happy that you're the friend of these admirable Christians.*

Here we find Mauriac giving Wiesel advice on his novel; that he does so suggests why Wiesel has suppressed the great bulk of the correspondence, especially the letters that concern Mauriac's role in editing *Night*, which, as we have shown earlier, was far more important in preparing *Night* for publication than Wiesel admits. Mauriac was able to advise him about *Dawn* – free of charge! – because Wiesel had sent him a copy of his work in progress. These were the days when he truly loved Wiesel, before their relationship soured over Zionism. As for Feuer, whom I have been unable to identify with absolute certainty, he seems to have been a Jewish convert to Catholicism and was possibly the son-in-law, referred to above, of the French journalist and literary critic Ramon Fernandez (1894-1944). Mauriac's reference to him here would support my contention that Wiesel was spinning a web around Mauriac in an effort to feed the old man's delusion about his possible conversion to Catholicism.

The third letter is dated December 7, 1960. Mauriac writes:[150]

Dear Friend: I don't know what could have given you the idea that I was supposed to go to Israel *for the* Eichmann *trial. I have received absolutely no invitation* [from a newspaper or magazine] *in this matter. It will come, perhaps, but I doubt, in that case, that I would accept: I don't have the courage to face up to the fatigue and emotion of this trial. Which doesn't mean that I won't take a trip some day to your country* [Israel]. *Warmest wishes*

It would be interesting to know why Wiesel wanted Mauriac to travel to Israel with him. It was understandable that Wiesel, an ardent Zionist, would want to attend the show trial. But he should have also known that Mauriac was sedentary by nature and that, except for a few brief trips abroad, he hardly ever ventured out of France.

---

[150] *Ibid.*, 332: "Cher ami, Je ne sais ce qui a pu vous faire croire que je devais me rendre en *Israël* pour le procès *Eichmann.* Je n'ai reçu absolument aucune invitation à ce sujet. Elle viendra peut-être, mais je doute bien, dans ce cas, que je l'accepte: je ne me sens pas le courage d'affronter les fatigues et les émotions de ce procès. Ce qui ne signifie pas que je ne rendrai pas un jour visite à votre pays. Croyez, je vous prie, à mes sentiments bien affectueux."

Before discussing the fourth and last letter from Mauriac to Wiesel to which we have access, I would like to comment on another document brought to light by Caroline Mauriac in this book. It is a letter that Mauriac wrote to Wiesel's publisher, Editions du Seuil, on February 8, 1966, on the subject of Wiesel's forthcoming book *Le chant des morts* (*Legends of Our Time*). It began:[151]

> *Dear Sir: Here are a few words that you could publish at the beginning of Elie Wiesel's novel. What gives Wiesel a unique place among the novelists of his generation is that all the others have the experience of life, but only he has the experience of death. He was brought back to life from a camp of horrors when he was still a child. He has come up from the bottom of an abyss in which he had seen his whole family disappear. This is what gives to everything that he writes a certain resonance that no other work in any literature gives me. He is Lazarus whose descent into the netherworld made him lose his faith, and who then recovers it as he starts to live again.* [...] *Best wishes.*

There is nothing surprising in this letter. It only serves to confirm that, no matter what disagreements Mauriac might have had with Wiesel about the Israeli conquest and occupation of the Palestinians, he did not let them interfere with his friendship and support of the young writer. By this time their political disagreements had been simmering since 1963, and would explode about a year and a half later.

As I have already shown, Mauriac made it clear in his 1963 "*Bloc-Notes*" column that he had no illusions about Israeli expansionism. When, in 1967, Israel attacked the Arabs and destroyed Egypt's air force on the ground in a matter of minutes, Mauriac felt betrayed by this "preemptive" strike, which reminded him so much of the Nazi blitzkrieg. He wrote a devastating critique of Zionist expansionism in his weekly column of June 12, 1967, in *Le Figaro*. One sentence in the article was particularly prophetic. In it, he referred to the "mysterious power" (*pouvoir mystérieux*) that he thought God had given to the Jews, and asked:[152]

---

151 *Ibid.*, 398: "Cher Monsieur, Voici les quelques mots que vous pourriez publier en tête du roman d'Elie Wiesel. Ce qui donne à Elie Wiesel une place unique entre tous les romanciers de sa génération, c'est que tous les autres ont l'expérience de la vie, mais qu'il a, lui, l'expérience de la mort. Il est ressuscité par miracle d'un camp d'épouvante alors qu'il était un enfant. Il est remonté du fond d'un abîme où il avait vu disparaître tous les siens. C'est ce qui donne à tout ce qu'il écrit une résonance qu'aucune autre œuvre dans aucune littérature ne me donne. C'est Lazare à qui sa descente aux enfers aurait fait perdre la foi et qui la retrouve à mesure qu'il recommence à vivre. [...] Veuillez trouver ici, Cher Monsieur, l'expression de mes sentiments les meilleurs."

152 Mauriac, *Bloc-Notes*, vol. 4, June 2, 1967, 466: "S'en servira-t-il désormais pour une possession et pour une domination toute matérielle, et pour satisfaire sa volonté de puissance? Alors il s'étonnera lui-même de la haine qu'il aura suscitée et de la jalousie des peuples qu'il aura humiliés ou qui le redoutent et le rejettent parce qu'il est inassimilable."

> *Will Israel now use this power in order to occupy and to physically dominate* [the Palestinians] *while also satisfying its lust for power? If so, it will be amazed at the hatred it will arouse among the peoples it humiliates and who fear and reject it because it cannot be assimilated.*

In his next "*Bloc-Notes*" column, on June 18, 1967, he referred to the pouting friends of Israel who, like Wiesel, owed their primary allegiance to the Zionist state. Such readers were writing him letters of protest about his previous article. He wrote:

> *Friends of Israel write me letters full of sadness, or attack me in newspaper articles.*

To criticisms of Charles de Gaulle, France's president, he responded that de Gaulle's vocation was to put France before all else, including Jews and Arabs:[153]

> *He evaluates everything in terms of how it affects France's place in the world. But what do you expect! That is his vocation in life. If you look at his heroic role in* [France's] *history, he has been brought into this world for no other reason than to restore France, a conquered nation* [in 1940], *to the place it held before its defeat.*

Thus, a full six months before de Gaulle's famous press conference of November 27, 1967, in which he referred to the Jewish people as a "*peuple d'élite, sûr de lui et dominateur*" ("an elite people, sure of itself and domineering"), Mauriac was on record in strong and courageous opposition to Israeli Jewish imperialism.

According to Mauriac's conformist biographer, Jean Lacouture, on the basis of what Wiesel allegedly told him much later, in November 1979, Wiesel came to visit Mauriac the day after de Gaulle's 1967 remarks, and demanded that he publicly condemn de Gaulle. According to Wiesel's version of events, as supposedly told to Lacouture, Mauriac appeared on a television show shortly thereafter and "expressed, in opposition to what the general had said, a most fraternal expression of sympathy [for the Jewish people]."[154] Unfortunately, Lacouture is playing a linguistic game here, for while Mauriac continued to be a friend of French Jews and a firm supporter of de Gaulle's policy toward Israel, he remained until the end of his life an opponent of Israeli Jewish racism. Lacouture implies that Wiesel only con-

---

[153] *Ibid.*, June 18, 1967, 468: "Les amis d'Israël m'écrivent des lettres attristées, ou m'attaquent dans des feuilles[…] " "[…] ramène tout à une question de rang pour la France. Mais quoi! Telle est sa vocation. Il n'est venu au monde, à en juger par l'histoire dont il est le héros, pour rien d'autre que ce rétablissement d'une nation vaincue à la place qu'elle occupait avant sa défaite[…] ."

[154] Lacouture, *François Mauriac,* 623: "[…] opposa aux mots du général l'expression de la sympathie la plus fraternelle."

sented to renew his friendship with Mauriac on condition that the latter publicly condemn de Gaulle:[155]

> *Wiesel became his friend again, and profoundly renewed Mauriac's understanding of both the Old Testament and Judaism. To such a degree – Wiesel told me in November 1979 – that the aging Catholic writer wondered at the end of his life about the possibility of a profound altering of the relationship between Judaism and Christianity: "For me, it's too late.* [...]*"*

Lacouture is unable to document this claim for the simple reason that Mauriac never publicly condemned de Gaulle. His idyllic version of events, in which Mauriac rallies to Wiesel's call for support of Israel and the Jewish people, is contradicted by the fact of Mauriac's constant and unwavering support of de Gaulle. Thus, it would seem that the two did indeed exchange letters on this subject, but in the end Mauriac refused to let Wiesel dictate to him. From this point until Mauriac's death, their relationship was cold and distant. It was probably about this time that the wily Wiesel managed to get his letters back from his friend in order to suppress them.

Saint Cheron is much more vague and cautious on the subject of de Gaulle. In the end, however, he manages to invent a whopper of a lie, writing, without any proof whatsoever:[156]

> *Wiesel demanded that Mauriac protest against these remarks. Finally, the day came when he had an opportunity to express his disagreement with the general about the little phrase. It's easy to understand how difficult it must have been for him, since he admired de Gaulle so much. But once again, his gesture gave testimony to what an exemplary man and friend he was.*

Wiesel biographer Kolbert avoids the subject completely, and makes no mention of Wiesel's ever making demands on Mauriac about de Gaulle's comment.

In *Tous les fleuves*, Wiesel severely downplays this quarrel with Mauriac. In doing so, he backpedals from the myths contained in Lacouture's and Saint Cheron's fantasies and, in their place, substitutes a private disagreement. Of course, with Mauriac long dead, he can continue to say whatever he wants about his alleged private conversations without fear of contradiction. He told Harry Cargas:[157]

---

155 *Ibid.*, 623: "Wiesel redevint son ami, renouvelant profondément la vision qu'avait Mauriac de l'Ancien Testament et du judaïsme. Au point que – m'a raconté Wiesel en novembre 1979 – le vieil écrivain catholique s'interrogeait à la fin de sa vie sur la possibilité d'une révision profonde des rapports entre judaïsme et christianisme: 'Pour moi, il est trop tard[...] '"

156 Saint Cheron, *Elie Wiesel,* 157: "Wiesel exigea une protestation de Mauriac. Le jour vint où il lui fut donné de faire état de son désaccord avec le général sur cette petite phrase. Pour lui, qui l'admirait tant, on imagine ce que cela dut coûter. Une fois de plus, ce geste témoigne pour l'homme exemplaire et pour l'ami qu'il fut."

157 Harry James Cargas, "After Auschwitz: A Certain Script. An Interview with Elie Wiesel," *The Christian Century*, September 17, 1975, 791.

> *I thought I had to criticize the President, and Mauriac defended him, saying: "Nobody will make me believe that de Gaulle is anti-Semitic." To which I responded: "A man in his position is responsible not only for what he says, but also for the way in which his words are interpreted, and his little phrase is interpreted as anti-Jewish." Our disagreement didn't last long.*

In other words, the reality is that Mauriac, despite Wiesel's urging, never publicly turned against de Gaulle for this remark. He simply did not budge. He also remained a firm supporter of de Gaulle and his foreign policy with regard to Israel right up to the latter's resignation on April 28, 1969.

Barré's treatment of this subject offers a completely new interpretation of Mauriac's alleged quarrel with Wiesel about de Gaulle's words. First, Barré does not make it clear that it was de Gaulle's November 1967 "*petite phrase*" about the Jews being a "*peuple d'élite, sûr de lui, et dominateur*" that caused the problem between the two men. In fact, somewhat incredibly, he does not even mention that event. Clueless on this subject, Barré blames the "*Bloc-Notes*" column of June 12, 1967, cited above, for Wiesel's ire. As a result, he situates their disagreement in June 1967, and not in November of that year. He writes that Wiesel, in the days immediately following the June 12 column, put pressure on Mauriac and that, as a result, Mauriac "at Wiesel's request, agreed to sign a petition circulated by a committee organized to defend Israel."[158] Barré offers no further information about either the originators of this alleged petition or its content. Having eliminated the "petite phrase" from the discussion, Barré argues that the quarrel between the two men was about Mauriac's expression of blind devotion to de Gaulle in that June 12 column. He writes:[159]

> *His* [Mauriac's] *Jewish friends, feeling let down* [by Mauriac's column], *and led by Elie Wiesel, who immediately ceased to have any further contact with Mauriac, protested against what they considered to be, on his part, a betrayal of Israel and yet another proof of his blind devotion to de Gaulle.*

Barré's take on the "quarrel" not only removes de Gaulle's alleged anti-Semitism (and Mauriac's passive acceptance of it) from this legend, it also presents Wiesel as a somewhat traitorous partisan of a foreign country, Israel.

The fourth letter from Mauriac to Wiesel dates from January 7, 1970. It was written only nine months before his death. The brief note seems to have been written in answer to a greeting card or note that Wiesel sent

[158] Barré, *François Mauriac,* vol. 2, 435: "[…Mauriac] a accepté, à la demande d'Elie Wiesel, de donner sa signature à un comité de défense d'Israël."

[159] *Ibid.*, 436: "Se sentant lâchés, ses amis juifs, Elie Wiesel le premier, qui prend aussitôt ses distances avec Mauriac, protestent contre ce qu'ils estiment être, da sa part, une trahison d'Israël et une preuve supplémentaire de sa soumission aveugle à de Gaulle."

Mauriac to wish him a happy new year, and consists of only one sentence:[160]

> *I am very touched by your note, dear Elie Wiesel, and I hope, as you do, that peace will finally prevail in that place in the world which belongs to all of us, Jews, Christians, and Muslims. Yours truly.*

The fact that peace in the Middle East is the subject of Mauriac's note indicates the extent to which the issue had hijacked their relationship. It might also have been the last letter that Mauriac ever wrote to him. In it, Mauriac mentions peace in the Middle East, but probably only because Wiesel had brought up the subject in his own note, which indicates that it was he, Wiesel, who felt a need to mend fences with a by-now-disenchanted Mauriac.

Wiesel Insults the Memory of His Benefactor

Since Mauriac's death in 1970, Wiesel has continued to talk about his special relationship with his benefactor, adjusting the lighting depending on the circumstances. In his conversations with Harry Cargas, the guilt-ridden Catholic liberal who made a living as a Catholic journalist by being ever ready to accuse Pius XII and the Catholic Church of guilt for "the Holocaust," Wiesel always felt at ease. He could say anything he wanted about the Holocaust, and at this point in his career he continued to use his friendship with Mauriac as a weapon against the legacy of Pius XII:[157]

> *Mauriac returned again and again to this theme* [Catholic guilt for the Holocaust]. *And we became very close because of his recognition. He understood the part Christianity had played, and he was the first to come out against Pius XII. It wasn't Rolf Hochhuth, it was Mauriac who did it.*

A year later, in another interview, he again emphasized his debt to Mauriac:[161]

> *The fact is that, practically, I owe François Mauriac my career. He was a Christian, and we were very close friends. Had it not been for Mauriac, I would have become or remained an obscure writer, a journalist.*

In 1985, out of the blue and for reasons that were probably intended to strengthen his relationship with certain fellow Holocaust obsessives, Wiesel launched an attack on Mauriac for things he had written in the foreword to *La Nuit*. Wiesel most likely launched this assault against his erstwhile "friend" as a cold and calculated step in his Nobel campaign. Although, as I have shown above, Wiesel had thanked Mauriac for his

---

160 Mauriac, *Nouvelles Lettres,* 334: "Je suis très touché par vos vœux, cher Elie Wiesel, et j'espère comme vous que la paix finira par régner sur cet endroit du monde qui nous appartient à tous, juifs et chrétiens, et musulmans [...]. De tout cœur vôtre."

161 Cargas, *Conversation,* 33.

foreword to *Night*, as Mauriac's letter of May 5, 1958, attests, he could still write in 1985:[162]

> *We separated at one point. I did not like his preface to* Night. *It was very generous of him to write it. Whatever success I had in France was really due to him. He meant it. He was sincere, he was an* ohev Yisrael – *a lover of the Jewish people. Of course, as a Catholic he had to see the book through his own viewpoint. Therefore, there are some Christological overtones in the preface which I don't like. But it is his preface – not mine.*

What hypocrisy! If Wiesel disliked the foreword so much and had so many theological problems with it, why did he not have the courage to tell Mauriac that he would prefer not to have it? If the two men "separated at one point," it was clearly not over the foreword to *Night* in 1958, but over Mauriac's opposition, expressed as early as 1963, to Israeli aggression and disregard for Palestinian rights.

Wiesel continued his attacks on Mauriac, always with a view toward distorting the historical record. The next topic on which he chose to launch a polemic was the issue of Mauriac's dedication to him of his biography of Christ, entitled *The Son of Man*. Wiesel was determined to find fault with Mauriac's simple, kind and loving gesture in having dedicated the book to his young Jewish friend whom he saw as a Christ-like figure: Wiesel wrote (*ibid.*):

> *Then he wrote a book called the* Son of Man [Le fils de l'homme]. *It was published in French, in English, in many languages – he was a great man. It is his personal biography of Jesus. He sent me the book, and when I opened it, I was shocked. It was dedicated to me in a way which moved me to protest, because he dared to compare me to Christ, and that was a bit too much. He said, "This book I dedicate to Elie Wiesel, who was a crucified Jewish child who stands for many others." And then I had to say it. I said, "I accept your present. It is very nice of you, but the comparison with Jesus Christ is surely not applicable to me because of my background, because of my attitude, and because of my belief." That is when we decided to start our disputations. And when they will be published, they will create some stir.*

Once again, Wiesel is creating a problem where there was none. Here is what Mauriac actually wrote in his foreword to *The Son of Man*:

> *To Elie Wiesel, who was a crucified Jewish child, his friend, F. M. (A Elie Wiesel, un enfant juif crucifié, son ami. F. M.)*

That was it. There was nothing in Mauriac's dedication of his book to Wiesel that includes the term "who stands for many others." Wiesel is once again telling a lie, claiming that his relationship with Mauriac soured in 1958, when *The Son of Man* was published. Nothing could be further from the truth, for they remained friends at that time, and all the available evi-

[162] Abrahamson, *Against Silence*, vol. 3, 110.

dence shows that they remained firm friends until Mauriac's column of 1963 denouncing Israeli racism. That is when their "disputations" began. I might add that one finds no reference in Wiesel's autobiography to either his correspondence with Mauriac or to the "disputations" contained therein. He refers instead to his diary as the source of his recollections of Mauriac:[163]

> *In my diary, I made many notes about my conversations with François Mauriac. They are all concerned with religion, politics, history and literature.*

Significantly, Wiesel deleted this sentence from the English "translation" of *Tous les fleuves*. Its disappearance indicates that, in the English-speaking world, Wiesel's diary joins his correspondence with Mauriac, including the problematical "disputations" contained therein, as non-existent texts. Their erasure is consistent with the use of "retroactive continuity" in the Holocaust narrative as a whole. In this case, since Wiesel considers both the diary and the correspondence to be incriminating documents, he has simply written them out of the Mauriac-Wiesel story, as if they had never existed.

Mauriac's Death and State Funeral

Wiesel's culturally ingrained hatred of Catholicism was revealed in an unexpected way on the day of Mauriac's state funeral, which was held on Saturday, September 5, 1970. With regard to this event, which Wiesel deliberately made a point of *not* attending, he later wrote:[164]

> *I happened to be in Paris on the day of his funeral. Paul Flamand* [the Catholic intellectual who was his editor at Editions du Seuil] *and I went over to Notre Dame. But there were too many people, so we stayed outside. In silence.*

Mauriac had broken his right shoulder as the result of a fall, at home, in April 1969. He was never the same afterward, and was in and out of the hospital for about the next fifteen months. He died in the early hours of Tuesday, September 1, and plans were set in motion by the French government to organize a state funeral in his honor over the following weekend. The day after he died, the *New York Times* published an editorial honoring him. On Friday evening, September 4, a memorial ceremony was held at the Institut de France, where the Académie Française meets, with the other 39 "immortals" in attendance. The following day, Saturday, September 5, the State Funeral, including a solemn high mass, was held at Notre Dame with President Georges Pompidou in attendance. Although

---

163 *Tous les fleuves*, 343: "Dans mon journal, j'ai conservé de nombreuses notes sur mes conversations avec François Mauriac. Elles touchent toutes à la religion, la politique, l'histoire et la littérature."

164 *Ibid.*: "Je me trouvai par hasard à Paris je jour de ses obsèques. Paul Flamand et moi sommes allés à Notre-Dame. Il y avait trop de monde. Nous restâmes dehors. Silencieux."

Wiesel had received an invitation and actually traveled to Paris for the event, he still could not bring himself to enter Notre Dame Cathedral. Despite the fact that Mauriac, his benefactor, had almost single-handedly made his career as a writer, Wiesel still did not enter the church.

In behaving this way, he showed that he was still under the influence of the ultra-orthodox rabbis who had taught him in childhood to never enter a Catholic church. Since the men under whose tutelage Wiesel had grown up considered the statues routinely found in Catholic churches to be the equivalent of pagan idols, he would be committing a sin in the eyes of the rabbis if he ever entered such a place. Thus, to this day, there exists no oral or photographic evidence to the effect that Wiesel has ever attended an event of any kind held in a Catholic church. Since Wiesel's aversion for Catholicism is both religious and cultural in nature, and since he apparently did not want to admit this fact to his many naïve non-Jewish readers, he had to invent a plausible reason for not setting foot in the church. No problem, he simply invented the pretext that he remained outside Notre Dame because of the large crowd in attendance. Yet, given the load of inherited prejudices that he carries around within himself due to his religious upbringing, his decision to remain outside "in silence" was the only means available to him to pay homage to his deceased friend.

Postscript on Mauriac and de Gaulle

Jean Lacouture's myth, supported in his own way by Saint Cheron, according to which Mauriac publicly rebuked de Gaulle at Wiesel's insistence for having called the Jews a "*peuple d'élite, sûr de lui et dominateur*," is just that: a myth. This event never happened, and, if anything, the bond between de Gaulle and Mauriac strengthened as the latter's death approached.

Michel Droit, the former French Resistance member, biographer and confidant of de Gaulle, novelist, man of letters and member of the Académie Française, mentions Mauriac many times in his diary covering the closing years of the 1960s. When news began to spread that Mauriac was about to die, Droit noted that de Gaulle, who had been out of power since April 28, 1969, had sent a telegram and asked to be kept up to date on Mauriac's condition. Even more important, however, was the discussion that Droit had with de Gaulle about Mauriac's deteriorating state of health and his accomplishments as a writer, including the astonishing success of his 1967 novel, *Un adolescent d'autrefois* [Engl.: *Maltaverne*, 1970]. De Gaulle had read the book and, according to Droit, ranked it among Mauriac's greatest works of fiction. While discussing the subject, he had also blurted out rather unexpectedly, "Well, what do you expect, he's our greatest living writer."[165] Two days later, Droit wrote a note to Mauriac telling him what de Gaulle had said about him. Jeanne Mauriac brought it to the hospital, read it to Mauriac, and reported back that he had been deeply moved by de Gaulle's words. Droit then reflected on what had happened and, referring to de Gaulle's haughty and distant manner with most people, including those he liked and admired, such as Mauriac, he wrote:[166]

> *In telling him scrupulously what the General had said, without omitting even one detail, I had probably told Mauriac more* [about how much de Gaulle admired him] *than the General had ever expressed personally.*

---

[165] Michel Droit, *Les Feux du Crépuscule, Journal 1968 -1969 -1970* (Paris: Plon, 1977), 118: "Et puis, que voulez-vous, c'est notre plus grand écrivain vivant!"

[166] *Ibid.*, 119: "En lui rapportant scrupuleusement les propos qui venaient de m'être tenus, sans en omettre un seul, peut-être ai-je dit à François Mauriac davantage que le Général ne lui a jamais directement exprimé."

Chapter V
Wiesel at Auschwitz

Is Wiesel Guilty of Identity Theft? Was He Ever a Detainee at Auschwitz or Buchenwald?

In March 2009, an article about a former Auschwitz detainee, Miklós Grüner, appeared in a Hungarian newspaper.[167] Grüner, a Hungarian Jew, was a boy of fifteen when he was deported to Auschwitz, where he worked in a factory in the Monowitz industrial complex. He claims that, while there, he was befriended by two older men, the Wiesel brothers, Lazar and Abraham, who had been friends of his father. He has also retained a vivid memory over the years that the number tattooed on Lazar Wiesel's arm was A-7713. Later, in 1986, when Wiesel was awarded the Nobel Peace Prize, a Swedish journalist allegedly invited Grüner to meet Wiesel in order to renew their acquaintance. However, the meeting did not go well.

Miklós recalls that during this strange meeting, Elie Wiesel refused to show him the tattooed number on his arm, saying he didn't want to exhibit his body. Miklós adds that Elie Wiesel showed his tattooed number afterward to an Israeli journalist whom Miklós met and this journalist told Miklós that he didn't have time to identify the number but […] was certain it wasn't a tattoo. Miklós says:[168]

> *After that meeting with Wiesel, I spent twenty years of research and found out that the man calling himself Elie Wiesel has never been in a Nazi concentration camp, since he was not included in any official list of detainees.*

If this accusation is true, it is an extremely serious one. But is it true? Or is Grüner just another Holocaust profiteer trying to carve out a victimhood space for himself? The two questions have inspired the revisionist re-

167 www.haon.hu/hirek/magyarorszag/cikk/meg-mindig-kiserti-a-halaltabor/cn/haon-news-FCUWeb-20090303-0604233755.

168 www.henrymakow.com/translated_from_the_hungarian.html.

Ung. Jude

Konzentrationslager Art der Haft: Gef.-Nr.:

Name und Vorname: WIESEL Lazar
geb.: 4. 9. 13 zu:
Wohnort: Maramarossziget
Beruf: Schlosserlehrling Rel.:
Staatsangehörigkeit: Ungarn Stand:
Name der Eltern: Rasse:
Wohnort:
Name der Ehefrau: Rasse
Wohnort:
Kinder: Alleiniger Ernährer der Familie oder der Eltern:
Vorbildung: 26.1.45 KL. Auschwitz
Militärdienstzeit: von — bis
Kriegsdienstzeit: von — bis
Grösse: Nase: Haare: Gestalt:
Mund: Bart: Gesicht: Ohren:
Sprache: Augen: Zähne:

Illustration 3: Personal file card for Lázár Wiesel (KL Buchenwald)

searcher Carlo Mattogno, whose knowledge of Holocaust-related archival resources in Germany, Poland, Russia, and elsewhere is second to none, to launch an inquiry. What Mattogno has discovered is interesting: the man who calls himself Elie Wiesel, and who has always claimed that his Auschwitz ID number was A-7713, which was issued on May 24, 1944, might have actually usurped the identity of Grüner's friend. This person, Lazar Wiesel, who shared his last name with Wiesel, was also a Jew from Sighet, but was born on September 4, 1913. Mattogno found his file card from Buchenwald and reproduces it in his article (see Illustration 3).[169]

What this card revealed was that Lazar Wiesel arrived at Buchenwald and was registered there on January 26, 1945. At that time, he was given a new Buchenwald serial number, 123565, but his Auschwitz number, A-7713, also appeared on the form, and is written in at the top center. The date of January 26, 1945, indicating the date on which Lazar Wiesel's train from Auschwitz arrived at Buchenwald, is also stamped on the form. If Mattogno is right, Elie Wiesel, in taking over someone else's ID number, is not the man he claims to be, and was thus never a detainee at either Auschwitz or Buchenwald. These findings by Mattogno make it all the more ur-

[169] Carlo Mattogno, "Elie Wiesel, 'The Most Authoritative Living Witness' of the Shoah?," *Inconvenient History: An Independent Revisionist Blog*, February 24, 2010; www.revblog.codoh.com/2010/02/elie-wiesel-the-most-authoritative-living-witness-of-the-shoah/; see the updated version of this paper in the Appendix to this book.

gent for the authorities at the USHMM to release the full personnel files for Wiesel and all his family members.

Fundamental Dishonesty of *Night*'s Conformist Critics

Since *Night* contains so many historical falsehoods, the conformist scholars and teachers who comment on the book must quickly learn to present it in a way that avoids discussion of its problematical pages and passages. Generally speaking, there are two major categories of deception. First, there is the utterly mendacious, or implausible. Then there are the plausible claims that are weakened because they contradict the Holocaust's master narrative. One or the other assertion can be true, but both cannot be true. As an example of what I call the mendacious and implausible, we have Wiesel's burning trenches, their smoke visible outside the area of the camp compound and possibly for miles around, in which he claims to have seen children burnt alive. Conformist critics accept this eyewitness claim as true. But since the aerial photos, widely available on the Internet these days, show that this mass open-air burning of living multitudes of people never happened, such a belief is unfounded. Thus, the conformist critics simply avoid discussion of the subject.

An example of the second general category, in which a Wiesel claim contradicts the master narrative of the Holocaust, is offered by the episode involving his sore foot. In fact there are two contradictions here. In January 1945, Wiesel allegedly suffered from a case of frostbite, although the reader must construe this malady, since he does not use this word in his novel. Since his feet were sensitive to the cold, one of them began to swell. This event is quite plausible. In a word, it could have happened. Logically speaking, however, and in accordance with the vulgate version of the Holocaust, as it is repeated endlessly in the Zionist media, Wiesel ought to have been sent to the alleged gas chamber at Birkenau, or otherwise executed, for the simple reason that he could not work. (The Holocaust vulgate also claims that by January 1945 an order had been given to stop the alleged extermination program, but no documentary proof has ever been offered in support of this claim[170]). But this did not happen. He was not killed. Yet another contradiction of the Holocaust master narrative in this episode is found in the fact that he was not only spared gassing, he was operated on and restored to health by a Jewish surgeon at the camp hospital! This episode implies that German medical care, a very scarce commodity during

[170] The only evidence ever cited is the testimony by SS-Standartenführer Kurt Becher, IMT document PS-3762; *IMT*, vol. 33, 68f. However, Becher clearly made it up to save his neck, as he confessed to an acquaintance; see Göran Holming, "Himmlers Befehl, die Vergasung der Juden zu stoppen," *Vierteljahreshefte für freie Geschichtsforschung*, vol. 1. no. 4, 1997, 258f.; www.vho.org/VffG/1997/4/HolHim4.html.

the war years, was routinely given to sick or injured Jews. Yet the Holocaust master narrative states that medical care for inmates at Auschwitz was a sham, if not completely lacking.

There exists a multitude of books, articles and online resources that studiously evade such issues in order to deceive readers, especially young ones. Examples of this method can be found in the many manuals that are available in book form, such as the *Student Companion to Elie Wiesel* by Sanford Sternlicht or the *Sparknotes Guide to Night.* Then, of course, there are the Internet resources. They range from *Oprah's Book Club Guide to Night*, in which Wiesel himself is featured as a narrator, to the study guide on *Night* in the series called *Cliff Notes*, which usually contain a plot summary, biographical information on the author, and critical commentary. Such books are intended for high school students who must read the book in class as part of the state-supported indoctrination program that is administered to them in support of our state religion, the Holocaust.

These and other Internet guides all have one thing in common: avoiding direct questioning of the passages in the book that contradict the basic tenets of our state religion. Students read *Night* as part of their initiation into a state-imposed belief system, not into independent thinking. Thus, passages that provoke thought are avoided or passed over rapidly without comment. And since the Holocaust is our state religion, the instructors who actually teach this book to students on the high school level must engage in a self-imposed process of mental gymnastics even before they face a class. In so doing, they internalize the untenable belief that everything in Wiesel's book is true and really happened, because the book is an autobiography. Thus, on encountering events in *Night* such as those mentioned above, whether plausible or implausible, they must first flip a mental switch, that of voluntary blindness, before setting to work brainwashing their charges.

In order to help such teachers, as well as other readers, who want to understand *Night* for what it is, a work of fiction, I have created the following list, not exhaustive by any means, of historical problems.

Problem #1: Botched Chronology and Possible Identity Theft

Date of Departure from Sighet

The traditional *bildungsroman*, or novel of initiation into adulthood, always involves travel away from home as an essential part of the young man's journey to adulthood. Wiesel's novel is consistent with this pattern. The hero's travels will result in the creation of a new man, one who is ready to enter into the adult world. However, in his novel, Wiesel is extremely careless with regard to the basic question of a coherent chronology, and his carelessness extends even to the key issue of his departure from his hometown of Sighet and his arrival at Auschwitz. In an autobiography, in which everything is supposedly true, as Wiesel has claimed many times for *Night*, something as basic as an internally coherent chronology should be a given.

But that is not the case here. Wiesel seems to have invented dates as he went along, with the result that his story is a hodgepodge of events that take place in an internally contradictory time frame. I suspect that one reason for this problem is that Wiesel may have plagiarized other former detainees' texts, probably written in Yiddish, for his own Yiddish account, *Un di velt hot geshvign*. When he published his Yiddish book, his principal intention was to attack Germans and other gentiles, so he paid little or no attention to chronological detail. The main thrust of *Un di velt hot geshvign* involved Jewish racial hatred and the need to keep it alive. He had no idea at the time that the book would become the basis for one of the most sacred texts of the Holocaust. Thus Wiesel may well have never even bothered to stitch his various borrowings together into a coherent whole. Later, when Mauriac rewrote *Un di velt* on the basis of the bridge text that Wiesel had prepared for him, and, in the words of Holocaust theologian Naomi Seidman, "radically transformed" it into a French novel, he apparently concerned himself only with questions of language and style. He left everything else alone. As a result, *Night* is marred by a serious disconnect between the historical record and Wiesel's alleged experiences within the context of that record.

When did Wiesel leave Sighet for Auschwitz? The basic textual reference for establishing the novel's timeline is the Jewish Feast of Pentecost. Wiesel writes:[171]

> *On the Saturday before Pentecost (Shavuot), in the spring sunshine, people strolled, carefree and unheeding, through the swarming streets. They chatted happily.*

In 1944, the first day of Shavuot fell on Sunday, May 28. Thus, the day described above was May 27. According to Wiesel, the first trainload of Jews bound from Sighet for Auschwitz left the next day, Sunday, May 28, on the Jewish feast day of Pentecost. Wiesel then speaks of Monday ("*lundi*," *Nuit*, 37), then of dawn ("*aube*," 38), and then of another dawn ("*aube*," 41). He then writes:[172]

> *Saturday, our day of rest, had been chosen for our departure.*

The Jews of Sighet ate their ritual dinner on Friday evening, June 2, and then, the next morning ("*le lendemain matin*," 43), that is, on Saturday,

[171] *Nuit*, 29: "Le samedi précédant la Pentecôte (Shavuot), sous un soleil printanier, les gens se promenaient insouciants à travers les rues grouillantes de monde. On bavardait gaîment."

[172] *Ibid.*, 42: "Samedi, le jour du repos, était le jour choisi pour notre expulsion."

June 3, 1944, they left for Auschwitz. Since the trip usually took three to four days, they would have arrived on June 6 or June 7. Yet Wiesel writes as follows about his first full day in Poland:[173]

> *It was a beautiful April day. Springtime's sweet perfume floated in the air. The sun was setting in the west.*

This chronology is nonsensical, for if Wiesel left Sighet in June, he could not have arrived in April. It is this incoherence that leads me to suspect a botched job of plagiarism.

Marion Wiesel's Deceptive "New" Translation of *Night*

This botched chronology, possibly resulting from Wiesel's plagiarism of other Yiddish-language texts, helps to explain why a new translation of *Night* was deemed necessary by Wiesel and his Holocaust fundamentalist backers. With a breathtaking Orwellian stroke of the pen, Wiesel's wife has attempted to cover over a number of glaring defects in Wiesel's *Night*. Thus, the passage quoted above, and on which the chronology of the whole novel is based, "the Saturday before Pentecost (Shavuot)" ("*le samedi précédant la Pentecôte*"), has now been translated as "some two weeks before Shavuot."[174] By moving the whole chronology of the novel back two weeks, Wiesel and his wife are striving to have Wiesel leave Sighet on or about May 21, 1944, not June 3.

One of the reasons why Marion Wiesel has done this is to bring Wiesel's arrival at Auschwitz into line with that of the man whose identity Wiesel appears to have stolen, Lazar Wiesel, also from Sighet, but born in 1913. In keeping with the use of retroactive continuity, Wiesel's wife passes off this mendacious translation as if it were faithful to the original text from *La Nuit*, for there is no footnote alerting the reader that the original text has been altered through the use of this deliberate mistranslation.

Then, for consistency's sake, Wiesel's original description of his arrival in Auschwitz – "it was a beautiful day in April" ("*c'était une belle journée d'avril*") – has also been doctored in the new translation to "it was a beautiful day in May."[175] Once again, this has been done without a note to alert the reader to this deliberate mistranslation. It is truly shocking that a widely respected publishing house like Farrar, Straus & Giroux would actually lend its name to such a travesty.

Unfortunately, Marion Wiesel is not the first person to have tampered abusively with her husband's text in order to make it say what it most emphatically does *not* say. There is a precedent for what she has done, and the

[173] *Ibid.*, 69: "C'était une belle journée d'avril. Des parfums de printemps flottaient dans l'air. Le soleil baissait vers l'ouest."

[174] Elie Wiesel, *Night*, tr. Marion Wiesel (N.Y.: Farrar, Straus & Giroux, 2006), 12.

[175] *Ibid.*, 40.

culprit, as far as is known, is the publishing house that brought out the original German translation of *La Nuit* in 1962.[176]

In both cases, the counterfeiters seem to have acted in an attempt to correct the strong impression given by Wiesel of never having actually been in either Auschwitz or Buchenwald. In his novel, Wiesel claimed to have seen outdoor burning operations of live victims, while the master narrative of the Holocaust story, by 1962, was centered on the mythical gas chambers. The German falsifiers seem to have been concerned about two things: Wiesel's overall lack of verisimilitude in his description of killing operations, and his failure to even mention the gas chambers. Thus, the words crematory/ies and crematory oven(s) were simply translated as "gas chamber(s)" in 15 instances. This was done so systematically that the translator by accident even turned the Buchenwald crematory into a gas chamber, although everybody agrees that there was no homicidal gas chamber at the Buchenwald camp.[177] In this way, by a simple swipe of the pen, the text of what Wiesel had supposedly seen became more compelling and, at the same time, was brought into conformity with the Holocaust master narra□ive. On the other hand, Mrs. Wiesel, preoccupied with other matters some 40 years later, concentrates on the narrative blunders relating to the novel's botched chronology.

Carlo Mattogno's Accusation of Identity Theft

Carlo Mattogno, in his claim regarding Wiesel's possible theft of someone else's identity, emphasizes that the ID number in question was assigned on May 24, 1944. Thus, the dates of June 6 or 7, which I have extrapolated from Wiesel's chronology in the novel, are off by about two weeks. Furthermore, Mattogno, citing extant records, goes even further, stating that two thousand numbers, from A-5729 through A-7728, were distributed on that day, and suggests that Wiesel stole the identity of a man from Sighet named Lazar Wiesel, a person who might have been a distant relative and who might possibly have been known to Wiesel. Lazar Wiesel is listed in Buchenwald records as born in 1913, and was tattooed at Auschwitz with ID # A-7713 on May 24, 1944.

Such an impersonation would help to explain why Wiesel's French language biographer, Saint Cheron, tells us that Wiesel, whose name was Eliezer, or Elie, was actually called "Lazar," a diminutive of Eliezer, through the end of the 1940s. Saint Cheron wrote of Wiesel that "for many

176 *Die Nacht zu begraben, Elisha*, tr. Kurt Meyer-Clason (Berlin: Ullstein, 1962).

177 See the comparison of the three language editions (French, English, German) by Jürgen Graf in: Robert Faurisson, "Witnesses to the Gas Chambers of Auschwitz," in: Germar Rudolf (ed.), *Dissecting the Holocaust: The Growing Critique of "Truth" and "Memory,"* (Chicago, Ill.: Theses & Dissertations Press, 2003), 144.

years, until the end of the 1940s, [he] was called Lazar."[178] Thus, what seems like a gratuitous fact of no particular importance in Saint Cheron's authorized biography of Wiesel could have actually been an attempt to provide a cover story for Wiesel's theft of someone else's identity.

Here is what Wiesel writes about his tattoo in *La Nuit*:[179]

> *The three veteran detainees, with needles in their hands, engraved a number on our left arm. I became A-7713. From this point on, I had no other name.*

Yet, Wiesel's tattoo cannot be discerned on any extant photograph or film of him.[180] Nor have Elie Wiesel's personal and medical records ever been made public – if they exist; are they being withheld by the various Holocaust museums and record centers? Thus, there is no way of knowing for sure where Wiesel spent the war years.[181]

Did Wiesel Assign another Inmate's Identity to His Father?

In a follow-up article on Wiesel's theft of Lazar Wiesel's identity, Mattogno discusses the contents of Miklós Grüner's Hungarian language website. Of particular interest for the purposes of the present study is the fact that Wiesel has claimed that his father was registered at Auschwitz under the ID # A-7712. Yet the documents shown on Grüner's website, which came to him uncensored because he is a former detainee, clearly indicate that ID # 7712 did not belong to Wiesel's father (Shlomo Wiesel), as he has claimed, but to a man named Abram (Abraham) Wiesel (Viesel), born in 1900. Mattogno then concludes:[182]

> *The Auschwitz ID number A-7712 was assigned on 24 May 1944 to Abraham Viezel, born on 10 October 1900 at Maromarossziget, registered at Buchenwald on 26 January 1945 under the ID number 123488, who died in this camp on 2 February.*

Mattogno's allegation of identity theft only adds further justification to the task I have undertaken. This question of whether or not Wiesel was actually deported to Auschwitz and Buchenwald is of vital importance not only

[178] Saint Cheron, Elie Wiesel, 16: "[…] que l'on appela longtemps Lazar jusqu'à la fin des années 1940 […]"

[179] Wiesel, *La Nuit*, 72: "Les trois 'anciens,' des aiguilles à la main, nous gravaient un numéro sur le bras gauche. Je devins A-7713. Je n'eus plus désormais d'autre nom."

[180] As mentioned in my Introduction, there exists a website devoted to the question of Wiesel's tattoo and identity: www.eliewieseltattoo.com.

[181] Jean Robin, "Elie Wiesel n'a pas le tatouage qu'il prétend avoir." *Enquête et Débat*, December 24, 2012. www.enquete-debat.fr/archives/elie-wiesel-na-pas-le-tatouage-dauschwitz-quil-pretend-avoir-94416 . Robin presents the texts of an email exchange he engaged in with Wojciech Płosa, the head of archives at Auschwitz. In the exchange, the latter confirmed the truth of Mattogno's reading of the Grüner and Wiesel ID cards.

[182] Carlo Mattogno, "Elie Wiesel: New Documents," *Inconvenient History: An Independent Revisionist Blog*, March 26, 2010; www.revblog.codoh.com/2010/03/elie-wiesel-new-documents/; see the updated version of this article in the Appendix to this book.

with respect to his personal identity, but also to the Jewish Holocaust story as a whole. Given the pre-eminent status that the Holocaustian establishment has bestowed upon Wiesel as the most authoritative and trustworthy eye-witness to the Holocaust, solid proof that he is an imposter would both destroy his credibility and represent yet another nail in the coffin of the orthodox Holocaust narrative.

Wiesel Depicts Young Orthodox Jews' Sexual Orgy on the Train

One of the most subversive passages about the specifically Hasidic world of Orthodox Jewry to be found in Wiesel's novel concerns his brief description of the young Orthodox Jews copulating on the train after their departure from Sighet. It is truly shocking. He writes:[183]

> *Freed from any social constraint, the young people let themselves go and yielded to their base instincts. Under the cover of night, they copulated with one another in our very midst, without any concern about who might be watching, as if they were all alone in the world. The others pretended not to notice.*

This passage has caused a great deal of concern among rabbis and other Jews over the years. Since it offers a window into one of the unsavory aspects of the world of Orthodox Jewry, such people have wanted that window to be closed. Although Wiesel uses the words "*les jeunes*," or "young people," we must not interpret this term as referring only to heterosexual copulation, for it could have also included acts of sodomy between boys. Since this passage states that these Jewish "young people" were openly copulating while the adults looked the other way, the Holocaustian fundamentalists succeeded in convincing Wiesel, in 2007, to change the verb "*s'accoupler*" (to copulate) to "*s'attoucher*" (to caress one another). Since then, as unbelievable as it might seem, but in keeping with the use of the deceptive narrative technique of retroactive continuity in the telling of the Jewish Holocaust story, the original French text of the novel has been changed in all subsequent re-editions in order to accommodate these rabbinical objections. Marion Wiesel readily accepted this new word, "*s'attoucher*" (which she translated as "caressed one another," 23), and incorporated it into her translation. She did so as if the original verb, "*s'accoupler*" (to copulate) had never existed. These changes demonstrate once again that Wiesel's book is actually a novel and not an "autobiography," in which every event recounted is represented as true and having really happened.

183 Wiesel, *Nuit*, 45: "Libérés de toute censure sociale, les jeunes se laissaient aller ouvertement à leurs instincts et à la faveur de la nuit, s'accouplaient au milieu de nous, sans se préoccuper de qui que se fût, seuls dans le monde. Les autres faisaient semblant de ne rien voir."

Problem #2: Wiesel "Saw" Eichmann at Sighet

Gestapo Officers on the Platform

The first chapter of *Night* ends with a depiction of German soldiers walking on the train platform at Sighet. The text reads:[184]

> *Two Gestapo officers, with big smiles on their faces, strolled along the platform. On the whole, the operation had gone well.*

The only reason why Wiesel could have assumed that the two men were officers would have been that they wore uniforms. Unfortunately, Wiesel is confused here between the Gestapo, the Nazi-state secret police, and the SS. The former, whose principal responsibility was to spy on the civilian population, did not wear uniforms. Thus, on a basic point, Wiesel shows that he does not know what he is talking about.

Wiesel makes no mention of Adolf Eichmann in this scene or anywhere else in the novel. This caution has served him well. But Wiesel also had no way of knowing, as he wrote in 1954/55, whether Eichmann had been in Sighet in May 1944. It must be recalled that Eichmann only became famous in 1960, after Israeli government Mossad agents kidnapped him. They then shipped him to Israel where he was forced to serve as the main attraction in a lugubrious Israeli version of a Stalinist show trial. Thus, there is no reason why the deportees in 1944, or Wiesel in 1954/55, should have attached any particular importance to the German officers on the platform. But that fact did not keep Wiesel from stating years later, in 1987, that he had seen Eichmann in Sighet on that day in 1944.

In 1987, three decades after this scene appeared in *Night*, the *New York Times* and the various Jewish organizations that represent Holocaust fundamentalism were cementing Wiesel's status as our nation's Holocaust High Priest. By then, having been recognized as such by the president of the United States in 1985, and then awarded the Nobel Peace Prize in 1986, Wiesel had truly become not only "a great man in Israel," as the Rabbi of Wizhnitz had predicted in 1936 (according to Wiesel), his bizarre fame also resonated throughout the world. This renown might perhaps explain why he seems to have felt a need to enhance his growing media image by claiming to have seen Eichmann, one of the foremost bogeymen of the Jewish Holocaust story, in 1944. Since by 1987 Wiesel was being billed as *the* eyewitness to the Holocaust, he was tempted to overreach. Thus, out of the blue, he told Fanny-Brigitte Cohen, whose interview book with him appeared in conjunction with his testimony as a Holocaust eyewitness at the 1987 Barbie trial, that one of the officers depicted in *Night* on the train platform had been Adolf Eichmann, and that he had only begun to realize

---

[184] *Ibid.*, 44: "Sur le quai déambulaient deux officiers de la Gestapo, tout souriants; somme toute, cela s'était bien passé."

this when he saw Eichmann in the courtroom at his show trial in Jerusalem:[185]

> *First of all, I did recognize him. Eichmann had come to Sighet, my home town, to supervise the departure of the last Jews; at this point in time there were only him and one other German to oversee a ghetto containing 15,000 to 25,000 Jews.* [...] *I had seen Eichmann the last day, at the railroad station. I observed this German officer with his melancholy air. He seemed to be sad at the thought that his work was finished. He must have really liked to put Jews into railroad cars, so much so that he would have liked to do it for the rest of his life.*

This claim to have seen Eichmann is mendacious for at least two reasons. First, Eichmann was not in Sighet on this day, and the master narrative of the Jewish Holocaust story has never claimed that he was. In this matter, therefore, the whole burden of proof rests on Wiesel's shoulders. Second, the German officers presented in *La Nuit* as having "big smiles on their faces" are now suddenly struck with melancholy.

Wiesel employs here the widespread Holocaust eyewitness trope according to which the self-identified eyewitness only finds out later the true meaning of what he had supposedly seen. The trope allows the mendacious eyewitness to interpose a narrative and exculpatory screen between his supposedly sincere testimony and the deliberate mendacity it contains. This drastic alternation offers further proof that Eichmann's presence in Sighet was completely imagined by Wiesel. Additional proof of the fact that Wiesel never saw Eichmann at Sighet is found in Wiesel's 1961 article in *Commentary*, the organ of the American Jewish Committee. Its subject was the Eichmann trial, which Wiesel covered for them as a reporter.[186] Logically, if he had actually seen Eichmann on the station platform in Sighet in 1944, he would have stated in that piece that he had recognized Eichmann at the trial. Yet he made *no* mention of recognizing Eichmann in that lengthy article, or anywhere else for that matter.

This omission was repeated in another article he published in *Commentary* the following year. Even though his subject was "hate," Eichmann's alleged presence at Sighet did not come up. Wiesel was nonetheless able to express therein his unequivocal hatred of Germans when he wrote:[187]

---

185 Cohen, *Qui êtes-vous?*, 56f.: "D'abord, je l'ai reconnu. Eichmann était venu à Sighet, ma ville natale, pour superviser le départ des derniers Juifs; il n'y avait, à ce moment, que lui et un autre Allemand pour surveiller un ghetto qui comptait de 15.000 à 25.000 Juifs. [...] J'avais vu Eichmann le dernier jour, à la gare. J'observais cet officier allemand qui avait l'air mélancolique. Il semblait triste en contemplant son travail terminé. Il devait tellement aimer fourrer des Juifs dans les wagons, qu'il aurait peut-être voulu continuer ainsi toute sa vie!"

186 Elie Wiesel, "Eichmann's Victims and the Unheard Testimony," *Commentary*, December 16, 1961, 510-516.

187 Elie Wiesel, "An Appointment with Hate," *Commentary*, December 1962. This article

> *Every Jew, somewhere in his being, should set apart a zone of hate – healthy, virile hate, – for what the German personifies and for what persists in the Germans. To do otherwise would be a betrayal of the dead.*

Thus, what Wiesel told Cohen in 1987 was a falsehood; gratuitous, unnecessary lies like this one have become more and more of a potential embarrassment for the Holocaust fundamentalists who dominate the Zionist media. By 1995, Wiesel had apparently been advised to give up his absurd and historically inaccurate claim about having seen Eichmann. Whatever the reason, he changed his story once again. In 1995, in *Tous les fleuves*, the sighting of Eichmann is displaced from the train station to his arrival in the town with the German forces. Also, Wiesel uses the "I only found out later" trope to screen his mendacity:[188]

> *The arrival of two senior Gestapo officers – later people will tell us that one of the two was Eichmann himself, and that's why I thought I had recognized him at his trial in Jerusalem.*

Wiesel later recycled the same lie for a large audience in America's mass circulation Sunday magazine supplement:[189]

> *Two high-ranking Gestapo officers arrived. (We later were told that one of them was Adolf Eichmann himself, which is why I think I recognized him during his trial in Jerusalem.)*

The use of the "we only found out later " trope, to which Wiesel has recourse once again, shows that it is easier for a liar to climb up a tree than to climb down.

Problem #3: Wiesel's Personal Encounter with Dr. Mengele

Dr. Mengele: An Overview

Dr. Josef Mengele, born in 1911 into a Catholic family in Günzburg, Bavaria, Germany, served as the chief physician of the gypsy family camp on the medical staff at Auschwitz-Birkenau from May 1943 until January 1945. Most, if not all, of the doctors under his command were Jewish. Having been wounded, and highly decorated, on the eastern front in 1942, Mengele was deemed medically unfit for combat and reassigned to duty in the German camp system. He was assigned to Auschwitz as a replacement for another physician who appears to have died of typhus. Mengele himself also contracted the disease but he was able to recover from it. After the war, he lived on a farm in Austria, with occasional trips back to Germany,

---

was later reprinted as a chapter in *Legends of Our Time* (New York: Holt Rinehart & Winston, 1968).

188 Wiesel, *Tous les fleuves*, 89: "Arrivée de deux officiers supérieurs de la Gestapo – plus tard, on nous dira que l'un deux était Eichmann lui-même, et c'est pourquoi je croirai le reconnaître lors de son procès à Jérusalem."

189 Wiesel, "Decision," 5.

from 1945 until 1949, when he fled to South America. He lived there until his accidental death in 1979, apparently of drowning. It is ironic that he should have died in the very same year when the release of the Allied aerial photos of Auschwitz showed not the slightest evidence to support the claim of an extermination of Jews in gas chambers.[190]

In Dr. Mengele's Vestibule: Wiesel's Silence about His Sisters Bea and Hilda

Wiesel begins the narrative of his entry into the Birkenau camp by describing, very quickly, his separation from his mother and his three sisters. In fact, just prior to what appears to be his imagined encounter with Dr. Mengele, the arriving men and women are separated into two separate groups. The men are ordered to march to the left, and the women to the right. This division foreshadows the coming meeting with Dr. Mengele, who will also send people to the left and the right. Wiesel writes:

> *In a fraction of a second, I could see my mother and my sisters go off to the right.* (*En une fraction de seconde, je pus voir ma mère, mes sœurs, partir vers la droite. Nuit*, 53)

Wiesel, seeking to confuse and mislead his reader, mentions neither the names (Bea and Hilda) nor the ages of these sisters here. In treating them in such a manner in a book that is supposed to be his autobiography, Wiesel arouses suspicion as he attempts to sneak them by us in plain sight, so to speak. He probably did not allow these two women to become full-fledged characters in the novel for a very important and specific reason: their survival at Auschwitz (as well as that of Wiesel and his father) raises serious questions about whether or not Auschwitz-Birkenau was in fact a so-called extermination camp in which all Jews were supposedly killed simply because they were Jewish.

Embarrassed and defensive about the fact that these two sisters did not die in Birkenau or anywhere else during their alleged captivity, as they logically should have, if the master narrative of the Holocaust were true, Wiesel in effect kills his two sisters in the novel by denying them their personhood as survivors. This glaring contradiction at the heart of the novel has been deliberately ignored by Wiesel's conformist critics and commentators, whether in academe or the Zionist media. From the Holocaust sophisticates at the *New York Times* all the way down to the high school teachers who actually do the dirty work of robotizing their students by im-

---

[190] A number of biographies exist about Mengele, but all of them are more or less infected by absurd, even grotesque Holocaust propaganda; see for instance Gerald L. Posner and John Ware, *Mengele: The Complete Story* (2nd ed., New York: Cooper Square Press, 2000); as a healthy counter-weight see Carlo Mattogno, "Dr. Mengele's 'Medical Experiments' on Twins in the Birkenau Gypsy Camp," *Inconvenient History*, vol. 5, no. 4, 2013; www.inconvenienthistory.com/archive/2013/volume_5/number_4.

posing Holocaust brainwashing on them, none of them has ever shown the slightest interest in this almost total omission of these older sisters from the narrative.

Setting the Stage for the Encounter with Mengele

As Wiesel and his father continue to walk toward Dr. Mengele, an unidentified detainee asks Wiesel and his father how old they are. Eliezer replies "not yet fifteen" ("*pas encore quinze ans*"; *La Nuit*, 54), which Marion Wiesel translates incorrectly as "fifteen," and his father replies "fifty." ("*cinquante ans*"; *Nuit*, 54). However, if Wiesel was born on September 30, 1928, as he claims, he would have been "not yet sixteen" in early 1944, so Marion Wiesel's mistranslation of the text of *La Nuit* may have been motivated either by her desire to correct Eliezer's mistake or to make his subsequent claim of being "eighteen" rather than "not yet fifteen" a bit more credible. Wiesel now describes the unidentified inmate as becoming quite angry when he hears the boy and his father state their true ages when asked; he orders them to say "eighteen" and "forty" instead, although he does not say why. The implication is clear, however, that both father and son will be more likely to be "exterminated," rather than assigned to a work detail, if they state their true ages. Within the context of the master narrative of the Jewish Holocaust story, this is supposedly so because the father would be too old to work and the son too young.

The inmate's voice, which actually represents the mind-numbing and robotic voice of the master narrative of the Holocaust itself, concludes angrily: "Even more furious, he repeated: 'No. Not fifty years old. Forty. Do you hear what I'm saying? Eighteen and forty.'" ("*Plus furieux encore, l'autre reprit. 'Non. Pas cinquante ans. Quarante. Vous entendez ? Dix-huit et quarante'*"; *Nuit*, 54) Shortly after receiving this advice, Eliezer continues walking straight ahead and finally encounters the legendary Dr. Mengele:[191]

> *We continued to walk until we reached an intersection, and there, in the middle of it, was Dr. Mengele, the notorious Dr. Mengele (typical SS officer, cruel face, although not without intelligence, and a monocle), an orchestra conductor's baton in his hand, as he stood amidst other officers. The baton kept moving, first to the right and then to the left.*

Before discussing the absurdity of this description of Mengele, comment is in order about yet another deliberate mistranslation of this passage by Marion Wiesel, in gratuitously adding a phrase to Wiesel's text not found in *La Nuit*. She writes: "Standing in the middle of it was, *though I didn't know it*

[191] *Nuit*, 56: "Nous continuâmes de marcher jusqu'à un carrefour. Au centre se tenait le docteur Mengele, ce fameux docteur Mengele (officier S. S. typique, visage cruel, non dépourvu d'intelligence, monocle), une baguette de chef d'orchestre à la main au milieu d'autres officiers. La baguette se mouvait sans trêve, tantôt à droite, tantôt à gauche."

Illustration 4: Richard Baer (left), Auschwitz camp commandant since late 1943; Dr. Josef Mengele (center), head physician of the gypsy family camp at Birkenau, and Rudolf Höss (right), Auschwitz camp commandant until late 1943.

then, Dr. Mengele" (31; italics added). Her addition of this phrase represents an admission by her that Wiesel, the author of an autobiography in which everything is supposedly true, would have had no way of knowing, at the time, who this man actually was. Unethically, and with the apparent (and shameful) support of her publisher, she employs the "I only found out later" trope, discussed above, to place a narrative screen between the reader and her husband's mendacity. In other words, since her husband's "autobiography" is actually a novel, Marion Wiesel has resorted to the use of this trope to keep the scam alive, according to which *Night* is "autobiographical." Her addition also indicates that, even within the community of Holocaust fundamentalists, Wiesel's magical ability to immediately identify Mengele is perceived as a problem. Finally, her emendation to the text of the novel is also a concession, and a pathetic one at that, to skeptical revisionist readers of this text.

I now move on from Wiesel's magical identification of Mengele to his imagined discussion with him. Wiesel would like us to believe that Mengele next asked him how old he was and what he did for a living. He writes:[192]

---

[192] *Ibid.*: "Déjà je me trouvais devant lui. 'Ton âge?' demanda-t-il sur un ton qui se voulait

> *Suddenly I was standing there in front of him. "Your age?" he asked in a tone of voice that seemed to be trying to sound paternal. "Eighteen." My voice was trembling. "In good health?" "Yes." "Your trade?" "Should I tell him I was a student?" "Farmer," I heard myself say.*

Wiesel includes these questions and responses because they belong to a literary commonplace, or an "in joke" that Jews often share among themselves about the Germans: that the latter are so stupid that they will believe just about any lie the Jews tell them. In American popular culture, such German fools were embodied in the characters Col. Klink and Sgt. Schultz (both TV roles actually played by Jews) in the 1965–1971 sitcom *Hogan's Heroes*. Needless to say, the gullible Mengele not only believes that Wiesel's father is forty and not fifty, he also believes that this pale-looking and sickly little mama's boy of "not yet fifteen" is actually eighteen, and an experienced field hand at that! Since Mengele is stupid enough to believe Wiesel and his father, his conductor's baton points to the left for both the father and the son.

There are several elements in this scene that raise once again the question of whether Wiesel actually lived this experience, plagiarized it, or simply made it up as he wrote his novel. To begin with, the man depicted by Wiesel bears no physical resemblance whatsoever to the real Dr. Mengele. As Illustration 4 shows, Mengele did not have a "cruel face," nor is there any evidence to support Wiesel's claim that he wore a monocle. In addition, the conversation between him and Wiesel is so implausible as to be ridiculous. Mengele could have determined Wiesel's age with a cursory glance at him. He was clearly not eighteen. As for Wiesel's trade, Mengele could have answered that question by simply looking at Wiesel's hands. After all, the likelihood that any of the Hasidic Jews getting off the train were farmers would have been very slim indeed. As for Wiesel's possible sources of inspiration for his faulty description of Mengele's physiognomy, he seems to be recycling the image of Erich von Stroheim, widely circulated during the interwar years, as the quintessential villainous Prussian officer. That image had been created for him by the Jewish-dominated silent film industry in the years following World War I, and reached its high point when he played the cold and detached German camp commander, von Rauffenstein, in Jean Renoir's 1937 film classic, *La Grande Illusion* [The Grand Illusion]. Wiesel might very well have seen that film as a young man in Paris. Von Stroheim fulfilled to perfection the stereotype of the monocle-wearing German officer who carries either a riding crop or a swagger stick. Wiesel, dismally ignorant of things military, puts that igno-

---

paternel. 'Dix-huit ans.' Ma voix tremblait. 'Bien portant?' 'Oui.' 'Ton métier?' 'Dire que j'étais étudiant?' 'Agriculteur,' je m'entendis prononcer.'"

rance on display when he calls Mengele's alleged swagger stick an orchestra conductor's baton.

Mengele Is the Major Satan Figure of the Holocaust Narrative

Perhaps the best way to understand the Jewish Holocaust narrative is as a pop culture phenomenon. Since it is a cultural product made to be consumed primarily either by children or by adults who think like children, it features stock characters. Human psychology is kept to a bare minimum, and the typical Holocaust narrative draws a sharp and simple line between good and evil. Heroes and villains are easily recognizable, and their acts are always consistent with their identities, as with an earlier pop cult manifestation, the stage melodrama. Jews, of course, are always depicted as virtuous. They also enjoy an exclusive right to victimhood. Germans are always evil, with some described as truly diabolical. In the latter category, Mengele plays the role of a major Satan figure. It can even be argued that he is more important to the Jewish Holocaust narrative than Hitler or any other top Nazi. Why? Because, in that narrative, these characters give orders from remote locations, while Mengele directly interacts with Jews, allegedly sending them to their deaths. Since he is also accused of torturing Jews and engaging in sadistic surgeries on them, his role is an essential part of what Gary Weissman calls the "fantasy" dimension of the Jewish Holocaust narrative.[193] In telling of their supposed experiences through the stock character of Mengele, who works in the "hell" of Auschwitz, some Jews are able to actually encounter Satan in an up-close and personal way.

Mengele in the Pages of the *New York Times*

It is for this reason that, over time, an encounter with Mengele has become *de rigueur* for any Jewish "survivor" who wants to boast about his or her experiences at Auschwitz. In fact, the repeated appearance of such encounters with Mengele in *New York Times* obituaries and articles over the years is an enduring sign of the fact that, among Jews, there are degrees of Holocaust celebrity, ranging from that of mere "survivors" to those who actually confronted Satan, in the person of Mengele, at Auschwitz. To be a true Holocaust celebrity, a "somebody," it has become almost mandatory that one have interacted with the man. Two examples of this particular form of Jewish narcissism and self-referentialism, each from the pages of the *New York Times*, typify the genre. An excerpt from a family folktale concerning one Pepi Deutsch comes from her *New York Times* obituary:[194]

---

[193] Gary Weissman, *Fantasies of Witnessing: Postwar Efforts to Experience the Holocaust* (Ithaca, N.Y.: Cornell University Press, 2004).

[194] Joseph Berger, "Pepi Deutsch, 101, Holocaust Survivor with Remarkable Tale," *New York Times*, November 8, 1999, A29.

> *The notorious Dr. Josef Mengele assigned the youthful-looking Mrs. Deutsch, then in her 40's, to a work group of younger women.* [...]

So you see, implies the obit, she was special: she looked so much younger than her actual age that even the devil himself, Mengele, unable to figure out how old she was, assigned her to work and not for "extermination."

Then there is the irrepressible Dr. Gisella Perl, who one-ups Pepi Deutsch by claiming to have actually been a member of Mengele's staff! When the *New York Times* reported on her alleged experiences at Auschwitz, it remained faithful, as ever, to the fundamentally lowbrow pop culture essence of the Holocaust narrative, writing:[195]

> *But all of medicine was her province in the camp. As one of five doctors and four nurses chosen by Dr. Mengele to operate a hospital ward that had no beds, no bandages, no drugs and no instruments, she tended to every disease wrought by torture, starvation, filth, lice and rats, to every broken bone or head cracked open by beating. She performed surgery, without anesthesia, on women whose breasts had been lacerated by whips and become infected.*

But that is not all! Working in accordance with the rhetorical commonplace, or Jewish "in joke," mentioned above, according to which a German like Mengele can always be tricked by a clever Jew, the wily Dr. Perl was up to the task. Since, according to Perl, "the greatest crime in Auschwitz was to be pregnant," she supposedly saved the lives of pregnant women by performing abortions on them "in the night, on a dirty floor, using only my dirty hands." Although the Labor Assignment Office at Birkenau listed over seven hundred children living in the Children's Block on the eve of the camp's liberation, where they were being raised as a matter of routine,[196] Perl's sick and lowbrow narrative is intended to show that Mengele was so stupid that neither he nor any other German ever heard the screams of the "hundreds" of women allegedly aborted by Perl, nor did he ever see a trace of the blood that these abortions must have left on the floor each morning as he entered his dispensary. For people like Deutsch and Perl, the addition of Mengele's name is a trope that adds a sense of authenticity to

---

[195] Nadine Brozan, "Out of Death, a Zest for Life," *New York Times*, November 15, 1982, C20.

[196] Hermann Langbein, *People in Auschwitz* (Chapel Hill, NC: The University of North Carolina Press, 2004), 239: "Some statistics about children at Auschwitz have been preserved. According to a compilation by the Labor Assignment Office, 619 boys ranging in age from six months to fourteen years were living in Birkenau on August 30, 1944. On January 14, 1945, shortly before the evacuation, 773 male children and youths were registered." See also: Robert Faurisson, "Enfants juifs: leur déportation ne signifiait pas leur extermination," February 23, 2008; http://robertfaurisson.blogspot.com/2009/03/enfants-juifs-leur-deportation-ne.html; see the Trip Advisor's photo of the Birkenau Childrens Children's Block at http://www.tripadvisor.com/LocationPhotoDirectLink-g274754-d275831-i62070793-Auschwitz_Birkenau_State_Museum-Oswiecim_Lesser_Poland_Province_Southern_P.html

the survivor's tale, and insures the bizarre kind of prestige and celebrity that such people crave as they raise themselves up above the masses of rather ordinary Jews who were mere "survivors." In reality, however, the use of this or similar tropes has turned out to be a cancer for Jews. In deforming and hyping their alleged experiences in such a transparent manner, such Jewish "eyewitnesses" have devalued their legitimate wartime sufferings.

Problem #4: Burning of Victims in Huge Trenches

Wiesel claims to have seen two massive, flaming trenches at Birkenau. He writes in *Night* that he saw a truckload of Jewish babies dumped into one of them. The other trench was for burning the bodies of adults, according to Wiesel. Wiesel's description of the nature of these pits and, even more critically, their very location, is extremely vague. His lack of specificity with regard to the emplacement of the novel's major atrocity is very troubling indeed, for it raises once again the question of whether he actually saw, plagiarized, or invented what he claims to have seen. In fact, when his description is read in terms of the Allied aerial photos of Birkenau, taken in May and August 1944 and declassified and published by the CIA in 1979, the only thing that can be determined is that his flaming pits would have been located near or adjacent to the ramp, that is, the railroad train debarkation area located between the front gate and the crematoria. Jean-François Forges, the well-known French Holocaustian, situates Wiesel's pits in precisely this area, and I agree with him on this point. Needless to say, Wiesel's imagined pits do not appear in the Allied aerial photographs of this area.

In the mid-1950s, Wiesel had no way of knowing that the Allies had taken extensive aerial photographs of Birkenau on selected dates in 1944. If the Allied prosecutors at Nuremberg knew about them, they suppressed these pictures for good reason: they would have helped the accused Germans to prove their innocence by raising embarrassing questions. But even if Wiesel had heard about these photographs, he could not have seen them, since they remained classified until 1979. Selected photos did not become available to the public until two CIA analysts published them for the first time.[197] If ten to twenty thousand people were being killed at Birkenau each day, an industrial undertaking of incredibly extensive magnitude and scale, it would have been impossible for the Allied aerial photography experts to have missed the unfolding of this project. The fact that this alleged

[197] Dino A. Brugioni and Robert G. Poirier, *The Holocaust Revisited: A Retrospective Analysis of the Auschwitz-Birkenau Extermination Complex* (Washington, DC: The Central Intelligence Agency, 1979). Many more air photos are more thoroughly analyzed by John C. Ball, *Air Photo Evidence*, 3rd ed. (Uckfield, UK: Castle Hill Publishers, 2015), in particular Chapters 5.9 and 5.10, 96-105.

program does *not* show up on the film is proof that it did not exist beyond the level of rumor. These photos demolish both the open-pit burning and gas chamber allegations.[198]

For Wiesel, the declassification and publication of these photos was a disaster, for they showed that his testimony was false. It was especially devastating coming as it did just a year or so after the NBC docudrama *Holocaust*. Since that made-for-TV series posited the gas chambers as the exclusive means of mass killing at Auschwitz, Wiesel's claim about the huge pits that he had seen, one for babies and one for adults, lost in the popular imagination its already tenuous validity as a historically credible event. While the two CIA analysts, Brugioni and Poirier, mention "external burning pits" (*Holocaust Revisited*, 10) at Birkenau, they are unable to identify even one such pit among the photographs. With regard to the smoke and flame that allegedly came from Wiesel's mythical pits and the crematoria, the authors are a bit more honest with their reader:

> *Although survivors recalled that smoke and flame emanated continually from the crematoria and was visible for miles, the photography we examined gave no proof of this.* (25)

Huge Trenches within View of the Gate at Birkenau

In *Night,* during the trip from Sighet to Auschwitz, a middle-aged woman, Madame Schächter, lapses into a state of delirium each evening. She imagines seeing huge fires in which Jews are presumably being burned. Wiesel writes:[199]

> *In front of us were the flames. In the air, that smell of burning flesh. It must have been midnight. We had arrived – at Birkenau.*

It is important to note here that Wiesel's insistence that mass murder could be witnessed from outside the main gate at Birkenau contradicts the master narrative of the Jewish Holocaust story on its most fundamental point. From Nuremberg on, the legend of the flames and the belching chimneys has been played down in favor of the gas chamber story. The Holocaustians have done this in order to maintain the fiction that the victims did not know they were going to die until the very last minute. For if flames and smoke could be seen for miles around, then there would have been no secrecy. And without secrecy, there would have been no surprise. And without the element of surprise, there would be no explanation for why tens of thousands of Jews waited patiently in line for many hours each day, day and

---

198 For a thorough analysis of claims about open-pit cremations at Auschwitz see Carlo Mattogno, *Auschwitz: Open Air Incinerations* (Chicago, Ill.: Theses & Dissertations Press, 2005).

199 Wiesel, *Nuit*, 52: "Devant nous, ces flammes. Dans l'air, cette odeur de chair brûlée. Il devait être minuit. Nous étions arrivés à Birkenau."

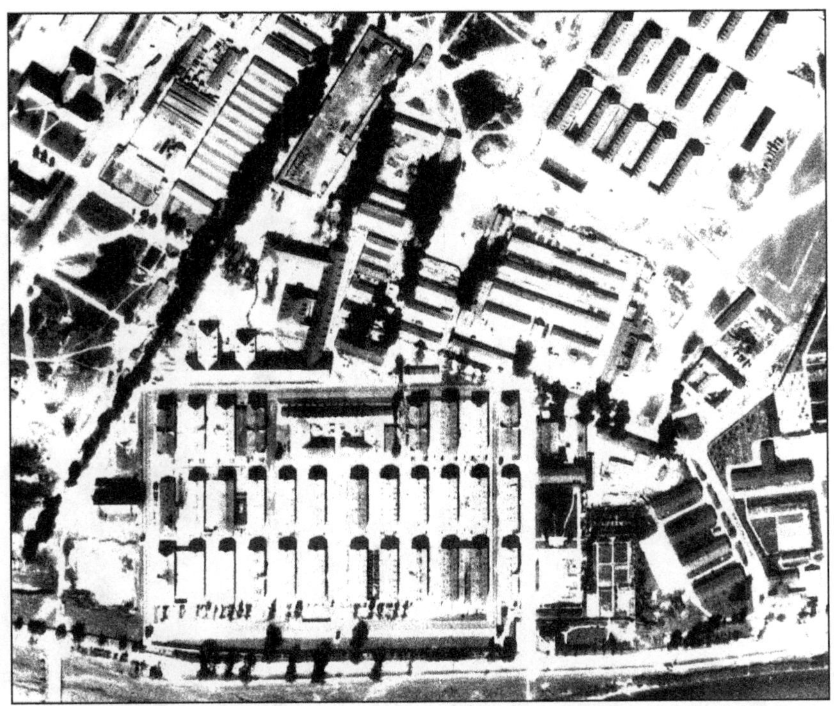

Illustration 5: Auschwitz I, Overview of Main Camp, August 25, 1944, as published by John C. Ball.

night, without causing any disturbances, to go into the legendary gas chambers. Since there seem to have been tens of thousands (if not hundreds of thousands) of Jewish survivors of Auschwitz, it is astonishing indeed that not one of them has ever explained the mechanism by which this alleged surprise was able to occur within the confines of such a narrow and cramped space. This problem of the silence of the survivors is dealt with at length in Chapters VII and VIII.

U.S.-born Jews, as well as the main Jewish organizations, who generally shunned the survivors when they started to move to the U.S. after the war, were of course onto their game, but remained silent out of feelings of Jewish group solidarity. These Jewish people knew better than anyone else that the idea of Jews waiting in line patiently for their turn to go into the gas chambers, ten thousand or more per day no less, was a scam from beginning to end. Thus, Wiesel's supposed autobiography, in positing the existence of smoke and flame visible from the outside, stands in utter contradiction to the master narrative of the Holocaust tale. In fact, only oil refinery and gas flare stacks give off flame and smoke as a matter of course; otherwise, flaming chimneys, including those from crematoria, are a sign of a severe emergency and must be extinguished immediately. It is impossible to profess belief in Wiesel's version of events without raising ques-

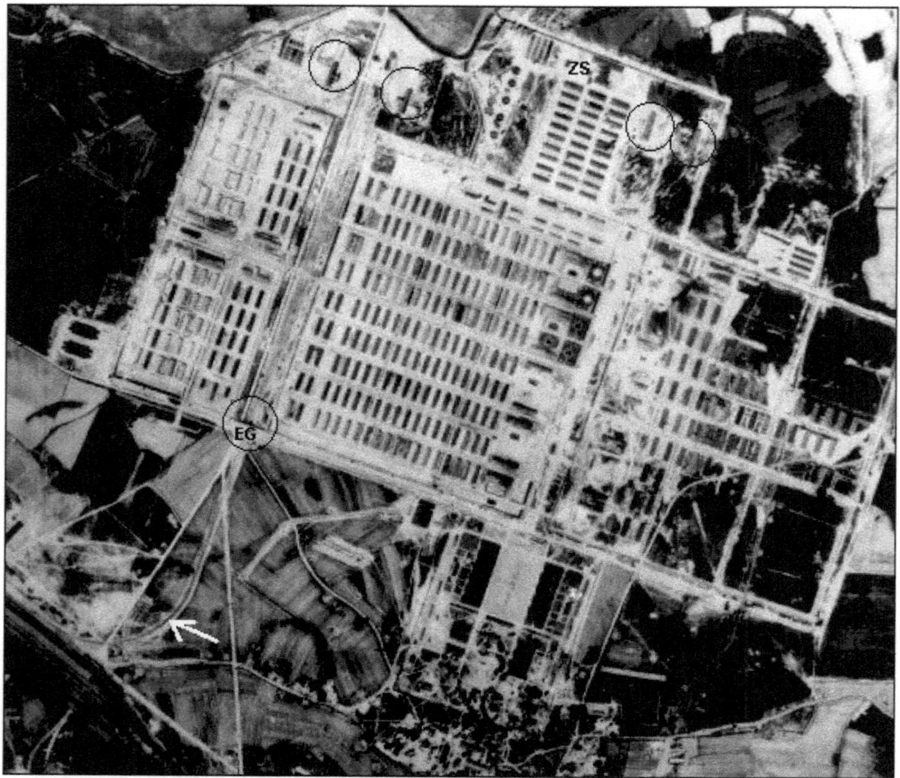

*Illustration 6: Aerial photograph of the Birkenau camp, taken on May 31, 1944 (NA, 60PRS/462, D 1508, Exp. 3056). The circles mark the crematoria: (left to right) II, III, IV, V. The building in the shape of a "T," marked "ZS," is the Central Sauna. "EG" is the entrance building (*Eingangsgebäude*). The arrow (at bottom) marks the railway spur.*

tions about the validity of that master narrative, with its emphasis on secrecy and surprise. In summary, the evidence provided by the Allied aerial photography shows that both Wiesel's tall story and the master narrative are rather crude lies.

Yet according to *Night*, Wiesel walks on with his fellow Jews toward an unknown destination following their selection by Mengele. Suddenly he sees before him a large ditch in which people are being burned alive:[200]

> *Not far from us, flames were leaping up from a ditch, gigantic flames. They were burning something. A truck drove up to the ditch and dumped its load – little children. Babies! Yes, I saw it – saw it with my own eyes* [...] *children in the flames.*

[200] *Ibid.*, 57: "Non loin de nous, des flammes montaient d'une fosse, des flammes gigantesques. On y brûlait quelque chose. Un camion s'approcha du trou et y déversa sa charge: c'étaient des petits enfants, des bébés! Oui, j'avais vu, de mes yeux vu. [...] Des enfants dans les flammes."

"Kitschman of genius" that he is, Wiesel now asks a rhetorical question: "So is it any wonder that I have not been able sleep since that time?"[201] But now, suddenly, the narrative voice realizes that "a little further along, there was a larger ditch, for adults."[202] Here, he employs another common Holocaust narrative trope, the one of not believing what one is supposedly seeing as an eyewitness to the Holocaust. In so doing, Wiesel is able to rhetorically distance himself from the absurd claim that he is about to make:[203]

> *I pinched my face: was I still alive? Was I awake? I just could not believe it. How could it be possible that they were burning men and children, and that the world remained silent? No, all this could not be true. A nightmare.* […] *Soon I was going to wake up with a jerk, my heart pounding, and find myself in my childhood bedroom surrounded by my books.* […]

Through the use of this trope, with its reference to a rhetorical dream state, Wiesel is able to claim simultaneously that he saw something that exists in the real, concrete world, yet actually saw nothing.

Another solid indication of the fact that Wiesel avoids direct descriptions that would call his veracity into question is the manner in which he treats the location of the crematoria chimneys. As groups of people are being lined up five abreast, an unnamed detainee tells them that they will soon be taken to the crematorium and burned alive:[204]

> *Do you see that chimney over there? Do you see those flames? (Yes, we did see the flames.) Over there – that's where you're going to be taken. That's your grave over there. Haven't you realized it yet? You dumb bastards, don't you understand anything? You're going to be burned. Burned to a crisp. Reduced to ashes.*

Wiesel has already indicated his ignorance of Birkenau's topography by placing his huge baby-and-adult-burning trenches adjacent to the ramp about seventy-five to a hundred meters inside the front gate. In reality, barracks were located there, as the aerial photos make clear. Now, since he apparently does not have the slightest idea as to where the crematoria buildings, with their tall smokestacks, were actually situated, he must mask his ignorance. But the best he can do for indicating where these chimneys were actually located is to say "over there" (*là-bas*), which displays once again his general ignorance of Birkenau's layout.

---

201 *Ibid.*: "Est-ce donc étonnant si depuis ce temps-là le sommeil fuit mes yeux?"

202 *Ibid.*: "Un peu plus loin se trouvait une autre fosse, plus grande, pour des adultes."

203 *Ibid.*, 58: "Je me pinçai le visage: vivais-je encore? Etais-je éveillé? Je n'arrivais pas à le croire. Comment était-il possible qu'on brûlât des hommes, des enfants, et que le monde se tût? Non, tout cela ne pouvait être vrai. Un cauchemar. […] J'allais bientôt m'éveiller en sursaut, le cœur battant et retrouver ma chambre d'enfant, mes livres […]"

204 *Ibid.*: "Voyez-vous là-bas la cheminée? La voyez-vous? Les flammes, les voyez-vous? (Oui, nous les *voyions* les flammes.) Là-bas, c'est là-bas qu'on vous conduira. C'est là-bas votre tombe. Vous n'avez pas encore compris? Fils de chiens vous ne comprenez donc rien? On va vous brûler! Vous calciner! Vous réduire en cendres!"

Now the narrative voice of his novel takes over once again and describes both the man who has just pointed to the flames and the Jewish detainees who have listened to his message. Wiesel writes:[205]

> *His rage became hysterical. We stood there motionless, petrified. Wasn't it all a nightmare? An unimaginable nightmare?*

Wiesel uses the dream state trope here once again (wasn't it all a nightmare?) to get around the fact that his novel's Jewish detainees, when they see the flames, do not make any attempt to resist. On the contrary, they go forward like so many sheep to the slaughter, which is not a credible behavioral response for Jewish (or any) characters in this situation. But how can the reader have any sympathy for people who are so passive and so stupid that they make no attempt to resist? Wiesel's solution to this problem is to resort once again to the same device he used to describe his reaction to seeing the burning babies in the trench. Thus, the Jewish detainees' passivity is excused because they thought it was a nightmare, or a bad dream. In other words, Wiesel's first-person narrator engages in double talk by saying simultaneously that what he saw was really happening, while also conceding that what he saw was actually just a bad dream. Wiesel invokes the "delirium" trope throughout his novel, and his conformist academic commentators have gone along with it for decades without questioning it.

Release of Aerial Photography Forces Wiesel to Change His Story

Since the release in 1979 of the aerial photography of Auschwitz, which represented yet another nail in the coffin of the orthodox Holocaust narrative as history, attacks on Wiesel have multiplied. These pictures did not offer any evidence to support his claims in *Night* as to open-pit burning at Birkenau. At the same time, the pictures also failed to confirm the existence of gas chambers there with their alleged lines of 10,000 to 20,000 people per day waiting to enter them in May 1944.[206] Nonetheless, despite the declassification and publication of these pictures, the Zionist media and their collaborationist allies in academe not only continued to endorse the narrative of mass murder in the gas chambers of Auschwitz, they also made it into the central metaphor of the Western world's secular religion of "the

[205] *Ibid.*: "Sa fureur devenait hystérique. Nous demeurions immobiles, pétrifiés. Tout cela n'était-il pas un cauchemar? Un cauchemar inimaginable?"

[206] Of course, those long lines would have been visible only for several hours on days when mass gassings are said to have happened, which may not have been every day. Hence, the lack of any such lines on existing air photos may simply be due to the aircraft having taken the photos at the wrong time. Be that as it may, the fact is that these photos cannot be used to undergird mass gassing claims. More important is the complete lack of any signs of the claimed huge pyres, which would have smoked for days, if not weeks, covering huge areas under a haze. Due to the enormous work being done around them, the ground cover in their vicinity would have been destroyed. Both traces should be clearly visible on every single air photo of Birkenau, but they are NOT.

six million." Since then, as the need to believe in the gas chambers has soared in youth-indoctrination classes worldwide, complete with pilgrimages to the camp under the close supervision of teachers, Wiesel's silence about these alleged killing machines in *Night* has become the Achilles heel of his status as a credible eyewitness among fellow Holocaustian Jews. As a result, he has attempted to confuse his reader as much as possible about what he actually saw. The following examples highlight this personal disinformation campaign.

Wiesel long claimed that he did not believe what he had seen until years later, when he read unnamed "documents" asserting that the pits containing the bodies of burning babies had actually been there. In 1976, for instance, he told Harry Cargas:[207]

> *When I saw it, I was convinced it wasn't true and I recorded it almost as a nightmare. Then I found the documents, the corroboration, and it was true. They had so many killings to do in those days – the Hungarian Jews, my Jews – that they did burn them alive. You imagine one million children* [...]

Since Wiesel did not specify in *Night* whether or not the Jewish children were dead or alive when allegedly thrown into the flaming pits, I now deal with that issue. On April 19, 1985, as he was in the process of becoming the High Priest of our state religion, he insisted that they were alive. On that day, when he addressed President Reagan at the White House, he stated:[208]

> *You spoke of Jewish children, Mr. President; one million Jewish children perished. If I spent my entire life reciting their names, I would die before finishing the task. Mr. President, I have seen children – I have seen them being thrown in the flames alive. Words – they die on my lips.*

Five years later, in *From the Kingdom of Memory* (1990), he invented a new location for the pits, since the aerial photography had rendered the location stipulated in *La Nuit* untenable. He still insisted, however, that the Jewish babies were burned alive. It came out like this:

> *What I saw is enough for me. In a small wood somewhere in Birkenau I saw children being thrown into the flames alive by the S. S. Sometimes I curse my ability to see. It should have left me without ever returning. I should have remained with those little charred bodies.* (*Kingdom*, 174)

By the mid-1990s, Wiesel brought the pits back out of the wood in which he had placed them in 1990 and also invented a new myth about "specially tended furnaces." It came out like this:[209]

---

[207] Cargas, *Conversation*, 39.

[208] "Remarks on Presenting the Congressional Gold Medal to Elie Wiesel and on Signing the Jewish Heritage Week Proclamation," April 19, 1985, www.pbs.org/eliewiesel/resources/reagan.html

[209] Wiesel, *Tous les fleuves*, 102: "Il m'a fallu du temps pour me convaincre que je ne m'étais pas trompé. J'ai vérifié auprès de compagnons arrivés la même nuit que moi, j'ai

It took me a long time to convince myself that I was not somehow mistaken. I have checked with others who arrived that same night, consulted documents of the Sonderkommandos, and yes, a thousand times yes. Unable to 'handle' such large numbers of Hungarian Jews in the crematoria, the killers were not content merely to incinerate children's dead bodies. In their barbarous madness, they cast living Jewish children into specially tended furnaces.

When Wiesel made this bizarre claim in the mid-1990s, he once again raised serious questions about his credibility as an eyewitness when he invented this special machine for killing Jewish babies that had never appeared before in the Holocaust master narrative. Finally, in apparent anticipation of reader skepticism about this new claim, about five decades late, which he repeated in the introduction to his wife's new translation of *La Nuit*, he made use of the "it must have been a nightmare" / "I could not believe my eyes" trope in doing so:

Have I used the right words? The infants thrown into fiery ditches. [...] *I did not say that they were alive, but that was what I thought. But then I convinced myself: no, they were dead; otherwise I surely would have lost my mind. And yet fellow inmates also saw them: they were alive when they were thrown into the flames.* (*Night*, xiii-xiv)

Now the unidentified "documents" that he cited fifteen to twenty-five years ago have been replaced by confirmations received from "fellow inmates" who, of course, also remain unidentified. At the same time, by focusing on the issue of whether or not these children were dead or alive when burned, he seeks to distract us from the fact that the whole scene is purely imaginary and never happened.

Mauriac's Friend, Léon Poliakov: A Possible Source for Wiesel

One book Wiesel almost certainly read before writing his novel was Léon Poliakov's *Bréviaire de la haine*.[210] The reader will recall that François Mauriac had provided the foreword for this volume, so Wiesel could have discovered both Mauriac's style and political commitments at the same time as he read Poliakov's book. In this work, Poliakov simply repeated the many nonsensical – and clearly invented – elements that he found in much of the evidence contained in his Nuremberg sources. He accepted without question the self-serving atrocity and propaganda charges that the Allies made against the Germans. Poliakov's claims with regard to the open-air burning of human bodies, which is precisely the claim that

---

consulté les documents des Sonderkommandos: oui, mille fois oui. Incapables de 'traîter' un si grand nombre de Juifs hongrois dans les crématoires, les tueurs ne se contentèrent pas d'incinérer les cadavres des enfants; dans leur folie barbare, ils jetèrent des enfants juifs encore vivants dans des brasiers spécialement entretenus."

[210] The English translation is entitled *Harvest of Hate* (Syracuse: Syracuse University Press, 1954), and all quotations from Poliakov used herein are taken from the English edition.

Wiesel would later make in *Night* (and which is in fact the basis of the word "Holocaust"), are of particular importance here. Poliakov asserts in his book that 12,000 to 15,000 Jews were killed each day in the gas chambers during May and June 1944, the period during which Wiesel allegedly arrived at Birkenau. Thus, for Poliakov, the imagined gas chambers were the primary weapon of destruction. He wrote:

> *The maximum of 12,000 to 15,000 a day was reached in May–June 1944 during the deportation of the Hungarian Jews.* […] *the four crematories were no longer adequate, and besides, the ovens were deteriorating, so enormous funeral pyres in the open made up the deficiency.* (*Harvest*, 202)

What Poliakov seems to be saying is that the people burned on these imagined pyres were already dead, not living.

Poliakov does not identify the location of these enormous pyres other than to state that they were in the open. However, there was actually no open space near the crematoria (where these alleged pyres would have had to be located for logistical reasons), as the aerial photography makes clear. Such fires, if they had existed, would have generated flames, smoke and very foul odors for miles around. They also would have required the use of a fleet of trucks to haul in the thousands of tons of timber required to construct the pyres, and then to haul out the hundreds of tons of ash left behind afterwards.[211] Such timber would have theoretically come from the pristine forests that surrounded the camp, but that were never touched and are still intact. These telltale signs would then have attracted the attention of the Allied intelligence agencies, since the Allies were conducting routine overflights of the camp at this time. Yet Poliakov maintains the official line put forward by the Allied prosecutors at Nuremberg to the effect that all these crimes were committed in secret. He writes:

> *A veil of absolute secrecy, however, hung over the actual work of extermination action, and the participants were sworn to silence on pain of execution.* (212)

Poliakov is forgetting that these crimes allegedly took place in the real world, and not just in the minds of those who imagined them. The claims of both Poliakov and Raul Hilberg, discussed below, about the secrecy surrounding these alleged mass murders are especially unconvincing in view of the fact that the purported killing area in the Birkenau camp was so small. Poliakov's error is understandable, though, when we recall that *he had not visited the place before writing his book.* Since he had never walked the terrain, as I have, he could not grasp that it would have been physically impossible for the Germans to hide such huge fires (not to mention the long lines of 10,000 to 20,000 people each day waiting quietly to

[211] On the size and fuel requirement of such cremation pyres see Heinrich Köchel, "Open Air Incineration of Corpses," *Inconvenient History*, vol. 7, no. 1, 2015; http://inconvenienthistory.com/archive/2015/volume_7/number_1.

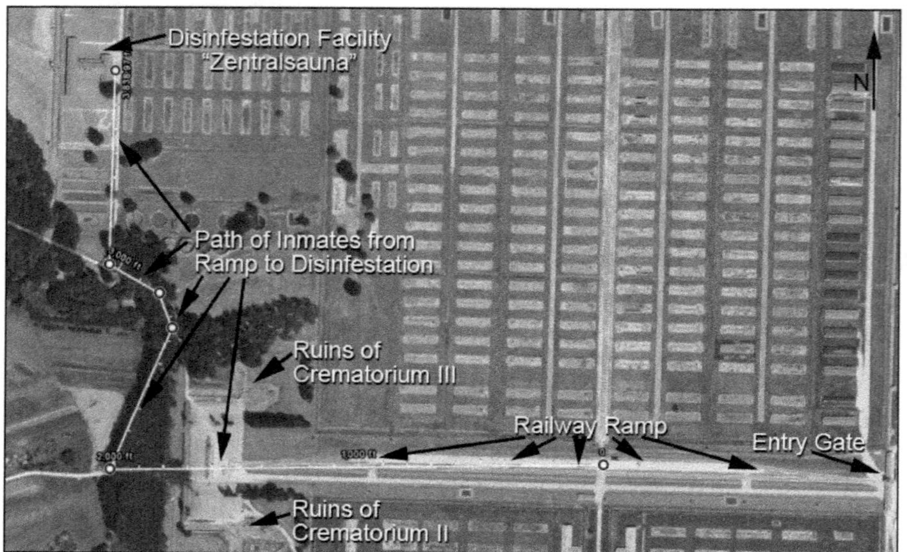

Illustration 7: This Google Earth photo of Birkenau shows the path thousands of inmates arriving at the railway ramp had to walk to reach the "Zentralsauna" for their obligatory shower and haircut. The path led them right by the two large Crematoria II & III, the alleged "epicenters" of the Holocaust.

go into the gas chambers) from newcomers arriving by the entrance building through which the railroad tracks passed.

Poliakov was also apparently unaware that all inmates arriving at the Birkenau railway ramp had to undergo disinfestation procedures at the "*Zentralsauna*" (see Illustration 7). To get there, they walked west for some 2000 ft (measured roughly from the middle of the ramp). On their way they would not only pass several inmate barracks, but also the two large Crematoria II & III, which are said to have housed the largest gas chambers.[212] These inmates would have been able to see those buildings in all their glory just a couple hundred feet away. The procedure the inmates had to undergo was documented by the SS when they took numerous photographs of Hungarian Jews being processed at Birkenau in 1944, from their unloading at the ramp via their way west, through their getting a haircut, getting showered and receiving inmate clothes. These photographs were published in the so-called *Auschwitz-Album* (edited by S. Klarsfeld). Hence, tens of thousands of inmates who were properly admitted into the camp, many of which survived the war, could observe closely what was going on.

Incredibly, Poliakov and later Hilberg, as I show below, want us to believe that the flaming pits remained a secret! They also neglect to mention

[212] The other two crematoria in this camp (Cremas IV & V) are said to have had two or three homicidal gas chambers each (depending on the witness), whereas Cremas II & III had only one each, but they were much larger.

the problem of outsiders looking in, for both historians also seem unaware that there was no visual barrier around the Birkenau camp, just barbed wire. Thus, anyone could observe from the outside what was happening on the inside. Also, there were hundreds of consultants, suppliers, technicians and other skilled tradesmen representing various German and Polish firms coming through the camp each day to conduct business before returning to their civilian lives outside the camp system.[213] Finally, how did the Germans manage to keep the amounts of smoke and flame secret? This claim is implausible since the prevailing winds blowing across the plain on which Auschwitz is located would have blown them far afield.

Birkenau Is also Located in a Flood Plain

Poliakov, like the other ersatz Holocaust historians who were to follow in his tracks, was ignorant of the fact that the Birkenau camp is located in what is called a "floodplain." This term designates a flat, low-lying area near a river or stream that tends to flood in heavy rains. The Auschwitz complex, located near the confluence of the Vistula and Sola Rivers, and, in particular, the Birkenau camp, is prone to flooding. Also, as in virtually all floodplains, Birkenau is characterized by a high water table.[214] For this reason, even outside the usual annual flood times of late winter and spring, one can usually find water just a few feet below ground level. This preexisting high water table in turn helps contribute to flooding when the rains come.

Poliakov's tall tale about the burning of bodies on enormous pyres in the open, an event which would have had to take place near the crematoria, even if a bit less absurd than Wiesel's claim of burning of Jewish babies in trenches, is still ridiculous. Both alleged operations would have required the digging of deep pits, but the deeper the pit, the higher the water would have been stood in it. When the heavy rains of May 18–19, 2010, hit the camp, they caused such a flood that "officials closed the Auschwitz-Birkenau memorial site Tuesday [May 18] to protect its Holocaust archives and artifacts"[215] (see Illustration 8). In fact, the flooding was so severe that the Museum's artifacts had to be moved from the first to the second floor. Two days later, it was reported that "the Birkenau section of the memorial

---

213 Carlo Mattogno, in *The Central Construction Office of the Waffen-SS and Police Auschwitz: Organization, Responsibilities, Activities Special Treatment* (Chicago, Ill.: Theses & Dissertations Press, 2005), 51-56, lists 46 civilian firms working at Auschwitz, with usually close to 1,000 (mainly German) civilians working there day in, day out.

214 For detailed studies of this topic see Werner Rademacher, Michael Gärtner, "Ground Water in the Area of the POW camp Birkenau," *The Revisionist*, vol. 1, no.1, 2003, pp. 3-12; Carlo Mattogno, "'Cremation Pits' and Ground Water Levels at Birkenau," *The Revisionist*, vol. 1, no. 1, 2003, pp. 13-16; www.codoh.com/library/series/1432/

215 "Flooding Causes Holocaust Site to Close," *Atlanta Journal-Constitution*, May 19, 2010, A4.

Illustration 8a, b: Flooding at the Birkenau camp, May 19, 2010

to Holocaust victims was reopened from the main gate to the ruins of the crematoria, which remain partly submerged by rising ground water.[216]

This is precisely the area in which, according to both my reading of *La Nuit* and that of Jean-François Forges, the French Holocaust scholar charged with training teachers to indoctrinate French youngsters about the Holocaust, Wiesel's pits would have had to be located. The pre-existing water table there is quite high indeed, and that is why the floodwaters remained in place for several days. Not surprisingly, the *New York Times*, in its self-designated role as the U.S. media custodian of the Jewish Holocaust narrative, perhaps sensing how threatening this important story was to their carefully crafted image of Auschwitz, passed over it in silence and failed to report it.

216 "Auschwitz Memorial Partly Opened, Water Receding," *Taiwan News*, May 20, 2010.

Poliakov's Pyres Become Hilberg's Massive Trenches

Raul Hilberg (1926-2007), the dean of the so-called Holocaust historians, published his book *The Destruction of the European Jews* in 1961, three years after the appearance of *La Nuit*. During his lifetime he was the reigning authority on the official historiography of the Holocaust, and thus merits being quoted here on the subject of the importance of secrecy at Auschwitz. Here is Hilberg on this subject:[217]

> *The success of the killing operations depended, in the first instance, upon the maintenance of secrecy. Unlike any other administrative task confronting the bureaucracy, secrecy was a continuous problem. Precautionary measures had to be taken before the victims arrived, while they went through the processing, and after they were dead. At no point could any disclosure be permitted; at no time could the camp management afford to be caught off guard. The killers had to conceal their work from every outsider, they had to mislead and fool the victims, and they had to erase all traces of the operation.*

With Hilberg's emphasis on secrecy in mind, let us now situate Wiesel's novel in relation to Holocaust historiography. When Wiesel wrote *Night*, he opted to carve out a rather unique victimhood space for himself by emphasizing the alleged burning of victims in flaming pits. In doing so, he was straying from the principal claim of the Holocaust master narrative, according to which Jewish victims at Birkenau were killed mostly, indeed overwhelmingly, in gas chambers.

In Hilberg's book, Poliakov's "enormous pyres" are replaced with massive pits. He writes:

> *During May and June the Hungarian Jews alone were being gassed at a rate of almost 10,000 a day, and higher numbers may have been reached when the Lodz transports arrived in the second half of August. Anticipating these developments, the Auschwitz specialist in charge of body disposal, Hauptscharführer Moll, a man described as a sadist with indefatigable energy, directed the digging of eight or nine pits more than forty yards in length, eight yards wide, and six feet deep. On the bottom of the pits the human fat was collected and poured back into the fire with buckets to hasten the cremations. Survivors report that children were sometimes tossed alive into the inferno. The rotten remains were sometimes cleaned up with flamethrowers. Although the corpses burned slowly during rain or misty weather, the pits were found to be the cheapest and most efficient method of body disposal. In August 1944, when 20,000 corpses had to be burned on some days, the open pits broke the bottleneck.* (*Destruction*, 978)

[217] Raul Hilberg, *The Destruction of the European Jews* (N.Y.: Quadrangle, 1961), 961f.

Illustration 9a-d: No matter which air photo we study: there are no huge smoking pits anywhere, in particular nowhere near the infamous Birkenau railway ramp, nor can victims be seen lining up in front of any crematorium/gas chamber.[197]

Auschwitz-Birkenau, May 31, 1944 *Auschwitz-Birkenau, June 26, 1944*

Auschwitz-Birkenau, July 8, 1944 *Auschwitz-Birkenau, August 20, 1944*

Hilberg's description is utter nonsense, for the distance from the main gate to the buildings that are said to have contained the gas chambers, as mentioned above, is only 1466 feet, or 451 meters. The Google Earth photography shows conclusively that there was simply no room to accommodate nine pits forty yards long and eight yards wide. There were already too many barracks buildings in the way, and those buildings are still standing today. In addition, no Holocaustian researcher is known to have ever looked for, much less found, evidence in the ground of such a huge industrial undertaking.

Poor Hilberg was also apparently unaware that the Birkenau camp was located in a floodplain. As a result, ground water would have not only impeded the burning process, it would have also diluted the alleged collection and recycling of human fats. Thus, the exact measurements that are provided by the Google Earth photos, when added to the Allied aerial photography of 1944, constitute yet another nail in the coffin of the Holocaust. Hilberg, his mind clouded, and his will driven by his commitment to Zionist Jewish ideology, made no attempt whatsoever to bring his narrative into line with what the laws of physics that govern the natural world will permit, recycling instead the testimonies of his unidentified eyewitnesses. He, like Poliakov, also apparently never gave any thought to the fact that, if there had been fires in these huge trenches, they would have required the consumption of hundreds of tons of timber, and that the personnel assigned to scooping the "human fat" out of the bottom of the pits would have had to wear protective gear (that did not exist in those days) just to approach fires that burned at hundreds of degrees centigrade! Finally, the aerial photography of Birkenau shows clearly that such a statement is totally mendacious, and that there were no fires, no smoke, and no lines of victims "at a rate of almost 10,000 a day" waiting patiently to go into either the mythical gas chambers or Wiesel's massive pits.[206]

Hilberg's historically faulty and deliberately mendacious (but politically correct) depiction of what happened at Birkenau in 1944 has not kept Yale University Press from issuing and promoting the Third Edition (2003) of *The Destruction of the European Jews*. Nor did it keep the American Library Association from recognizing his book as an "Outstanding Academic Title" in 2005. In Imperial America, in which the Holocaust is the state religion, all official educational and cultural entities are expected to follow closely the official imperial political line as laid down by the Holocaust fundamentalists and their allies. Thus, academic and professional groups line up behind their media counterparts in giving blind and unquestioning support to our state-sponsored religion, the Holocaust. No lie is too big.

RECOGNIZE SOMEONE?

A group of elderly Jewish men from Subcarpathian Rus who have been selected for death, walk along the road to the gas chambers.

Illustration 10: Wiesel claims that he was ordered to go with the men, who would have looked like these Hasids as they walk along a barbed-wire fence through which anyone on the outside could see. There is no secrecy, no smoke and no fire. The picture offers eloquent proof that there was no extermination program going on. Auschwitz Album *photo with mendacious caption by USHMM, photo #77335.*

Flash Forward to 2001: Jacques Mandelbaum of *Le Monde*

The historical and moral bankruptcy of both the open-pit and gas chamber theses would later be revealed quite succinctly in January 2001 at an exhibit organized by French Holocaustians at the Hôtel de Sully Museum in Paris. Entitled *Mémoire des camps* (Memory of the Camps), it was reviewed for *Le Monde* by staffer Jacques Mandelbaum. In his review, he noted that one of the unintended effects of the exhibit was to highlight the fact that there is no evidence that the gas chambers ever existed. He wrote:[218]

> *On the photography of the camp taken from an altitude of 7,000 meters on April 4, 1944, by American reconnaissance aircraft, the photo interpreters were able to see everything that was there, except the presence of the gas chambers.*

[218] Jacques Mandelbaum, "La Shoah et ces images qui nous manquent" (The Holocaust and These Missing Images), *Le Monde*, January 1, 2001, 17. "[…] des photographies du camp prises à sept mille mètres d'altitude, le 4 avril 1944, par des avions de reconnaissances américaines, dont les lecteurs déchiffrèrent toutes choses existantes, sauf la présence des chambres à gaz."

Illustration 11: A convoy of Hungarian Jews on the "Jewish Ramp" at Birkenau at the end of June 1944. The added arrows point to the chimneys of Crematoria II and III, without flames or smoke.
Source: Auschwitz Album *(USHMM, photo #77221)*

His statement contradicted the Jewish Holocaust narrative, which is based solely on the problematical testimony of supposed eyewitnesses. Mandelbaum might have added that Wiesel's flaming pits and belching smokestacks were also nowhere to be seen.

French Government-Endorsed Brainwashing Manual Admits the Burning Pits Are "Symbolic"

It is important to note how Jean-François Forges, the author of the French brainwashing manual for teachers, handles this claim by Wiesel. Not surprisingly, he falls back on the excuse that Wiesel is actually speaking in allegorical terms, not literal ones. First, completely ignoring the aerial photography which clearly shows that Wiesel's vision is a pure invention, Forges tries to validate Wiesel's vision by stating that other eyewitnesses also saw flames. This, of course, was an amazing achievement, especially since the cremation facilities at Auschwitz were fired by coke, which burns with little smoke, if any. Then, almost as if to admit that this is all a sad hoax, Forges adds:[219]

219 Jean-François Forges, *Eduquer contre Auschwitz* (Paris: ESF, 1997), 41. "On doit sans doute comprendre ces récits comme une description symbolique de l'enfer dans lequel les déportés se trouvent plongés selon les images traditionnelles du monde de la souffrance et de la damnation. "

> *We of course have to understand such stories as a symbolic description of the hell in which the deportees find themselves as expressed through traditional images of the world of suffering and damnation.*

In passing off Wiesel's description as merely symbolic, Forges is deliberately ignoring the fact that Wiesel's claim to have actually witnessed this burning scene lies at the very core of his identity as the U.S. public figure who is most closely associated with the Holocaust. This alleged experience is the basis for both the narrative strategy and the title of his novel, *La Nuit*, as well as the underlying justification for his financially successful brand, the Holocaust, under which he does business. Without the literal truth of this supposed vision, he had no right to tell Mauriac he had seen Jewish children who had suffered more than Christ, or to inform the president of the United States he had seen Jewish babies thrown into the flames, or to level the accusation of "silence" against Pope Pius XII, who correctly never believed in the Holocaust, a deliberately contrived exaggeration of the actual wartime sufferings endured by the Jews.

But the problem still remains for Forges. Since the aerial photography speaks clearly to the fact that Wiesel's open pits belching fire and smoke never existed, how does he reply? He bites the bullet and admits that Wiesel is a liar. Forges writes:[220]

> *The presence of such a pit on the ramp, within full view of the arriving deportees, is impossible. Blueprints of the area where the ramp was located, the American aerial photography, other* [eyewitness] *testimonies, the Germans' intention to keep the deportees in a state of calm and illusion as long as possible, all these elements invalidate this scene.*

Forges ends his attempt to justify Wiesel's mendacity by falling back once again on an allegorical explanation:[221]

> *Even if the act of burning children on the ramp is not a historical fact, the imagined scene,* if the reader is carefully prepared for it in advance, *represents the massacre of innocence at Birkenau, children burned elsewhere, and beyond this the massacre of all the Jewish children in the Shoah.*

In the final analysis, Forges's book is essentially a manual for the brainwashing and mind control of French children. His use of the phrase, "if the reader is carefully prepared for it in advance," makes this fact quite clear.

---

[220] *Ibid.*, 41: "La présence d'une telle fosse, sur la rampe, aux regards des déportés arrivant n'est pas possible: les plans de la rampe, les photos aériennes américaines, les autres témoignages, la volonté souvent affirmée des Allemands de maintenir le calme et l'illusion parmi les prisonniers le plus longtemps possible, tout infirme cette scène."

[221] *Ibid.*, 42. "Même si le fait de brûler les enfants sur la rampe n'est pas un fait historique, la scène imaginée, *si le lecteur en est soigneusement prévenu,* représente l'innocence massacrée à Birkenau, les enfants brûlés ailleurs et, au-delà, le massacre de tous les enfants juifs de la Shoah."

In summary, the aerial photography of Auschwitz proves beyond a shadow of a doubt that Wiesel's eyewitness account of open-pit burning of victims is false. In fact, this account is not something that Wiesel actually saw, but is merely a repetition of mendacious testimony given at Nuremberg. People with fertile imaginations invented this technical impossibility, and neither the Zionist media nor conformist academics have ever dared to question it.

Problem #5: The Deaths of Wiesel's Mother and Sister

The *Sparknotes* guide to *Night* treats Wiesel's mother and three sisters in a fashion rather typical of the scholastic brainwashing guides provided by other, similar, sources. Since these works are written for the same captive audience, the junior-high and high-school students who are forced to read *Night* as part of the state-mandated brainwashing program about the Holocaust, they all follow the same formula. In this case, little is said about Wiesel's mother and three sisters despite the fact that two of them, Wiesel's mother and little sister, probably died during the typhus epidemic of 1944, while his two older sisters, like Wiesel and his father, survived. With regard to these two deaths it would be a rather simple matter for the USHMM to allow scholars to have free access to their personal and medical files. But this has never happened.

As for the four who did not die at Auschwitz, their very survival offers important information, and it goes a long way toward supporting the revisionist argument that there were no gas chambers at Auschwitz. I say this because the master narrative of the Holocaust stipulates that all Jews were targeted for death, and that they were killed for the simple reason that they were Jewish. If we suppose for a moment that this master narrative is true, it would be illogical and self-defeating for the Germans to put Wiesel's mother and younger sister into the mythical gas chamber, while sparing the four other members of the family, who were also Jewish. It makes no sense. Another internal contradiction in the standard narrative is that the Germans, desperately in need of labor to support the war effort, went to the trouble of bringing in the Hungarian Jews at Armaments Minister Albert Speer's request and on Hitler's order in 1944, only to allegedly kill 90% of them as unfit for labor.

That is why the brainwashing guides simply suppress discussion of these people. Here is the excuse provided by the authors of *Sparknotes on Night* for a gross omission like this:[222]

---

[222] Sparknotes, *Night*, SparkNotes Literature Guide Series (N.Y.: SparkNotes, 2003), 3; www.sparknotes.com/lit/night/context.html.

RECOGNIZE SOMEONE?

Jewish women and children from Subcarpathian Rus who have been selected for death at Auschwitz-Birkenau, walk toward the gas chambers.

Illustration 12: La Nuit *is silent about what happened to Wiesel's mother and three sisters at Birkenau. They would have looked something like this, though more prosperous. Conspicuous by their absence are smoke, flame, or lines of up to 20,000 victims waiting to be gassed in the crematorium visible in the background, where one of the gas chambers was allegedly located. (*Auschwitz Album, *with mendacious caption from the USHMM, photo #77346)*

> *Whatever events lie outside the narrator's direct observation vanish from the work's perspective. After Eliezer is separated from his mother and sister* [sic], *for example, he never speaks about them again, and we never learn their fate.*

The editors thus claim that Wiesel's failure to speak of what became of his mother and three sisters (they seem to think he had only one sister) shows that the book is a memoir, or autobiography, and not a novel. But if it were actually a memoir, it ought to have chronicled the outcome of the Auschwitz experience for all the members of the family. At the very least, he should have told his reader whether or not they were put on a dump truck and dropped into one of the flaming pits. It should also be recalled that Wiesel says nothing in *La Nuit* about the gas chambers or the long lines of people allegedly waiting to go into them.

Wiesel is very cagey in the way he speaks of his mother's death in *Tous les fleuves*. He does so while speaking of the photo of the Rabbi of Wizhnitz (the man who had predicted in 1936 that he would become a "great man in Israel") that he had nailed to the wall above his bed in his home in Sighet. Wiesel writes:[223]

> *I had hung it there on the 2nd Day of the Month of Sivan.* [...] *As I write these words I suddenly remember that my mother died on exactly the same day, along with my little sister and my grandmother Nissel, but eight years later* [in 1944]. *I cried as I placed the Rabbi's photo above my bed.*

Wiesel dates his mother's and sister's deaths according to the Hebrew calendar. This date corresponds to May 24, 1944, in the Gregorian calendar. In this text, Wiesel makes no mention of the gas chambers in relation to his mother's death. However, two pages later, he hints that she had died in a gas chamber, but does so only in a very oblique manner:[224]

> *In the Jewish tradition, a person's death is his own personal business. As for the gas chambers, it's better that they should remain closed to prying eyes. As well as to the imagination. We'll never know what went on behind those steel doors.*

Before 1995, Wiesel had never given any specific date for his mother's death. However, we recall that, according to the internal chronology of *La Nuit* which I provided in my close reading above, Wiesel's family did not leave Sighet until June 3. With this as their departure date, they would not have arrived at Auschwitz until June 6 or 7.

Thus, when Marion Wiesel deliberately mistranslated all the relevant indications of time contained in the opening pages of the novel in order to move up the family's departure date from June 3 to May 21, she not only violated the basic presumption of trust that must exist between translator and reader, she also did so brazenly and with the deliberate intention to deceive. Her purpose was to have the Wiesel family arrive on the 2nd of Sivan, which fell on May 24 in that year, thus bringing the chronology of the 1958 novel into conformity with what Wiesel had written about his mother's death in his 1995 autobiography. This date, May 24, 1944, also dovetails with the arrival date at Birkenau of Lazar Wiesel, born in 1913, the man whose identity Wiesel appears to have stolen. In providing this deliberately deceptive and mendacious translation, Marion Wiesel, along with her editors and her publishing house, Farrar, Straus & Giroux, have simply trampled upon expected professional standards of trust and accuracy in the

---

223 Wiesel, *Tous les fleuves*, 95: "Je l'avais accroché le jour de son décès, le deuxième jour du mois de Sivan. Je me revois encore: avec un marteau très lourd, j'enfonce un clou et y suspends le cadre. En écrivant ces mots, je me rends soudain compte que ma mère mourut exactement à la même date, et ma petite sœur, et grand-mère Nissel, mais huit ans plus tard [1944]. C'est en pleurant la mort du Rabbi que j'avais placé sa photo au-dessus de mon lit. Le clou y est toujours. Une grosse croix y est suspendue."

224 *Ibid.*, 97: "Dans la tradition juive, la mort d'un être n'appartient qu'à lui. Les chambres à gaz, il vaut mieux qu'elles restent fermées au regard indiscret. Et à l'imagination. On ne saura jamais ce qui s'est passé derrière les portes d'acier."

name of the Holocaust. Sales over the years of millions of copies of Wiesel's *Night* to the captive audience of students in both the original translation and the new, utterly dishonest one,[225] are said to be FSG's principal revenue source. The firm's willingness to deliberately deceive their readers for financial gain speaks volumes about the corruption associated with Holocaust profiteering, and perhaps the publishing industry.

More Holocaustian Silence: Suppression of the Bad Arolsen Documents in the U.S.

In 2007, the documents held by the International Tracing Service in Bad Arolsen, Germany, were finally opened to select institutions in the eleven member states of its governing commission. Thereafter, tens of millions of pages of personal documents concerning some nineteen million concentration-camp-era people were sent to the USHMM in Washington. The practical effect of this huge international operation was to place these records in Jewish custody despite the fact that over 75 percent of them concern the lives of non-Jews. Since the USHMM continues to limit access to the records, despite their general historical interest, their intent seems to be to suppress the kind of evidence that would contradict Holocaust claims, including, quite probably, documented facts bearing on Wiesel's experiences in 1944 and 1945.[226]

Illustration 13: Arolsen: The personnel and medical records of Wiesel's mother and sister are contained in these suppressed archives.

As a result of this decision, gatekeepers at the museum have complete control over what can be seen and by whom. In practical terms, it means that there is no free access for all researchers. In fact, access to the archives is difficult even for those who make the effort to travel to the museum. But this reality is part of a larger policy, for the museum authorities will not even allow archival access through the open Internet or through terminals at libraries and universities around the country. This latter development is a shocking policy of censorship in a day and age when university researchers routinely have access to esoteric databases of all kinds. In this sense, the

225 http://en.wikipedia.org/wiki/Elie_Wiesel; see also http://archive.sltrib.com/article.php?id=3476960&itype=NGPSID

226 Edwin Black, "Survivors Oppose the Transfer of Holocaust Archive to D. C.," *JTS Wire Service*, May 10, 2007; Edwin Black, "Survivors Outraged at Holocaust Museum over Bad Arolsen," *History News Network*, May 13, 2007. http://historynewsnetwork.org/article/38788.

Bad Arolsen documents from the International Tracing Service have never really been released to the public. Thus, one of two things must happen:

1) either another copy of these files be provided to the National Archives; or
2) the copy in the possession of the USHMM be transferred to the National Archives, where free access would be guaranteed.

Problem #6: Wiesel's Medical Treatment at Auschwitz

Possible Plagiarism in This Section of *Night*

Wiesel claims that he stayed at the Auschwitz main camp for three weeks before being sent to Monowitz, the adjoining industrial complex, which is also sometimes called Auschwitz III. He states that "our group included a number of children between the ages of ten and twelve. The officer took an interest in them and ordered that food be brought to them."[227] This statement sends up a red flag, for it raises questions about the master narrative of the Jewish Holocaust story, according to which 1.5 to 2 million Jewish children were killed. If this is so, why then would German soldiers be going out of their way to feed these youngsters? This contradiction between what Wiesel wrote and the master narrative of the Holocaust story shows once again that Wiesel did not succeed in giving internal coherence to his narrative, despite his alleged ten-year vow of silence. It also hints at the possibility that the novel is a cut-and-paste job in which different sections were plagiarized from the testimonies of other survivors, but not properly edited and incorporated into the book. This problem of incoherency is salient in the section of the novel that deals with the medical care he claims to have received.

Wiesel Goes to the Hospital in *La Nuit*

In January 1945, Wiesel's right foot begins to swell, for he seems to have a case of frostbite, a disorder caused by abnormal sensitivity to cold. He has been living at the Monowitz industrial complex since the previous spring, and now decides to visit the clinic and have a doctor look at his foot:[228]

> *It was toward the middle of January, and my right foot began to swell up because of the cold. I could no longer stand on it, so I went to sick call. The doctor, an eminent Jew, a prisoner like myself, made no bones about it: "You need*

---

[227] *Ibid.*, *Nuit*, 79: "[…] notre convoi comportait quelques enfants de dix, douze ans. L'officier s'intéressa à eux et ordonna qu'on leur apporte quelque nourriture."

[228] *Ibid.*, 124: "Vers le milieu de janvier, mon pied droit se mit à enfler, à cause du froid. Je ne pouvais plus le poser à terre. J'allai à la visite. Le médecin, un grand médecin juif, un détenu comme nous, fut catégorique: il faut l'opérer. Si nous attendons, il faudra amputer les doigts du pied et peut-être la jambe.'"

> *to be operated on. If we wait, I'll have to take off your toes and maybe even your leg."*

Working backward from the date on which, according to the historical record, the entire Auschwitz camp complex began to be evacuated, which was at 6:00 AM on January 18, 1945, this reference to mid-January can be taken to have occurred on January 14, 1945. Wiesel then describes the comforts offered by the hospital, which would have been a complete waste of resources, if the Germans were planning to actually exterminate the Jews, which they clearly did not do. Next, he mentions the patient in the bed next to him, who is "a Hungarian Jew suffering from dysentery."[229] Once again, the reader sees that the diabolical Germans actually offered a wide range of care, and not just surgery. If the master narrative of the Holocaust folk tale were true, this man would have been a likely candidate for the mythical gas chamber before even getting to the hospital. But now Wiesel pushes even further beyond the bounds of credibility when he has this character state:[230]

> *They also have selections here, more often actually than on the outside.*

In claiming, as he does here, that selections for the mythical gas chambers also took place at the hospital, Wiesel is making an utterly absurd statement. For if such an assertion were true, it would mean that the Germans deliberately planned to spend scarce medical resources on sick Jews, even though the latter were scheduled to be gassed immediately afterwards!

Wiesel's Jewish doctor comes back into the room and tells him that the operation will take place the next morning at 10 AM. This "next day" is January 15.[231] He is completely anesthetized, and the procedure lasts one hour. After he awakens, the doctor tells him:[232]

> *Everything went fine. You've got guts, kiddo. Now you're going to stay here for two weeks, get some bed rest, and then your treatment will be completed. You'll eat well and relax both your body and your nerves…*

If Wiesel had in fact spent the medically recommended two weeks resting his body and healing his foot, his hospital stay would have lasted until January 29. However, Wiesel now tells us that, "beginning two days after my operation,"[233] rumors began to spread that the camp would soon be abandoned. He now spends his "last night,"[234] that is, the night of January 17-18, at Monowitz. Thus, instead of getting the two weeks of bed rest in the SS hospital that his surgeon had prescribed, Wiesel leaves the camp volun-

---

229 *Ibid.*: "un Juif hongrois atteint de dysenterie."
230 *Ibid.*: "Ici aussi, il y a la sélection. Plus souvent même que dehors."
231 *Ibid.*, 125: "le lendemain."
232 *Ibid.*, 126: "Tout s'est bien passé. Tu es courageux, petit. Maintenant tu vas rester ici deux semaines, te reposer convenablement, et tout sera fini. Tu mangeras bien, tu détendra ton corps et les nerfs…"
233 *Ibid.*, 127: "dès le surlendemain de mon opération."
234 *Ibid.*, 131: "dernière nuit."

tarily to join in on the forced march to Gleiwitz, some fifty-five kilometers distant from Auschwitz, in the middle of winter. In asserting that he was able to participate in this march just three days after his operation, Wiesel once again severely tests his readers' credulity. That march will be discussed in detail below.

Wiesel's Foot Injury Becomes a Knee Injury in *Tous les fleuves*

Wiesel returned to this subject in *Tous les fleuves*:[235]

> *January 1945. Every January brings me back to that one. I see myself sick. My knee is swollen.* [My emphasis] *I'm in pain and I'm walking with a limp. It's wintertime, and winters in Upper Silesia are severe, in fact merciless. The snow is burying us. My body is half frozen. It's difficult to walk while dragging a body that's exhausted. Impossible to go out on a work detail with the fever I've got, which is wearing me out and grinding me down. I'm at the end of my rope.*

Wiesel now seems to have forgotten that in his "autobiographical" *Night* he had suffered from a case of frostbite, and that it was his foot that was swollen, not his knee! Liars have a way of forgetting their previous tall tales, and Wiesel certainly fits that pattern. He then discusses with his father the possibility of going on sick call, claiming illogically, however, that to do so is "dangerous, few patients ever walk out of there, except to be taken to [the gas chamber] of Birkenau."[236] After he reports for sick call, he is screened by an orderly, and then led into a doctor's office. After the latter checks out Wiesel's knee, he tells him that it has to be operated on right away, and that is exactly what the camp doctors do! In *La Nuit*, Wiesel has to wait twenty-four hours for the operation on his foot, but in *Tous les fleuves* the Germans operate on his knee right away! Wiesel writes:[237]

> *Finally, my turn comes. A doctor takes a quick look at my knee, palpates it, and somehow I hold back my cry of pain.*

Not only is Wiesel spared a trip to the mythical gas chamber, but he actually receives top-quality emergency medical care. Then, the icing on the cake comes when his surgeon reassures him before his knee operation (not after it, as in *La Nuit*):[238]

> *It won't hurt, or not much anyway. Don't worry, kiddo, you'll be okay!*

---

235 Wiesel, *Tous les fleuves*, 117: "Janvier 1945. Chaque janvier me ramène à celui-là. Je me vois malade. Mon genou est enflé. J'ai mal. Je me déplace en boitant. C'est l'hiver. Ils sont sévères, impitoyables, les hivers silésiens. La neige nous ensevelit. Le corps est à moitie gelé. Difficile de marcher en traînant un corps qui vous abrutit. Impossible to sortir en commando avec la fièvre qui me secoue et m'assomme. Je suis à bout."

236 *Ibid.*, 117: "Dangereux. Peu de malades en sortent, sauf pour être conduits à Birkenau."

237 *Ibid.*, 118: "Finalement, mon tour arrive. Un médecin jette un coup d'oeil sur mon genou, le palpe, je réprime un crie."

238 *Ibid.*: "Tu n'auras pas mal, ou très peu, ne t'en fais pas, petit, tu vivras."

Illustration 14: German medical staffers in 1944 at the SS Hospital at Birkenau. Clearly, there is no Holocaust going on in the background.[239]

Wiesel's change of the story about his operation from his foot to his knee offers further proof that the original version of this tale in *La Nuit* had probably been plagiarized. After all, that operation, if it had actually taken place, would have left one or several scars on his foot and toes. These scars in turn would have served as a reminder, as Wiesel wrote *Tous les fleuves*, that he had undergone a foot operation, not a knee operation! In summary, Wiesel received excellent hospital care at Auschwitz, seems to have plagiarized the tale about the operation for frostbite, and offers more proof that there was no extermination program in place at Auschwitz.

Problem #7: Wiesel's Alleged Loss of Religious Faith at Auschwitz

Wiesel's references to his alleged loss of religious faith at Auschwitz are too numerous to mention. He began this deception in *La Nuit*:[240]

Never will I forget the flames that consumed my faith, once and for all.

This deception continued when he met Mauriac. In fact, Mauriac's impression of Wiesel's loss of his Jewish faith was so strong that he later came to believe that he could convert Wiesel to Catholicism. This bizarre wish, in addition to the old man's physical attraction to Wiesel, remains hidden for now in the letters that the two men exchanged and that Wiesel will not release. His desire to convert Wiesel helps to explain why Mauriac dedicated his 1958 version of the life of Christ, *Le fils de l'homme* (*The Son of Man*, 1960) to Wiesel, calling him "a crucified Jewish child" (un enfant juif crucifié).

If Wiesel milked his alleged loss of faith in order to deepen his bonds with Mauriac, he exploited it later as a part of his effort to market the Holocaust. To cite but two examples, Lawrence L. Langer reflected the approved interpretation of this issue when he referred to the "apostate narrator" of *La Nuit*,[241] and Irving Halperin offered a further orthodox Holo-

[239] http://img.dailymail.co.uk/i/pix/2007/09_03/auschwitzpics4_800x531.jpg

[240] Wiesel, *Nuit*, 60: "Jamais je n'oublierai ces flammes qui consumèrent pour toujours ma foi."

[241] Lawrence L. Langer, in: Harry Cargas (ed.), *Responses to Elie Wiesel* (N.Y.: Persea,

caustian opinion when he wrote that Wiesel allegedly lost his faith because he had supposedly seen children being burned alive in the trenches, and spoke of "his turning away from God on witnessing the mass burning of children at Auschwitz."[242]

Yet Wiesel never ceased to practice his "faith," whatever that word means for him. In the camps, he actually devoted time each day to study the Talmud, not to be confused with the Jewish Pentateuch. His Talmud study continued uninterrupted in 1945:[243]

> *In the camps, I worked with a Rosh-yeshiva, a tutor; as we carried stones, we would recite the Talmud by heart. And the first thing that I asked the children's camp director when I got to France was to be able to study the Talmud.*

Despite the "God is dead" tone of *La Nuit*, which is a theme that Wiesel latched onto after he had gotten a taste of life in Paris in the early 1950s, he admitted to Brigitte-Fanny Cohen not only that he had remained a believer while in the camps, but that he had prayed every day there:[244]

> *In the camps, I prayed almost every day* [...and] *the real questioning began after the camps.*

In other words, despite his hagiographers' claims about Wiesel's loss of faith, he remained an observant Jew without interruption. Thus it should come as no surprise that once he reached France and was free to do what he wanted, he returned immediately to the formal life of Orthodox Jewry:[245]

> *Strangely, when I got to France in 1945, I took up my religious life once again. And I took it up with a great deal of fervor, as if I had wanted to see in the war a kind of hiatus. I wanted to close that hiatus, return to 1944 and open up the Talmud on the page where I had left it.*

Wiesel was able to wear his phylacteries, an outward sign of his identity as an Orthodox Jew, every day of his life in the camps, and continued to do so for years afterward. This is an astonishing admission for a man who supposedly lost his faith there! In the "interview book" on the subject of

---

1978), 41.

242 Irving Halperin, in Cargas, *Responses,* 54.

243 Cohen, *Qui êtes-vous?*, 77: "Dans les camps, je travaillais avec un *Rosh-yeshiva*, un maître d'étude: nous portions des pierres et nous récitions par cœur le Talmud. Et la première chose que j'ai demandée au directeur du camp d'enfants en arrivant en France, c'était de pouvoir étudier le Talmud."

244 *Ibid.*, 86: "Dans les camps, j'ai prié presque tous les jours [...] la véritable interrogation s'est produite après les camps."

245 *Ibid.*: "Etrangement, lorsque je suis arrivé en France, j'ai tout de suite repris ma vie religieuse. Et je l'ai reprise avec beaucoup de ferveur, comme si j'avais voulu voir dans la guerre une sorte de parenthèse. Je voulais refermer la parenthèse, revenir en 1944 et retrouver le Talmud à la page où je l'avais laissé."

memory that he did with French president François Mitterrand, Wiesel stated:[246]

> *Me, I remember the first time I didn't put on my phylacteries. It was in Israel in 1949. I was with a journalist. I was so busy that day that I completely forgot to put them on. And for me that was terrible because I'm very pious. But the world didn't fall apart. Yet, I was convinced that if I ever did such a thing I would die right away from a heart attack!*

Finally, despite his considerable pains to seem open to the "God is dead" academic critics who, in the 1970s and 1980s, explicated his novel as an existential cry of anguish, he came clean in *Tous les fleuves* when he wrote that in Auschwitz "I needed God."[247]

In summary, Wiesel's claim of a loss of faith in the camps was a deliberate fabrication. He later used this misrepresentation as bait to lure Mauriac, who was strangely attracted by this particular aspect of Wiesel's persona. Imputing a facile, and false, religious crisis to Wiesel during the war years has become a staple of the contemporary scholastic guidebooks that U.S. youngsters consult in conjunction with their reading of *Night*.

Problem #8: The Famous Hanging Episode

The Boy on the Rope Represents the Six Million and Replaces Christ

The so-called "hanging scene" is the most famous one in *Night*. Wiesel invokes Christian imagery in this scene, specifically the crucifixion of Christ, by depicting a boy being hanged between two grown men. (The three had hidden weapons and attempted to sabotage electrical equipment.) Since the boy is not heavy enough to pull the noose tight, he does not die within a few minutes, as the two men do. Instead, he dangles for half an hour between them, reminding us of Christ hanging on the cross between two thieves for three hours. The prisoners are then forced to walk past the three victims. Wiesel wrote:[248]

> *Then we began to walk by. The two adults were already dead, their swollen, bluish tongues hanging out of their mouths. But the third rope was still mov-*

---

246 Mitterrand and Wiesel *Mémoire*, 53: "Moi, je me souviens de la première fois où je n'ai pas mis les phylactères. C'était en 1949, en Israël. Je me trouvais avec un journaliste. J'étais tellement occupé, ce jour-là, que j'ai complètement oublié de les mettre. Et pour moi, c'était terrible, parce que je suis très pieux. Mais le monde ne s'est pas effondré. Pourtant, j'étais convaincu que je si je commettais un tel acte, je mourrais sur-le-champ d'une crise cardiaque."

247 Wiesel, *Tous les fleuves*, 109: "J'avais besoin de Dieu."

248 Wiesel, *Nuit*, 104: "Puis commença le défilé. Les deux adultes ne vivaient plus. Leur langue pendait, grossie, bleutée. Mais la troisième corde n'était pas immobile: si léger, l'enfant vivait encore. […] Plus d'une demi-heure, il resta ainsi, à lutter entre la vie et la mort, agonisant sous nos yeux. Et nous devions le regarder bien en face. Il était encore vivant lorsque je passai devant lui. Sa langue était encore rouge, ses yeux pas encore éteints."

> *ing; the child being so light he was still alive.* [...] *He stayed like that for more than half an hour, struggling between life and death, as we witnessed his agony. And we had to look directly at his face. He was still alive when I walked by. His tongue was still red, and the light had not yet gone out of his eyes.*

This scene is dramatically heightened by Wiesel's expropriation of two Gospel texts from Christianity. In the first, the unidentified kapo who is ordered to remove the chairs on which the three condemned stand awaiting hanging refuses to do so:[249]

> *This time, the* Lagerkapo *refused to obey the hangman's order, and was replaced by three SS men.*

Let us first ponder the absurdity of such a gesture: the public refusal – in front of hundreds of other prisoners – by a man assigned to lead other prisoners, to obey a direct order from a superior. Here, as so often in *Night*, Wiesel expects his reader to believe the unbelievable. But he is forced to create this implausible scene in order to serve a higher purpose, for he wants the unnamed *Lagerkapo* to remind us of Pontius Pilate in the Gospels (Matthew 27:24). In refusing to remove the three chairs, he is in effect saying, like Pontius Pilate: "I do not want to be involved in this injustice." Similarly, Pilate had refused to take part directly in the condemnation of Christ. He did so by publicly, in front of a large crowd, "washing his hands of the blood of this just man." The second thing that Wiesel does to subvert the Christian crucifixion story in order to use it for his own ends is to have someone in the crowd cry out: "Where is God?" The answer comes back: "Where is he? He is right here hanging in the gallows."[250] Here Wiesel is adapting and subverting Matthew 27:46, in which Christ cries out to heaven: "Why hast thou forsaken me?" Or, in Wiesel's words, "Where is God?" The answer to this question is that darkness covered the earth, and the veil of the Temple was split in two (Matthew 27:45; 51-54). These apparent miracles are traditionally interpreted in Christian theology as the reply from heaven that Christ has not died in vain, for his death serves a redemptive purpose for all mankind. Wiesel adapted this response, somewhat didactically, in the reply found in his novel: "Where is he? He is right here hanging in the gallows."

In this scene, the boy in the middle, presumably an Orthodox Jewish boy like Wiesel, becomes a Christ figure, and the novel's narrative voice works hard to drive this message home. It is thanks in large part to this scene that the absurdist (at first glance, there is no apparent meaning to the scene) and existential (but it has paved the way for the creation of Israel) sacrifice of the Six Million has been able to replace the completely spiritu-

---

[249] *Ibid.*, 104: "Le *Lagerkapo* refusa cette fois de servir le bourreau. Trois S.S. le remplacèrent."

[250] *Ibid.*: "Où donc est Dieu?[...] . Où il est? Le voici, il est pendu ici, à cette potence."

al Christian notion of the sacrifice of Christ. In Holocaust indoctrination classes, this replacement of Christ by the Six Million is intended to affect those youngsters who come from a Christian background. As it artfully subverts what they have been taught, it posits the Six Million as the modern-day equivalent of, and replacement for, Christ. For youngsters from a non-Christian background, the Zionist message, although purely political and not feeding off a prior cultural subtext, is no less clear: the boy in the gallows stands for the Six Million who, in turn, stand for Israel.

Mauriac and the Hanging Scene

Mauriac was so struck by the hanging scene (which of course he had also helped to shape into its final form) that he referred specifically to it in his foreword to the novel. His statement is not at all vague, and hints at one of the main points I have sought to make throughout this study about his troubled relationship with Wiesel: that the aging writer sensed (naively and wrongly) that Wiesel was interested in converting to Catholicism. Thus, Mauriac claims that he saw in Wiesel's eyes the "angelic sadness which had appeared one day upon the face of the hanged child."[251] In other words, Mauriac sensed that Wiesel was still carrying with him a remnant of some sort from the experience of this boy, the novel's Christ figure. Is this why Wiesel had presented the hanging scene in Christian terms in the first place? Did he do this in order to attract people like Mauriac to his book? Confronted by this glimpse of Christ in Wiesel's "angelic sadness," Mauriac then asks himself two rhetorical questions. First:

> *What did I say to him? Did I speak of that other Jew, his brother, who may have resembled him, the crucified one, whose cross has conquered the world?*

Of course, the very fact that Mauriac frames the issue in the form of a rhetorical question is his way of revealing that he had in fact talked with Wiesel about his interest – or at least professed interest – in converting to Catholicism. Mauriac, after all, wrote this text in 1958, just before the publication of *La Nuit*. Three years had passed since he had first met and become attached to Wiesel. As we have seen, in all likelihood he had offered to rewrite the young man's Yiddish book and prepare it for publication. By so doing, he had offered Wiesel an example of Christian humility by hiding his own major role in the transformation of the Yiddish polemic into a more finely crafted French novel. Doubtless he had hoped by his generosity to encourage in some way Wiesel's religious conversion.

Now we come to the second rhetorical question:[252]

---

[251] Mauriac, foreword to *La Nuit*, iii: "[…] le reflet de cette tristesse d'ange apparue un jour sur le visage de l'enfant pendu."

[252] *Ibid.*: "Que lui ai-je dit? Lui ai-je parlé de cet Israélien, ce frère qui lui ressemblait peut-être, ce crucifié dont la croix a vaincu le monde? Lui ai-je affirmé que ce qui fut pour lui pierre d'achoppement est devenu pierre d'angle pour moi et que la conformité entre la

Did I tell him that the stumbling block to his faith was the cornerstone of mine? And that the relationship between the Cross and human suffering was, in my eyes, the key to the impenetrable mystery on which the faith of his childhood had foundered?

Here Mauriac is stating that he had discussed with his young Jewish friend an even more difficult subject: the fact that, for Christians, suffering has a meaning in so far as it can help to procure their eternal salvation, whereas the Jewish religion in which Wiesel had been raised has no such dimension.

Ruth R. Wisse, a specialist in Yiddish literature at Harvard, has provided an English translation of part of the Yiddish version of the hanging scene. For her, the book is a novel, not a memoir, and this particular scene is clearly a literary creation. First, regarding the fictional nature of *Night*, she writes:[253]

Although he [Wiesel] *resists the description of his work as fiction, readers have no trouble distinguishing the book's principal tropes – night and father-son – its recurrent imagery and coherent plot.*

She also situates *Un di velt* in the Yiddish series in which it appeared. In doing so, she mentions that, not only is Wiesel the youngest author to have published in it, his approach is also quite different from those of the one hundred and sixteen others who came before him. While they, in keeping with the genre, try to name and document the fates of as many dead relatives, friends and acquaintances as possible, the cautious Wiesel, who talks only about his father, "creates a highly selective and isolating literary narrative" (*Canon*, 212). In other words, Wiesel's failure to provide supporting details about his experiences has caused Wisse to suspect that he might be hiding something. She also points out that, in the transformation of the Yiddish text into French, the hanging scene was compressed to "half its length" (214). Yet despite this overall compression, the four most important and "literary" sentences in the French version are not present in the Yiddish original. Rather, they have been added to the original. They are:

He stayed like that for more than half an hour, struggling between life and death, as we witnessed his agony. And we had to look directly at his face. He was still alive when I walked by. His tongue was still red, and the light had not yet gone out of his eyes.

These sentences, which utilize a detached, authoritative, third-person narrative voice to sum up what has just happened, describe in an objective manner the effect of the event on the onlookers. To me, Mauriac's fingerprints

croix et la souffrance des hommes demeure à mes yeux la clef de ce mystère insondable où sa foi d'enfant s'est perdu."

253 Ruth R. Wisse, *The Modern Jewish Canon: A Journey through Language and Literature* (Chicago: University of Chicago Press, 2003), 212f.

are all over this emendation, yet Wisse – lamely and illogically – attributes it to Wiesel, despite what she concedes is "the thinness of his artistic heritage" (216).

Finally, in the last two sentences of the hanging scene, Wiesel once again shows his ignorance of what life was really like at Auschwitz. This time, however, Wisse does not play along with him. Wisse translates Wiesel's Yiddish as follows:

> *That evening the soup had no taste. We hid it away for the next day.*

Wisse then observes wryly (214):

> *The closure of this passage was also rendered more credible* [in French]. *The French text reads: "Ce soir-là, la soupe avait un goût de cadavre."* [That night, the soup tasted of corpses.] *By all accounts, no one at Auschwitz could have left his soup for the next day.*

Wisse, in making it clear that Wiesel's claim about hiding soup at Auschwitz is utterly absurd and stands in contradiction to the master narrative of the Jewish Holocaust story, wryly raises the question of the authenticity of Wiesel's alleged wartime experiences. At the same time, she validates the superiority of the French version of the text, which I attribute to Mauriac.

Alfred Kazin Questions the Historical Validity of the Hanging Scene

Alfred Kazin (1915–1998), a well-known "New York intellectual" in his day, was the first mainstream media literary critic to question Wiesel's credibility in *Night*. To him, the hanging scene was sheer fiction. In 1989, he wrote about Wiesel:[254]

> *The more I learned about him, the more I pursued the vast literature about Auschwitz, the less surprised I would have been to learn that the episode of the boy struggling on the rope had never happened.*

Kazin also wrote a letter to a friend in which he called Wiesel a "mystifier." Alexander Cockburn, in his by now famous article on Wiesel as a "fibber" in *Night*, referred to that letter when he wrote:[255]

> *In a letter to David Hirsch dated October 6, 1994, Alfred Kazin writes that at the beginning of their friendship, "I liked him* [Wiesel] *enormously, and I was in awe of him because of his suffering in Auschwitz." But at the same time "[…] when he expanded at length about his experiences under the Nazis, it was impossible to miss the fact that he was a mystifier."*

---

[254] Alfred Kazin, "My Debt to Elie Wiesel and Primo Levi," in: David Rosenberg (ed.), *Testimony: Contemporary Writers Make the Holocaust Personal* (New York, Random House, 1989), 123.

[255] Alexander Cockburn, "Did Oprah Pick another Fibber? Truth and Fiction in Elie Wiesel's *Night*: Is Frey or Wiesel the Bigger Moral *Poseur*?" Counterpunch.com, April 1-2, 2006. www.counterpunch.org/2006/04/01/truth-and-fiction-in-elie-wiesel-s-night-is-frey-or-wiesel-the-bigger-moral-poseur/

In 1989, when Kazin expressed his suspicion that *Night* was not a memoir but a novel, the two men were supposedly friends. However, as a result of Kazin's comment, Wiesel severed the relationship. For Wiesel, Kazin had not only dared to question his integrity, he had also violated a powerful Jewish taboo: Jews, especially those who are not survivors, must never question any aspect of the Holocaust. Even worse, Kazin, like Alan Greenspan, Abe Rosenthal, Saul Bellow, and so many other Jews of that era, had been able to successfully avoid direct military service during World War II.

Wiesel attacked Kazin in two different sections of *Tous les fleuves.* In the first he addresses directly Kazin's declaration of disbelief of the hanging scene in *Night*, while in the second he deals in generalities with their former personal relationship. In the first instance, he doesn't mention Kazin by name, referring to him only as a "Jewish American literary critic." Wiesel, the supreme false Holocaust witness, was obviously quite sensitive about being called out by a fellow Jew on a specific – and rather flagrant – act of mendacity. Here is what he wrote of Kazin, without mentioning his name:[256]

> *I reported precisely the hanging of three prisoners. I described the agony of the youngest among them. Forty years later, a Jewish American literary critic would say that, if he learned that this scene had been invented, he would not be surprised. Unhealthy skepticism? Mentally disturbed? Contagious Holocaust denial? This critic must be a lowlife to attribute such an underhanded act to me.*

The unidentified "translators" of *Tous les fleuves* into English deleted this whole passage. The avowal by Wiesel that a New York Jewish intellectual had doubts about the authenticity of the hanging scene was apparently deemed too explosive to publish. In another section of *Tous les fleuves*, he attacked Kazin again, but mentioned him by name this time:[257]

> *The witness has nothing but his memory. If people reject that, what does he have left? In the final analysis, a man like Kazin gives support to those who deny the Holocaust. If he refuses to believe someone like me, why would Holocaust deniers believe other survivors?*

Good question.

---

256 Wiesel, *Tous les fleuves*, 117: "J'ai rapporté avec précision la pendaison de trois prisonniers. J'ai décrit l'agonie du plus jeune. Quarante ans plus tard, un critique littéraire juif américain dira que, s'il apprenait que cette scène était inventée, il ne serait pas surpris. Scepticisme malsain? Raisonnement perturbé? Négationnisme contagieux? Ce critique doit vivre bien bas pour m'attribuer sa bassesse."

257 *Ibid.*, 437: "Le témoin n'a que sa mémoire; si on la récuse, que lui reste-t-il? A la limite, un homme comme Kazin apporte son soutien à ceux qui nient l'Holocauste. S'il refuse de me croire, moi, pourquoi, les négationnistes croiraient-ils d'autres survivants?"

Raul Hilberg on the Hanging Scene

In his 2006 article on Wiesel as a "fibber," Alexander Cockburn wrote of *La Nuit*:

> *The trouble here is that in its central, most crucial scene,* Night *isn't historically true, and at least two other important episodes are almost certainly fiction. Below, I cite views, vigorously expressed to me in recent weeks by a concentration camp survivor, Eli Pfefferkorn, who worked with Wiesel for many years; also by Raul Hilberg.*

Due to limitations of space, I shall only deal with the comments made to Cockburn by Hilberg about *Night*. First, with regard to a translation of the Yiddish original, Hilberg told Cockburn:

> *From a purely academic viewpoint, it would be interesting to have a scholarly edition, comparing the Yiddish version with subsequent translations and editions, with appropriate footnotes, Wiesel's comments, etc. He was addressing two entirely different audiences, the first being the Yiddish-speaking Jews, members of the world of his youth whom he addressed in nineteenth-century terms. There's more detail, more comment. I made that suggestion to Wiesel and he didn't react favorably.*

Second, regarding the historical reality of the hanging scene, Hilberg commented to Cockburn:

> *I have a version of the hanging from an old survivor with the names of all three adults.*

Third, Hilberg apparently expressed his skepticism on this point in a review of *Night*. He told Cockburn:

> *I made no secret of our differences. But whereas it* [the age of the central figure in the hanging] *may seem somewhat small, it makes a very big difference to Christians, particularly Catholics, because it's very clear that mystics are intensely interested in the scene because it seems to replicate the crucifixion. It made a considerable impact. So the fact that this figure may not have been a boy at all is disturbing.*

One last comment by Hilberg is also pertinent here:

> *It would appear, from the record I have, that some witnesses have questioned whether this scene took place at all.*

While Hilberg called for a parallel scholarly translation of the Yiddish and French versions of *La Nuit* in this interview, the Holocaust fundamentalists, with Wiesel in the lead, continue to oppose such a project. They have too much to lose, so here, as so often elsewhere, the revisionists will have to take the initiative. Second, like Alfred Kazin before him, Hilberg believes that the scene did not actually happen as it is described in *Night*. Finally, Hilberg correctly observes that this scene is an element in the book that clearly appeals to Catholics and other Christians. But that does not mean the tale has no appeal to Holocaustians, especially since Christians who see the boy as a Christ figure must overlook the fact that Jesus was not a child when he was executed.

Whether Wiesel actually wrote this scene or borrowed it from another text, the dying child image actually fits in quite well with Wiesel's conception of himself as a child-victim representing the six million. The image also dovetails with his oft-repeated claim, now a rather absurd embarrassment, that 1.5 to 2 million Jewish children died in the Holocaust without leaving a trace.

Jean-François Forges: The Scene Is Pure Invention

Jean-François Forges, whose book guides teachers charged with brainwashing French children about the Holocaust, agrees with Kazin and Hilberg against Wiesel on the hanging scene. He writes:[258]

> *This scene of a child tortured and killed in this manner is, as far as I can determine, unique in books about the concentration camps. It seems to me to have been constructed as a kind of parable intended to focus on a metaphysical problem. I see this child as an allegorical icon, and I cannot bring myself to believe that it is based on a historical fact.*

In conclusion, the hanging scene raises many questions about the supposed autobiographical element in *Night*. These difficulties also help us to understand why Hilberg told Cockburn that, when he suggested to Wiesel that a bilingual edition of the two books should be made available, Wiesel "didn't react favorably." Hilberg is speaking volumes here about Wiesel's deceit as an eyewitness, and *La Nuit* as an "autobiography."

Problem #9: Wiesel Shuns Liberation, Leaves Auschwitz with Germans

Wiesel Joins in Auschwitz Evacuation

On January 17, 1945, two days after his foot surgery, Wiesel tells us in *La Nuit* that he is hearing a rumor to the effect that the camp is about to be evacuated. As he discusses the rumor with others in the hospital who have just benefited from German medical care, he is told that the very same people who just saved his life will now kill him, and he expects the reader to believe such nonsense. He then has two of his characters mention possible ways in which all the detainees could be killed. One detainee speculates that "all the sick will be finished off at point-blank range,"[259] while another states that "the camp is surely mined, and as soon as the evacuation is

---

[258] Forges, 42: "Cette scène qui, à ma connaissance, est unique dans la littérature concentrationnaire, de l'enfant torturé et tué de cette manière, me paraît construite comme une parabole pour poser un problème métaphysique. Je vois cet enfant comme une icône allégorique. Je ne parviens pas à croire à sa réalité factuelle."

[259] *Nuit*, 129: "Tous les malades seront achevés à bout portant."

completed, it will all be blown up."[260] Wiesel goes to his father and asks what he would like to do:[261]

> *He was lost in his meditations. The choice was in our hands. For once, we could decide for ourselves what our own fate would be. Both of us could stay at the hospital, where I could have him admitted either as a patient or a nurse, thanks to my doctor. Or we could go with the others.*

But when his father remains silent and does not express a preference, it is Wiesel himself who takes the initiative and suggests one to him: "Let's allow ourselves to be evacuated with the others,"[262] he tells his father. Faced with this suggestion from his son, the father, who is supposedly very sick and quite weak, and who has not been able to work at Auschwitz for even one day, looks at the boy's foot (and not his knee) and asks: "Do you think you can walk?"[263] Wiesel responds: "Yes, I think so."[264] It is clear in this exchange that the father, first through his silence, and then by expressing his doubt about his son's ability to engage in the forced march that would be part of the evacuation plan, does not want to go. He wants to stay, but his son wants to leave.

Without giving any explanation for his decision, and in contradiction to everything that has come before, Wiesel chooses to do just the opposite of what, logically, he should do: escape from the Germans at all cost! How can his act be defended? This decision is simply inexplicable within the context of the "autobiography" – or novel – up to this point, since it simply defies reason and turns our basic notions about cause and effect on their head. Thus, we must once again analyze the factors, mentioned above, that made the decision to remain behind seem like the obvious one. First, with regard to his father's health, we must conclude that, by leaving with the Germans, Wiesel in fact hastened his father's death instead of saving his life. Thus, in retrospect, Wiesel's act was clearly irrational. Secondly, by leaving, he also needlessly risked his own life in the forced march. This was another irrational act that makes no sense in the context of the novel's narrative to that point.

We now come to the third element that must of necessity be figured into his decision: German atrocities and overall brutality as part of an alleged extermination policy. The problem here is that Wiesel's freely made decision to go with the Germans explicitly contradicts the anti-German rhetoric

---

260 *Ibid.*: "Le camp est sûrement miné. Aussitôt après l'évacuation, tout sautera."

261 *Ibid.*, 129f.: "Il était perdu dans ses méditations. Le choix était entre nos mains. Pour une fois, nous pouvions décider nous-mêmes de notre sort. Rester tous deux à l'hôpital où je pouvais le faire entrer comme malade ou comme infirmier, grâce à mon docteur. Ou bien suivre les autres."

262 *Ibid.*, 130: "Laissons-nous évacuer avec les autres."

263 *Ibid.*: "Tu crois que tu pourras marcher?"

264 *Ibid.*, 30: "Oui, je crois."

that characterizes *La Nuit* from its opening pages. This decision rocks the whole foundation on which the novel is based. The accusatory Jewish narrative voice, so stridently anti-German throughout, is completely contradicted by this act. In other words, this decision to voluntarily remain in German custody raises suspicions in the reader's mind that the anti-German diatribes found in the preceding pages might not be true. If they were, Wiesel would have never agreed to go along with the Germans. Alternatively, his decision could be interpreted by a skeptical reader to mean that Wiesel knew that the anti-German rhetoric he had used in the preceding parts of the novel had no basis in fact.

Wiesel's Existential Act Speaks Louder than Words

This decision by Wiesel raises several serious questions about him as both a moral agent and a novelist. First, from a moral point of view, it is he, and not his father, who suggests this course of action. Even worse, he also insists on leaving with the Germans, even though such a choice represents the moral equivalent of signing his father's death certificate. Given the detailed description of the father's medical condition that is provided throughout the text of the novel, the son clearly understands that the decision to leave with the Germans involves serious risks for the father's survival. What kind of a son is this?

Second, Wiesel, as the narrator and protagonist of this novel, seems to have already forgotten that his doctor had ordered two weeks of complete bed rest, that is, until January 29. By taking part of his own free will in a forced march and arduous travel by train when he supposedly could not even stand, Wiesel tests his reader's ability to believe him. This is especially true when we recall that he was risking his father's life as well as his own. It was also widely believed that anyone who fell out of the march for any reason was liable to be shot. This episode makes no sense, unless of course Wiesel was much healthier than he claims. On the other hand, if he really was unable to walk, he simply invented, or plagiarized, the whole story.

This basic inconsistency in Wiesel's narrative offers a further explanation for why his camp medical records have been suppressed. Sadly, the evidence in the text suggests that Wiesel, as narrator, never even considered such issues, hinting yet again that this episode is pure invention. In fact, Wiesel's whole novel, up to the point of this pivotal discussion with the father, argues in favor of staying behind to be liberated. In doing so, he and his father would not only be escaping from the satanic Germans, Wiesel himself could have also gotten those two weeks of needed rest, and his father's life would have been spared.

Illustration 15: January 27, 1945: Perfectly healthy Jews at Auschwitz greet their Soviet "liberators".[265]

If Wiesel's book is an autobiography, it must reflect life's basic realities, including the relationship between cause and effect, as ordinary people understand that link. If not, his story cannot be taken seriously as a lived experience. Alternatively, if Wiesel's book is a novel, which I believe to be the case, it should nonetheless contain the all-important quality of verisimilitude, that is, the quality of being in conformity, as a work of art, with that same understanding of cause and effect shared by ordinary folk.

In high-school and college literature classes, students hear the expression "willing suspension of disbelief," which refers to the implicit bargain that any reader of a realistic work (excluded here are science fiction, fantasy literature and the like) strikes with an author. The reader will suspend disbelief, or skepticism, about the veracity and believability of the tale in exchange for entertainment or instruction. But should that reader conclude that the characters' actions are arbitrary and do not make sense, then the pact is broken. The reader allows his skepticism to get the better of him and might even stop reading. In other words, suspension of disbelief implies a *quid pro quo* arrangement between author and reader. But skeptical school students who are forced to read this book cannot break the pact out of fear of reprisal from their teachers. After all, they are reading it "for credit," and sometimes "for extra credit."

Those who justify Wiesel's decision to remain in German custody, including of course the teachers who administer Holocaust brainwashing at the grassroots level in the nation's schools, are forced to justify Wiesel's decision by citing the rumors mentioned in his discussion with the two other patients at the SS hospital. As shown above, one rumor had it that, if inmates remained behind, the Germans would shoot everyone at point-blank

265 https://furtherglory.files.wordpress.com/2012/05/auschwitzliberation.jpg.

Illustration 16: Auschwitz, January 1945: Soviet photo of healthy Jewish children disproves myth that all Jewish children at Auschwitz were gassed [still shot from Soviet film footage].[266]

range, while the other predicted that the whole camp would be destroyed. Yet there are at least two reasons why it is difficult, if not impossible, to take these rumors seriously.

First, they were being circulated by people whose lives were being saved by fellow Jews working in a thoroughly normal and professional manner for the German government in a German military hospital. It would have made no sense for the Germans to save these patients, if they had intended to kill them the next day. Jewish proponents of the Holocaust faith have never been able to answer this massive contradiction at the heart of the master narrative of the Holocaust story, so they simply ignore it. Unfortunately, the collaborationist historians and literary scholars of academe give them a pass on the issue.

The second reason why these rumors cannot be taken seriously involves the sheer magnitude of the task they describe, killing thousands of people in a few hours!

Wiesel's Decision Is Consistent with the Reality of Life in the Camps, Not the Holocaust

While there were no doubt individual instances of German brutality toward Jewish detainees in the camps, there was no German government-

266 http://upload.wikimedia.org/wikipedia/commons/5/51/Child_survivors_of_Auschwitz.jpeg

ordered extermination plan at Birkenau. Thus, Wiesel's decision to remain with the Germans makes sense only if he believed that the German program involved the ethnic relocation of Jews to work camps in Germany and farther to the east in order to force them to work on behalf of the German war effort, and not to kill them. His decision to remain in German custody makes no sense, however, within the context of the Holocaust.

In summary, Wiesel's decision to evacuate the Auschwitz camp with the retreating German "war criminals," instead of remaining behind to be liberated by the Soviets, offers yet another insight into what was actually happening at Auschwitz. Many Jews were in fact deported from Germany and other European countries, spent time in camps, and were then transported farther to the east. In Wiesel's case, he and his family were imported into the Reich to work in support of the German war effort, and if they were not always treated as humanely as in this episode, they were certainly not subjected to an industrial-scale extermination policy, as the Holocaust myth claims.

Thus, Wiesel's decision to leave Auschwitz with the Germans is quite consistent with the reality of wartime Jewish suffering, but not with that of Holocaust fantasy. The latter is an exaggeration of the historical facts in order to justify, among other things, 1) German payment of restitution to Jews, 2) Jewish conquest and confiscation of Palestine, and 3) placement of guilt for war crimes solely on Germany. Thus, Wiesel's decision, made within the horrible context of total war, signals his conviction at the time that the Germans had treated him relatively well. Not only had they provided him with medical care, they also offered the same level of care to his ailing father, even though the latter was never able to work.

Primo Levi and Lili Jacob Were Also Treated in the SS Hospital

One detainee who stayed behind was Lili Jacob. She later discovered the collection of photos that would come to be called *The Auschwitz Album.* By her own admission, she appears to have been treated well by the Germans before they left. According to the *New York Times*:[267]

> *On the day Auschwitz was liberated by Allied troops in December 1944* [sic], *Lili Jacob was ill with typhus, lying in a camp hospital.*

Primo Levi, who had worked as a lab assistant at the Buna synthetic rubber factory in the Monowitz complex, was also in the hospital with scarlet fever when the Germans left. Although sick and unable to work, he had not been sent to a gas chamber or killed by other means by the Germans either![268] Here again, the story peddled by Holocaust fundamentalists to the

---

[267] Jo Thomas, "'Holy Document' of Auschwitz Found: Closing the Past, Knew Her Tattoo Number," *New York Times*, August 14, 1980, A16.

[268] Primo Levi, *If This Is a Man* (New York: Orion, 1959); see also Illustration 17, grateful-

effect that sick people were routinely put to death in a gas chamber has proved to be false, for both Lili Jacob and Primo Levi, like Wiesel and his father, were well cared for.

Lfd. Nr.	Häftl. Nr.	Name	Zugang	Abgang	Bemerkungen
21641	167615	Plech, Bernhard Isr.	30.3.44	27.4.44	nach Birkenau
21642	171313	Kotschernik, Grigor	"	17.4.44	Entlassen
21643	151003	Meyer, Eduard Isr.	"	3.4.44	Entlassen
21644	172352	Kupferwasser, Hersch Isr.	"	17.4.44	Entlassen
21645	172719	Israel, Leon Isr.	"	5.4.44	Entlassen
21646	E 7156	Sepitalny, Kasimierz	"	6.4.44	Entlassen
21647	173174	Domogalla, Alfred	"	12.4.44	
21648	127503	Kowalski, Josef	"	14.4.44	Entlassen
21649	174486	Coen, Giuseppe Isr.	"	11.4.44	Entlassen
21650	135658	Gemel, Zygmunt	"	3.4.44	Entlassen
21651	156975	Bonomo, Marco Isr.	"	15.4.44	Entlassen
21652	121590	Ahn, Benedikt	"	20.5.44	
21653	157139	Sternberg, Paul Isr.	"	22.4.44	Entlassen
21654	106999	Markus, Erwin Isr.	"	25.5.44	nach Birkenau
21655	137486	Rapaport, Israel	"	22.5.44	Entlassen
21656	167086	Israelski, Michel Isr.	"	27.4.44	nach Birkenau
21657	169854	Kriwatsy, Thomas Isr.	"	20.4.44	Entlassen
21658	174522	Luria, Cesare Isr.	"	8.4.44	
21659	171837	Lagodzinski, Aron Isr.	"	30.4.44	nach Birkenau
21660	161264	Kornreich, Roman Isr.	"	15.4.44	Entlassen
21661	158255	Marek, Paul	"	13.5.44	nach Birkenau
21662	115437	Ziabicki, Zygmunt	"	20.5.44	
21663	172409	Tasma, Benjamin Isr.	"	11.4.44	Entlassen
21664	168012	Marcaria, Raffaele Isr.	"	1.4.44	Entlassen
21665	117546	Glotzer, Kive Isr.	"	"	Entlassen
21666	76347	Krzeczanowski, Abraham Isr.	"	7.4.44	Entlassen
21667	171989	Hiron, Israel	"	7.4.44	Entlassen
21668	144055	Kohn, Josef Isr.	"	"	Entlassen
21669	174517	Levi, Primo Isr.	"	20.4.44	Entlassen
21670	108182	Kranz, Bronislaw Isr.	"	16.5.44	Entlassen
21671	167697	Westreich, Benjamin Isr.	"	1.4.44	Entlassen
21672	151057	Root, Meyer Isr.	"	8.4.44	Entlassen
21673	172667	Chrzanovski, Paul Isr.	"	6.4.44	Entlassen

Illustration 17: Register of the inmate hospital at the Monowitz camp with the entry no. 21669 of April 20, 1944, about Primo Levi, inmate no. 174517 (fifth line from the bottom): "Entlassen" = discharged and sent back to the camp, like thousands of others who were successfully treated and healed at this hospital. (Source: I.G.-Farben Trial, document NI-10186, p. 360)

ly received from Carlo Mattogno.

Chapter VI
Wiesel at Buchenwald

Problem #10: Travel to and Arrival at Buchenwald

Wiesel Offers No Coherent Chronology for This Trip

Just as Wiesel had offered his reader a botched chronology at the beginning of his novel, he repeats the same mistakes in recounting 1) the trip to Buchenwald, and 2) the early days after his arrival there, up to and including the death of his father. I shall deal first with the chronology of the trip.

Incredible as it might seem, Wiesel provides neither the departure nor the arrival dates for this momentous experience. Although he neglects to provide the departure date from Auschwitz, he does state that the detainees left at 6:00 AM in the middle of a snowstorm. As mentioned in the previous chapter, the historical record indicates that the Germans abandoned the Auschwitz camp complex during the night of January 17–18, 1945. Since those units most crucial to supporting the war effort left after nightfall on January 17, some historians date the beginning of the exodus as January 17, while others prefer January 18, when the operation was completed. Having already used the date of January 18 for the calculation of the time that Wiesel spent in the hospital, I retain it here as the date *a quo*, that is, the beginning date for calculating the time involved in the trip to Buchenwald. Although Wiesel offers no specific date for his arrival at Buchenwald, he does provide a date for his father's death. That date, the night of January 28-29, 1945, must therefore be taken as our date *ad quem* for establishing the novel's chronology.

The detainees leave Auschwitz at 6:00 AM on January 18. They march all day and into the evening. At that point "the commander announced that we had already traveled seventy kilometers."[269] Wiesel is exaggerating

[269] Wiesel, *Nuit*, 138: "Le commandant annonça que nous avions déjà fait soixante-dix kilomètres depuis le départ."

here, for by this point they had only marched about two-thirds of the way to Gleiwitz. Since the total distance between the two points is 55 kilometers [34 miles], they would have marched about 36-37 kilometers [20 miles], not 70 [43 miles]. Marion Wiesel translates "seventy kilometers" (*soixante-dix kilomètres*) as "twenty kilometers." (*Night* [2006], 87) She deliberately presents this mistranslation to her reader, no doubt in accord with the author, in order to bring Wiesel's absurd exaggeration more into line with the ascertainable fact that the whole trip could only amount to about fifty-five kilometers.

Wiesel then continues to walk well beyond midnight, but does not indicate how far. Once again, one would think that this experience would have been recalled in more precise detail. Furthermore, there remains the strange anomaly that he is able to walk these long distances two days after having undergone a serious foot operation for which two weeks of bed rest had been prescribed. Wiesel then sleeps for a very short time. He awakens after sunrise.[270] Wiesel then writes:[271]

> *We remained at Gleiwitz for three days. Three days without food or drink.*

If this assertion about an imposed three-day fast in the middle of winter were true, many of the prisoners would have become terribly weakened, and even died.

On the morning of the third day, they are marched outside the town of Gleiwitz to await a train, which does not come until "quite late in the evening."[272] After they climb aboard, they then travel for ten more days and nights before reaching Buchenwald.[273] Thus, according to Wiesel's chronology, a total of fourteen days (one day of walking, three days of imposed starvation while waiting for the train, and a ten-day train trip) are required for the trip. When Wiesel wrote his novel (or at least this episode), he was apparently unaware that the Auschwitz camp had been abandoned on January 18, as mentioned above. This ignorance about a basic historical fact, a fact that should have remained firmly embedded in his memory during his alleged ten-year vow of silence, because he had actually lived it, speaks volumes about the *in*-authenticity of his autobiography.

These fourteen days of travel mean that he must have arrived at Buchenwald on February 2. But such an arrival date is simply impossible, because our date *ad quem*, the only firm date Wiesel offers after the end of the trip, is the one he provides for the death of his father, the night of January 28-29. In other words, he could not have arrived on February 2 on a train with his father, *and* have his father die at Buchenwald about a week

---

[270] *Ibid.*, 150: "Je m'éveillai, à la clarté du jour."
[271] *Ibid.*: "Nous demeurâmes trois jours à Gleiwitz. Trois jours sans manger et sans boire."
[272] *Ibid.*, 152: "[…] fort tard dans la soirée"
[273] *Ibid.*, 156: "Dix jours, dix nuits de voyage."

earlier. For this reason, Marion Wiesel has mistranslated the very specific "ten days and nights of travel" (*dix jours, dix nuits de voyage*) as "there followed days and nights of traveling." (*Night* [2006], 100) Once again, the reader is not informed of this deception, and through the use of retroactive continuity, this mendacious translation serves to justify the date given for the death of Wiesel's father.

Absurd Chronology and Narrative Incoherence after the Arrival at Buchenwald

I now turn to the problem of *Night*'s chronology following Wiesel's arrival at Buchenwald. The first indication of time that Wiesel gives us comes in his statement that he and the others who had arrived from Auschwitz were obliged to take a shower on the third day after their arrival.[274] Thereafter, he writes of "the next day."[275] Then, a day after the trip's eighteenth day, he writes that "a week went by."[276] This additional week brings the total number of days since Wiesel's departure from Auschwitz on January 18 to twenty-five.

Thus, according to the novel's internal chronology, the date for the death of Wiesel's father would be February 13. Nonetheless, Wiesel tells us in the novel that his father died during the night of January 28-29, 1945. He writes:[277]

> *I climbed into my bunk above my father, who was still alive. It was January 28, 1945. I awoke at dawn on January 29. Another patient was lying there in my father's place.*

Working backward twenty-six days from January 29, the morning on which he finds his father missing from his bunk and presumed dead, establishes that Wiesel would have had to leave Auschwitz on January 3, 1945. But such a date would be a complete absurdity, for it would mean that he left Auschwitz even before undergoing foot surgery! This is why Marion Wiesel deliberately mistranslated "ten days and ten nights of travel" as "days and nights of travel."

Records of Three Trains from Gleiwitz to Buchenwald in January 1945 Analyzed

The Italian researcher Carlo Mattogno has found evidence that three trains left Gleiwitz and traveled to Buchenwald on January 18, 1945. The

---

274 *Ibid.*, 168: "Le troisième jour après notre arrivée à Buchenwald, tout le monde dut aller aux douches." [The third day after our arrival at Buchenwald, everybody had to take a shower."]

275 *Ibid.*, 171: "le lendemain."

276 *Ibid.*,: "Une semaine passa."

277 *Ibid.*, 173f.: "Je grimpai sur ma couchette, au-dessus de mon père, qui vivait encore. Je m'éveillai le 29 janvier à l'aube. A la place de mon père gisait un autre malade."

time it took each train to travel from Gleiwitz to Buchenwald varied: four days for the first train, five days for the second, eight days for the third. No trip took fourteen days, as Wiesel claims was his experience in *La Nuit*:

Date of departure	Date of arrival	ID numbers	Number of detainees
18 January	22 January	117195-119418	2,224
18 January	23 January	119419-120337	919
18 January	26 January	120348-124274	3,927

There is a serious discrepancy between Wiesel's supposed experiences and the actual historical reality. This basic contradiction suggests that Wiesel either plagiarized this episode, or simply invented it.

Mattogno shows that both the former Jewish detainee Miklós Grüner (Buchenwald ID # 120761), and his friend Lazar Wiesel (Buchenwald ID # 123565), whose identity Grüner accuses Wiesel of having stolen, were given ID numbers at Buchenwald on January 26, the day on which their train arrived, and on which they entered the Buchenwald camp. Mattogno has also studied the lists of Buchenwald detainees, and states that there is no mention of Elie Wiesel being assigned a Buchenwald identification number. Wiesel wrote *La Nuit* as if unaware of the very existence of these ID numbers, and Mattogno concludes on the basis of this evidence that Wiesel was never a detainee at Buchenwald. He may be right, but more information seems needed before coming to a definitive conclusion.

That said, I must add that Mattogno's assertion is firmly supported by the evidence provided in the very text of the novel. According to *Night*'s internal chronology, as I have shown above, the only firm date provided is the one for his father's death, January 28-29, 1945. If we work back twenty-five days from that date, we arrive at January 3 for his departure date from Auschwitz. But this date is impossible for two reasons: 1) historically, we know the camp was not abandoned until January 17-18; and 2) this date also contradicts Wiesel's other assertion that the operation on his foot took place "toward the middle of January" (see Chapter V), just before the camp was evacuated.

The contradictions derived from this internal evidence of the novel indicate that, when Wiesel wrote of the trip from Auschwitz to Buchenwald, his version of events could not have been based on personal experience. Thus the novel fully supports Mattogno's contention that he was never at Buchenwald.

Mattogno on Mortality aboard Wiesel's Train to Buchenwald

Finally, with regard to the mortality rate for those who made the trip from Auschwitz to Buchenwald, Wiesel offers testimony only about the railroad car in which he and his father traveled. He writes:[278]

> *The last day saw the highest death toll. About a hundred of us had gotten onto this railroad car, and only a dozen of us, including my father and myself, got off.*

These numbers indicate a death rate of 88 percent, and Wiesel implies that such a figure is also valid for the other cars in the train. Mattogno, on the other hand, relying on the original manifest for the convoy that reached Buchenwald on January 26, states that, of the 3,987 detainees who began the trip, 3,927 were logged into Buchenwald. Assuming that the missing sixty inmates died *en route*, these sixty deaths represent a mortality rate of 1.5 percent, which is a far cry from Wiesel's claimed death rate of 88 percent.[279] I might add that Wiesel claims more deaths in his car alone than were recorded for the whole train. This fact not only raises yet another question about Wiesel's actual presence on this train, it also offers another example of the systemic cancer of exaggerations that afflicts Holocaust computations at all levels.

After recounting the death of his father, Wiesel announces that he will not have anything to say about the period that extends from that event, on January 28-29, to his liberation on April 11. He then offers a lame excuse for this strange silence when he writes:[280]

> *I won't speak about my life during this time period. Living no longer mattered to me. After my father's death, nothing touched me anymore.*

This alibi is not only unconvincing, it also reinforces the impression he has already given to the reader: that he might not have ever been at Buchenwald. If that is the case, his silence about daily life among the other children in the *Kinderblock* is natural and understandable.

About life with the other children and adolescents, he writes:[281]

> *I was transferred to the Children's Block, where there were six hundred of us.*

However, he once again raises our suspicions about whether he actually experienced this event when he fails to mention the important fact that these children were placed in the by-now famous Block 66 which, in turn, was located in a section of Buchenwald called the "Little Camp." This

---

[278] *Ibid.*, 161: "Le dernier jour avait été le plus meurtrier. Nous étions montés une centaine dans ce wagon. Nous en descendîmes une douzaine. Parmi eux, mon père et moi-même."

[279] Mattogno, "Elie Wiesel, 'Most Authoritative,'"

[280] Wiesel, *Nuit*, 75: "Je ne parlerai pas de ma vie durant ce temps-là. Elle n'avait plus d'importance pour moi. Depuis la mort de mon père, plus rien ne me touchait."

[281] *Ibid.*, 175: "Je fus transféré au bloc des enfants, où nous étions six cents."

omission is especially strange in so far as Block 66 has taken on an almost legendary importance in the saga of the Buchenwald camp's last days. Here is how the official Holocaust history, as found on the Buchenwald website, puts it:[282]

> *In January 1945, political inmates succeeded in convincing the SS to set up a further shelter for the adolescents arriving on mass transports – Barrack 66 in the Little Camp. Here particularly Jewish adolescents found refuge, among them the later Nobel Prize laureate Elie Wiesel.*

Ironically, the official Holocaust history of the event now places Wiesel there, without any documentation, of course. But Wiesel, writing in the 1950s, referred neither to Barrack 66, nor to the larger space in which it was located, the "Little Camp" (*kleines Lager* or *le petit camp*). Once again, Wiesel's ignorance of basic details speaks volumes about this alleged experience.

Problem #11: Liberation Day at Buchenwald

Wiesel's Nobel Campaign Requires More Falsehoods

On July 4, 2004, *Parade* magazine featured an article by Wiesel. The piece included what is probably one of the most famous propaganda pictures from World War II. Taken by Private H. Miller of the Civil Affairs Branch of the U.S. Army Signal Corps at Buchenwald concentration camp on April 16, 1945, five days after the Americans arrived there on April 11 (see Illustrartion 19, p. 166), the photo has been altered in the *Parade* version to include a circle drawn around the face of a man identified as Elie Wiesel. This photo, showing inmates, some emaciated and half-naked, crammed into crude bunks, was not taken on the spur of the moment on April 11, but was one of a larger group of about a dozen photos in which professional montage and *mise en scène* techniques were used.[283] It is also worth noting in passing that there are scores of photos of men in bunks available for viewing on the official Buchenwald website, but somehow none of them manages to show the crowding alleged to have been normal. The shot was then released to the media to be used for the usual propaganda purposes: to project an image of the Germans as war criminals while distracting the American public from the horrible war crimes then being committed by Allied forces. That it was still being exploited almost seventy years after it was taken shows how successful and adaptable it has proved to be.

In *La Nuit*, Wiesel writes:[284]

---

[282] www.buchenwald.de/english/index.php?p=140.

[283] Jonathan Heller, *War and Conflict: Selected Images from the National Archives*, (Washington, D.C., National Archives and Records Administration, 1990), 253.

[284] Wiesel, *Nuit*, 178: "Trois jours après la libération de Buchenwald, je tombai malade; un

Three days after the liberation of Buchenwald, I fell sick. Food poisoning. I was taken to the hospital and spent two weeks between life and death.

Since this mysterious illness occurred "three days after the liberation of Buchenwald," the date would be April 14. He was immediately hospitalized and, in his words, "spent two weeks between life and death." According to this scenario, the *first* of several that he would provide over the years, Wiesel should have been in the hospital from April 14 to April 28. Since the Signal Corps propaganda picture was taken on April 16, Wiesel could not have been in it.

Wiesel later changed this basic story a number of times. Here is the *second* version of events, which he invented in 1976:[285]

After the liberation I became sick, and it's strange how it happened. I hinted at it in Night, *but it's not the full story. April 11, 1945, when the Americans came, we were some 20,000 left in Buchenwald out of some 60,000 or 80,000, and we hadn't had food for a week or so. Suddenly the Americans came and brought their food, but they really didn't know what they were doing; they gave fats. 5,000 people died immediately from food poisoning.* [...] *and my body rebelled; I lost consciousness immediately and was sick for ten days or so – unconscious, in a coma – blood poisoning or something.*

In this second version, Wiesel says that he ate the food "an hour or two after the liberation," which contradicts his original claim in *Night* that he only got sick three days after liberation. Also, in this new version he is sick, unconscious and in a coma for ten days, or from April 11 until about April 21. In this scenario, once again, he could not have been in a picture that was taken on April 16.

As for Wiesel's claim of 5,000 deaths from food poisoning, it is not mentioned in *La Nuit,* nor is it supported by the historical record. The closest he comes in *La Nuit* to implying large numbers of deaths at the liberation of Buchenwald occurs when he writes:[286]

Each day, several thousand detainees would go through the camp's gate and wouldn't return.

He later provided further information about this subject when, on February 1, 1978, he spoke at Washington University in St. Louis. In answer to a student's direct question on this issue, he stated:[287]

On April 5, when they began to evacuate my camp, 80,000 inmates remained. And every day they would select 10,000 and kill them outside the gate. Somehow, I was always among those left behind.

---

empoisonnement. Je fus transféré à l'hôpital et passai deux semaines entre la vie et la mort."

285 Cargas, *Conversation*, 88.

286 Wiesel, *Nuit*, 176f.: "Chaque jour, quelques milliers de détenus traversaient la porte du camp et ne revenaient pas."

287 Abrahamson, *Against Silence*: vol. 3, 253.

Strangely, but in accordance with the ever-changing Jewish Holocaust narrative, we are now left to wonder why the liberating GIs, upon their arrival at Buchenwald's gates on April 11, never saw or commented upon the 60,000 dead bodies which, according to Wiesel, must have accumulated there since April 5. Apparently they had all mysteriously disappeared!

The Mendacious Role of the *New York Times* in the Barracks Photo Affair

The Buchenwald barracks picture first appeared in the *New York Times* on May 6, 1945, several weeks after it was taken. The caption read: "Crowded Bunks in the Prison Camp at Buchenwald" (see Illustration 20, p. 166).The caption does not date the photo, but it implies that it was taken on April 11, the day Buchenwald was liberated. The media has always implied that the picture was taken on that date, and it is this basic untruth on which other misinterpretations are based.

The original *New York Times* story did not identify any of the men in the picture, which did not so much portray the chaotic reality of Buchenwald on April 11, as the carefully staged recreation and repackaging of that reality. The photo appeared in conjunction with an article by correspondent Harold Denny, in which he communicated the official U.S. Government propaganda line. Entitled "The World Must Not Forget: What was done in the German prison camps emphasizes the problem of what to do with a people who are morally sick,"[288] his piece was a distraction from the war crimes that the Allies were then committing against the Germans.

As Denny wrote in the pages of the Jewish-owned *New York Times*, Germany was a smoldering ruin as a result of Allied carpet bombardment of civilians; Dresden, Hamburg and hundreds of other German cities had been bombed to a pulp; the dams on numerous rivers had been destroyed, drowning untold numbers of innocents and destroying their homes; hundreds of thousands of German soldiers were both being starved and caged in the open, without shelter, day and night, by Gen. Eisenhower; countless German civilians whose families had lived in East Prussia and Poland for centuries were being forcibly evicted by the advancing Soviets; the Volga Germans, who had been settled in Russia since the eighteenth century, had been deported to Siberia and elsewhere, where many of them would perish; the valiant men of the Red Army were in the process of raping millions of German women as they advanced through Germany; and, most dreadful, Hiroshima and Nagasaki were on the drawing board.[289] For the *New York*

[288] Harold Denny, "The World Must Not Forget," *New York Times*, May 6, 1945, 42.

[289] See two basic studies by James Bacque: *Other Losses: The Shocking Truth behind the Mass Deaths of Disarmed German Soldiers and Civilians under Gen. Eisenhower's Command* (Rocklin, Calif.: Prima Publishing, 1989), and *Crimes and Mercies: The Fate of German Civilians under Allied Occupation, 1944-1950* (Vancouver: Talonbooks, 2007).

Times, however, with its scarcely concealed obsession with Jewish suffering, it was the Germans who were "morally sick." Had the Allies not saved civilization?

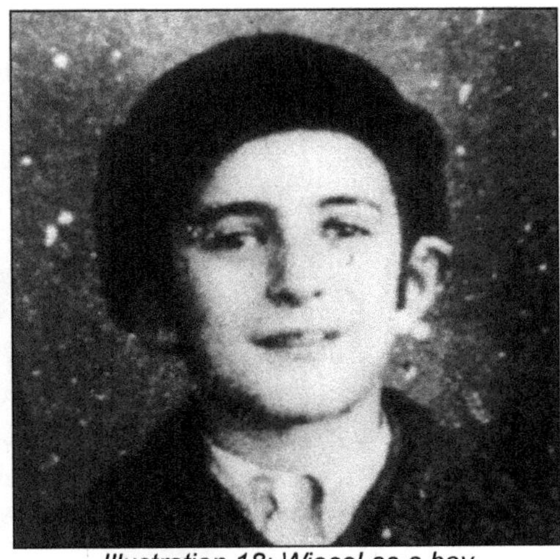

Illustration 18: Wiesel as a boy

The *third* version of Wiesel's liberation from Buchenwald is linked to the same photo. In 1983, almost forty years after the barracks picture was taken, the *New York Times* published it with this caption:

> *On April 11, 1945, American troops liberated the concentration camp's survivors, including Elie, who later identified himself as the man circled in the photo.*

It is important to note here that Wiesel had never claimed to be in this famous picture before 1983. Why not? And why did the *New York Times* suddenly want to associate Wiesel with this picture, especially since the individual circled in it was clearly a grown man, and not a boy of sixteen? In fact, this man does not resemble in any way other pictures said to date from Wiesel's teenage years (see Illustrations 21f., p. 167). Obviously, the "newspaper of record" had not fact-checked Wiesel's claim. In retrospect, however, it is clear that this bogus claim was a first step in the *New York Times*'s campaign to secure a Nobel Prize for Wiesel. The picture was published in the high-circulation Sunday *New York Times Magazine*, and with the following statement:[290]

> *His name has been frequently mentioned as a possible recipient of a Nobel Prize, for either peace or literature.*

After the *New York Times* had manufactured history by mendaciously declaring that Wiesel was pictured, the *Times* had the nerve a few years later to castigate the administration of the Buchenwald museum, at that time part of the Communist East German regime, for not repeating the *New York Times*'s lie as fact! In 1989, a *New York Times* reporter visiting Buchenwald, wrote:[291]

> *A large photograph in the* [Buchenwald] *museum shows Mr. Wiesel, among others, on the day of liberation. He is not identified in a caption. And the guide*

---

290 Samuel G. Freedman, "Bearing Witness: The Life and Work of Elie Wiesel," *New York Times*, October 23, 1983. The picture appeared on p. 34.

291 Henry Kamm, "No Mention of Jews at Buchenwald," *New York Times*, March 25, 1989, A8.

> *who has shown visitors around Buchenwald for 14 years had never heard of the author, who has written eloquently* [sic] *about that camp.*

Nowadays, the USHMM follows in the footsteps of the *New York Times* by making the same fraudulent claim about this picture on its website.

With regard to this picture, Professor Kenneth Waltzer first became involved in the subject around 2010-11. He had already begun writing a book to be entitled *The Rescue of Children and Youths at Buchenwald*, and was determined to include his friend Wiesel as one of those children of Buchenwald. In a Michigan State University press release about him and his project, he was quoted as writing the following about Wiesel:[292]

> *He* [Wiesel] *was too weak at liberation on April 11 to leave his barracks (hence he was photographed in a famous picture in the barracks on April 12 or 13), and he came to understand he was free only days later.*

In writing such nonsense, Waltzer revealed that he had obviously not even done basic archival research on this picture. A Holocaustian imagination does not get much more inventive than Waltzer's does here!

In due course, that press release, an embarrassment to all concerned, was removed from the web. But the damage had already been done. Why? Because by 2011 Wiesel's absence from this picture had sparked a wider discussion of the fact that there is in fact no pictorial record of any kind of Wiesel at Buchenwald.

When the announced book failed to appear in 2011, the noted U.S. revisionist Bradley Smith devoted several blog entries to the subject. Unfortunately, they have all been rendered inaccessible on the web. At the same time, Carolyn Yeager, working from her www.eliewieseltattoo.com website, has continued to heap ridicule on Waltzer, and her relentless attacks appear to have had an effect on his book project.[293] As of early 2015, it has still not appeared in print.

In addition to Wiesel's earlier claims that he was sick when the picture was taken, another major problem with the photograph is the disparity between the facial features said to be Wiesel's in this picture and those that appear in the boyhood photo.[294] This picture has been cropped from a photo that appears in both *Tous les fleuves* and *All Rivers* in which he is shown as a boy of about nine to twelve (1937 to 1940) years of age with his mother and little sister. The caption reads:

---

[292] "Ken Waltzer on Elie Wiesel's *Night*," http://special.news.msu.edu/holocaust/wiesel.php?wiesel.

[293] On June 29, 2013, she wrote: www.eliewieseltattoo.com/is-ken-waltzer-on-the-outs-no-longer-cited-as-a-holocaust-expert/; on June 30, 2011, she wrote: www.eliewieseltattoo.com/ken-waltzer-replies-to-my-question/; and on September 8, 2013, she wrote: www.eliewieseltattoo.com/ken-waltzer-inadvertantly-supplies-proof-that-elie-wiesel-was-not-at-buchenwald/.

[294] Elie Wiesel, "Le jour où Buchenwald a été libéré," *Paris-Match*, April 10-16, 2003, 116.

> *Elie with his mother and his sister Tziporah, shortly before the Nazis entered Sighet.*

Since Wiesel was fifteen and a half in April 1944, the editor of Wiesel's autobiography is attempting to deceive and confuse the reader when he states that the picture was taken "shortly before the Nazis entered Sighet." Clearly, this picture had been taken several years before 1944. Likewise, the picture that supposedly shows Wiesel as a boy of about sixteen also bears a misleading caption in *All Rivers*. It states:

> *Elie, age fifteen, not long before the deportations.*

But how could the boys shown in the two pictures, their ages being at least three years apart, both date from the spring of 1944? Even worse, the second picture not only appears to date from the postwar period, the boy presented in it bears little if any resemblance to the boy in the earlier one. In any case, whether or not this picture of an adolescent actually shows Wiesel, it offers ample proof that this photo, and that of "the man in the bunk," who appears to be about thirty years old, if not older, do not depict the same person. Thus, the pictures of Wiesel that I show here, coupled with the fact that, prior to 1983, he had always stated that he was sick on April 16, offer solid proof that his claim to be shown in the Buchenwald propaganda picture is merely another example of his mendacity.

As Wiesel's Nobel campaign went forward, the *New York Times* usually tried to present him in dramatic terms, even if it meant telling more fibs about him. His image as a Holocaust survivor needed to be enhanced. Thus, for example, when he made a trip to Berlin in January 1986 to attend a Holocaust conference, the *New York Times* reporter declared solemnly:[295]

> *Elie Wiesel returned to Germany this week for the first time since he was released from the Buchenwald concentration camp almost 41 years ago.*

Unfortunately, this dramatic statement was nonsense. The *Times* should have done its homework. When Wiesel was beginning his career as a New York Jewish journalist, he published a hate-filled article in December 1962 appropriately entitled "An Appointment with Hate" in *Commentary*, the organ of the American Jewish Committee (see Chapter V). Its subject was a recent trip he had made to Germany.

Likewise, even after the Nobel award was announced on October 14, 1986, the *New York Times* continued to embroider the facts, always trying to dramatize Wiesel's life experience. For instance, on November 2 they triumphantly republished a severely cropped version of the barracks photo with the caption:[296]

---

295 John Tagliabue, "Elie Wiesel Back in Germany after 41 Years," *New York Times*, January 23, 1986, A4.

296 Martin Suskind, "A Voice from Bonn: History Cannot Be Shrugged Off," *New York Times*, November 2, 1986, D2.

Illustration 19: Photo taken in the Buchenwald camp on April 16, 1945; filed by the Office of War Information. Overseas Operations Branch; official caption: "These are slave laborers in the Buchenwald concentration camp near Jena; many had died from malnutrition when U.S. troops of the 80th Division entered the camp." First published in the Los Angeles Times, *April 29, 1945. Source: http://commons.wikimedia.org; NARA 535560*

Crowded bunks in the prison camp at Buchenwald.

Illustration 20: Interstingly, The New York Times Magazine, *published this image on May 6th, 1945 (p. 42) with the naked man removed from the image, perhaps for reasons of "decency."*

Source: Winston Smith, "The Most Famous Holocaust Photo a Fraud," Jan 17, 2013; http://winstonsmithministryoftruth.blogspot.com/2013/01/the-most-famous-holocaust-photo-fraud.html

> *Elie Wiesel, the winner of the Nobel Peace Prize (at far right in the top bunk) in the Buchenwald concentration camp in April 1945, when the camp was liberated by American troops.*

The *New York Times* cropped the picture in such a way as to remove parts of the two upper bunks and to make the man who is now supposed to be Wiesel barely visible. At the same time, the newspaper airbrushed the naked man on the right completely out of the picture (see Illustration 20). The *New York Times* also suggests the picture was taken on April 11, 1945, without, of course, actually saying so. Then, in January 1987, the *Times* erroneously claimed that Wiesel had been "freed from Auschwitz" during the war.[297]

Illustration 21: Wiesel as an adolescent after the war

Illustration 22: Allegedly Wiesel's face in the 1945 Buchenwald photo

A year later, in connection with a Wiesel trip to Auschwitz, the *New York Times* wrote:[298]

> *Mr. Wiesel was a prisoner at Auschwitz and witnessed the killing there of his father and one of his sisters.*

Of course, Wiesel has always claimed that his father died in Buchenwald, and information on his mother's and youngest sister's fates continues to be effectively withheld by the USHMM and other authorities. But the word "Auschwitz" is one of the three Jewish Holocaust terms that have been pushed as slogans over the years in the pages of the *New York Times.* These eternally repeated or sloganized terms are designed to set off a "brand recognition" reaction among the New York Jewish readers in the newspaper's customer base. The terms "Auschwitz," along with "six million" and "gas chambers," constitute the essence of this triad, but Buchenwald doesn't make the cut.

In 1987, after cashing his $270,000 Nobel prize check, Wiesel testified at the trial of Klaus Barbie in Lyon, France. On the fringes of the trial, the well-known (in France) Jewish Holocaust profiteer and publicity seeker Marek Halter announced his intention to stage a parallel trial of France's World War II Vichy regime. How-

297 "A Survivor's Prize," *New York Times*, January 4, 1987, XIII, 3.

298 Clyde Haberman, "Wiesel and Walesa Visit Auschwitz," *New York Times*, January 18, 1988, A3.

ever, the Jewish lawyers who were staging the Barbie show trial correctly saw this plan as a publicity stunt, and rejected it as a "political show."[299] Undeterred, Halter and his followers set up a large tent in Lyon's main square about a mile from where the Barbie show trial was taking place. There, they presented an exhibit called "The Children of Memory." It was in Halter's bizarre tent that the Signal Corps photo was exhibited for exploitation once again by the Zionist media.[300] It is not clear, however, to what extent Wiesel was involved in this particular display of what was by now a Holocaust icon.

On June 3, 1987, the *Chicago Tribune* published an AP photo containing a cropped version of the men in the bunks at Buchenwald. What was completely new in this *fourth* tall tale about his liberation was that Wiesel, accompanied by two unidentified people, was shown standing in front of a blown-up version of the picture and pointing to himself in it (Illustration 23). The caption read:

> *Nobel Prize winner Elie Wiesel points to a picture of himself, taken by a German at the Auschwitz death camp in 1945. The photograph is part of the Holocaust Memorial in Lyon, France.*

In this instance, the Zionist media was probably guilty not so much of deliberate disinformation as of slovenly reporting, a recurring problem in articles dealing with the Holocaust. Since the Barbie show trial focused on deportations to Auschwitz, not Buchenwald, and since Auschwitz, not Buchenwald, was being trumpeted in the Zionist media every day, the mendacious caption made the picture more relevant. In fact, the only problem we have with it is in determining who created this example of Holocaust-related media deception: Shoah-businessman Halter, someone in the employ of the media, or Wiesel. When one recalls that he stated early in his career, and has repeated many times since then, that "some events do take place but are not true; others are true although they never occurred,"[301] Wiesel's possible involvement in this media caper in the opening stages of the Barbie trial cannot be ruled out.

In retrospect, there can be no doubt that this heavily-trafficked picture was an important ingredient in the overall package designed to bolster Wiesel's Nobel candidacy. In this regard, Carolyn Yeager makes a good point when she states that Wiesel recognized the picture's importance in

---

[299] Judith Miller, *One by One by One, Facing the Holocaust* (N.Y.: Simon & Schuster, 1990), 129.

[300] Halter has seen his false claims about his alleged wartime experiences questioned and exposed in recent years. See Piotr Smolar, "Marek Halter, le bonimenteur," *La Revue XXI*, 4, autumn 2008, 142–153; Grégoire LeMénager, "Les Mensonges de Marek Halter," *Le Nouvel Observateur*, October 15, 2008. http://bibliobs.nouvelobs.com/actualites/20081015.BIB2187/les-mensonges-de-marek-halter.html

[301] Wiesel, *Legends*, viii.

AP Laserphoto

Nobel Prize winner Elie Wiesel points to a picture of himself, taken by a German at the Auschwitz death camp in 1945. The photograph is part of the Holocaust memorial in Lyon, France.

Wiesel testifies at Barbie trial

Illustration 23: Ludicrously false caption published in the Chicago Tribune, *June 3, 1987*

the Nobel campaign when he flew to Jerusalem in the month following reception of the prize to have his picture taken in front of it.[302] Thankfully, that picture encapsulates perfectly Wiesel's mendacity and, as long as the USHMM keeps on claiming that Wiesel is seen in it, their mendacity as well.

Wiesel Claims the Men in the Bunks Are Children from the *Kinderblock*

In 1995, Wiesel offered a *fifth* version of his liberation experience in an interview published in the German weekly *Die Zeit*. It contained two new pieces of information. The first was the claim that the picture had been taken the day after the liberation, that is, on April 12, 1945, not on April 11, as

302 Carolyn Yeager, "Gigantic Fraud Carried Out for Wiesel Nobel Prize" ; www.eliewieseltattoo.com/the-evidence/photographic-evidence/gigantic-fraud-carried-out-for-wiesel-nobel-prize/

the media had always implied. This new date not only contradicted the date of April 16 given by the U.S. Army, but it also made it impossible for Wiesel to be in it, if we believed his second claim, mentioned above, according to which he had been put in the hospital for ten days immediately upon eating American food on April 11. The second new assertion to emerge from this interview was that the picture had been taken in the children's barracks, or *Kinderblock*, at Buchenwald, where Wiesel was allegedly lodged. The following statement to this effect appears twice in the article, once in the text and once again as the caption to the picture (in which the person alleged to be Wiesel is circled, as in the *New York Times* photo in 1983):[303]

> *On the day after the liberation the picture was taken in the Children's Block at Buchenwald by an American soldier. It shows old men. But these old faces are the faces of men who, in truth, were 15 or 16 years of age as I was.*

Since 1945, when the *New York Times* first made propaganda use of this picture, no one had ever claimed that it depicts children. In fact, it does not depict children. It depicts adults. Yet Wiesel actually expects us to believe that these men, some of whom are heavily bearded or partially bald, were mere boys. Finally, when Wiesel states that the picture was taken "by an American soldier," he gives the impression that it was a spur-of-the-moment event and not one that was carefully orchestrated for propaganda purposes.

Wiesel Claims He Saw Black Soldiers at Buchenwald on Liberation Day

A *sixth* version of events at the liberation of Buchenwald was concocted by Wiesel in 1989, when he claimed to have seen black soldiers on liberation day, April 11, at Buchenwald. He told a *New York Times* interviewer:[304]

> *I will always remember with love a big black soldier. He was crying like a child – tears of all the pain in the world and all the rage. Everyone who was there that day will forever feel a sentiment of gratitude to the American soldiers who liberated us.*

As will be amply demonstrated below, Wiesel simply made up this ridiculous claim, like so much of what he claims to remember about the Holocaust, out of whole cloth. Nonetheless, this claim seems to have provided the spark that would lead to the creation of a 90-minute documentary film telling the story of this completely imagined event. A black filmmaker and a Jewish producer launched this new Holocaust myth, according to which a

---

[303] Elie Wiesel [interviewed by], Werner A. Perger, "1945 und Heute: Holocaust," *Die Zeit*, April 21, 1995, 16: "Am Tag nach der Befreiung wurde das Bild aus dem Kinderblock von Buchenwald von einem amerikanischen Soldaten aufgenommen. Darauf sind alte Männer zu sehen. Doch diese alten Gesichter sind die Gesichter von Menschen, die in Wahrheit wie ich um fünfzehn oder sechzehn Jahre alt waren."

[304] Kamm, "No Mention," 8.

black unit, the 761st Tank Battalion, had actually liberated the Jews at Buchenwald! Their announced intention in doing so was to increase black and Jewish mutual "understanding" in Brooklyn through a movie to be shown on PBS called *Liberators: Fighting on Two Fronts in World War II.*

The reality, however, was that they also wanted to produce a film that could later be shown in predominantly black schools as a means of sucking innocent and unsuspecting black children into the Holocaust vortex. Wiesel's 1989 lie had given birth to this film, and one can imagine the Holocaust fundamentalists quietly rejoicing in the background as they added yet another layer of disinformation to the Holocaust. It is important to remember here that, just as the Holocaust myth had been initially created, under the brand name of "genocide," for very specific political reasons as mentioned above, so also this new story was being invented to fulfill a very specific political need for the New York Jewish elite: restoration of Jewish political control over the city's black mayor and its other black politicians.

Sadly, black politicians, from Mayor David Dinkins on down, allowed themselves to be manipulated by the Holocaust fundamentalists who were behind the film. It was premiered on November 9, 1992, at a gala event staged at New York's Lincoln Center. Some seven hundred mostly black and Jewish dignitaries were in attendance. Then, on November 11, the film was broadcast on WNET, the local PBS station.[305]

A month later, Jesse Jackson, who from the beginning had given full support to this absurd film in order to ingratiate himself with New York's wealthy Jews, most of whom had been shunning him since he had referred to New York City as "Hymietown" in 1984, introduced the film at the Apollo Theater in Harlem.[306] At the beginning of 1993, the Holocaust fundamentalists of Hollywood, pulling their oar in the overall Jewish effort, made sure that the film was one of five documentaries nominated for an Oscar.[307]

Yes, there seemed to be something in this crude hoax for everybody. Indeed, since this event was yet another true and authentic exercise in mendacity, but on a colossal scale, Wiesel's involvement is perfectly understandable. Yet the historical scam could not go on forever. Jeffrey Goldberg, breaking the Jewish code of silence, spoke for many New York Jews and others, when he denounced this media fabrication, so strongly supported by the *New York Times*.[308] Within a week after his article appeared, the

---

305 John J. O'Connor, "America's Black Army and a Dual War Front," *New York Times*, November 11, 1992, C24.
306 Ari L. Goldman, "Blacks and Jews Join Hands for an Even Brighter Future," *New York Times*, December 18, 1992.
307 Ann Hornaday, "Documentaries and the Oscars: No Cinderellas at the Ball," *New York Times*, March 14, 1993, H13.
308 Jeffrey Goldberg, "The Exaggerators," *New Republic*, February 8, 1993, 13f.

film had to be withdrawn.[309] Disgraced, it failed to win an Oscar, finishing fourth out of five. *Liberators: Fighting on Two Fronts in World War II* has now disappeared down the Orwellian memory hole. In accordance with the use of the narrative technique of retroactive continuity in the telling of the Holocaust story, this exercise in dishonesty, brainwashing and propaganda, after being added, however briefly, to the master narrative of the Jewish Holocaust story, has now been erased from it, as if it had never existed.

Wiesel Weasels on Having Seen Blacks at Buchenwald

In 1995, Wiesel repeated this particular tall tale in the first volume of his autobiography, but he did so in such a way as to suggest that his memory had been faulty. By this time it was clear that Jeffrey Goldberg and the other New York Jews who had denounced this film as a fraud were also, by extension, and of course in petto, rejecting Wiesel's bogus and suddenly "recovered" Holocaust memory in support of it. After all, it is these fellow Jews who know better than anyone else what a faker he actually is. Thus, realizing that he needed to backtrack in order to preserve some semblance of credibility with these people, his core supporters, he wrote his *seventh* version of what happened that day. He offered:[310]

> *I remember the American soldiers and the horror that could be read in their faces. I will never forget that black sergeant – was he in fact a sergeant? Someone must have told me later on that he was. Was he black? I think that's the way I remember him. A muscle-bound giant and full of humanity, he wept tears of impotent rage and shame, shame for the whole human race, to which we all belonged. He spewed curses and insults that, coming from his lips, became holy words. We tried to lift him onto our shoulders to show our gratitude, but we didn't have the strength. We were too weak to even applaud him.*

Sadly, Wiesel's portrayal of black people as inarticulate, muscle-bound bozos offers a fair description of his prejudices. In addition, his use of the shopworn Holocaust trope, "I only found out later," as a screen for his mendacity and deception is a further insult to all of his readers.

---

309 Joseph B. Treaster, "Film Halted on Blacks Freeing Jews: Movie Is Withdrawn on Unit's War Role," *New York Times*, February 12, 1993, B3.

310 Wiesel, *Tous les fleuves*, 129: "Je me souviens des soldats américains, de l'horreur qui se lisait sur leurs visages. Je n'oublierai jamais ce sergent noir – était-ce un sergent? On a dû me le préciser plus tard. Etait-il noir? Je crois me le rappeler. Géant tout en muscles et plein d'humanité, il versait des larmes de colère impuissante, des larmes de honte: il avait honte pour l'espèce humaine, dont nous faisions tous partie. Il proférait des malédictions et des injures qui, sur ses lèvres, devenaient des paroles sacrées. Pour lui manifester notre gratitude, nous essayâmes de le porter en triomphe, mais la force nous manquait. Nous étions trop faibles même pour l'applaudir."

Two More Pictures: The Boys from the *Kinderblock*

Another utterly absurd statement in Wiesel's seventh version of the story is that the boys in the *Kinderblock* had been too weak to even applaud the black American soldier, let alone lift him up. Yet the two photos (Illustrations 24f.) of the boys marching out of the "Little Camp," in which the *Kinderblock* was located, tell a completely different story. These boys, even under the arduous circumstances occasioned by total war, had clearly been well fed by the Germans. In fact, these pictures, taken by AP photographer Byron H. Rollins on April 21, 1945, or ten days after their liberation, give the lie to the existence of a German plan to eradicate all Jewish children. It also reminds us of how mendacious Wiesel's oft-repeated claim is that 1.5 million Jewish children died in the Holocaust. Amazingly, even though Wiesel's story was known to be false, he was nonetheless able to incorporate it into his stand-up routine on the lecture circuit.

Illustration 24: As the boys from the "Little Camp" emerge, they appear to have been well fed by the German "war criminals." (USHMM photo #69158)

Illustration 25: Another view of the boys from the Kinderblock *marching out of Buchenwald*

One example of the use of such deliberate deception in the telling of the Jewish Holocaust story occurred in an appearance he made before a largely student audience at the University of Massachusetts at Amherst in 1995. At that time, he told African-American poet and Nobel laureate Maya Angelou the same tall tale about having seen black soldiers on liberation day at Buchenwald.[311] The man has no shame, and is not worthy of belief.

---

[311] "Maya Angelou and Elie Wiesel on Love, Hate and Humanity," *Massachusetts*, Spring 1995, 4.

Two pictures of boys marching out of Block 66, where they had been lodged in the final days of the camp's existence, further erode claims by both Wiesel and the USHMM that he is one of the men in the barracks picture.

I deal first with the picture shown above, the one taken from above and from a distance, and which shows how lengthy the column was. It is important to note that neither Wiesel nor the USHMM claims that he is pictured therein. The USHMM apparently refrains from doing so for two reasons. The first is that, just as they do not identify Wiesel in the picture of the Jewish refugee boys in France, they also fail to identify him here for the simple reason that he is not in the picture. The other reason is because the museum continues to give support on their website to Wiesel's false claim that he is shown in the Buchenwald barracks picture. Yet Professor Kenneth Waltzer claimed in the internet article that has now been taken down that Wiesel is seen in both this picture and another one, shown below. He wrote:[312]

> *But another picture* [than the one of the men in the bunks] *taken after liberation, on April 17, when the boys were led to the former SS barracks outside the camp, shows Wiesel marching out, fourth on the left, among a phalanx of youth moving together, heads held high, a group together guided by prisoners who had helped save them.*

There are two quite erroneous assertions made here by Waltzer. The first concerns the date on which the picture was taken. Although the Buchenwald museum clearly provides the date as April 21, Waltzer displays once again his sloppy scholarship by stating that it was taken on April 17. Another thing that is troubling about Waltzer's claim is that he does not specify who is actually "fourth on the left" in this picture. Is it the tall boy wearing the beret or the boy in front of him? In the final analysis, however, there is no resemblance between either of these boys and the man in the bunk.[313]

Problem #12: After Liberation: Interaction with the Germans

As mentioned in Chapter V, Naomi Seidman pointed out in her 1996 article that the two versions of Wiesel's novel were written for two different audiences, the first being Yiddish-speaking Jews from Eastern Europe and the second for more sophisticated non-Jewish readers in Western Europe.

---

[312] Waltzer, Wiesel's *Night.*"

[313] In addition to Carolyn Yeager, an anonymous blogger by the name of "further glory" has also helped to illuminate this subject with several important posts about the lack of pictorial proof that Wiesel was ever at Buchenwald https://furtherglory.wordpress.com/2013/07/17/whatever-happened-to-ken-waltzers-proposed-book-about-the-buchenwald-orphans/

She also argued that François Mauriac played an important role in helping Wiesel to "transition" his book from one audience to the other, although she seems not to fully appreciate the extent to which Mauriac rewrote Wiesel's Yiddish book. Even before Seidman's article appeared, Eve Kessler, an editor with the New York Jewish newspaper *Forward*, published her own commentary about it. Concerned that Seidman's article transgressed the limits of orthodox Holocaust fundamentalist discourse, Kessler wrote:[314]

> *The article, "Elie Wiesel and the Scandal of Jewish Rage," charges that Mr. Wiesel sanitized his reminiscences, purging them of uncomfortable references to Jewish vengeance when they later appeared in French, in order to position himself not as a Yiddish memorialist but as a writer in the European existentialist tradition.*

In using the accusatory word "charges" to describe what she took to be Seidman's attack on Wiesel, Kessler obviously read Seidman's article as an act of aggression against him. In fact, she also anticipated that the article "which will appear in November, seems likely to ignite a major intellectual controversy." She was right, for Seidman's article has turned out to be a solid contribution to Holocaust revisionism.

When the essay appeared a month later, it did not disappoint. In *La Nuit*, the young Jews, after their liberation from Buchenwald, go to the nearby town of Weimar. Wiesel, presenting his fellow Jews as quasi-angelic creatures, insists that they did not exact vengeance on the defeated Germans:[315]

> *Our first act as free men was to throw ourselves on the food supply. That's all we thought about. Neither about vengeance, nor about our parents. Only about bread. And even after we had had our fill, not one person thought about vengeance. The next day* [after liberation], *several young men ran off to Weimar to gather up potatoes and clothing, and to sleep with girls. But there was not a trace of vengeance.*

Seidman offers the following translation of the equivalent passage in Yiddish:[316]

> *The first gesture of freedom: the starved men made an effort to get something to eat. They only thought about food. Not about revenge. Not about their parents. Only about bread. And even when they had satisfied their hunger, they still did not think about revenge.*

---

314 E. V. Kessler, "The Rage That Elie Wiesel Edited Out of *Night*," *Forward*, October 4, 1996.

315 Wiesel, *Nuit*, 178: "Notre premier geste d'hommes libres fut de nous jeter sur le ravitaillement. On ne pensait qu'à cela. Ni à la vengeance, ni aux parents. Rien qu'au pain. Et même lorsqu'on n'eut plus faim, il n'y eut personne pour penser à la vengeance. Le lendemain, quelques jeunes gens coururent à Weimar ramasser des pommes de terre, des habits – et coucher avec des filles. Mais de vengeance, pas de trace."

316 Seidman, "Elie Wiesel," 5.

Until this point, the final version of *La Nuit* coincides quite closely with the Yiddish text. From this point on, however, we clearly see the extent to which Mauriac toned down Wiesel's text. It is important to recall that, as he did so, Wiesel remained in New York, supposedly bed-ridden, killing time while his lawyer worked out a maximum settlement on his insurance claim. But Mauriac not only toned down Wiesel's Yiddish text, he radically changed it, as Seidman points out in her article. Here is the continuation of Seidman's translation of the Yiddish text:

> *Early the next day, Jewish boys ran off to Weimar to steal clothing and potatoes. And to rape German girls. The historical commandment of revenge was not fulfilled.* ("Elie Wiesel," 5)

As we see, Mauriac made three huge changes in Wiesel's original Yiddish text, which was presumably faithfully translated by Wiesel in the "bridge text" that he provided to his benefactor. Seidman, seemingly oblivious to the fact that her article was helping to demolish the image of Wiesel as a reliable eyewitness to the Holocaust, makes the following observation about Mauriac's transformation of *Un di velt*:

> *In the Yiddish version, the survivors are explicitly described as Jews and their victims (or intended victims) as German.*

But this is not all:

> *The implication in the Yiddish text is that rape is a frivolous dereliction of the obligation to fulfill 'the historical commandment of revenge'; presumably fulfillment of this obligation would involve a public and concerted act of retribution with a clearly defined target.* Un di velt *does not spell out what form this retribution might take, only that it is sanctioned – even commanded – by Jewish history and tradition.* ("Elie Wiesel," 5)

Is it any wonder that Eve Kessler was upset when she read this article prior to its publication? With regard to what Seidman calls "lawless retribution," one cannot help but think of the "lawless retribution" that the Jews of Israel have been exacting from the Palestinians for the last six decades for the simple crime of being non-Jews.

Mauriac obviously could not let this passage remain in *La Nuit*. Thus, he rewrote it and, in doing so, introduced three major changes. The first was to delete Wiesel's insistence that these young men were Jews. The second change he made was to delete any reference to Jewish racism. Thus the phrase "the historical commandment for revenge was not fulfilled" was completely deleted. The third thing that Mauriac did was to delete the verb "rape" and replace it with "sleep."

Yes, Kessler was right, for Wiesel had indeed "sanitized his reminiscences, purging them of uncomfortable references to Jewish vengeance." But it was Mauriac who did that for him. Why? There is one major and obvious reason why Mauriac had to do this. He knew that "lawless retribution" is a war crime. Although Wiesel saw no problem with this particular war crime as long as Jews were committing it and Germans were its victims, Mauriac knew that such crimes can never be condoned under any circumstances. As a philo-Semite, he would also have wanted to avoid giving any scandal to non-Jewish readers. His implementation of these emendations is quite possibly mentioned in his correspondence with Wiesel, a correspondence much of which has unfortunately disappeared from view, analogously to the use of retroactive continuity in the telling of the Jewish Holocaust story.

Problem #13: Mauriac and the Face in the Mirror

The closing scene of *La Nuit* is drastically different from the corresponding scene in *Un di velt*. It offers convincing proof of the fact that, without Mauriac's rewrite, Wiesel's book would have had little or no chance to be successful. After the liberation of the camp, Wiesel falls sick and spends two weeks in the hospital. Mauriac then closes Wiesel's novel with the following sentences:[317]

> *One day I was able to get up, gathering all my strength. I wanted to see myself in the mirror that was hanging on the wall across the room. I hadn't seen myself since the ghetto. From deep inside the mirror, a cadaver was staring back at me, and I have not been able to rid myself of his gaze.*

Mauriac liked to bring his novels to a clear ending, to have his characters' probable future clearly delineated rather than leaving them up in the air. He was a great writer, and his hand is quite visible here, especially when we compare the ending that he gave to *La Nuit* with the ending found in the Yiddish text. Naomi Seidman has translated that ending for us, and the contrast between the two texts speaks volumes:

> *One fine day I got up – with the last of my energy – and went over to the mirror that was hanging on the wall.*
> *I wanted to see myself. I had not seen myself since the ghetto.*
> *From the mirror a skeleton gazed out.*
> *Skin and bones.*
> *I saw the image of myself after my death. It was at that instant that the will to live was awakened.*
> *Without knowing why, I raised my balled-up fist and smashed the mirror, breaking the image that lived within it.*
> *And then – I fainted.*
> *From that moment on my health began to improve.*

---

[317] Wiesel, *Nuit*, 178: "Un jour je pus me lever après avoir rassemblé toutes mes forces. Je voulais me voir dans le miroir, qui était suspendu au mur d'en face. Je ne m'étais plus vu depuis le ghetto. Du fond du miroir, un cadavre me contemplait. Son regard dans mes yeux ne me quitte plus."

I stayed in bed for a few more days, in the course of which I wrote the outline of the book you are holding in your hand, dear reader.
But -
Now, ten years after Buchenwald, I see that the world is forgetting. Germany is a sovereign state, the German army has been reborn. The bestial sadist of Buchenwald, Ilse Koch, is happily raising her children. War criminals stroll in the streets of Hamburg and Munich. The past has been erased. Forgotten.
Germans and anti-Semites persuaded the world that the story of the six million Jewish martyrs is a fantasy, and the naïve world will probably believe them, if not today, then tomorrow or the next day.
So I thought it would be a good idea to write a book based on the notes I wrote in Buchenwald.
I am not so naïve to believe that this book will change history or shake people's beliefs. Books no longer have the power they once had. Those who were silent yesterday will also be silent tomorrow. I often ask myself now, ten years after Buchenwald:
Was it worth breaking that mirror? Was it worth it?

The differences between the two endings are striking. First, Mauriac brings a clean sense of closure to the book, while Wiesel's version wanders and sputters. What is Wiesel getting at? He is dealing with too many subjects at the end of his book, and the reader can easily become confused.

Second, Mauriac uses the silent image in the mirror to encapsulate the true and unjust wartime suffering of innocent Jews. He understands that, despite its silence, this image speaks more loudly than the disorganized flood of words that constitute Wiesel's anti-German rant.

Wiesel, on the other hand, goes off on a pseudo-existentialist tangent. I say this because, in the 1950s, when existentialism was the opium of many Paris intellectuals, the "Sartrean gaze" (*le regard sartrien*) was much discussed. This expression reflected Sartre's contention that people all too often allow their own perceptions of themselves to be unduly influenced by the way in which others "gaze" upon them. In so doing, they lose their own freedom and allow "the other" to impose an unwanted identity on them. As a Communist, Sartre also saw the gaze as one of the ways in which those in power look at those whom they dominate and, in doing so, impose this subservient identity.

In addition, the sentence "The bestial sadist of Buchenwald, Ilse Koch, is happily raising her children" is a deliberate lie, which he repeats even in the foreword to Marion's latest version of *Night*. The fact is that "The Bitch of Buchenwald" was sentenced to life in prison and committed suicide in 1967. The editors at FSG were aware of this lie but refused to correct it or speak to Wiesel about it, because "he is our best-selling author."

It is also interesting that Karl-Otto Koch, Ilse's husband, was executed at Buchenwald a week before it was liberated by the Americans, while

Wiesel was allegedly there. (Perhaps he heard the firing squad.) The charges were mistreatment of prisoners and embezzlement. Not surprisingly, Wiesel does not mention this.

It is for this reason, a philosophical and political one, that Wiesel's narrator must break the mirror. In this way, he symbolized his break with the past. Although Wiesel acted in a manner consistent with Sartrean existentialism, his didactic strategy as a writer still ends in failure, just as the existentialist novels that Sartre wrote in the 1940s and 1950s are quite unreadable today. Those works are pitifully boring because didacticism and good intentions do not necessarily make art. Mauriac, who had been crossing swords with Sartre over a number of issues since 1939, surely saw Wiesel's bungling of this scene for what it was and thus drastically modified it.

Wiesel's Yiddish version ends with a philosophical question: was it worth it for me to try to break the image in the mirror, the image that my enemies, the Germans, had imposed on me? Or was it a futile gesture because "Holocaust denial" was already on the rise? These questions emphasize Wiesel's obsession with himself as both a victim and alleged eyewitness. As such, he is isolated from the many Jewish deportees who underwent similar experiences. In contrast to Wiesel, Mauriac universalizes this closing strategy through the use of the image staring back at the young man. In this way, Mauriac emphasizes the memories that all Jews retained of their wartime sufferings (but not of the exaggerated form of that suffering as found in the orthodox Holocaust narrative), and the young man's link to them.

Chapter VII
The 1960s: Wiesel in New York while Mauriac Rewrites *Night*

Wiesel Launches His Career

Just as François Mauriac had "discovered" Wiesel in France, it was also Catholic intellectuals who first publicized his work in the U.S. As Wiesel told Harry Cargas in 1976, Jews rejected him at first:[318]

> *I was received beforehand by the non-Jewish world which is rather sad to say for a Jew. Once the non-Jewish world listened to me and read me, the Jews began reading my work. In fact, I practically owe François Mauriac my career. He was a Christian, and we were very close friends. Had it not been for Mauriac, I would have become or remained an obscure writer, a journalist.*

One of the themes of the present study is that many Jews were onto Wiesel's game from the very beginning. American-born New York Jews, in particular, knew instinctively that it was highly unlikely that Jews would stand in line patiently as they waited their turn to go meekly into the mythical gas chambers because the Germans had tricked them into doing so! Many of them knew that the genocide charge was a deliberate exaggeration, if not an outright fabrication, told with the good intention of fighting anti-Semitism.

It was also implicitly understood that there were not supposed to be any "stars" playing roles in the genocide story, much less basing their careers on it. That is why, as Wiesel candidly admits here, fellow Jews suspected him, at the very least, of being a profiteer and a grandstander, if not an outright fraud. He was just too syrupy, too much over the top in his delivery. But when Catholic liberals, attacking Pius XII as the symbol of the "old Church" that they wanted to sweep away and replace with a "new church,"

[318] Cargas, *Conversation*, 33.

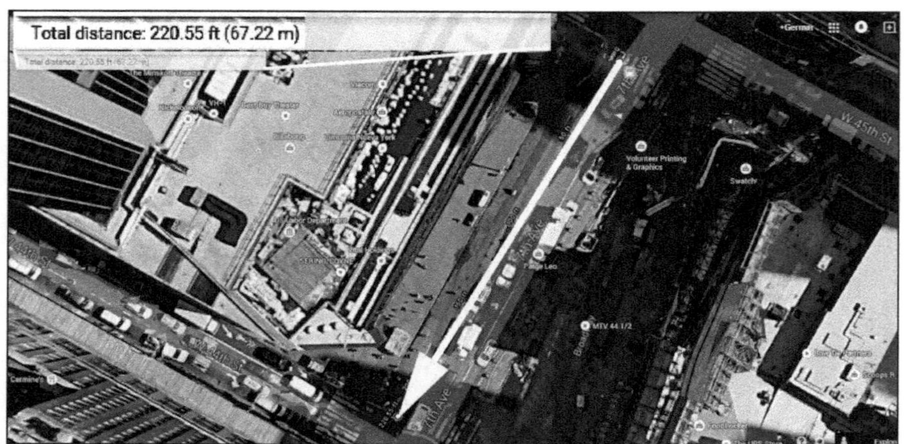

Illustration 26: Measured with Google Earth: 220.5 ft from Forty-Fifth to Forty-Fourth Street along Seventh Avenue. To fly such a distance when hit by a cab requires a vehicle impact so strong that it kills anyone instantly. Hence, Wiesel is at least exaggerating.

started expressing feelings of guilt over what would soon come to be called the Holocaust, it became more and more difficult for self-proclaimed survivors and other Jews who looked askance at Wiesel not to take advantage of what the Catholic liberals were giving them. Thus, to the extent that Wiesel incarnates the Holocaust, it must be understood that the seeds for this cultural phenomenon first blossomed in the fertile soil of the anti-papal, guilt-ridden imagination of liberal Catholic intellectuals. Little did they realize that, half a century later, popes like John Paul II, Benedict XVI and Francis would feel compelled to make ritualized and highly public visits to the sites of former German concentration camps in order to worship at the altar of the Six Million.

During the Suez Crisis in the summer of 1956, Wiesel was hit by a taxi in the Times Square area of New York City:[319]

> *As we crossed Times Square at Seventh Avenue and Forty-Fifth Street, I was hit by a taxi. The impact hurled me through the air like a figure in a Chagall painting, all the way to Forty-Fourth Street. Twenty minutes later, an ambulance came to pick me up and take me to the hospital.* (See Illustration 26.)

This accident allegedly left Wiesel so badly injured that he wound up in a full body cast, then a wheelchair. He told Harry Cargas in 1976:

> *I came here as a journalist on a stateless document, a French travel document. I had the accident, and for almost a year I was an invalid. I had to prolong my American visa.* (*Conversation*, 63)

---

[319] Wiesel, *Tous les fleuves*, 372: "En traversant Times Square, au croisement de la VIIe Avenue et de la 45e Rue, je suis renversé par un taxi. Le choc soulève mon corps et, pareil à un personnage de Chagall, je vole jusqu'à la 44e Rue. C'est là que, vingt minutes plus tard, l'ambulance viendra me ramasser pour m'emmener à l'hôpital."

Twenty years later, in *Tous les fleuves*, he put it this way:[320]

> *The entire left side of my body was shattered. It took a ten hour operation to put me back together, leaving me in a cast from head to foot. All I could move was my head.*

Yet, miraculously, Wiesel supposedly finished writing *Night* while in this state, and over the years he has never walked with a limp or required the use of a cane to move around. In any case, according to Wiesel, after a number of complications occasioned by the requirement of the French administration that he return to France to have his visa renewed, he was simply granted U.S. citizenship. In other words, he was already politically connected and did not have to adhere to immigration rules that applied to others. He later stated:[321]

> *For years and years I remained stateless. Do Americans, the American-born, know what it means to be stateless? It means to feel unwanted everywhere. It means to arouse suspicion at every border.* […] *That is why I also remember the day – January 1963 – when I stopped being stateless. I became a citizen of this country.*

It is ironic indeed that such words could be written by a man who has remained untouched over the course of more than five decades in public life by the tragic statelessness of the Palestinian people in their own country. But since it is fellow Jews who are imposing this outrageous injustice on the Palestinians, their plight doesn't count.

Why did Wiesel decide to live in New York, instead of in France or Israel? After all, he was a French novelist. Would it not have made more sense for him to reside in Paris, where the action was for a man who writes in French? Harry Cargas asked Wiesel this question and was told that he lived in New York for "very practical reasons" – in other words, mostly for money. Wiesel hastened to add that he hoped someday to get out of New York, and live in a "small village" where he could write full time without distraction. (*Conversation*, 64) This, of course, was utter nonsense, for Wiesel had already come to understand how, as a Jew with powerful Jewish backers, being in New York could work to his advantage. He was already aware that, as a professional survivor, he would be well provided for by his wealthy and influential New York Jewish friends.

The insurance settlement his Jewish attorney had arranged for him after his accident was proof of that. When the insurance company offered him $250,000, he was ready to accept, but then his lawyer told him he could get a million if he hired a really big-time attorney. That is what he did, and on

[320] *Ibid.*, 372: "Tout mon côté gauche avait été fracassé. Il fallut dix heures d'opération pour me recoller et me laisser dans le plâtre jusqu'au cou, seulement capable de bouger la tête."

[321] Elie Wiesel, "What It Means to Be Stateless: 'How Could a People Expel and Disown Its Citizens?'" *New York Times*, July 6, 1986, E13.

his counsel's advice waited out the insurance company for two more years while Mauriac worked on his novel in Paris. He settled his claim in 1958. Wiesel tells us only that he gave his attorney 30 percent of the take – while concealing the amount of the settlement (*Tous les fleuves*, 377). Whatever it was, it must have been more than the $250,000 he had been offered two years earlier, which works out to about $2.4 million in today's dollars. Not a bad deal. Is it any wonder that he wanted to stay in New York?

As for Wiesel's claim that he longed to live in a "small village" away from New York City, only a naïve Catholic liberal like Harry Cargas could possibly believe such nonsense. When Wiesel made this absurd assertion, it was probably with the model of the Russian intellectual Alexander Solzhenitsyn in mind. On February 13, 1974, the latter had left the Soviet Union, flying from Moscow to Frankfurt. Shortly after that flight, he announced plans to come to the U.S. and take up residence in the Vermont countryside. But Solzhenitsyn was a real writer, not a self-promoter like Wiesel, and he really *did* want quiet and solitude in order to develop his *œuvre*. Around this time, Wiesel did indeed acquire a second home. To be sure, it was on Long Island, but it was an investment property that his agent rented out for him, not a refuge for serious writing.

At the end of 1960, Wiesel made the pages of the *New York Times*, perhaps for the first time, when *Night* was reviewed in that paper. The task was given not to an established author or critic, but to Gertrude Samuels, "a member of the *Times* Sunday staff [who had] reported from many displaced persons camps after World War II." The book was presented not so much as a work of literature, but rather as a human testimony in the face of hardship and adversity, which is precisely how Mauriac had seen it. Samuels tells us that the novel chronicles the struggle of a young Orthodox Jewish boy to retain his faith in God while "the forces for good and evil fought for supremacy"[322] within him. Interestingly, Samuels's approach to the novel remains the predominant one in today's Holocaust indoctrination classes.

Vatican II and *The Deputy*

Wiesel's first years in New York dovetailed with the period leading up to the Second Vatican Council (1962-65). From early 1959, when Pope John XXIII announced that he intended to convoke a Council, until the fall of 1962, when the first of four sessions convened, there was a great feeling of optimism, even euphoria, among Catholic liberals. In New York, the Catholic liberals at *Commonweal* and the Jesuits at *America* led the way in proclaiming that the Church was about to "enter the modern world." These

---

[322] Gertrude Samuels, "When Evil Closed In," *New York Times*, November 13, 1960, BR20.

liberals would emerge from the Council with a string of victories that they never could have anticipated a decade earlier. Their intention was quite simply to replace the so-called Tridentine Church, that is, the one that Catholics had known since the Council of Trent in the sixteenth century, with a new, secularized one. They wanted to replace the "old Church," with its code of spirituality, its intellectual links to Thomism, and its devotion to Mary.

They especially wanted to end the Church's justified policy of skepticism and suspicion toward Jews and Jewish organizations because of the negative ways in which the latter had used their economic and media power over the centuries against both the Church and its adherents. These liberals wanted to rebrand the Church to make it more acceptable to the anti-Catholic secularists, among whom Jews played a disproportionate role, now firmly in control of all the Western societies of Europe and North America. The Catholic Church had remained the last holdout against the secularist drive to posit protection and advancement of Jewish interests as the prime responsibility of all non-Jewish Americans. As the various traditional Christian sects declined in importance, the Zionist media subtly reminded people that they must never even allow Jewish people to feel "uncomfortable," much less entertain critical attitudes towards them.

Thus, one of the main purposes of media coverage of the Council became to make Catholics revere Jewish people. This press coverage was epitomized by the detailed "Letters from Vatican City" written by a Catholic priest from the Redemptorist order, Francis X. Murphy, which appeared in *The New Yorker* over the course of the Council's four sessions.[323] His access to inside information and his obsession with the need for the Church to make a "statement on the Jews" that would absolve them of the historic responsibility for killing Christ, which is clearly specified in various New Testament texts, echoed throughout the rest of the Zionist media, including the many Catholic publications that were now being taken over by the liberals. His articles were so unfaithful to traditional Church teachings on the Jews – as well as to the Church that he served as a priest – that he wrote under the pseudonym of Xavier Rynne.

But Murphy, later showered with awards from the various Jewish organizations, was not alone. Between the third and fourth sessions, in early 1965, another priest, Edward H. Flannery, became an even noisier tool of the Jewish organizations when he published an absurdly biased and contrived book entitled *The Anguish of the Jews: Twenty-Three Centuries of Anti-Semitism* (N.Y.: Macmillan, 1965). In 1967, the American bishops put

---

323 Xavier Rynne, *Letters from Vatican City* (N.Y.: Farrar, Straus and Giroux, 1963). The second, third and fourth sessions were later chronicled in subsequent editions of Rynne's *Letters*.

this man in charge of "dialogue" with the leaders of the same Jewish organizations that had been pulling his strings for years; he would render them faithful service for the next nine years.

Wiesel, ever the opportunist, could not help but observe that these U.S. Catholics were behaving like so many little Mauriacs, forever proclaiming their philo-Semitism and their love of Israel. He seems to have determined then and there to put their fervor to good use in fueling his career. Meanwhile, the ascendant Catholic liberals took their cue from their newfound Jewish "friends," and labeled Pope Pius XII the principal symbol of the pre-Vatican II Church that they were determined to denigrate, overhaul and replace. They attacked him relentlessly – and with neither charity nor justice.

It was in the midst of this period of crisis for the Church that *The Deputy* made its international debut in Berlin on February 20, 1963, just after the close of the Council's first session. The importance of this theatrical event, both for the U.S. Jewish community and world Jewry, cannot be overemphasized: it was a huge propaganda victory against the Catholic Church in general and the papacy/Pius XII in particular. In fact, in terms of its use of the preferred Zionist tactic of surprise, it can be compared to Israel's military attack on the Arabs in 1967, resulting in the conquest of the West Bank and Gaza. In large part because of the impact of this dramatic presentation (one hesitates to call *The Deputy* a play) on the Council fathers, the Zionist media in the U.S. were able to present the anticipated "statement on the Jews" as the only topic of interest at the Council.

In tandem with the Jewish media campaign, the American Jewish Committee hired a Catholic priest, the Jesuit Malachi Martin, to serve as a mole within Cardinal Bea's staff at the Council. According to Edward D. Kaplan, who was later given access to private and other internal AJC documents, Martin used that position to spy shamelessly on his superior, betraying his Church as he "provided logistical intelligence and copies of restricted documents" to his AJC spymasters.[324] Martin's handler at the AJC was one Zachariah Schuster, to whom he routinely sent copies of internal documents from Bea's office, in exchange for payments that were sent to Martin's secret Swiss bank account. Thus, every time Bea's office was ready to make a move of any kind with regard to "the statement on the Jews" or any other pertinent issue, the AJC knew about it in advance and had a response ready to send over to their cohorts at the *New York Times.* Incredibly, during the Council Martin also wrote a book at the behest of this same Zionist organization, a task for which he was paid by the perfidious Schuster. Entitled *The Pilgrim* (N.Y.: Farrar, Straus and Giroux, 1964),

[324] Edward D. Kaplan, *Spiritual Radical: Abraham Joshua Heschel in America* (New Haven: Yale University Press, 2007), 243.

the book appeared – again – under a pseudonym: Michael Sarafian. After the Council ended, this sad story of Catholic betrayal and Jewish subterfuge was summarized quite well in one of the best articles ever published on the Council's "statement on the Jews." Written by Joseph Roddy, *Look* magazine's senior editor at the time, it offered a penetrating contemporary insight into the colossal scope of the betrayal that had taken place. Roddy wrote:[325]

> *There are Catholics close to what went on in Rome who think that Jewish energy did harm.*

Then, referring to the fact that the much stronger declaration that the Jewish groups had lobbied for was eventually voted down at the Council and replaced with one that was very much watered down (something that has rarely been mentioned since), Roddy cited Cardinal Cushing's expression of disgust with what the Jews had done at the Council: writing that "in his usual gruff way Cardinal Cushing said that the only people who could beat the Jewish declaration were the Jewish lobbyists." (Roddy, 23)

Mauriac Blindsided by Hochhuth

Hochhuth's *The Deputy* was based on the alleged testimony of the enigmatic Kurt Gerstein, who claimed to have seen the gas chambers in operation at Belzec and Treblinka.[326] Its political message was clear: that Pope Pius XII had been a silent accomplice of the Nazis in the alleged extermination of the Jews during World War II. The play was in fact a transparent propaganda work in the style of Bertolt Brecht. Complete with one-dimensional characters, a simple-minded plot unredeemed by the slightest amount of subtlety, mind-numbing dialogue and constant repetition of the play's message, the production owed more to Soviet Realism than to the Western dramatic tradition. It is also a faithful reflection of the overall mediocrity of Hochhuth's work as a dramatist. In fact, the rest of his career, if one can call it that, is characterized by a long series of theatrical failures. However, thanks to the strong and unquestioned support that the play received from the Zionist media worldwide, it succeeded in placing the issue of the supposed World War II "silence" of Pius XII about what would soon come to be called the Holocaust squarely before the public's consciousness.

Wiesel, still unknown in 1963, watched and waited as he observed the media completely reverse what had been, until that time, the prevailing –

---

[325] Joseph Roddy, "How the Jews Changed Catholic Thinking," *Look*, vol. 30, no. 2, January 25, 1966, 23.

[326] On this issue see Henri Roques, *The Confessions of Kurt Gerstein* (Costa Mesa, Calif.: Institute for Historical Review, 1989).

and correct – media image of Pius XII as an enemy of Hitler and an ally of Roosevelt.

Ironically, the reprimand that Mauriac had directed at Pius XII in his 1951 foreword to Poliakov's ersatz work of history, *Bréviaire de la haine* [*Harvest of Hate*], now turned up again in 1963 in the theater program for Hochhuth's play in truncated form (see Chapter I), and has been reprinted at the beginning of every printed edition of the play since then:

> *We have never had the consolation of hearing the successor of the Galilean, Simon-Peter, condemn clearly, openly and not by diplomatic allusions, the crucifixion of innumerable "brothers of the Lord."* [...] *the guilt for a crime of this size falls to a certain extent upon those who did not cry out, whatever might have been the reasons for their silence.*

It is not difficult to imagine the intensity of Mauriac's dismay as he suddenly found the words he had published in 1951 now being used against the papacy, and the Church as a whole, by Hochhuth.

Mauriac understood, of course, that there was foul play involved here. He had not been provided with any advance warning that he would be quoted in the playbill in support of Hochhuth's thesis; he only learned of it from the Paris newspapers, after the Berlin opening. What made things worse was that Hochhuth, clearly acting in bad faith, had also deleted the whole middle section from Mauriac's original text, including these words:

> *there can be no doubt the occupiers* [Vatican City lay squarely in the center of German-occupied Rome] *had irresistible means of bringing pressure to bear, and that the silence of the Pope and the hierarchy was in fact a horrible duty; they wanted to avoid even worse misfortunes.*

The words Mauriac had written to boost sales of Poliakov's book, and thus, in part, to placate his Jewish friends about a decade earlier, in a completely different context, were now being used by them in a way to which he never would have given his approval. Printed at the head of the playbill given to spectators, his words seemed to give his blessing to the whole sordid enterprise. In a word, Mauriac had been stabbed in the back by his Jewish "friends."

But how did he react to this betrayal? Paradoxically, the man who had criticized Pius XII for his supposed silence now answered his betrayers by a silence of his own. From 1963 until the end of his life in 1970, Mauriac never made any attempt to explain away – or to complain about – this obvious betrayal. He neither demanded that this quotation be stricken, which would have angered his Jewish friends, nor stated outright that he had not given his blessing to this use of his work; nor did he endorse Hochhuth's play. In a word, Mauriac remained silent.

Yet on one occasion, in May 1963, about halfway between the play's German debut in February and its subsequent opening on the Paris stage in

December 1963, Mauriac did seem to refer to the appropriation of his words, but only indirectly, when he wrote:[327]

> *Whether I was right or wrong, during the last war, to have expected a statement or a gesture of some kind from the Holy Father, and whether I was right or wrong to have been disappointed* [at not receiving it], *my expectations were high only because my love* [for the Church] *was so great.*

The word "silence" as an accusation against Pius XII disappears completely here, for how could Mauriac dare to use that word when he himself was in the process of remaining silent and not protesting the use to which Hochhuth had put his words?

Since the Holocaust fundamentalists apparently preferred that the lead attacker against Pius XII be a Jew and not a Protestant, the media dismissed Hochhuth, and gradually replaced him with Wiesel. As a result, the former slowly disappeared back into the deserved obscurity from which he had been briefly lifted. The world has been no worse off for his absence. After all, he had served his purpose and could now be replaced by Wiesel in the role of the accuser who constantly laments the alleged silence of Pius XII. Wiesel later expressed his awareness of the fact that Mauriac had served as a link between him and Hochhuth:[328]

> *François Mauriac returned again and again to such themes. And we became very close because of this recognition. He understood the part Christianity had played, and he was the first to come out against Pius XII. It wasn't Rolf Hochhuth, it was Mauriac who did it.*

Like a Trojan horse, Wiesel was wheeled into the very bosom of the Catholic Church, first by Mauriac and then, in the U.S., by the Catholic liberals. Once inside, there was no way to get him out. In fact, if the number of awards, including honorary doctorates, given to him by Catholic institutions is any measure of support, Holocaust con man Wiesel was and probably still is deeply respected by such people.

Wiesel Starts His Career at *Commentary*

As the 1960s progressed, the various Zionist-dominated media entities were busy pumping out concentration-camp-related writing. Israel, as Pius XII had feared and predicted, was rapidly becoming an apartheid state, even before 1967, and World War II horror stories served as both an alibi for, and a distraction from, this process. As just one example of such absurd journalism intended to justify Israeli barbarism, the British Jew A. Al-

---

[327] Mauriac, *Bloc-Notes*, vol. 3, 386: "Que j'ai eu tort ou raison, durant la dernière guerre, d'avoir attendu une certaine parole, ou un certain geste du Saint-Père; que j'aie eu tort ou raison d'avoir été déçu, mon exigence en tout cas était à la mesure de mon amour."

[328] Cargas, "After Auschwitz," 791.

varez wrote with a straight face, in one of the major organs of the controlled media, that "altogether 4,500,000 million people died" at Auschwitz, and that "the gas chambers at Auschwitz-Birkenau were designed for 2,000 at a time; in theory, they could 'process' 40,000 victims a day."[329]

Wiesel, always ready to exploit an opening, could not help but notice that "Auschwitz" was becoming the new symbol of Hell to an increasingly secular society, and that he, as a "survivor," could possibly profit from this development. Crass Zionist Jewish propaganda articles like this one are an embarrassment to the Holocaust fundamentalists today when the official death toll at Auschwitz has been officially downsized from 4.5 million to under 1 million, and when the gas chamber shown to Holocaust tourists at the Auschwitz main camp is admitted to be a fake[330] – although the Auschwitz Musum calls it a "reconstruction," albeit one not based on any solid evidence.[331] But it was against the background of such propaganda that Wiesel began to emerge and to start on his way to becoming our present-day high priest of the Holocaust.

---

329 A. Alvarez, "The Concentration Camps," *The Atlantic Monthly*, December 1962, 70.

330 Éric Conan, "Auschwitz: la mémoire du mal," *L'Express*, January 19-25, 1995, 68 (www.lexpress.fr/actualite/societe/la-memoire-du-mal_487340.html):

> *"Autre sujet délicat: que faire des falsifications léguées par la gestion communiste? Dans les années cinquante et soixante, plusieurs bâtiments, qui avaient disparu ou changé d'affectation, furent reconstruits, avec de grosses erreurs, et présentés comme authentiques.* […] *En 1948, lors de la création du musée, le crématoire-I fut reconstitué dans un état d'origine supposé. Tout y est faux: les dimensions de la chambre à gaz, l'emplacement des portes, les ouvertures pour le versement du Zyklon B, les fours, rebâtis selon les souvenirs de quelques survivants, la hauteur de la cheminée."*
>
> *"Another delicate subject: What to do with the falsifications left behind by the communist administration? In the 50s and 60s, several buildings which had either disappeared or been repurposed were rebuilt with gross errors and presented as authentic.* […] *In 1948, when the museum was created, Crematory I was supposedly restored to its original state. Everything in it is wrong: the dimensions of the gas chamber, the locations of the doors, the openings [in the roof] for pouring in Zyklon B, the furnaces, rebuilt according to the recollections of some survivors, the height of the chimney."*

See Robert Faurisson's analysis in "Les falsifications d'Auschwitz d'après un dossier de 'L'Express'," January 19, 1995 (www.robertfaurisson.blogspot.com/1995/01/les-falsifications-dauschwitz-dapres-un.html); see also Robert van Pelt, Deborah Dwork, *Auschwitz: 1270 to the Present* (New Haven/London: Yale University Press, 1996) 363f.: "[…] the reconstruction of Crematorium I just outside the northeast perimeter of the present museum camp. With its chimney and its gas chamber, the crematorium functions as the solemn conclusion for tours through the camp. Visitors are not told that the crematorium they see is largely a postwar reconstruction. […] A chimney, the ultimate symbol of Birkenau, was re-created; four hatched openings in the roof, as if for pouring Zyklon B into the gas chamber below, were installed, and two of the three furnaces were rebuilt using original parts. There are no signs to explain these restitutions, they were not marked at the time, and the guides remain silent about it when they take visitors through this building that is presumed by the tourist to be the place where *it happened*."

331 For a thorough review of all the extant evidence see Carlo Mattogno, *Auschwitz: Crematorium I and the Alleged Homicidal Gassings* (Chicago, Ill.: Theses & Dissertations Press, 2005).

From November 1947 to January 1949, Wiesel had worked for *Zion in Kanf*, the newspaper published by the Israeli terrorist faction headed by Menachem Begin, the Irgun. That group's extermination of innocent Arabs at the village of Deir Yassin took place on April 9, 1948, while Wiesel was on the payroll. This background as a Jewish journalist who did not bat an eyelash at terrorism, as long as Jews were committing it, must have stood him in good stead as he used his growing connections among influential Jews in New York to launch his journalistic career in this country.

Wiesel's earliest important articles were published in the Zionist monthly *Commentary*, edited at the time by Norman Podhoretz, and financed by the American Jewish Committee. It is at *Commentary* that an important percentage of the racist "blood and soil" (*Blut und Boden*) segment of American Jewry congregates. Wiesel's first article in *Commentary* was entitled "Eichmann's Victims and the Unheard Testimony"; it appeared in December 1961. *Night* had only been in print for about a year in the U.S. market, and was going nowhere. There was no interest in it. It was perhaps for this reason that Wiesel decided to adopt a more strident tone, one to which Mauriac would have never given his approval. His article pursued a very strong line of hatred against gentiles, while at the same time twisting the facts of the Eichmann case. Wiesel had covered the trial as a journalist and, as we recall, had wanted Mauriac to attend it with him. The trial came at a perfect time for Wiesel's career, and he knew how to take advantage of it. In fact, Samuel G. Freedman of the *New York Times* later noted:[332]

> [...] *circumstances and timing also helped Wiesel. When the trial of Adolf Eichmann and the Six Day War in 1967 spurred interest in the Holocaust, Wiesel was already an established author on the subject.*

One of the first things that the trial did for Wiesel was to enable him reach the *Commentary* audience of like-minded Jews. They were very much on his wavelength, and shared basic convictions about Israeli policies in Palestine. Today, these same "blood and soil" Jews strongly support the racist Jewish "settlers," who currently spearhead Israel's insatiable expansionist policy.

The Eichmann trial also played an important role in helping Wiesel to define for himself exactly how he would exploit his experience of the camps. After all, he had little, if any, formal education, as he would later admit in 1973 when he wrote:[333]

> *Shushani was probably the decisive teacher in my postwar years. He taught me Talmud again and he taught me philosophy. He taught me secular sciences and prepared me for the Sorbonne. Whatever I knew, I got from him.*

---

[332] Samuel G. Freedman, "Bearing Witness," 33.

[333] Elie Wiesel, "My Teachers after the War," in Abrahamson, *Against Silence*, vol. 2, 21.

Despite this handicap, he still needed to think about earning a living. What was he going to do with his life? Exactly how was he going to be a "witness"? Here, in the case of Eichmann, lay a possible solution to his problem. Already gaining a reputation as a "survivor," Wiesel realized that he would be able to channel his personal hatreds and carve out a niche as a journalist and commentator by inserting confrontational language against Pius XII and non-Jews in general when writing about what the media still called the "genocide" of the Jews. Here was an opportunity to become a media personality who could upbraid the gentiles for insufficient philo-Semitism. His first *Commentary* article was a good start in this direction.

Wiesel's second *Commentary* article, "An Appointment with Hate," appeared in December 1962, and developed the same themes. In relating a visit he had made to Germany the previous summer, he tells his reader that the only decent Germans are the ones who feel guilty about World War II. But the granting of such a dispensation doesn't mean that he personally cannot hate all Germans, even those wracked by guilt feelings. It was the intransigence, indeed the blatant Jewish racism, expressed in this article that must have caught the eye of like-minded Jews at the *New York Times*. In fact, the recruitment of Wiesel by the *New York Times* as a contributor of note was, and is, part of an ongoing process of importing Jewish extremists from the racist fringe of Jewish small-magazine writing into the "mainstream." The addition of columnist David Brooks as a regular contributor several years ago to the *Times* op-ed page is just one recent example of this policy.

In "Appointment with Hate," Wiesel laid bare his hatred of all Germans:

> *It was, indeed, not until I re-entered Germany that I understood about hate, a hate that was more than desirable, justified.* (471)

It is his conclusion to the article, however, that exposes his core racist convictions, to which a man like Mauriac would never have given his blessing, had he known of them. Wiesel wrote:

> *Every Jew, somewhere in his being, should set apart a zone of hate – healthy, virile hate – for what the German personifies and for what persists in the German. To do otherwise would be a betrayal of the dead. I shall not return to Germany soon again.* (476)

If a Palestinian public figure or an American gentile were to write something like this about Jews, there would be a storm of protest, and the offender would, short of issuing a groveling retraction, be barred for life from access to a public forum. Yet Elie Wiesel not only wrote this half a century ago, he has been acting on those expressed convictions for at least that long, without arousing the slightest protest from the nation's elites.

The British Jewish literary critic and intellectual A. Alvarez, mentioned above, reviewed *Night* in *Commentary*, writing:[334]

> *As a human document,* Night *is almost unbearably painful, and certainly beyond criticism. But like* [...] *dozens of other equally sincere, equally distressing books, it is a failure as a work of art.*

Alvarez simply wrote the plain truth about Wiesel's book. A few years later, however, as the term "Holocaust" was being developed after 1967 to justify Israel's latest war crimes and crimes against humanity, the *New York Times* and the rest of the Zionist media would transform the book that Alvarez had correctly seen as "a failure as a work of art" into a masterful depiction of what would soon be called "the Holocaust."

In a *Commentary* article that appeared in March 1965, Wiesel widened his field to express hatred not only for Germans, but for all Christians. The subject of "The Last Return" is his native town of Sighet, in Romania, to which he had recently made a short visit.[335] As Wiesel recounts the days in 1944 before the deportation of the Jews in the ghetto, he superciliously asserts that, "although a minority in a town of twenty-five thousand, Sighet's ten thousand Jews had set the tone in everything." ("Last Return," 46) Jews, he seems to be saying, were culturally and economically superior to the largely Catholic and Orthodox Romanians among whom they lived. Such talk, as we have seen, is typical of Wiesel. Since, for him, the Jews are always the best people, when the Germans arrived, "the Christian population dropped its mask – and declared its thirst for Jewish blood" ("Last Return," 48). Again, a non-Jew writing such words about Jews would be roundly condemned by the Jewish thought police.

During the 1960s, the term "survivor" began to leave the confines of the Jewish community and enter other strata and enclaves of society. It originally designated people who had survived the Nazi camps, and rapidly expanded to include any Jew who had lived in Europe during the war years. Wiesel immediately became *the* spokesman both to and for such people, and was presented as such in the pages of the *New York Times.*

The "survivors" had previously kept a rather low profile since the war, generally keeping their claimed experiences to themselves. This was a prudent tactic on their part, for they sometimes encountered difficult questions from other Jews if they declared themselves "survivors." To paraphrase Hannah Arendt in *Eichmann in Jerusalem*, they asked questions like: Why did you allow yourself to be deported? Why did you work for the German war machine? Why did the Jewish Councils work so efficiently with the Germans by actually organizing the Jews for deportation? Why didn't you fight back? How could you stand in line so patiently for two to three hours,

---

[334] A. Alvarez, "*Night*," *Commentary*, October 1964, 65.
[335] Wiesel, "Last Return," 43-49.

even days at a time, waiting your turn to go into the gas chamber? New York Jews would never behave like that! If there were really gas chambers, why did you go into them so meekly?

And then, of course, there were countless Jews who understood that the whole story of the Holocaust had been nothing but a big Jewish reparations scam from the very beginning. Yes, it was better for such people to keep a low profile and to remain silent.

The situation in which the veterans of the camps found themselves was compounded by the fact that so many wildly different – and contradictory – stories circulated in the immediate postwar years in the various veteran communities around the world. These stories were in essence a faithful reflection of the multitude of rumors of various kinds that had circulated in Europe during the war years, especially if they had been invented and nourished by the Allied propaganda services.

It was not until 1953, when the Israeli government created its Yad Vashem state propaganda museum, and 1954, when the Soviets opened the Auschwitz State Museum at the site of the former concentration camp, that there were any official, state-supported versions of events.

Luckily for us today, the bound volumes of the Nuremberg trials, although seriously flawed in certain respects, still stand as an irreplaceable monument to the lies contained in the various survivor stories presented there as unquestioned fact. Most of these lies were already being erased from the nation's collective memory in the 1960s, for it was plain that almost all of these horror stories were not true, and that some selection would have to be made.

Would it be death to millions through electrocution in massive vats of water?[336] How about those deadly steam chambers?[337] Would Justice Jackson's claim that the Germans had used an atomic bomb on 20,000 Jews a few miles from Auschwitz survive the cut?[338] Or how about rapid-assembly portable gas chamber sheds to gas Jews on the spot wherever they were found?[339] Would it be through the burning of millions of living victims in the cremation ovens used to dispose of dead typhus victims? Would it be

---

[336] IMT document USSR-93; quoted in IMT, vol. 7, 576f.; once claimed to have been the primary murder weapon at the Belzec camp, it was later silently abandoned by historians; see Carlo Mattogno, *Bełżec in Propaganda, Testimonies, Archeological Research, and History* (Chicago, Ill.: Theses & Dissertations Press, 2005), 11-26, 35-41.

[337] IMT document 3311-PS; reproduced in IMT, vol. 32, 153-158; here, too, this initially claimed murder weapon at the Treblinka camp was later tacitly abandoned; cf. Carlo Mattogno, Jürgen Graf, *Treblinka: Extermination Camp or Transit Camp?* (2nd ed., Chicago, Ill.: Theses & Dissertations Press, 2005), 51-62.

[338] IMT, vol. 16, 529f.

[339] That nonsense was claimed by Adolf Eichmann during his trial; see Rudolf Aschenauer (ed.), *Ich, Adolf Eichmann* (Leoni, Bavaria: Druffel, 1980), 179f. For a collection of further absurd claims see Rudolf, *Dissecting*, 128-131.

the burning of millions of victims in large open pits day and night with smoke and flame seen for miles around? Or would it be slaughter in "gas chambers" that would survive the cut?

Since the Allies had made all these absurd accusations in 1945/46, the veterans were in fact behaving quite prudently in keeping silent about their own personal sufferings. Wiesel, as one of them, would later explain this period of silence dictated by prudence as one that he had deliberately chosen. He called it his "ten-year vow of silence." But even he eventually fooled himself. When he began writing his novel in earnest in 1954, he opted for the open-pit burning thesis to the detriment of the gas chamber thesis. There are no descriptions of the functioning of gas chambers in *Night.* If such monstrous machines really had existed at Auschwitz-Birkenau, one is entitled to wonder how Wiesel, if he had actually been there, missed seeing them or, at the very least, hearing about them.

As the official history developed after the reopening of Auschwitz in 1954, the open-pit burning thesis was quietly downplayed (after all, the OSS, forerunner of the CIA, had multitudes of aerial photos, never seen at Nuremberg, that proved that no such thing had ever happened), while the gas chamber thesis was gaining general acceptance as *the* principal means of extermination. This fundamental inconsistency at the heart of Wiesel's superstar status could be glossed over for a while. But once the aerial photographs of Auschwitz were declassified, their failure to confirm the existence of either Wiesel's flaming pits or the long lines of people going into the gas chambers offered support and comfort to the dreaded revisionists.[206] Henceforth, the media and academic elites would be forced to engage in a particular kind of silence of their own, as they generally played down the very existence of these pictures.

Wiesel Gradually Becomes the Spokesman for the "Survivors"

Fellow New York Jews generally shunned the veterans, and were skeptical about their tall tales. Abe Foxman, for instance, who arrived on the lower East Side of Manhattan in 1950 at the age of ten, after he and his parents had "miraculously" lived through the war years, has offered the following description of this skepticism:[340]

> *I think that the survivors felt guilty that they had survived. They were embarrassed about things they had to do to live through those years. But their isolation, or whatever else they felt, was reinforced by our* [Jewish] *neighbors. They expected us to look like we had come right out of a camp – emaciated, wounded. They hinted that they wanted to know what we had gone through, only they*

[340] Quoted in Miller, *One by One,* 221.

> *didn't really. My parents tried to explain at first. But they stopped. It simply wasn't worth it.*

The leaders of the traditional Jewish organizations, who perhaps understood better than anyone else the fraudulent manner in which documentable Jewish wartime persecution had been hyped into "genocide" at Nuremberg, also shunned them. After all, these were the very same people who had proclaimed that the pictures of emaciated typhus victims *were typical of all the people who had survived the camps*, even though they knew for a fact that the overwhelming majority of them were healthy when the conflict ended.

This general indifference of organized Jewry, an indifference which no one disputes actually occurred, to the supposed plight of the veterans speaks volumes, for these same Jewish leaders knew there had been no Holocaust of millions of people. Likewise, the average American-born Jewish person on the New York City subway, like the gentiles who lived among them, strongly suspected that the genocide claim was largely a scam intended to generate reparations. In fact, many non-Jewish New Yorkers also suspected that the genocide story was intended in part to drown out and paper over the many rumors circulating about the multitudes of Jewish draft dodgers who had sat out the war years in plain sight in New York City.

In any case, here is the spin that Judith Miller puts on the indifference of Jewish leaders and ordinary New York Jews to the supposed "pain" of these "survivor" Jews:[340]

> *Outside their homes, there was little support for these victims. Their pain was not recognized by organized American Jewry. Survivors were not exactly excluded as a group; but they were not included either. Neither the Jewish community – nor Gentiles – were interested in their harrowing tales.*

Ironically, as the Jewish organizations remained silent in the immediate postwar years with regard to the "harrowing tales" of the camp veterans, their measured behavior reminds us that, during the war years, Pius XII had also empathized with those Jews who truly suffered. However, by remaining silent both during and after the war, and never voicing any support for the clearly exaggerated veterans' testimonies that would later become part and parcel of the Holocaust narrative, he indicated by that silence his skepticism about the veracity of such claims.

Yet, Pius XII did break this silence on one occasion. It occurred in his long message to the assembled delegates meeting in Rome for the Sixth International Conference on Penal Law from September 27 to October 4, 1953.[341] In his message, he specifically addressed a wide range of legal is-

[341] The Congress's Proceedings were later published; see: Association Internationale de Droit Pénal, *VIe Congrès International tenu à Rome du 27 septembre au 3 octobre 1953*

sues that had arisen during the war and had still, in his view, not been settled.[342] This message was in essence a rather long critiques of the judicial injustices implemented against the German side in the postwar trials conducted by the Allies. At one key point, he made it clear that, in his opinion, the particular group that was still claiming, almost a decade after the end of the war, to have lost "millions" of its people during the conflict did not have his support. He stated:[343]

> *In recent decades, we have seen massacres driven by racial hatred; the toll of horror and cruelty associated with the concentration camp system has been revealed to us; we have heard of the "removal" by the hundreds of thousands of "human beings unfit for life."*

The Pope did not of course refer to any particular group by name in these remarks. He was first and foremost a diplomat, but it is rather clear that in this particular case he was referring specifically to the Jews and to the claims their representatives had made and were still making with regard to their wartime sufferings. By 1953, the Zionist propaganda figure of the mythical "six million" was already very well established in the western world, and was routinely cited in the media and official history books. Nonetheless, Pius XII, in a public statement at an international forum, counted Jewish losses in the "hundreds of thousands," not in "millions."

Also, to make his thought clear on this subject, he referred to the German resettlement program of the Jews by using the French word *suppression* and not by the word *extermination*, which he could have done. By adding to *suppression* the phrase *"d'êtres inadaptés à la vie,"* Pius XII made allowances for large numbers of Jewish deaths to be related to the German resettlement program but, once again, he stopped short of using the words "millions" and/or "extermination." His remarks on this occasion make it clear that, despite the many wartime rumors generated by the Allies, Pius XII never believed – either during or after the war – that the German resettlement program aimed at Europe's Jews was an extermination program.

---

sous les auspices du Gouvernement de la République Italienne. Comptes rendues des discussions (Milan: Giuffré, 1957), 58 (sect. I), 179-182 (sect II), 218-220 (sect III), 309-310 (sect IV). Translation in English: K. Ligeti.

342 Jose Luis de la Cuesta (ed.), *Resolutions of the Congresses of the International Association of Penal Law (1926 – 2004)* (Toulouse: Érès, 2009.); www.penal.org/sites/default/files/files/RICPL%201953.pdf.

343 "Ces dernières dizaines d'années, on a vu massacrer par haine de race; on a mis à jour devant le monde entier les horreurs et les cruautés des camps de concentration; on a entendu parler de la 'suppression' par centaines de milliers 'd'êtres inadaptés à la vie.' " *Discours du VIe Congrès international de droit pénal* in R. Kothen (ed.), *Documents Pontificaux de sa sainteté Pie XII*, vol. 15, 1953 (Paris: La Bergerie, 1954), 468f. I have used the French translation of these documents: Simon Delacroix (ed.), *Les Documents pontificaux de S.S. Pie XII*, 21 vols. (Saint-Maurice (Switzerland): Ed. Saint-Augustin, 1962/63).

1959: Yad Vashem Policy Privileges "Memory" over History in Witness Testimony

One of the principal reasons why so many truly ridiculous Jewish survivor stories have become the norm rather than the exception over the years is because of a change of regime that took place at Jerusalem's Yad Vashem Museum and Holocaust Memorial in 1959. As Professor Faurisson has pointed out in one of his most important blog entries,[344] the institution was founded in 1953 by Professor Ben Zion Dinur who, at the time (1951-1955), was Minister of both Education and of Culture. Since Dinur was skeptical, as are most historians and legal professionals, of the automatic validity of "eye-witness testimony," he soon found arrayed against him the forerunner of today's Holocaust lobby, which was determined to present Jewish wartime suffering through the lens of "memory."

According to the Israeli historian Arielle Rein, this "memory" lobby was composed mainly of eastern European, mostly Polish Jews, like the ones that Wiesel was now working for in New York. She described them as "survivors of Polish origin, trained in history before the war, and motivated with a sense of mission."[345] These people were afraid that the "memory" of their "experiences" would not survive the process of traditional academic analysis. Rein continues:[346]

> *Likewise, these Jews engaged in a lengthy and acrimonious debate with Dinur on the roles to be played respectively by historians and witnesses. For survivor historians, the Shoah was a unique and incomparable event. Thus, it required a special methodology in which survivor testimonies had to take precedence because they had lived it. In their eyes, scientific study and analysis of these testimonies by professional historians could not do justice to such sources. As a result, they demanded of the institution that it adopt a publication policy completely based on witness testimony: newspapers, memoirs and correspondence. In opposition to them, Dinur maintained that research on the Shoah*

[344] http://robertfaurisson.blogspot.com/2009/03/memoire-juive-contre-histoire-ou.html

[345] Arielle Rein, "L'historien, la mémoire et l'Etat / L'œuvre de Ben Zion Dinur pour la commémoration et la recherche sur la Shoah en Israël," *Revue d'histoire de la Shoah*, no. 182, January-June 2005, 276: "des rescapés de la Shoah d'origine polonaise, formés à l'histoire avant-guerre ou autodidactes mus par un sentiment de mission."

[346] *Ibid.*, 276: "De même [ces juifs] engagent-ils avec Dinur une polémique de longue durée sur la place respective des historiens et des témoins dans la recherche sur la Shoah. Pour les historiens rescapés, la Shoah est un événement unique et incomparable. De ce fait, elle exige une méthodologie particulière, dans laquelle doivent être privilégiés les témoignages de ceux qui l'ont vécue. A leurs yeux, la reprise scientifique et l'élaboration de ces témoignages par les historiens professionnels ne peuvent que trahir les sources. En conséquence de quoi, ils demandent une politique de publication qui soit tout entière concentrée sur la littérature du témoignage: journaux, mémoires et correspondance. Face à ces positions, Dinur maintient la nécessité d'établir la recherche sur la Shoah sur des bases rigoureusement scientifiques. Il considère que le témoignage, s'il est essentiel, constitue pour l'historien, seul formé et habilité à son traitement, une matière brute, n'ayant de valeur qu'après avoir été passée au crible de la critique historique."

> *needed to take a rigorously scientific approach. He held that personal testimonies, while essential, are, in the eyes of the professional historian, who alone is trained and capable of evaluating them, nothing more than uncorroborated assertions, and only attain meaning after being vetted by* [traditional] *historical criticism.*

Rein then goes on to explain that with Dinur's resignation from his leadership post at Yad Vashem in 1959, the dispute over Holocaust historiography was settled: "memory" had won out over history:[347]

> *Faced with growing opposition to his policy inside the Yad Vashem Institute as well as in a segment of Israeli popular opinion, which took sides with the survivor historians, Dinur resigned from office in 1959.*

This policy has been supported wholeheartedly for decades by the Zionist-controlled media in the western democracies. As a result, testimony from purported veterans is generally never questioned. Only in outrageous instances of mendacious survivor testimony yoked to a desire for monetary gain is any media or academic questioning allowed. In the 1990s, for example, the Wilkomirski and Defonseca scams had to be exposed in the media in order to control damage to the overall Holocaust enterprise.[348]

Wiesel Rises to Fame amidst Concern of Some Jews

Wiesel felt compelled to address the widespread and growing Holocaust skepticism that had existed since 1945 not only among many gentiles, but also among fellow Jews. The problem was exacerbated by the fact that Hannah Arendt had broken the Zionist media taboo by giving voice to these skeptics' doubts in her 1963 book on the Eichmann show trial.[349] At first Wiesel tried to placate such doubters, in his 1966 book of essays and stories, *Le chant des morts*. (*Legends of Our Time*, 1968). Clearly referring to Arendt, although not by name, he wrote:[350]

> *In recent times, people just about everywhere are beginning to ask themselves about the problem of the incomprehensible, even enigmatic, behavior of Jews in what was concentration-camp Europe. Why did they march into the night the way cattle go to the slaughterhouse?*

---

[347] *Ibid.*, 277. "Face à l'opposition croissante que suscite sa politique, à l'intérieur [de l'institut] Yad Vashem et dans une partie de l'opinion publique israélienne qui prend parti pour le camp des historiens rescapés, Dinur démissionne de ses fonctions en 1959."

[348] See Chapter XI for a discussion of these two cases, starting on p. 340.

[349] Hannah Arendt, *Eichmann in Jerusalem: A Report on the Banality of Evil* (N.Y.: Viking Press, 1963).

[350] Elie Wiesel, *Le chant des morts* (Paris: Seuil, 1966), 194: "Dernièrement, l'on commence à s'interroger un peu partout sur le problème que pose le comportement incompréhensible, voire énigmatique, des Juifs en ce qui fut l'Europe concentrationnaire. Pourquoi sont-ils entrés dans la nuit comme le bétail va à l'abattoir?"

In other words, the Jews had behaved throughout the war as if no Holocaust was happening – and of course they did so, because there was no Holocaust, as such, happening. But in the post-Nuremberg world, in which every normal, everyday action from those years had to be re-interpreted, this particular behavior could not be twisted and distorted to mean something else. No, the passivity of the Jews had spoken volumes. Referring to the taboo that Arendt had broken, Wiesel continues:[351]

> *Sometimes one has to regret the passing of the good old days when this subject, which still belonged to the domain of sacred memory, was considered taboo.*

Wiesel then tells those fellow Jews like Arendt who are asking questions in an attempt to understand the Holocaust narrative, in the same way they would seek to study and comprehend any other historical event, that their efforts are in vain:[352]

> *The events that took place in those days obeyed no law, and no law can be derived from them. The subject matter to be studied consists of death and mystery; it slips between our fingers, it runs faster than our perception, it is everywhere and nowhere.*

Wiesel's Shoah-merchant chutzpah, as he peddles these self-serving and defective wares, is simply astounding. He concludes by stating:[353]

> *I still don't understand what happened, or how, or why.*

For the last forty-five years, the Zionist media and innumerable conformist academics have accepted such Holocaust mumbo jumbo without question. In doing so, they have not only brought shame to their professions, they have also betrayed their obligation to seek and to disseminate the truth.

As the 1960s went forward, the veterans gradually blended into mainstream Jewry. During this complex historical period characterized by unsettling and largely unforeseen social change, there were many more reasons for Jews to pull together than to stand apart. In the years between the Eichmann trial and the 1967 war, many found common cause in embracing their Jewish identity as they rallied around Israel or gave support to the Civil Rights movement.

Against this background, the various veteran groups began to organize and were becoming more visible and powerful, each one making more exaggerated claims than the other. Thus, in 1965, for instance, the Bergen-Belsen veterans met and declared that their camp "was the worst horror

---

[351] *Ibid.*, 195: "On en arrive à regretter le bon vieux temps où ce sujet, encore du domaine du souvenir sacré, était considéré comme tabou."

[352] *Ibid.*, 200: "Les événements d'alors n'obéissent à aucune loi, et aucune loi n'en découle. La matière étudiée est faite de mort et de mystère, elle glisse entre les doigts, elle court plus vite que notre perception: elle est partout et nulle part."

[353] *Ibid.*, 201: "Je ne comprends toujours pas ce qui s'est passé, ni comment, ni pourquoi."

story of the war."[354] At this, their very first meeting, they established a "Remembrance Award," and of course the first prizewinner, to the tune of $2,500, was a young Jewish con man named Elie Wiesel. The veterans were giving Wiesel money, but he was giving them something that was much more valuable: credibility. His in-your-face belligerence and chutzpah with regard to doubters, whether Jewish or not, were worth millions to these people.

A pattern was being established. On the one hand, Wiesel would henceforth show no compunction about exploiting for his own benefit residual Jewish collective memory of Germany's wartime resettlement program. At the same time, however, he both hyped and transformed that memory into what would soon come to be called "the Holocaust," and he did so in such a way that the veterans suddenly had credibility, especially among U.S.-born Jews, who could not be conned as easily as the average gentile. Wiesel obviated the need for these Eastern European Jews, who spoke with an accent, to justify their passivity in the face of the mythical gas chambers. Thus, the money trees that were available to him for the shaking began to multiply at a dizzying pace. By the end of the 1960s, a would-be veteran had only to say that he had been there, and no fellow Jew would dare to snicker, even to himself. Albert H. Friedlander, writing in the 1960s, put it this way:[355]

> *Of all the witnesses, Wiesel is the most sensitive one, with the most accurate vision and the clearest recall.*

Such a statement was, and remains, utter nonsense, but the creation of an aura of veracity around Wiesel helped him in turn to stipulate over and over again that "silence" was his principal means of communicating. It was a shell game. Instead of trying to explain to skeptical fellow New York Jews what it was like to see that truck dumping its load of little babies into the flames, and to have marched obediently to within a few feet of a flaming pit without attempting to resist in any way, he now boasted that "silence" was his answer. Thanks to Wiesel, the ordinary, run-of-the-mill, non-celebrity Jewish "survivor" who, like Wiesel, spoke English with a heavy accent, but lacked his incredible chutzpah, would now automatically enjoy the same dispensation. If Wiesel could answer skeptics with "silence," and be proud of doing so, then they could too. There was no longer any need to explain.

Wiesel's cultivation of the veteran community in turn generated a great deal of support among U.S.-born rabbis, for he quickly revealed himself to

---

[354] "1,000 Nazi Death Camp Survivors Meet Here; Honor British Liberator of Belsen as They Observe 20th Year of Freedom," *New York Times*, November 25, 1965, 61.

[355] Albert H. Friedlander, *Out of the Whirlwind: A Reader of Holocaust Literature* (Garden City, N.Y.: Doubleday, 1968), 400.

be an expert at laying guilt on U.S.-born Jews, that is, Jews who had not "been there." He shamed them, claiming that they were "killing the dead a second time," if they were not responding generously to fund-raising efforts. As he did so, he made them dig deeper and deeper into their pockets to compensate for their skepticism, voiced of course behind closed doors, about the passivity of the veterans. As a result, his name quickly became synonymous with fundraising.

From a humble beginning, Wiesel developed his business by playing the Jewish lecture circuit. Like the numerous Jewish vaudeville entertainers Milton Berle, Sid Caesar, and Ed Wynn, among so many others, who had worked for years, even decades, on the stage before finally striking it rich on TV, Wiesel also started out small. The man who nowadays commands upwards of $25,000 for a mere appearance also started out as a smalltime operator. His big break came with the 1967 Israeli sneak attack on the Arabs, which enabled Israel to invade and annex the West Bank. Once Elie Wiesel had appropriated the term Holocaust as a justification for Israeli Jewish war crimes and crimes against humanity, the Zionist-directed media took care of the rest.

Wiesel's Career Greased by Abe Rosenthal at the *New York Times*

Wiesel's rise was greatly abetted by his close personal relationship with Abe Rosenthal, for a quarter century a key editor at the *New York Times*. Without Rosenthal's support, Wiesel's name would not have become a household word among the U.S. social elites with quite the same speed. But with Rosenthal and the *New York Times* pro-Zionist propaganda machine solidly behind him, there was no obstacle that he could not surmount.

Ari L. Goldman would later comment that "Wiesel had a life-changing effect on Abe."[356] Goldman seems to be alluding to the fact that Rosenthal, who had successfully avoided military service during World War II, suddenly became a Holocaust fundamentalist after befriending Wiesel.

Rosenthal had gone to work at the *New York Times* in 1943, after graduation from City College. But if, as Wiesel has claimed in recent years, the whole world allegedly knew as early as 1943 that the Holocaust was happening at Auschwitz, that puts Rosenthal in the same existential situation of silence as Pius XII. While Rosenthal is said to have received a medical deferment, one may still wonder why, in the face of the alleged Holocaust, he was content to remain in his comfortable office in New York.

Sadly, Rosenthal was not the only draft-age Jewish man to sit out the war, yet the *New York Times* has never shown the slightest interest in this

---

[356] Ari L. Goldman, "A. M. Rosenthal: New York Times Editor and Advocate for Israel," *New York Times*, May 19, 2006.

particular form of Jewish silence in the face of the Holocaust. After the war, Rosenthal worked his way up the ladder at the *New York Times*. In 1963, when Rosenthal became metropolitan editor, through 1970, when he was promoted to managing editor, he perhaps did more than anyone else to shape Wiesel's career. Then, serving from 1970 to 1977 as managing editor, and from 1977 to 1988 as executive editor, he pulled out all the stops to ordain Wiesel as the undisputed "High Priest" of our secular religion, the Holocaust.

The Frankfurt Show Trial of 1963 – 65

The Auschwitz show trial that was organized in Germany in the mid-1960s also helped Wiesel, for it kept the subject of German war guilt and the need for reparations in the public's consciousness. The ostensible purpose of the trial was to prosecute twenty former Auschwitz guards and functionaries, but it was more than a simple coincidence that this trial, which lasted for the better part of two years, from December 1963 to August 1965, happened to coincide with the shakedown of the German government by various Jewish leaders from around the world. The latter, with the tacit support of the Communist regime in East Germany, wanted West Germany to 1) increase the amount of money that it was already paying to Jews who claimed to have suffered during the National Socialist era, and 2) allow new claims to be made. Since the original indemnification law had stipulated that all those making claims would have to come forward before October 1, 1953, the many Jews who left Communist-controlled countries after that date were refused compensation. Thus, the Frankfurt show trial can be seen, in part, as a means used by Jewry to pressure the West Germans to pay up.

Officially, at least, these trials were not organized by the Bonn government. Nor were they held in response to popular demand. In fact, the average German, who had little or no voice in the Zionist media apparatus that had been imposed on his country since 1945, could not criticize the trials for fear of being fined or imprisoned. Rather, it was supposedly the local law enforcement agencies that took the initiative and went forward with the prosecution under laws that dated back to the Second Reich. Arthur J. Olsen, reporting for the *New York Times*, made it quite clear that the trial had been brought about through outside pressure, for the Germans themselves had no stomach for it. He wrote:[357]

357 Arthur J. Olsen, "The Auschwitz Trial: It Holds the West Germans' Attention although They Disagree on Its Value," *New York Times*, April 3, 1964, 2; cf. *idem.*, "Auschwitz Trial Enters Second Year: 20 Defendants in Frankfort Arouse Strong Emotion," *New York Times*, December 22, 1964, 11.

> *Independent observers, relying on impressions obtained from public discussions, letters to newspapers and conversations, tend to agree that the West Germans' consensus is reluctant support for the distasteful prosecutions. They are accepted as an unavoidable, painful step toward 'mastering the past.' But the prospect of five more years of trials is scarcely welcomed by responsible West German leaders.*

In retrospect, however, we are fortunate to have at our disposal the sordid record of a trial that took place before the sudden appearance and precipitous rise of international revisionism.[358] As one reads today the transcripts and press coverage generated by the trial, it is obvious that, just as at the Nuremberg show trial, most of the defendants would have to be found guilty, but some would be let go. A similar script, designed to give the impression that justice had been served, was used here. In this case, seventeen were condemned, with six of them receiving life sentences, while three were allowed to go free for lack of evidence.[359] Each one had been denounced by specially trained and rehearsed eye-witnesses, with an occasional archival document thrown in for good measure.

The resemblance between the Eichmann show trial of a few years earlier and these proceedings is truly eerie. The German government, with the trials going on in the background, and facing the prospect that they would continue for another five years, was easy prey for Jewish shakedown artists. Wanting to maintain good relations with the U.S. and its other allies, West Germany agreed to pay another 600 million marks ($150 million) to the various Jewish claims organizations. But this was not enough. The Jewish claimants wanted more money, demanding three billion marks, and they got it.[360]

Adolph Schalk, a Catholic intellectual of German-American heritage, covered the trial for the Holocaustian Catholic liberals at *Commonweal.* Although Catholic soldiers had died out of proportion to their numbers in the U.S. population during World War II, a war that had clearly served

---

[358] Although Paul Rassinier (1906-1967) was still publishing revisionist books and articles as he had been since 1947, his work did not yet reach beyond a small circle of readers in France. Nonetheless, his revisionist classics, *Le mensonge d'Ulysse* (1950/1961), *Le véritable procès Eichmann ou les vainqueurs incorrigibles* (1962; Engl.: *The Real Eichmann Trial*), and *Le drame des juifs européens* (1964) have lost none of their sting, while his detailed demolition of the Zionist Jewish disinformation campaign against Pius XII, entitled *L'opération vicaire* (1965), remains a masterpiece. A collection of some of Rassinier's books was published in English as *Debunking the Genocide Myth: A Study of the Nazi Concentration Camps and the Alleged Extermination of European Jewry* (Los Angeles, Calif.: Noontide Press, 1978). Revisionism can be said to have become an international movement only after the *New York Times* reported on the existence of Prof. Arthur Butz's *Hoax of the Twentieth Century* in 1976, as described below in Chapter VIII (p. 225).

[359] Philip Shabecoff, "17 Auschwitz Aides Get Prison Terms; 6 Must Serve Life," *New York Times*, August 20, 1965, I, 8.

[360] Olsen, "Auschwitz Trial," 11.

Jewish interests, ordinary U.S. Catholics in the pew were nonetheless deemed by such Catholic liberals to be anti-Semitic, and thus in need of re-education.

Schalk was delighted to report on the Frankfurt show trial, for he had attended one session with a "good" German family, the Kohlers. Their supposed goodness consisted in the fact that they were "willing to accept fully the burden of responsibility and atonement for the sins of the Nazi regime against the Jews."[361] In other words, they were willing to pay. But, Schalk lamented, the Kohlers were definitely in the minority because "the lawyers on the small prosecution staff of the Auschwitz trial reportedly believe that as many as 90 percent of the German people are opposed to such trials."

He illustrated the objections to the trials that were being made by the overwhelming majority of Germans with the following quotes: "Who can believe such statistics?" Or "We suffered too. Millions of Germans were driven from the homeland, and look what the Allies did to Dresden." Ironically, now, fifty years later, as the Auschwitz death figures are in freefall, plunging from 4.5 million to just under a million and still falling as I write, the rejection of the inflated death figures for Auschwitz by the overwhelming majority of Germans seems more than justified.

The transcripts of the 1965 trial make for terrifying reading today, for they demonstrate that, a mere twenty years after the war, a Stalinist official history had already been put in place. The statistics provided by the puppet prosecutors about deaths at Auschwitz were nothing but a rehash of Soviet propaganda, but in Germany it was, and of course remains, a crime to question them.

The more or less official version of the trial is found in Bernd Naumann's *Auschwitz*.[362] Naumann covered the trial for the influential German daily *Frankfurter Allgemeine Zeitung*. He was thus in a good position to turn his notes into a book. In this country, Sybille Bedford's article in *The Saturday Evening Post*, entitled "The Worst That Ever Happened," captured the bizarre flavor of the event, as if the trial was one of the last and most absurd examples of the theater of the absurd, then in its death throes.[363] Her article, like Naumann's book, offers several sublime passages of Holocaust kitsch, and unwittingly shows the extent to which the trial took place in a wholly imagined never-never land. We are told, for in-

---

361 Adolph Schalk, "Return to Auschwitz," *Commonweal*, July 9, 1965, 500.

362 Bernd Naumann, *Auschwitz: Bericht über die Strafsache gegen Mulka u.a. vor dem Schwurgericht Frankfurt* (Frankfurt: Athanäum Verlag, 1965); Engl.: *Auschwitz: A Report on the Proceedings against Robert Karl Ludwig Mulka and Others before the Court at Frankfurt* (N.Y.: Praeger, 1967).

363 Sybille Bedford, "The Worst That Ever Happened," *The Saturday Evening Post*, October 22, 1966, 92.

stance, that "four thousand people could be killed at one time" in "the subterranean gas chambers of Auschwitz," rooms that had actually served as morgues when the number of dead, as during the several typhus outbreaks, temporarily exceeded the capacity of the crematories. In fact, it would have been difficult to accommodate even a thousand persons in these morgues, let alone four thousand.[364]

The trial's Kafkaesque dimension is perhaps best illustrated by the fact that everyone, including the defendants, had been well rehearsed, and everyone was allowed to claim victimhood. Since the existence of the gas chambers was assumed without investigation or context, witnesses and prosecutors jockeyed back and forth as to whether those defendants who had been at the ramp had actually doomed those deemed to have been gassed, and were thus villains, or had saved the others, and were thus heroes!

An Unintended Result of the Frankfurt Show Trial: The Birth of Holocaust Revisionism

One of the unforeseen consequences of this grotesque exercise in "justice" was the subsequent publication of what can be called the first major Holocaust revisionist book to appear in Germany. Its author, Wilhelm Stäglich (1916-2006), had served as an officer in an anti-aircraft unit of the German Luftwaffe at Auschwitz in 1944. By 1965, he was a widely respected judge, but was denounced by judicial colleagues for having privately expressed skepticism about the Frankfurt trial to some of them. When his wartime experiences during his time at Auschwitz were published by a small German magazine in 1973,[365] the German authorities initiated disciplinary measures against him, since his version contradicted the official dogma.[366] To avoid punishment, Stäglich decided to retire early

[364] Technically, some 1,500 people could have been cram-packed into the largest of these claimed homicidal gas chambers, the Morgues #1 of Crema I & II (wartime numbering) with their floor area of 210 m², but only with the victims' disciplined, choreographed cooperation. Realistically, half of this number may still be optimistic. For a detailed study of the alleged Birkenau gas chambers see Carlo Mattogno, *Auschwitz: The Case for Sanity. A Historical and Technical Study of Jean-Claude Pressac's "Criminal Traces" and Robert Jan van Pelt's "Convergence of Evidence"* (Washington, D.C.: The Barnes Review, 2010).

[365] Stäglich had written it earlier, but he gave permission to publish it only in the wake of the scandal, in Germany, caused by Thies Christophersen's revisionist brochure *Die Auschwitz-Lüge* (*The Auschwitz Lie*; Mohrkirch: Kritik-Verlag, 1973). Engl.published *i.a.* as *Auschwitz* (London: Steven Books, 2007). Christophersen's experiences were similar to Stäglich's, hence encouraging the latter to come forward.

[366] *Nation Europa*, vol. 22, no. 10, October 1973, 50-52. For an English translation of this document see Appendix II in Wilhelm Stäglich, *Auschwitz: A Judge Looks at the Evidence* (3rd corrected ed.: Uckfield, UK: Castle Hill Publishers, 2015), 380f.

with a reduced pension. Yet instead of deterring him from causing more trouble, these persecutorial acts accomplished the exact opposite:[367]

> *However, the reaction* [my letter] *provoked made me realize for the first time what importance is placed on the Auschwitz taboo by the powers that have for decades been determining the destiny of my German nation. That realization awakened in me an irresistible urge to research the historical sources for the allegation that Auschwitz was an "extermination camp," and come to grips with it. I believe my findings deserve to be brought to the attention of the general public.*

Later, after the publication of his book,[368] his 1951 Ph.D. degree in law from the University of Göttingen was taken from him. German government leaders simply could not tolerate such a show of independence on the part of an eminent jurist. Stäglich's book appeared after Butz and Faurisson had made important revisionist breakthroughs in the U.S. and France.

The Auschwitz trial and a series of subsequent Holocaust hearings served Wiesel's purposes insofar as they kept the subject of Auschwitz before the German and U.S. public for the years to come. Thanks to the Frankfurt show trial, the Jewish playwright Peter Weiss wrote a play entitled *The Investigation*, which the Holocaust fundamentalists had no problem in bringing to Broadway. Not only did the Zionist Jewish media produce it there in late 1966, they also made sure that it was followed by a 90-minute television production on NBC the following year. In each case, there was a howl of protest from official Jewish individuals and groups because the word "Jew" was not mentioned even once in Weiss's play.

This wholly contrived controversy was simply a repeat of a tried and true Zionist media ploy. Weiss, who was a Marxist, claimed that the alleged millions of dead at Auschwitz should be seen as victims of "capitalism's bestial nature."[369] He had left out the word "Jew" from the text because, according to Uli Grosbard, the Belgian Jew who directed the TV adaptation of the play, he wanted to give his play universal validity.[370] Through the use of maneuvers of this kind, the Holocaustians distract their readers from the utterly ridiculous and contradictory content of the Jewish Holocaust story itself, and implicitly assume that the supposed facts of the narrative are true and beyond dispute, but that there still remain a few disagreements among the cognoscenti, say, over the motives of "the perpetrators" or the meaning that should be ascribed to the event itself. This absurd media-

---

367 W. Stäglich, *Auschwitz* (2015), 13f.

368 *Der Auschwitz Mythos: Legende oder Wirklichkeit*? (Tübingen: Grabert Verlag, 1979); 1st Engl. ed.: *The Auschwitz Myth: A Judge Looks at the Evidence*, tr. Thomas Francis (Costa Mesa, Calif.: IHR Press, 1986).

369 Oliver Clausen, "Auschwitz: It Still Stands," *New York Times*, October 16, 1966, B1.

370 John Keating, "Memories from the Living Dead," *New York Times*, April 9, 1967, B17; Irving Spiegel, "Inaction Charged to Western Jews on Soviet Issue; Dr. Heschel of the Theological Seminary Scores Americans," *New York Times*, May 17, 1966, 10.

driven controversy about the absence of the word "Jew" in Weiss's play is best understood in this context. Several more examples of the use of this trope will be noted below.

At the time, in 1965, the broad masses of the U.S. public were undergoing a kind of quick refresher course in Holocaust brainwashing. The people needed to learn once again, as they had in the World War II era, that they must remember to automatically insert the word "Jewish" when prompted by terms like "concentration camp," "six million," or "Auschwitz." In this refresher, we are reminded that François Mauriac had written of the "children on the train" in his *Black Notebook* in 1943 without mentioning that they were Jewish. But he knew full well that his British and American readers, already subject to intense state-sponsored propaganda, would be able to fill in the blank by automatically inserting the word "Jewish" to complete the phrase.

Wiesel Searches for a New Issue: Soviet Jewry

In September 1965, Wiesel spent several weeks visiting with various Jewish communities in the Soviet Union. The result of this experience was his book *The Jews of Silence* (N.Y.: Holt, Rinehart & Winston, 1966). He returned to Moscow in October 1966 and, not surprisingly, his trip was chronicled in a *Commentary* article entitled "Will Soviet Jewry Survive?"[371] In tandem with Dr. Abraham Heschel of the Jewish Theological Seminary of America in New York, who, we recall, had financed the dishonorable and ethically repugnant spying operations against Cardinal Bea by Malachi Martin at Vatican II, Wiesel seized upon "the plight of Soviet Jewry" as an issue that would enhance his status as a survivor. The *New York Times* dutifully supported the joint efforts of the American Jewish Committee, Heschel, and Wiesel to suggest that a new Holocaust was about to take place in the USSR. The newspaper reported Wiesel's preposterous claim that there existed "parallels between what he [Wiesel] regarded as the abandonment of European Jews during the Nazi period and the West's present attitude toward Soviet Jews."[372] Wiesel would continue to milk this issue for about the next two years, until the Israeli surprise attack on the Arabs in June 1967 opened up newer and more fertile opportunities. Gradually, he and Abe Rosenthal would phase in the term "holocaust," first in lower case and then capitalized, as the all-purpose distraction from and justification for Israel's ongoing commission of war crimes and crimes against humanity.

---

[371] Elie Wiesel, "Will Soviet Jews Survive?," *Commentary*, February 1967, 47-52.
[372] Spiegel, "Inaction Charged,"10.

Wiesel Adapts Pius XII's Term "Church of Silence" for Zionist Purposes

With regard to Wiesel's use of the term *Jews of Silence* for the title of his 1966 book, it is useful to recall that, during the Cold War, Pius XII had repeatedly used the term "Church of Silence," from 1951 until his death in 1958, to describe the Catholic Church under Communism in Eastern Europe. In countries like Poland, Czechoslovakia, Romania and Hungary, the native Catholic populations had been dominated and brutally persecuted by the Communist secret police and state security apparatus, in which numerous Jewish figures were often perceived to play important roles.

Feeling frustrated and disappointed that the human-rights guarantees contained in the Atlantic Charter and in Roosevelt.'s "Four Freedoms" had not been extended to these captive populations, and harboring a personal sense of guilt over the fact that he had indeed been silent during the war about the unscrupulous and immoral Anglo-American alliance with Communism, the Pope first used this term in his Christmas message of 1951, when he stated:[373]

> *Hands tied, lips sealed, the 'Church of Silence' responds to our invitation. As she beholds the still freshly dug graves of her martyrs, and the chains of her faithful, she is confident that her silent holocaust and her sufferings will be a solid contribution to the cause of peace.*

To Pacelli, the silence involved was the one imposed on the hierarchies, clergy, lay groups and the faithful generally, in all the largely Catholic countries that had come under Communist rule after the war. Pius XII was also unequivocal in characterizing the sufferings of the Church of Silence as "a holocaust." In fact, he used the word repeatedly throughout his pontificate, yet neither the Holocaust fundamentalists nor those Catholics who claim to be "defenders" of Pius XII have ever noticed this fact.

Wiesel unabashedly expropriated and adapted the term "Church of Silence" and used it for the title of his book. He not only replaced the word "Church" with the word "Jews," he also radically altered the identity of the group associated with silence. In his usage, the word referred not only to the supposedly persecuted Jews under the Soviet regime, but also to Jews in the U.S. who, in his opinion, were not protesting loudly enough to their congressmen and in the Zionist media about this alleged persecution.

---

[373] R. Kothen, "Radio message au monde du 24 décembre 1951," in *idem*, *Documents Pontificaux*, vol. 13, 1951, 567: "Tout en ayant les mains liées et les lèvres closes, 'l'Eglise du silence' répond à notre invitation. Elle indique du regard les tombes encore fraîches de ses martyrs, les chaînes de ses confesseurs, dans la confiance que son holocauste muet et ses souffrances seront les plus solides renforts à la cause de la paix."

The *New York Times* and the Unveiling of the Auschwitz Propaganda Monument

On April 16, 1967, the Soviets and their Polish puppets dedicated a monument at Auschwitz. It declared in eighteen languages that "four million people suffered at the hands of the Nazi murderers between 1940 and 1945."[374] Since no specific mention of the number of Jewish dead was made on this monument, the U.S. ambassador was instructed by his pro-Zionist superiors in Washington not to attend the ceremony. The *New York Times*, in its article, claimed that "the preponderance" of victims were Jews, but refrained from asserting a specific figure.

[374] Henry Kamm, "Monument Unveiled for 4 Million Killed at Auschwitz Camp," *New York Times*, April 17, 1967, 1.

Chapter VIII
The 1970s: Wiesel Rises to Fame amidst Concern of Some Jews

Wiesel Triumphant

In just a few short years, Wiesel emerged as the undisputed spokesman for world Jewry. Virtually unknown in 1960 when the English translation of *La Nuit* first appeared in New York, his name had become a household word by the early 1970s. Remarkably, he had achieved this recognition not because he was chosen by his fellow Jews, or was admired and respected by them, but because the media, the *New York Times* in the lead, had simply created Wiesel as a new brand name.

He now began projecting, and assiduously so, the image of a man in a state of perpetual sadness. No picture would henceforth appear unless it conformed to this new image. This look rapidly became, in the hands of the *New York Times*'s Abe Rosenthal and cohorts, an essential feature of the Wiesel brand and, in retrospect, beautifully encapsulates the essence of what can be termed "Holocaust kitsch." His outward demeanor denotes Wiesel's eternal sadness as an unending victim and, by extension, a living symbol of the victimhood of all Jews.

Significantly, during these years, the Holocaust fundamentalists were engaged in the rebranding of Catholics from the status of victims, which had been accorded to them at the Nuremberg show trial and which they had been allowed to keep for some twenty years, to that of bystanders or perpetrators, with Pius XII serving as the icon of this new, demoted status.

It was at this time that Wiesel officially and authoritatively declared that not only Catholicism was dead, but indeed all of Christianity. In 1971 he told Harry Cargas:[375]

[375] Harry Cargas, "What is a Jew? Harry Cargas Interviews Elie Wiesel," *U.S Catho-*

> *The sincere Christian knows that what died in Auschwitz was not the Jewish people but Christianity.*

Parallel to this important media shift in the treatment and perception of Catholics was the solidification of the media image of the Palestinians: despite the ongoing crimes being committed against them by the Jews of Israel, they continued to be portrayed as terrorists rather than victims.

In 1970, as the *New York Times* was trying to encourage sales of Wiesel's latest book, *A Beggar in Jerusalem*, he was interviewed in the *New York Times* by Israel Shenker, a member of the newspaper's metropolitan staff from 1968 to 1979. Read today, the interview demonstrates the deep connection that already existed, in the years immediately following the 1967 war, between the Jewish Holocaust story, on the one hand, and the justification for Israeli racism and imperialism on the other. Speaking of Wiesel as if he were a messianic figure, Shenker tells us that "on June 4, 1967, he was giving the commencement address at the Jewish Theological Seminary here – when it occurred to him that it was ridiculous to be talking about philosophy when, as he told his audience, 'There may be a war tomorrow." Shenker continues:[376]

> *'If there is a war,' he said, 'forget your exams. Go to Israel.' When war broke out on June 5,* [when Israel launched a surprise attack against Egypt], *Mr. Wiesel took his own advice and went to Israel.*

Shenker unabashedly presented Wiesel as a Jewish intellectual who was steadfast in his support for Israel. The *New York Times* continued to promote Wiesel's career, never missing a chance to portray him as the poster boy for Jewish suffering at Auschwitz.

When Germany's foreign minister Walter Scheel went to Auschwitz in November 1970, "to honor the memory of four million victims of Hitler Germany," the *New York Times* covered his visit.[377] The embrace of the number four million for the total of dead at Auschwitz is striking today, for it reminds us again of the deep bonds between Zionism and Communism still evident at the time. It should be recalled that it is only since 1991 that the Auschwitz museum authorities (followed by many other Holocaustians) have been using the figure of about one million Jewish dead for Auschwitz, and of course this revised figure was adopted only because the revisionists had effectively demolished the four-million figure. Thus, for some forty-five years, the Holocaust fundamentalists publicly and authoritatively endorsed the mendacious four-million figure, even though they knew there was no credible evidence for it.

---

lic/Jubilee, September 1971, 28

[376] Shenker, "Concerns," 48.

[377] James Feron, "A Bonn Minister Visits Auschwitz; Scheel Lays Wreath during Tour of Nazi Death Camp," *New York Times*, November 9, 1970, 16.

The bonds between Zionism and Bolshevism were indeed strong, and the Zionist myth makers did not want to embarrass their Communist allies. One of the true gems in this 1970 *Times* article is the author's comment about the *wooden doors* to the gas chambers:

> *The scratch marks on the inside of the heavy wooden doors testified to panic within the chambers as the air slowly ran out.*

The *New York Times* could get away with such irresponsible kitsch some forty years ago – as if "heavy wooden doors" would have been technically possible on any but completely imaginary gas chambers! Before revisionists like Butz and Faurisson began to publish their work and slowly deconstruct the Holocaust as history, Holocaustian insouciance knew no limit. The wooden doors on the gas chambers were accepted for some thirty years as a normal part of the master narrative of the Jewish Holocaust story but, like the four-million death figure, have now been "retconned" out of the tale as a result of revisionist arguments.[378] As for the existence of "scratch marks on the inside of the door," Feron's fevered imagination might have played a role in their genesis.

Thomas Lask Questions Wiesel's Notion of "Causality"

The identification of Wiesel as the embodiment of the link between increased use of the Holocaust as a justification for Israeli imperialism was noted a few months later by Thomas Lask.[379] In 1970, as Wiesel was making his media breakthrough with the help of Abe Rosenthal, many important U.S. Jews, outside of the media's glare of course, were resisting the imposition of the Holocaust on their fellow Americans as a justification for blind support of Israel. In a review of Wiesel's *One Generation After*, the poet Thomas Lask, who was also a regular book reviewer and poetry editor at the *New York Times*, conceded that Wiesel was "a powerful and articulate defender of the new state of Israel." He went on, however, to voice concerns that many, including numerous Jews, had about Wiesel's message:

> *He refuses to establish a causality between the German actions and the founding of the state, except to say that those who survived did not bother with revenge, but devoted their energies to building a new country. But in his books there is a disturbing and confusing shift that somehow lays the guilt of the Germans at the feet of the Arabs, as if what happened in Germany justifies what is happening in the Middle East. It is an attitude that is hard to differentiate from a narrow nationalism.*

---

378 On the utter inadequacy of the wooden doors allegedly used – they were anything but heavy – see Hans Jürgen Nowak, Werner Rademacher, "Some Details of the Central Construction Office of Auschwitz," in: Germar Rudolf (ed.), *Dissecting*, 324-336.

379 Thomas Lask, "The Stain That Won't Go Away," *New York Times*, December 15, 1970, 43.

Lask concluded:

> *Is the suffering in Auschwitz to be interpreted to mean that Jerusalem must be in Israeli hands? Mr. Wiesel suggests that it does. Has all that learning and all that wisdom been reduced to this?*

Of course Lask was on target in analyzing what Wiesel was up to. Ironically, he was making the same point that Iranian President Mahmoud Ahmadinejad made repeatedly during his term in office (2005-2013): that the Palestinians have been forced to pay for the alleged German war crimes of World War II. At the same time, Lask was making it clear that, within a larger framework, the Jewish Holocaust narrative was being exploited as a justification for the uprooting and ethnic cleansing of the Palestinian people.

Wiesel Addresses Jewish Skepticism about the Holocaust

In *One Generation After*, Wiesel displayed his sensitivity to the fact that some New York Jews remained equivocal about him, his message and his way of delivering it. Either they did not believe his tall tales about the Holocaust or, if they did, they disapproved of his exploitation of Jewish suffering as a justification for what fellow Jews in Israel were doing to the Palestinians. Referring to these Jewish skeptics, Wiesel wrote:[380]

> *People* [fellow Jews] *wanted to know everything, resolve all questions, leave nothing in the dark. What frightened them was the mystery. The survivors were reticent, their answers vague. The subject: taboo. They remained silent. At first out of reserve; there are wounds and sorrows one prefers to conceal. And out of fear as well. Fear above all. Fear of arousing disbelief, of being told: Your imagination is sick, what you describe could not possibly have happened.*

Since the Holocaustian power brokers would not allow either media or academic voices to do their jobs properly and to publicly express skepticism about the absurd eyewitness accounts then being put forth by veterans of the camps, no discussion of the Holocaust was permitted in mainstream outlets or academe in the critical years between 1945 and 1970 (nor has there been more than a handful of revisionist articles published in the mainstream since then). Thus, a chance to impede the imposition of the Holocaust as the state religion of the American people was lost. From the

[380] Elie Wiesel, *One Generation,* 7. This text is a more or less faithful translation of what Wiesel had written earlier that year in *Entre Deux Soleils,* 246. The only addition to the English text consists of the words “the subject, taboo.” “On voulait tout savoir, résoudre toutes les questions. Ne rien laisser dans le noir; le mystère faisait peur. Réticents, les survivants répondaient à côté, tournaient autour du sujet. Ou gardaient le silence. Par pudeur d’abord: il y a des blessures, des deuils qu’on préfère cacher. Par crainte aussi. Crainte de susciter l’incrédulité, de s’entendre dire: vous avez l’imagination malade, ce que vous décrivez n’a pas pu se produire.”

beginning, the incessant, retributive vigilance of the Holocaust fundamentalists drove legitimate questions about the historicity of the Holocaust underground. This intolerance and censorship led in turn to the creation of a whole "samisdat," or underground, culture outside the bounds of the censored and controlled media and academic venues. That is how Holocaust revisionism began. Before long, the reprobate revisionists were circulating the results of their research among themselves and, in doing so, gradually improved the quality of that work. As the 1970s began, the Holocaust fundamentalists remained in complete control of the Holocaust narrative, but within a few years the revisionists would begin to erode their control. As they did so, they would force the Holocaustians to scale back the Holocaust accordingly, but of course the real reason for the various downsizings was never mentioned to the public.

From the Beginning, Skeptical Jewish Voices Question the Holocaust

Another *New York Times* interview with a triumphant Wiesel appeared in a 1973 article by Edward B. Fiske, who later served as education editor of the *New York Times* from 1974 to 1991.

The early 1970s were the high-water mark of Wiesel's career. The revisionist attacks on his credibility had not yet begun, and the aerial photography of Auschwitz had not yet been declassified and published. By 1979, when it would become possible to compare Wiesel's description of the atrocities he had claimed to see at Auschwitz with the Allied aerial photos that showed that no such things had ever happened, the dam would begin, albeit slowly, to crack. But for now he was secure. He enjoyed complete and total adulation from the media, with no academic or Jewish person daring – publicly and on the record – to question his credentials. However, there was still reasoned resistance among highly assimilated and influential U.S. Jews to the growth of Holocaust fundamentalism. These Jews did not see the point, in general, of alienating their Christian neighbors by a growing obsession with the Holocaust folktale and, in particular, of poking fingers in the eyes of their Catholic friends over Pius XII's alleged silence. The *New York Times*, as a kind of parish bulletin for New York Jews with regard to things Jewish, took note of this discussion, although in coded terms. Fiske wrote:[381]

> *Mr. Wiesel tells stories about the Jewish past in his novels, from lecture platforms and in the classroom – and he tells them well. So well, in fact, that the 44 year old survivor of two Nazi concentration camps has become not only a*

[381] Edward B. Fiske, "Elie Wiesel: Archivist with a Mission; Charisma without a Beard," *New York Times*, January 31, 1973, 43.

major force in American letters but also something of a spiritual phenomenon among Jews of all ages.

Fiske, seeking to illustrate that there was serious resistance to what would soon become the full-blown social cancer of Holocaust fundamentalism, added that there was a substantial number of Jews who could see through Wiesel and who understood clearly what he was up to. He refers to them as follows:

Some people have accused Mr. Wiesel of "exploiting" his identification with the holocaust for personal gain, yet no one does this publicly. Even his detractors acknowledge that he remains that rarity in Jewish culture, a charismatic figure without a beard.

He goes on:

Some Jewish leaders have accused Mr. Wiesel of going beyond the bounds of good taste in building his career on the interpretation of the holocaust. "He has cheapened the memory of the six million martyrs," said one prominent rabbi who did not want his name mentioned. "Many survivors would prefer silence to overstatement."

Whoever this sensitive, but unidentified rabbi was, he understood the discrepancy between what Wiesel was claiming to have seen at Auschwitz and what had actually happened there. In other words, he sensed that Wiesel was a living time bomb waiting to go off. The rabbi's use of the word "overstatement" is a resounding slap in the face to Wiesel, and the distance from "overstatement" to the outright mendacity of which I accuse Wiesel in the present study is not far. In other words, many New York Jews were already onto Wiesel's game.

Fiske then goes on to tell us that Wiesel's annual fall lectures at the 92nd Street Young Men's Hebrew Association "are sold out months in advance," and that "Wiesel has become a virtual symbol of those who survived the 'holocaust' [note the lower case "h" and the quotation marks] – the Nazi extermination of six million Jews – at a time when this tragedy is becoming a major theme of Jewish life and literature." Fiske then quotes several of Wiesel's admirers. One rabbi tells him that "No major Jewish organization feels it has arrived until it has had Elie Wiesel address a meeting," while another assures Fiske:

He [Wiesel] *is the closest thing we have in the Jewish community to a superstar. He is the only person who, by his name alone, can produce a crowd of people and an aura of anticipation. People come to him already emotionally charged. He is a tremendous energizer to American Jewry.*

In summary, Wiesel's showmanship made the wealthy Jews to whom he spoke get out their wallets and contribute to Jewish causes, and this ability was what was driving his ascent to the status of superstar in the U.S. Jewish community.

Finally, Fiske tells us that "one of the principal characteristics of what has been termed the 'Elie Wiesel phenomenon' is that, with the exception of literary reviews of his writings, virtually all criticism is said privately. 'He's the one person in the Jewish community that you can't knock publicly,' Rabbi Borowitz said. 'He's still beyond public criticism.'" Fiske concludes with a reference to Wiesel's carefully managed stage presence:

> *Mr. Wiesel's soft voice and stark clothing give an air of controlled theatricality to his public lectures. As a result, Mr. Wiesel's talks become spiritual events for many of his listeners.*

Fiske was right, of course, but he did not realize that the Zionist media barons would soon take these Wiesel-inspired feelings of quasi-religious fervor among New York Jews and redirect them toward the American people as a whole in the state religion of the Holocaust.

More and more, it would be wealthy – and loud – "survivor" Jews, that is, people who claimed to know firsthand that there had been a great deal of Jewish suffering during the war years because they had lived it, who would bankroll Wiesel and his movement. But such people were also generally aware that those sufferings, as presented in an exaggerated form through the Jewish Holocaust narrative, had been based largely on rumor and hearsay. For this reason, assimilated U.S. Jews, always liable to the rejoinder of "How can you criticize the survivors? You weren't even there!," preferred not to make waves within the Jewish community, and tended to remain silent.

Felix Frankfurter, while hardly an anti-Zionist, remains an emblem of those Jews who, putting reason before emotion, resisted pressure to blindly support the propaganda efforts of the Jewish organizations and their allies during the war. In opposition to his reasoned stance, Wiesel seeks first and foremost to stir Jewish emotions, indeed latent hatred, in his exploitation of the Holocaust. When Jan Karski, who claimed to be an eyewitness to the Holocaust, was brought from wartime Poland to convince Justice Frankfurter and other officials of the truth of the propaganda being spread by the Polish Government in Exile and U.S. Jewish groups, Frankfurter refused to believe him. He told Karski directly:[382]

> *Mr. Karski, a man like me talking to a man like you must be totally frank. So I must say: I am unable to believe you.*

Rabbi Jacob Neusner, born in 1932, taught Judaism in the religion department at Bard College in Annandale-on-Hudson, New York, from 1994 until

---

[382] E. Thomas Wood and Stanislaw M. Jankowski, *Karski: How One Man Tried to Stop the Holocaust* (N.Y.: John Wiley, 1994), 188; in later statements, Karski seems to have turned around and supported the revisionist claim that what he saw at Belzec was not an extermination camp but rather a transit camp; see Friedrich Jansson, "Jan Karski's Visit to Belzec: a Reassessment," *Inconvenient History*, vol. 6, no. 4, 2014.

his retirement a few years ago. In 2006, Bard awarded him with an endowed chair which, since his retirement, is named in his honor. Neusner, watching the Holocaust buildup taking place during the 1970s, had some rather harsh words at the end of that decade, because he felt that the growing cult was doing great harm to traditional Jewish culture. He saw the emerging movement as something that was basically a cultural phenomenon of the late 1960s and 1970s, not something that was essential to Judaism as a religion. To Neusner, the Holocaust story was "corrupted by sentimentality, emotionalism and bathos," and was infected with "vacuous mysticism on the one side and mindless sloganeering on the other."[383] Quoting Wiesel's statement that the dead of Auschwitz "must forever [...] be wounds, immeasurable pain at the very depth of our being," Rabbi Neusner rejected it as kitsch. The rabbi then distinguished between the Jewish theological tradition, to which he belonged, and the Holocaust. He wrote:

> *For those for whom the classic Judaic symbolic structure remains intact, the wisdom of the classic piety remains sound.*

He went on:

> *The currently fashionable "Jewish assertion" draws on the Holocaust, to be sure, as a source of evocative slogans, but it is rooted in America and in the 1970s, not in Poland and in the 1940s. It has come about in response to the evolving conditions of American society, not to the disasters of European civilization. Proof of its shallowness and rootlessness derives from its mindless appropriation of the horrors of another time and place as a rationale for "Jewish assertion," – that, and its incapacity to say more, in the end, than "Woe, woe." "Jewish assertion" based on the Holocaust cannot create a constructive, affirmative and rational way of being Jewish for more than ten minutes at a time. Jews find in the Holocaust no new definition of Jewish identity because we need none. Nothing has changed. The tradition endures.*

In subsequent decades other Jews have also seen fit to question the Holocaust. But of course the Holocaust fundamentalists will not allow the views of such people to be aired in the tightly controlled "mainstream" media. Such people were never interviewed by Larry King, and do not appear on Fox News and CNN. Within the U.S. Jewish community there are in fact many who are appalled by Wiesel and what he represents. Professor Marc H. Ellis, for instance, has also pointed out how the Holocaustians exploit "Holocaust theology" as a weapon. In 1990, he wrote:[384]

> *Then too one instantly saw that the term* [the Holocaust] *was a part of a polemic and that it sounded more comfortable in certain speakers' mouths than*

[383] Jacob Neusner, *Stranger at Home: "The Holocaust," Zionism and American Judaism* (Chicago: University of Chicago Press, 1981), 80.

[384] Marc H. Ellis, *Innocence and Redemption: Confronting the Holocaust and Israeli Power* (N.Y.: Harper & Row, 1990), 33.

> *in others'; the Holocaustians used it like a club to smash back their opponents. [...] Sometimes it almost seems that "the Holocaust" is a corporation headed by Elie Wiesel, who defends his patents with articles in the Arts and Leisure section of the Sunday* Times.

Ellis taught at Baylor University from 1988 until he was forced into retirement in 2012. The university president, Kenneth W. Starr, who assumed office in 2010, worked together with off-campus Christian fundamentalist stalwarts and the Zionist power structure to oust Ellis because of his criticism of Israel. Ellis's many books and essays on the topic, culminating in *Judaism Does Not Equal Israel: A Call for a Return to Prophetic Jewish Value* (N.Y.: New Press, 2009), was probably the last nail in his coffin at Baylor. Once Starr arrived, he went after Ellis because of allegations that the latter had been guilty of "abuse of authority" during his years as a teacher and administrator at the school, whereas the real reason, many suspected, was the content of his scholarship and personal opinions.[385] Ellis left the school at the end of the 2011-12 academic year and, on December 11, 2012, published a scathing internet article on Wiesel entitled "Exile and the Prophetic: Elie Wiesel and the History of the Court Jew."[386]

Rabbi Michael Goldberg of Los Angeles has also critiqued the Holocaust, calling it a "cult" within Judaism. In 1996 he wrote:[387]

> *As the Holocaust has become many contemporary Jews' master story, so, too, its perpetual observance has become their paramount Jewish practice, its veneration their religion. And as with any organized church, this Holocaust cult has its own tenets, rites, and shrines.*

Rabbi Goldberg has no doubts about Wiesel's role in this cult, writing that

> *the Holocaust cult's High Priest is Elie Wiesel. His blessing is sought for every Holocaust museum and memorial, from the local hamot to the central hechal in Washington. [...] Wiesel has found that being High Priest is not without its benefits. [...] Lionized by Jews and non-Jews alike, he can command five figure fees for his speaking engagements, to which he has been known to fly by private plane.*

Finally, Rabbi Goldberg adds:

> *Nor has Wiesel ever publicly preached the cult's core gospel – "No silence ever again in the face of evil!" – to those who need to hear it most: Jews who stood by and said nothing as Palestinians during the intifada were beaten, tortured and worse.*

---

[385] Lawrence Swaim, "Ken Starr's Pogram: Religious Right and NeoCons Gang Up on a Progressive Jew," June 20, 2012; www.counterpunch.org/2012/06/20/ken-starrs-anti-semitism.

[386] http://mondoweiss.net/2012/12/exile-and-the-prophetic-elie-wiesel-and-the-history-of-the-court-jew

[387] Michael Goldberg, *Why Should Jews Survive? Looking Past the Holocaust toward a Jewish Future* (N.Y.: Oxford University Press, 1996), 59.

The Jewish writer Norman G. Finkelstein, who is mistakenly considered by some to be a revisionist, has also expressed doubts about Wiesel and his claims in his book *The Holocaust Industry*, first published in 2000 and expanded in the 2003 edition. There, he wrote about the Holocaust and Wiesel:[388]

> *Only a flea's hop separates the claim of Holocaust uniqueness from the claim that The Holocaust cannot be rationally apprehended. If The Holocaust is unprecedented in history, it must stand above and hence cannot be grasped by history. Indeed, The Holocaust is unique because it is inexplicable, and it is inexplicable because it is unique. Dubbed by* [Peter] *Novick "the sacralization of the Holocaust," this mystification's most practiced purveyor is Elie Wiesel. For Wiesel, Novick rightly observes, The Holocaust is effectively a "mystery" religion. Thus Wiesel intones that The Holocaust "leads into darkness," "negates all answers," "lies outside, if not beyond, history," "defies both knowledge and description," "cannot be described nor visualized," is "never to be comprehended or transmitted," marks a "destruction of history," and a "mutation on a cosmic scale." Only the survivor-priest (read: only Wiesel) is qualified to divine its mystery. And yet, The Holocaust's mystery, Wiesel avows, is "noncommunicable,"* [for] *"we cannot even talk about it." Thus, for his standard fee of $25,000 (plus chauffeured limousine), Wiesel lectures that the "secret" of Auschwitz's "truth lies in silence."*

Finally, Tova Reich's 2004 novel, *My Holocaust*, directly parodies Wiesel. The character who represents him, Maurice Messer, is both a Holocaust false witness and a director of the USHMM in Washington, D.C. When we recall the fact that Reich is the wife of Walter Reich, the former director of that museum (1995 – 1998), we begin to get an idea of the extent of skepticism about Wiesel and the Holocaust that exists within the U.S. Jewish community. Her book is discussed in detail in Chapter XI.

In summary, one of the main contentions of the present study is that there remains a small group of people within the U.S. Jewish community who, if not skeptical about some aspects of the Jewish Holocaust story, are at least cautious about embracing it fully as something that is "good for the Jews." While they may not dare to directly question the extent of the Holocaust, their concern does cover its exploitative use by Wiesel and the Zionist media as a justification for Israeli war crimes in occupied Palestine. While I argue that this undercurrent has been present among U.S. Jews since 1945, I would not go so far as to say that it is a large or growing movement. But it does exist. In fact, one could argue that the growth of Holocaust-obsessed groups like the Simon Wiesenthal Center indicates a perceived need by such extremists to squash intramural expressions of such concern, caution, or questioning. In fact, one of the goals of these Jewish

---

[388] Norman G. Finkelstein, *The Holocaust Industry: Reflections on the Exploitation of Jewish Suffering* (London: Verso, 2003), 45.

extremists might be to push the ADL, AJC and other established groups into even more strident support of Holocaust doctrine and intransigence, and thereby assure that any skeptical Jewish voices will remain silent.

New York Jewish Chicanery: Wiesel Becomes a "Distinguished Professor" at CUNY

Thanks to his success as a Holocaust huckster, Wiesel "gave up journalism" (*Conversation,* 64), that is, the life of a reporter for a small Yiddish language newspaper, in the mid-1960s. His contacts now included some big fish in the City University of New York (CUNY) system. Thus, despite his lack of higher educational credentials of any kind, he received an appointment as a faculty member at CUNY. After serving for a time as a "visiting professor" in the Jewish Studies Department teaching courses in Hasidism and Jewish literature, he was given a permanent position as a full professor with tenure in the fall of 1972. Wiesel's ascent as an academic took one step further when he was named shortly thereafter to a chair as a distinguished professor. The typical salary at the time for such appointees was $31,250 plus another $5,000 annual supplement.[389] Thus, despite his lack of preparation and training, and without holding a Ph.D., Wiesel seems to have possessed a magical quality that most mere mortals at CUNY did not. His academic career was advancing nicely, although he had no refereed publications in learned journals, the official criterion for advancement. As academic honors came to him more or less automatically, he steadily built his personal wealth on top of the insurance killing he had made a few years earlier.[390]

Wiesel recounts the details of his professionally questionable appointment at CUNY in *...et la mer*. However, when the time came to translate that book into English, his Holocaust fundamentalist handlers saw what he had written for a French audience, and simply decided to airbrush part of this information out of that alleged translation. Wiesel's frank description of the policy of Jewish nepotism from which he benefited is quite startling. As he tells it, fellow Jews gave him a job, even though he lacked the most elementary qualifications for it. Even worse, when told of his appointment, he didn't even know that the job existed! He wrote:[391]

---

[389] M. S. Handler, "Lillian Hellman Is among Nine Named to City University Chairs," *New York Times*, September 26, 1972, 38.

[390] James F. Clarity, "Brandt to Visit Israel; Notes on People," *New York Times*, April 3, 1973, 39.

[391] Wiesel, *...et la mer*, 65: "Comme cela est arrivé chaque fois que je me suis trouvé à la croisée des chemins, c'est au hasard que je dus ma nomination en tant que 'distinguished professor of jewish studies' à l'université de la Ville de New York. Je ne l'ai pas sollicitée, je ne savais même pas que le poste existait."

As it has happened each time I've been at a crossroads, it was by chance that I was made a Distinguished Professor of Jewish Studies at City University of New York. I didn't apply for it; in fact, I didn't even know the job existed.

The editors of the English-language version, not translation, of that book apparently perceived his admission to be a bit too forthright. As a result, they translated only the first two sentences:[392]

Once again, fate intervenes at the crossroads. I owe my appointment as Distinguished Professor of Jewish Studies at the City College of New York purely to chance.

The sentence "I didn't apply for it; in fact, I didn't even know the job existed" was deleted for obvious reasons: the manner in which Wiesel was hired was unethical, and possibly illegal.

Wiesel then goes on to explain that the chairman of the department, a rabbi by the name of Yitz Greenberg, had put the fix in for him, and all Wiesel had to do was to sign the contract. Of course, when Greenberg got around to telling him about the details of this deal, moral ambiguities included, Wiesel accepted it on the spot. Here again is what Wiesel meant when he told Cargas that living in New York had certain "practical advantages."

Two days after Greenberg told Wiesel that he would soon be a "Distinguished Professor," Wiesel went to see his dean, Ted Gross, also Jewish, to sign his new contract. He then concluded, in the French version:[393]

I'm really proud. I don't deny it. City College isn't just any university. It's really one of the best. People compare it to Harvard and Yale. And here I am at the top of the hierarchy without having had to work my way up through the ranks as the rules stipulate.

Significantly the English translation of this statement includes only the first two sentences:[394]

I am proud, I don't deny it. City College is not just any college. It is a place of real distinction.

Wiesel's comparison of that school, with its policy of open admissions, to Harvard and Yale, is an absurd exaggeration designed to deceive his French readers. Thus it is deleted here as an embarrassment. The English-language editors also deleted the rest of the passage, in which Wiesel states that, thanks to Yitz Greenberg and Ted Gross, he had been able to start at the top and did not have to pass through a period of academic probation as spelled

---

[392] Wiesel, *And the Sea,* 49.

[393] Wiesel, *…et la mer*, 66: "Je suis fier. Je ne le nie pas. City College, ce n'est pas n'importe quelle université. Elle compte parmi les meilleures. On la compare à Yale et Harvard. Et me voilà tout au sommet de la hiérarchie, sans avoir dû franchir les étapes réglementaires."

[394] Wiesel, *And the Sea,* 49.

out in accordance with the American Association of University Professors (AAUP).[395] Nor did he have to produce refereed publications, or demonstrate his ability as a scholar; his renown as a Holocaust survivor was apparently sufficient to get him the job. The clincher for the decision to delete this part of Wiesel's text was probably his use of the phrase "*étapes réglementaires*" in French. That phrase, referring to the existence of widely acknowledged stages of professional advancement in both French and U.S. universities, revealed that Wiesel himself knew that something was wrong here.

The following spring, in April 1973, Wiesel gave the commencement address at the City College graduation ceremonies. His career was advancing, and the *New York Times* continued to profile him as a Jewish folk hero standing up to the fascists in the Vatican. In an article about his Holocaust literature class at City College, Wiesel said that the Jewish students in his class "never cease to astonish me with their thirst to know." He then went on to state that "they knew in the Vatican that Treblinka meant industrialized murder and that Majdanek was drawing entire communities toward an inferno whose flames touched the sky."[396] From today's perspective, at a time when the revisionists have completely demolished such myths as Treblinka[337] and Majdanek[397] being so-called extermination camps, Wiesel's statement seems laughable. But he and the *New York Times* were not really talking about history, but about power and control. The *Times* was also preparing Wiesel for his future role as High Priest of the Holocaust by having him specifically attack the papacy and the Vatican. Since, in attacking the Pope, he had unilaterally ratcheted himself up to papal level as the high priest of the Holocaust, these attacks did not take place on any genuine merits, but as a career move.

The efforts of the *New York Times* and other Jewish publications to augment Wiesel's celebrity status were seconded by the Catholic liberals in their various publications and public pronouncements. By the 1970s, the liberals were firmly in control of the apparatus of Church governance in the U.S., and they continued to be unconcerned about Wiesel's ritual condemnations of Pope Pius XII for his alleged silence during the war. During the supposed media uproar over *The Deputy* in the early 1960s, no Catholic writer or spokesman ever made a serious attempt to defend Pius XII by asking for proof that the Holocaust had actually occurred as claimed. A

---

395 www.aaup.org/report/recommended-institutional-regulations-academic-freedom-and-tenure

396 Elie Wiesel, "Survivors' Children Relive the Holocaust," *New York Times,* November 16, 1975, 36.

397 Jürgen Graf, Carlo Mattogno; *Concentration Camp Majdanek. A Historical and Technical Study* (3rd ed., Washington, DC: The Barnes Review, 2012); see also the documentary based on this book: Eric Hunt, *The Majdanek Gas Chamber Myth* (20th Century Hoax, 2014); http://holocausthandbooks.com/index.php?page_id=1009

decade later, his guilt overwhelmingly assumed and accepted, except by some non-revisionist Catholics who defended him on the basis of having saved Jews, Pius XII had become the official symbol, in the Zionist media, of the "old Church" that the ascendant Catholic liberals were quite properly in the process of dismantling. As these liberals remained silent while Wiesel attacked the memory of Pius XII, that same silence earned them further points in the Zionist-controlled mainstream media, and facilitated, for some of them, a step up into more lucrative levels of mainstream journalism.

In a 1975 interview published in the *Christian Century*, under questioning from Catholic Holocaustian Harry James Cargas, Wiesel stated correctly that Mauriac had been "the first to come out against Pius XII."[398] Wiesel also took this occasion to attack the Catholic Church as a whole:

> *Auschwitz would not have been possible without Christianity – and this is something that John XXIII understood: the fact that Hitler was never excommunicated, the fact that more than 20 percent of the S.S. killers were practicing Christians, the fact that Pius XII never spoke up.*

A year later, John B. Breslin, S. J., literary editor of the Jesuit weekly *America*, piled on by repeating such nonsense.[399] In retrospect, it was almost as if the editors of *Commentary* had fed Breslin his lines, and that he was working under cover for the American Jewish Committee, just as Malachi Martin had during Vatican II.

The next step up for Wiesel was his 1976 appointment as Mellon Professor in the Humanities at Boston University. At the same time, Wiesel, enjoying the unearned and unmerited backing of powerful Jewish theater owners and operators, was able to try his hand at writing and staging a Broadway play. He was given this opportunity despite his already well-documented and conspicuous lack of literary talent. Entitled *Zalmen, or the Madness of God*, his play debuted at the famous Lyceum Theater on West 45th Street in the fall of 1976. Brendan Gill reviewed it for the *New Yorker*. His comments are valid not only for this play, but for all of Wiesel's fiction with the exception of *Night,* which, of course, has Mauriac's fingerprints all over it. Gill wrote:[400]

> *The play is well made, in an old-fashioned and, to me, irritating way; it is literally didactic, and on occasion I felt that I was hearing certain statements for the third and fourth time as well.*

Gill's words sum up quite well why Wiesel has never attracted attention as a serious writer from literary critics in France, the U.S. or anywhere else.

---

398 Cargas, "After Auschwitz," 791.

399 John B. Breslin S.J., "Elie Wiesel, Survivor and Witness," *America*, June 19, 1976, 537ff.

400 Brendan Gill, "Zalmen," *The New Yorker*, November 29, 1976, 64.

The exaggerated and simple-minded didacticism of his work is almost completely bereft of literary qualities.

Arthur Butz's *Hoax of the Twentieth Century* Exorcized at Northwestern University

A particularly difficult time for Wiesel must have been the interval between the publication of Arthur Butz's revisionist masterpiece, *The Hoax of the Twentieth Century*, in 1976, and the declassification of the Auschwitz aerial photography in 1979. Butz's book contradicted the official history of the Holocaust as written by the Holocaust historians, who wrote with the tacit support of both the U.S. Government and Zionist academe. This state-mandated version of history, with its contradictions, gaps and inconsistencies, had remained – and still remains today – uncontested by the cowardly and conformist academic historians. Yet, to date, none of these Holocaust historians, academic or not, has ever been able to respond to Butz's demolition of the myth of Auschwitz as an extermination camp. Thus, they simply ignore his book, as if it had never been written. By doing so, they have dealt powerful blows to both the integrity and credibility of public discourse and to intellectual life in America. It is in large part because of this betrayal of public trust by the U.S. academic community that the Holocaust fundamentalists have been able to establish the Holocaust as our state religion, and enabled its use in driving the warfare state in its execrable wars of aggression for the benefit of Israel.

In *The Hoax* Butz raised the possibility that the Allies had made aerial photos of Auschwitz, which, if ever declassified, would prove him right in asserting that the claim that millions had died in gas chambers at Auschwitz was a hoax.[401] Three years later, his prediction became historical fact. The photos existed and were published; none gave evidence of gassing at Auschwitz. Yet, academic historians, in the face of such evidence, continue to pretend that the Holocaust really happened at Auschwitz. Unfortunately, the nation's intellectuals and academics have willingly bowed to the imposition of self-censorship. Thus, no free, open or public discussion on this subject is permitted, and Israel's puppets among the nation's intelligentsia meekly accept it.

The *New York Times* reported the publication of Butz's book in early 1977. Arrogantly, the *Times* did not even bother to check the book's title, calling the work *Fabrication of a Hoax*. How could anybody question the Holocaust? It is probable that no one on the staff even bothered to read the book, for the newspaper's concerns in announcing the existence of Butz's

---

[401] Section headlined "Where are the pictures?"on pp. 202f. of the latest, updated and expanded edition (Uckfield, UK: Castle Hill Publishers, 2015).

book lay elsewhere: to reassure its core readership, New York's Jewish community, which included many survivors, that a Jewish counterattack was already underway. As was, and is, so often the case at the *New York Times*, Abe Rosenthal and his acolytes were less interested in conveying news than in stimulating and directing the indignation of their base.

Since Butz was a tenured professor at Northwestern University, he could not be fired outright. Yet the Hillel rabbi there was already leading a signature campaign demanding that Butz be dismissed:[402]

> *Petitions were circulated this week and signed by many faculty members and students.*

Despite the signature campaign to oust Butz, cooler heads in the administration apparently took the time to actually read the book. Confronted by Butz's utter demolition of the claim that Auschwitz had been a death camp, they apparently understood that such a step would be inadvisable. Their refusal to take action against Butz offered firm evidence that, in one stroke, he had inflicted serious harm on the Holocaust myth. If Northwestern fired him and he sued, a likely outcome at the time, no matter what happened to Butz, it would be impossible for the legend of the Holocaust to avoid incurring serious damage. Butz was determined to fight and would not back down. In a court test, many self-proclaimed eyewitnesses, starting with Wiesel himself, would have had to testify under oath, and such a scenario would have been disastrous for both the Holocaust fundamentalists and the Holocaust, even with the aerial photography still conveniently suppressed.

Thus, the Holocaustians adopted the policy that Deborah Lipstadt refers to these days as "dynamic silence." This term, as Lipstadt currently uses it, means no mention whatsoever of the offending book or article in the mainstream media.[403] In Butz's case, direct references to the book's title were virtually nonexistent, while mentions of his name, very rare, sometimes included mention of his place of employment. The Holocaustians, of course, can impose such a policy for the simple reason that they control the media. Thus, if they give the order that a particular person and his book are "anti-Semitic" and therefore cannot even be mentioned in polite society, they are obeyed. For the great majority of Americans, the author and the work will thereby automatically disappear into a "dynamic silence" just as enveloping as Orwell's "memory hole."

The Holocaustians of Northwestern, centered in the school's local Hillel branch, fearing they might lose a public debate with Butz on the merits of the case, chose instead to organize a ritual ceremony of denunciation. It

402 Seth S. King, "Professor Causes Furor by Saying Nazi Slaying of Jews Is Myth," *New York Times*, January 28, 1977, 10.

403 E. Michael Jones, "Holocaust Denial and Thought Control: Deborah Lipstadt at Notre Dame University," *Culture Wars*, May 2009, 14. www.culturewars.com/2009/Lipstadt.htm.

was decided that Elie Wiesel, the emerging High Priest of the Holocaust, would be flown in to be the lead speaker in this ritual chastising of a faculty member. Since there was no professional historian – at Northwestern or elsewhere – who would dare to engage in debate with Butz on whether Auschwitz had been an extermination camp, and whether four million Jews had died there in the gas chambers and flaming pits, reasoned discourse, the supposed hallmark of a U.S. university, was displaced by an emotional ritual redolent of the tribal ceremonies of primitive societies. Ironically, Zionist-controlled Northwestern, conscious of its office in a Judeocentric nation, willingly sponsored this latter-day exorcism of a "possessed" faculty member. The Holocaust myth had been seriously wounded, and might be *in extremis*. But Elie Wiesel, the emerging high priest of the Holocaust, would be the shaman who would make it whole again.

There was a great feeling of anticipation among the predominantly Jewish audience as Wiesel rose to speak. What would he say? Oddly, the self-designated "great man in Israel" turned out to be quite cagey. First, he made no mention of Butz by name and, secondly, did not speak about the Holocaust as if it were historical fact. Instead, his speech was entitled "The Holocaust as Literary Imagination," which hinted that this supposedly indisputable historical event had actually been the product of someone's imagination. Wiesel was playing dodge ball with his audience; this was not what the Jews of Northwestern and their non-Jewish allies had expected! Wiesel had been brought in as an out-of-town hit man. He represented Big Money and Big Media, and he was expected to use his principal weapon, his status as an eyewitness to the Holocaust, to provide his audience with irrefutable proof of what had really happened at Auschwitz. His assignment was to slay the unknown and insignificant Butz in exactly the same way that Israeli thugs and storm troopers slay Palestinians: without mercy.

Unfortunately for the audience, Wiesel's boring talk consisted mostly of quotes from other alleged eyewitnesses, most of them obscure. Such quotes were supposed to prove that Butz's immense scholarly achievement was somehow wrong, but the people in the audience had come to hear about what he, Wiesel, had seen with his own eyes. Finally, at the end of his talk, Wiesel sprang to life and got around to telling his audience what it wanted to hear. The message came in two parts: first the anti-Catholic hate, then the Jewish Holocaust kitsch. Thus, Wiesel asked rhetorically "why all the killers were Christians, bad Christians surely, but Christians. Somebody will have to explain why so many killers were intellectuals, academicians, college professors, lawyers, engineers, physicians, theologians."[404] His historically unsupported accusation is especially ironic today, at a time when

[404] Elie Wiesel *et al.*, *Dimensions of the Holocaust* (Evanston, Ill.: Northwestern University Press, 1977), 17.

the Jewish social and intellectual elites worldwide have been "silent" for decades about the unspeakable crimes that their fellow Jews in Israel have been methodically inflicting on the Palestinians, without penalty and mostly without media coverage, for over half a century. With his anti-Catholic message of hate taken care of, Wiesel, who has never been able to furnish proof that he actually was a detainee at Auschwitz, was now ready to speak about his own supposedly eye-witness experience:

> *As for myself, I do not know. The boy that began to talk to you tonight, where is he? Did he dream or live his dreams of fear and fire? Did he really witness the agony of mankind, through the death of his community? Did he really see the triumph of brutality, did he hear or imagine the laughter of the executioner? Did he really see killers throwing children, Jewish children, into the flames alive? I rarely speak about this; but in this place we must. For a very long time I resisted accepting the story as mine. For years and years I clung to the belief that it was all a dream, a nightmare. No, I did not see the children. I did not see the flames.*

Then, going beyond the all-too-familiar game of playing hide-and-seek with his audience by entertaining the possibility that what he thought he had seen was actually a nightmare, Wiesel effortlessly reached those heights of Holocaust kitsch for which he is famous when he intoned:

> *It was no dream. It was real. Jewish children, living Jewish children were thrown into the flames in order to save money because the gas was costly.*

True to form, and determined not to disappoint his audience, Wiesel, in the end, behaved as the "kitschman of genius" that he really is! Yes, that was why these huge imaginary pits had been dug! What he called "the gas," presumably Zyklon B, had apparently become very "costly;" this new fact about the steep rise in gas prices in 1944 was one that the Holocaust historians had never mentioned before. Somehow the subject of German concern for cost effectiveness during the Holocaust had been neglected by the Holocaust historians all these years!

Wiesel's performance, and the support given to this ritualized denunciation of Butz and his book by Northwestern University, offer ample proof of the extent to which prominent research universities have abdicated their responsibility to seek the truth, no matter where it leads. Jewish megadonors, backed by the Zionist media, do indeed matter, and Northwestern, like other major research universities, did not dare to cross them. Compounding its betrayal of its mission, Northwestern University Press hastily produced a pamphlet entitled *Dimensions of the Holocaust*, which contained the texts of the speeches made on that occasion. Today that document stands as concrete proof of Northwestern's betrayal of academic standards for the presentation of evidence in learned discourse. *Dimensions* was dishonest in its essence, for it provided only one point of view, and did not allow Butz a single word of rebuttal. Even worse, the Holocaustians were so afraid of the truthful message contained in Butz's book that they did not even permit his name or the name of his book to be printed in *Dimensions*. Had they been so certain that the Holocaust had happened as mythologized, and that Butz was a "flat earther" or, even worse, a "neo-Nazi," why did they go to such lengths to suppress any information about the man and his work?

Northwestern University incurred further shame and embarrassment when, just two years later, the declassification and publication of the aerial photography of Auschwitz proved beyond a shadow of a doubt both that Butz had been right and that Wiesel was a liar.

A few years later, in 1983, Wiesel stated why he had gone to Northwestern:[405]

> *There are sixty-five books now trying to prove that the Holocaust is nothing but an invention, that Jews did not die, that Jews did not suffer. They are saying these things while we are still alive. What can be more vicious than to deprive the victim of his suffering? I went to Northwestern to protest, and the president of the university told me, "What can we do to Butz? He has tenure." I said, "Why didn't the faculty at least sign a declaration of moral condemnation?" They did, and out of twelve hundred members of the faculty only four hundred signed it. This is what hurts me. This is the enemy. Those who let Butz get away with it, they frighten me. I am terribly disturbed by the Butz thing.*

Not surprisingly, various Zionist media outlets rushed to the defense of the Holocaust in the wake of the appearance of Butz's book. *Time,* in a review of Wiesel's 1978 book, *A Jew Today*, intoned:[406]

> *Wiesel's hottest outrage is reserved for the so-called scholarship of revisionists who call the Holocaust a myth, or in the words of Northwestern Professor Arthur Butz, "the hoax of the century." Replies Wiesel: "Where has a people disappeared? Where are they hiding?" In fury, he asks why academics have not boycotted Butz and why students have not walked out on his classes.*

These are very good questions, indeed. As for the silence of the conformist historians, they know that Butz is right, but they fear Jewish payback if they say so publicly.

As a result of the self-censorship involved in *Dimensions of the Holocaust*, some thirteen years later, a second edition had to be produced that offered footnotes, including one that indicated who Butz was and what he had done to trigger this anti-intellectual exorcism ritual. But the new edition continued to offer no information about the content of Butz's book, the nature of his argument, or the fact that no conformist historian, at Northwestern or elsewhere, had dared to rebut rather than condemn him.

---

[405] Elie Wiesel, "Questions and Answers at Brandeis-Bardin," in Abrahamson, *Against Silence*, vol. 3, 251-2

[406] "Jeremiah II," *Time*, December 25, 1978, 81.

Wiesel, His Credibility in Doubt, Defends the Veterans Again

Wiesel's less-than-satisfactory performance at Northwestern caused him to be a bit more cautious about what he said publicly. Whereas the *New York Times* had just a few years earlier boasted about his Holocaust literature course at City College, he by now had apparently stopped talking to students about his own alleged experiences as a part of that course. In 1977, he told one interviewer, for instance, "I rarely talk to them about the war or about myself."[407] This was quite a reversal for *the* eyewitness to the Holocaust, especially if we recall that he had no formal education to speak of and was clearly not an intellectual. If Wiesel was not going to speak about what he had seen, what was it then that he was going to speak about?

This reticence on his part about what he had supposedly seen at Auschwitz quickly extended to a similar reticence about the Holocaust as a whole. Fellow Holocaustian Michael Berenbaum would later say of him:[408]

> *Wiesel virtually rules out any discussion of the Holocaust. He relates to it as an Event, unlike any other event, as a world apart from this world. Any comparison, any invocations of the ordinary categories of history or of art is a sacrilege.*

The very word "Event," which Wiesel had used at his Northwestern performance, and as used here by Berenbaum, would be employed by Wiesel more and more frequently in the future as a distraction from the fact that the word "Holocaust" was now becoming an embarrassment to him. Since the word referred directly to the nonexistent burning pits that he claimed to have seen, he gradually stopped using it, using terms like "event," "whirlwind," and "catastrophe" instead.

Another reason that might explain why Wiesel was beginning to pull back a bit was because of his growing concern that, due to his having gone to Northwestern to condemn Butz, fellow Holocaustians might look to him in the future as a kind of SWAT team to defend the Holocaust. As such, they might even, under certain circumstances, call upon him to offer court testimony, presumably under oath, against those who would later come to be called "Holocaust deniers." Wiesel, knowing that his personal Holocaust narrative was largely fabricated, must have privately shuddered at such a possibility.

On April 1, 1977, just days before Wiesel's appearance at Northwestern, his essay "A Plea for the Survivors" appeared in France as a chapter in his book *Un juif aujourd'hui* (*A Jew Today*, 1978). In it he defended once again the absurd eyewitness testimonies of notional veterans of the camps,

---

[407] Cohen, *Qui êtes-vous ?*, 54: "Je leur parle rarement de la guerre et je parle rarement de moi-même."

[408] Michael Berenbaum, "The Spoken Word and the Temptation of Silence," *America*, November 19, 1988, 413.

as he had done in 1966 in *Le chant des morts* (*Legends of Our Time*, 1968), as discussed in the previous chapter, and in 1970, in *Entre Deux Soleils* (*One Generation After*, 1970), quoted at the beginning of this chapter. His return to this subject for the third time since 1966 suggests that Hannah Arendt had indeed touched a raw Jewish nerve in 1963. In giving voice to the widespread Jewish skepticism that existed with regard to the difficult-to-believe passivity of Jews as they waited patiently to go into the gas chambers, she had let the cat out of the bag. In fact, why would Wiesel have even broached this subject if he felt that all Jews were safely aboard the Holocaust train that he was driving? Published as the final chapter in *Un juif*, this piece is probably Wiesel's most troubled essay, for it acknowledges, once again, the general skepticism with which the testimony of the veterans was generally received by other Jews.

In fact, in comparison with his defense of the veterans in the two previous essays, "A Plea for the Survivors" represents further retrenchment. What? Jews standing patiently for ten to twelve hours at a time while they waited their turn to go into the gas chamber? Who ever heard of Jews, 10,000 to 20,000 of them at a time, being duped by the *goyim* on that scale? The whole story was totally ridiculous! Wiesel, addressing these skeptical fellow Jews, writes:[409]

> *They had hardly come to live among you, when you started berating them in your living rooms and your periodicals. Inquiries, discussions, debates. Why were the Jewish Councils created? Why was there a special Jewish Police Force? Why were there Jewish* kapos*? Why did the victims walk like cattle into the slaughterhouse? Why this and why that?*

This reference by Wiesel to the Jewish Councils (*Judenräte*) touched a raw nerve among postwar European Jews. In France, the 74,000, mostly stateless Jews who were deported under Germany's resettlement program were identified, arrested and sent to camps in the East by fellow, mostly native-born French Jews working for the various Jewish Councils in cooperation with the umbrella group, the *Union Générale des Israélites de France* (*UGIF*). Yet after the war these collaborators were not arrested or prosecuted for their allegedly lethal "collaboration" with the enemy. The immunity tacitly granted to them by the French Communists who had the dominant role in the *épuration*, the government-driven policy of vengeance against wartime "collaborators," offers further eloquent testimony to the fact that, despite all the lies cooked up mostly by the Soviets at Nuremberg about an alleged extermination program, Jews tacitly understood among themselves that no such thing had really happened. These thousands of Jews who had

[409] Wiesel, *Un juif*, 199: "A peine se trouvaient-ils parmi vous, que déjà on s'acharnait contre eux dans les salons, dans les revues. Enquêtes, discussions, débats: pourquoi les Judenräte? Pourquoi la police juive? Pourquoi les kapos juifs? Pourquoi les victimes marchaient-elles comme le bétail à l'abattoir? Pourquoi ceci et pourquoi cela?"

worked with the Germans – of whom many were either anti-Communist and/or pro-German, for whatever reason – got off scot-free and were conveniently overlooked during the *épuration*. One of the supreme ironies of this situation was that any particular boatload of European "displaced persons" arriving in New York right after the war would have contained not only Jews who had been deported under the resettlement program, but also Jewish agents of the German government who had helped to round them up and send them there. This subject is so explosive that it has been excluded from the Jewish Holocaust narrative from Day One. Needless to say, no conformist historian has ever touched it either.

Yes, the Holocaust story was just too much for critical-minded Jews to believe. New York Jews generally did not behave in such a docile manner nor, as far as they could remember, had their immigrant parents.

If anything, it was, as Wiesel wrote in this essay, the element of passivity and collaboration in the Holocaust narrative that tipped his fellow Jews off to the fact that the gas chamber story was a hoax made up after the fact. In the face of such whisperings, Wiesel made the argument, clearly addressed to other Jews, that, since the self-qualified "survivors" were the only ones who knew what had really happened, other Jews, who were not there, such as Alfred Kazin and Saul Bellow discussed above in Chapter V, should hold their peace. By this reasoning, the testimonies of self-identified veterans like himself should not be studied or analyzed too closely because anyone who had not been there would never understand anyway. Having demanded Jewish self-censorship, Wiesel resorts to one of his familiar rhetorical devices, denying having said what he just said:[410]

> *Let no one misunderstand me: in no way do I suggest that the concentration camp phenomenon must not be studied. On the contrary, I am saying that it must be studied, again and again, every aspect of it, and everything that has been written about it.*

Having rebuked fellow Jews for their irreverence toward, and skepticism about, the survivors, Wiesel finally gets around to his real reason for asking these fellow Jews to stop questioning the Holocaust. The rapid growth of revisionism had completely changed the situation, and this new threat could only be confronted if all Jews fell into lockstep against it. So what, Wiesel seemed to be saying in coded terms, if the Holocaust never happened the way the survivors said it did? There was a bigger threat now, Holocaust revisionism, and Jews had to stick together to fight it:[411]

---

[410] *Ibid.*, 196: "Que l'on me comprenne bien: je ne suggère nullement qu'il ne faille pas étudier le fait concentrationnaire. Je dis, au contraire, qu'il faut l'étudier, encore et encore, sous toutes ses formes et dans toutes ses expressions."

[411] *Ibid.*, 197: "Fini le temps où l'on retenait son souffle dès que l'on évoquait l'holocauste. Fini le temps où les morts incitaient au recueillement et non à la profanation."

> *The days when people held their breath at the mention of the Holocaust are gone. As are the days when the dead elicited meditation rather than disrespect.*

In this essay, in an attempt to make the revisionists seem simple-minded, Wiesel distorted what they were actually saying:[412]

> *There are dozens and dozens of satirical tracts, published in a dozen languages, which categorically deny that European Jews died in the camps.*

The revisionists did not in any way question the fact that Jews had died in the camps, but stipulated that their deaths were part of the total war that afflicted victims of every nationality, and were not the result of a German government-organized extermination plan. He also attacked Professor Robert Faurisson, although not by name. In doing so, he was finally forced to admit how serious the threat actually was, for Faurisson was assaulting the gas chambers, the very foundation of the Holocaustian belief system:[413]

> *And a French university professor adds: there exists no proof that there were ever gas chambers at Birkenau.*

Wiesel ended his essay by calling upon his fellow Jews once again to close ranks behind the veterans instead of constantly carping at them:[414]

> *This, then, is their request: leave them alone; and, for the love of heaven, cut them some slack. If they can't bring you up to their level, don't try to bring them down to yours.*

Yes, the revisionists were exerting a powerful and immediate influence on the development of the Holocaust narrative. They had mounted a grassroots intellectual insurgency against the forces of Zionist Jewish hegemony, and were winning. But, as in any guerrilla war, the media in government-controlled areas was not permitted to let the people know what was happening.

1978: *Annus Horribilis* for the Emerging "Holocaust"

In 1978, the airing of the NBC television series *Holocaust* marked another major turning point in Wiesel's career. On one level, it signaled an absolute triumph for him. *His* subject, the Holocaust, was used as the title of a propaganda series aired on the Jewish-owned and -operated NBC network. Millions of people saw it. The series claimed to be the definitive version of that "Event," and would notionally fix forever in the minds of the

---

412 *Ibid.*: "Des dizaines et des dizaines de pamphlets, publiés dans une dizaine de langues, nient catégoriquement la mort des juifs européens dans les camps."

413 *Ibid.*: "Et un universitaire français ajoute: il n'existe pas de preuve que les chambres à gaz aient vraiment existé à Birkenau."

414 *Ibid.*, 203: "Voici donc leur requête: laissez-leur en paix, pour l'amour du ciel, accordez-leur un peu de répit. S'ils ne peuvent pas vous élever à leur niveau, n'essayez pas de les abaisser au vôtre."

public the use, by the evil Germans, of monstrous gas chambers to kill millions of Jews. Of course, the media reviews were overwhelmingly positive. But Wiesel, alone among the Holocaust fundamentalists, was not pleased. Although he could not say so directly, he refused to go along with the Zionist-media-driven euphoria for one simple reason: the media, in insisting on the primacy of the gas chambers in the Holocaust, were implicitly condemning his flaming pits to oblivion.

For Wiesel, this was very serious business. After all, when he had insisted on the use of the word "Holocaust," and slowly but surely had seen it capitalized in the pages of the *New York Times* and, from there, spread to the rest of the controlled media, his goal was to emphasize his personal witness of burning, not of gassing. Thus, it was in part for this reason that Wiesel would not go along with the official euphoria. Since the appearance of Butz's book, as his pleas in *A Jew Today* confirm, doubts were spreading about the veracity of his testimony among fellow Jews, including powerful ones whose opinions mattered. This was not what he had had in mind when he and Abe Rosenthal launched the Holocaust as his proprietary brand in the pages of the *New York Times* in the early 1970s. Things were slipping out of his hands. He was losing control.

The mass media, despite all their good intentions in wanting to emphasize Jewish suffering above and beyond the suffering of any other group, were part of American culture, with its religion of boosterism and its Barnum and Bailey antics. While he could comfort himself with the thought that the media would always give primacy to Jewish suffering, there already seemed to be too many people (other than himself) making money off the Holocaust cash cow. While he had not legally patented the trademark "Holocaust," he had expected that other Jews would recognize that it was his shtick and back off. What he had pictured in his mind as a story of tragedy in which he, with his long, sad face, would forever have the lead role, was now being vulgarized and infringed.

Various Holocaustians would in fact later refer to this packaging, exploiting and profiting from the Holocaust as the "Americanization of the Holocaust," but that fact offered little if any comfort to Wiesel.[415] Even worse, perhaps, than all the unauthorized profiteers jumping on the bandwagon was the fact that the supposed lessons of the Holocaust were now beginning to be adapted and applied to all sorts of non-Jewish types of suffering, as in terms such as "Cambodian holocaust." This was a develop-

---

[415] Alvin H. Rosenfeld, "The Americanization of the Holocaust," in *idem* (ed.), *Thinking about the Holocaust* (Bloomington: Indiana University Press, 1997), 119-150; Peter Novick, *The Holocaust in American Life* (N.Y.: Houghton-Mifflin, 1999); Hilène Flanzbaum (ed.), *The Americanization of the Holocaust* (Baltimore: Johns Hopkins University Press, 1999).

ment that Wiesel had not foreseen and, as a Jewish racist, simply could not tolerate.

Thus, unexpectedly, Wiesel decided to attack the NBC television series *Holocaust*. The blockbuster "docudrama" premiered at 8:00 PM on Sunday evening, April 16, 1978, and continued for three successive Sundays. It chronicled the fictional lives of people in two families, one Jewish and one German, between 1935 and 1945. It was to be the supreme achievement in the realm of Holocaust kitsch but, as mentioned above, the series slighted Wiesel's burning thesis, encapsulated in his word "Holocaust," in favor of the gassing thesis. However indirectly, the series undermined his authority as the premier eyewitness to the Holocaust. The fact that this damage came so soon after Butz's demolition of the myth of Auschwitz as an extermination camp made the series doubly toxic for him.

When Wiesel launched his attack, in the pages of the *New York Times* of course, his was virtually the only important media voice that dared to criticize that terribly flawed, melodramatic and propagandistic docudrama. Since he could not say outright what I have just stated above, he opted to fault the Jewish media barons, and in particular Gerald Green, the Jewish novelist and propagandist who had written the script of the series, with having turned the Holocaust into a soap opera. He added for good measure the legitimate accusation that the producers had presented as factual certain events that could not have happened as they are portrayed. *How ironic that a first class prevaricator like Wiesel should be taking fellow Jews to task for misrepresenting the Holocaust*!

Wiesel was also upset that Green and his staff had conned many groups into supporting his docudrama even before seeing it. Wiesel wrote:[416]

> *Many Jewish and non-Jewish organizations supported the project and promoted it among their members. But they did so even before they could view the programs.*

Green and his team had also produced a study guide to accompany the series, so that students could undergo further Holocaust brainwashing in their school classrooms. Wiesel also averred that he had been asked to write the introduction to this study guide without having first seen the program, but refused. He wrote:[417]

> *I did take Mr. Green's advice in one respect. I "addressed* [my] *views about* [his] *untrue, offensive and cheap" program to Rabbi Irving Greenberg* [the same man who a few years earlier had hired Wiesel at City College and then made him a Distinguished Professor], *who, interestingly, reminded me that he had asked me long before the first screening to write the introduction to the*

416 Elie Wiesel, "Trivializing the Holocaust: Semi-Fact and Semi-Fiction," *New York Times*, April 16, 1978, 75.

417 Elie Wiesel, "Wiesel Answers Green," *New York Times*, April 30, 1978, D39.

> *now much-touted interagency study guide and that I had agreed to do so, if I liked the film. Well, I saw the film; he did not. I wrote no introduction; he did. To his regret.*

Here again, there is a wonderful jewel of irony hidden in Wiesel's statement. After all, such study guides for *Night* generally offer a very shallow and superficial discussion of the novel and its historical context. Yet Wiesel has never condemned these exercises in Jewish propaganda and brainwashing.

This media controversy, like others that are cooked up by the *New York Times*, and already alluded to above, was intended to reinforce the idea that, while the Jewish Holocaust narrative was basically true, there still existed honest differences of opinion among Holocaustians as to how to communicate that supposed truth. This game has been replayed in the pages of the *New York Times* a seemingly infinite number of times for one simple reason: it is needed as a distraction from the essential issues.

As for Wiesel's behavior when confronted by this TV series, the main issue was whether or not the elimination from the series of his flaming pits, whence had come the current and prevailing use in popular culture of the very word "Holocaust," was an oversight. In other words, why is the word "Holocaust" used to describe killings in gas chambers?

Wiesel's violent attack should also be read as an expression of his frustration at being pushed to the side as other, newer people took over the franchise. In a word, he had tangible proof that he was indeed losing control of the business he had launched, and various members of the "board" of what Prof. Norman Finkelstein has called "the Holocaust Industry" were pushing him out. As they were taking over Wiesel's market, they were also deleting any reference to his original vision of the Holocaust as consisting of vast open pits in which multitudes of Jews were burned!

Like any entrepreneur who comes up with a new idea and a new product, Wiesel had been forced to bring in large capital investors like Abe Rosenthal and the *New York Times* in order to go public. In the process, he knew that he would surely amass enormous wealth for himself, but he does not seem to have understood that, at the same time, with new investors on board, his version of the Holocaust would be airbrushed out of existence simply because most of the investors did not believe him. And this is exactly what Wiesel saw taking place before his eyes. Although he had indeed developed and then hyped the Holocaust as a product, the corporate marketing men, working for and implementing the agendas of the extremist Jewish billionaires who represent the very summits of Holocaust fundamentalism, were taking over, and Wiesel, along with his vision of the Holocaust, was being pushed aside.

Alfred Kazin, Self-Professed "New York Jew," Mocks Wiesel

As we have seen, one of the first people to express disbelief about the hanging episode in *Night* was the New York intellectual Alfred Kazin. Thirteen years Wiesel's senior, he had published a positive review of *Night* in a small intellectual weekly called *The Reporter*. Wiesel, always seeking to advance his career, contacted Kazin. The son of Yiddish-speaking immigrants, Kazin, like many such people, had successfully avoided military service during the war years. Wiesel appears to have initiated the friendship, but it would eventually end in an acrimonious breakup. As in the earlier breakups with his kabbala teacher in Sighet during the war, his mystical master, "Shushani," and later Mauriac, Wiesel's imperious personality and congenital mendacity played pivotal roles. It appears to have happened gradually over time.

In 1978, Kazin wrote of having attended a lecture by Wiesel in which "everything Wiesel said was pitched high, stabbed you and was meant to stab you with the impossibility of finding words for Jewish suffering." Kazin, who was seated opposite his friend Saul Bellow, whom he described as "bored by the flow of words" coming from Wiesel's mouth, noted that Wiesel lacked any sense of irony or detachment about the Holocaust. Wiesel's insistence caused Kazin to conclude, quite rightly, that "the Jews could not state their case without seeming to overstate it. The world was getting tired of our complaint."[418] Kazin, in writing such words, was violating a major taboo among New York and other Jews: he was publicly mocking Elie Wiesel, which no one else had ever dared to do until then. He would later draw more blood from Wiesel, as I have discussed in more detail above, on the issue of the hanging scene in *Night*, and would be severely rebuked for it in the pages of *Tous les fleuves*. However, Kazin's attack on Wiesel in 1978 happened to coincide with the advent of major revisionist criticism of the alleged Auschwitz gas chambers, and was thus especially painful to him.

1978: Zionist Media Campaign on "Why Auschwitz Was Not Bombed"

Ironically, at the same time as the Zionist media controversy about the NBC Holocaust docudrama was dying down, the Holocaust fundamentalists at the American Jewish Committee came up with a new topic with which to assail the American public about the Holocaust. The subject was a simple one: if 10,000 to 20,000 people a day were being killed in Auschwitz in 1944, the Allies, through their overflights of the camp, must have

---

[418] Alfred Kazin, *New York* Jew (N.Y.: Alfred A Knopf, 1978), 285.

known about the supposed atrocities occurring there. Thus, why did they not bomb Auschwitz? David S. Wyman, writing in the group's monthly magazine, called the Auschwitz camp a "killing installation." He assured his readers that "gas was a far more efficient means of mass murder than shooting, and it caused much less of a psychological problem to the killers. The operation of the gas chambers, which killed over 2,000 people in less than half an hour, required only a limited number of SS men."[419] The man's imagination, which could not be bothered with the technical problems that would have been involved with such a huge industrial undertaking, had taken possession of his mind. There was nothing new about this ridiculous assertion, for it was standard Holocaustian boilerplate. Wyman, an excellent example of a gentile whose academic career benefitted greatly from his unquestioning adherence to Holocaust orthodoxy, would later publish *The Abandonment of the Jews: America and the Holocaust, 1941-1945* (N.Y.: Pantheon Books, 1984). He was also rewarded by the Holocaustians when, in 1991, they named the David S. Wyman Institute for Holocaust Studies after him.

About six months later, the Catholic liberals at *Commonweal* dutifully followed the Jewish myth propagated by *Commentary* when Roger M. Williams repeated Wyman's piece. He added a few details not found in Wyman's article, emphasizing a different set of claims that are also a part of the orthodox Holocaustian version of events. He told his readers, for instance, that in 1944 "the crematoria were renovated, the chimneys strengthened with iron bands, and large pits [for mass cremations] were dug behind the buildings."[420] Two months later, in January 1979, the aerial photography of Auschwitz would reveal that these articles were without merit: simply put, there had been no killing installations at Auschwitz to bomb. Taken when the extermination was supposedly at its height, the photos gave no sign of gas chambers or the burning pits needed to deal with the thousands of corpses allegedly produced each day. The publication of these pictures justified, in one stroke, the suspicion with which Pius XII had greeted anti-German rumors and allegations made by the various U.S. Jewish groups during the war. Ironically, the CIA's publication of these pictures showed in a strong, forthright and definitive way the fact that the Pontiff's silence about the purported Holocaust had been more than justified.[421]

---

[419] David S. Wyman, "Why Auschwitz Was Never Bombed," *Commentary* (May 1978), 38.

[420] Roger M. Williams, "Why Wasn't Auschwitz Bombed?" *Commonweal*, November 24, 1978, 747.

[421] In Germany, the world's foremost Orwellian state, the appearance of the aerial photography showing that there had been no Holocaust at Auschwitz and thus no need to bomb the railway lines leading to the camp did not impede the publication of an absurd book on the subject. See: Heiner Lichtenstein, *Warum Auschwitz nicht bombardiert wurde* (Cologne: Bund-Verlag, 1980). Judging by the fact that Lichtenstein's book has never

As 1978 came to a close, Professor Robert Faurisson, a chaired professor at the University of Lyon, whose specialty was close reading of literary texts, published an article in the prestigious Parisian daily *Le Monde*. Entitled "Le Problème des chambres à gaz, ou la rumeur d'Auschwitz," [The Problem of the Gas Chambers: or the Auschwitz Rumor] it appeared on November 19, 1978. A second article, with the same title, also appeared in *Le Monde* on January 16, 1979. It contained Faurisson's response to a series of articles and editorials in *Le Monde* denouncing him, and appeared under the French media's traditional recognition of a "droit de réponse," a right to respond.[422] About five weeks after the publication of Faurisson's response, *Le Monde* allowed itself to have the last word on this polemical exchange when it published a public letter from thirty-four historians denouncing Faurisson again (see on p. 305 below).

Also in January 1979, Wilhelm Stäglich published *Der Auschwitz Mythos: Legende oder Wirklichkeit?*[368] Before long, the German judicial authorities, under strictly enforced Zionist occupation, ordered the book to be confiscated and destroyed in Germany, which meant that any copy found by the authorities anywhere had to be burned in waste incinerators under police supervision. Within just a few years, starting with Butz's book in 1976, a societal doctrine that had been accepted without question since 1945 was suddenly being subjected to very serious scrutiny.

Between the appearance of Butz's *Hoax* and Stäglich's and Faurisson's publications, Yehuda Bauer, an Israeli professor and, some would say, currently dean of the conformist historians who specialize in the Holocaust, published a book entitled *The Holocaust in Historical Perspective*. In it, he dismissed both Butz and his predecessor Paul Rassinier as examples of people who engage in "Nazi gutter historiography."[423] Butz was consigned to the gutter because he had violated the rule that one may only consult the official Nuremberg record when studying the Holocaust. In writing his ground-breaking study, Butz had consulted new and different types of available information, thereby violating Holocaustian control over historiography, that is, the evidence that one is allowed to use in dealing with this topic. Bauer had no means of rebutting Butz on the facts of his case, so he had to resort to this *ad hominem* assault, which has since become the default setting for Holocaust fundamentalists like Bauer. When the revisionists use facts, like the aerial photos of Auschwitz, to make their point, the

---

been translated into English, one can conclude that the Holocaust Fundamentalists take a dim few of its probative value.

[422] This "affaire Faurisson" is documented in Serge Thion (ed.), *Vérité historique ou vérité politique?* (Paris: La Vielle Taupe, 1980); see also Robert Faurisson, *Mémoire en défense* (Paris: La Vieille Taupe, 1980).

[423] Yehuda Bauer, *The Holocaust in Historical Perspective* (Seattle: University of Washington Press, 1978), 38; cf. also Bauer's *A History of the Holocaust* (New York: Benjamin Watts, 1982).

Holocaustians, who control discourse in both the media and academe, have the choice of either labeling them "Holocaust deniers" or ignoring them altogether. They usually take the latter course.

Israel Loyalist Stuart Eizenstat Plans a "Holocaust Museum"

Stuart Eizenstat served on Jimmy Carter's White House staff in various key capacities from 1977 to 1981. These were the years in which the Holocaust, centered in the alleged extermination at Auschwitz, was beginning to succumb to the results of revisionist scholarship. The release of the aerial photography might be called the metaphorical last shovel full of dirt that closed its grave. The Holocaust, including Wiesel's eyewitness claims, as factual history was dead. The Holocaust fundamentalists, understandably, were not about to allow their myth to be destroyed without a fight, though.

These attacks on the Holocaust from outside the U.S. Jewish community, as noted above, followed upon and complemented the ongoing doubts among American Jews about what the survivors were claiming to have endured. As Hannah Arendt had observed in 1963, their behavior had not only been passive, it had also included collaboration with the Germans. Wiesel's essays, directed to such Jewish Holocaust skeptics, culminate, as I have shown, in his appeal to such doubters to stop directing pointed questions to the "survivors." Now that revisionism was growing, he argued, such questioning only helped the revisionists.

It is within this context of challenges from both within and without that we can best understand the strong reaction of powerful Holocaust fundamentalists like Eizenstat. Understandably, they were not about to let their myth be destroyed without a fight. After all, the justification for the very existence of Israel, which had already become an apartheid state in 1967, depended in large part on the Holocaust. But if the Holocaust, centered on the myth of the gas chambers of Auschwitz, were to be proved false, then Israel's most important *raison d'être* would be lost. It was for this reason that Eizenstat and his fellow Holocaust fundamentalists hatched the idea of buttressing the Holocaust by building in the nation's capital a place of veneration for Jewish victimhood. In doing so, they would transform their self-serving myth into the state religion of an increasingly secularized America. Unfortunately, due to the cowardice and collaboration of President Carter, they were able to get their plan off the ground.

According to Wiesel's biographer Mark Chmiel, discontent with Carter's views on the Mideast in the U.S. Jewish Community was such that "one aide in particular felt that Carter could begin to make amends for his alleged Middle East miscues by visiting a Holocaust studies center in New

York."[424] Carter apparently refused to do this, so more drastic medicine was recommended to bring him into line. According to Judith Miller:[425]

> *The idea of a national Holocaust memorial was initially promoted in mid-1977 by three Jewish officials in Jimmy Carter's Administration: Stuart Eizenstat, Carter's chief domestic policy adviser; Mark A. Siegel, a liaison with the Jewish community who worked on the White House staff, and Ellen Goldstein, another staff member.*

Eizenstat had been concerned, she says, not only about the erosion of memory of the war among people of his generation, but also about the growing incidents of Holocaust revisionism.

According to Miller, Carter was not interested in the idea, so it languished for a year. But as a result of Carter's having spoken out in favor of a "homeland" for the Palestinians and having approved the sale of F-15 fighter jets to Saudi Arabia (actions that were in the national interest of all citizens of the United States), the leaders of the U.S. Jewish Lobby, driven by their passionate attachment to Israel, went into overdrive. As a symbolic gesture and a slap in the face to Carter, Holocaust fundamentalist Siegel resigned from his job as liaison to these unregistered agents for Israel. Carter then panicked, for American Jews were the main bankrollers of the Democratic Party. Without their financial and media support, he would face grave difficulties in the next election cycle. As a result, as Miller tells us, he caved in and gave them what they wanted:[426]

> *In March 1978, Goldstein sent a second memorandum about a national Holocaust memorial, this time to Eizenstat, who in turn discussed the matter with the President. Three months later, Carter surprised a group of rabbis he was meeting in the Rose Garden by saying he had decided to appoint a commission to explore the construction of a Holocaust memorial.*

Naively, Carter insisted that, since this project was what Miller calls "specific" to the U.S. Jewish community, "they would have to finance it" (Miller, *One by One*, 259). Hyman Bookbinder of the American Jewish Committee agreed:

> *After $3 billion a year for Israel, it would have been unseemly to beg for $100 million for a museum.* (*Ibid.*, 258f.)

But the catch is that the Holocaustians did not "beg" for their money; they simply waited a few years and then ordered their puppets in the U.S. Congress to allocate it to them. Under our Judeocentric form of government, in which the members of the U.S. Congress are held hostage by Jewish media and financial power, the U.S. taxpayer must now pay for this absurd "mu-

---

[424] Mark Chmiel, *Elie Wiesel and the Politics of Moral Leadership* (Philadelphia: Temple University Press, 2001), 117.

[425] Miller, *One by One*, 255.

[426] *Ibid.*, 255f.

seum" that is "specific" in its service to one ethnic group. Carter's final concern was to find someone to lead his Commission. He decided on Wiesel, since his advisors had assured him that "his appointment would not be controversial" (*Elie Wiesel*, 118). Thus, on November 1, 1978, the Commission on Remembering the Holocaust was created with Elie Wiesel as its Chairman. He presided over a group of thirty-four people, most of them Jewish.

Robert F. Drinan's Unholy Alliance with Wiesel

As these events were taking place, they were supported by yet another betrayal of Catholic tradition and culture by a Catholic priest. For just as priests like Francis X. Murphy (Xavier Rynne), Edward H. Flannery and Malachi Martin (Michael Sarafian) had worked day in and day out on the American Jewish Committee plantation for the greater glory of Israel and "the Holocaust" during Vatican II, a Jesuit priest, Robert F. Drinan, now became their successor as a standard bearer for such causes. Drinan, who had been representing the heavily Jewish 4th Congressional District of Massachusetts since 1970, sold his soul to the Holocaustians when he published *Honor the Promise: America's Commitment to Israel*.[427] The book can be seen as one that established a new paradigm for Catholic intellectuals willing to compromise core beliefs and ignore the weight of Catholic tradition in order to find a larger and overwhelmingly approving audience in and around the Zionist media and collaborationist academe. The book should also be seen clearly in the context in which it appeared: the Holocaust, the justification for Israel's very existence, was now under attack by revisionism, and Drinan, beholden to the wealthy Jewish liberals from Brookline and Newton who had financed his campaigns, was most likely catering to their whims, if not following their orders.

In addition, Wiesel, after working at City College for four years, moved to Boston University in the fall of 1976. Once there, although he commuted back and forth to New York by plane, he befriended Drinan, writing the foreword to the Jesuit's pro-Zionist screed. Finally, it is important to remember that revisionists have vigorously defended Pius XII against his attackers: for instance, Arthur Butz, in his *Hoax of the Twentieth Century*, devoted an appendix to a vindication of the Pope with regard to the charge that he had been silent during the Holocaust.

Drinan's book, with Wiesel's imprimatur, unabashedly defended the indefensible: the imposition of a Zionist state on the native population of Palestine. It was a pure piece of Zionist propaganda that staffers at the American Jewish Committee could have penned. But Drinan, an opportun-

---

[427] Garden City, N.Y.: Doubleday, 1977.

ist who wanted to see his name mentioned approvingly in the Zionist media as someone who had "courage" and who did not fear to "speak out," had already compromised his integrity as a Catholic priest by supporting abortion.

With regard to Pius XII and his alleged "silence" during "the Holocaust," Drinan fudged his position, neither strongly defending nor strongly accusing Pius XII. He did, however, accuse that Pontiff – correctly I might add – of opposing the creation of Israel. Drinan wrote, without mentioning Pius XII by name:

> *Whatever one might conclude about the Holy See's attitude toward the Holocaust, it is unfortunately impossible to conclude that the Holy See gave very much encouragement to the next struggle of the world's Jews – the establishment of Israel.* (*Honor*, 53)

But what the Zionist stooge Drinan saw as a reason for blame, history has shown to be a reason for praise. Ironically, as time goes by, Pacelli's ability to see the future apartheid State of Israel for what it was speaks volumes about the man's wisdom, foresight, courage, integrity and sense of justice.

Drinan's words are those of a sycophant trying to curry favor with his Jewish bankrollers, and not those of a man possessing a sense of either history or justice.

January 1979: the Month When the Holocaust Died

In January 1979, out of the blue and for reasons unknown, two CIA staffers published several aerial photographs of Auschwitz, taken on four different dates in 1944. For reasons unknown, the Allied aerial photography as a whole had remained hidden from view for forty-five years. These pictures were taken over a period from spring 1944 through January 1945, including the months from May through July when, according to the conformist historians, the Hungarian Jews were allegedly being slaughtered to the tune of 10,000 to 20,000 per day. The mendacity and cynicism of those who had been making this baseless claim since 1945 was shattered by this revelation.[428] When this little book by two former CIA analysts, Dino A. Brugioni and Robert G. Poirier, appeared, several of these pictures became available to the public for the first time. In their general discussion, the authors talk about "external burning pits" (*Holocaust Revisited*, 10) at Birkenau, but are unable to identify even one such "pit" in their photography. With regard to the alleged smoke and flame that Wiesel has claimed to have seen, they are a bit more honest with their reader:

---

[428] Brugioni and Poirier, *Holocaust Revisited.*

> *Although survivors recalled that smoke and flame emanated continually from the crematoria and was visible for miles, the photography we examined gave no proof of this.* (25)

These pictures proved beyond a shadow of a doubt that the vast open pits in which Wiesel had supposedly seen truckloads of children and adults being burned alive were completely imaginary. Nor did these pictures show the long lines of 10,000 to 20,000 Jews waiting patiently each day to be taken to the "gas chambers," or the masses of dead bodies that would have had to be lying about waiting for disposal as successive groups waited to be "gassed."[206]

Mendacity of the *New York Times* and *Washington Post* about the Aerial Photos

It was one thing for the CIA to allow the publication of these pictures that destroyed, once and for all, the myth of Auschwitz as an "extermination camp" where "four million" people had died. But since we live in a Judeocentric "mediacracy," in which the owners of the Zionist media, the Holocaust fundamentalists, actually control the everyday political reality of the world in which Americans live, it would be another thing to see what meaning the Zionist media would assign to this revelation. The answer did not take long in coming, for both the *Washington Post* and the *New York Times*, both owned by wealthy Jewish families who set the "mainstream" media parameters of what right-thinking and respectable people will be allowed to say about "the Holocaust," published their official interpretations within days of each other. In each case, no mention was made of the glaring fact that the pictures revealed that the "eyewitnesses" who had spoken of 10,000 to 20,000 people a day being killed there and, like Wiesel, of massive open pits in which truckloads of Jewish babies were burned alive, were revealed to have been outrageous liars.

Also, in each case, the silent testimony of the pictures about the Holocaust was avoided by orienting the reports around the subject of the "failure to bomb" theme that the Zionists had introduced during 1978. In addition, both newspapers employed this theme in exactly the same way the "failure to mention the word Jew" trope is used when needed as a distraction. This was done even though the pictures showed clearly that there was in fact no reason to bomb!

On February 23, 1979, the *Washington Post* reported[429] that the pictures

> *clearly show the camp's gas chambers and crematoria where victims' bodies were burned. Several photos show prisoners undergoing disinfection and*

[429] Thomas O'Toole, "44 Photos Showed Auschwitz Camp," *Washington Post*, February 23, 1979, A1, 14.

> *standing in line to be tattooed. One photo shows a line of 1500 prisoners being led into the camp from 85 railroad boxcars parked at the end of the rail line just outside the camp.*

Of course, the pictures showed no such thing. What they did show, however, was that the allegation that up to 20,000 Jews a day were waiting in line, stolidly and without incident, to go into the "gas chamber" was a myth. There were no lines of people waiting to go into the "gas chambers," nor was there any evidence of the huge industrial apparatus that would have been necessary to kill and dispose of thousands of people at a time. As for the massive pits that Wiesel claims to have seen, there was no flame and no smoke to be seen. Thus, Wiesel's own personal myth went up in nonexistent smoke, as it were.

The *New York Times* article was more cautious, for the author of its article was not even identified. This fact offered an excellent example of what Pius XII had referred to in his Christmas message of 1951 as the mendacious "anonymous voice" ("*voix anonyme*") of the Western media.[430] In this case, that voice tells us that the two authors of the book, Brugioni and Poirier, had worked on the project on their own time starting in April 1978.[431]

> *The analysts said that the television series* Holocaust*, which included several scenes on a set meant to simulate Auschwitz, had motivated their project.*

Just as in the *Washington Post* review of the book, the narrative voice of the *New York Times* completely avoided the fact that the photos gave no evidence of what the "eye-witnesses" – for years – had been telling us had been there. He wrote:

> *They said that they could identify camp officers marching a newly arrived group of prisoners to the open gates of the gas chamber-crematorium compound. The analysts also pointed to a second group that they said was waiting to be disinfected and tattooed.*

Despite the claim by these two CIA analysts, recycled by the *Washington Post* and *New York Times*, to the effect that these pictures reinforced the Jewish holocaust narrative, both the revisionists and the Holocaust fundamentalists now knew who was right and who was wrong about the allegation that Auschwitz had been an extermination camp. In just a few short

[430] Pope Pius XII, "Radio message au monde, du 24 décembre 1951," in Kothen, *Documents Pontificaux*, vol. 13, 1951, 565. Referring to the millions of individuals who, in the "free world" in the postwar years, had become lazy and were allowing the media to speak for them, he warned that they must not accept the media's pre-packaged opinions as their own, and cautioned specifically against the danger of the "anonymous voice" ("*voix anonyme*") that always speaks through the media, pretending to be objective, but always in the service of its hidden master.

[431] Special to the *New York Times*, "Photos of Auschwitz Extermination Unit Produced," *New York Times*, February 24, 1979, A2. In my opinion, "Special to the NYT" is code for "directly from the CIA."

years, the revisionists had mortally wounded and, with the release of these pictures, slain the Holocaust beast. They were jubilant for the simple reason that their position on the Holocaust had been vindicated.

On the other side, the Holocaust fundamentalists, unhappy that their historical scam had been revealed as such, decided to redouble their efforts to increase pressure on their owned and/or controlled politicians in order to enshrine the Holocaust as the new revealed dogma of the U.S.. By elevating the Holocaust to the level of an article of civic faith, and by imposing it on the U.S. population as the state religion, the Holocaust fundamentalists would be able to contain the revisionists and silence the doubters within the U.S. Jewish community while also using their new religion to justify the unlawful wars for Israel's security that were to come.

1979: British Code Breakers: Another Nail in the Coffin of the Holocaust

By coincidence, at about the same time as the aerial photography of Auschwitz was declassified by the CIA, the distinguished British historian F. H. Hinsley of Cambridge University published his monumental study of British intelligence operations during the war years. It included documentation on the work that British code breakers had done in intercepting and deciphering encrypted German military communications. Hinsley wrote, with reference to the legendary gas chambers that so many "survivors" later said they had seen:[432]

> *From the spring of 1942 until February 1943* [...] *the returns (reports) from Auschwitz, the largest of the camps with 20,000 prisoners, mentioned illness as the main cause of death, but included references to shootings and hangings. There were no references in the decrypts to gassing.*

Hinsley's conclusions dovetail perfectly with the information provided in the Allied aerial photography: there was no "gassing."

Wiesel and Carter Clash over the "Eleven Million"

As the Holocaust was dying as history in February 1979, Wiesel made his first formal statement as the Chairman of the President's Commission on Remembering the Holocaust. Employing the usual chutzpah, Wiesel made it clear that the Commission's members must never ask any probing questions about the Jewish Holocaust narrative. According to Chmiel,

[432] F. H. Hinsley, *et al.*, *British Intelligence in the Second World War: Its Influence on Strategy and Operations* (London: H. M. Stationary Office, 1979), 673; for a detailed analysis of the German radio messages pertaining to Germany's wartime concentration camps, as intercepted and decrypted by the British, see Nicholas Kollerstrom: *Breaking the Spell: The Holocaust, Myth & Reality* (Uckfield, UK: Castle Hill Publishers: 2014).

Wiesel pulled this off by describing "the Holocaust as an unimaginable mystery such that the commission must proceed slowly with fear and trembling" (*Elie Wiesel*, 120). Two months later, at a Holocaust Remembrance Day in the Capitol Rotunda on April 24, Carter stunned Wiesel when he defined "the Holocaust" as consisting of eleven million victims of whom six million were Jews. Since Carter wanted to placate various other non-Jewish ethnic groups, including Poles and Ukrainians, whose voters were mostly Democrats, he had apparently adopted a suggestion offered by Wiesel's arch-enemy, Simon Wiesenthal, enshrining the figure of "eleven million" in his Executive Order # 12169. Wiesel, of course, was "furious" at this turn of events. Thus, a new, but quite small and manageable "controversy" ensued. Since Wiesel's "anger" was purely ritual and completely staged, after the usual posturing had taken place, the "controversy" blew over, and it was back to business as usual – Shoah Business, to be sure.

June 7, 1979: John Paul II at the Auschwitz Monument

As the plan for the Holocaust museum advanced in Washington, Pope John Paul II visited the Auschwitz-Birkenau camp on June 7, 1979. While there, he stopped in front of its infamous propaganda display, mentioned above, that claimed, in eighteen languages, that four million people had perished there. Pausing in front of the Hebrew language version of the inscription, the Pope said:[433]

> *In particular, I pause with you* [...] *before the inscription in Hebrew. This inscription awakens the memory of the people whose sons and daughters were intended for total extermination. This people's origins spring from Abraham, our father in faith, as was expressed by Paul of Tarsus. The very people who received from God the commandment 'Thou shalt not kill,' here experienced in a special way what is meant by killing. It is not permissible for anyone to pass by this inscription with indifference.*

The monument's message, which officially enshrined the Soviet claim of four million dead made at Nuremberg and embraced there by both the U.S. prosecutors and the Zionist-controlled media, was of course completely mendacious. All the concerned parties, including and especially the Holocaust fundamentalists, knew that "four million" people had not died at Auschwitz, yet they remained silent about this deliberate fraud. The Holocaustians' silence about this particular Holocaust lie speaks volumes, for it underscores the deep commonalities that existed between the twin tyrannies of Communism and Zionism. This Soviet-sponsored monument would

---

433 John Vinocur, "Pope Prays at Auschwitz: 'Only Peace,'" *New York Times*, June 8, 1979, A1; also "Homily at Auschwitz, June 7, 1979," in: Eugene Fisher, Leon Klenicki (eds.), *Pope John Paul II, Spiritual Pilgrimage: Texts on Jews and Judaism 1979–1995* (N.Y.: Crossroad, 1995), 7.

remain in place until 1991. But then, because revisionist attacks had transformed its continued presence into an ongoing embarrassment for the Holocaustians, it was quietly removed and replaced with a new one.

The Pope, while speaking of Jewish suffering, had not specifically used the word "Jew" in his remarks. If Wiesel had noted this omission, he held his tongue and had nothing to say for the time being, probably because he was in the process of being hoisted into position as the High Priest of our state religion, the Holocaust. However, nine years later, he would play the tried and true game, so dear to the editors of the *New York Times*, of invoking the "failure to say the word Jew" trope. At that time, he would express "outrage" at John Paul II over this alleged omission. I would argue that Wiesel remained silent about this issue in 1979, but attacked the Pope for it in 1988, because his personal status had changed in the interim. By 1988, he was himself the "Holocaust Pope" of the United States. As such, his attack served to burnish his own credentials as a peer of the Roman Pope.

Wiesel Submits His Report to Carter

Illustration 27: U.S. President Jimmy Carter in thrall to Elie Wiesel

On September 27, 1979, Wiesel's Commission submitted its report to President Carter at the White House. It contained four recommendations. The first was to build a propaganda center, officially labeled as a "Holocaust Museum," in Washington, D. C., in order to brainwash the people of the U.S., especially the nation's children, about the Holocaust. They wanted this facility for "education" purposes in lieu of a monument. The second recommendation called for Carter to find and donate federal land for this propaganda center, which would be paid for by private donations. The third recommendation was that the Holocaust be instituted as the state religion, and for this task to be accomplished by having the Federal Government set aside certain days each year for official "Holocaust Remembrance," with parallel commemorations sponsored in state capitals across the country. The fourth recommendation called for the creation of a standing "Committee on Conscience" to report on human-rights abuses around the world. This last, super-hypocritical proposal was eventually rejected because it endangered the ongoing U.S. policy of engaging in human-rights violations across a wide range of countries around the globe, while simultaneously looking the other way as the Israeli Jews ethnically cleanse the Palestinians from their (the Palestinians') homeland.

It is important to understand that President Carter's designation of Wiesel as the high priest of the emerging Holocaust cult had monumental implications for both Wiesel and for the U.S. people. As Mark Chmiel has correctly pointed out, while using terminology borrowed from the French philosopher Pierre Bourdieu, any sovereign state has a monopoly on the exercise of what he calls "legitimate violence." Thus, when the government of such a state designates an individual as an official representative, that individual inherits a share in the exercise of legitimate violence that the state monopolizes. Chmiel writes:

> *In light of the politics of such official naming and authorizing, then, Wiesel became not only the servant of the state by virtue of his agreement to serve on this Carter-created commission, but he was also a beneficiary of 'the strength of the collective' conferred by the U.S. government itself.* (*Elie Wiesel*, 123)

Chmiel goes on to point out that "by undertaking this unprecedented memorial venture, the U.S. government established the authorized perspective of the "worthy victims" (*Elie Wiesel*, 123), that is, Jews. Thus, Jewish Americans officially became in effect the sacred cows of American culture. As such, they are always victims and never perpetrators, and the state must protect their interests ahead of those of other citizens.

Wiesel Travels to Auschwitz, the "Golgotha" of the Holocaust

In November 1979, Wiesel traveled to Auschwitz, leading a group of forty-four dignitaries who "had been charged by President Carter with the mission to recommend an appropriate program for remembering the victims of the Holocaust."[434] This trip had two major goals: to replicate the visit that John Paul II had made to Auschwitz just five months earlier; and to establish Wiesel's credentials as the emerging Holocaust High Priest of the United States. The *New York Times Magazine* was along for the trip, of course, and that newspaper was now launching, in cooperation with the Holocaust fundamentalists in the various Jewish organizations and the U.S. Government, the campaign to transform the Holocaust, now dead as history, into the mystical national religion of the United States. In a perverse sort of way, and as a parody of Christianity, it would be "resurrected" from the dead and turned into the faith of the nation. Its victims, "the six mil-

---

[434] Elie Wiesel, "Pilgrimage to the Country of Night," *New York Times*, November 4, 1979, VI, 37.

lion," would collectively replace the sacrifice of Christ and, as this process took place, the United States would be transformed from a Christian nation into a Zionist Holocaust nation. Gradually, as the existentialist religion of the Holocaust became the operative faith of the United States, its problematical "lessons" would be banged into the heads of U.S. school children. They would be taught not only that they must never question any dogma of the new faith (for to do so would offer *de facto* proof that they were guilty of "anti-Semitism," the ultimate social transgression), but also that they must remain ever-vigilant in order to "prevent another Holocaust."

Chapter IX
1980s: Wiesel Becomes America's Holocaust High Priest

1980: United States Holocaust Memorial Council Founded in Part to Fight Revisionism

On October 7, 1980, the U.S. Congress voted unanimously to establish the United States Holocaust Memorial Council and, at the same time, named Elie Wiesel as its chairman. In doing so, the U.S. government granted Wiesel's three main requests: the creation of a museum to serve as a propaganda center for the education (brainwashing) of U.S. citizens and others; the selection and donation of federal land on which this propaganda center would be built; and the designation of special Jewish holy days to be called the "Days of Remembrance," to be observed not only in Washington's most sacred civic spaces, but also in all the nation's state capitals. This truly comprehensive legislation, based on the religious belief that "Auschwitz becomes Sinai," imposed the Holocaust as the official state religion of the United States of America.

It should be clearly understood by the reader that for many Christian and Jewish Holocaustians the Holocaust cult is religious, not secular, in nature. As Wiesel's friend, Steven T. Katz, director of the Elie Wiesel Center for Judaic Studies at Boston University, points out, the slogan "Auschwitz becomes Sinai" refers to the idea that "the Shoah marks a new era in which the Sinaitic covenantal relationship was shattered; now, if there is to be any covenantal relationship at all, an unprecedented form of it must come into being."[435] In other words, in imposing the Holocaust on U.S. citizens, the

---

[435] Steven T. Katz, "The Holocaust as Revelation: Fackenheim and Greenberg. According to Some Jewish Thinkers, Events of the Nazi Era Initiated Changes in the Nature of Judaism."
www.myjewishlearning.com/beliefs/Theology/Suffering_and_Evil/Responses/Modern_

U.S. government is funding the Jewish religion in its most recent manifestation.

Illustration 28: Steven T. Katz

Thus, about a year after Wiesel had submitted his report to President Carter, his requests, essentially religious in nature, were enacted by Congress. Wiesel's admirer Mark Chmiel pointed out that, although this was a great personal victory for Wiesel, it came at a cost for all other U.S. citizens:[436]

> [...Wiesel] *received a tremendous boost for his mission when he consented to participate in a project that reinforced the "authorized perspective" of state power to define and divide the social world – in the present instance, by privileging more useful, now worthy victims over other, more disturbing, unworthy victims.*

What Chmiel was trying to say was that this new law effectively ended the mythical separation of church and state that supposedly exists in the U.S., for by this vote the U.S. Congress officially designated Jews as the state's official "worthy victims." If this law had imposed Catholicism as the state religion, Jewish and Jewish-funded organizations like the ADL, ACLU and SPLC would have immediately filed suit to stop it. In this case, however, their silence gave resounding assent.

This legislation thus places the full force of the State behind the supposed veracity of the Jewish Holocaust narrative, despite the fact that the latter is riddled with lies, internal contradictions and exaggerations from beginning to end. Likewise, its designation of Jews as "worthy victims" in the eyes of the state also means that those groups that are not so designated must of necessity be "unworthy." Foremost among the unworthy we must list Catholics, for one of their popes, Pius XII, has been designated, since 1963, as a major villain and "bystander" in the Jewish Holocaust narrative.

More specifically, President Carter, in another betrayal of the trust of the U.S. people, gave these "worthy victims" 1.9 acres of prime real estate adjacent to the Mall in Washington, D. C., for the site of the Holocaust Museum. This abominable decision, which was hurtful and discriminatory

---

Solutions/Holocaust_as_Revelation.shtml.

[436] Mark Chmiel, *Elie Wiesel,* 124. Chmiel, in making the distinction between "worthy" and "unworthy" victims, was adapting to the Zionist context a distinction first made by Chomsky with respect to "unworthy" victims of U.S. oppression in Latin America. See Edward S. Herman and Noam Chomsky, *Manufacturing Consent: The Political Economy of the Mass Media* (N.Y.: Pantheon, 1988).

toward all non-Jewish U.S. citizens, was unrelated in any compelling way to U.S. history or to the U.S. people as a whole. Carter wanted the museum to be built as a sop to the lobbyists and propagandists of the nation's wealthiest and most powerful ethnic group, the Jews. Even worse, he gave away public land, that is, land that belonged to all the people, to one small group, and he did so precisely because he needed Jewish financial and media support in his reelection campaign. He had no right to do this, which is why he never discussed with anyone the construction of a monument to what Chmiel calls "unworthy victims" – such as black people as victims of slavery or Americans Indians as victims of genocide. No, Carter's decision was made solely for personal political gain: to court the wealthy and politically influential Jews whose money he would need to maintain himself in power.

When Congress unanimously established the Holocaust Council, it made no mention of the fact that the revisionist threat was one of the main reasons for the establishment of both the museum and the "Days of Remembrance."[437] Once the legislation had been signed by President Carter, the mask came off. In the Council's meeting in New York on December 10, 1980, Wiesel made it clear that he perceived Holocaust revisionism to be a grave threat both to himself and to the Jewish Holocaust narrative as a whole. He told the members of the Council:[438]

> [...] *the denial of the Holocaust is a very serious problem. As some of you may know, I was probably the first to alert the American Jewish community to that danger. In the beginning there were only a few articles and two or three books, and nobody listened. Then I said: "You know, there are already ten books." Somewhat later I said: "There are already twenty-four books." Year after year, the number has increased. The problem has finally caught up with us. I must say that I feel impure when I touch these books. I don't know what to do. Debate them? I would not dignify them with a debate. I would not dignify them with a dialogue.*

Wiesel then asked in his still wobbly English:

> *What should be done with them. To ignore them? I do not know how. We cannot. The best thing to do is what we are doing: to write more books, to speak more about the Holocaust in more authentic voice.*

In other words, since 1980, unable to answer the revisionists, Wiesel, the museum authorities and the Zionist media have simply turned up the volume on their one-sided and propagandistic presentation of the Holocaust.

---

437 www.ushmm.org/m/pdfs/20100816-orig-council-charter.pdf

438 Elie Wiesel, "Remarks on Anti-Semitism and on Revisionism," in Abrahamson, *Against Silence,* vol. 3, 174.

Founding of the Institute for Historical Review

In late 1978, the lobbyist and activist Willis Carto founded the Institute for Historical Review as an independent think tank. Its purpose was to provide a central place in which independent historical researchers scattered about the country – and the world – could establish contact with each other, share their research findings, and have them published. In September 1979, the IHR held its first colloquium, at which scholars from the U.S., Germany, France, Britain and Sweden read papers and exchanged views. At the same time, a book publishing arm was created and the Noontide Press was born.

Concurrently, a scholarly quarterly, the *Journal of Historical Review*, was also founded. From the beginning, it took aim at what were still some of the most absurd claims still surviving from Nuremberg and warmly embraced by the Holocaustians. Thus, in the first four issues of Volume I, which appeared in 1980, among other things the myth of soap made from the flesh of dead Jews was demolished. These revisionist pioneers also argued that it had been the Soviets, and not the Germans, who had committed the Katyn atrocity. Of course, on both counts, they were right. But if it had not been for these courageous scholarly pieces, these myths – which have now been completely and quietly "retconned" out of the Holocaust master narrative – might still be in existence. Those first issues also began attacking the technical impossibilities inherent in the gas chamber myth at Auschwitz, and that early technical questioning would later lead to much more powerful and substantial studies.[439]

From the outset, the IHR was under attack from the Holocaustian establishment, which sought to quash it in the bud. Thus, a campaign of violence was unleashed against its offices in Torrance, California, and this harassment culminated in the arson attack of July 4, 1984, which destroyed the organization's offices and bookstore, wiping out its inventory. The Jewish Defense League, recognized by the FBI as an extremist group under the command of the notorious Jewish thug Irv Rubin, was suspected of the attack, but never prosecuted.[440] This reaction proved, if proof were necessary, that the same people who were at that time forcing the creation of their Holocaust Museum on the U.S. people in the name of "tolerance" were speaking out of both sides of their mouth.

As is the case with many small, controversial groups, the IHR was not immune to internal dissension. It lives on today, but its heyday was the first thirteen years or so, from its founding in late 1978 into the early 1990s.

---

439 The first volume's contents are accessible at www.ihr.org/jhr/v01/v01index.html.

440 Institute for Historical Review, "How Jewish Terrorists Fire-Bombed the Institute for Historical Review," May 2013; www.ihr.org/other/jdl1984arson.html.

Another Blow to the Holocaust: Serge Klarsfeld Publishes the *Auschwitz Album*

As the U.S. Holocaust Memorial Museum was coming into being, Serge Klarsfeld, who was still a rather obscure French lawyer and Jewish Holocaustian activist, published the so-called *Auschwitz Album*, which is also known as Lili Jacob's Album, after the name of the Jewish deportee who discovered it. It is also important to remember that she did not find it at Auschwitz-Birkenau, but at the Dora-Mittelbau camp in south central Germany. The fact that Jacob suppressed the album from 1945 until 1980, when she donated it to the Yad Vashem museum in Israel, helps to explain what its pictures really show: that there was no Holocaust at Auschwitz-Birkenau. But with the rise of revisionism in the 1970s, Klarsfeld apparently thought that by publishing the pictures, often misleadingly captioned, he could use them as a weapon against the revisionists.[441] Lili Jacob had suppressed these pictures for over three decades because they exposed to ridicule the utter mendacity of the Jewish survivors. In fact, anyone who looks at them with a critical eye today cannot help but conclude that they establish that there was no Holocaust at the Birkenau camp. But by the time Klarsfeld and the Holocaustians took over the pictures in 1980, in the Orwellian world in which we live – a world in which up is down, black is white and peace is war – these pictures could be published with highly deceptive captions in the certainty that no official historian or other recognized expert would dare to publicly question that they documented mass gassing at Birkenau.

Nonetheless, like the aerial photography of the Auschwitz camp, published in 1979, this album is yet another nail in the coffin of the Holocaust. The 193 pictures contained in the original album were probably taken by two German members of the Birkenau staff, Ernst Hoffmann and Bernhard Walter. The pictures are as down-to-earth and as matter of fact as can be, for these German men were trying to capture on film a contingent of Orthodox Jews from Hungary. The shots and angles they selected indicate that they must have considered themselves amateur sociologists or anthropologists. Their intent was most likely to take the pictures home with them after the war. They sought to document as much as possible the nuts and bolts of the day-to-day processing of the large numbers of people who were being imported into the German Reich. If anything, Hoffmann and Walter's pictures prove that the Jewish claim of an extermination program at Birkenau is utterly mendacious, for these mundane shots, taken between May 15 and July 8, 1944, show just the opposite. No smoke and flame rise from the chimneys of the crematoria. Nor is there any trace of Wiesel's im-

[441] Serge Klarsfeld (ed.), *L'Album d'Auschwitz* (Paris: Fils et Filles des Déportés Juifs de France, 1980).

agined "open pits" that burn truckloads of adults and babies. In fact, the pictures show how tightly packed the reception and processing area actually was, for the main rail line split into three tracks after passing through the entrance building. These three train tracks were closely surrounded by barracks. There was simply no room available for the alleged long lines of 10,000 to 20,000 people to line up patiently each day while awaiting their turn to go into the "gas chambers."

The German editor of the original album divided them according to theme or subject. They include 1) "Arrival of a Transport Train" [Ankunft eines Transportzuges]; 2) "Newly Arrived Men" [Männer bei der Ankunft]; 3) "Newly Arrived Women" [Frauen bei der Ankunft]; 4) "Division into Groups" [Aussortierung]; 5) "After Division into Groups: Men Still Fit for Labor" [Nach der Aussortierung: noch einsatzfähige Männer]; 6) "Women Still Fit for Labor" [Noch einsatzfähige Frauen]; 7) "After Delousing" [Nach der Entlausung]; 8) "Assignment to the Labor Camp" [Einweisung ins Arbeitslager]; 9) "Personal Effects" [Effekten]; 10) "Men No Longer Fit for Labor" [Nicht mehr einsatzfähige Männer] and 11) "Women and Children No Longer Fit for Labor" [Nicht mehr einsatzfähige Frauen und Kinder].

There is nothing sinister or secret about the events depicted in this album, for the historical record indicates that there were untold thousands of Jews who, like Wiesel's father, were not exterminated although they were never able to work. Even the order of events speaks to the lack of an extermination plan, for everybody, even those who would not be able to work, went through the delousing process. Why would the Germans waste scarce and expensive resources like this on people they were planning to exterminate a few minutes later? Such nonsensical events are routine, however, in the Holocaust.

Zionist Media Use of Retroactive Continuity in the Holocaust Narrative

As the decade began, the Holocaust fundamentalists were growing more and more concerned that the success of the revisionists was undermining belief in the Holocaust.

They were pleased with themselves for having secured Congressional approval for their planned Holocaust museum, but this support had never really been in doubt, because the Jewish Lobby exercises complete control over the U.S. Congress. Yet the Lobby was still worried about the threat represented by Butz, Faurisson and the other revisionists. The essence of this threat resided in the fact that the revisionists had successfully raised, albeit to a small audience, many unanswered questions about the overall veracity of the various Jewish Holocaust eyewitnesses, in general, and Elie Wiesel in particular. It is in the context of the Holocaust narrative's deterioration that we are best able to understand the widely publicized comment that the Israeli cultural commentator Boaz Evron made about the Holocaust at this time. While of course genuflecting to the Holocaust as history, Evron made an important point with regard to what Butz, Faurisson and the other revisionists were in the process of doing to the Jewish folktale, when he wrote:[442]

> *Two terrible things happened to the Jewish people during this century. First, the Holocaust and the lessons drawn from it. Second, the non-historical and easily-refutable commentaries on the Holocaust made either deliberately or through simple ignorance, and their use for propaganda purposes among non-Jews and Jews both in Israel and the diaspora constitute a cancer for Jews and for the State of Israel.*

Evron might have added that no other Jewish false witness incarnated this cancer for Jews better than Wiesel did. Then again, presently no official, media-recognized eyewitness has anything approaching the stature of Elie Wiesel.

Despite the fact that the Allied aerial photography showed no immense fires at Auschwitz emanating from Wiesel's imagined flaming pits, the Zionist media continued to lie to their readers about this issue. For instance, in September 1981, in a very long article in the *Atlantic Monthly*, its author, a senior editor at the Zionist bastion *Time* since 1971, stated that "these fires were burning in the summer of 1944, fires that could be seen from as far as thirty miles away."[443] Of course, if such fires had ever existed, they would have eliminated the need for the alleged secrecy and surprise that had supposedly been necessary to dupe 10,000 or more Jews per day into walking quietly into the gas chambers. This need for secrecy had been part of the Holocaust narrative from the very beginning, but the Zionist media manipulators of the early 1980s were acting as if it had never been part of the Jewish Holocaust master narrative. Why did they do it, and how did they get away with it?

Thanks to the Holocaustians' use of retroactive continuity, as noted earlier, a narrative technique routinely used in comic books, serials of various kinds, soap operas and professional wrestling, among other types of pop culture narratives, they did not have to worry about the internal coherence of their narrative over time. The "retcon" procedure, which involves the deliberate changing of previously established details of a narrative in order to adapt it to changed circumstances, is essential to the master narrative of

---

442 Boaz Evron, "Holocaust, a Danger for the Jewish People," *Yiton*, no. 77, May – June 1980.

443 Otto Friedrich, "The Kingdom of Auschwitz," *The Atlantic Monthly*, September 1981, 54.

the Holocaust. Its use enables the Holocaust mythmakers to get rid of potentially damaging story elements without cost.

Examples of the use of this technique abound. In fact, as noted in the previous chapter, Wiesel's claim of having seen open-pit burning of living victims at Auschwitz, as showcased in *Night*, had already been phased out of the Holocaust master narrative by the time the 1978 TV series *Holocaust* was presented. As a result, Wiesel's term "Holocaust," which specifically denotes the complete burning of a given substance, was used to designate a story in which people were gassed, not burned! The disconnect between the denotative and connotative meanings given to the word was huge. Yet, thanks to retroactive continuity, the series was shown to a gullible U.S. public as if the Holocaust burning thesis, which is at the heart of the word "Holocaust," had never even existed, and as if the word "Holocaust" denoted gassing and not burning!

As the Jewish Holocaust narrative was emerging at Nuremberg in 1945, U.S. Prosecutor Thomas Dodd, behaving like a latter-day P. T. Barnum, claimed at the opening of the trial that the Germans had not only mastered the bizarre art of shrinking human heads, but also of making lamp shades out of tattooed skin and soap from the fat of dead Jews. Until recently, these Jewish propaganda fabrications were a central element of the Holocaust narrative. As such, they were beyond question. After the revisionists began to criticize such Jewish myths in the 1970s, the Holocaustians gradually began to realize their potential vulnerability in light of such tales. It was too dangerous to maintain such fables at the center of the Holocaust myth. Stressing outlandish claims like the skin and soap legends could result, like a peripheral infection that goes untreated, in the spread of the contagion – in the case of the Holocaust myth, disbelief – thus menacing the entire organism. For this reason the Holocaust fundamentalists decided – in truth: were forced – to delete these tall tales from the Holocaust master narrative, gradually and without ever mentioning that they were doing so under duress from revisionist scholarship. The Holocaust mythmakers' dilemma is complicated by the fact that, unlike doctors, they must contend with the consequences of negating what were long held as inflexible truths. This is probably why such barbaric impostures as the lamp shade and human skin absurdities continue to eke out a twilight existence on the fringes of the Holocaust master narrative.

Later, as I will show below, the development of the Internet would drastically shorten the amount of time existing between the birth of a new, mendacious Holocaust claim and the onset of revisionist criticism leading to its demise – and forced withdrawal – as if the claim had never existed in the first place!

The Holocaust Narrative Is a Form of Lowbrow Culture

The use of "retconning" in the Holocaust narrative positions it firmly within the ambit of other forms of lowbrow and middlebrow culture, in which the technique is also essential. As noted earlier, these include comic books, professional wrestling, movies with sequels and prequels, and soap operas, among others. Significantly, in each of these cases, the unsophisticated mass audience accepts the changes, which are clearly violations of verisimilitude, for the simple reason that "it's just a story, anyway." The one difference is that, in the case of the Holocaust, the audience is overwhelmingly involuntary. It consists primarily of U.S. school children who are forced to undergo brainwashing classes about the Holocaust. While some of them might be able to figure out by themselves that the whole story is a scam, they likely tell themselves "it's just a story, anyway." Yet, none would dare to express such an opinion in class for fear of harsh retribution from their teachers.

Another lowbrow aspect of the Holocaust narrative is reflected in its continuing emphasis on sex and violence. This strategy is apparently deemed necessary, because the Jewish movie moguls have concluded that non-Jews will not attend a Holocaust film without strong doses of either sex or violence. For this reason, Roman Polanski's Holocaust propaganda film *The Pianist* was extremely vulgar. Its fornication scenes were not only unnecessary, they were so crudely done that they were essentially pornographic in nature: the characters portrayed exhibited no sense of either love or intimacy. As if that were not enough, the film included repeated nude scenes, including several in which two characters argue, one of whom is un-clothed! In a word, the film was an excellent exhibition of the strong relationship that exists today between visual representation of the Holocaust and resolutely lowbrow culture. Yet not surprisingly, the predominantly Jewish Oscar voters gave *The Pianist* three Oscars in 2002, for Best Actor, Best Director and Best Film Writing, while at Cannes it was selected as Best Picture. A few years later, when Kate Winslet signed on to act in the nude in many scenes in the Holocaust propaganda film entitled *The Reader*, her decision offered further proof of the fact that Hollywood's Holocaustians must now stoop to baser and baser levels of lowbrow entertainment in order to sell their wares.[444]

In addition to sex, there is also violence. In early 2009-10, the mayhem-packed Holocaust film entitled *Inglourious Basterds* exemplified the role of violence in Holocaust film narration. This film, which utterly lacked anything remotely related to esthetic content, received eight Oscar nomina-

444 John Harlow, "Winslet Nude Scenes Trivialise Holocaust," *The Sunday Times*, December 7, 2008; Manohla Dargis, "Innocence Is Lost in Postwar Germany: Film Review," *New York Times*, December 10, 2008, C1.

tions, and was widely expected to win several of them. At the last minute, however, a reaction seems to have set in among the Holocaustian insiders who were to make the final, secret decisions. First, they seem to have realized that this 153-minute exercise in vulgarity was glaringly unworthy of being nominated for even one Oscar. Second, they finally came to understand that by heaping awards on this film they would only be ratifying the revisionist mockery of the film that had already been circulating on the Internet for months. After all, the pre-adolescent script was pure fiction, and trashy fiction at that. But since this was a Holocaust film, its sick narrative of Jewish racial revenge had already become part of the Holocaust's master narrative, and thus passed for true.

With the Holocaust now enshrined as our state religion, the Holocaustians finally seem to have realized why the revisionists were laughing so hard. The inclusion of so trashy a narrative in the canon of the Holocaust was already a disaster for Jews, for it laid bare the lowbrow nature of the Holocaust story. The bestowal of Oscars on this train wreck of a movie would have proved that the Holocaustians are not only vulgar and tasteless, but also utterly corrupt. Suddenly, they understood that they were walking into a trap of their own making. Thus, on Oscar night, a strange thing happened. Despite all the "can't miss" Oscar predictions that their various media stooges had been paid to predict for the film, *Inglourious Basterds* won only one Oscar (for best supporting actor, Christoph Waltz).

In the end, though, the film's very existence had revealed the tight bonds that link the Holocaust narrative to lowbrow culture, while also suggesting that Hollywood's Jewish masters realize that the Holocaust is a tough sell on its own, and now needs this strong lowbrow ingredient to attract an audience.

One last point to be made about these recent films on the Holocaust is the fact that they stray as far away as possible from dealing directly with the alleged crimes committed at Auschwitz and the other "extermination camps." The Jewish moguls know that they cannot show gas chambers because there were none. Nor can they show Wiesel's flaming pits because there were none. In fact, Steven Spielberg's 1993 failure to show the mythical gas chambers in operation in *Schindler's List* appears, in retrospect, to have been one of the most significant concessions that the Jewish Holocaustians of Hollywood have ever made to the revisionists. In that film, as a number of Jewish women fear that they are about to enter a gas chamber, the dreaded gas chamber turns out to be an ordinary disinfestation facility, just like the one that had really existed in the Sauna building at Birkenau. Spielberg stayed true to contemporary Hollywood Holocaust standards by mining this scene for maximum titillation from the women's nakedness. The Jewish moguls of Hollywood have not dared to touch the subject of

Auschwitz since then. (See my comments in Chapter XI on *Amen*, a film version, made in France, of *The Deputy.*) They still undertake money-making, lowbrow, pornographic flights of Holocaust fancy, as witnessed by films like *The Pianist*, *The Reader* and *Inglorious Basterds*, but they have learned to stay away from Auschwitz.

The *New York Times* Finally Mentions Prof. Faurisson by Name

In early 1981, the *New York Times* publicized a poorly made TV documentary film about a self-identified Auschwitz veteran named Kitty Hart. Entitled *Kitty: Return to Auschwitz*, the film was shown on a New York City PBS station, and the *New York Times*, not unexpectedly, sought to promote it. Kitty's Holocaust story was soon published in book form in London, with a New York edition by 1982. It turned out, however, that Kitty's story dovetailed nicely with the *New York Times*'s desire to launch an attack on Prof. Robert Faurisson of the University of Lyon-II. The *Times* reported:[445]

> *Last December, Robert Faurisson, a suspended Lyon University lecturer, published a book in France maintaining that the Holocaust never happened. The German concentration camps, he claimed, were not death camps at all. Preposterous as this thesis is – it has attracted very few adherents – that it could even be stated and argued is evidence of the surprising fact that many people today know little or nothing about the Nazi genocide during the Second World War.*

According to this opinion piece masquerading as news, the rise of revisionism had set off alarm bells of concern among the Holocaust fundamentalists. As a result, there was now a new urgency to flood the media with Holocaust propaganda as an antidote to revisionism.

This was the context in which the Hart film, produced in Britain, was brought to New York: to reassure New York Jews that the Holocaust was beyond cavil, and to propagandize anyone else who might have had doubts about the tall tales told by the survivors. It was perhaps because of this sense of urgency about combating revisionism that the *New York Times* decided to modify its policy of never mentioning the dreaded revisionists by name. Deborah Lipstadt, Holocaust orthodoxy enforcer and enemy of free speech, calls that particular Jewish media policy "dynamic silence."[446] The very fact that the Jewish Holocaustians are able to engage in, indeed impose, such a policy, speaks volumes about their control over the mainstream media.

---

445 Gene Lambinus, "Television Week: Poignant Pilgrimage," *New York Times*, February 1, 1981, D39..

446 Michael Jones, "Holocaust Denial," 19.

But here was the *New York Times* mentioning Faurisson's name! Their reason for doing so was evident: they wanted to spread disinformation about the man. Thus, Faurisson was presented as a lecturer at the University of Lyon-II, whereas in fact he was a tenured and chaired professor, whose publications, previous to the publication of his writings on the Holocaust, had been highly praised. Nor had he been suspended by the university for his writings; rather, the administration had informed him that he could no longer teach his classes: a Jewish student group was threatening to cause a riot if he was not silenced. Finally, Faurisson did not say in so many words that the "Holocaust never happened." On the contrary, he had pointed to the many concededly false testimonies about the alleged gas chambers of Auschwitz by supposed eyewitnesses, including German concentration camp personnel, and had also raised searching technical questions about the functioning of these alleged killing machines. Faurisson's conclusion was that the crime the survivors claimed to have seen and to which various SS men confessed was physically and chemically impossible, and therefore could not have happened.

As for the documentary *Kitty: Return to Auschwitz*, the *Times* not only promoted it in advance, but also ran a favorable review of it three days later. Like so many of the other documentaries that the Holocaustians have produced and promoted over the years, this one illustrates quite well that important Jewish media moguls have no shame when it comes to exploiting the Jewish dead of Auschwitz (real and imaginary).

So crude was *Kitty* as propaganda that, if the film were shown on television today, it would be an embarrassment to the Holocaustians. Nonetheless, the *Times* review pulled out all the stops of Holocaust kitsch. After assuring readers at the outset that "this is a more extraordinarily touching program than so many others that have tried to capture the evil spirit of Auschwitz," the anti-revisionist message was delivered:[447]

> *She wanted to return, she explains, so that her son, now a doctor in Canada, would know that there really was such a horror, that such things happened, despite attempts in some quarters to minimize them.*

Kitty actually claims at one point to be showing the location of Wiesel's imaginary flaming trenches. That the Allied aerial photography had made it clear that no such pits could be found did not keep Kitty from claiming that she had seen them:

> *Here are the pits where people were burned alive. Look, here are ashes, human ashes, still here, maybe of your relatives.*

Holocaust kitsch seldom plumbs such depths. Undaunted, Kitty also remembers that the grassy fields on screen "were all mud then; a blade of

[447] Richard F. Shepard, "TV: Story of Auschwitz by a Survivor," *New York Times*, February 4, 1981, C22.

grass would have been eaten by the victims, whose most precious possession was a bowl that served both as soup-plate and toilet bowl."[448] Sadly, Kitty's anal obsession leads her to an outright lie, for the Germans were fanatical about maintaining hygiene at Auschwitz, as the Holocaust fundamentalists have now been forced to admit. When Kitty's book appeared the following year, its pages gave evidence that her imagination had swung into even higher gear:[449]

> *Up to 2,000 corpses at a time were burnt on wood pyres, and more were burnt on top of the moldering bodies dumped in the pits from earlier killings. Vaster than medieval plague burials, these mass graves contained over 100,000 corpses by the end of November 1942.*

One can only imagine how many more thousands of bodies must have been buried there when Kitty arrived in the summer of 1944. Strangely, it never dawns on Kitty that, if these pits had actually existed, they would have been excavated many, many years ago.

Wiesel Begins to Positions Himself as the Holocaust Antipope

Wiesel's five-year campaign to secure the Nobel Prize for himself, either for Literature or Peace, began in 1981. As that effort was taking shape, he was also being elevated to new heights due to his chairmanship of the Holocaust museum project. Wiesel was headed for big things, and he knew it. It was in this context that he began to project himself in interviews as the Jewish equivalent of a pope. In fact, with the Holocaust becoming more and more a recognizable and freestanding religious offshoot of the main Judaic trunk, this pretension made sense.

But by 1981, Wiesel had competition. Since there were other Jewish academics milking the Holocaust under the banner of "Holocaust theology," while deploying the slogan "Auschwitz becomes Sinai," as mentioned above, he had to define himself more clearly. For instance, while Holocaust theologian Emil Fackenheim stressed a pro-Israel and hardcore Zionist message in his brand of Holocaust theology, Richard Rubenstein worked the "death of God" angle. Thus, Wiesel had to position himself and his par-

---

[448] See also Friedrich, "Kingdom." Friedrich recycles the same nonsense, claiming that the Germans forced people to use the same bowl for eating and as "chamber pots at night" (40). Incredibly, he also wants us to believe that there were 1,500 women in one barracks, with just twenty bowls from which to eat (*ibid.*). This Jewish obsession with excrement reached its sick and demented zenith in Joseph Tenenbaum's now long-forgotten work *In Search of a Lost People: The Old and the New Poland* (N.Y.: Beechhurst Press, 1948), 145. Tenenbaum claims therein that at Auschwitz, Jewish deportees mated in the dung under the latrines.

[449] Kitty Hart, *Return to Auschwitz: The Remarkable Story of a Girl Who Survived the Holocaust* (New York: Atheneum, 1982), 89.

ticular Holocaust product against such competition, without disavowing the work of his competitors.

This awareness of the need to stay on message as he perfected his own unique selling proposition helps to explain a gratuitous attack he made on Pope Pius XII in the pages of the mainstream Protestant magazine *Christian Century* in 1981. In a piece published there, he intoned:[450]

I was angry at Pope Pius XII: How could he have kept silent?

No, Wiesel did not "do theology" *per se*, but did do "traditional Jewish anti-Catholicism." However, as he engaged in these gutter tactics, he reminded any and all Catholic Vatican haters worldwide, especially those who might have seats on the Nobel committee in Oslo, that his future and evolving mission would put the theme of hostility to the papacy front and center. As Wiesel moved in this direction, the words of Robert McAfee Brown, written within a month of the *Christian Century* smear, now seem prophetic. Brown wrote concisely:[451]

Wiesel is very fond of questions. He is not fond of answers.

1982: Anti-Faurisson Conference at the Sorbonne

In France, the Holocaustians reacted to Professor Faurisson's work by organizing a conference on the Holocaust, at the Sorbonne. Entitled "National Socialism and the Jews" (*Le National-Socialisme et les Juifs*), which took place from June 29 to July 2, 1982. In attendance were eminent historians, generally well-established specialists on World War II, who had been charged with publishing a statement at the end of their deliberations that would demolish once and for all both Faurisson and his fellow revisionists. Their utter failure to achieve this declared objective was reflected in the fact that the volume containing their debates and discussions did not appear until three years later. Even worse, the bad faith of the conformist historians who compiled this volume can be gauged from the fact that they did not make room for a contribution from Faurisson or any other revisionist. This book thus offered no evidence of a debate on the Holocaust, and proved to be just another exercise in propaganda from the collaborationist historians.[452]

---

450 Wiesel, "Recalling," 606.

451 Robert McAfee Brown, "The Power of the Tale," *The Christian Century*, June 30, 1981, 650.

452 Ecole des Hautes Etudes en Science Sociale (ed.), *L'Allemagne nazie et le génocide juif* (Paris: Gallimard/Le Seuil, 1985).

1983: Walter N. Sanning's Revisionist Study of Overall Jewish Wartime Losses

By the late 1970s/early 1980s, a number of scholars had tried to estimate the numerical losses of European Jewry during the Second World War,[453] but a thoroughly researched monograph on this important topic was still lacking. Although there is disagreement about how many Jews died where and for which reasons, and even though the number of victims claimed for the various alleged crime scenes kept changing over the decades,[454] all Holocaustians seemed to invariably agree that some six million Jews lost their lives in the Holocaust.

The U.S. revisionist Don Heddesheimer was the first researcher to thoroughly document the fact that the six-million figure had long since been used by world Jewry as a metaphor for persecution and annihilation as far back as the late 19th century.[455] As such, it predates not only World War II, but also World War I. This fact demonstrates that the figure is essentially symbolic, imaginary and political, with no documentary evidence to support it.

Prof. Butz stated in his *Hoax* that it would be close to impossible to determine by demographic means how many Jews actually died during World War II as a result of the German resettlement program.[456] Spurred on by this assertion, the German demographer Wilhelm Niederreiter, writing under the pen name of Walter N. Sanning, tried to do just that: establish an accurate death figure on the basis of available evidence. He published his first research results on the subject in 1980.[457] Three years later his work appeared as a book, and was published simultaneously in English and German.[458]

While Sanning confirmed in his study that after the war millions of Jews were indeed missing in countries that had come under the German sphere of influence, he was able to locate many of these missing Jews in other countries – mostly the U.S. and Israel – as a result of a new Jewish

[453] The most prominent tallies can be found in Gerald Reitlinger, *The Final Solution* (London: Mitchell, 1953), as well as in Hilberg, *Destruction.*

[454] See Thomas Dalton's attempt to nail down the numbers in *Debating the Holocaust,* (New York: Theses & Dissertations Press, 2009) 67-81; *idem*, "The Great Holocaust Mystery: Reconsidering the Evidence," *Inconvenient History*, vol. 6, no. 3, fall 2014.

[455] Don Heddesheimer, *The First Holocaust*, (reprint of 2nd ed., Washington, D.C.: The Barnes Review, 2011).

[456] In the 2015 edition, at the end of his chapter "How Many Jews?", 38: "Believing that the task is not possible, I will offer here no definite estimate of Jewish losses."

[457] Walter N. Sanning, "Die europäischen Juden. Eine technische Studie zur zahlenmäßigen Entwicklung im Zweiten Weltkrieg," 4 parts, *Deutschland in Geschichte und Gegenwart*, vol. 28, nos. 1-4, 12-15, 17-21, 17-21, 25-31.

[458] Walter N. Sanning, *The Dissolution of Eastern European Jewry* (Torrance, Calif.: Institute for Historical Review, 1983; 2nd ed., Uckfield, UK: Castle Hill Publishers, 2015); *Die Auflösung des osteuropäischen Judentums* (Tübingen: Grabert 1983).

exodus which had occurred during and after the war. He also discovered that the Soviet Union had deported and evacuated the majority of Polish and Soviet Jews within its reach to Siberian labor camps prior to and shortly after the outbreak of the German-Russian war in June 1941. He concluded therefore that only some 200,000 to 300,000 missing Jews could not be accounted for within the context of known and normal attrition rates for any group of people. (2015 edition, 193f.)

In deviation from the normal practice of "dynamic silence," two mainstream historical periodicals "reviewed" Sanning's book,[459] although rather unfavorably and without addressing any of his arguments.[460] That his work had nonetheless struck a sensitive Holocaustian nerve can be gleaned from Henry Huttenbach's review:[459]

> *The danger of this book (and of those that will doubtlessly follow) is its clever veneer of scholarship.* [...] *Not one in a thousand undergraduates could find fault with it; only a few more graduates would be competent to identify its flaws and to convincingly question its credibility. The ultimate danger lies in the lack of a serious response to this continuing wave of attacks on history itself.*

A group of conformist historians replied to Sanning eight years later in a dismissive and somewhat halfhearted manner.[461] Sanning's book is only mentioned in passing in a footnote on the next to last page, while none of his main arguments are mentioned, let alone addressed. Not surprisingly, the editor of this exercise in conformist history, Wolfgang Benz, determined that the mythical six-million figure was historically accurate! (17)

Three years later, in reply to Benz, the revisionist historian Germar Rudolf established that Benz's anthology does not provide a solid basis in fact for his six-million figure.[462] Rudolf showed that Benz *et al.* calculated this number in essence by simply adding up the Jewish population differences between the last pre-war and the first post-war censuses in the countries of the German sphere of influence. Hence Benz wants to make his readers believe that no considerable emigration of Jews from Europe ever occurred during and right after the war. He also ignored the already mentioned mass

---

[459] John S. Conway, "History, Hitler, and the Holocaust," *The International History Review*, vol. VII, no. 3, August 1985, 441-450, here 450f.; Henry R. Huttenbach, *Martyrdom and Resistance*, vol. 11, Sept.-Oct. 1984, 2, 12.

[460] See Dan Desjardins's "Critique of John S. Conway's Review," *The Journal of Historical Review*, vol. 7, no. 3, 1986, 375, 379; see also the exchange of letters by W. D. Rubinstein – making similar unfounded accusations – and W. N. Sanning as well as A. R. Butz in response, *The Journal of Historical Review*, vol. 5, nos. 2-4, 1984, 367-373.

[461] Wolfgang Benz (ed.), *Dimension des Völkermords* (Munich: Oldenbourg, 1991).

[462] G. Rudolf, "Statistisches über die Holocaust Opfer – W. Benz und W.N. Sanning im Vergleich," in: Ernst Gauss (ed. = Germar Rudolf), *Grundlagen zur Zeitgeschichte* (Tübingen: Grabert, 1994), 141-168; Engl.: "Holocaust Victims: A Statistical Analysis · W. Benz and W. N. Sanning – A Comparison", in: G. Rudolf (ed.), *Dissecting the Holocaust* (2nd ed., Chicago, Ill.: Theses & Dissertations Press, 2003), 181-213.

evacuations of the Soviet Union, stating simply that all victims of Stalinist wartime policies have to be counted as German Holocaust victims as well, since Germany had started the war (560).

1985: Wiesel Does Not Testify as Expert Witness at Ernst Zündel's Trial in Toronto

In the 1980s, the German-born Canadian writer and publisher Ernst Zündel came under attack by the Holocaust fundamentalists of Canada for his revisionist activity as a publisher and publicist. Unable to answer his valid and legitimate questions about the Holocaust, these powerful Jewish militants decided to exploit their influence on the Canadian judicial system and other organs of the Canadian government in order to silence Zündel.

Wiesel, who did not testify at this trial – there exists no evidence to prove that he was ever asked to testify – has maintained a discreet silence on the subject for years. In Wiesel's absence, Raul Hilberg, author of *The Destruction of the European Jews*, served as the state's main expert witness. However, Hilberg's testimony was thoroughly demolished by Zündel's attorney, Douglas Christie, who was ably supported by Professor Faurisson, in charge of gathering and presenting Zündel's historical evidence against the Holocaust. Time and time again Christie was able to employ advice from Faurisson, by his side throughout the trial, to devastating effect against Holocaust eyewitnesses and savants.[463] The stakes were huge, for the confrontation between the Holocaust fundamentalists and their arch-enemies, Zündel and Faurisson, could not have been more direct. After the inevitable guilty verdict was reached by the judge, it was reversed on a legal technicality. So Zündel was tried anew.

During the second Zündel trial in 1988, Raul Hilberg, seriously embarrassed and discredited as an utter incompetent when questioned under oath on the subject of the Holocaust during round one in 1985, refused to return for Zündel II. Hilberg's decision not to testify at the retrial was probably linked to two key assertions he had made under oath during Zündel I. The first was his claim to have discovered a written order from Hitler to unleash the Holocaust. Having been unable to produce such an order in the first edition of *Destruction*, he promised to publish this proof in the forthcoming second edition of the book. This new edition did indeed appear several months after the close of the trial, but it did not contain the promised material. As a result, if Hilberg had returned for Zündel II, he risked being exposed to ridicule (and possibly accusations of perjury) by Christie

463 For a summary of the proceedings see Michael A. Hoffman II, *The Great Holocaust Trial* (Torrance, Calif.: Institute for Historical Review, 1985; 2nd ed.: Coeur d'Alene, Idaho: Independent History and Research, 2010); the complete transcript of the trial can be found at www.codoh.com/library/document/3355.

and Faurisson on this issue. Thus, not unlike another famous fibber, Falstaff, Hilberg came to the realization that "discretion is the better part of valor," even in service to the Holocaust.

Prudently, he decided to stay home. His place was taken by the young non-Jewish conformist historian Christopher Browning. Like Hilberg, he had never inspected an alleged gas chamber before writing about the Holocaust, nor had he ever conducted research at an alleged extermination camp. Even worse, during the trial his knowledge and understanding of the German language proved to be embarrassingly shaky, at times even inadequate.[464] As expected, however, the judge once again found Zündel guilty, and sentenced him to fifteen months in jail. But, once again, upon appeal to the Canadian Supreme Court, that verdict was also overturned.[465] As for the conformist Browning, the Holocaust fundamentalists made sure that he was later well compensated for his efforts on behalf of the Holocaust. After teaching for twenty-five years at a very small and, in terms of research, insignificant college, Pacific Lutheran University, Browning was suddenly catapulted into a position as the occupant of an endowed chair, and named Frank Porter Graham Professor of History at the University of North Carolina in 1999.

The first Zündel trial would have offered Wiesel a perfect opportunity for a dramatic performance like that at Northwestern University in 1977. There was one major problem, however: in Toronto Wiesel would have been cross-examined under oath, and he dared not risk such an experience, especially with Professor Faurisson sitting at Zündel's attorney's side. In conclusion, the failure of the man who had become the spokesman for the veterans of Auschwitz to testify under oath at the Zündel trials speaks volumes. Since Wiesel's career is based on lies, he had everything to lose and nothing to gain.

While Hilberg's failure was the highlight of the first Zündel trial, Browning's testimony in Toronto during Zündel II was overshadowed by the testimonies of two other expert witnesses who testified on behalf of the defense: the U.S. expert for execution technologies Fred A. Leuchter, Jr., and the British historian David Irving, at that time probably the world's best-selling author on Third Reich history.

Leuchter had accepted a commission by Zündel's defense team to prepare an expert report about the alleged extermination facilites (crematories and homicidal gas chambers) at the former Auschwitz and Majdanek

---

[464] For a compilation of the transcript see Barbara Kulaszka (ed.), *Did Six Million Really Die? Report of the Evidence in the Canadian 'False News' Trial of Ernst Zündel – 1988* (Toronto: Samisdat Publishers, 1992).

[465] See Robert Faurisson's inside story, "The Zündel Trials (1985 and 1988)," *The Journal of Historical Review*, vol. 8, no. 4, winter 1988/89, 417-443 (www.ihr.org/jhr/v08/v08p417_Faurisson.html).

camps in Poland. Although Leuchter's expert report was submitted during the trial, the court rejected Leuchter as an expert witness. However, the *Leuchter Report*, as it was later titled,[466] swayed David Irving to testify on behalf of the defense, stating that Leuchter's technical report had convinced him that no gassings had taken place at either Auschwitz or Majdanek. Both testimonies taken together proved highly explosive, as they convinced thousands of individuals in subsequent years that the orthodox Holocaust narrative was not kosher at all. In the wake of Zündel II, scholars like Germar Rudolf, Jürgen Graf, John C. Ball and many others joined the ranks of revisionism. With their subsequently published in-depth studies they gave revisionism a tremendous boost which lasts to this day.

1985: Wiesel Testifies before the Senate Foreign Relations Committee

Instead of facing "the enemy" in Toronto during the Zündel trial, Wiesel did what he does best: cater to the wealthy and powerful. On March 7, 1985, he was called upon to testify before the Senate Foreign Relations Committee on the proposed Genocide Treaty. He had become in the eyes of the senators the equivalent of a government official, with his particular portfolio the Holocaust. As Wiesel's Jewish admirer Mark Chmiel puts it, by this time Wiesel had become "a discreet and solicitous advisor to American power" (*Elie Wiesel*, 128). Having attained this exalted capacity, Wiesel knew that the U.S. government was never going to question his veracity. This was because the lies he told served to justify the lawmakers' blind support of Israel, helped bloat Pentagon budgets that enriched the "defense" industries, and fostered under-the-radar CIA mischief and interventionism.

During his appearance before the Foreign Relations Committee, the man who to this day has never shown the public his A-7713 tattoo from Auschwitz, inflated his Holocaust kitsch to rhetorical levels never before attained. At a moment when carefully measured words and very precise speech were required from the quintessential eyewitness to the Holocaust, Wiesel actually revealed his disdain for both self-control and precision about the Holocaust when he stated:[467]

> *Mr. Chairman, I have seen the flames, I have seen the flames rising to nocturnal heavens. I have seen parents and children, teachers and their disciples, dreamers and their dreams, and woe unto me, I have seen children thrown*

---

[466] Leuchter later wrote three more reports about related topics. All four texts are summarized and critically commented in a new edition: Fred A. Leuchter, Robert Faurisson, Germar Rudolf, *The Leuchter Reports: Critical Edition* (3rd ed., Washington, D.C.: The Barnes Review, Washington, DC, 2011).

[467] *Congressional Record* (7 March 1985), S2857.

Illustration 29: Wiesel meets U.S. President Ronald Reagan at the White House

> *alive in*[to] *the flames. I have seen all of them vanish in the night as part of a plan, part of a program conceived and executed by criminal minds that have corrupted the law and poisoned the hearts in their own land and the lands that they had criminally occupied.*

Wiesel's White House Investiture as Holocaust High Priest

About a month after Wiesel's testimony before the Senate Foreign Relations Committee, President Reagan awarded him the Congressional Medal of Freedom at the White House. The ceremony took place on April 19, in the Roosevelt Room, despite Wiesel's previous criticisms of Reagan for his plan to visit a cemetery in Bitburg, West Germany, where a few S.S. soldiers were buried. The award recognized Wiesel for the totality of his "lifetime achievement," and was televised nationally by both CNN and NBC. Such coverage was highly unusual for this award, but the Zionist media barons who made the decision to broadcast the event knew much more about its actual significance to the nation's elites than they let on to their general audience.

According to Chmiel, once again reading the event through the prism of Bourdieu's theory of power and legitimacy, the award enabled Wiesel to reach the apex of legitimacy as a consecrated representative of the Imperial State, or what I call in the present study the exalted status of High Priest of the Holocaust, our national religion. Chmiel writes:[468]

[468] *Elie Wiesel*, 133. Pierre Bourdieu, *La Distinction. Critique sociale du jugement* (Paris:

> *The bestowing of the Congressional Medal during the Bitburg crisis ironically constituted the apex of Wiesel's "consecration" by the state. Pierre Bourdieu argued that such "cultural consecration does indeed confer on the objects, persons and situations it touches a sort of ontological promotion akin to transubstantiation."*

Chmiel is right, but I would argue that it was not only Wiesel who was undergoing transubstantiation; it was also, by extension, the Holocaust itself that was being transubstantiated into the nation's official secular faith. Expressing the same idea in slightly different terms, Judith Miller writes:

> *Representative Stephen J. Solarz, Democrat of Brooklyn, whose district is home to more Jews than Jerusalem, said he had never believed that Jews would be so successful in transforming the Holocaust into part of the nation's officially recognized civic culture.* (*One by One*, 227)

Now, some thirty years later, at a time when the Imperial State is defined by moral bankruptcy as it bombs, tortures, maims and kills innocent civilians in its attacks on Israel's rivals, the meaning of the "transubstantiation" of Elie Wiesel can be seen more clearly for what it was.

We must recall that this award to Wiesel was based on the assumption that the alleged events to which he had claimed to be an eyewitness, that is, the absolute evil of the Holocaust, was actually true and had really happened. This assumption has now become a fundamental dogma of the U.S. Imperial State. It justifies wars of both "choice" and "necessity" for Israel's "security," while also allowing the U.S. government to turn a blind eye to the war crimes and crimes against humanity that the Israelis routinely inflict on the Arabs of Palestine. The Holocaust dogma also undergirds the Israeli and U.S. policy of extraterritoriality, that is, the right to attack anyone, anywhere, and at any time on the basis of secret evidence or information. This policy has made both countries fully functioning terror states.

The brainwashing campaign of our nation's youth about the Holocaust flows directly from this dogma.[469] It does not differ in intent, in any discernible way, from the youth ideological components of the propaganda programs that existed in former times in Hitler's Germany and the Soviet Union and its satellites. Not surprisingly, it also evinces tenets of the Zionist youth movements that flourished in many areas of Eastern Europe in the early years of the twentieth century. As with its forerunners, the goal of this modern-day brainwashing program for non-Jewish youth is to heighten "awareness" and "understanding" of the Holocaust in order to facilitate the work of the Holocaust fundamentalists on behalf of Israel.

Minuit, 1979), vii.

[469] Joseph Berger, "Once Rarely Explored, the Holocaust Gains Momentum as a School Topic," *New York Times*, October 3, 1988, A16.

Inspired by the new honors being heaped on Wiesel, one of his admirers, Irving Abrahamson, gathered together copies of Wiesel's essays, lectures, speeches and stories, and published them in a three-volume set entitled *Against Silence: The Voice and Vision of Elie Wiesel* (New York: Holocaust Library, 1985). This work sought to offer further evidence of Wiesel's importance as a writer as his Nobel campaign sped along. After all, since Wiesel's collected works were already being published, he must of necessity be an important writer. As to the title, with its emphasis on silence, Wiesel commented:[470]

> *I entered literature through silence. I felt I needed ten years to collect words and the silence in them, to purify every word in silence.*

Ironically, Abrahamson's title could also be interpreted as referring to the many other silences in Wiesel's life. Among them is his silence about his alleged tattoo, A-7713. Why won't he show it? Then there is his silence about the fact that the aerial photography of the Birkenau camp fails to confirm the existence of the fires he claims to have seen there. Third, he also remains silent when it comes to publishing his correspondence with Mauriac. Finally, his ongoing silence with regard to Israeli crimes in occupied Palestine is truly resounding.

The Nobel Prize Campaign

The campaign to secure a Nobel Prize for Wiesel ran concurrently with the efforts made by the Holocaust fundamentalists to have him named as the head of the U.S. Holocaust Memorial Museum and, later, to receive formal investiture from President Reagan as the nation's Holocaust High Priest. The Nobel campaign, to put it simply, sought worldwide recognition for the man. It was intended not only to increase Wiesel's personal prestige but also, in so doing, to universalize the new, emerging Holocaust faith. The plan seems to have originated early in that decade, and to have gathered steam thereafter. Given the cordial relationship that has historically existed between the major international Jewish organizations and the Nobel committee, the campaign got off the ground quite easily, encountering little if any resistance. In addition, since the Holocaustians felt that Wiesel was qualified for both the literature and peace prizes, they were unconcerned about which of the two he would receive. Thus, the Wiesel candidacy had a flexibility to it that few if any others have possessed.

A letter-writing campaign was already underway when, in 1983, the *New York Times* informed the public of it:[471]

---

[470] Herbert Mitgang, "Wiesel to Be Honored for 3-Volume Work," *New York Times*, December 5, 1985, C17.

[471] Freedman, "Bearing Witness," 34.

> *These are retrospective and cautiously positive times for Elie Wiesel. His name has been frequently mentioned as a possible recipient of a Nobel Prize, for either peace or literature.*

Accompanying that article, as described in Chapter VI, was the famous U.S. Army Signal Corps propaganda photo of "the men in the bunks" at Buchenwald. The newspaper's editors had drawn a circle around one of the men in the background of the photo, and claimed in the picture's caption that the adult male clearly visible is in fact the adolescent Wiesel:

> *On April 11, 1945, American troops liberated the concentration camp's survivors, including Elie, who later identified himself as the man circled in the photo.* (*Ibid.*)

It must be reiterated here that it was not until 1983 that Wiesel ever claimed to be in this widely recognized picture. How to explain this silence until then? And why did the *New York Times* suddenly, in 1983, seek to associate him with this picture, especially since the individual it identified as Wiesel is a full-grown man, and obviously not a boy of sixteen?

Furthermore, the man identified as Wiesel in no way resembles adolescent pictures that Wiesel has provided of himself. It would seem that the *New York Times* failed to fact-check Wiesel's claim to be in the picture, but the *Times* knows that in matters relating to the Holocaust, other media voices will challenge it at their peril. Thus, they are quite free to tell Holocaust fibs whenever necessary.

It should be noted in passing that the author of this article, Samuel Freedman, mentions there, as Edward Fiske had done in the *Times* a decade earlier, that many Jews took a dim view both of Wiesel and of his exploitation of the Holocaust to propel his career. Freedman also lamented that such people would not speak on the record:

> *And with Wiesel's fame has come, on the one hand, a dehumanizing sort of adulation and, on the other, a criticism of his writing and his personality – little of it rendered in public – from some leading American Jewish intellectuals. One Jewish historian and critic told the* Times *that, beneath the civil surface, Elie Wiesel arouses passions as strong as those that divided Jews during Israel's 1982 invasion of Lebanon.* (*Ibid.*)

These are strong words indeed. Freedman also conceded in this article that the campaign to canonize Wiesel as a cultural saint and living icon of the Holocaust was linked to the Zionist Jewish determination to silence the revisionists, whom he describes as "a handful of scholars [who] have arisen to proclaim the killing of six million Jews an exaggeration or a fraud." (*Ibid.*)

As part of the international campaign for Wiesel's reputation as a man of peace, the Holocaustians next proceeded to position the Holocaust within a constellation of related, but non-Jewish, humanitarian issues. To facilitate this positioning, Wiesel had embarked for Cambodia on a humanitarian mission in 1980. A month before his departure, the *New York Times* announced:[472]

> *Joan Baez, the singer, Bayard Rustin, the civil rights leader, and Elie Wiesel, the author and chairman of the President's Commission on the Holocaust, will be among a dozen Americans who will attempt to accompany a convoy of food and medicine into Cambodia next month, according to the International Rescue Committee.*

A month later, however, after arriving in Cambodia, Wiesel gave vent to his usual rhetoric on the uniqueness of Jewish suffering. When he prayed for the Cambodian dead, he did so by reciting the Jewish prayer for the dead in memory of his father, who is alleged to have died in Buchenwald in 1945. Here Wiesel was simply engaging in Jewish cultural imperialism, for his prayer had nothing directly to do with Cambodia in 1980. His prayer and remarks, not surprisingly, caused some grumbling among the other travelers in his entourage. But in positing the primacy of Jewish suffering by making that prayer, Wiesel laid bare his personal hypocrisy for all to see. This was the same man, after all, who had been "outraged" when François Mauriac had called him a "crucified Jewish child" and, in doing so, had spoken of his Jewish suffering in Christian terms.

The *New York Times*, as usual, sped to Wiesel's defense. The Holocaust was in the process of becoming the new secular faith of America, while being universalized as the new world religion. This new and utterly racist paradigm – Jewish suffering can metaphorically express the suffering of others, but the suffering of others can never be a metaphor for, let alone be compared to, Jewish suffering – required justification:[473]

> *But he* [Wiesel] *and many marchers agreed that at the edge of a country where several millions are feared to have died under Pol Pot's regime, the war that preceded it, and the war and famine that followed its ouster, the Kaddish had a wider appropriateness.*

The *Times*, in using this affair to unveil the new Holocaust doctrine of "wider appropriateness," was now justifying the imposition of Holocaust indoctrination on the youth of the Western democracies. Since the Holocaustians assume that Jewish suffering possesses universal symbolic value, it subsumes the sufferings of all other peoples. Given this dogmatic assumption, it flows logically that the imposition of Holocaust brainwashing on U.S. teenagers benefits from a wider appropriateness, and is thus the best antidote to "hate."

---

472 "Mission to Cambodia," *New York Times*, January 16, 1980, B2.

473 Henry Kamm, "Marchers with Food Aid Get No Cambodian Response," *New York Times*, February 7, 1980, A3.

As the Nobel campaign went forward, Sigmund Strochlitz, a New London, Connecticut, Ford dealer and – like Wiesel – a claimed veteran of the Holocaust, led the lobbying effort. A multi-millionaire in his own right, Strochlitz devoted five years of his life and traveled many thousands of miles in support of the project. Perhaps most important, he also coordinated the letter-writing campaigns. Wiesel, of course, knew all about the campaign. An ambitious man, more than ever questing for fame and wealth, he had quietly given his blessing to his friend's work.

When informed that the Nobel committee had awarded him the prize, Wiesel proclaimed, his English still rusty after thirty years in America, that "in Jewish history there are no coincidences. If it happened after Yom Kippur here, then some of my friends and myself have prayed well."[474] The actual amount paid to Wiesel for his Peace Prize was $287,769.78, tax-free,[475] a considerable sum even by today's standards. There was also plenty of kitsch to go around. Recalling the flaming pits he claimed to have seen as an eyewitness, he told *Time*:[476]

> *The child that I was had been consumed in the flames. There remained only a shape that looked like me. A dark flame had entered my soul and devoured it.*

Two weeks later, the *New York Times* stated plainly that there had been a major political reason behind Wiesel's selection, reporting that the Nobel Committee "chose precisely Elie Wiesel for the award" because they wanted to send a message to the Kohl government in Germany, which had not demonstrated sufficient guilt in 1985 in commemorating the fortieth anniversary of the end of World War II.[477]

In January 1987, the *Times* continued its policy of conflating the terms "Wiesel" and "Auschwitz" by erroneously claiming that Wiesel had been "freed from Auschwitz" at the end of the war.[478] Here was yet another deliberate use of disinformation about the "Great Man in Israel," but it sounded so much better than the truth, which was that (if in fact he had actually been there) he had been freed from Buchenwald.

A year later, when Wiesel made a trip to Auschwitz, the *New York Times* told yet another other whopper when it wrote:[479]

> *Mr. Wiesel was a prisoner at Auschwitz and witnessed the killing there of his father and one of his sisters.*

In reality, Wiesel did not witness any of his family members or friends from Sighet being killed. Furthermore, according to Wiesel, his father died

---

474 Joseph Berger, "Witness to Evil," *New York Times*, October 14, 1985, I, 10.

475 "Keeping Up With the Stallones: What To Remember About 1986," *Newsweek*, December 29, 1986, 66.

476 Zoglin, "Lives," 66.

477 Suskind, "Voice."

478 "A Survivor's Prize."

479 Haberman, "Wiesel and Walesa…"

at Buchenwald, not Auschwitz. The *Times*'s false assertions, whether deliberate or the fruit of shabby journalism practices, raise uncomfortable questions about that newspaper's commitment to printing the truth about Wiesel and the Holocaust.

After the Fact: Wiesel's Nobel Prize Campaign Revealed

After the announcement that Wiesel had won the Peace Prize, information about Sigmund Strochlitz's shameless campaign began to trickle out. One critic wrote:[480]

> *Wiesel's supporters have concentrated much of their energy on the U.S. Senate. One Senate aide described their energy as "relentless and heavy-handed." Strochlitz would show up every winter and say it's time to write letters again, one staffer said. He'd say, "You did it last year, it's time to do it again." He'd get the senators to send "Dear Colleague" letters to each other in an ever-widening circle.*

Strochlitz, a close friend of Wiesel's, denies doing any campaigning. This statement offers a valuable insight into the inner workings of our Israelocratic form of government. It depicts U.S. senators mindlessly – and obediently – taking orders from the likes of Sigmund Strochlitz and the Israel Lobby that stands behind him. There is no hint here that any of the senators who complied ever even entertained the thought of saying no.

The Zionist weekly *U.S. News and World Report* tried to justify the excessive zeal and money spent on Wiesel's Nobel campaign by arguing that in lobbying for the prize Wiesel did no more than what all the other candidates had done. Ironically, its article devoted to the subject disproved this very contention, for Wiesel's campaign had been excessive by any criterion, but especially on the extent to which members of the U.S. Congress, dominated by the Israel Lobby, had fallen into line:

> *Nearly all the candidates had prominent backers, but none matched Wiesel's list. It showed appeals from 170 U.S. lawmakers, 80 in West Germany, 12 in Sweden,* [and] *the heads of state in France, West Germany and Israel.*

Quoting a close friend of Wiesel, the report also made it clear that he personally wanted the prize, for he "always made it clear privately that the award was important to him, not only for recognition of Elie Wiesel, but [also] for the subject to which he had devoted his entire life – the [sic] Jewish memory, the Holocaust."[481]

The most serious outright criticism of the Nobel committee's selection came from investigative journalist Alexander Cockburn. He focused his at-

---

480 Jacob Weisberg, "Pop Goes Elie Wiesel," *New Republic*, November 10, 1986, 12.

481 Susanna McBee, "These Glittering Nobel Prizes," *U.S. News and World Report*, October 27, 1986, 67.

tention on the statement made in the award ceremony to the effect that Wiesel is a "messenger to mankind." Cockburn rejected such a description of Wiesel as patently absurd, and pointed to his ongoing silence (that word again) about Israel's war crimes against the Palestinians:[482]

> *It is difficult to find examples of Wiesel sending any message on behalf of those victimized by the policies of the United States, and virtually impossible when it comes to victims of Israel.*

Cockburn's article triggered letters of indignation from readers of *The Nation*. After all, by verbally assaulting Wiesel, he had dared to attack the most sacred of all the Jewish sacred cows of U.S. society. In his reply, Cockburn pointed out that Wiesel had received the award in part because of his "servility to power," adding:[483]

> [...] *Wiesel's role in the world is mostly to shut people up: to stop thinking or asking any questions that might discommode the powers that be. In every sense of the word, he is one of the exploiters.*

In a reply to another letter writer, Cockburn blurted out the truth of the matter in a way that no one in the mainstream media had ever done before (or has done since):[484]

> *Let us say, therefore, clearly: Wiesel cannot be considered as a real writer, but neither can he be regarded as a real thinker or a real social fighter.*

Simon Wiesenthal on Wiesel's Nobel

In a bizarre postscript to Wiesel's sordid exercise in self-aggrandizement, "Nazi hunter" Simon Wiesenthal claimed that he had always been under the impression that the fix had been put in for both of them, and that the Nobel Committee had been instructed in 1986 to act accordingly. "For him to get the Nobel Prize, one of his friends went around to lobby for it," Wiesenthal said bitterly. Vying with Wiesel as a champion user of broken English, he went on:[485]

> *I never made a propaganda* [for the prize]. *When the announcement was made that it went to Elie Wiesel, I walked out of my office, and my secretaries were crying. I said nothing. I thought the prize was going to be shared.*

When asked whether he had any reaction to Wiesenthal's comments, the Nobel laureate graciously responded:

> *I don't comment on hatred*

---

[482] Alexander Cockburn, "Beat the Devil," *The Nation*, November 8, 1986, 478.
[483] "Letters: Cockburn Replies," *The Nation*, December 20, 1986, 690.
[484] *Ibid.*, 716.
[485] Beth Landman, Deborah Mitchell, "A Bitter Battle over Nobel Pursuit," *New York Magazine*, vol. 29, no. 3, January 1996, 9

1985: Claude Lanzmann's *Shoah*

In October 1985, Claude Lanzmann's crude propaganda film *Shoah* opened in New York. It had been financed by the Israeli government to the tune of $850,000. Menachem Begin, Israel's prime minister at the time, justified this expenditure of state funds by calling the film "a project in the national Jewish interest."[486] At least he was honest about its propaganda value for Israel. This connection, however, went unmentioned either in the movie's film credits or in the Zionist media outlets that feed naïve non-Jews disinformation such as the *New York Times*, the *Washington Post* and the lesser ones that follow their lead.

With a running time of nine and a half hours, the film defied the patience of even the most hardcore true believers in the Holocaust. Strangely, it consisted entirely of interviews, and used no archival film footage. In retrospect, given the decade of revisionist victories since the publication of Butz's *Hoax* in 1976, Lanzmann really had no other strategy available to him. He could not use archival footage of either the gas chambers or of Wiesel's flaming pits, because none exists. And no such footage exists because these pseudo-events never happened. They are symbolic narratives of Jewish collective wartime suffering, and nothing more. Yes, Jews *were* deprived of their civil rights in Nazi Germany, they *were* deported from the country and they *were* held in concentration camps, where they *were* forced to work for the German war effort while the German armed forces struggled to secure the land on which these Jews would be resettled at the end of the war.

Since Lanzmann was unable to document either a plan for, or an implementation of, a massacre of Jews on an industrial scale, which is what the Holocaust supposedly involved, he had to be content with a series of often absurd and usually redundant interviews.

French Jewish Holocaustian Attacks Wiesel

It is worth noting in passing that Lanzmann chose to call his film *Shoah*, and not *Holocaust.* I would argue that he did so because at the time there was a growing discontent with both Wiesel and his word "Holocaust" among French intellectuals. By the mid-1980s, at precisely the time when his handlers were raising him to unimagined heights of prestige for the edification of the gullible *goyim*, Wiesel was causing concern among Holocaustians on both sides of the Atlantic. At issue was not only his abrasive personality, but also his pomposity, self-righteousness and overt Jewish

---

[486] "Report 'Shoah' Got Grant from Israel," *The Jewish Journal* (New York), June 27, 1986, 3; Paul Attanasio, "Resurrecting the Horror on Film: Claude Lanzmann's Long Struggle With the Holocaust and 'Shoah,'" *The Washington Post*, November 20, 1985, B1.

racism. And these problems were just the tip of the iceberg. The worst part of it was that the deadly combination of the revisionist attacks and the declassified aerial photography of Auschwitz had already proven him to be a false witness. Furthermore, France's Holocaustian Jews were embarrassed by his word "Holocaust," which referred directly to his mendacious claim to have witnessed the open-pit burning of large numbers of victims. Such criticism was generally kept strictly within Holocaustian circles.

Finally, Pierre Vidal-Naquet, the renowned historian of ancient Greece, unable to contain his frustration with Wiesel, publicly attacked him. In an interview with the French satirical magazine *Zéro*, Vidal-Naquet stated:[487]

> *For example, you have Rabbi Kahane, the Jewish extremist, who is less dangerous than a man like Elie Wiesel, who says anything that comes to mind.* [...] *You just have to read parts of* Night *to know that certain of his descriptions are not exact and that he is essentially a Shoah merchant* [...] *who has done harm, enormous harm, to historical truth.*

This statement revealed that the Holocaustians were seriously split between those who realized that Wiesel was a loose cannon that must be brought under control, and others, mostly fellow claimed veterans, who continued to champion him. Vidal-Naquet's words had additional impact in that they were uttered shortly after Wiesel had received the Nobel Peace Prize. Indeed, Vidal-Naquet was accusing Wiesel, with due circumspection, of lying about what he had witnessed during the Holocaust. These words of the late French scholar, confirmed Holocaustian, and bitter foe of Robert Faurisson, still stand as a crushing indictment of Wiesel and the fraud that he embodies.

December 1986: Wiesel Resigns as Chairman of the U.S. Holocaust Memorial Council

In December 1986, a month after cashing his Nobel check, Wiesel resigned from his position as chairman of the U.S. Holocaust Memorial Council. He had needed that position to enhance his credentials as a candidate for the Nobel Peace Prize, but once the money was in his pocket, he resigned. The timing of this rather abrupt departure involved not only the Nobel windfall, but also his frayed relations with fellow Jews involved in creating the museum. Many of them had become fed up with Wiesel; the reality is that they forced him out. First, there was his resentment that five

---

[487] Pierre Vidal-Naquet, "Une entrevue avec Pierre Vidal-Naquet," *Zéro*, April 1987, 57: "Par exemple, vous avez le rabbin Kahane, cet extrémiste juif, qui est moins dangereux qu'un homme comme Elie Wiesel qui raconte N'IMPORTE QUOI [...] Il suffit de lire certaine description de *La Nuit* pour savoir que certaines de ses descriptions ne sont pas exactes et qu'il finit par se transformer en marchand de Shoah [...] Eh bien, lui aussi, porte un tort, un tort immense, à la vérité historique."

million non-Jews had been accorded victim status by President Carter. Wiesel's racist stance on this issue was unyielding and, for those outside the immediate hothouse world of the Holocaust, his position seemed mean-spirited.

The present-day reality of the U.S. Holocaust Memorial Museum is that Jews receive close to ninety-nine percent of the victimhood coverage, while virtually nothing is said, in comparison, about President Carter's five million non-Jewish victims, or almost fifty percent. Yes, today the Jews monopolize the show and, as they do so, they rather arrogantly thumb their nose at Carter's original intent – the sharing of victimhood – when he gave them the land – land that belonged to the U.S. people – for their museum.

In 1986, with memories still fresh, especially among the aggrieved non-Jewish groups, about what Carter had actually mandated, Wiesel's continuing public insistence on the primacy of Jewish victimhood generated negative publicity. Then, when Gypsies were proposed for enshrinement in the USHMM as "worthy victims," Wiesel also opposed their inclusion and vigorously resisted it. In doing so, he once again shone an unwelcome and embarrassing light on the reality of Jewish racism. "Only Jews are allowed to sit in the front of the victimhood bus," he seemed to be saying.

In addition, he was a very poor administrator and extremely suspicious of people, even fellow Jews, if they were not Holocaust veterans. He justified this exclusivist desire to allow only (claimed) veterans into his inner circle by claiming that they were the only people who could understand the mystery of the Holocaust. This latter point is quite understandable when it is recalled that many of the veterans share a terrible secret: indeed, they were living proof that there had been no Holocaust. Thus, by the mid-1980s, Wiesel's continued insistence on his version of events seems to have been a principal reason, if not the main one, that his enemies among the Holocaust fundamentalists began to work tirelessly to remove him from his position as chairman of the museum council.

After the dust had settled, a cover story was invented for public consumption, and Michael Berenbaum, a well-known fundamentalist and one of the original staffers at the museum, made the case publicly that Wiesel's dismissal was due to a dispute between him and Simon Wiesenthal, and that this hostility in turn mirrored "the rivalry between New York's Museum of Jewish Heritage and the United States Holocaust Memorial Museum."[488] Berenbaum also knew that the Zionist media would never question this lame excuse for Wiesel's dismissal.

---

[488] Michael Berenbaum, "The Struggle for Civility: The Auschwitz Controversy and the Forces behind It," in: Carol Rittner, John K. Roth (eds.), *Memory Offended: The Auschwitz Carmel Controversy* (N.Y.: Praeger, 1991), 85.

Another Revisionist Insurrection: Henri Roques and *La Thèse de Nantes*

As mentioned above, Poliakov's *Bréviaire de la Haine*, for which Mauriac had written the foreword in 1951, had taken seriously the bizarre testimony of Kurt Gerstein, and had quoted from it in a highly selective manner. The revisionist historian Henri Roques demolished Poliakov's presentation of Gerstein as a credible witness (and in the process Poliakov's book as a serious work of history) in a doctoral thesis that he presented at the University of Nantes in 1986. After the thesis was accepted by the university, the Holocaust fundamentalists in France's Jewish community went into action, pulled the usual political strings, and had Roques's thesis annulled from above by administrative decree.

The extent of the damage that this Jewish-sponsored political subversion had inflicted on the integrity of the French university system became truly visible for all to see when Roques's doctoral thesis was later published.[489] Since then, the Holocaustians have neither been able to refute Roques's destruction of Gerstein's credibility, nor to rehabilitate Poliakov, who relied heavily on it as a historian.

Thanks in part to their utter inability to rebut Roques, Faurisson and the other revisionists, France's powerful Jewish Holocaust fundamentalists decided on stronger medicine against the revisionists. In July 1990, two months after Roques became editor of the revisionist journal *Revue d'Histoire Révisionniste*, the French parliament passed the Gayssot Act, which made it a crime punishable by severe penalties to publicly express doubt, let alone denial, of any kind about the official, state-mandated version of "la Shoah," as the Holocaust is known in France. Needless to say, this law also constituted the death sentence of the *Revue d'Histoire Révisionniste*, whose last issue, its sixth, appeared in May 1992.

Noted Historian Michel de Boüard Supports Henri Roques' Right of Inquiry

After the dust settled, a second controversy revolving around Roques' work erupted when Michel de Boüard, a distinguished medieval historian who held a professorship in medieval history at the University of Caen before World War II, and was also a member of the prestigious French learned society known as the Institut de France, expressed support for Roques' revisionist inquiries. He expressed this view in an article he penned in the daily newspaper, *Ouest-France*, which covers the geograph-

[489] Roques, because of his prior experience with Holocaustian censorship, published the book under a pseudonym: André Chelain, *La Thèse de Nantes et l'Affaire Roques* (Paris: Polémiques, 1989). Engl.: *The 'Confessions' of Kurt Gerstein.*

ical area in which the city of Nantes is located. It appeared as a feature article in the paper's weekend, Saturday-Sunday issue.[490]

Its power and importance derived from the fact that Boüard, both a fervent Catholic and a Communist, as unlikely as such a combination might seem, had been arrested by the Germans for his Resistance activities in 1944 and imprisoned in the Mauthausen Camp in what is today Austria. While there, he played a leadership role among his fellow prisoners, and was also tortured by his captors. After the war, as time went by, he slowly began to realize that, in the euphoria of liberation in 1945 and thereafter, many claims about alleged German crimes at Mauthausen had been terribly overinflated and consisted, for the most part, of nothing more than rumor. As a professional historian, he realized that, in the name of historiography and truth, these bogus claims, especially the one about an alleged homicidal gas chamber at Mauthausen, needed to be corrected. Still Dean of the Faculty at the University of Caen at the time, he went out on a limb with the regard to the powers that be, and wrote:[491]

> *On the one hand, I found myself torn between my conscience as a professional historian and the responsibilities that go with it, and, on the other hand, the fact that I had belonged to a group of comrades whom I deeply love but who refuse to recognize* [as a group] *the need to treat the historical fact of wartime deportation in accordance with traditional historical methods of inquiry.*
> *I am haunted by the thought that in a 100 years, or even 50, those historians who ask, with regard to this particular aspect of the Second World War, what in fact the concentration camp system was actually like, will be able to determine with certainty* [what it actually consisted of]. *The record is rotten to the core. On one hand you have a considerable number of fantasies, inaccuracies, obstinately repeated (in particular concerning numbers), a hodgepodge of unrelated facts, and generalizations. On the other hand, however, there are the (revisionists') critical studies, which are tightly argued and demonstrate the utter inanity of those exaggerations.*
> *I fear, finally, that these historians* [of the future] *will conclude that the deportation phenomenon must have been nothing more than a myth.*

---

490 Michel de Boüard, "Où ai-je acquis la conviction qu'il y avait une chambre à gaz à Mauthausen?," *Ouest-France*, August 2/3, 1986, 3.

491 "Je me trouvais déchiré entre ma conscience d'historien et les devoirs qu'elle me fait et l'appartenance à un groupe de camarades que j'aime profondément, mais qui ne veulent pas reconnaître la nécessité de traiter ce fait historique qu'est la déportation selon les méthodes d'une saine Histoire.
Je suis hanté par la pensée que, dans cent ans ou même cinquante, les historiens s'interrogent sur cet aspect de la Seconde Guerre mondiale qu'est le système concentrationnaire et de ce qu'ils découvriront. Le dossier est pourri. Il y a, d'une part, énormément d'affabulations, d'inexactitudes, obstinément répétées, notamment sur le plan numérique, d'amalgames, de généralisations et, d'autre part, des études critiques (les études négationnistes) très serrées pour démontrer l'inanité de ces exagérations. Je crains que ces historiens ne se disent alors que la déportation, finalement, a dû être un mythe. Voilà le danger. Cette idée me hante."

Therein lies the real danger, and this idea haunts me.

As might be expected, M. de Boüard came under fire from France's Holocaustian extremists, but stood his ground and never disavowed his statement. In fact, the same sentiments were expressed a year later in a learned journal.[492] Roques later brought closure to this controversy when he wrote:[493]

> *We won't succumb to the temptation to claim that, near the end of his life, M. de Boüard became an ardent revisionist* [...but] *he was an* "honnête homme," *a* "juste," *and especially a courageous historian.*

June 1987: Wiesel's Bungled Testimony at the Klaus Barbie Trial

One of the best-kept secrets in the life of Elie Wiesel is the manner in which he bungled his testimony at the Klaus Barbie show trial in Lyon, France, in 1987. As mentioned above, he had been sure *not* to appear at the Zündel trial in Toronto in 1985, precisely because he would have been questioned under oath about his experiences as an eyewitness. That was a real trial about the historical truth of the Holocaust. But in Lyon, he apparently thought, the situation would be somewhat different. After all, Barbie was already a convicted war criminal, and the event in which Wiesel was scripted to appear would be a classic example of a Stalinist show trial from beginning to end. Thus, he apparently thought he had nothing to fear. Yet, in his confrontation with Barbie's defense attorney, Jacques Vergès, Wiesel would be severely gored. Vergès, instead of taking a revisionist stance and questioning the Holocaust as fact, zeroed in on Wiesel's hypocrisy, including his use of double standards as an unapologetic supporter of Israel. When Vergès attacked, he threw the courtroom spectators and the three presiding judges into panic: he achieved the same effect with the Zionist media. As a result, the official history of the trial includes an elaborate cover-up of Wiesel's shoddy performance.

Prior to the trial, the Zionist media of France had announced that the government intended to capture the courtroom drama on film for the future education of the nation's youth, and that the resultant videos would be freely available to all. The reality today, however, in the age of the Internet, is that there is no readily-accessible video of the argument that took place

---

492 Michèle Cointet *et al.*, "Histoire, déontologie, médias: à propos de l'affaire Roques," *Revue d'Histoire Moderne et Contemporaine*, vol. 34, no. 1 (Jan-Mar 1987), 174-184.

493 Henri Roques, "Le doyen Michel de Boüard et les chambres à gaz homicides," *Revue d'Histoire Révisionniste*, vol. 1, no. 2, August-October 1990, 49; www.histoireebook.com/index.php?post/2012/07/31/Roques-Henri-Revue-d-Histoire-Revisionniste-1990-1992: "Nous ne céderons pas à la tentation de prétendre que M. de Boüard était devenu, à la fin de sa vie, un révisionniste convaincu [...mais il] était un honnête homme; c'était un juste; il fut surtout un historien courageux."

between Wiesel and Vergès, nor is there a verbatim text of this clash to be found anywhere. France's Holocaustian fundamentalists have succeeded in suppressing everything, and the French government has allowed them to get away with it. Instead, they have only allowed publication of the text that Wiesel read at the trial before Vergès began his interrogation. Published in an anthology of short texts entitled *From the Kingdom of Memory*, it gives no hint whatsoever of what transpired after Wiesel read his statement. As usual, Wiesel refers in this statement to the burning pits he claims to have seen and that had already become his particular and identifiable brand name among the pantheon of Holocaust eyewitnesses. He wrote:[494]

> *What I saw is enough for me. In a small wood somewhere in Birkenau I saw children being thrown into flames alive by the S.S.*

In order to fully explain the significance of this fiasco, I must start at the beginning. In 1983, Klaus Barbie was extradited from Bolivia, where he had long lived under the assumed name of Klaus Altmann. President François Mitterrand, anxious to reward the wealthy Jewish supporters who had given him both financial and media support during his election campaign in 1981, paid Bolivia's military dictator Hugo Banzer $50 million, and sent Bolivia a planeload full of arms, plus 3,000 tons of wheat.[495] In return, Banzer simply kidnapped Barbie, a law-abiding citizen, and shipped him off to France. Once in French custody, France's Holocaustians demanded that he be exhibited in a show trial in much the same way as Eichmann had been in Jerusalem in 1961. Since Barbie, who had been a Gestapo leader in wartime Lyon, had already been condemned to death twice in absentia by French courts, the outcome of his trial could not be in doubt. Thus, this was to be the new, updated version of the Eichmann trial, for its major purpose was to indoctrinate a new generation about the Holocaust. Eichmann had been locked in a glass booth at his show trial, and a similar fate was planned for Barbie. He would be exhibited before his accusers as if he were an animal, and would stand as a symbol of all those Germans who had deported Jews from France to the East during the war years.

To that end, the media kept on repeating, day in and day out in advance of the trial, that about 76,000 Jews had been deported from France to German camps during the war, claiming without proof that over 90 percent of them had been killed there. Yet there is an important fact regarding this issue that is almost never revealed: in 1941 – 1942 there were about 320,000 Jews living in France, including those without passports. Such figures are disturbing to the extermination legend, for they show that it is scarcely

---

[494] Wiesel, "Testimony at the Barbie Trial," in *Kingdom*, 181.

[495] Erna Paris, *Unhealed Wounds* (New York, Grove: 1985), 108.

likely that there could have been an extermination program in place, if only 25 percent of the Jews in France were deported. That the Holocaustian Jews of France and the captive French media refrain from mentioning this fact betrays their bad faith. In a word, if the Vichy government deported 76,000 Jews out of a total of 320,000, the question is "Why these Jews and not others?" Was it because they were stateless and undocumented? Or was it because they were Communists and, as such, considered to be security risks? Or was their deportation due to their membership in a Resistance group, or even to their (individual) status as common criminals? Finally, although Serge Klarsfeld, other Holocaustians and the media assert that only a couple of thousand of the 76,000 deportees survived, their claim is vitiated by their insistence that the only French Jewish survivors who can be officially recognized are those who later registered at a government office in France after the war.

After years of legal delays, the trial finally began on May 11, 1987, and lasted through July 4. The Zionist scriptwriters were dealt a serious setback at the outset of the trial when, on May 13, after all the charges against Barbie had been read, he announced that, in accordance with French law, he would no longer come to the courtroom. He considered the trial to be a political farce and stated:

> *If I am here before you, it's because, as a Bolivian citizen, I have been the victim of an illegal deportation. It is therefore my intention to no longer appear before this court. (Si je me trouve devant vous, c'est parce que j'ai été victime, étant Bolivien, d'une expulsion illégale. Je n'ai donc plus l'intention de paraître devant ce tribunal.)*

The various Jewish groups (*les parties civiles*) orchestrating this event were thrown into confusion; some of them wanted the presiding judge, André Cerdini, to force Barbie to appear. Although the law gave him that power, the judge decided, for reasons that have never been made clear, to allow Barbie to remain in his cell for the rest of the trial. This decision, which robbed the show trial of its intended theatrical effect, only served to heighten expectations of Wiesel and his much-awaited performance. Nonetheless, Barbie and his attorney had made their point: the show trial was essentially a Zionist media stunt, and those who were pulling the strings behind the scenes were making a mockery of legal procedures. Even Ted Morgan, a Christian Zionist writing in defense of the trial, had to admit that it was a judicial farce:[496]

> *The conduct of the trial, in its pretended adherence to the judicial principles of the French Republic, was a necessary travesty.*

But a show trial, even when labeled a "necessary travesty," is still a show trial in which the guilt of the defendant is assumed beforehand.

---

[496] Ted Morgan, *An Uncertain Hour* (N.Y.: William Morrow, 1990), 24f.

Before considering Wiesel's appearance in court, it is worth recalling that in the year of the Barbie trial, 1987, the Zionist media arranged for the publication of Wiesel's interview book with Brigitte-Fanny Cohen, *Elie Wiesel: Qui êtes-vous?* To sharpen the book's relevance to the trial, it was published in Lyon. Its purpose was to serve as a backup to Wiesel's appearance on the witness stand. Although by 1987 Wiesel was well known in the U.S., he enjoyed only limited brand recognition in France, and apparently this was why the French Holocaustians deemed this book to be a necessity. Its very title bespoke its subject's obscurity: "Who are you, Elie Wiesel?" Wiesel owed his lack of recognition in France to infrequent exposure there; as a writer he enjoyed little if any respect in the eyes of the French intelligentsia. French critics found his novels boring, repetitive and patently didactic to the point that they were considered almost unreadable. As for Wiesel's essays, his lack of a formal education hampered his ability to argue a point in the traditional French manner, that is, with references, made in an authoritative manner, to thinkers and philosophers of previous generations. Despite the myth about Wiesel's studies at the Sorbonne, this was an insurmountable handicap. The only subject about which Wiesel knows anything is the Talmud, and his writing style in French is, to put it charitably, plodding.

Wiesel's appearance had been scripted for June 2, 1987, for two basic reasons. First, each of the thirty-nine Jewish groups, "co-plaintiffs," bringing a complaint against Barbie had an opportunity to state its case in court in the weeks before Wiesel's testimony. Klarsfeld & Co. had apparently figured out in advance that this mind-numbing and repetitive performance would be a waste of time that would risk killing off whatever interest non-Jews in France might have had in the trial. Thus Wiesel's role as a big name Nobel Prize winner was designed to refocus attention. Second, in the days immediately preceding his appearance, the court was informed of the supposed fate of the Jewish children from the orphan's home in the small town of Izieu, not far from Lyon. These children, who had all been placed there by the Jewish organization that the Pétain government had set up at the beginning of the war, the *UGIF* (*Union Générale des Israélites de France*), were deported to Auschwitz on April 13, 1944. They arrived at the camp two days later, on April 15. There, according to the official historiography, they were immediately placed in the mythical gas chambers at Birkenau (Morgan, 274).

The supposed fate of these children had only begun to be exploited in 1984 with the publication by Serge Klarsfeld of his polemical booklet, *Les enfants d'Izieu: une tragédie juive*.[497] Klarsfeld had published this book

[497] Serge Klarsfeld, *Les enfants d'Izieu: une tragédie juive* (Paris: Les Fils et les Filles des Déportés Juifs de France, 1984).

shortly after Barbie's extradition to France, in anticipation of the show trial. The USHMM brought out a translation of this book in 1985 under the title *The Children of Izieu, a Human Tragedy*. No effort was ever made, however, either by Klarsfeld or any of his Holocaustian cohorts on the one hand, or by Vergès and his legal team on the other, to consult the archives of the International Tracing Service with regard to the fate of the forty-three children under the age of seventeen who had been deported. Located in the town of Bad Arolsen, in what was still West Germany, these personnel files contain authoritative information on millions of individuals who had passed through the German camp system. To this day, the myth of "*les enfants d'Izieu*," just like the myth of nearly all of the 76,000 Jews deported from France perishing in the Holocaust, remains in place only because the evidence concerning the children's fates remains suppressed. Since those files are now in the possession of the USHMM and not in the U.S. Archives, where they rightly belong, there is now no way for me to check on their fate.

As Wiesel read his statement before being cross-examined by Vergès, he played his familiar game of not believing what he had supposedly seen. He stated:[498]

> *I cannot recall my mother or my little sister. With my eyes, I still look for them, I will always look for them. And yet I know* […] *know everything. No. Not everything.* […] *one cannot know everything. I could imagine it, but I do not allow myself to. One must know when to stop.* […] *My gaze stops at the threshold of the gas chambers. Even in thought, I refuse to violate the privacy of the victims at the moment of their death.*

This was the same old charlatan using the same old doubletalk.

I now follow the account of this cross-examination as found in the online narrative provided by the Jewishvirtuallibrary.org.[499] Referring to the children of Izieu, Vergès asked Wiesel if he had ever done anything to help the thousands of Algerian children who had died in French internment camps before and during the Algerian war of Independence (1954-1962). Wiesel replied that "when I see an injustice, I protest and I have done it." Having walked right into Vergès's trap, he was then asked:

> *Have you ever heard of the massacre of the children at Deir Yassin* [in the village of that name by the Israelis in 1948]*?*

Vergès had struck a raw nerve, exposing in one breath the utter hypocrisy on which the whole "trial" was based: that Jews are always "worthy victims," while those who are killed by Jews must always remain "unworthy victims," about whose fate not a word may be uttered. Vergès's thrust broke the calm that had existed in the courtroom until then, and "at this

---

498 Wiesel, *Kingdom*, 182.

499 www.jewishvirtuallibrary.org/jsource/Holocaust/barbietrial.html#court

point, [presiding judge] Cerdini, sensing the increased tensions not only on the courtroom floor but all around the chamber, tried to intervene." When calm was finally restored, Wiesel said:

> *Yes. I stand with Israel. I'm proud of it. It's the only country in the world that was ready to recognize a Palestinian Arab. The Arabs did not want to. They wanted to make a war with Israel.* [...] *That does not justify the brutalities. I am against such things wherever they occur.*

Vergès now delivered his next blow to Wiesel:

> *One cannot be unconditionally for Israel. I asked a question about Deir Yassin and nobody answered it!*

Wiesel, shocked, had no immediate reply. Then, after trying to compose himself, his voice cracking, he said:

> *I find it especially regrettable that the lawyer for the defense dares to accuse the Jewish people of the very crimes committed against them. Is that all he has to say today in 1987?*

Now the knockout blow was about to be delivered both to Wiesel and to all the string pullers, from Serge Klarsfeld on down, who had orchestrated this legal charade, but it would not be Vergès who would deal that blow directly. No, it would be the chief judge himself, who would let the cat out of the bag with regard to the true nature of this show trial. I quote from Jewishvirtuallibrary.org once again:

> *Cerdini, seeing that the argument was going to spin out of control, and wanting to avoid national embarrassment over what might happen next, shouted: "We are getting distracted from our trial!"*

It is impossible to know exactly what Cerdini was thinking when he used the ambiguous expression "our trial." In retrospect, however this supposedly judicial event was obviously a classic example of a show trial. In light of the fact that there was no doubt that Barbie would be found guilty, it had been organized for the sole benefit of the Jewish co-plaintiffs as well as to serve the propaganda needs of the international Jewish community, which was determined to show the world that Jewish suffering is greater than the suffering of any other people on the planet. And this was precisely how Vergès interpreted Cerdini's remark. He had already become disgusted with the avalanche of Jewish propaganda that had been allowed at the trial with the complicity of the three French judges. On several occasions, he had been interrupted by the judges when comparing Jewish suffering to that endured by Blacks and Asians, in exactly the same time period, as a result of French colonial policy. Thus, when Barbie's lawyer Vergès drowned out judge Cerdini's last words ("...our trial") and exclaimed:

> *"All peoples are considered the same!"*

– he was giving public expression to this feeling of frustration.

The conduct of the show trial deteriorated after Wiesel's aborted testimony. The evidence, prepackaged and repetitive, continued to be presented. Thereafter, each of the thirty-nine lawyers for the various Jewish groups was given an opportunity to sum up the case against Barbie. Even the fiercely Jewish Zionist Alain Finkielkraut had to admit, in an essay he later wrote in an attempt to whitewash these vile proceedings, that the "thirty-nine closing speeches talked the audience into a stupor without interruption from the 17th to the 26th of June. The irritation building up against the plaintiffs in the course of the hearing was unleashed on Mr. Zaoui [one of the Jewish lawyers] when he tried to interrupt his Algerian colleague [a member of the Barbie defense team]:[500]

> *Enough, you windbag! Shut up! We have already heard more than enough from you! You have expounded shamelessly for eight days; you are not going to add to this by drowning out the voice of your opponents!*

Wiesel's performance was of course covered by the *New York Times*, but with very delicate tweezers as to Vergès's withering cross-examination of "the great man in Israel." The *Times* report stated that Wiesel had testified about "what he called the unique nature of the Nazi campaign against the Jews,"[501] while also claiming that the survivors represent what he called the "collective consciousness" of the Holocaust. The reporter went on, taking pains to spare Wiesel:

> *But his* [Wiesel's] *testimony also became the occasion of a long anticipated effort by Mr. Barbie's defense lawyer, Jacques Vergès, to argue just the opposite – that what he called 'other atrocities,' comparable to the Nazi persecution of the Jews, had taken place in the 20th century, and they remain unpunished.*

1987: Stage One of Wiesel's Abusive Relationship with Cardinal O'Connor of New York

During a trip to the Middle East in the summer of 1986, Cardinal John Joseph O'Connor of New York called for the creation of a Palestinian state.[502] Impelled by Catholic teachings on social justice, he issued that statement in his capacity as president of the Catholic Near East Welfare Association, a papal agency that dates back to 1926, and that offers humanitarian and pastoral support to the Catholics of the region. He did nothing

---

500 Alain Finkielkraut, *Remembering in Vain: The Klaus Barbie Trial and Crimes against Humanity* (N.Y.: Columbia University Press, 1992), 63; for a revisionist take on the Barbie trial see A. Chelain (Henri Roques), *Le procès Barbie, ou le shoah-business à Lyon* (Paris: Polémiques, 1987).

501 Richard Bernstein, "Wiesel Testifies at Barbie's Trial," *New York Times*, June 3, 1987, A7.

502 E. J. Dionne, Jr., "O'Connor Calls for a Homeland for the Palestinians," *New York Times*, June 19, 1986, A2.

wrong in making that statement, and in fact at least half of America's Jews reportedly supported the creation of such a state at the time.[503] But influential Jews in New York were angry about what he had said. Knowing that O'Connor was a good-hearted man, but a diplomatic fool, they saw an opportunity to make a point – that only Jews can be "worthy victims" – by embarrassing him. Since O'Connor's statement had provided implicit proof that he thought Jews were in the wrong in Palestine, he had to be brought back under control. The cardinal needed a lesson in what Elie Wiesel's consecration as our Holocaust High Priest a year earlier signified: that the Jews are perpetual "worthy victims," whereas the Palestinians are perpetual "unworthy victims."

The first thing the Jewish leaders did, following the Holocaust fundamentalist script to the letter, was to invite Cardinal O'Connor to visit the Yad Vashem Holocaust museum in Jerusalem, which he did in January 1987. O'Connor's symbolic recognition that Jews are the world's eternal "worthy victims" should have been the end of the affair, but his lack of diplomatic skill worked against him once again. When he emerged from the museum, he was in tears at the thought of the suffering that the Jews had endured in the Holocaust, that is, the deliberately inflated and distorted version of their actual wartime sufferings. President George W. Bush was similarly moved to tears there a decade later.[504] But the hapless prelate immediately angered Jews anew by saying that "it might well be that the Holocaust may be an enormous gift that Judaism has given to the world."[505]

What he meant was that, in Catholic terms, it was possible that some spiritual good could come from it. O'Connor's words were meant to express sympathy for Jews in the most earnest terms he knew, those of his Catholic religion. Mauriac had done the same thing in 1958, when he called Wiesel a "crucified Jewish child." Wiesel had not done any differently when, on his trip to Cambodia, he had prayed for the dead Cambodians by using the Jewish prayer for the dead. While there had been some grumbling over Wiesel's prayer as an expression of Jewish cultural and religious hegemony over others, the *New York Times* concluded that there is actually a "higher appropriateness" when a Jew like Wiesel says the Jewish prayer for the dead for non-Jews.

But this doctrine of higher appropriateness obviously did not apply to O'Connor's remarks, and he once again was pilloried by his Jewish critics.

---

[503] Steven M. Cohen, "Half of U.S. Jews for Palestinian Homeland," *New York Times*, July 1, 1986, A22.

[504] Aron Heller, "Bush Visits Israel's Yad Vashem Holocaust Memorial," *AP Worldstream*, January 11, 2008.

[505] Joseph Berger, "O'Connor Tours the Holocaust Museum," *New York Times*, January 3, 1987: "The Cardinal said he has also discussed his visit to Yad Vashem with Mr. Hammer. 'I mentioned to the Minister,' he said, 'that it might well be that the Holocaust may be an enormous gift that Judaism has given to the world.'"

No sooner had the cardinal touched ground in New York than he was greeted by a statement of condemnation signed by the leaders of fifty-three Jewish organizations. The *New York Times* reported:[506]

> *The statement was unusual not only for its criticism of the Cardinal – Jewish officials have until now tried to hold him blameless in other critical comments on the trip – but also because of the wide spectrum of Jewish opinion that it encompassed.*

A few days later, Wiesel, in his new role as the nation's Holocaust High Priest, made what can be termed a pastoral call on O'Connor. The latter, badly battered by the ongoing media assault, welcomed this visit, which represented a complete role reversal for the two men. Abused people always like the ostensibly kind side of their abusers. They met privately on January 29 "at the initiative of Mr. Wiesel, who said he was concerned about the critical reaction that Jewish leaders had expressed to the Cardinal's trip."[507] The naïve O'Connor then became friends with Wiesel, whom he called "the Prophet of the Holocaust." Unbeknownst to Cardinal O'Connor, he was entering into an abusive relationship, one that would last until his death in 2000.

O'Connor was not the first of Wiesel's victims, but he offers a chilling example of a much larger and ongoing pattern of abuse. The specific precursors of the O'Connor-Wiesel relationship date back to the years just after Vatican II, when well-intentioned bishops dispatched "experts" to "dialogue" with the Jewish organizations. But as the dialogue continued, through intermediaries like Eugene Fisher, the longtime expert on Catholic-Jewish relations for the National Council of Catholic Bishops, these spokespersons brought shame upon both the Church and themselves, as they allowed a supposed dialogue to degenerate into a monologue in which their Jewish interlocutors routinely scolded them. Even worse, Catholics in the pews have had to look on as the princes of the Church, from the Bishop of Rome on down, groveled at the feet of the Holocaust fundamentalists who lead the principal Jewish organizations.

In the end, O'Connor probably did no worse than popes like John Paul II and Benedict XVI, who, as part of this sick and ongoing "dialogue," have felt compelled to visit the sites of former German concentration camps in order to kneel in obeisance to the secular sacrifice of the six million who allegedly died in the Holocaust. With modern popes trying to serve two masters, is it any wonder that the Church has entered into such a spiral of decline?

---

[506] Ari L. Goldman, "Jewish Groups Fault O'Connor on Mideast Trip," *New York Times*, January 11, 1987, A1.

[507] Ari L. Goldman, "For Cardinal, Wiesel Visit Proved a Calm in Storm over Trip," *New York Times*, February 15, 1987, I, 67.

During the decade or so that Wiesel and O'Connor engaged in dialogue, observers were able to witness the unfolding of a classic scenario of abuse: the perpetrator, with his quick temper, is bossy and possessive. He pressures the victim to do things that dishonor him and to speak untruths. The worst feature of this syndrome is that the abused party, having grown accustomed to this treatment, no longer even thinks about escaping this degrading situation. An early example of such submission in the decade of abuse came when O'Connor, trying to score points with New York Jewish leaders, ordered that the Catholic Church in New York commemorate the night of November 9–10, 1988, as the fiftieth anniversary of *Kristallnacht*, the pogrom against Jews across Germany in 1938. O'Connor ordered that the bells of St. Patrick's Cathedral, his church, be rung, and that the lights be left on all night in archdiocesan buildings! On the same evening, the local PBS station in New York City (which had aired *Kitty* a few years earlier), broadcast a propaganda film entitled "Elie Wiesel: A Self Portrait," in which a voice from off camera lobbed Wiesel softball questions about his life.[508] Yes, O'Connor learned quickly how to submit unquestioningly to the demands of his abuser, even as Wiesel was enjoying adulatory exposure on a local, Zionist-controlled TV station. For any of its readers too obtuse to grasp it, a *Times* reporter explained the reason for O'Connor's ridiculous and expensive gesture:[509]

> *Many Jews chafed at a remark the Cardinal made during his already controversial Middle East trip. Upon leaving the Yad Vashem Holocaust museum in Jerusalem, he said the Holocaust "may be an enormous gift that Judaism has given to the world."*

Now O'Connor was obediently putting the concerns of all those New York Jews who had allegedly "chafed" ahead of those of the Catholics whose shepherd he was. His reckless gesture meant that the Catholics in the pews, mostly ordinary working folk, would bear the cost of O'Connor's waste of electricity in his needless gesture of appeasement to the New York Jewish community.

1988: Wiesel, as Holocaust High Priest, Attacks John Paul II

In June 1988, the First Intifada had been underway for about six months; the *New York Times*, trying to present the 1986 Nobel Peace laureate in a favorable light, published an opinion piece by Wiesel on that subject. Although Wiesel's article was not overly strident in its denunciation of the Palestinians, it dripped with Jewish hypocrisy by arguing, dishonestly

---

508 Walter Goodman, "Elie Wiesel: A Self-Portrait," *New York Times*, November 10, 1988, A10.

509 Joseph Berger, "The View from St. Patrick's," *New York Times*, March 28, 1989, SM38.

and mendaciously, that it was *only* the Jews of Israel who were the victims of terror and unjustified violence.[510] This was the "official," not the real Wiesel, who was being advertised by the *New York Times* for public consumption. But not all New York Jews were sympathetic to Wiesel's brand of Holocaustian sanctimony.[511] One of them, New York intellectual Arthur Herzberg, replied to Wiesel's article in the pages of the *New York Review of Books*, accusing him – and rightly so – of silence about what the Jews of Israel were doing to the Palestinians. While it took a while for Herzberg's rejoinder to make it into print (after all, he was attacking New York's most sacred Jewish cow), his article was clearly intended to answer Wiesel's *New York Times* op-ed of June 23. Herzberg's piece offered further proof of the festering disgust that many U.S. Jews harbored with respect to Wiesel's hypocrisy and grandstanding.

A day after the appearance of Wiesel's op-ed, Pope John Paul II embarked on a state visit to Austria, where he was received by President Kurt Waldheim, whom Jewish groups had sought to turn into an international pariah following unsubstantiated charges that the former UN secretary general had committed war crimes while serving in the Wehrmacht. Simultaneously, the Holocaust fundamentalists, in an effort to insult both the Pope and the papacy, staged a revival of *The Deputy* in Vienna, although by then that propaganda piece was already twenty-five years old and showing its age. Worse, it had been repeatedly debunked and deconstructed over the years by the revisionists who, although they are for the most part not Catholics, continued to resolutely defend Pius XII against the accusation of silence.

The Pope's meeting with Waldheim was enough to send the Pope's detractors at the *New York Times* into overdrive. They watched his every move in Austria with a highly critical eye. The *Times*'s first report from Austria was intended to stir up outrage among its "congregation," New York City's Jews. The Pope had as yet made no verbal *faux pas* about the Holocaust, so the meeting with Waldheim would have to suffice for stirring up indignation in the newspaper's first dispatch.[512] The next day, during a visit to the Mauthausen camp, the Pope mentioned the names of four victims, all of whom had been Catholics. Since he did not mention any Jews by name, the *New York Times* fulminated in rage over the alleged insult. The reader will recall that this ploy is a standard feature of *New York Times* reporting on the Holocaust. When Jewish primacy in suffering is not driven home to the satisfaction of some Jewish leader or other, the *New York*

---

510 Elie Wiesel, "A Mideast Peace: Is It Impossible?," *New York Times*, June 23, 1988, A23.

511 Arthur Herzberg, "An Open Letter to Elie Wiesel," *New York Review of Books*, August 18, 1988, 13f.

512 Serge Schmemann, "John Paul II Meets with Waldheim Again: Arriving for Visit to Austria, Pope Avoids Mentioning Furor over President," *New York Times*, June 24, 1988, A3.

Times will at minimum express "concern," if not "chafe" or worse at more grievous affronts to "Jewish suffering." This policy was evident in the second dispatch, filed the next day.[513]

Illustration 30: Elie Wiesel at the White House visiting U.S. President George H.W. Bush

On the final day of his visit, the Pope dutifully mentioned Jewish suffering. There was, however, a verbal defect in his formula. Mischievously, the Pope had mentioned the suffering of Jews, but had also stipulated that the sufferings of all, both Christians and Jews, had been a "gift to the world."[514] This was obviously a reference to Cardinal O'Connor's remark seventeen months earlier at Yad Vashem, which as we have seen earned him furious attacks from Jewish leaders in New York. Yet in its third dispatch on the papal visit, the *Times* apparently decided, for reasons unknown, to miss the obvious connection when the Pontiff reprised the Archbishop of New York, his friend.

I now return to Wiesel, whose op-ed had appeared in the *New York Times* at the beginning of the week. On June 28, that is, at the culmination of the pope's trip to Austria, writing in the tabloid *New York Post*, Wiesel abandoned the tone of carefully simulated tolerance that had characterized his *Times* op-ed of June 23, and attacked John Paul II as an anti-Jewish bigot.[515] This diatribe was so virulent and hateful that, to the best of my knowledge, the *New York Times* has never touched this story. Doubtless the *Times* suppressed it because it revealed a side of Wiesel at odds with the image that this newspaper desires to project of the Nobel peace laureate. *Times* editors must have also been embarrassed to see Wiesel using one of their favorite tropes, failure to mention the word "Jew," almost a decade after the Pope's alleged infraction. Wiesel's delayed and staged outrage brought discredit to this shopworn journalistic contrivance. In his article, Wiesel lashed out savagely at John Paul II, saying that "this Pope has a problem with Jews, just as Jews have a problem with him." But, as if this insulting lie were not enough, he went on to level a specific charge against John Paul II that was totally false. Said Wiesel:

---

[513] Serge Schmemann, "John Paul Meets with Austrian Jews; Papal Remarks at a Death Camp Are Criticized," *New York Times*, June 25, 1988, A1.

[514] "John Paul Cites Suffering of Jews; Criticized, He Says Ordeal of All Nazis' Victims Was a 'Gift to the World,'" *New York Times*, June 26, 1988, A6.

[515] Elie Wiesel, "John Paul II and His Jewish Problem," *NY Post*, June 28, 1988, 27.

> *He never mentioned the Jewish victims during his first Auschwitz visit nine years ago.*

Wiesel had been silent about this alleged affront in 1979. But why? Was it because he was still feeling his way forward and had not yet received his formal investiture, at the hands of President Reagan, as our Holocaust High Priest? Now, however, with the enthusiastic imprimatur of the U.S. government, the Zionist-controlled media, and the nation's collaborationist university apparatus, Wiesel evidently felt he could say anything he wanted to, however reckless, without worrying about open criticism from the people who control public discourse.

As mentioned in the previous chapter, the fact is that, when Pope John Paul II visited Auschwitz on June 7, 1979, he stopped at the propaganda marker (since dismantled as an embarrassment by order of the Holocaust fundamentalists) that told visitors in eighteen languages that four million people had perished there (see p. 247). Although the Pope did not mention the word "Jew" in his speech, he certainly did refer to the Jews and to Jewish suffering.

Wiesel clearly wanted to pick a fight with the Pope, and merely selected this supposed slight, already nine years old, as the pretext for it. But readers of this study know by now that for Wiesel facts mean nothing. Since he is driven by a complex amalgam of hypocricy, hatred, Jewish racism, and self-interest, there is no way of predicting exactly how he will frame his arguments and attacks in any particular situation.

Wiesel's Attack Was Part of the "Softening-Up" of John Paul II

In retrospect it is clear that Wiesel's 1988 assault on the Pope was part of the media-driven Auschwitz Carmel controversy that was being used at the time as a club to beat John Paul II. As such, Wiesel's *Post* article was part of a softening-up process that had begun soon after John Paul's installation as Pope in 1978, and increased in intensity when, during his historic visit to the Auschwitz camp in 1979, he authorized that a large cross be erected on its grounds in honor of all the dead, whether Christians or Jews. In 1979 the Pope also expressed support of the Carmelites whose convent was located on the grounds of the former camp. These positions angered Jewish Holocaustians because, in their view, the Auschwitz-Birkenau camp was to be dedicated exclusively to Jewish "memory." They would not be satisfied until any and all manifestations of Catholicism on the grounds of Auschwitz were removed.

Yet it must be noted that, in terms of actual documented suffering, the Jewish side cannot claim a monopoly on suffering at Auschwitz. That claim is based either on dubious oral testimony or "affidavits" signed by tortured Nazis. Yet, we do have a tangible source of hard facts, the so-called "Death Registers" (*Sterbebücher*) of Auschwitz, which the conformist historians avoid citing at all costs in this context. Dr. Nicholas Kollerstrom has recently written about this issue and found that the extant registers, which cover the months from July 1941 to April 1943, indicate a very important fact: that of the approximately 65,000 deaths which occurred during this period, mostly from typhus, Catholics (mostly Polish) outnumbered Jews: 47% to 43%; and all Christian Auschwitz deaths together outnumbered Jewish deaths by some 55% to 43%.[516] Thus, on the basis of available historical evidence, the Holocaustians had no right to demand that Pope John Paul II's cross be removed.

Beginning in 1979, the major Jewish organizations and the *New York Times* commenced a relentless attack on the Pope aimed at forcing him to accept solely Jewish victimhood in the Holocaust. In July 1989, after Rabbi Avi Weiss of Riverdale, New York, along with six Jewish henchmen, scaled the walls of the Carmelite convent at Auschwitz to protest its presence there, the controversy gained momentum when the Zionist media depicted the invading Jewish thugs as victims.[517] When several local Polish men, outraged by their breach of the nuns' privacy, evicted them, they unwittingly stepped into a trap. Instead of helping the nuns, they wound up setting the stage for the nuns' eventual eviction by the Pope. By 1993, John Paul was so fatigued by the constant Zionist Jewish propaganda bombardment that he finally cracked. Although he had already betrayed the Church by ordering that both the cross and Carmelites be removed from the camp's grounds, he now committed an even more serious act of betrayal of Catholic tradition by granting formal Vatican diplomatic recognition to the Israeli apartheid state. As John Paul II gave his blessing to the Zionist caste that rules Israel, Pope Pius XII, a consummate Catholic diplomat, must have been turning over in his grave. After this unexpected and undeserved papal *volte-face*, the *New York Times* expressed its gratitude through a sudden change in how it covered John Paul II; the rest of the Zionist-controlled media followed. This positive coverage continued, culminating at the Pope's death in a sickening orgy of Zionist media adulation that lasted for days in both the U.S. and Europe. Nothing could better demonstrate the significance of what John Paul II had surrendered, without receiving anything in return.

---

[516] Kollerstrom, *Breaking the Spell*, 83. See also the Auschwitz Museum's data at www.auschwitz.org/en/museum/about-the-available-data/death-records/sterbebucher/

[517] See Avi Weiss, "Auschwitz is a sacred place of Jewish memory. It's no place for a Catholic church," *The Washington Post*, January 28, 2015; www.washingtonpost.com/posteverything/wp/2015/01/28/auschwitz-is-a-sacred-place-of-jewish-memory-its-no-place-for-a-catholic-church/; see also "Rabbi Fights Poles," New York Times, January 27, 1995, 5.

The Pope's abandonment of traditional papal caution resulted in many dire consequences for the Church, especially since he had made his concession to Israel without reciprocation from the Jewish side. As a result, crucial questions relating to taxation of the Church and the legal status of Church property in Israel were not addressed. Nor was there any settlement of the question of the legal status of Church officials, whether religious or lay people, so that now such people can be harassed at will by the Israeli authorities. All such questions were left for negotiation at a later date, but today, more than two decades later, none has been resolved.

By the end of his long reign, John Paul II had increased his personal philo-Semitism, in word and deed, to levels never before seen in a pope. As a result of his capitulation to the Zionists, apparently in the mistaken belief that he would build confidence by forfeiting the Church's legitimate prerogatives, the Zionist media, as noted above, went into a frenzy of commemoration after his death on April 2, 2005. Both in the U.S. and in Europe, the media indulged for days on end in a profane celebration of John Paul II's supposed legacy, with the accent on his commitment to the Jewish-Catholic dialogue. Jewish movie moguls also made three different movies about his life.[518] In conclusion, it can be argued that John Paul's lamentable process of surrender to Zionism accelerated following Wiesel's 1988 attack on him in the pages of the *NY Post*.

Wiesel and the Catholic Holocaustians

As Wiesel's credibility was eroding among his fellow Jews, the "great man in Israel" sought increased support among Holocaustians within the U.S. Catholic community. After all, Harry Cargas, an obscure but ambitious *Commonweal* Catholic, had made a name for himself in the 1970s when he "discovered" Wiesel and then made him palatable to a Catholic audience in a series of interviews.

More and more doubts were being expressed among prominent Jews as to 1) whether or not the Jewish media barons were correct in transforming the Holocaust into the national religion of the United States, 2) and on the wisdom of promoting Wiesel, with his many character flaws, as the High Priest of the new faith. The internal colloquy was already underway and would later find some expression in 1999 with the publication of Peter Novick's *The Holocaust in American Life*. Novick's answers to both of these questions would be no. Such Jewish doubts about Wiesel, while usually expressed in private, impelled him to court support from Holocaustian Catholics. Such Catholics found that promoting the Holocaust was an at-

518 These films are: 1) *Have No Fear. The Life of Pope John Paul II*; 2) *Pope John Paul II*; and 3) *Karol: A Man Who Became Pope*.

Illustration 31: Carol Rittner

tractive avenue for advancing their careers. Since this particular group generally saw Vatican II as a great moment in Church history precisely because it swept away the vestiges of the "old Church," symbolized by Pius XII, they were naturally attracted to the Jewish Holocaust narrative as a new paradigm in which to work. Holocaustian Catholics could thus transform their dislike of Pius XII into something positive. By embracing the Jewish Holocaust narrative as their own, they were not only better positioning themselves to fight for women's ordination, full and open admission of homosexuals into the clergy, and Holocaust brainwashing in Catholic schools, they were also able to benefit from the very tangible financial support from the powerful Zionists who support Wiesel.

As soon as Wiesel had received the windfall payment for his Nobel Prize, he used some of the money to create the Elie Wiesel Foundation for Humanity. Shrewdly, he appointed a nun, Sr. Carol Rittner, RSM (Religious Sisters of Mercy), as his first executive director. Although the origins of their relationship remain obscure, Rittner soon became the poster child for Catholics eager to achieve success and recognition in the Zionist-dominated mainstream culture by making a cult of the Holocaust. Rittner served Wiesel's purposes by making important Catholic connections for him. In 1988, during her tenure with Wiesel, the Jesuits, under then-editor John B. Breslin, S. J., did the unthinkable and devoted a whole issue of their weekly magazine, *America*, to Wiesel and the Holocaust. These are men who are ordained to preach Christ, not the absurdist Holocaust allegory of the six million, and who, in addition to the normal priestly vows, take a special vow of fidelity to the pope. Here they abandoned both truth and the cause of Pope Pius XII to serve the emerging state religion of the Holocaust.

Rittner's overall influence in this project is probably reflected by the fact that the Jesuits' Holocaust issue was intended to be a sixtieth birthday present for Wiesel. As for Rittner's article, it consisted of an interview with her employer in which she asked the expected softball questions. One question, however, stands out, and we must read it within the context of the quotation from the anonymous Jewish historian that Samuel Freedman had included in his 1986 *New York Times* article two years earlier:[471]

> *Elie Wiesel arouses passions as strong as those that divided Jews during Israel's 1982 invasion of Lebanon.*

In light of this statement, it is apparent that Rittner was going after such Jewish detractors when she asked Wiesel if he had "ever regretted writing *Night*." It is difficult to conceive of the liberal Catholic readers of *America*, for whom Wiesel was a saint, ever asking themselves this question. But there is an ongoing resistance movement (whose size, admittedly, is difficult to gauge) against Wiesel within the ranks of U.S. Jewry. Wiesel was able to respond to Rittner from a position of strength, surrounded as he was by gullible liberal Catholics offering him adulation bordering on subservience. He told Rittner, in veiled terms but almost certainly with such Jews in mind:[519]

> *I stand by every word, every comma, every silence in that book.*

No, he wasn't backing down or becoming less abrasive, even though he "arouses passions" among fellow Jews.

Another article was penned by Vienna-born Eva Fleischner, who later played the role of the submissive Catholic involved in the "Jewish-Catholic dialogue" to such perfection that she was awarded, incongruously, a position as a Catholic theologian at a secular institution, Montclair State University in New Jersey. Her piece reveals succinctly the self-imposed and irrational guilt in which the Catholics involved in this special issue were wallowing. Fleischner, who had become an acquaintance, if not a friend of Wiesel, wrote her *America* article in the form of a personal letter. First, she had to cleanse herself of her feelings of Holocaust guilt by simultaneously projecting herself as a "righteous gentile:"

> *For us Christians the sense of guilt at our corporate history of persecution of Jews becomes, at times, almost too heavy to bear. The burden is lightened when we discover, or remember, that there have been through the centuries Christian women and men who did not run with the mob, even – also – during that darkest of times that will forever be known as the Holocaust.*

Now unburdened, she could express her naiveté about the Mauriac-Wiesel correspondence, which, as we recall, Wiesel had claimed in 1985 that he was planning to publish:[520]

> *Permit me to end these reflections with a wish. Won't you, please, as you promised in* A Jew Today, *publish your conversations with Mauriac, which continued over the years? Then we would know a little more of the relationship between you, of what enabled you both to transcend your religious and political disagreements. Only you can give us the answers to this and, by doing so, shed further light on one of the most remarkable friendships of the century.*

More than twenty-five years later, we are still waiting.

---

519 Carol Rittner, "An Interview with Elie Wiesel," *America*, November 19, 1988, 401.

520 Eva Fleischner, "Mauriac's Preface to *Night*: Thirty Years Later," *America*, November 19, 1988, 419.

The Holocaust fundamentalists had bigger and better things in store for Rittner, and were generous in rewarding her. In 1990, she edited a collection of essays in praise of Wiesel that bordered on hagiography. Entitled *Elie Wiesel: Between Memory and Hope* (N.Y.: NYU Press), it brought together seventeen short articles that are remarkable for their meekness in accepting Wiesel's claims about his experiences during the Holocaust. The reader will find no hint therein of doubt as to Wiesel's credibility, let alone its dissection as in the present study. Published by a prestigious university press, the work shows the extent to which the Holocaust faith had already become Imperial America's established religion. Rittner's book should be seen as an important contribution by an official and publicly committed Catholic person to the imposition of the Holocaust religion on the United States of America. Replete, from cover to cover, with lies of omission, *Elie Wiesel* contains none of the most basic and obvious questions that ought to be asked about Wiesel and the Holocaust.

Rittner's public servitude to the dogma of the Holocaust grew stronger. After she left Wiesel's employ, she was rewarded with a position as Distinguished Professor of Holocaust and Genocide Studies at Richard Stockton College, a unit of the university system of New Jersey. (Like Fleischner, Rittner struck pay dirt in the Garden State.) That prestigious position, at least in terms of service to our state ideology, allowed her to render further services – as a Catholic front – to the Zionist cause. In 2000, she was presented as the lead editor of a book entitled *The Holocaust and the Christian World* (N.Y.: Continuum, 2000). On the book's title page, the names of two major Holocaust propaganda institutions, the Beth Shalom Holocaust Memorial Center in Nottingham, England, and the Yad Vashem International School for Holocaust Studies, appear alongside that of Continuum Books. Their inclusion as co-publishers suggests that these institutions might have also subsidized publication of the book. Finally, Rittner's status as a Catholic stooge for this Holocaustian project was further indicated by the fact that the book's copyright is held by the two above-mentioned organizations, and that conformist historian Yehuda Bauer, in his capacity as "Consulting Editor," apparently orchestrated the operation. Not surprisingly, one of her co-editors, Stephen D. Smith, established his academic credentials by founding the UK Holocaust Centre in Nottingham in 1995, and has by now moved up in life: he is presently the director of the USC Shoah Foundation in Los Angeles, a far more lucrative situation. Rittner's other co-editor was Irena Steinfeldt, who now heads the Righteous among the Nations Department at Yad Vashem. The book is a patent work of pro-Israel propaganda of the most one-sided sort, as might be expected, given its co-creators. It asks no questions about the revealed truths of the Holocaust, and contains predictable attacks upon both Pius XII and the Catholic

Church. When Rittner agreed to put her name to this book as lead editor, she betrayed the religious and cultural roots from which she had sprung, for one of the main objectives of the Jewish Holocaust myth is to weaken if not destroy Catholicism. But she got her thirty pieces of silver: media recognition and a chaired professorship

As the 1980s came to an end, with the First Intifada continuing in Palestine, other Catholics decided to jump on the Holocaustian gravy train. Conor Cruise O'Brien launched a virulent attack on Pius XII, writing, among other things, that "Pius XII never, while Hitler was alive, published anything that could have angered Hitler." He continued:[521]

> [...] *Hitler, understandably, took* [...] *Christian silence for consent. It gave the green light for the preparation of the Holocaust.*

Such utter nonsense, especially when looked at twenty years later, demonstrates the depths of self-abnegation to which ambitious Catholic intellectuals can stoop when seeking to appeal to the narcissistic impulse of their Zionist Jewish editors and publishers.

O'Brien's article in the ardently Zionist *New York Review of Books* prefigured later assaults, launched in the midst of the Palestinian Second Intifada, by three Holocaustian foot soldiers: former Jesuit Gary Wills in *Papal Sin: Structures of Deceit* (2000),[522] ex-priest James Carroll in *Constantine's Sword* (2001),[523] and British historian John Cornwell in his *Hitler's Pope* (2002).[524]

These blasts from O'Brien, Wills, Carroll and Cornwell not only provided cover for Jewish war crimes in suppressing the First and Second Intifada movements, they followed the revisionists' demolition of the Holocaust myth. These traitors to their church could look back for consolation at the examples of cultural and religious betrayal by men like François Mauriac and Robert Drinan. With regard to the content of their diatribes against Pius XII, Prof. Faurisson responded in his 2006 book, *Le révisionnisme de Pie XII*, which was translated into English that same year.[10] Unfortunately, Zionist media power is such that his book could not even be mentioned, much less reviewed, in mainstream outlets.

---

521 Conor Cruise O'Brien, "A Lost Chance to Save the Jews," *New York Review of Books*, April 27, 1989, 28.

522 Gary Wills, *Papal Sin: Structures of Deceit* (N.Y.: Doubleday, 2000).

523 James Carroll, *Constantine's Sword* (Boston: Houghton-Mifflin, 2001).

524 John Cornwell, *Hitler's Pope* (London: Penguin, 2002).

1989: Wiesel Deeply Wounded by French Catholic Writer Jean-Marie Domenach

I close my discussion of Wiesel in the 1980s with a reference to the French left-wing Catholic intellectual Jean-Marie Domenach (1922-1997) and the controversy that he sparked over Wiesel and the Holocaust. Domenach, who had been deeply involved in the Resistance in France from 1943 to 1945, and had later edited for some twenty years the Catholic literary review *Esprit* while also teaching social science at the prestigious Ecole Polytechnique in Paris, accused "*certains Juifs*" (certain Jews) of seeking to exploit the Holocaust in order to enrich themselves or, as he put it, to receive financial dividends – "*les dividendes d'Auschwitz*" – as a reward for their sufferings.

Apparently fed up by the endless propaganda in which France's Zionist media had indulged from 1983 on, starting with the return of Barbie to France, his ridiculous 1987 show trial, and then the Auschwitz Carmel Affair from 1987 to 1989, Domenach rightly took aim at Wiesel, and did so in a manner that unquestionably denoted him as the principal recipient of the *dividendes d'Auschwitz*.[525] In a discussion with the Jewish public intellectual Alain Finkielkraut, which was published as an article in the weekly newspaper *L'Événement du jeudi*, Domenach represented a Catholic point of view, and his comment exploded like a bomb on the Parisian cultural and political landscape.

France's Zionist media overlords, panicked over what Domenach, a certified member of the Parisian establishment, had done, decided to take a page out of the Orwellian playbook, and completely censored any further reference to the event. As a result, references to this assault on Wiesel have been systematically erased from the Internet in an attempt to make it seem as if Domenach's magnificent critique had never occurred, and the term *les dividendes d'Auschwitz* had never been used against the Holocaustians.

Wiesel, however, writing about this assault almost a decade later in the second volume of his autobiography, still smarted from Domenach's words. He wrote:[526]

> *In France, our common adversary, and by "our" I mean all of us survivors, the one who has made the most noise, is Jean-Marie Domenach.*

Wiesel's diatribe against Domenach goes on:[527]

---

525 Michel Labro, *et al.*, "Juifs-cathos: le face à face, Finkielkraut-Domenach," *L'Evénement du jeudi*, September 28 – October 4, 1989, 86-90.

526 Wiesel, *...et la mer*, 167: "En France, notre adversaire à tous, je veux dire à tous les survivants, celui qui a fait le plus de bruit, c'est Jean-Marie Domenach."

527 *Ibid.*, 168f.: "Ce qui l'agace dans la France d'aujourd'hui? Il le dit sans mâcher ses mots: 'Les dividendes d'Auschwitz,' que 'toucheraient' certains Juifs pour des raisons politiques, littéraires et autres. J'ignore lequel des écrits de J.-M. Domenach sera protégé de l'oubli, mais cette petite phrase fort 'originale' restera. On dira 'Domenach' et on

> *What bothers him in today's France? He says so without mincing his words: it's "the Auschwitz dividends" that are "allegedly cashed in" by certain Jews for political, literary or other reasons. I don't know which of Domenach's writings will withstand the test of time, but this highly "original" little phrase will remain. People will say "Domenach" and others will reply: "Oh yes, the Auschwitz dividends." He'll give birth to a school of thought, no doubt about it. Whoever writes a book about the Jewish tragedy in the days to come will do so at his own risk. Historians and theologians, philosophers and psychologists, novelists and poets: beware, a Domenach is lying in wait for you at the bend in the road.*

Since Wiesel is the figurehead for a whole army of Jewish schemers, conmen and profiteers, the so-called survivors, his vehement reaction to Domenach's well-warranted accusation that he sought to reap *les dividendes d'Auschwitz* was understandable. Yet Wiesel's overreaction against Domenach gave the game away. Although Domenach had not accused the self-designated veterans of deceit, only of profiteering, his charge brought welcome attention to the terrible cost of the Holocaust to French society as a whole.

New, Obvious, Holocaust Fraudsters Reap *les dividendes d'Auschwitz*

Domenach's sarcasm, impatience, even outrage at the Jewish exploitation of the Holocaust for financial gain was completely justified. In the years that followed his remark, which was essentially revisionist in tone if not precisely in content, the works of new, up-and-coming Holocaust profiteers continued to appear. In 1995, Benjamin Wilkomirski's absurd autobiography, *Fragments*, originally published in German, and Misha Defonseca's equally ridiculous *Misha: A Mémoire of the Holocaust Years,* which appeared in 1997, were both put on the market in a naked attempt to reap the "Auschwitz dividend." These books were clearly novels whose stories had been made up from scratch, but the Holocaustians cynically insisted that, like Wiesel's *Night*, they were eyewitness accounts of actual experiences. The fact that such rubbish could even be published showed that, within the Holocaust fundamentalist community, the lust for, indeed the obsession with, money was all-pervasive. Yes, Domenach, through the term "Auschwitz dividend," had beautifully summed up and encapsulated their greed and lust for power. It is noteworthy that Wiesel wrote a blurb for Defonseca's book cover – "very moving."

---

ajoutera: 'Ah oui, les dividendes d'Auschwitz.' Il fera école, n'en doutons pas. Quiconque rédigera un ouvrage sur la tragédie juive le fera désormais à ses risques et périls. Historiens et théologiens, philosophes et psychologues, romanciers et poètes, un Domanach vous attend au tournant."

After all, the Holocaust® was essentially a Jewish-owned business. As the various Holocaust museums were being built during the 1990s, each one containing a gift shop, new products were needed to keep the cash registers ringing. Once school teachers dutifully placed new Holocaust titles on their required reading lists, sales totals would soar. Accordingly, the Holocaust fundamentalists canonized Wilkomirski with an appearance on *60 Minutes*, a laudatory profile in *The New Yorker*, and of course a literary prize. Even worse, Defonseca's fraudulent book would be turned into a French-language feature film at great expense. And each time the Jewish media barons forced such ridiculous books on the public, they would give further justification to Domenach's sarcasm.

Over the course of the 1980s, Wiesel had indeed been established as the living, state-endorsed Holocaust High Priest of the United States. But, as the decade came to an end, there was as well a growing dissatisfaction with the Holocaust at the grassroots level in both the U.S. and France. This ongoing but largely subterranean rebellion was, and remains, difficult to document, because it could not be spoken of objectively, let alone analyzed accurately, in the tightly-controlled Zionist media. Nonetheless, Wiesel's 1989 evocation of a recent, recurring nightmare reflected his awareness of this growing sense among ordinary folk that the Holocaust was essentially a Jewish scam:[528]

> *I have an occasional nightmare now. I wake up shivering, thinking that when we* [the veterans] *die, no one will be able to persuade people that the Holocaust occurred.*

---

[528] Miller, *One by One,* 220.

Chapter X
1990s: Growing Jewish Doubts about Wiesel

1990: Orwellian Removal of the Four-Million-Dead Figure on the Auschwitz Monument

By 1990, a little more than a decade had elapsed since the publication of Faurisson's 1979 article in *Le Monde.* In it, he had argued that the alleged gas chambers of Auschwitz were nothing more than what he called "the rumor of Auschwitz." At the time, France's Holocaust fundamentalists assembled a group of thirty-four scholars who signed and published in *Le Monde*, on February 21, 1979, a reply to Faurisson's earlier articles and letters to the editor questioning the existence of the gas chambers. The essence of their Orwellian statement asserted:[529]

> *One must not ask how,* technically, *such mass murder was possible. It was technically possible since it happened.* […] *There is not, nor can there be, any debate on the existence of the gas chambers.*

The French Holocaustian establishment then turned up the pressure by taking legal action to silence the man, to no avail. Nothing seemed to work, and by the end of the 1980s revisionism was still on the march. As a result, France's Holocaustians concluded correctly that they could never prevail over the revisionists in a free and open debate. In other words, to the extent that the Zionist media had allowed a debate to take place, the revisionists had won. Therefore, they decided to take the extreme measure of forcing

[529] "Déclaration de trente-quatre historiens," *Le Monde*, February 21, 1979, 23: "Il ne faut pas se demander comment, *techniquement*, [italics in original] un tel meurtre de masse a été possible. Il a été possible techniquement puisqu'il a eu lieu. […] Il n'y a pas, il ne peut pas y avoir de débat sur l'existence des chambres à gaz."

Illustration 32a, b: At the left the old, at the right the new English language memorial plaque at Auschwitz-Birkenau

their controlled politicians, in July 1990, to pass the Gayssot Act, which criminalizes questioning of *la Shoah*.

One of the Holocaustians' many handicaps as they attempted to defend the orthodox view of the Holocaust was the Auschwitz monument. By this time, the orthodox Holocaust historians had been forced to reduce the Auschwitz death figure, which at Nuremberg had been set at four million, to about one and a half million. But the lingering presence of the monument was a constant reminder of the fact that the Western Allies had endorsed a Soviet lie at Nuremberg. Thus, the Holocaustians sought to work their way out of this uncomfortable position by blaming the erroneous figure on the easily implicatable Poles. France's Holocaustian Jews and their allies had long tried to evade the anomaly of the grossly exaggerated Auschwitz death figure of four million, invented by the Soviets and on exhibit at the supposedly historically accurate Auschwitz State Museum. By 1990, however, the four-million claim, which Soviet experts had arrived at by multiplying the actual capacity of the cremation ovens by about tenfold, had become an object of revisionist ridicule. It was simply dead weight that the tall tale of the Holocaust could no longer bear.

If the preceding four decades of Holocaust exploitation to blackmail Germany and to justify the continuing horrors the Jews of Israel were imposing on the Palestinians were to continue, accommodations would have to be made. Thus, by 1990, after the Holocaustians came to the realization that the revisionist onslaught was making them look like mendacious manipulators, the old plaques showing four million victims were replaced with new ones.

The 1991 monument remains in place, but it does not account for the 2.5 million victims who were "retconned" out of existence from the previous monument The message chiseled onto the new monument was nothing less than an admission to the world that the previous message had been a crude propaganda lie. It reads in nineteen languages (see Illustrations 32):

> *Forever let this place be a cry of despair and a warning to humanity, where the Nazis murdered about one and a half million men, women and children, mainly Jews from various countries of Europe. Auschwitz-Birkenau 1940–1945.*

Now, more than twenty years later, as Germany continues to be blackmailed into funding the preservation of the crumbling barracks and other buildings at Birkenau, the 1.5 million figure has been ratcheted down by a factor of about one third, or about another half million:[530]

> *More than 1 million people, mostly Jews, died in the camp's gas chambers or through forced labor, disease or starvation.*

Like the publicly traded security of a company in which investors have lost trust and confidence, the death figure for Auschwitz & Co. continues to plummet with no new buyers in sight.[531]

Main Components of Retroactive Continuity Applied to the Holocaust

The dismantling on April 3, 1990, of the Auschwitz monument that for decades had proclaimed a death toll of four million offered an excellent example of Zionist Jewish media control. Enjoying a near total monopoly over what constitutes news, and how that news is presented, the Holocaustians engaged – with impunity – in an outrageous act of retroactive continuity. Since 1945, the Holocaust had consisted of the hallowed and mystical figure of six million dead Jews, but with the important proviso that most of those deaths had occurred in the imaginary gas chambers of Auschwitz. Now, not the least as a result of revisionist criticism, the number of Jewish deaths at Auschwitz had been downsized to between 1.1 and 1.5 million, while the mystical overall figure of 6 million dead Jews remained in place! In so doing, the Holocaustians demonstrated anew that the Holocaust is just another generic Jewish-scripted cultural artifact, like TV series, soap operas, cartoons or comic strips. The story line can always be rewritten retroactively, with previous characters and events simply cast down the memory hole as needed. With one Orwellian stroke, history was completely rewritten. Henceforth, the Zionist-controlled mainstream media would tell the Auschwitz story as if the four-million figure had never existed. As official history was being rewritten, Orwell was probably turning over in his grave.

---

[530] Monika Scislowska, "Germany Pledges Funds to Preserve Auschwitz," *AJC*, December 16, 2010, A18.

[531] Some mainstream scholars claim even lower death tolls, cf. footnote 129 on page 71.

Credibility of the Jewish Holocaust Tale Continues to Disintegrate

The Holocaustians were in fact now so desperate in the faltering defense of their myth that they were already planning to criminalize any questioning of it. As belief in the Shoah became more difficult to justify on the basis of evidence, individual Holocaustians did what they could to save whatever remnants of credibility or respectability could be scraped together for Wiesel. Thus, for instance, in 1990 Jean-Claude Favez, in a book designed to sing Wiesel's praises, referred to the Holocaust as "the Event," so as not to even have to evoke the imaginary flaming trenches that are implicit in Wiesel's word Holocaust. He wrote:[532]

> *Wiesel's testimony is about the Event, not specific events. Precision in descriptions and factual exactitude are of less importance than the quest for meaning. Thus, certain specialists have raised questions about certain scenes, particularly in* Night. *But for the writer* [Wiesel], *that's not what is essential. Rather it's in the power of the work to bear witness.*

Favez does not identify the specialists who had raised embarrassing questions about *Night*, but he might have been thinking of Pierre Vidal-Naquet, cited above, a Holocaustian who had turned against Wiesel. Nor did Favez tell his readers exactly which assertions in Wiesel's book were being questioned. But his concession was a dramatic departure from the official line on *Night*, according to which the book's power is said to derive from the fact that the whole story is true.

At the same time, the people behind Favez and Wiesel stooped to new lows when, during the spring of 1990, they launched a powerful arm-twisting campaign aimed at French politicians, surreptitiously calling in IOUs from those under their influence, while conducting a huge media offensive aimed at the public. The resulting Loi Gayssot (Gayssot Act, named after the Communist member of the National Assembly of that name) criminalizes any publicly expressed doubt about the Holocaust. It does so by treating such skeptical questions as a *de facto* display of racism or anti-Semitism. The revisionists had won the argument, but now were being persecuted for telling the truth. Heavy fines and serious jail sentences have been imposed in France since 1990 for such "crimes."

If the Zionist Jewish power brokers had been winning the historical argument against the revisionists in 1990, they would not have had to resort to such an extreme measure. It is one thing to refuse to give the revisionists access to the tightly-controlled Zionist media with the excuse that such

---

[532] Jean-Claude Favez, "Elie Wiesel et la Shoah," in Banon, *Présence*, 69: "Le témoignage de Wiesel est celui de l'Evénement, non des événements. La précision dans la description, l'exactitude du fait comptent moins que la recherche du sens. Ainsi les spécialistes ont pu mettre en doute certaines scènes, notamment dans la *La Nuit*. Mais pour l'écrivain, l'essentiel n'est pas là. Il est dans la force de l'œuvre qui témoigne."

people are liars. But when Holocaust fundamentalists use their power over national legislative and judiciary systems to imprison and fine people for the "crime" of simply questioning the certitudes on which Holocaust dogma is based, they show how barbaric, and truly Stalinist, they actually are.

Bradley R Smith Emerges as a Major Figure in U.S. Revisionism

By 1990, Bradley R. Smith, born in 1930, had emerged as a major figure in the revisionist movement. In 1979, after reading Professor Faurisson's essay "The Problem of the Gas Chambers," Smith gradually became active in revisionism through his association with the Institute of Historical Review. To further his unique revisionist outreach via radio, television and the campus press, Smith created a new revisionist organization, the Committee for Open Debate on the Holocaust, in the late eighties. Then, in 1990, he began publishing a monthly newsletter called *Smith's Report*, which is still appearing a quarter-century later. One of his regular targets over the years was Wiesel, and perhaps his most memorable piece on the subject appeared in April 1997 (no. 42) when he mocked "the great man in Israel" for his exaggerated retelling of his automobile accident in New York City in 1956, as recounted above in Chapter VII (p. 182).[533] The many projects that Smith has accomplished through CODOH, include the placement of revisionist ads in U.S. college newspapers, mass mailing campaigns to U.S. conformist academics, and the creation of the many-faceted CODOH website. Perhaps most importantly, Smith, patient and even-tempered (as well as being a gifted writer and editor), has served as the unofficial face of U.S. revisionism in a calm, deliberate and professional manner for the past quarter century.

1990: Wiesel and Cardinal O'Connor Collaborate on *A Journey of Faith*

In New York, as the decade began, Wiesel continued his abuse of his newly discovered friend, Cardinal O'Connor, when he convinced him to collaborate on an interview book. The hapless cleric was still quite unaware that he had been involved in an abusive relationship since 1987. O'Connor of course had no inkling of why Wiesel and his powerful New York Jewish backers wanted this interview so much. In retrospect, however, it is clear that the continuing revisionist attacks on the Holocaust, which were taking their toll on the Holocaust fundamentalist community, were the driving force behind the book. General skepticism about the Holocaust was

533 "Elie Wiesel: sometimes the truth is an accident," *Smith's Report*, no. 42, April 1997, 3f.; www.codoh.com/library/categories/2132.

growing worldwide, and the Holocaustians were discovering that they were unable to counter revisionist arguments.

There was another worry: O'Connor, as the head of the Catholic Near East Welfare Society (CNEWS), had expressed too much sympathy for the Palestinians, and had to be brought back under control. We recall that, a few years earlier, he had made his sympathy for the Palestinians quite clear. At an airport news conference hours after he had visited a squalid beachfront refugee center in the Israeli-occupied Gaza Strip, the Cardinal had said:

> *They don't have a real identity, they don't have a passport, they don't have a piece of land they can call their own. They can hardly be called a people who have the right of self-determination.*

A little later, he stated that he was ending his trip "with a much better understanding of the Palestinians and the Arab world. I feel we have a stereotype in the U.S. of Arabs and Palestinians," and added that too many Americans see Palestinians as terrorists and not as an "ancient, honorable and noble people."[534]

The book project was conceived not only as a means of tethering O'Connor, it was also intended as a sign to other prominent Catholic clergymen that no similar display of political courage in the name of justice would be tolerated. New York Jewish leaders shared a suspicion of, indeed an outright hostility to, the organization that O'Connor headed. The latter's words, both blunt and truthful, must have reminded them of his combative predecessor as national director of the CNEWS in the late 1940s and 1950s, Msgr. Thomas J. McMahon. The latter, having been delegated by Cardinal Spellman, Archbishop of New York, to represent the interests of Palestine's Christians in the face of the Zionist Jewish conquest and occupation of Palestine, represented both Spellman and Pius XII on the ground in New York and Washington. While Pius XII spoke in diplomatic terms to express his misgivings about the creation of a Jewish homeland in someone else's country, McMahon's style was more confrontational. For him, the Zionists' media slogan at the time, "a land without people for a people without land," was beneath contempt.

When David Ben-Gurion, the head of pre-state Israel, came to New York in May 1947 to justify Jewish depredations against the Palestinians before the UN's Political and Security Committee, McMahon was there and requested well in advance the right to speak at the hearing. With the full support of Pius XII, he wanted to document Zionist atrocities in the Holy Land and, in so doing, refute Ben-Gurion's assertions, but he was banned from speaking. The UN authorities justified the silence imposed on

[534] Joseph Berger, "O'Connor, Ending Visit to Israel, Stresses the Plight of the Palestinians," *New York Times*, January 6, 1987, A12.

him because, they said, the people he represented did not constitute a "considerable portion" of the population of Palestine. McMahon protested this exclusion, claiming that 45,400 Catholics (out of 130,750 Christians) did indeed represent a considerable portion of the population, to no avail.[535] A month later he complained directly to the UN's Secretary General, Trygve Lie, that the Catholics under Jewish control did not in fact enjoy "'factual freedom' from 'discrimination'" by Jews.[536]

After the creation of Israel in 1948, over 750,000 Palestinians were forced to flee their homes. McMahon, as the leader of the CNEWS, went to Palestine in the fall of that year to coordinate Catholic relief efforts. Then, in early 1949, after Pius XII established the Pontifical Mission for Palestine, he was also appointed leader of that group. For nearly another decade, until his retirement, he continued to do all he could to relieve the suffering that all Palestinians were being forced to endure at the hands of their Zionist Jewish conquerors. Due to limitations of space, it will be impossible to describe in more detail McMahon's valiant defense of the interests of all Palestinians, not only those who were Christians, as the Zionist siege against them played out. However, as O'Connor spoke out so courageously against what Jewry was doing in Palestine in 1987, his words must have echoed, in Zionist ears, both the tone and conviction of McMahon's rugged determination to defend the world's most enduring "unworthy victims."

The Wiesel/O'Connor interviews were conducted by New York City's Channel 4 (NBC) newsman, Gabe Pressman; the book appeared under the title *A Journey of Faith.* My discussion will deal briefly with four issues that are germane to the present study: 1) the Holocaust fundamentalists' counterattack against revisionism, 2) Wiesel's continuing attacks against Pius XII as a means of enhancing his own "papal" status in the Zionist media, 3) the aerial photography of Auschwitz, which, a decade earlier, had revealed Wiesel to be a liar about his eyewitness claims, and 4) O'Connor's maladroit remark in 1987 that the Holocaust had been a "gift."

In the book's introduction, Pressman announced that "it was Elie Wiesel's idea to do this program. And both the Cardinal and WNBC-TV readily agreed it was a good idea."[537] Pressman began by telling Wiesel that "you have been described as a prophet," alluding thereby to the term that O'Connor used to describe him: "the Prophet of the Holocaust." This "prophet" status for Wiesel also referred to his virtual ordination by the President of the United States in 1985 as America's Holocaust High Priest. Pressman started the discussion by attacking the revisionists, but without

---

535 "Ben-Gurion Here to Lead Zionists," *New York Times*, May 10, 1947, 4.

536 Nancy MacLennan, "Lie Forwards Plea on Palestine Curb," *New York Times*, June 7, 1947, 5.

537 O'Connor, Wiesel, *Journey*, v.

using the pejoratives "Holocaust denial" or "Holocaust deniers" for the simple reason that Deborah Lipstadt had not yet invented them:

> *But you heard just this month, and you hear it frequently, a meeting, a so-called meeting on the West Coast, I believe, by a revisionist historian who claimed that the Holocaust didn't exist.* (*Journey*, 15)

Wiesel, picking up the cue, replied:

> *Those are the most wicked of all people. There is anti-Semitism in the world, racism in the world. But the most wicked of all are these so-called Revisionists. They are morally ugly, morally perverted, morally sick.* (15f.)

At this point, Cardinal O'Connor, apparently referring to Arthur Butz's study *The Hoax of the Twentieth Century*, replied:

> *It's a cyclical kind of thing. Remember about fifteen years ago, there was a move in the same direction. Some college professor* [Butz] *somewhere* [Northwestern University] *wrote what was allegedly a scholarly book that said the whole thing was made up.*

To which Wiesel replied:

> *Unfortunately, the Revisionists are all over the world. While the ceremony of the Nobel Prize was being held* [...]

Pressman, correcting Wiesel's lamentably broken English, "When you received the Nobel Prize?"...

> *There was a demonstration outside in the streets. There were people who said that it never happened, that the whole thing was a hoax. Those people have lots of money. I don't know from where. But they do. And their books are being translated into almost every language in the world. You find them in Germany, in South Africa, in Norway and even in Australia. Wherever I go, I find them. Just as we are committed to preserve memory, they are committed to distort it.* (16)

Hearing Wiesel's statement about the revisionists, O'Connor asserted immediately that anyone who rejects or has doubts about Holocaust propaganda is an anti-Semite. In fact, in the short time since he had fallen under Holocaustian control, fighting anti-Semitism had become an obsession for him. He proclaimed:

> *It gives me great concern. I preach about it a great deal. I seize every opportunity to get at it publicly. I can't count the number of times in my past five years in New York* [since becoming Archbishop in 1984] *I have lectured on or preached about anti-Semitism. And most of the time, I'm trying to get at unconscious anti-Semitism.* (18)

Pressman then introduced the second reason for the book: desecration of the Catholic memory of Pius XII. He thus asked Wiesel if he "feels strongly" (33) about the man. Pressman did not ask about facts, only feelings. Wiesel replied:

But I'm afraid that in the case of Pius, too, the Cardinal and I don't agree, because I feel that Pope Pius XII did not do enough. I hear occasionally that there are documents in the Vatican that can show otherwise, but they have not been made public. Maybe if I were to see those documents, I would change my mind. I have probably read everything that has been written on the subject. And I'm afraid my conclusion is that Pope Pius did not do all he could have to help the Jews during World War II. (33f.)

Wiesel, demanding access to Vatican archival documents, is the same man who supports the continued suppression of the documents from the International Tracing Service (ITS), and who has also suppressed publication of his correspondence with Mauriac, while also making sure that no English or French translation of *Un di velt* will be appearing any time soon.

In fact, with regard to the suppression of ITS sources, about 75 percent of the detainee records now under the control of the USHMM concern non-Jews. This museum not only suppresses information, it also engages actively in deliberate deception. For instance, in its main exhibit, it presents photos of dead non-Jewish typhus victims as if they were Jewish victims of the Holocaust. Professor Richard Evans, the Cambridge University historian who had served as an expert witness for Lipstadt's legal team in the lawsuit brought against her by British historian David Irving (see Chapter XI), has commented on this fact:[538]

Visiting the Holocaust Memorial Museum in Washington, D. C., for example, I was struck by its marginalization of any other victims apart from Jews, to the extent that it presented photographs of dead bodies in camps such as Buchenwald or Dachau as dead Jewish bodies, when in fact relatively few Jewish prisoners were held there.

President Carter's wish – that U.S. Jews share victimhood with non-Jews at their museum – has obviously been ignored and, in fact, reversed.

Third, Pressman introduces the subject of the aerial photography of Auschwitz. He shows Wiesel an unidentified shot from the summer of 1944 and asks "what your thoughts and feelings are now." (63) (Once again, the Holocaust is all about feelings.) Wiesel begins by claiming – falsely – that these pictures were taken by accident:

By chance, the navigator forgot to shut the camera, and that is how the camera took pictures of the camp. (64)

He then recounts how he had allegedly discussed these pictures with President Carter:

So I sat with the President and became his guide, and I showed him what the pictures meant. They were clear, everything in them was clear. (64)

---

538 Richard J. Evans, *Lying about Hitler: History, Holocaust and the David Irving Trial* (N.Y.: Basic Books, 2001), 261.

There is a huge difference, of course, between what these pictures actually showed and what a Holocaust fundamentalist like Wiesel says they meant. It is exactly the same difference that exists between history in its traditionally accepted meaning (that is, when it is based on a rigorously analytic method that establishes facts with great care, and not merely on the basis of hearsay and "feelings") and the Jewish cult of "memory" as it is used with respect to the Holocaust. The crowning irony of Wiesel's statement comes when he states that the pictures are "clear," which in effect confirms the fact that they show neither the smoke nor the flame that would have emanated from his imagined flaming pits. But he is nonetheless able to see the Holocaust in these pictures, because he is looking at them through the lens of "memory," not history.

Wiesel concludes his statement about his feelings by claiming against all evidence that over a million Jewish children died in the Holocaust:

> *I think of all the children. I am always at the edge of the abyss, when I am confronted by these children, one million or one-and-a-half million children. I don't know, it drives me to rage. Why? Why children? How could the world do that to children?* (64)

Ironically, according to *Night*, Wiesel, as a child, had received a life-saving operation while at Auschwitz. But his hypocrisy does not stop there, for as he was speaking, the Israeli occupation forces were slaughtering Palestinian children armed with stones and slingshots. Wiesel has never expressed sympathy for these maimed and slaughtered Palestinian children, because they are "unworthy victims."

I conclude with the Jewish Holocaustian abuse of O'Connor for his statement that the Holocaust was a "gift."[539] We recall that, before O'Connor had even gotten off the plane back from Israel, various Jewish leaders had published a statement condemning him.[540] He had been upset by this attack and apparently associated this hostile statement with Wiesel. He says:

> *I was utterly astonished at the resentment, the bitterness that this statement aroused. I "blamed" part of it on Elie Wiesel, because he writes so much about suffering.* (65)

He then reiterates, to Wiesel:

> *My statement was theological. But I must confess, I was deeply hurt.* (67)

Now Wiesel and Pressman have the pathetic O'Connor, a sick victim of abuse, feeling sorry for himself. O'Connor, supposedly a man, is behaving like a child. They have him right where they want him. As a victim of abuse, he is grateful for any crumb that his powerful abuser will let fall

---

539 Berger, "O'Connor Tours," 3.

540 Ari L. Goldman, "O'Connor Is Upset by Critics of Trip," *New York Times*, January 12, 1987.

from the table. He thus blurts out to Wiesel, apparently referring to the fact that, the day after his return, Wiesel came to visit him at his residence:

> *That was one of the most touching things that you did, to come see me the next day, and* [...]

But before O'Connor can finish his sentence, Gabe Pressman interrupts and finishes it for him:

> *You compared the Holocaust, or the suffering of the Jewish people, to the Crucifixion at one point, too.* (68)

Yes, the two religions are now equal, at least in New York City. There would be more to come. The Holocaust fundamentalists were not yet finished with O'Connor, for their plan was to eventually manipulate him into blaming Catholics, including Pius XII, for the Holocaust.

More Apologies from a Dying Cardinal

In 1997, the next phase in this sad story of abuse ensued when Wiesel invited O'Connor to help him dedicate New York City's new Holocaust museum, the Museum of Jewish Heritage. There, the cardinal took it upon himself to apologize for all Catholics who had contributed to past Jewish suffering.[541] O'Connor had no right to do any such thing, especially when one remembers the roles played by prominent Jews, under Communism, in the imposition of misery, suffering and death on untold millions of Eastern European Catholics. But this remark did offer positive proof that O'Connor, as a victim of psychological abuse, was a very sick man.

Two months later, he reiterated his belief that Jewish suffering is superior to Catholic suffering when his own archdiocesan newspaper quoted him as saying:[542]

> *Although many Christians were persecuted by the Nazis, the cardinal said, only Jews were killed mainly because of their ethnic background. He stressed that he is "passionately committed" to making the truth about the Holocaust known.*

Of course his statement is absurd, for Nazi ideology was equally scornful of the Catholic Poles, parts of whose country were supposed to provide living space for the Germans. Furthermore, an archbishop's primary responsibility is to proclaim Christ, not to play the role of a wandering bard telling the Jewish Holocaust story.

Two years later, on September 8, 1999, the final stage of Wiesel's abuse of O'Connor played out when the sick clergyman, recovering from brain

---

541 Brian Caulfield, "Holocaust Memorial: Cardinal Asks Forgiveness for Christians Who Turned Their Backs on Jews," *Catholic New York*, September 18, 1997, 14f.

542 Brian Caulfield, "University Award: Cardinal Honored for Promoting Catholic Jewish Relations," *Catholic New York*, November 13, 1997, 12.

surgery, wrote Wiesel a personal letter in which he made the same kind of apology. Wiesel and the Jewish Holocaustians then rather unscrupulously paid $99,000 to turn the cardinal's private missive into a full-page ad in the Sunday *New York Times* ten days later. Strongly implied in each of O'Connor's gestures was the idea that the Jewish suffering of World War II replicates in a modern context the sufferings of Christ, an idea that a faithful Catholic, no matter how sympathetic to Jewish wartime sufferings, simply cannot accept.

Wiesel's Continuing Offensive against the Papacy

In 1992, the New York Jesuits provided Wiesel with yet another forum, their quarterly review, in which to attack Pius XII. There, he wrote:[543]

> *I have been hurt by the silence of Pope Pius XII during the extermination of my people under Nazism, by Pope John Paul II's meetings with Arafat and Waldheim, by the installation of a convent at Auschwitz. Am I to keep silent, lest I be accused of being anti-Catholic?*

Wiesel launched this attack simply because the Pope had spoken to Kurt Waldheim (who had never been convicted of any crime, and who was later found by the European Court of Justice to have been lynched in the Zionist media), and to Yasser Arafat (who spoke for all Palestinians, including Christian Palestinians, who suffered under the harsh yoke of Israeli occupation).

This attack on Pope John Paul II was typical of Wiesel's animosity to the man before 1993, when the Pope stunned the world by offering Vatican diplomatic recognition to Israel. The treatment accorded to John Paul II after that *volte-face* by both Wiesel and the Zionist media was dramatic. On December 26, 1994, for instance, the Pope would be declared "Man of the Year" by *Time*, an event that would have been impossible before he gave diplomatic recognition to the Jewish apartheid state. Although Wiesel would also become, outwardly at least, an admirer of the man after 1993, his rhetorical tone was inexcusable here.

The Pollard Affair

Also in 1992, Wiesel became involved from the start in the drive to commute the life sentence of the Israeli spy Jonathan Pollard, a U.S. citizen who had stolen sensitive classified information and passed it to his Israeli handlers. Wiesel demanded that Pollard be freed immediately for time already served. One of the many problems with this scenario was that the information taken by Pollard and given to Israel was then peddled to the

---

[543] Elie Wiesel, "*Nostra Aetate*: An Observer's Perspective," *Thought*, December 1992, 370.

USSR and China by his Israeli paymasters. From there, the nuclear secrets went to both North Korea and Iran. Of course, Wiesel, in his zeal to free a traitor simply for racist reasons, *i.e.*, because he was a fellow Jew, has ignored these unpleasant aspects of the Pollard case. But Wiesel's position was perfectly logical, since his primary allegiance has always been to Israel, not to the United States.

The Pollard affair also offered him another opportunity to generate headlines for himself by alleging that somehow Pollard was a victim of anti-Semitism. The fact that Pollard did far more damage to U.S. security than any other American traitor, for money, is irrelevant to Wiesel. So too are the U.S. and foreign operatives who were exposed and killed as a result of the information Pollard sold to Israel and Israel later sold to the Soviet Union.

Wiesel justified his special concern for Pollard by saying that "just before Passover, I went to see him in jail and told him that I was totally opposed to what he did. I told him that Israel was wrong to accept his services, and he was wrong to offer them. But this has become a matter of humanitarianism."[544] Not surprisingly, Wiesel's commitment to humanitarianism applies only to Jews. Palestinian political prisoners, some of whom have been held in Israeli jails for decades without due process, remain "victims" unworthy of such humanitarianism.

Not surprisingly, Wiesel's old friend, the Jesuit priest Robert Drinan, who had shown his dedication to the Zionist cause when he published the propaganda essay *Honor the Promise: America's Commitment to Israel* in 1977, supported Wiesel's campaign on behalf of Pollard. Since 1981, Drinan had been a Professor of Law at Georgetown University where he specialized in ethics, yet his ethical sensibilities did not extend to the Palestinians. A true example of what some Democrats call a "PEP liberal," that is, a liberal who is "progressive except for Palestine," Drinan would continue to serve as a faithful Catholic foot soldier in the service of Zionism until his death in 2007. In exchange, he would be showered with praise in the Zionist media.

1992: John Clive Ball's Groundbreaking Work on the Aerial Photography of Auschwitz

In 1992 the orthodox Holocaust narrative suffered further damage to its credibility and, as some would say, was fatally wounded. This happened when the photographic evidence taken by German and Allied reconnaissance planes during the war became available in a more accessible format. Many of these photos had become officially accessible to the public during

[544] Nadine Brozan, "Chronicle," *New York Times*, June 20, 1992, A24.

the 1980s, so it was only a matter of time before a revisionist author qualified in this field would locate them in the National Archives' Air Photo Library in Alexandria, Virginia, draw the inevitable conclusions, and facilitate access to them.

The man who accomplished this Herculean task was John Clive Ball, a Canadian mineral exploration geologist who had been analyzing air photos as part of his professional activities for many years. In 1992 he published his seminal book on the aerial photography of Auschwitz and other alleged Nazi crime scenes under the title *Air Photo Evidence: Auschwitz, Treblinka, Majdanek, Sobibor, Bergen Belsen, Belzec, Babi Yar, Katyn Forest.*[545] It was a 120-page letter size book full of reproductions of wartime photos of the places mentioned in the book's subtitle, accompanied by Ball's critical comments and analyses. The CIA had acknowledged the existence of some of these photos in 1979 and declassified a few of them at that time, as noted above. However, the revisionists had not been able to make full use of them in the intervening decade other than to see in these pictures confirmation that there had been no gigantic smoking outdoor pyres or lines of 10,000 people a day queuing up for entry into the Auschwitz gas chambers.[206]

A little more than two decades later, Ball's book is now an acknowledged revisionist classic, and has recently appeared in an updated and expanded 3rd edition entitled *Air Photo Evidence: World War Two Photos of Alleged Mass Murder Sites Analyzed.*[546]

This study continues to be an incontrovertible stumbling block for the Holocaustians, for it portrays in graphic terms that so many of the victims' supposedly eye-witness experiences were completely imaginary. The same can be said for the book's lethal effect on the work of the dean of the Holocaustian historians, Raul Hilberg. His claim, noted above, that just inside the main gate the Germans had dug "eight or nine pits more than forty yards in length, eight yards wide, and six feet deep" for the burning of bodies is revealed to be utter nonsense. Yes, a picture can be worth a thousand words, and even more when those words contain deliberate falsehoods.

1992: François Mitterrand Creates a High Priest Position for Wiesel

In 1992, President François Mitterrand of France took a page from President Reagan's playbook and created, in response to a request from Wiesel, a pro-Israel propaganda podium for him in France. It was called the *Académie Universelle des Cultures*. We recall that Mitterrand had paid millions to Bolivia's strongman in 1983 to have Klaus Barbie kidnapped by the Bo-

---

[545] (Delta: Ball Resource Services, 1992).
[546] *Holocaust Handbooks*, vol. 27 (Uckfield, UK: Castle Hill Publishers, 2015).

livian government and shipped to France for a show trial in order to please France's Jewish lobby. In creating this podium for Wiesel, Mitterrand was appeasing his Jewish supporters once again, in the middle of his second seven-year term in office. The appointment, which made Wiesel an official spokesman for the French government, meant that he could 1) pose as a friend of the downtrodden people of the world, while also 2) assuring that the Palestinians would never be included in this group of "worthy victims."

To cite but one example, in 1997, Wiesel organized the *Forum International sur l'Intolérance* in Paris on March 27-28. In the course of the two-day event, various governments around the world were accused of intolerance, while Zionist Israel remained free of any such accusation. In this way, Mitterrand dutifully carried out the orders that had been given to him by his Zionist Jewish bankrollers. He also paid that group public obeisance through his subservience to their lobby, called *CRIF* (*Conseil Représentatif des Institutions Juives de France*). This service included attendance at their banquets for French politicians and other social elites. As a result of Mitterrand's cozy relationship with *CRIF*, France's media treated him with kid gloves, both before and after his death.

Wiesel Launches the USHMM Campaigns against "Hate"

As the Holocaust continued to deteriorate as history, the Holocaust fundamentalists in the U.S. became more and more desperate to silence the dreaded revisionists. Therefore, they decided to adapt with slight modifications what the French government had done in 1990 to criminalize questioning of the Holocaust myth. We must bear in mind that the infamous Gayssot Law did not specifically outlaw revisionism, but rather criminalized the questioning of the definition of crimes against humanity as spelled out in Article 6 of the London Charter of 1945. In this way, France's Jewish lobby sought to mask the blow that they were dealing to free speech and free inquiry in the country that had invented the concept of the rights of man.

The Gayssot Law specifically stated that it intended to "repress all racist, anti-Semitic or xenophobic acts" (*une loi tendant à réprimer tout acte raciste, antisémite ou xénophobe*), but behind this rather vague and seemingly high-sounding language, the Holocaustians of France had taken a drastic step to maintain their control over how the Holocaust myth could be portrayed in public discourse in France. The practical effect of this law was inescapable, for the very act of questioning the official, state-mandated version of the Holocaust would henceforth constitute the crime of "racism," "anti-Semitism," or "xenophobia," and possibly all three at once. The law allows Jewish groups in France to bring suit against revisionists without having to prove that their claims about the truth of the Holocaust have any merit. Finally, this deeply flawed law presumes that the London Charter, a document prepared by the Allies, including the Soviet Union, to undergird a simulacrum of justice in the postwar trials of German leaders, represented some kind of divine revelation, and these Jewish plaintiffs have been able to milk it accordingly.

The Holocaust fundamentalists of the United States set about laying the groundwork for passing a similar law in this country. However, they faced a problem that the Jewish lobby of France had not encountered: the First Amendment to the U.S. Constitution, which guarantees the right to free speech. In order to work around the First Amendment and, in effect, to subvert one of the strongest commitments of the Founding Fathers, the ADL launched a campaign to criminalize "hate." Their intent was, and remains, to link questioning of the Holocaust with "hate." As the First Intifada continued, Wiesel convened a conference on "The Anatomy of Hate" at Boston University in 1989. The same conference theme was developed in Haifa, and in Oslo in 1990. Then, in late 1991, as the old Soviet Union was dying, even Moscow played host to a conference on "hate." Abe Rosenthal and the *New York Times* backed the ADL push for an anti-hate law in the U.S. that was intended to silence the revisionists once and for all. Rosenthal attended Wiesel's Moscow conference and sang his praises for having organized it.[547] In November 1992, the conference was slightly rebranded, the title changing to "The Anatomy of Hate: Saving Our Children." Mario Cuomo, governor of the State of New York and a man beholden to Jewish financial support to keep his career going, appeared at the event, which was held at New York University.

Against the background of the ongoing campaign against "hate," on April 22, 1993, Wiesel attended the dedication ceremony of the U.S. Holocaust Memorial Museum in Washington. In his capacity as Holocaust High Priest, he stood beside President Clinton and was the principal speaker. The *New York Times* played up, quite ironically, "the somber testimony of Elie Wiesel, who spoke of his mother's murder at Auschwitz." Yet, some seventeen years after the opening of the museum, no proof that Wiesel's mother was ever listed on a train manifest taking her from Sighet to Auschwitz has ever been provided. Nor has proof been offered that she and the other members of her family actually entered the camp. Wiesel may tell us that his mother died, allegedly in a gas chamber at Auschwitz. Yet sixty-five years after the war there is no tangible evidence of such gas chambers – and how could she have been gassed if she was never there anyway? In all likelihood, if she was interned at Auschwitz, and did die there, her death

[547] A. M. Rosenthal, "On My Mind: Detesting the Haters," *New York Times*, January 14, 1992, A23.

Illustration 33: Elie Wiesel together with former U.S. President Bill Clinton.

would have resulted, not from the mythical gas chambers, but from typhus or some other disease. In any case, her personnel records from the International Tracing Service remain suppressed by the USHMM and cannot be viewed by revisionist researchers like me.

The *New York Times* report also looked ahead to the brainwashing of America's children that would result from the museum's creation:[548]

> *The Museum opens as Holocaust survivors enter their final years, many of them troubled by a recent survey indicating a majority of high school students know of the Holocaust only as a chapter of death and tragedy, not necessarily connected to Jews, Nazis or Hitler.*

The article also conveniently overlooked and was silent about the hundreds of U.S. citizens from across America who appeared there to protest the opening of this state-sponsored propaganda center. A week later, the *New York Times* attacked the demonstrators and those who shared their opinion as anti-Semites. The hatchet job was given to Michiko Kakutani, who had started out at the newspaper as a reporter in 1979 and became the in-house book reviewer and literary critic in 1983, a job she still holds. She wrote:[549]

---

548 Diana Jean Schemo, "Holocaust Museum Dedicated in Payment to Dead," *New York Times*, April 23, 1993, A1, A14.

549 Michiko Kakutani, "When History Is a Casualty: Holocaust Denial," *New York Times*, April 30, 1993, C1.

> *The contentions of these "Revisionists" are shocking, anti-Semitic ones that fly in the face of all historical facts and viciously mock the suffering of survivors. Some of them argue that the Holocaust never occurred at all, that, in the words of one "revisionist historian," it was all a "gigantic politico-financial swindle whose beneficiaries are the State of Israel and international Zionism." The gas chambers never existed, say these deniers, and the deaths at Auschwitz and other camps simply resulted from disease.*

The Term "Holocaust Denial" Is Born

The Holocaustians timed the publication of Deborah Lipstadt's book *Denying the Holocaust* with the opening of the Washington museum. Simultaneously, Columbia University Press prostituted itself by publishing an English translation of a selection of articles written by the French Jewish Holocaustian Pierre Vidal-Naquet in an attempt to respond to Professor Faurisson's debunking of the Holocaust. Entitled *Assassins of Memory: Essays on the Denial of the Holocaust*, the book is one-sided and intellectually dishonest. Instead of debating directly with Faurisson and allowing him to state his arguments, Vidal-Naquet sets up a straw man called Faurisson, and then argues against this fictitious and artificial entity.[550] Ironically, the book stands today as a monument to the fact that by 1993 the Holocaust had already collapsed as history, while also testifying to the moral bankruptcy of a university press that places dedication to its Jewish financial benefactors ahead of its commitment to the search for historical truth.

Lipstadt's new term for the revisionists, "Holocaust deniers," immediately became a household word in the controlled media, while its sister term, "Holocaust denial," also began to be mainstreamed to the U.S. public as itself a virulent form of "hate." Leaving nothing to chance, the *New York Times* made sure that both books were reviewed by a man who was not only a close and trusted Holocaustian friend, but also a future director of the USHMM.[551] The invention of the term "Holocaust denial" marked the beginning of Lipstadt's rise to a bizarre sort of notoriety in U.S. academe as the Holocaustians' chief enforcer of Holocaust orthodoxy.

On the Road with Wiesel's "Hate" Train

Wiesel's "hate" train made a stop at the University of Massachusetts at Amherst on March 28, 1995. The event was entitled "Crossworlds: Maya Angelou and Elie Wiesel in Conversation," and seems to have been part of the Holocaustians' effort to link U.S. blacks to the Holocaust by enabling

---

[550] See Faurisson's rebuttal: *Réponse à Vidal Naquet* (Paris: La Vieille Taupe, 1982).
[551] Walter Reich, "Erasing the Holocaust," *New York Times*, July 11, 1993, BR1.

Wiesel to tell audiences about the black American soldiers he had seen at Buchenwald on liberation day. Angelou, like Wiesel, was born in 1928 and had no college degree. She was also the author of seven separate autobiographies, which often contradict each other. According to a printed report of the event, Wiesel began the evening by asking Angelou: "Maya, what is hate?" He then went on to recount meeting his first black person: "an American soldier among the liberators of Buchenwald."[552] History – not "memory" – records that there were no blacks present on the day that Buchenwald was liberated, but that has not kept Wiesel from claiming, since the mid-1980s, that he saw black soldiers there.

Wiesel continued to lash out blindly on the subject of "hate" in one of his preferred forums, the weekly *Parade Magazine*, edited at the time by his friend Walter Anderson. Over the years, Wiesel enjoyed free rein to push his personal agenda in *Parade*. In a 1992 article entitled "When Passion Is Dangerous," he attacked the revisionists and the damage they were doing to the Jewish Holocaust narrative. He wrote:[553]

> [...] *political anti-Semitism is followed in its turn by an historical anti-Semitism* [revisionism] *that seems to me the most vicious and injurious of all. For historical anti-Semitism assaults the memory* [again, memory is not history] *that Jews hold of their own past suffering, as in the Holocaust.*

He concluded:

> *If these new anti-Semites succeed in imposing their will, a Jew will no longer be able to speak of the Jewish tragedy.*

Ironically, as Wiesel struggled in this article to define the word "fanatic," he was blind to the fact that he was actually defining himself. The ardent Zionist offered a chillingly precise description of himself when he wrote:

> *I would say that an idea becomes fanatical the moment it minimizes or excludes all the ideas that confront or oppose it. In religion, it is dogmatism; in politics, totalitarianism. The fanatic deforms and pollutes reality. He never sees things and people as they are* [...]

Who more than Wiesel minimizes and excludes from consideration ideas that are different from his own? Who is more dogmatic than Wiesel, with his insistence on what we are allowed to think and to say? Who is more out of touch with reality than Wiesel, with his refusal to recognize that the Palestinians are human beings too, and that we cannot be indifferent to what the Jews of Israel are doing to them?

---

552 "Maya Angelou..."

553 Elie Wiesel, "When Passion Is Dangerous," *Parade Magazine*, April 19, 1992, 20.

Changing of the Guard at the Holocaust Museum

Less than two years after the creation of the USHMM, its founding director, Jeshajahu "Shaike" Weinberg, who had emigrated from Germany to Israel in 1933 at the age of fifteen, retired. In January 1995, the name of Weinberg's replacement, Professor Steven Katz, a historian at Cornell University, was announced. Not surprisingly, Katz was a hard-core Holocaustian who, like his friend and sponsor Wiesel and USHMM board chairman Miles Lerman, insisted on the "uniqueness of the Holocaust."[554] But, as it turned out, Cornell University had concerns about Katz's professional behavior. In March 1995, just two weeks before he was supposed to assume his new job, Katz was forced to withdraw when reports circulated that he had been censured by Cornell for lying about his scholarly achievements, and for taking another job while on sabbatical leave from Cornell.[555] As a result of these transgressions, Katz's salary had been frozen for three years and he had been barred from taking future sabbaticals.[556] Once this information became public, the museum had to withdraw the appointment. Katz remained at Cornell four more years, until 1999. By then, Boston University had created the Elie Wiesel Center for Judaic Studies, and Wiesel made sure that Katz was appointed as its first director. The appointment was a grim reminder of the Holocaust cronyism involved in Wiesel's academic career.

As a result of Katz's withdrawal, the museum appointed Walter Reich to succeed Weinberg. As a psychiatrist, Reich had no experience as a curator, a fact that offers further proof of the odd uniqueness of the Holocaust Memorial Museum. When Reich proved to be too independent-minded, clashing openly and often with Wiesel's fellow veteran board chairman Miles Lerman, his tenure was cut short, and he resigned in protest in 1998.

New York Jewish Intellectual Takes a Dim View of Wiesel's Autobiography

In 1995, the English translation of the first volume of Wiesel's autobiography, *Tous les fleuves vont à la mer*, appeared. The *New York Times* called upon New York Jewish intellectual Daphne Merkin to review it.[557]

---

[554] Larry Judelson, "New Holocaust Museum Director Promotes the Uniqueness of the Jewish Genocide," *Jewish Telegraph Agency*, January 3, 1995. www.jta.org/1995/01/03/archive/new-holocaust-museum-directorpromotes-the-uniqueness-of-the-jewish-genocide.

[555] Judith Weinraub, "Holocaust Museum Chief Forced Out before Starting," *Washington Post*, March 4, 1995, 6.

[556] Karen De Witt, "Holocaust Museum's New Chief Resigns," *New York Times*, March 4, 1995, 11.

[557] Daphne Merkin, "Witness to the Holocaust: A First-Person Look at the Shy Boy Who

Merkin pointed out that Wiesel, near the beginning of his book, tells the story, recounted here in Chapter II, about how his future eminence as "a great man in Israel" had been foretold by the Rabbi of Wizhnitz when Wiesel was only eight years old. She writes, cutting to the heart of Wiesel's pathetic narcissism:

> *But most people who wear a halo of greatness tend not to point it out; certainly most people who write literary autobiographies are at pains to let their character speak for itself.*

As if such a statement were not enough, she also accuses Wiesel of mendacity and underhandedness. She writes:

> *Along the way to finding out very little about Elie Wiesel, we also find out a lot.*

Merkin then lists some of the things she learned: that he is "thin-skinned" and cannot take criticism, that he supposedly suffers from "migraines," and that, amazingly, Wiesel, his father and two sisters had survived Auschwitz while one sister and his mother did not. Merkin was thunderstruck by this news: how could some members of a family be gassed while others were not?

She directs most of her scorn at Wiesel's lies of omission, lamenting his refusal to discuss all the fixes that had to be put in place over the years by his Jewish and Zionist handlers to build his career. Sardonically, she calls Wiesel "the shy boy who became a cautious man who became Elie Wiesel." She then cuts to the jugular of our Holocaust High Priest:

> *There is a beguiling, if not entirely convincing lack of individual will throughout this recounting, as though the author has intuited that ambition yoked to moral purpose is so problematic that it is best to act as though he simply wandered into the Nobel Prize.*

Merkin's review demonstrates once again the degree to which fellow New York Jews look askance at Wiesel. This negative portrait was apparently strident enough to keep the *New York Times* from asking her to review the second installment of Wiesel's autobiography when it appeared a few years later.

1995: Official Remembrance of Auschwitz

In January 1995, the Zionist media began its retrospectives on the fiftieth anniversary of the liberation of the various German concentration camps, and Auschwitz, overrun by the Soviets in January 1945, was at the top of the list. Wiesel had originally been listed as one of the speakers to

---

Became the Cautious Man Who Became Elie Wiesel: *All Rivers Run to the Sea*, Memoirs," *NY Times Book Review*, December 17, 1995, BR7.

appear at the ceremonies planned by the Polish government at Auschwitz. But the Polish authorities had not taken into account the fact that Wiesel dislikes the Polish people, whom he considers, in comparison to the Jews, culturally inferior. Thus, they were surprised when he discovered something objectionable in the calendar of events planned for Friday, January 27. Using a variation on the usual theme of taking offense over the failure to mention the word "Jew," described above, he was now "offended by what he called sloppy organization and the failure of the Polish Government to include the Kaddish, the prayer for the dead. Mr. Wiesel had said he was not sure he would attend, even though he was listed as one of the main speakers."[558] Since the Holocaust fundamentalists are not exactly happy about having to share victimhood with the Catholic Poles at Auschwitz, it should come as no surprise to us that Holocaust High Priest found their preparations "sloppy." Also, the *New York Times's* reporter was merely reflecting her employer's Judeo-centric bias when she wrote:[559]

> *The organizers have no comprehension of the Jewish component, which is central, really.*

When Wiesel finally got to Auschwitz, he was still unhappy. As the leader of the U.S. delegation to this commemoration and as the man who, according to Chmiel, had undergone "transubstantiation" when President Reagan had made him the High Priest of the Holocaust, he represented all U.S. citizens, not just Jews. Yet he brazenly threatened to lead an alternate ceremony to protest what he and fellow Jews said was Poland's de-emphasis of Jewish suffering in the Holocaust.[560] As usual, Wiesel knew that no politician, public figure, or member of the Zionist media would dare to question his unilateral making of such a threat. By doing so, he once again offended the Polish people in the name of the United States, and showed his utter contempt for both the Poles and for all non-Jewish Americans.

The *New York Times*, committed as always to the uniqueness of Jewish suffering and thus to the higher appropriateness of Jewish prayers over those of other people, added additional disinformation to its news reporting when it editorialized:[561]

> *That the killings continued even to the last moment darkens the blot on Germany's reputation. Yet it is also a matter of record that when the Americans and British learned what was happening at Auschwitz, senior officials rejected pleas to bomb the death camp and its rail approaches, a failure of imagination*

---

558 Jane Perlez, "Confusion Marks Polish Plan to Commemorate Auschwitz," *New York Times*, January 16, 1995, A2.

559 Jane Perlez, "Wiesel Now Agrees to Take Part in Auschwitz Rites," *New York Times*, January 20, 1995, A4.

560 Jane Perlez, "Separate Auschwitz Services Highlight Jewish-Polish Dispute," *New York Times*, January 26, 1995, A10.

561 "Remembering Auschwitz," *New York Times*, January 26, 1995, A20.

> *that today seems incomprehensible. The only preventive for a repetition of Auschwitz is remembrance. That is why the Polish Government was so wrong in its initial decision to prevent the recitation of the Jewish prayer for the dead at commemoration ceremonies, and why Elie Wiesel and others were so right to insist on its inclusion.*

As we see, this particular Holocaust scam, the failure to mention specifically the word "Jew," or to recite the specifically Jewish prayer, mixed in with the failure-to-bomb trope, is an eternally repeatable formula that the *New York Times* cynically recycles year in and year out.

Chirac in France, Like O'Connor in New York, Forced to Apologize

Elie Wiesel's friend François Mitterrand never apologized during his fourteen years in power (1981-1995) for the involvement of the Vichy government in the deportation of a minority of Jews resident in France during the war years. Opinions vary as to why France's Jewish Holocaustians accorded him this dispensation, but he rendered them so many services, including the organization of the Barbie show trial and the appointment of Wiesel to a quasi-ambassadorial position with the *Académie Universelle des Cultures*, that they most likely did not want to cause any unnecessary political trouble for a trusted friend. But when Jacques Chirac came to power in 1995, the Zionist media began a campaign to elicit such an apology from him. As a result, he had to move this issue to the top of his agenda. Since Chirac had opposed passage of the Gayssot Law in 1990 on the grounds that it would establish a government-approved, official or authorized version of history, as had been the case under Communism, the Holocaustians did not trust him. Thus, as they had done with Cardinal O'Connor a few years earlier in New York, they sought to bring him into line through their media campaign.

In 1990, as a member of the French Senate, the upper house of France's bicameral legislature, Chirac had attended the debates and voted against this law three times. On each occasion, June 11, June 29 and June 30, 1990, he had done so because it threatened "freedom of expression" (*la liberté d'expression*).[562] By 1995, when France's Jewish-dominated media beat their media drums for him to make this symbolic recognition of Jewish victimhood under the Vichy government, Chirac realized that he would never be able to govern effectively if he did not make amends to France's Holocaustian Jews for having placed his country's interests ahead of their narrow ones when he had cast these three votes. Thus, one of Chirac's first acts on becoming president was to apologize for the deportation and al-

---

[562] http://fr.wikipedia.org/wiki/Loi_Gayssot

leged deaths of nearly 74,000 French Jews.[563] This gesture, which was purely political, had little historical basis in fact. Until the names of all the deportees alleged to have died are checked through the now-suppressed files of the International Tracing Service, there is no reason to believe that the death toll among these deportees was anywhere near as high.[564] Chirac's act of subservience to *CRIF* and the other groups composing France's Jewish Lobby forced the bishops of France to apologize in a similar manner on September 30, 1997.[565]

1997: Wiesel's Hypocrisy at De Paul University, Chicago

On June 15, 1997, Wiesel delivered the commencement address at De Paul University, a Catholic institution in Chicago. It was entitled "Learning and Respect," and he was able to impart his core message while keeping a straight face:[566]

> *Furthermore, humiliation. Always remember, my good friends, that there is one sin we must never commit, and it is to humiliate another person or to allow another person to be humiliated in our presence without us screaming and shouting and protesting.*

Incredibly, the man who has never uttered a word of protest against the daily humiliation of the Palestinians by his fellow Jews in Israel went unchallenged by his largely Catholic audience for this expression of hypocrisy.

1998: More Hypocrisy at Boston University

In October 1998, a symposium on the subject of "The Claims of Memory" was held at Boston University to celebrate Wiesel's 70th birthday. One of the speakers was Prof. Susan Suleiman of Harvard University. As the New York Times reported:[567]

> [She] *spoke about the "institutional boundary" between fiction and nonfiction. It is notable, she said, that it can really only be violated in one direction. "If a*

---

[563] Marlise Simons, "Chirac Affirms France's Guilt in Fate of Jews," *New York Times*, July 17, 1995.

[564] That said, an analysis of the Auschwitz Death Registers indicates that a large percentage of these deportees did in fact die as a result of various diseases, especially typhus, in the catastrophic epidemic that decimated that camp from July 1942 until well into 1943; see Enrique Aynat, "Die Sterbebücher von Auschwitz: Statistische Daten über die Sterblichkeit der 1942 aus Frankreich nach Auschwitz deportierten Juden," *Vierteljahreshefte für freie Geschichtsforschung*, vol. 2, no. 3, 1998, 188-198.

[565] Roger Cohen, "French Church Issues Apology to Jews on War," *New York Times*, October 1, 1997.

[566] Elie Wiesel, "Learning and Respect," June 15, 1997; http://archive.humanity.org/printview.php?page=wiesel_at_depaul§ionName=voices

[567] Sarah Boxer, "Giving Memory Its Due in an Age of License," *New York Times*, October 28, 1998, C1, C6.

> *memoir is felt to be fraudulent, there are shockwaves," especially if the events described are traumatic. If a novel turns out to be a memoir, she said, people don't care as much. "I don't think there should be limits on what one can do with the Holocaust in literature," she said. But, she added, "I think the category of memoir implies a kind of contract."*

Prof. Suleiman implies, but does not state specifically, what this supposed "contract" involves, but she does seem to say that a memoir writer is expected to tell the truth and refrain from making up stories. Not one of the Holocaust profiteers invited to speak at this symposium condemned Wiesel or confessed to feeling "shockwaves" from the many lies found in *Night*. Not surprisingly, the last word in this article was given to Wiesel himself, who confided:

> *Memories, even painful memories, are all we have. In fact, they are the only thing we are. So we must take very good care of them.*

Sadly, Wiesel's mendacious "memory" functioned to perfection when he imagined Dr. Mengele as looking very much like Erich von Stroheim. And then of course there is his clear "memory" of a foot injury that later turned – rather magically – into a knee injury.

1999: Faurisson's *Ecrits Révisionnistes* Appear as an Underground Publication

When Jacques Chirac became president of France in 1995, he made a symbolic gesture, as explained above, to the Holocaustians who rule France from behind the scenes by offering a public apology in his capacity as head of state for the deportation of 25 percent of France's Jews under the Vichy regime. This act, by a man who had opposed the Gayssot Act of 1990, set the tone of subservience to a foreign lobby for his remaining twelve years in office.

In 1999, Professor Faurisson published a monumental four-volume collection of his revisionist writings under the title *Ecrits Révisionnistes*. But thanks to Holocaustian censorship, enforced by the subservient Chirac, Faurisson could not offer the book for sale in public without incurring a serious jail term for *négationnisme*, the Orwellian word the French use for "Holocaust denial." Thus, the four volumes were circulated privately, around the world, with the words *édition privée hors-commerce* (private publication not for sale) prominently emblazoned on their covers. In this way, Faurisson avoided having his work fall under the purview of the Gayssot Act. That he had to do so offers further proof of two important facts: that the Holocaustians of France know that Faurisson is right and that they are wrong on this historical question, and that France's politicians have brought incalculable shame upon themselves by adopting the Shoah as their nation's state religion.

1999: Peter Novick on Wiesel and "the Holocaust"

In 1999, Peter Novick's *The Holocaust in American Life* appeared. Novick, like Finkelstein, whose *Holocaust Industry* would appear a year later, claimed to believe that the Holocaust is a true story, and that it really happened. Like Finkelstein, he also attacked Wiesel, but his mockery was more ironic and nuanced than Finkelstein's. Toward the end of his book, he writes of Wiesel's theatrics:

> *Elie Wiesel, of course, became the emblematic survivor. His gaunt face, with its anguished expression, seemed to freeze time – to be staring out from a 1945 photograph of the liberation of the camps.* (273)

Novick quickly adds that Wiesel's media image is not only contrived; the hypocrisy contained in it also drives innumerable Jews crazy. Regarding this hypocrisy, he writes:

> *Numerous Jewish critics – occasionally in print, more often in private – have been acerbic about what they see as Wiesel's carefully cultivated persona as a symbol of suffering, as Christ figure.* (274)

Although Novick at least mentions this taboo subject, he does not have the courage to explore it and to ask: "Why is it that so many fellow Jews despise Wiesel?" However, his statement does support one of the major themes of the present study, which is that many, if not most, U.S. Jews are skeptical, perhaps even "acerbic," about Wiesel. Their concern is not only with the man's exploitation of the Holocaust in the Zionist media to advance his career; it also relates to Wiesel's persona as a professional Jew.

An unknown factor that might explain this overall Jewish silence about Wiesel, even though many if not most of them know he is a fraudster, is the Jewish principle of *mesirah*. According to this tradition, Jews are enjoined to never inform on another Jew to secular authorities about fraudulent activities.[568]

Rabbi Neusner: Wiesel's "Holocaust-and-Redemption" Cult Turns off Young Jews

As the century came to an end, Rabbi Jacob Neusner, quoted above at a time when the Holocaust was just beginning to take over Jewish life in the United States, issued a further assessment of the effect that Wiesel's self-aggrandizing obsession with the Holocaust was having on young U.S.

---

[568] http://en.wikipedia.org/wiki/Mesirah

Jews. As the game of ethnic politics in the defense of Israel had replaced traditional Jewish belief and practice, young Jews began to be turned off by Jewish identity in unprecedented numbers. Neusner wrote:[569]

> *Now, 25 years later, an entire generation of Jews has grown up with the ethnic Jewishness of Holocaust and Redemption. Don't trust the Gentiles; do depend for psychic security on Israel.*

He continues:

> *And how have the children responded to this Judaism consisting of only memory? The same years that mark the triumph in American Jewry's civil religion of Holocaust and Redemption also have witnessed an unprecedented wave of intermarriage between Jews and unconverted gentiles. In the past eight years alone, more than half of all Jews entering marriage did so with gentiles.*

Neusner concludes, obviously, that gentiles want to marry Jews, so U.S. society is not Nazi Germany. On the Jewish side, however, he notes:

> *Jews vote not only with their feet – choosing not to live in Israel – but also with their heart – choosing not to raise another generation of Jews. Holocaust-and-Redemption Judaism simply has failed in its chosen mission to keep Jews Jewish.*

---

569 Jacob Neusner, "American Jews Embrace a Religion of Memory," *St. Petersburg Times*, April 12, 1999, A11.

Chapter XI
2000s: Wiesel, His Credibility Eroding, Is Satirized by Tova Reich, and Denounces "Deniers"

New Elements in Second Volume of Wiesel's Autobiography

The second volume of Wiesel's autobiography, entitled *And the Sea Is Never Full*, appeared in 2000. James Carroll, by then a well-established Catholic Judeophile and Zionist, reviewed it for the *New York Times Book Review*.[570] An ex-priest, he now holds the post of Distinguished Scholar in Residence at Suffolk University in Boston and continues to write opinion pieces for the *Boston Globe*. In 2000, he was apparently considered to be a safer bet to review Wiesel's autobiography than Daphne Merkin, who had reviewed the first volume.[571] Although Carroll predictably heaped praise on both Wiesel and his book, he nonetheless managed to include a few critical comments. Alluding obliquely to those many Jews who detest Wiesel's exploitation of the Holocaust, Carroll wrote that Wiesel "has become an even more passionate and, to some, problematic voice, obsessed with the subject." He also lists some of the objections that are made with regard to Wiesel's sanctimony:

> *He has been rebuked for being too attached to Israel and for not living there (an American citizen, he has made his home in the United States since 1956). His insistence on the uniqueness of the Holocaust has been taken to denigrate*

---

570 James Carroll, "Witness: For Elie Wiesel Silence Is Not an Option: *And the Sea Is Never Full,* Memoirs," *New York Times Book Review*, January 2, 2000, BR10.

571 One must also remember that the *New York Times* completely transformed the *Boston Globe* during the twenty years (1993-2013) it owned that newspaper. In 2001-2, when the last members of the Taylor family, the previous owners, were being eliminated from the management team, the paper's transformation into a full-fledged Zionist propaganda entity was completed.

> *the suffering of others, like the millions of Ukrainian victims of Stalin's terror-famine.*

Finally, Carroll gets around to mentioning Wiesel's utter failure as an intellectual and as a writer:

> *His writing has been neglected by critics even as his fame has been exploited by the self-interested.*

Carroll is an approved Catholic voice in the Zionist media. For this reason, his editors at the *Times* allowed him to criticize Wiesel, but only within permissible parameters. The most serious critique that he makes of Wiesel is that, although he is widely criticized – even despised – in the U.S. Jewish community, Jewish rabbis, intellectuals, and other leaders generally do not dare to criticize him publicly. Carroll is repeating here what Novick had written a few years earlier to the effect that "numerous Jewish critics – occasionally in print, more often in private – have been acerbic about what they see as Wiesel's carefully cultivated persona as a symbol of suffering [...]" (see p. 330 here). Novick, in turn, was merely repeating what Samuel Freedman had written in 1986 when he stated that "with Wiesel's fame has come, on the one hand, a dehumanizing sort of adulation and, on the other, a criticism of his writing and his personality – little of it rendered in public – from some leading American Jewish intellectuals" (see p. 273 here). Freedman, of course, was recycling what Edward B. Fiske had reported at the beginning of Wiesel's career in the 1970s about "some Jewish leaders" accusing "Wiesel of going beyond the bounds of good taste in building his career on [...] the holocaust" (see p. 216 here).

The silence of the Jewish elites, with their privileged and often direct access to the Zionist media's gatekeepers, with whom, in addition, they share various biases and predispositions, is truly deafening. They refuse to speak out about Wiesel, for the benefit of their non-Jewish fellow citizens, and to denounce his chicanery in public. This behavior suggests they might feel compelled to do so by the Jewish tradition of *mesirah*.

The title to Carroll's review opens with the words "[...] For Elie Wiesel Silence Is Not an Option." It would have been more accurate if it had read "For Elie Wiesel Silence Is Always an Option." Examples of Wiesel's various silences have already been given to the reader. A truly classic silence on his part, however, has been the one he has employed with respect to the repeated written requests he has received for over two decades from the Palestinian human rights organization, Deir Yassin Remembered. That organization has asked him to apologize for the massacre and ethnic cleansing of the Arab village of Deir Yassin on April 9, 1948. This terrorist attack was carried out by Wiesel's employer, the Irgun, for whom he proudly worked, allegedly from late 1947 to early 1949. His answer is always the same: no answer. In response the group has coined the phrase "Wieselian Silence."

Wiesel Testifies under Oath That Everything in *Night* Is True

On February 1, 2007, Wiesel attended a conference at the Argent Hotel in San Francisco on the theme of "Facing Violence: Justice, Religion and Conflict Resolution." While he was there, a young man named Eric Hunt accosted him, and was arrested. Since I strongly oppose the use of violence or coercion of any kind in opposition to the Holocaust fundamentalists, I unequivocally condemn what this young man allegedly did when he is said to have placed hands on Wiesel. At his trial, Hunt was found guilty and served an eighteen month prison sentence. However, the trial also included sworn testimony by Wiesel on one important aspect of his Holocaust claims. On July 8, 2008, Judge Robert Donder questioned Wiesel and received the following answers:[572]

> *Q. And is this book* Night *that you wrote a true account of your experience during World War II?*
> *A. It is a true account. Every word in it is true.*
> [...]
> *Q. And what was your – what day were you born in Sighet, Romania?*
> *A. September 30th, 1928.*
> [...]
> *Q. And what* [number] *was tattooed on your left arm?*
> *A. My number was A7713. My father's number was 7712.*

If Wiesel was not in fact prisoner A-7713, and if his father was not prisoner number A-7712, then he is guilty of perjury.

Holocaust Museum Gift Shops Encourage More Faux "Memoirs"

The dreaded revisionists would never have been able to demolish the Holocaust as history without the help of the Holocaustians themselves. The latter, driven by their lust for both money and control, remained in perpetual need of new products, however ridiculous. As this need burgeoned, the Holocaust fundamentalists revealed not only that the Holocaust is a business, "Shoah Business," but also that they needed to discover new eyewitnesses and new "survivors" in order to develop this market. Their books and videos are sold in the gift shops housed at all the Holocaust museums, and are also utilized by those teachers who deliver state-mandated Holocaust brainwashing instruction in the nation's schools. The Holocaustians

---

[572] Superior Court of California. County of San Francisco. Before the Honorable Robert Donder, Judge Presiding, Department Number 23. *People of the State of California, Plaintiff, v. Eric Hunt, Defendant. Testimony of Elie Wiesel*, July 8, 2008, pp. 7, 13.

also need scripts, no matter how absurd, for Holocaust-related movies. Thanks to the tightly controlled distribution and reward system, such movies receive advertising support, and positive reviews are assured in advance, since no corporate-employed reviewer would risk his or her job by criticizing a Holocaust film. Likewise, such productions automatically receive primary consideration for Oscars and other awards. By the beginning of the twenty-first century, the only caveat seemed to be that such books, videos, and films avoid direct treatment of Auschwitz.

<u>Revisionist Researchers Germar Rudolf and and Carlo Mattogno</u>

Although Professor Lipstadt insists that there is no "other side" to the debate on the historicity of the Holocaust, her view contains a greater dose of wishful thinking than she would probably be willing to admit. To be sure, the revisionists are silenced by the Holocaustians and their stooges wherever possible. They are ostracized and persecuted in every imaginable way, and in many countries they are even prosecuted, fined and sent to prison for their peaceful dissent. Hence it is not surprising that only very few individuals have dared to openly and publicly voice their dissent on this subject. With these harsh facts in mind, I would like to briefly profile two of the most prolific revisionists of the past twenty years. The totality of their work is simply monumental. Even better, it is ongoing.

Although the saga of Germar Rudolf's persecution by the German government for his revisionist views and publications began in the 1990s, it extended into the early years of the new century, and so will be treated here. Carlo Mattogno's career has followed a similar arc. Although he began publishing revisionist essays in the mid-1980s, his productivity reached its pinnacle only after the turn of the millennium.

In 1993, Germar Rudolf (b. 1964) was a young German chemist preparing his PhD thesis at the Max Plank Institute for Solid State Research in Stuttgart. He would soon become a redoubtable addition to the forces of revisionism. Unfortunately, he would also pay dearly for his courage in searching for the truth. Asked by a fellow German citizen, who had been indicted for expressing doubts about the Holocaust, to present an expert opinion on his behalf in court, Rudolf agreed to do so. Not surprisingly, however, Rudolf's expert opinion was disallowed by the judge because its conclusions not only questioned but disproved the gassing myth at Birkenau. Rudolf was then fired from his job, and shortly thereafter forced out of the doctoral program at the University of Stuttgart.[573]

---

[573] For details see his autobiographical notes in the Appendix of his expert report: Germar Rudolf, Wolfgang Lambrecht, *The Rudolf Report: Expert Report on Chemical and Technical Aspects of the "Gas Chambers" of Auschwitz* (2nd ed., Washington, D.C.: The Barnes Review, 2011), 283-437.

In April 1993, Rudolf published a book containing the essence of his technical research on the gas chambers of Birkenau. Entitled *Gutachten über die Bildung und Nachweisbarkeit von Cyanidverbindungen in den 'Gaskammern' von Auschwitz* [*Expert Report on the Formation and Detectability of Cyanide Compounds in the 'Gas Chambers' of Auschwitz*].[574] For this *Expert Report*, Rudolf was indicted by the German judiciary and tried in 1994/95.

Also in April 1993, Rudolf published a less technical book titled *Vorlesungen über Zeitgeschichte: Strittige Fragen im Kreuzverhör* [*Lectures on Contemporary History. Controversial Issues Cross Examined*], which is based on presentations of revisionist research results made by Rudolf before German academic audiences in 1992.[575] The book also appeared in an expanded and updated form in English.[576]

While being tried for his *Expert Report* in late 1994, Rudolf published another work in collaboration with other revisionists including Udo Walendy, John Clive Ball, Carlo Mattogno and Professor Faurisson. It appeared under the title *Grundlagen zur Zeitgeschichte: Ein Handbuch über strittige Fragen des 20. Jahrhunderts*[577] [*Foundations of Contemporary History: A Handbook on Disputed Issues of the Twentieth Century*]. It was later published in English under the title *Dissecting the Holocaust*.[578]

In early 1995, while Rudolf's first trial was still in session, the German authorities once more emphasized their commitment to freedom of thought and expression by initiating criminal investigations against Rudolf, several of his co-authors and his publisher for his 1994 *Grundlagen* book.

At the end of his first trial in June 1995, Rudolf was found guilty of what was essentially a thought crime and sentenced to fourteen months in prison for his *Expert Report*.

In November 1995, Rudolf published yet another revisionist anthology together with Serge Thion, Robert Faurisson and Carlo Mattogno: *Ausch-*

---

[574] This first printed edition (Bad Kissingen: Remker-Heipke, April 1993) was later replaced by a slightly revised second edition bearing as editors the made-up names Rüdiger Kammerer and Armin Solms (eds.), *Das Rudolf Gutachten: Gutachten über die Bildung und Nachweisbarkeit von Cyanidverbindungen in den 'Gaskammern' von Auschwitz* (London: Cromwell Press, July 1993). A third revised and expanded edition (although it is labeled the second) appeared in 2001 (Hastings, UK: Castle Hill Publishers). The first English edition appeared in 2003: *The Rudolf Report: Expert Report on Chemical and Technical Aspects of the "Gas Chambers" of Auschwitz* (Chicago, Ill., Theses & Dissertations Press); for the 2nd Engl. ed. see the previous footnote.

[575] Tübingen: Grabert Verlag, 1993; 2nd ed.: *Vorlesungen über den Holocaust* (Hastings, UK: Castle Hill Publishers, 2005; 3rd ed.: Uckfield, UK: Castle Hill Publishers, 2012).

[576] *Lectures on the Holocaust: Controversial Issues Cross Examined* (Chicago, Ill., Theses & Dissertations Press, 2003; 2nd ed.: Washington, D.C.: The Barnes Review, 2010).

[577] Tübingen: Grabert Verlag, 1994; published under Rudolf's pen name Ernst Gauss.

[578] Edited under the pen name Ernst Gauss (Capshaw, Al.: Theses & Dissertations Press, 2000), 2nd ed., edited as Germar Rudolf (Chicago, Ill.: Theses & Dissertations Press, 2003).

witz: Nackte Fakten—Eine Erwiderung an Jean-Claude Pressac[579] [*Auschwitz: Naked Facts—A Response to Jean-Claude Pressac*], which also appeared in English ten years later.[580]

In March 1996, Rudolf's appeal against his first verdict was rejected, his second trial for his *Grundlagen* book was scheduled to start in June of that year, while another criminal investigation was prepared for his *Auschwitz* book. Fearing that he would actually have to serve a much lengthier jail term under Germany's Orwellian judicial system – there were additional criminal investigations pending for magazine articles Rudolf had authored – he fled to England in early 1996. While in England, the German court sentenced the publisher of Rudolf's *Grundlagen* book to pay a fine of 30,000 DM, issued an arrest warrant against the absent Rudolf, and ordered that the book's printing plates and all existing copies be destroyed. They were burned in waste incinerators under police supervision.

In England, Rudolf started his own little publishing company focusing exclusively on scholarly revisionist material in the German language. When the British media initiated a campaign to have Rudolf extradited to Germany in late 1999, he fled to the United States where he eventually applied for political asylum.

Rudolf's publication output was prolific during his next six years in the U.S. One of the major works produced at this time was the English translation of his already mentioned book *Vorlesungen.* While in the U.S., he also launched the series *Holocaust Handbooks*, in which thirty-one titles have already appeared.[581] These studies, which are based on scientifically sound, evidence-based studies of data, systematically dismantle many of the Holocaust's standard myths. In doing so, they stand in sharp contrast to the standard works on the Holocaust produced by the conformist and self-censoring U.S-American university presses and other publishers. Perhaps the best proof of their validity is the fact that their very existence cannot even be mentioned in the Zionist media.

Rudolf remained in the U.S. until October 2005, at which time he was arrested and four weeks later deported to Germany, where he was found guilty in a trial that was a travesty of justice, sentenced and imprisoned for 30 more months for having written his *Lectures* book and for revisionist texts posted online. After his release in 2009, he returned to England. In

---

579 Edited under the pen name Herbert Verbeke (Berchem, Belgium: Vrij Historisch Onderzoek, 1995); this was a revisionist rebuttal of Jean-Claude Pressac's second book on Auschwitz: *Les Crématoires d'Auschwitz: la Machinerie du Meurtre de Masse* (Paris: Editions du CNRS, 1993).

580 Germar Rudolf (ed.), *Auschwitz: Plain Facts—A Response to Jean-Claude Pressac* (Chicago: Theses & Dissertations Press, 2005)

581 http://holocausthandbooks.com/index.php?main_page=1

2011, he immigrated again to the U.S. where he presently resides with his U.S. wife and children.

Carlo Mattogno, born in 1951, ranks among the most important living and active revisionists. His work on Wiesel, quoted above in Chapter V and printed in an updated version in the Appendix, is an essential feature of the arguments presented in this study about Wiesel's false identity as an Auschwitz survivor.

Starting with his first revisionist book published in 1985,[582] Mattogno's revisionist writings have ever since been published primarily in Italian in his native country Italy. When Mattogno contacted the Institute for Historical Review a few years later, his *œuvre* was discovered by the U.S. revisionist and IHR supporter Russ Granata, a decorated U.S. Navy veteran and retired school teacher of history, literature and German. After becoming aware of Mattogno's work, Granata initiated a correspondence with him and began translating his works into English.[583] As a result of these efforts, Mattogno's monumental work *The Myth of the Extermination of the Jews* appeared in two parts in 1988, and is now available online.[584] This paper fulfilled all the promises implicit in the earlier works, and hinted at more detailed studies to come, first on the Auschwitz-Birkenau camp, and then on the mythical extermination camps in eastern Europe associated with "Operation Reinhardt." *Myth* was breathtaking in range, and brought to its readers sources of information that the conformist historians had dutifully avoided so as not to upset their own, cherry-picked narrative of the Holocaust.

At his own expense, Granata published and promoted several seminal early works by Mattogno, including *My Banned Holocaust Interview* (1996), and *The Crematories of Auschwitz: A Critique of Jean-Claude Pressac* (1993). In bringing the latter work to the attention of the Anglophone revisionist community, he paved the way for the publication of a revised version of this book by the IHR entitled *Auschwitz: The End of a Legend.*[585]

In 1989, Mattogno made his first visit to the U.S. in order to attend the 9th International Revisionist Conference. He read a paper in Italian, with Granata translating it piece by piece. He returned to the U.S. again for the 12th International revisionist Conference in 1994. There he met the multi-

[582] *Il rapporto Gerstein: anatomia di un falso*, (Monfalcone: Sentinella d'Italia, 1985); reviewed by Robert A. Hall in *The Journal of Historical Review*, vol. 7, no. 1, 1986, 115-119.

[583] www.revisionists.com/revisionists/granata.html

[584] *The Journal of Historical Review*, vol. 8, nos. 2f., 1988, 133-172, 261-302; online *e.g.* at www.archive.org/details/TheMythOfTheJewishExtermination.

[585] Newport Beach, Calif.: Institute for Historical Review, 1994; this book is now a chapter in vol. 14 of the series *Holocaust Handbooks*: Rudolf (ed.), *Auschwitz: Plain Facts*, 117-190.

lingual Swiss revisionist Jürgen Graf and discussed with him the possibility of conducting research in the Russian archives, which were just becoming available at that time. Then, beginning in 1995, Mattogno, Graf and Granata actually traveled to Russia, rented two apartments in Moscow, and settled in for a lengthy period of work in the archives captured by the Soviets in 1945 and suppressed until then.[586] As they did so, they were doing work that the conformist historians, with their automatic access to archives, should have conducted years earlier, but never did and still have not.

The total number of Mattogno's published pages on the Holocaust legend is simply massive, and numbers in the tens of thousands.[587] Fortunately, however, his work has been brought to the attention of all World War II researchers through the ambitious publication program launched by Germar Rudolf's series *Holocaust Handbooks*. To date, about half of the thirty books to have appeared in the series have been authored by Mattogno.[588]

Prof. Deborah Lipstadt, Emory University, and the Collapse of *Fragments*

As indicated in Chapter IX, the best-selling British historian David Irving testified on behalf of the defense during the second Zündel trial. This brought upon on him the wrath of organized Zionism, which has been trying hard ever since to destroy the man's reputation and livelihood. One important step during this process of character assassination was Deborah Lipstadt's 1993 book *Denying the Holocaust*, which is almost completely devoid of any scholarly content, but replete with *ad hominem* attacks. David Irving was one of Lipstadt's main targets in that work, and her attack on him consisted mainly of name-calling. That did not go down well with the belligerent Irving, who subsequently sued her and her British publisher Penguin Books for libel. The public hearing of the ensuing court case started in early 2000 and attracted the attention of the world's mass media.[589]

During his preparation for this trial, David Irving made the fatal mistake of assuming that the trial would not be about the Holocaust, but only about whether or not Lipstadt's remarks were libelous. A few months before the hearing, however, Irving was confronted with a massive expert report on the alleged mass exterminations at Auschwitz. It was submitted by Prof. Dr. Robert J. van Pelt, a Jewish cultural historian who had been asked by

---

586 Carlo Mattogno, "Obituary: Memories about Russell Granata (Aug. 22, 1923 – Aug. 14, 2004)," *The Revisionist*, vol. 2, no. 4, 2004, 442f.; www.codoh.com/library/document/1742.

587 Most of his writings translated into English can be found at www.codoh.com/library/authors/1464; many of his Italian papers are posted at www.studirevisionisti.myblog.it

588 www.holocausthandbooks.com/index.php?author_id=5

589 See for instance the compilation by Institute for Historical Review, "Media Coverage of the Irving-Lipstadt Trial," *The Journal of Historical Review*, vol. 19, nos. 1&2, 2000, 40-52, 47-53.

Illustration 34: Prof. Dr. Deborah Lipstadt, emerging victoriously from her court battle with British historian David Irving

the defense team to testify against Irving. Irving was utterly unprepared for this surprise attack, the preferred Zionist *modus operandi*, both because he was not a Holocaust expert at all – he even admitted that he had never read a single revisionist book on the topic – and because he had little time left to mount a counterattack. Hence he lost the case, and the Holocaustians were jubilant, claiming that they had scientifically refuted Holocaust revisionism.[590]

Nothing could be farther from the truth, though, because no Holocaust revisionist was ever present in that court room. The real battle of arguments was yet to follow, first when Prof. van Pelt published his revised and expanded expert report as a book,[591] which was then followed by a thorough and devastating revisionist critique of it authored by Carlo Mattogno.[592] While van Pelt's book was showered with the usual uncritical praise in the media and academe, Mattogno's response – delayed for five years due to his publisher's – Germar Rudolf's – imprisonment for thought crimes (see the previous section) – was met with deafening silence.

Lipstadt's battle against, and victory over, Irving turned her into a Holocaustian heroine, although her contribution to Holocaust research is basi-

---

590 See for instance Don D. Guttenplan, *The Holocaust on Trial: History, Justice and the David Irving Libel Case* (London: Granta Books, 2001); Deborah E. Lipstadt, *History on Trial: My Day in Court with a Holocaust Denier* (New York: Ecco, 2005).

591 Robert J. van Pelt, *The Case for Auschwitz: Evidence from the Irving Trial* (Bloomington: Indiana University Press, 2002).

592 Mattogno, *Auschwitz: The Case for Sanity* (2010); this book is not only a comprehensive rebuttal of van Pelt's tome but also of both of Jean-Claude Pressac's works: *Auschwitz* (1994), and *Auschwitz: Technique and Operation of the Gas Chambers* (N.Y.: Beate Klarsfeld Foundation, 1989).

cally zero. But that was no obstacle for her growing fame, for her mission was obviously not one of education but rather of indoctrination and enforcement, as we will soon see.

As the new millennium began, Holocaust media frauds that had been concocted during the 1990s were publicly unraveling. A man born with the name Bruno Grosjean, who later went by the name of Bruno Dössekker, published an autobiography in 1995 under the name of Binjamin Wilkomirski. Entitled *Bruchstücke: Aus einer Kindheit 1939–1948* (*Fragments: Memories of a Wartime Childhood*), the book was so utterly lacking in credibility that it was clear to revisionists from the beginning that it was a botched attempt at deception. Originally published in Switzerland, the book was hyped by the Holocaustian media as a new and important eyewitness account by someone who had been a child at Auschwitz! Fawning reviewers fell over each other comparing this bogus memoir to Wiesel's *Night*, while Wiesel, not exactly happy that someone was poaching on his private preserve, kept his distance from the book and did not publicly endorse it.

Another reason for Wiesel's negative reaction to the book was that, as the Zionist media were still hyping it and various Jewish groups were awarding it literary prizes, there was speculation that *Fragments* would make an excellent Hollywood movie. This was of course a strong slap in the face to Wiesel, since, as is well known, the Jewish moguls of Hollywood have never dared to invest the millions that would be needed to bring Wiesel's "memoir" to the screen. They maintain a safe distance from *Night* because they know that the book is toxic. In fact, their rejection of it for the last fifty years offers firm proof that they fear that its lies would be evident on the screen.[593]

Wilkomirski hit the jackpot when the Holocaust fundamentalists arranged a national tour for him, including a $150-a-plate luncheon sponsored by the USHMM at a fancy New York hotel. Wilkomirski's tour featured a personal visit with the emerging Holocaust commissar, Professor Lipstadt, in Atlanta. Meanwhile, in the background, the revisionists were having a merry time of it as they went about disemboweling Wilkomirski's faux memoir while it was still being treated in the Zionist media with awe and admiration.

Before long, however, thanks to the revisionists' revelations, the more prudent Holocaustians began to suspect that there was something seriously wrong with Wilkomirski and his memoir. Slowly, and very late, they realized that *Fragments* was indefensible. Thereupon, the Holocaustians threw in the towel and admitted that Wilkomirski and his book were complete

---

[593] Jay Geller, "The Wilkomirski Case: Fragments or Figments?," *American Imago* 59 (Fall 2002), 343-365.

frauds. Tom Gross, covering the affair after the fact in the *Wall Street Journal*, asked:[594]

> *What does Deborah Lipstadt, author of* Denying the Holocaust, *think of the fact Dössekker* [Wilkomirski] *has become (against his wishes) a hero for Holocaust deniers? Professor Lipstadt assigned* Fragments *to her class reading list, and spent a whole day with "Wilkomirski" when he came to Atlanta as part of his speaking tour.*

Gross ought to have added the fact that, even after the Holocaust fundamentalists were obliged to acknowledge that *Fragments* had been just another Holocaust scam, Professor Lipstadt still kept his book as a classroom text for discussion in her Emory University course on the Holocaust. She later justified her position by stating that it "might complicate matters somewhat, but it's [the book] still powerful."[595] For Lipstadt, like Wiesel, emotion and feeling are more important than established fact. Like Wiesel, Lipstadt accepts fiction as historical truth as long as it has the right political spin, that is, posits fellow Jews as victims.

Wiesel's Endorsement Propels a New Holocaust Scam, *Misha*

Misha Defonseca received an important endorsement from Wiesel in 1997 when she published her purported autobiographical account of her experiences during World War II. Entitled *Misha: A Mémoire of the Holocaust Years*, the book appeared in Boston and probably would have gone nowhere except for the fact that Wiesel had penned a publicity blurb for it. Wiesel's statement to the effect that Defonseca's "memoir" was "very powerful" appeared on the back cover and surely enabled the book to gain traction, especially at the beginning.

Another advantage that the book enjoyed was that it recounted Holocaust-related events that had allegedly taken place far away from Auschwitz, which is the Holocaust fundamentalists' preferred approach these days. Misha claimed to be a Belgian Jew who had been separated from her parents during the war. Just a little girl, she then spent years trekking 1800 miles across Europe on foot in search of them. Incredibly, she claimed that she eluded capture by living in the wild with packs of friendly wolves. In a word, the book was utter nonsense.

Misha became a bestseller in Europe, however, and was translated into eighteen languages. The Holocaust gravy train was rolling, and the Zionist media got on board. The Holocaustians arranged for the book to win an impressive number of literary prizes. The book next became the basis of a French movie called *Survivre avec les loups* (*Surviving with Wolves*). It

---

594 Tom Gross, "Real Horrors: Phony Claims: Duping the Holocaust Experts," *WSJ*, February 6, 2002.

595 www.fpp.co.uk/Auschwitz/Wilkomirski/index.html.

was filmed in a short sixteen weeks in 2006 and released in 2007. From its publication in Boston in 1997 through the release of the film in 2007, the revisionists, just as they had done in the case of Wilkomirski and his bogus memoir *Fragments*, exploited the burgeoning Internet to mock the book, and then the movie, as a ridiculous Holocaust scam. Then, suddenly, the dam broke. Defonseca, whose actual name turned out to be Monique de Wael, and who was not even Jewish, was forced to admit that the whole story had been a hoax. Her excuse was that, although the story existed only in her mind, it was still true. When the scam collapsed for good in February 2008, there had already been 540,000 paid admissions to the movie, which was immediately shut down and withdrawn from circulation.

Illustration 35: Misha Defonseca / Monique de Wael

As for Wiesel, the complaisant Zionist media, including the *New York Times* and the *Washington Post*, excused his enthusiastic endorsement of the fraudulent memoir, although it was important to its success. When the dust had settled, a reporter reached Wiesel on the phone and asked about the scandal. He said: "It is sad. It's just very sad." He went on:[596]

> *In truth I don't recall reading it. You see, when I speak with Holocaust survivors,* [sic] *I am always urging them to write, write, write. So whenever I receive a memoir, I am willing to say something about it. But it doesn't mean I have read every page.*

Incredibly, "sad" was the most damning word that Wiesel had for this ridiculous Holocaust deception. But what did the Holocaust High Priest mean by "sad?" Was it sad that Defonseca had lied, further diminishing the rapidly shrinking credibility of the Holocaust story as a whole? Or was it just sad that she had been caught?

Herman Rosenblat's "Memoir," *Angel at the Fence*, Turns out to be a Novel

As a result of the collapse of these two media scams, the Holocaustians seem to have realized that their policy of publishing ridiculous Holocaust horror stories was helping to create cynicism about the Holocaust among non-Jews. This growing awareness of their own guilt in promoting the sen-

596 "Boston Author's Book a Holocaust Hoax," *Providence Journal*, April 27, 2008, I, 1.

Illustration 36: Herman and Roma Rosenblat

sationalization of the Holocaust dovetailed with their realization that the explosive growth of the Internet was also sapping whatever credibility the Zionist mainstream media still retained regarding the Holocaust. A policy change was needed, and its implementation became apparent when a new Holocaust swindler, Herman Rosenblat, was just about to cash in with a big book and movie contract. His story, eventually titled *Angel at the Fence*, had first been publicized by Oprah Winfrey in 1996, when he appeared on her show. Predictably, since it pertained to the Holocaust, Oprah called it "the single greatest love story" she had ever heard. The ridiculous tale deals with two Jewish people who met on a blind date in Coney Island. At the time, they had no inkling that they had met during the Holocaust when she, Roma, had tossed an apple to Herman each day over the fence at Buchenwald. Among the story's ludicrous details was Herman's appointment, in advance, to enter Buchenwald's gas chamber on a particular day – not even Holocaustians claim the camp had such a chamber. As for the camp's layout, including the location of the *Kinderblock*, Herman didn't have a clue. In summary, the story, like Wiesel's *Night*, was clearly a fabrication.

The Rosenblats made two more appearances on Oprah's show in 2007, and the book was scheduled to appear in February 2009. The fix had been in from day one at Berkley Books, a division of Penguin, to launch yet another money-making book and movie project exploiting – indeed trivializing – the Holocaust. Leslie Gelbman, editor and publisher at Berkley, in cahoots with Rosenblat's editor, Natalie Rosenstein, had cynically exploited their Jewish media power to push this book forward. They had also hired a New York ghostwriter, Susanna Margolis, "who polished Mr. Rosenblat's manuscript."[597] This need for polish reminds us of, and corre-

[597] Motoko Rich, Joseph Berger, "False Memoir of Holocaust Is Cancelled," *New York Times*, December 28, 2008, A12.

sponds to, Mauriac's involvement in the redaction, or perhaps I should say polishing, of *La Nuit*. But what these deliberate deceivers did not understand is that, in the wake of the collapse of both the Wilkomirski and Defonseca scams, the Holocaustians were apparently reconsidering the advisability of continuing along this path. By publishing such rubbish, they were strengthening the revisionists' hand, while also displaying contempt for the non-Jews who were expected to consume these ersatz cultural products.

After his story was called into question, Rosenblat stoutly defended it, but did so with Elie Wiesel doubletalk, that is, defended the story's alleged truth as based on "memory." He told one interviewer: "This is my personal story as I remember it."[598] In another interview, he phrased it a bit differently, claiming:[599]

> *I saw things through a young child's eyes. But I know and remember what I saw. What I offer in this memoir are the images, sounds, smells and feelings that have stayed in my mind for some seven decades.*

A day later the story collapsed when Rosenblat admitted his deception. Then it was learned that Rosenblat's children and relatives had known that the story was false from 1996 through his fall from grace in 2008, but never said anything. The relatives' silence corresponds to the similar, tribal silence referred to above, *mesirah*, according to which vehement, even acerbic criticism of Wiesel by other Jews is rarely if ever made publicly. In self-defense, Rosenblat then took another page from the Elie Wiesel playbook when he began comparing his alleged experience to a dream. Like Wiesel, who has been trying to figure out for decades if the flaming pits were real or a dream, Rosenblat played the same game, stating:[600]

> *My mother came to me in a dream and said that I must tell my story so that my grandchildren would know of our survival from* [sic] *the Holocaust.*

He went on:

> *In my dreams, Roma will always throw me an apple, but I now know it is only a dream.*

In conclusion, it was only after the smoke had cleared that the Holocaust gatekeepers at the *New York Times* publicly informed their readers that Holocaustian watchdogs were now trying to prevent the repetition of such egregious scams. The newspaper of record explained solemnly (*ibid.*):

---

598 Hillel Italie, "Oprah's Holocaust Memoir Recommendation, *Angel at the Fence*, Defended by Author, Publisher, Following Scrutiny," *Huffington Post*, December 26, 2008. www.huffingtonpost.com/2008/12/26/oprahsholocaust-memoir-r_n_153565.html

599 "Author Defends Disputed Holocaust Memoir: Herman Rosenblat Says Love Story, Promoted by Oprah, Is Based on Vivid Childhood Memories," *CBS News*, December 26, 2008.

600 Rich and Berger, "False Memoir."

> *Holocaust survivors and scholars are fiercely on guard against any fabrication of memories because they taint the truth of the Holocaust and raise doubts about the millions who were killed or brutalized.*

This statement, with its reference to "the fabrication of memories," was a major concession to the revisionists, although of course the latter could not be mentioned by name. This new media policy is probably intended to protect Wiesel, for there is a creepy similarity between Wiesel's and Rosenblat's lies. But since the Holocaustians have invested heavily over many years in order to create and maintain the Holocaust High Priest as a man of unquestionable integrity, he must be protected. In addition, his memoir is a dogmatic text in our state religion. It plays a major role in the Holocaust brainwashing of America's vulnerable youth. On the other hand, the Holocaustians owed nothing to the grasping Rosenblat, so he could be cut loose. The only question that remains is not if, but when, Wiesel's inevitable fall from grace will occur. Time will tell.

By the end of the decade, the publication and promotion of these deliberately mendacious memoirs had badly damaged the master narrative of the Holocaust. In an apparent attempt to engage in damage control, Ruth Franklin, senior editor at the ardently Zionist *New Republic*, published a book entitled *A Thousand Darknesses: Lies and Truth in Holocaust Fiction.*[601] In doing so, she broke a taboo by admitting that most, if not all, Holocaust narratives, whether fiction or memoir, contain "lies." Thus, it would seem, the "scholars who are fiercely on guard against any fabrication of memories," alluded to above by the *New York Times*, are wasting their time. Lamely trying to explain away the fact that many prominent Jewish intellectuals, including Deborah Lipstadt of Emory University, had heaped praise on Wilkomirski's and Defonseca's clearly fraudulent memoirs, Franklin argues that Holocaust writers have the dual task of remaining truthful overall while also presenting an entertaining story, even if it contains lies on supposedly minor points. She concedes that even Wiesel, whom she calls "by any estimation the most influential Holocaust survivor in America if not the world," (*Thousand*, 5) tells lies. Incredibly, she claims that "the only real challenge to *Night*'s credibility as a memoir" came from Alfred Kazin. Why? He did not believe that Wiesel had really lost his faith during the war, as claimed in *Night*, and he turned out to be right. Franklin actually wants her reader to believe that this is the only credibility issue contained in the novel. As for the revisionists, she admits their existence, but dismisses them: "I am discounting the Revisionists, who have leaped like hyenas on each perceived discrepancy" (80) in the novel. The bottom line is that Franklin's book consists essentially of pious readings designed

---

[601] Ruth Franklin, *A Thousand Darknesses: Lies and Truth in Holocaust Fiction* (N.Y.: Oxford University Press, 2011).

to reassure the Holocaust faithful of the truth of their religion and of the sanctity of their Holocaust High Priest.

Fatelessness Poses a Threat to *Night*'s Hegemony

One final point to be made about these three attempts at creating new memory-driven Holocaust consumer products to be sold to gullible non-Jews is that, in each case, the story line took place far from Auschwitz. U.S. Holocaustians, aware that the legend of Auschwitz as a death camp is, itself, quite dead, seem to want to stay as far away from it as possible. Further proof of this fact emerged when the Hungarian movie *Fateless*, dealing with the alleged experiences of a teenage boy at Auschwitz and Buchenwald, did not exactly receive a warm welcome from these powerful Jewish arbiters of what can be read or seen in the "mainstream" media.

In 2002, the Hungarian novelist Imre Kertész won the Nobel Prize for Literature. Although the total impact of his work had been, and remains, rather unremarkable, he had published a "semi-autobiographical" novel entitled *Sorstalanság* (*Fatelessness*) in 1975. In it, Kertész trespassed on Wiesel's subject matter in *Night* by telling the story of a fifteen-year-old boy who had been deported to both Auschwitz and Buchenwald. Even worse, he wrote a kind of modern day *Candide*, in which a naïve Voltairian hero discovers a concentration camp. Although the book had apparently been written with the best of Holocaustian intentions, it lends itself quite readily to a revisionist interpretation.[602] This fact helps to explain why the Holocaust fundamentalists have been wary of it; that wariness resulted, outside of Hungary, in an almost complete silence about the book's existence. As a result, the novel was not translated into German for fifteen years, first appearing in that language in 1990 under the title *Roman eines Schicksallosen* (*A Novel of the Fateless*). In the Holocaustian-dominated English-language publishing world, the censorship policy was even stronger, for it was ignored for almost two decades, and did not appear in English translation until 1992. Even when it did, no commercial publisher would touch it, and it had to be published by a university press.[603] After Kertész, who is, after all, a veteran of the camps who writes about the Holocaust, received his Nobel Prize in 2002, a new and supposedly improved translation of the novel came out in New York in 2004.[604] At this time the book was finally translated into French under the title *Être sans destin (To Be Fateless)*.

602 For a revisionist review of the book see Markus Springer, "The New Face of the 'Holocaust'," *The Revisionist*, vol. 2, no. 3, 2004, 297-300; www.codoh.com/node/1730

603 Imre Kertész, *Fateless*, tr. Christopher C. Wilson and Katherina M. Wilson (Evanston, Ill.: Northwestern University Press, 1992).

604 Imre Kertész, *Fatelessness*, tr. Tim Wilkinson (N.Y.: Knopf, 2004).

The momentum generated by the Nobel Prize continued into 2005 as a film version of the novel was launched and completed in Hungary. That film, entitled *Fateless*, opened in American theaters on January 6, 2006; the reviews, as expected, were overwhelmingly positive. After all, this was a film about the Holocaust. In fact, many critics, assuming that it would be among the five films selected as contenders for an Oscar as Best Foreign Language Film, naively believed that it had a strong chance to win. But such people did not take into account the fact that *Fateless* would have to overcome several major hurdles in order to do so.

First, Wiesel is America's established Holocaust High Priest, and his novel *Night* is a basic text in Holocaust brainwashing classes, with millions of copies already sold to indoctrinate the young. He and his book are the established brand name as far as the subject of teenagers at Auschwitz is concerned. If an Oscar were to be awarded to the new film, it would only cause confusion, especially since its appearance in DVD was scheduled for May 9. One can easily imagine that the last thing the Holocaustians wanted was for overzealous and misguided Holocaust teachers to show that film to students in conjunction with the reading of *Night*!

The second problem was that the very appearance of this movie about a teenager at Auschwitz risked reminding people of the fact that *Night* has never been turned into a film and, given the narrative's improbabilities (conceded even by Holocaustians), probably never will be.

The third problem, discussed below, had to do with the new translation of *Night* that Wiesel's wife had just prepared for publication, which was to be marketed in conjunction with a nationwide essay contest in which teachers would assign students to write essays stating why *Night* is still relevant today.

Fourth, at that very moment, amidst the snows of January, Wiesel and Oprah Winfrey were filming a propaganda documentary about Auschwitz at the Birkenau camp.

Thus, despite the proliferation of overwhelmingly positive reviews of the film following its January 6 release, with many reviewers calling it a "can't miss" for an Oscar, the wardens of the Oscar system, seeing the dangers described above, made sure that *Fateless* was not one of the five Oscar-nominated films announced on January 31. Thus, the danger to Wiesel's primacy was nipped in the bud, and all further discussion of the film's Oscar eligibility ceased. Now, several years later, the Zionist media have succeeded for all practical purposes in "disappearing" both the novel and the film. It has been almost completely "retconned" out of existence.

Wiesel, the Catholic Church, and the Holocaust

Wiesel and John Paul II Offer Bush Conflicting Advice on Iraq

In the run-up to the invasion of Iraq, Wiesel, in his priestly capacity, made a lightning visit to the White House on February 27, 2003. The Holocaust fundamentalists were pushing for a needless, immoral and illegal war. Vice President Cheney was on board, but Bush seemed to be wavering.

The *New York Times*, which since late 2001 had been running Judith Miller's deceitful articles on Saddam Hussein's alleged plan to acquire nuclear and biological weapons, heartily endorsed the U.S. drive toward war.[605] Miller's newspaper fables also helped to spur sales of her 2001 book *Germs*.[606] When Wiesel visited Bush on that day in February, the *Times*, instead of reporting the event, suppressed coverage. This was business as usual for both the *New York Times* and the Zionist media in general; this particular lie of omission, or silence, contributed, as is often the case, to more U.S. non-Jews dying for Israel.

Fortunately, however, Robert Woodward did mention Wiesel's surreptitious visit to the White House in his 2004 book *Plan of Attack*. Ironically, Woodward was writing at a point in time when the invasion and occupation were supposedly going well. Thus, his intent in mentioning Wiesel's dramatic performance at the White House was not to criticize the man, but rather to praise him, while also offering an honest portrayal of his immense power. In doing so, Woodward made it clear that this "war of choice" was as much about Israel as it was about oil.

Woodward stressed that Bush had been wavering about his decision to unleash the dogs of war until he received Wiesel's blessing. Wiesel had told him that Iraq was a "terrorist state and that the moral imperative was for intervention." Israel's security was supposedly at stake. He asked: "In the name of morality, how can we not intervene?"[607] Woodward concludes:

> *In the days after, Bush routinely repeated Wiesel's comments.*

He leaves it to us to fill in the winks and nods that must have gone with that statement, for what Bush in effect was saying was that by launching a proxy war for Israel he was averting another "Holocaust." Colin Powell, apparently referring to our High Priest's influence on Bush, later stated sardonically that the president had relied on "divine guidance" in deciding to go to war, as if the mendacious Wiesel were some kind of a holy man.

At about the same time that Wiesel was giving Bush his blessing for the invasion, Pope John Paul II sent Cardinal Pio Laghi, who had formerly

---

605 Alexander Cockburn, "Judy Miller's War," *Counterpunch.com*, August 18, 2003.

606 Judith Miller, Stephen Engleberg and William Broad, *Germs: Biological Weapons and America's Secret War* (N.Y.: Simon & Schuster, 2001).

607 Bob Woodward, *Plan of Attack* (N.Y.: Simon & Schuster, 2004), 320.

Illustration 37: U.S. President George W. Bush and the Dalai Lama with the Holocaust High Priest

Illustration 38: Elie Wiesel and Colin Powell: brother in war.

been the Vatican representative in Washington, to the White House. His charge was to argue against undertaking a disastrous war. Since Laghi had enjoyed cordial relations with the Bush family over the years, he was a trusted friend. He brought with him a letter from the Pope, and both the contents of that letter and his own verbal exhortations affirmed that the coming war would be unjustified on both moral and legal grounds.[608]

The difference between the Catholic position, as voiced by Laghi, and the one espoused by the Holocaust fundamentalists, as voiced by Wiesel, could not have been more radically different. Bush, of course, aware of who has power in this country and who does not, ignored the advice of John Paul II and his emissary, for their opinion was irrelevant – as was that

608 "Cardinal Pio Laghi, RIP," *The Catholic World Report*, March 9, 2009, 6.

of the millions of believing Catholics in the U.S. Since he realized that Wiesel spoke for the Holocaust fundamentalists, he understood that the man's very presence at the White House – uninvited – offered proof that the Zionist media would support him in this reckless gesture on behalf of a foreign country, Israel.

Now, over a decade later, tens of thousands of American men and women – and countless Iraqis – have been killed and maimed in a needless war. Their blood is on Elie Wiesel's hands.

Wiesel Attacks John Paul II over Israel's Apartheid Wall

In November 2003, as Israel was building its apartheid wall in occupied Palestine, Wiesel expressed his support for the project, even though it would impose additional inhuman hardships on the Palestinians. Then, when Pope John Paul II stated on November 16, 2003 that "the Holy Land does not need walls, but bridges," Wiesel erupted in defense of Israel's latest crime against humanity:[609]

> *From the leader of one of the largest and most important religions in the world, I expected something very different, namely a statement condemning terror and the killing of innocents, without mixing in political considerations and above all comparing these things to a work of pure self-defense. To politicize terrorism like that is wrong.*

Ironically, the same man who accuses Pius XII of silence wanted John Paul II to be silent about Israel's so-called separation barrier.

The Strange Fate of *Amen*, a French Film Version of *The Deputy*

In 2002, some forty years after the original stage production of *The Deputy*, which the Zionist media had hailed as a masterpiece, even though ordinary folk could see that it was a rather pathetic piece of Zionist propaganda, the Holocaust fundamentalists decided to revive it for a new generation. Filmed in 2001, the movie *Amen* opened in France on February 27, 2002. France's Holocaustians spent a large sum of money on their new product, which deals directly with the alleged extermination program at Auschwitz. They were aware that in making the movie they were going against the policy that the Jewish moguls of Hollywood had been imposing since *Schindler's List* in 1993. They went ahead anyway since their primary market, France, was quite different from the U.S. market. The reader will recall that *Schindler's List*, in which Schindler's Jewish women were shown entering simple disinfestation showers rather than gas chambers, revealed that Steven Spielberg did not dare to take the revisionists head-on by attempting to physically portray the totally imaginary gas chambers of Auschwitz. Despite the multiplicity of Academy Awards that were ritually

[609] "Wiesel Slams Pope's Comments," *News24.com*, November 17, 2003.

showered upon *Schindler's List*, the film can be seen in retrospect as the Stalingrad of the Holocaust as far as visual representation of the alleged gas chambers is concerned. In a word, Spielberg had capitulated to the revisionists, and since then Hollywood has avoided making any Holocaust film that deals directly with Auschwitz and its problematical gas chambers.[610]

While *Amen* alluded to Auschwitz only from a distance, and no attempt was made therein to recreate the gas chambers, the strategy made absolutely no sense. After all, the whole point of the play on which the film was based was that Pius XII had been silent about the gas chambers. Since one of the key differences between stage and film is the latter's superior capacities in terms of representation, this refusal by the makers of *Amen* to touch the subject of Pius XII's alleged silence turned out to be yet another surrender to the revisionists.

As might be expected, in France, where public expression of doubt about any aspect of the Holocaust is a crime punishable by severe fines and prison terms, the Holocaust fundamentalists had no trouble lining up top awards for their film. *Amen* won awards for Best Writing, Best Actor, Best Cinematography and Best Director. It was also nominated for Best Film, Best Sound and Best Music for a Film. This list of awards, and the obvious manipulation that went into it, help to explain why the movie was made in the first place. Since belief in the Shoah is mandated with the force of law in France, the French Holocaustians seemed to have had a triple goal in making their film: 1) to use their money and media power to increase their mind control over the French population as a whole; 2) to produce a film for use in state-organized brainwashing classes for students; and 3) to provide a distraction as the Second Intifada continued in full swing in Occupied Palestine.

Despite the film's many awards and its apparent success in indoctrinating a new generation of French children on the alleged silence of Pius XII during the Holocaust, Wiesel held his tongue about this particular propaganda operation. One searches in vain for any comment from him about it. Once again, Wieselian silence was resounding.

In the U.S., *Amen*'s fate was quite different. Released in the American market in late January 2003, it was shown in a small number of theaters and withdrawn from circulation shortly after release. The Jewish-dominated film distribution network treated *Amen*, which was presented in French with English subtitles, like a generic foreign-language art-house movie.

---

[610] Editor's remark: The one major movie about Auschwitz, including staged gassing scenes, which has been produced since then was a controversial German production: *Auschwitz* by Uwe Boll (2011); see http://en.wikipedia.org/wiki/Auschwitz_(film); see also the documentary *Auschwitz: The Surprising Hidden Truth* by Mike Smith aka DenierBud; www.holocausthandbooks.com/index.php?page_id=1005

Given the work's subject matter, however, one wonders why a dubbed version in English was not made for a mass audience. During its 26-week run, it was never shown in more than eight theaters at any one time. *Amen* grossed a paltry $274,299 in the U.S., which was a miniscule portion of its worldwide receipts.[611] In France and elsewhere, mostly in countries where it is a crime to question the Holocaust, it sold 1,320,000 tickets and grossed €15,800,000.[612] The film was clearly a work of propaganda; doubtless it was too shrill for the Zionist moguls of Hollywood to deem worthy for a mass gentile audience, which explains why a dubbed version in English has not been released.

By 2003, there was also a factor peculiar to the U.S. market, and thus absent from France in 2002. The Holocaustians in the U.S. were already attacking Mel Gibson's *The Passion of the Christ*, which was in the pipeline. A major publicity campaign for *Amen* might have offended many Christians and in turn further justified Gibson's film. As it was, Gibson was forced to finance *The Passion of the Christ* himself, and find an independent distributor for it on his own. Released on February 24, 2004, just thirteen months after *Amen*, Gibson's film opened on 4,400 screens in 3,170 theaters and grossed $125 million in its first week, dwarfing the performance of the French Holocaust film.

Benedict XVI Visits Auschwitz as Wiesel Attacks Pius XII on CNN

Joseph Ratzinger was elected pope on April 19, 2005; he took the name Benedict XVI. As a native of Germany who had been a member of the Hitler Youth at the end of World War II, he risked, from the very first day of his pontificate, being pressured by the Holocaustians to apologize for both his nation of origin and the church he now headed. The former had supposedly carried out the Holocaust, while the latter, personified by Pius XII, had remained silent while this alleged event unfolded. Such an apology would give formal, papal recognition to the Holocaustian religion of the six million. The stakes were huge. It did not take long for the Holocaustian pressure that was being brought to bear on the pope, presumably in the name of Jewish-Catholic relations, to bear fruit. In fact, a little more than a year after his election, on May 28, 2006, Benedict XVI visited the Auschwitz camp complex.

Benedict clearly made the trip to demonstrate his recognition (though not necessarily his approval) of the reality of Zionist Jewish media, political and economic power. In doing so, he must have pondered the possibil-

---

611 www.imdb.com/title/tt0280653/business.

612 www.leboxofficepourlesnuls.com/2014/12/26/box-office-mathieu-kassovitz-est-il-lacteur-francais-le-moins-bankable.

Illustration 39: Benedict XVI entering the Auschwitz I camp

ity that he might be seen by some as establishing an extremely dangerous precedent for future popes.

In any case, his act mirrored Jacques Chirac's trip to the Vélodrome d'Hiver, the indoor skating rink in Paris, on July 16, 1995, at the very beginning of his first term in office. While Ratzinger's baggage, mentioned above, consisted essentially of the fact that he was a German national who now held the job that Pius XII once had, Chirac's revolved around his three 1990 votes against the Gayssot Law criminalizing revisionist questioning of the Shoah in France. Chirac explicitly apologized for the role played by the French state, the Vichy government, in arresting and deporting about 25 percent of France's Jews, most of whom were either foreigners or stateless, or they had been naturalized only recently, hence were considered security risks by the Germans. In doing so, he showed that he did not possess the personal political capital that major figures like de Gaulle and Mitterrand had enjoyed, for the latter had never allowed France's Jewish community to publicly manipulate them on this issue, and thus had never apologized on behalf of people who were no longer living. From the very moment when Benedict XVI's travel plans were announced, the major question was whether or not he would apologize.

Benedict XVI visited both the Auschwitz main camp and the Birkenau camp, spending a total of two hours in an act of public commemoration of the victims of the Holocaust. His every word and gesture was watched closely by the Zionist media in order to interpret their meaning. Although many Holocaustians expected an apology on both the German and the Catholic accounts, none came. The *New York Times* had to admit as much when their reporter wrote that Benedict "spoke eloquently about 'forgiveness and reconciliation,' but he did not beg pardon for the sins of Germans or of the Roman Catholic Church during World War II."[613]

Illustration 40: Benedict XVI bowing in memory of "the six million" at Auschwitz I

Since the Pope had failed to provide the response expected by so many Holocaustians, the newspaper of record consulted Rabbi David Rosen of the American Jewish Committee. Asked to evaluate the import of the day's events, Rosen called Benedict's "omission of a broader, national responsibility, 'lamentable,' but nothing new in the pope's often expressed interpretation of the war." Clearly, then, on the issue of national guilt and responsibility, Benedict XVI had not taken the bait, and thus failed to perform to the liking of the visit's Holocaustian stage managers.

On the second issue, the lack of an apology for supposed Catholic guilt, Rosen was asked if the visit would make any difference in Jewish-Catholic relations, his specialty. He responded:

> *No, because Jewish-Catholic relations anyway are no longer based upon our view of the past but on the nature of relations in the present, and from that perspective Benedict XVI is as good as it gets.*

Rosen's emphasis on the present over the past can be read as a possible indication that Zionist Jewish opposition to the canonization of Pius XII is weakening. If that is in fact the case, this change has not been caused by Pacelli's Church-approved Catholic defenders, who never question Holocaust dogma, but by the withering attacks that the revisionists have brought to bear on the Holocaust faith since 1976.

Rabbi Rosen's emphasis on the present also seems to refer to the ongoing success of the abusive relationship that exists between Jewry and the Vatican. In fact, the very fact that a pope now seems to feel that he must publicly bow to the memory of "the six million," if he wants to avoid Zionist media abuse and get his pontificate off to a good start, demonstrates the power that the Jewish side wields in this sick relationship. This abuse also includes the free access that the Jewish propagandists continue to have to Catholic youth. Brainwashing classes on the Holocaust, conducted in Catholic schools by rabbis, faux veterans, children of such veterans, or

[613] Ian Fisher, "A German Pope Confronts the Nazi Past at Auschwitz," *New York Times*, May 29, 2006, A7.

ADL and AJC staffers, are an ongoing feature of this systematic abuse taking place in Benedict XVI's domain. Sadly, these classes sometimes involve a very serious form of child abuse of highly impressionable Catholic youth.

For this and other reasons, the ongoing "dialogue" is at the very least misguided, and at the worst heretical. I say this because the Jewish side is allowed to present the martyrdom of "the six million" as a modern-day version of (and replacement for) the sacrifice of Christ. Strangely, this "dialogue" also fails to make any reciprocal provision for Catholics to tell young Jews about Christ. Rosen was right, this is "as good as it gets."

After the Pope's visit to the main camp, a convoy of vehicles drove the dignitaries about two kilometers to the Birkenau complex. One Zionist newspaper, caught in a time warp, as if the Jewish Holocaust narrative still claimed that the Germans had killed four million people at Birkenau, wrote:[614]

> *The convoy moved on to Birkenau, an adjoining camp, which was built with such grim efficiency that it could kill and incinerate 20,000 people every day.*

Of course, the aerial photos, coupled with revisionist research, have relegated to libel the very existence of such "grim efficiency."

The papal visit to Auschwitz on Sunday, May 28, happened to occur just after Wiesel had made his three appearances on the Oprah Winfrey Show. That evening, CNN saw fit to invite Wiesel to be interviewed by their staffer Carol Lin in order to comment on the Pope's visit. The fact that CNN called upon Wiesel, and not on one of the innumerable other Jewish experts who consult for them, to comment on Benedict's visit to Auschwitz illustrates quite clearly that in the Zionist media Wiesel and whoever happens to be pope at the time share equal status. The interview between Lin and Wiesel appears to have been carefully scripted in advance, with Lin tossing softball questions to the Holocaust High Priest. After commenting to Wiesel that people had been "brutally murdered" at Auschwitz, she said:

> *The Catholic Church in the past had been criticized for not doing more to stop the Holocaust. And here today, we see Pope Benedict visiting Auschwitz, saying a prayer. I am wondering how that moment struck you, and what you think the Catholic Church should do, needs to do, to prevent another Holocaust from happening again?*

This was an amazing question, for it posited as fact the totally unwarranted claim that the Catholic Church was guilty of not doing more to stop the Holocaust. Her query also presumed that the Catholic Church has within its

---

[614] Daniel McLaughlin, "Pope Bows down for the Victims of Auschwitz Killed by His Countrymen," *The Guardian*, May 29, 2006. www.theguardian.com/world/2006/may/29/secondworldwar.catholicism

power the ability to prevent another Holocaust in the future. Once Lin had set the stage, Wiesel, on cue, told his listeners that Jews died in the Holocaust for one simple reason. It was "because there was a pope who was silent, Pope Pius XII. And then came John XXIII, who was a great pope, and John Paul II was a great pope. I think this one is trying."[615] Of course, no dissenting voice was invited on the show to dispute Wiesel's absurd contention. The Holocaust High Priest had spoken.

Holocaustian Softening up Campaign against Benedict XVI

After the visit to Auschwitz, Benedict XVI continued to encounter Jewish enmity, just as John Paul II had in the early years of his pontificate before granting diplomatic recognition to Israel in 1993. In 2007, Benedict reinstated a traditional Latin prayer for the salvation of the Jews. Suppressed since Vatican II, the prayer's return was requested by Catholic conservatives. It is said only in the traditional Good Friday ceremony when the Church has historically prayed for the Jewish people. The words were:[616]

> *Lift the veil from the eyes of the Jews and end the blindness of that people so that they may acknowledge the light of Your truth, which is Christ.*

Predictably, the Holocaustians were outraged, with Abe Foxman speaking for them:[617]

> *We are extremely disappointed and deeply offended that nearly 40 years after the Vatican rightly removed insulting anti-Jewish language from the Good Friday Mass, that it would now permit Catholics to utter such hurtful and insulting words by praying for Jews to be converted.*

Here once again, a dominant bully in a one-sided, abusive relationship was informing his victim of an infraction of the code. Under this arrangement, Catholics are not supposed to express their faith among themselves as they see fit without express prior approval from the likes of Abe Foxman.

As the result of this Holocaustian criticism, in February 2008 Benedict published a change in the prayer that had been the cause of offense several months earlier. It read:[618]

> *Let us pray for the Jews. May the Lord Our God enlighten their hearts so that they may acknowledge Jesus Christ, the savior of all men. Almighty and everlasting God, you who want all men to be saved and to reach the awareness of*

---

[615] Carol Lin, "CNN Sunday Night," *CNN.com Transcripts*, May 28, 2006; http://edition.cnn.com/TRANSCRIPTS/0605/28/snn.01.html

[616] Micah Halpern, "In Defense of Pope Benedict XVI," *MicahHalpern.com*, July 18, 2007; http://archive.frontpagemag.com/readArticle.aspx?ARTID=27417.

[617] Ian Fisher, "Pope Eases Restrictions on Wider Use of Latin Mass: Stresses Current Rite to Remain Standard," *New York Times*, July 8, 2007, A4.

[618] Ian Fisher, "Pope's Rewrite of Latin Prayer Draws Criticism from 2 Sides," *New York Times*, February 6, 2008, A8.

the truth, graciously grant that, with the fullness of peoples entering into your church, all Israel may be saved.

Needless to say, this modification was also rejected immediately by the Jewish side. Even though a Catholic spokesman stated that the prayer would be heard only by "a tiny minority of Catholics and they will hear it in Latin," that was still not good enough.[619]

Tensions between Benedict and the Holocaustians continued in this vein into 2009 and heightened on the eve of Benedict's planned trip to Israel. In January, the Pope was attacked by Italian rabbis for having changed the prayer back in 2007. This rather tardy contrivance masked what was probably the real issue here: Benedict's plan to honor the "heroic virtues" of Pope Pius XII and to declare him ready to be considered for canonization. A newsman reported:[620]

Jews have asked the pope to freeze the procedure that could lead to Pius being made a saint.

Also at this time, Benedict reinstated Bishop Richard Williamson when he revoked the excommunications of four bishops from the Society of St. Pius X, a schismatic group founded by Archbishop Marcel Lefebvre in 1970 in opposition to the liberal reforms of Vatican II. (The Williamson "Holocaust denial" issue will be discussed below.)

Also in the background, the Jews of Israel launched a murderous criminal offensive against the civilian population of Gaza from December 27, 2008, to January 18, 2009. Their behavior reaffirmed once again Pius XII's wisdom in opposing the creation of a racially exclusive Jewish state in the Holy Land.

Israel's Yad Vashem Holocaust memorial has kept the propaganda campaign against Pius XII alive by means of a picture of the man, accompanied by a caption beneath it, accusing him of "silence and the absence of guidelines" during the Holocaust.[621] Various Vatican and other Catholic notables have protested this distortion of history, but to no avail, for the Jewish side maintains that the condemnation of Pius XII will remain in place until the Vatican releases all of its archival documents from the World War II era. As noted above in Chapter I, Pius XII was firmly supportive of the

---

619 Neela Banerjee, "Conservative Rabbis to Vote on Resolution Criticizing Pope's Revision of Prayer," *New York Times*, February 9, 2008, A9.

620 Philip Pullella, "Italy Rabbis Pull out of Dialogue, Accuse Pope," *reuters.com*, January 13, 2009; www.reuters.com/article/2009/01/13/us-pope-jews-idUSTRE50C7KF20090113; James Carroll, "The Pope's Big Holocaust Lie," *The Daily Beast*, December 24, 2009; www.thedailybeast.com/blogs-and-stories/2009-12-23/the-popes-big-holocaust-lie/full/.

621 Christoph Schult, Alexander Smoltczyk, "The Word Left Unspoken: For German Pope, Yad Vashem Is Everywhere," *derspiegel.de*, May 18, 2009. www.spiegel.de/international/world/the-word-left-unspoken-for-german-pope-yad-vashem-is-everywhere-a-625471.html

Allied cause, and his supposed "silence" is best understood in the context of many other "silences" observed by various Allied leaders and organizations at the same time. This Israeli position also expresses in a nutshell the extent of Jewish hypocrisy about the Holocaust, for it is the Jewish side that is actually exerting censorship, most recently by keeping the millions of documents from the International Tracing Service under lock and key.[622]

Benedict had apparently learned nothing about his detractors on his 2006 visit to Auschwitz, and so he went poorly armed into his grueling eight-day visit to Israel in May 2009. Throughout that year, the Vatican continued its policy of appeasement, some would even say of self-debasement, toward world Jewry. On his trip, Benedict XVI made the obligatory visit to Yad Vashem, but did not enter the room in which Pius XII is insulted. He made this bizarre pilgrimage as part of the "Catholic-Jewish dialogue" that calls for Church officials at all levels to bow down before the golden calf of the Holocaust. While there, he expressed his compassion for Jews who had died in the Holocaust, but he and his staff must have known in advance that, no matter how much he humiliated himself before Jewish media and economic power, his enemies would nonetheless play the "failure to say the word Jew" game, or the equivalent thereof with some other word. In making this gesture, he was also acting in a manner that contradicts his job description, which is to preach Christ, not the Holocaust. Yet, while his physical presence represented, on one level, surrender to Jewish power, his words, carefully chosen, hinted that he entertained doubts about the Holocaust narrative. The Holocaustian leadership, especially the notional veterans among them, was irked.

After the visit, the chairman of Yad Vashem, Rabbi Yisrael Meir Lau, himself a Holocaust veteran, complained of the Pope's usage of the word "millions" instead of the more specific "six million" in speaking of the Holocaust's Jewish victims, as well as his use of the word "killed" rather than "murdered." "There's a dramatic difference between killed and murdered, especially when a speech has gone through so many hands," Lau said.[623]

---

[622] Of course Yad Vashem ignores the fact that it sits on stolen Palestinian land and overlooks Deir Yassin, where Wiesel's employer, the Irgun, massacred men, women, and children and where today not even a signpost is allowed to acknowledge this pivotal event in Palestinian/Jewish history. Requests to Wiesel and other Holocaustians to petition Israel to release from its military archives the photographs of the massacre at Deir Yassin are consistently met with both Wieselian Silence and media indifference.

[623] Jack Khoury, *et al.*, "Survivors Angered by Pope's 'Lukewarm' Yad Vashem Speech," *Haaretz*, May 12, 2009; www.haaretz.com/news/survivors-angered-by-pope-s-lukewarm-yad-vashem-speech-1.275872. Of course Rabbi Lau made no mention of the museum having spent tens of millions of dollars to collect the names of Jews said to have died (killed, murdered, and otherwise expired) during World War II, only to end up with fewer than 3 million to date, many of these illegitimate or duplicative. The sacrosanct six-million figure must be preserved.

Rabbi Lau's ritualized objection is a variation on the "Olympics of Suffering" meme so dear to the *New York Times*. That newspaper uses it when the word "Jew" has either not been specified, or has been used in a way that conflates suffering that is specifically Jewish (worthy victims) with that of others (unworthy victims). This meme has proved to be a useful tool for controlling the public utterances of gentile public figures. Yet, Benedict's words were, in retrospect, subversive, especially his refusal to mouth the non-historical Zionist propaganda term "six million." Surely Rabbi Lau was not the only major Jewish figure to be upset by Benedict's show of independence, for which the latter would be made to pay.

Later in the year, almost to the day when Wiesel was in Hungary calling for jail terms for "Holocaust deniers," Benedict XVI offered yet further evidence of his refusal to completely knuckle under to the Holocaustians. Unexpectedly, although he knew in advance that the Zionist media would mete out serious payback for what he was about to do, he announced that he considered Pope Pius XII to be "venerable," and thus worthy of canonization as a saint of the Church. He paired the announcement of Pius's new status as "venerable" with that of John Paul II. The Holocaustians had no trouble with the John Paul II's proposed canonization, since they were already covertly lobbying for it. But they were still opposed to any softening of their line on Pius XII. Of course, Abe Foxman, the National Director of the Anti-Defamation League since 1987, was outraged. Reaching into his toolbox of Holocaust kitsch, he asked:[624]

> *Why the rush to open up the wound again before the opening of the archives?*

The *New York Times* echoed the same Holocaustian propaganda line, stressing the notion that Pius XII must be considered guilty of silence as long as Vatican documents allegedly remain suppressed. A reporter wrote:[625]

> *Pius XII, however, has been a point of contention between the Vatican and some Jewish groups, who say he did not do enough to stop the Holocaust. They have called on the Vatican to open the sealed archives from Pius' papacy, from 1939 to 1958, for examination by scholars. On Saturday, the American Gathering of Holocaust Survivors and their Descendants called the decision on Pius "profoundly insensitive and thoughtless" and said it would cause "an inevitable blow to interfaith relations." A spokesman for the group added: "Pairing the announcement on Pius – who remained publicly silent during the Holocaust – with that on John Paul II, himself a victim of the Nazis, is a particularly disturbing and callous act."*

It can be argued, however, that both Abe Foxman and the interest group calling itself the American Gathering of Holocaust Survivors and Their De-

---

624 Samuel Goldsmith, "Pope Benedict Declares Pius XII 'Venerable,' Angering Jewish Groups," *New York Daily News*, December 19, 2009.

625 Rachel Donadio, "Popes Move Closer to Sainthood," *New York Times*, December 20, 2009, A13.

scendants were also being insensitive to the wound that their ongoing silence is causing, both to historical truth about the Holocaust and to the reputation of Pius XII before the court of history. If they really wanted to know what happened during the Holocaust, they would call for a speedy release of all the documents recently given by the International Tracing Service to the USHMM. However, if these records of the personal fate of millions of individuals caught up in the Holocaust were made wholly and completely available to any and all researchers, the Holocaust fundamentalists would risk seeing their whole edifice collapse, and the true identity of Elie Wiesel revealed.

By the end of 2009, Benedict must have been weary of the constant barrage of criticism coming from his Jewish Holocaustian tormentors. Since the latter have multiple connections inside the Vatican government and church hierarchy with like-minded Holocaustian Catholics, the latter were also able to make trouble for Benedict on issues not directly related to the Holocaust in order to contribute to the overall softening-up process. Unlike John Paul II, who ended his own media persecution at their hands by granting Vatican diplomatic recognition to Israel, Benedict had nothing that his enemies wanted, other than his disappearance from the scene. In the end, that is what he was forced to give them.

Wiesel's New Protégé: French Priest Patrick Desbois

As skepticism about Auschwitz and the Holocaust continued to grow during the first decade of the twenty-first century (two decades after Wiesel's installation by President Reagan as our Holocaust High Priest), the Holocaustians sought to displace public attention as much as possible from Auschwitz and onto outlying elements of the master narrative of the Holocaust. This fact helps to explain how and why, seemingly out of nowhere, a Catholic priest named Patrick Desbois suddenly appeared on the scene in 2004. His mission, bizarrely reminiscent of that of Cardinal O'Connor, who wanted to teach the New York faithful about the Holocaust in the last years of his life, is to tell the world, through the bullhorn of the Zionist media, about what he calls *la Shoah par balles* (the Holocaust by bullets). His tale is risible, yet the various worldwide Zionist media outlets treat Desbois as if he were a true prophet.

The background of Desbois's *Shoah par balles* is the Holocaustian claim that between 1.3 and 3 million Jews were murdered during the war by the German *Einsatzgruppen* on the temporarily occupied territory of the Soviet Union.[626] The *Einsatzgruppen* were a task force officially set up to

[626] Raul Hilberg, *The Destruction of the European Jews*, (2nd ed., New York: Holmes & Meyer 1985), 1219, claims 1.3 million; Helmut Krausnick and Hans-Heinrich Wilhelm, *Die Truppe des Weltanschauungskrieges. Die Einsatzgruppen der Sicherheitspolizei und des SD 1938-1942* (Stuttgart: Deutsche Verlags-Anstalt, 1981), 621, claim 2.2 million;

combat partisans behind the German-Russian front, among other duties. The Holocaustians, however, claim that these groups were primarily engaged in doing something else: ethnically cleansing the German-occupied Soviet Union of its Jews by means of either mass shootings or gassings in so-called "gas vans."[627] This massacre is said to have left behind thousands of mass graves, and Desbois set out to locate some of them. Before examining Desbois's activities, some background information is required.

Holocaustians Seek to Brand Ukrainian Victims of the Holodomor as Unworthy

Since the breakup of the Soviet Union, the Ukrainian people have commemorated their own holocaust, which they call the "Holodomor." The word refers to Stalin's program, begun in 1932, of imposing systematic starvation on the Ukrainians because of their resistance to his efforts to force them to adopt collective farming. The man Stalin appointed to lead the effort, which culminated in the extermination of seven million people, or about twenty-five percent of the Ukrainian population, was a bloodthirsty Jewish fanatic named Lazar Kaganovitch.[628] Many of his key underlings were also Jewish. In retaliation against the nationalist Ukrainians for launching this campaign of remembrance that highlights the role of Jews as murderers, the Holocaust fundamentalists sought to stigmatize the Ukrainian people as "anti-Semitic," and Desbois is simply a cog in that machine.

Desbois's mission to locate mass graves containing Jews massacred by Germans inevitably encountered massive problems precisely because the Ukraine has been the location of so many human disasters ever since the Russian Revolution. Even before the "Holodomor," Lenin's and Stalin's previous waves of forced collectivization had created many victims, and the millions of victims of these disasters were followed by millions of military and civilian casualties during the German-Russian war between 1941 and 1944. To this we have to add the uncounted victims of Stalin's mass reprisals, right after the war, against those Ukrainians accused of having collaborated with the Germans.

Thus, considering the fact that the Ukrainian countryside must be littered with mass graves that perhaps hold as many as 10 million victims, or maybe even more, it is a challenging task indeed to attempt to single out the mass graves of Jews allegedly murdered by Germans. This job is rendered even more difficult by the fact that such graves in that particular re-

Solomon M. Schwarz, *Jews in the Soviet Union* (Syracuse, N.Y.: Syracuse University Press, 1951), 220, claims 3 million.

627 For a critique of the gas van claims see Santiago Alvarez, *The Gas Vans: A Critical Investigation* (Washington, D.C.: The Barnes Review, 2011).

628 On this see Robert Conquest, *The Harvest of Sorrow: Soviet Collectivization and the Terror-famine* (Oxford: Oxford University Press, 1987).

gion of the former Soviet Union probably hold no more than a few hundred thousand victims. In other words, unless proven otherwise, any mass grave found in the Ukraine is at least ten times more likely to hold – usually Christian – victims of Communist massacres and war casualties than Jewish victims of German atrocities. Distinguishing the one from the other, if even possible, requires careful, professional forensic methods. What Desbois did, however, was the exact opposite, as we will see below.

While there seems to be no interest, let alone an initiative, to locate and forensically examine the tens of millions of preponderantly Christian victims of Communist mass crimes of the 20th century, any search for the claimed one million plus Jewish victims of alleged Nazi atrocities is always worthy of praise and publicity.

The Holocaustians also attempt to diminish the Ukrainian claim to victimhood in the Holodomor by emphasizing that the Jews were allegedly killed not so much by Germans but by Ukrainian neighbors who were hostile to Jews.

In other words, this campaign is really all about seeking to make sure that the Ukrainians will remain "unworthy victims" like the Palestinians, while the Jews retain primacy in suffering as the world's foremost "worthy victims."

<u>Desbois: First-Class Catholic Holocaustian</u>

Patrick Desbois started out as a seminary teacher and follower of Mother Teresa. Later, for reasons unknown, the bishops of France appointed him as their delegate to France's Jewish lobby. From 1992–1999, Desbois served as Secretary for Jewish Relations under Cardinal Decourtray of Lyon. In 1999, he was appointed as Secretary of the French Bishops' Committee for Relations with Judaism.

In 2004, as he neared fifty, the Jewish organizations took full control of him. They appointed him the figurehead leader of a new interfaith group called "Yahad – In Unum," which means "together" in both Hebrew and Latin. Real power in the organization was actually wielded by the notorious Israel Singer, who was also head of the World Jewish Congress from 2001 to 2007, at which time he was unceremoniously sacked by Edgar Bronfman amidst accusations of theft and embezzlement. Simultaneously, Desbois, who had never been to the Ukraine, was shipped off to that country by the Holocaustians. The alleged reason for the trip was to see the place where his grandfather had been a prisoner of war during World War II.

While Desbois was there, his Jewish handlers informed him that, although upwards of 1.5 million Jews had been killed there in 1941/42, not a single Jewish victim's grave had ever been marked. Desbois perhaps considered that one possible reason for the absence of markers above ground was the lack of bodies below-ground, but he seems to have swallowed any such doubts. Thus began Desbois's journey to media celebrity, a pilgrimage that has led directly to his current friendship with the Holocaust's ultimate charlatan, Elie Wiesel.

This story gets even better, in a perverse fashion. Desbois's new priestly vocation became to find and to mark these alleged graves! One wonders what this job has to do with his priestly commitment to preach Christ. And how could Desbois carry out this Herculean task, especially since he couldn't speak the local language and has no expert knowledge of Ukraine's history or geography? Thanks to his Holocaustian backers, Desbois suddenly became capable of finding and paying very old peasants capable of remembering 65 to 70 years in the past to tell him where the unmarked graves of some 1.5 to 2 million Jews are located.

According to the Zionist media:[629]

> *Desbois cross-checks every statement* [from a peasant] *with Soviet Archives at the Holocaust museum in Washington and German records. He registers an event or new grave site only after obtaining three independent witness accounts.*

One can only imagine the vast number of hours that would be required to carry out such research, if indeed it were possible. But then Desbois dug up the bodies, right? Wrong. First of all, there is no proof that Desbois has ever located the remains of even one Jewish victim, because he did not undertake any kind of forensic examination of the human remains he did find in order to determine the victim's identity and their probable time and cause of death, as is standard practice in similar cases.[630] Worse still, he did not even record the size of the mass graves he located nor determine how many victims they contained, as he stopped digging as soon as he reached the upper layer of bones. He then simply refused to dig up remains because rabbis had told him that he would be committing a sin if he disturbed the Jewish dead. Here is how Desbois explains this problem in his bizarre book:[631]

---

[629] Angela Charlton, "Ukraine Killing Fields Not Forgotten: Elderly Provide Chilling Details," *Atlanta Journal-Constitution*, July 6, 2007, C1, C4.

[630] For a revisionist response to Desbois's activities see Carlo Mattogno, "Patrick Desbois e le 'fosse comuni' di ebrei in Ucraina," ("Patrick Debois and the 'mass grave' of Jews in the Ukraine") 2009; http://ita.vho.org/052_Desbois_Fucilazioni.htm. The forensic research conducted by the Germans at the mass graves of Katyn and Vinnitsa containing Polish victims of Soviet massacres may serve as examples as to how to do it properly: Auswärtiges Amt, *Amtliches Material zum Massenmord von Katyn* (Berlin: Franz Eher Nachf., 1943); *idem*, *Amtliches Material zum Massenmord von Winniza* (*ibid.*, 1944); for a more modern approach see *e.g.* Tosha L. Dupras, *et al.*, *Forensic Recovery of Human Remains: Archaeological Approaches* (2nd ed., Boca Raton, Fl.: CRC Press, 2012).

[631] Patrick Desbois, *Porteur de Mémoires: sur les Traces de la Shoah par Balles* (Neuilly-sur-Seine: Ed. Michel Lafon, 2007), 186. "Il a été statué [par les rabbins] que les Juifs

> *It has been decreed* [by the rabbis] *that all the Jews assassinated under the Third Reich were tsaquidim, that is, 'saints,' and that eternal life has been granted unto them. For this reason, their graves* [...] *must remain intact so as not to upset their tranquility.*

It is for this reason, a hoary rabbinical statute, that Desbois can claim to have found proof that over a million Jews were shot to death in the Ukraine without having to produce the remains of even one victim! Carlo Mattogno has shown, however, that this alleged law has not prevented proper exhumations in many other cases.[632] This "law" therefore seems to be a mere smokescreen behind which the Holocaustians want to hide what they don't want to be seen: the lack of hard forensic evidence for the claimed mass murder. This suspicion is supported by the fact that the mass graves Desbois had opened were later filled with bitumen, allegedly in order to prevent grave robbers from digging for gold.[633] As unlikely as that is, this act surely impedes any future forensic research.[634]

Desbois's particular scam includes some of the tried and true staples of Holocaust kitsch. According to the *New York Times*:[635]

> *There are stories of how the Nazis drummed on empty buckets to avoid having to listen to the screams of their victims, how Jewish women were made sex slaves of the Nazis and then executed. One witness said that as a 6-year-old he hid and watched as his best friend was shot to death. Other witnesses described how the Nazis were allowed only one bullet to the back per victim, and that the Jews sometimes were buried alive. "One witness told of how the pit moved for three days, how it breathed," Father Desbois recalled.*

Here we observe once again the *Times*, in service to the Holocaust religion, casting aside its obligation to check facts before going to print and debasing itself to the lowbrow level of a tabloid.

In the course of this ongoing program to distract the public from the collapse of the Auschwitz gas chamber myth, it did not take long for

---

assassinés par le IIIe Reich étaient des *tsaquidim*, des 'saints,' et que la plénitude de la vie éternelle leur a été accordée. En ce sens leurs sépultures [...] doivent être laissées intactes afin de ne pas déranger leur quiétude."

632 Carlo Mattogno, Thomas Kues, Jürgen Graf, *The "Extermination Camps" of "Aktion Reinhardt": An Analysis and Refutation of Factitious "Evidence," Deceptions and Flawed Argumentation of the "Holocaust Controversies" Bloggers* (Uckfield, UK: Castle Hill Publishers, 2013), 1087-1092.

633 Patrick Desbois, *Porteur de Mémoires*, 227.

634 The same is true for the Belzec and Treblinka camps, where inconclusive excavations confirming revisionist claims resulted in massive concrete "memorials" being built on these sites in order to forever bury the victims – and the truth under them; on this, in addition to the massive study cited in footnote 632, see also Mattogno, *Belzec* (2004); Mattogno, Graf, *Treblinka* (2005); and also Eric Hunt's documentary *The Treblinka Archeology Hoax* (20th Century Hoax, 2014; www.holocausthandbooks.com/index.php?page_id=1008).

635 Elaine Sciolino, "A Priest Methodically Reveals Ukrainian Jews' Fate," *New York Times*, October 6, 2007, A1.

Illustration 41: Desbois (right) with Wiesel observing Holocaust Day in Geneva, Switzerland, on April 20, 2009.

Desbois to make Wiesel's acquaintance. Now the two men routinely make public appearances together. On April 20, 2009, on the opening day of the so-called "Durban II" Conference on racism held in Geneva under the auspices of the UN, the madcap Desbois spoke about "*la Shoah par balles*," stating that "more than two million Jews were killed like animals and buried like animals in ditches, behind churches and in parks. That was the holocaust by bullets."[636] Here he was pushing the upper limit past the inflated two-million figure, even though he has not yet produced even one dead body! A few weeks later, on May 8, 2009, Wiesel and Desbois appeared together at a Holocaust remembrance event at Touro College in New York City.

As 2009 came to a close, the English translation of Desbois's bizarre book, *The Holocaust by Bullets: A Priest's Journey to Uncover the Truth behind the Murder of 1.5 Million Jews* (N.Y.: Palgrave Macmillan, 2009), appeared. Its publisher stated that it had been "published with the support of the United States Holocaust Memorial Museum," which is tantamount to admitting that it is a work of pure propaganda. Desbois provides absolutely no forensic evidence for the historical claims that he makes, but his book does serve a very important purpose for today's Holocaust fundamentalists. It distracts both the Holocaust faithful and the *goyim* who pay taxes and trustingly send their children to Holocaust brainwashing classes from the fact that at Auschwitz the Holocaust is now in a state of utter collapse. The Holocaustians want the public eye to be focused as far away as possible from Auschwitz as they slowly, over time, "retcon" the Holocaust master narrative by downsizing the scope and importance of the non-existent gas chambers, and by completely eliminating Wiesel's untenable flaming pits.

Desbois has received a long list of Jewish prizes and awards, much like the ones that had been conferred upon Wilkomirski and to Defonseca be-

636 Zenit.org, "La Shoah par Balles: Intervention du Père Patrick Desbois," *Zenit*, April 24, 2009; www.zenit.org/fr/articles/la-shoah-par-balles-intervention-du-p-patrick-desbois. "Plus de deux millions de juifs ont été tués comme des animaux et enterrés comme des animaux dans des fossés, derrière les églises, dans des parcs. C'était la Shoah par balles."

fore their collapse as eyewitnesses to the Holocaust. They include honorary doctorates from at least two universities in Israel and a nomination by President Sarkozy of France to the rank of *Chevalier de la Légion d'Honneur* for his service… to Israel! In his newly acquired exalted status, he has become a traveling companion not only to the Holocaust High Prist, but also to Pope Benedict XVI, as when the latter visited the Jewish synagogue in Rome on January 17, 2010.

Wiesel Accuses Bishop Williamson of "Holocaust Denial"

One of the most refreshing events to take place in many years in Catholic-Jewish relations was the revelation that Father Richard Williamson, a British-born traditionalist bishop and a member of the Society of St. Pius X (SSPX), had told an interviewer for a Swedish television station in November 2008 that he thought there had been no gas chambers in the German camps and that only 300,000 Jews had died in the Holocaust, not six million. The Zionist media, tightly-controlled and disciplined, sat on this information for two months as they waited for Pope Benedict XVI to formally lift the excommunication that had been in effect against the SSPX clergy. When the news was announced that Benedict XVI had brought the SSPX back into the Church, the Zionists released the two-month-old "news" that Williamson was a "denier." It was a classic Zionist media trap.

Of course Wiesel had been informed in advance by his media friends about what was likely to happen, so he had his press statements ready at hand. Speaking as one "pope" about another, he verbally attacked Benedict XVI:[637]

> *What does the pope think we feel when he did that? That a man who is a bishop and Holocaust denier – and today of course the most vulgar aspect of anti-Semitism is Holocaust denial – and for the pope to go that far and do what he did, knowing what he knows, is disturbing.*

When asked in the same article if perhaps the Pope did not know that Williamson was a "denier," Wiesel replied:

> *Oh no! The Church knows what it does, especially on that level for the pope to readmit this man, they know what they are doing. They know what they are doing and they did it intentionally. What the intention was, I don't know.*

Then, asked if this rather old news would have an effect on Catholic-Jewish relations, which had experienced a supposed golden age during the papacies of John XXIII and John Paul II, Wiesel replied:

> *The Vatican created the situation. It's up to them to resolve it. As it is, it is a very sad situation. So unexpected because we had high hopes for the relations*

---

[637] Philip Pullella, "Elie Wiesel Attacks Pope over Holocaust Bishop," *Reuters.com*, January 28, 2009. http://in.reuters.com/article/2009/01/28/idINIndia-37701220090128

> *between Jews and Catholics because they had been so good under those two popes* [...] *and now it's the opposite.*

Wiesel concluded:

> *One thing is clear. This move by the pope surely will not help us fight anti-Semitism. Quite the opposite.*

Illustration 42: Elie Wiesel at the World Economic Forum on Jan 28, 2009, where he was given the opportunity to influence the flow of Big Money worldwide.

As one looks back on Wiesel's words, they have a premonitory ring to them. When he stated that "it is up to them to resolve it," it is almost as if the Holocaust High Priest was issuing a warning to his liberal supporters in the Catholic Church that they had better get rid of Benedict XVI.

The Catholic press in the U.S. immediately echoed the Holocaustian line on this issue. Since the U.S. bishops have sold their souls to the Zionist cause, and are locked in an abusive relationship with the ADL, the AJC and various other Jewish groups and individuals, they espouse, almost to a man, the teaching of Holocaust brainwashing classes in their schools. Thus, the reaction that came from Archbishop Wilton D. Gregory of Atlanta, chairman of the Catholic Bishops' Committee on Ecumenical and Interreligious Affairs, was not surprising. In fact, in his own newspaper, he accused Bishop Williamson of anti-Semitism for daring to entertain doubts about the gas chambers, stating that "there is no place in the church for anti-Semitism or racism. None. Absolutely none."[638]

While Gregory was correct in principle, the problem with his comment was that there was not the slightest trace of anti-Semitism in Bishop Williamson's remarks. In fact, the man was simply telling what he believes to be the truth about a historical matter – one on which the Zionist media monopolists will allow no discussion. The article stated, correctly, that Bishop Williamson "has claimed that reports about the Holocaust were exaggerated and that no Jews died in Nazi gas chambers." But it also highlighted the state of abuse in which Archbishop Gregory finds himself when it quoted, approvingly, a Jewish abuser, one Rabbi Gary Greenebaum, who referred to "Williamson's disgraceful remarks" as proof of his "Holocaust denial." Abuser Greenebaum then put the cherry on the cake when he stated:

> *Doubtless this will contribute to the deterioration of the excellent relations between Jews and the Catholic Church.*

---

638 Andrew Nelson, "Bishop's Remarks on Holocaust Repudiated," *The Georgia Bulletin*, February 5, 2009, 3.

Here was a textbook case of a Jewish Holocaustian heaping abuse on his willing Catholic victim, Archbishop Gregory. In a threatening, bossy and possessive manner, he was ordering Archbishop Gregory to criticize a fellow bishop for reasons that had nothing whatsoever to do with Catholic belief and practice. Of course, the "excellent relations" to which Rabbi Greenebaum refers are excellent for the Jewish side because they have total control, while the Catholic side is afraid to even make a request, for fear of angering the abuser.

Wiesel's Public Persona as Holocaust High Priest

Holocaust High Priest's 75th Birthday Celebration

In May 2004, the ADL celebrated Wiesel's seventy-fifth birthday, even though his birthday falls on September 30, and the party was about six months too late. But the date did not really matter, for the event was actually about money and power, as four hundred powerful and wealthy people gathered at New York's Waldorf Astoria Hotel.[30] The master of ceremonies for the evening was Tom Brokaw, an ever-faithful servant of Zionism throughout his career. Fittingly, he introduced himself as "your *Shabbos goy* for the evening." Abe Foxman, not surprisingly, outdid all the other speakers for the evening's Holocaust kitsch award when he said:[639]

> *Elie, you have given voice and continuity to a million and a half children who were murdered.*

Wiesel and Oprah, Redux

In early 2006 Wiesel appeared on Oprah Winfrey's television show. According to the official story, she had invited him in part because a previous guest, James Frey, had been accused of using her show to spur sales of his supposed autobiographical book, even though it contained many fictional elements. Winfrey thus sought to redeem herself from this accusation of fraud by bringing in a man who, according to the Zionist media, represents the absolute essence of truthfulness.[640]

Winfrey's first step was to select Wiesel's supposed autobiography, *Night*, to be read by her book club in January 2006. The catch here was that Wiesel's wife had just prepared a new English translation of *Night*; it was to be published later that month by Farrar, Straus & Giroux with a first printing of a million copies in paperback and hardcover. Oprah's selection of Wiesel's book meant that tens of thousands of copies of the new transla-

---

[639] "Anti-Defamation League: Wiesel Spends Lifetime Searching for Words," *15 Minutes Magazine*, July/August 2004. http://15minutesmagazine.com/archives/issue_60/leica.htm

[640] Cockburn, "Did Oprah…?"

Illustration 43: Holocaust kitsch at Auschwitz in January 2006

tion would probably be sold as a result of her endorsement. Oddly, this huge printing took place despite the fact that the original 1960 translation by Stella Rodway was still adequate. In addition, Rodway's translation had been published by Hill & Wang, which, by 2006, was owned by Farrar, Straus & Giroux. This meant that the parent company was launching a new product, even though its subsidiary still had tens of thousands of copies of the original translation in its inventory. The justification for this expense, however, was that the new translation by Wiesel's wife would be "closer to the original."[641]

As I have shown above, however, Marion Wiesel's many mendacious translations of various words, phrases and sentences found in the original version of *La Nuit* had actually taken the English-language reader further away from the French original. She had done this to rectify factual absurdities and to cover up evidence of Wiesel's possible plagiarism in the writing of *La Nuit.* She had also begun collecting the royalties that had formerly been paid to Rodway.

In order to boost sales of the new translation, Wiesel and Winfrey traveled together to Auschwitz in late January 2006. The trip was filmed, and a Holocaust "documentary" was presented on her TV show on May 24. The day before, Wiesel had appeared on Oprah's show to hype both the film and the new translation of his novel. When the film was aired, out of deference to its religious nature, network and corporate overlords decreed that there would be only "limited commercial interruptions." After all, it dealt with our nation's Holocaust High Priest, and his visit to the Holocaust's Golgatha. Wiesel reappeared on the show the following day, May 25, when the names of the winners of a nationwide essay contest were announced.

[641] Edward Wyatt, "Oprah's Book Club Turns to Elie Wiesel," *New York Times*, January 16, 2006, E1, 8; cf. *idem*, "It's a Matter of Timing," *New York Time*, January 19, 2006, E7; *idem*, "The Translation of Wiesel's 'Night' is New, but Old Questions Are Raised," *New York Times*, January 19, 2006, E1.

The Zionist media gave these events wide coverage. For example, after the trip, but before Wiesel's appearances on her show, Oprah published an op-ed piece in *Time* about her several days with the Holocaust High Priest at Auschwitz. Of the man who has borne a heart of stone throughout his public career to the inhuman suffering that the Jews of Israel have imposed on the Palestinians, she wrote:[642]

Illustration 44: Elie Wiesel with U.S. President Barack Obama

> *He is my hero not only for what he has endured, but for what he has become – a teacher, a sage, an activist, a humanitarian, a great spirit. Despite the horrors he has survived, he is one of the most loving spirits I have ever known.*

If this expression of hypocrisy were not enough, Oprah, in her obsequious servitude to Zionism, went on:

> *Evil is never the end of the story; the end of the story is still ours to write. Wiesel, 77, has taught us that we must not forget; that there is no greater sin than that of silence and indifference.*

Yet, despite Winfrey's words of praise, the reality is that her hero has not only lied about virtually every aspect of his so-called experiences during the Holocaust, he has also actively supported and made excuses for Israeli war crimes during his five decades in public life.

Perhaps the most sickening aspect of this whole affair is the fact that, behind Wiesel's TV appearances, the apparatus of the organized Holocaust state religion was at work. At the grassroots level, teachers encouraged and helped students to write about *Night* and its effect on their life, with the best essays submitted to the contest judges. Students were strongly encouraged to display emotion, not to employ reason. Backing up the teachers in each state were curriculum committees, school boards, and the various state commissions on the Holocaust. Wiesel is said to have read some of the essays and helped choose the winners. In a word, it was a major religious event for the young scholars, while for Wiesel and his wife it was another payday, since many, if not most, of these youngsters bought a copy of his wife's new translation of his "autobiography." Many school systems had to stock up on the new translation, now that the old one was suddenly

[642] Oprah Winfrey, "Elie Wiesel," *Time*, April 30, 2006, 117.

outdated. This large-scale exploitation of credulous children by an arch con man continued on May 25, when the winners were paraded before Wiesel and Winfrey on national television.

The Holocaust High Priest Presides over Holocaust Remembrance Day in 2009

President Barack Obama came into office in January 2009. Three months later, on April 23, 2009, Holocaust Remembrance Day, he played to perfection the role of sycophant to Holocaust High Priest Elie Wiesel in the Capitol Rotunda. In his speech, Obama warned of the danger represented by those who seek to discuss the Holocaust in a free and open manner. He stated:[643]

> *To this day, there are those who insist the Holocaust never happened, who perpetrate every form of intolerance – racism and anti-Semitism, homophobia, xenophobia, sexism and more – hatred that degrades its victim and diminishes us all.*

It was distressing indeed that the President chose to disparage in this way the integrity and sincerity of revisionist researchers and to distort their quest for historical truth with "intolerance, racism and anti-Semitism." After Obama's speech, the same source reported that "Wiesel waded into present day politics as well, condemning Iranian President Ahmadinejad as a Holocaust denier and thanking President Obama for boycotting the recent Durban II U.N."

Wiesel Joins Obama on Sacred State Pilgrimage to Buchenwald

Obama then reportedly invited Wiesel to accompany him on a trip to Buchenwald in June. But even before that trip took place, Wiesel assured the media that Obama would play the role assigned to him without a hitch:[644]

> *Based on my sense of him, what I know about him, I am sure of it. He is the sixth American president I have met, whom I see regularly – I am sure that with him* [the visit] *will be very powerful.*

True to Wiesel's prediction, Obama proclaimed, with the Holocaust High Priest standing nearby:[645]

---

643 Lynn Sweet, "Obama on Holocaust Remembrance Day: 'Contemplate the Obligations of the Living,'" *Chicago Sun-Times*, April 23, 2009. http://blogs.suntimes.com/sweet/2009/04/obama_and_holocaust_and_united.html.

644 Agence France-Presse, "Elie Wiesel Expects Obama to Be 'Very Moved' by Visit in Buchenwald," *European Jewish News*, June 5, 2009. http://ejpress.org/index.php?option=com_content&view=article&id=14777&catid=9:germany&Itemid=5

645 Jeff Keleny, Nicholas Kulish, "At a Holocaust Site, Obama Calls Denial 'Hateful,'" *New York Times*, June 5, 2009, A8.

To this day, there are those who insist that the Holocaust never happened – a denial of fact and truth that is baseless and ignorant and hateful. This place is the ultimate rebuke to such thoughts, a reminder of our duty to confront those who would tell lies about our history.

Illustration 45: Elie Wiesel with German Chancelor Angela Merkel and U.S. President Barack Obama at the Buchenwald memorial.

The legend of the Holocaust as history was slowly shriveling before the eyes of the world as the worm of mendacity devoured its innards. Panicked, Holocaust fundamentalists were forcing the President of the United States to come to their rescue. Ironically, no Holocaustian has ever claimed that the Buchenwald camp was a part of the so-called "Final Solution." No gas chambers or other means of mass annihilation existed there. Hence Obama's words that "this place is the ultimate rebuke" to "those who would tell lies about our history" hit the nail on the head.

Wiesel in Performance of His Official Priestly Duties

Throughout the decade, Wiesel continued to carry out his office as Holocaust High Priest on both the national and international levels. For example, in the United States he spoke at the opening of a new Holocaust museum in Skokie, Illinois, on April 19, 2009; on the international level he was the guest of honor at a dinner hosted by Prince Albert of Monaco on May 6, 2009. Yet, behind the Holocaust High Priest's glittering façade of success, the corpse of the official and state-mandated Holocaust continued to decay. While Wiesel increasingly basked in the adulatory light the Zionist media shone upon him, his duplicity about his life, including his very identity, and the double standards implicit in his values, were becoming, to a growing number of Americans, glaringly evident.

Traveling to Chicago in his capacity as Holocaust High Priest, Wiesel celebrated the fifteenth anniversary of the U.S. Holocaust Memorial Museum. In one of his typical "Kafka meets Orwell" speeches, he stated that "the 20th Century was a failure [despite] all the good things that happened – the end of colonialism, the end of official racism, the end of imperialism, communism, fascism." The three thousand people gathered at the posh Sheraton Hotel and Towers were also able to hear him invoke the most co-

Illustration 46: President Shimon Peres seen awarding Nobel Peace Prize recipient Elie Wiesel the Presidential Medal of Distinction. The Times of Israel, November 26, 2013.

lossal lie of the twentieth century as if it were something that had actually occurred:[646]

> *The dominant element, the dominant event, the dominant fact of the 20th Century was* [the Holocaust], *and that was a failure of humanity.*

Wiesel's venality plays a major role in both his private and public life. On October 25, 2009, he delivered a speech before a crowd of six thousand Christian Zionists. The event was entitled "Night to Honor Israel," and took place at Pastor John Hagee's Cornerstone Church in San Antonio. Hagee, whose lobbying group is called Christians United for Israel, had previously given Israel a check for $9 million. In the course of the evening, Hagee presented Wiesel with an additional $500,000, with the money supposedly earmarked for the Elie Wiesel Foundation for Humanity.

Obama Serves the Holocaust High Priest a "Good Kosher Lunch" at the White House

As President Barack Obama's presidency went forward, he sought to court the Holocaust fundamentalists whose support for Israel is unconditional. Since many of them thought his foreign policy was not sufficiently pro-Israel, he needed to reassure them. As a part of that campaign, he invited Wiesel to have lunch with him on May 3, 2010, in his private dining room at the White House. Wiesel, after all, is a living symbol of what these Israel-loving extremists stand for. The Holocaust High Priest emerged af-

646 Ryan Hagerty, "Calling Holocaust a 'Failure of Humanity,' Scholar Also Targets Iranian President," *Chicago Tribune*, October 17, 2007. http://articles.chicagotribune.com/2007-10-17/news/0710160876_1_elie-wiesel-holocaust-denier-holocaust-museum

terward and decreed not only that the president had provided a "good kosher lunch" for him, but also that he had given his guest sufficient assurances that his devotion to the interests of a foreign country, Israel, remained intact and unshakable.[647] The union between synagogue and state remained as rock solid as ever. Yes, presidents come and go in the United States of America, but its state religion, the Holocaust, and its Holocaust High Priest, endure.

Wiesel Recommends Jail for "Holocaust Deniers" in Hungary

In March 2009, an article about Miklós Grüner and his allegation that Elie Wiesel was not Auschwitz detainee A-7713 appeared in a Hungarian newspaper (see Chapter V). Although it was translated almost immediately by a Canadian revisionist and then flashed around the world over the Internet, the tightly controlled Zionist media buried it. But Wiesel must have been rankled by the fact that a Hungarian newspaper had dared to publish an article that questioned his identity as detainee A-7713, for it revealed that skepticism of the official Holocaust story was very much alive in that country.

Illustration 47: Elie Wiesel teaches U.S. President Barack Obama a lesson.

Thus, when Wiesel visited Hungary in December 2009, he demanded that the Hungarian government criminalize questioning of the Holocaust. "I ask you," he said, "why don't you follow the example of France and Germany and declare Holocaust denial not only indecent, but illegal? In those countries Holocaust deniers go to jail."[648] This statement was tantamount to an admission by Wiesel that the Holocaust as history is dead. For if the Holocaust were in fact a historical narrative based on fact, it would not need laws to protect it. Furthermore, if his eyewitness testimony were true, he would not be demanding jail sentences for those who contend that his story is largely imagined. When the most egregious of all the mendacious eyewitnesses to the Holocaust demands a jail sentence for anyone who questions the Holocaust narrative, he is only offering further proof that the Holocaustians are unable to furnish historical proof that the gas chambers or the flaming pits ever existed. This explains Wiesel's

[647] Helene Cooper, "Obama Tries to Mend Fences with American Jews," *New York Times*, May 4, 2010, A6.

[648] Reuters, "Elie Wiesel Tells Hungary to Ban Holocaust Denial," *Yahoo! India News*, December 9, 2009. http://in.reuters.com/article/2009/12/09/idINIndia-44603620091209

and the others' embrace of the Stalinist option: reliance on censorship and legal repression of revisionist dissidents to keep their myth afloat.

To put Wiesel's words in perspective, it is important to recall that he has stated on a number of occasions his utter hatred of the Hungarian nationalists. In 1995, he wrote of the day on which his family was deported from Sighet: "It would be hard to exaggerate the maliciousness of the Hungarian gendarmes," who treated Wiesel and his neighbors with "a zeal and brutality that will forever remain the dishonor of the Hungarian army and nation."[649] This is the same hatred he had already expressed about the Hungarian people in *Night* when he wrote:[650]

> *It was from that moment that I began to hate them, and my hate is still the only link between us today.*

But the Hungarians have the right, notwithstanding Wiesel's hatred of them, to create their own, non-Zionist, version of history, and they have been doing just that since the fall of Communism. Not only has historical revisionism made major inroads in Hungary, the whole Zionist worldview is under assault there. One major factor in this turn of events is the memory that the Hungarians have of the leading role played by Jewish political commissars under Communism in persecuting the country's native, largely Catholic, population.

The new Hungarian Holocaust-denial law may actually have backfired, as a public debate unfolded in Hungary in early 2010 about revisionist arguments, triggered exactly by this new law.[651] That debate might otherwise not have happened.

Wiesel Advocates Denial of Free Speech Rights for U.S. "Holocaust Deniers"

In June 2010, Wiesel called for the selective denial of the First Amendment guarantee of free speech to U.S. Americans. This suspension of a fundamental Constitutional right would apply only to "Holocaust denial;" such speech, he claimed, causes "pain" to the children of "survivors." Quoting Wiesel on the basis of a personal interview, Canadian journalist Joseph Brean wrote:[652]

> *His argument about free speech is compassionate, focused on the "pain, humiliation and agonies" of the children of Holocaust survivors. "When I think*

---

649 Wiesel, "Decision," 5.

650 Wiesel, *Nuit*, 39: "C'est en cet instant que j'ai commencé à les haïr, et ma haine est la seule chose qui nous lie encore aujourd'hui."

651 See Jürgen Graf, "Hungarian Holocaust Debate: Otto Perge vs. Dr. Laszlo Karsai," juergen-graf.vho.org/articles/hungarian-holocaust-debate.html.

652 Joseph Brean, "Salman Rushdie: 'We Are in Danger of Losing the Battle for Freedom of Speech,'" *National Post*, May 31, 2010; originally at www.nationalpost.com/news/story.html?id=3094760, but now (re)moved.

> *of them, I accept that freedom of speech in this case should be against the law," he said*

Brean also asked Wiesel about free speech for those who defame Muslims and their religion:

> *Mr. Wiesel agreed to a point that religious defamation should not be illegal. He said religion is like money and love. "It all depends what you do with it," he said. "It can and should be noble, but it can also be a vehicle for fanaticism." He said the sole exception should be Holocaust denial, which must be banned.*

The demand by Wiesel that "Holocaust denial" be criminalized, and the declaration by Benedict XVI that Pius XII could be considered "venerable," indicated that the Holocaustians were meeting resistance. Had they been able to prove that the Holocaust actually happened as they say it did, Wiesel would not have been offering the world a parody of himself by demanding that the United States of America criminalize free speech on the Holocaust.

As for Pope Benedict's decree, it offered reassurance that he had not abandoned the need for the rehabilitation of Pius XII. But his courageous December 2009 announcement of support for Pius XII, coupled with his refusal to mention the "six million" during his visit to Auschwitz in 2006, sharply increased Holocaustian animosity against him. In retrospect, it is possible that his Jewish enemies played a role, as yet unclear, in Benedict's subsequent decision to "resign" from his papal office.

Wiesel's Holocaust Gradually Formalized as New Global Religion

United Nations Creates Holocaust Remembrance Day

As sincere belief in the Holocaust continued to wane and as its historical basis continued to falter in the face of revisionist research findings, the United Nations took formal steps to make the Holocaust the world's official and universal religion. Needless to say, Wiesel actively promoted this project from the beginning, since its primarily beneficiary is Israel. Those who supposedly lead the world body, following orders from Zionist states like the U.S., Israel, and their allies, thus elevated the Holocaust from its status as secular religion of the Western democracies to that of secular religion of the whole world. Their intention was to support the ongoing campaign to criminalize any questioning of the Holocaust as history.

Thus, in December 2005, the UN General Assembly passed a resolution on Holocaust Remembrance which designated "27 January" – the day the Auschwitz camp was occupied by the Red Army – "as an annual International Day of Commemoration in memory of the victims of the Holocaust," thus instituting a holiday for the new world religion to be observed annually throughout the world. The resolution also included the statement that the

UN General Assembly "rejects any denial of the Holocaust as an historical event, either in full or part."[653] If this affront to freedom of thought and inquiry were not bad enough, about fourteen months later, in January 2007 and in reaction to Iran's organization of a revisionist conference in Tehran in December 2006,[654] the Zionist puppets in the UN General Assembly passed a new resolution stating that it "*condemns without reservation* any denial of the Holocaust."[655]

Illustration 48: Holocaust High Priest Elie Wiesel preaches to the world's leaders at the UN General Assembly.

Rothschild Financial Backing for the New Faith

By 2009, the Holocaustians took a further step toward the institutionalization of the Holocaust as our world religion when, on January 27 of that year, the UN conducted its first quasi-religious ceremony marking that date as the world's official "feast day" in the Holocaust's world religious calendar.[656] On that occasion, UN General Secretary Ban Ki-moon reminded the world's leaders that they all "must combat Holocaust denial."[657] This was a statement which, in effect, offered a blank check for the world's Holocaust infidels and heretics to be prosecuted anywhere and everywhere on the planet.

Two months later, on March 27, a new project, this one under the aegis of UNESCO, was launched. Called "Project Aladdin," it is the UN-endorsed Inquisition of the twenty-first century, for it is designed specifically to combat the Great Heresy of our time. According to its Zionist sponsors, "the Aladdin Project was founded primarily because of the growing prob-

653 United Nations, General Assembly, "Resolution adopted by the General Assembly on the Holocaust Remembrance," A/RES/60/7, 1 November 2005; www.un.org/en/holocaustremembrance/docs/res607.shtml.

654 George Michael, "Deciphering Ahmadinejad's Holocaust Revisionism," *Middle East Quarterly*, summer 2007, 11-18; www.meforum.org/1704/deciphering-ahmadinejads-holocaust-revisionism.

655 United Nations. "Resolution adopted by the UN General Assembly on Holocaust denial," A/RES/61/255, 26 January 2007; www.un.org/en/holocaustremembrance/docs/res61.shtml.

656 http://en.wikipedia.org/wiki/International_Holocaust_Remembrance_Day.

657 United Nations. "Ban calls on world to fight Holocaust denial, anti-Semitism and bigotry," 27 January 2009; www.un.org/apps/news/story.asp?NewsID=29679.

lem of Holocaust denial."[658] The project is funded by David de Rothschild, whose lobbying group, *La Fondation pour la Mémoire de la Shoah* (Foundation for Holocaust Remembrance), serves as his front organization. In this manner, private funds disbursed by a Zionist Jewish self-interest group are used to purchase the UN's stamp of approval for the Zionist Aladdin Project as a morally worthy project.

When Jacques Chirac, during his last two years in office (2005-2007), became a strong supporter of Aladdin, he also suddenly became a friend of Wiesel, with whom he had never been close in the past. After stepping down as France's president, he has continued to serve as a Rothschild front man for the Aladdin Project.

It should be noted that each of the UN initiatives on the Holocaust mentioned above stands in total contradiction to the Universal Declaration of Human Rights promulgated in Paris on December 10, 1946. Article 18 of that document reads:

> *Everyone has the right to freedom of thought, conscience and religion; this right includes freedom to change his religion or belief, and freedom, either alone or in community with others and in public or private, to manifest his religion or belief in teaching, practice, worship and observance.*

Sanctification of the Auschwitz Holocaust Pilgrimage Site

On December 18, 2009, it was announced that the Auschwitz pilgrimage site had been violated when the famous "*Arbeit Macht Frei*" sign at the entrance to the Auschwitz I camp had been stolen.[659] The details of the crime remain suspiciously murky, and the Zionist media so far have shown little interest in elucidating them. To understand the true meaning of this event, two important pieces of background information are necessary. First, in 2009, the Auschwitz camp complex broke all attendance records. Most visitors came from Poland, Great Britain, Israel, Italy and Germany, with the total amounting to 1.3 million, of which 821,000 were young people. Thus, Auschwitz plays an important role in the brainwashing of Europe's youth about the Holocaust. In fact, the museum's director, Piotr Cywinski, who announced the figures, stated correctly that "these young people represent the world's future. Without a solid understanding of Auschwitz, today's Europe is incomprehensible."[660]

---

[658] http://religious-activism.suite101.com/article.cfm/aladdin_project_seeks_end_to_holocaust_denial; last accessed in 2012, but now removed; see instead www.projetaladin.org and www.unesco.org/education/aladin.

[659] Judy Dempsey, "Sign over Auschwitz Gate Is Stolen," *New York Times*, December 18, 2009, A6; *idem*, "Perplexity after Auschwitz Sign Theft," *New York Times*, December 24, 2009, A6.

[660] "Nombre record de visites à Auschwitz," *7sur7* (Belgian TV news station), January 3, 2010. "Ces jeunes sont l'avenir du monde. Sans une bonne connaissance d'Auschwitz, – l'Europe d'aujourd'hui ne peut pas être comprise."

Illustration 49: Entry gate to the Auschwitz Stammlager *with the notorious sign "Arbeit macht frei" – labor liberates.*

The second thing that must be understood about this event is that Poland still remains, even as a member of the EU, a very poor country, and that the buildings at the Auschwitz pilgrimage site are falling apart. Given this situation, it was perhaps no accident that, on the day before the theft, the German government, in an Orwellian press release, announced that it would pay sixty million euros toward the cost of the upkeep necessary to maintain the Holocaust pilgrimage sites of Auschwitz I and Auschwitz II. Yet even more money was needed. Both camps now constitute a Disneyland of horror that brings in badly needed tourist dollars to Poland, while also demonstrating to the satisfaction of the Holocaustians that Germany is ever-willing to assume its burden of "guilt."

It could be argued therefore that it might not be pure coincidence that the theft dovetailed so nicely with the need, in the eyes of the Holocaustians, to get other countries to contribute to this effort. Not surprisingly, over the following weeks and months various government entities in Europe, at different levels, announced that they would donate taxpayer-confiscated funds to pay for the maintenance of the Auschwitz Holocaust pilgrimage sites. In France, for example, not only President Sarkozy and the national government, but local entities such as the City of Paris (€310,000), as well as France's 22 mainland regions (€1 to €2 million), announced that they would chip in.[661] These gifts are completely consistent with the status of the Holocaust as the religion of the West, that is, for all practical purposes, the world. In comparison to the Catholics' Rome and the Muslims' Mecca, which are beautifully maintained and which also offer excellent hotel facilities, Auschwitz lags far behind. Thus, this suspiciously timely theft lent new impetus to refurbishing and promoting the Holocaust cult's holiest shrine.

Wiesel's Achilles Heel: Holocaust-Doubting Fellow Jews

Jewish Revisionists

Even though it is usually taken for granted that Holocaust revisionism and Jewish interests are in irreconcilable opposition to each other, this is not necessarily true. As a matter of fact, it is the opposite position which must be argued, for the orthodox Holocaust narrative teaches Jews that all gentiles are a potential and permanent threat to their very existence.[662] It is therefore the Holocaust narrative itself which pits Jews against gentiles, while its revision should tend to reconcile the two groups.

It can moreover be argued that Israel, which among Jews is considered the Zionist answer to the Holocaust, is not the only safe haven for Jews in the world, but rather the exact opposite: it is the biggest threat to Jewish survival. Never before in their history have so many Jews lived on such a small piece of land surrounded by a sea of hundreds of millions of potentially lethal enemies: the Arabs alienated by 70 years of brutal Zionist conquest and expansion. And never before have "the Jews" antagonized more people on this planet – including the sycophantic, yet resentful gentiles who are officially in power – since Zionists have hijacked the foreign policy of the United States and other western countries in order to provide unconditional support to Israel's racist imperialism in the Middle East.

Anyone who is truly interested in making sure that Jews are safe should argue that the mousetrap called Israel be abandoned. But as long as the orthodox Holocaust narrative is used as a means to frighten Jews into maintaining this trap and, even worse, to force many of them to actually remain in it, the trap will remain set until, one day, it snaps on them.

Many Jews understand this. Yet, only a few dare to go the distance and speak out against *both* this Zionist menace to Jewry *and* the root cause that fuels Zionist power: the mendacious and deceitful Holocaust narrative.

---

[661] "L'aide des régions pour rénover Auschwitz pourrait être de 1 à 3 M euros," *La Croix*, February 7, 2010; once at www.la-croix.com/afp.static/pages/100207160139.p034rc0f.htm, but now (re)moved.

[662] See on this the excellent 2009 documentary *Defamation* by Yoav Shamir, http://wideeyecinema.com/?p=7208

The first Jewish voice to openly do both was that of Josef Ginsburg, who wrote a number of books in German, each one more revisionist and anti-Zionist in nature than the previous. Unfortunately, none of his books has ever been translated into English.[663]

The most prominent Jewish revisionist in the U.S. is, without a doubt, David Cole. In 1993, wearing a yarmulke, he went to Auschwitz to record the lies told by the Polish Auschwitz Museum guides to the visiting tourists. After taping his Polish tour guide as she confirmed repeatedly that the alleged gas chamber on display at the Auschwitz Main Camp was authentic in all details, Cole spoke to Dr. Franciszek Piper who, at the time, was the museum's curator. Prodded by Cole in the course of a filmed interview, he admitted on camera that the alleged gas chamber was not authentic at all, but rather a crude postwar "reconstruction."[664] Cole later appeared on a number of high-profile U.S. TV shows where he managed to argue his revisionist take on the Holocaust.[665] What happened next was typical: Cole was labeled a "self-hating Jew" and "traitor" by Zionist extremists and, after receiving death threats, changed his identity in 1998 and disappeared from public view. He remained in hiding for some fifteen years until, in 2013, a disgruntled girlfriend blew the whistle on him.[666]

Since the turn of the century, the number of Jews converting to revisionism has seemed to swell. The most prominent figures today are Paul Eisen with his courageous initiative "Jews for Justice for Germans,"[667] Gilad Atzmon[668] and Gerard Menuhin.[669]

And make no mistake: it is certain that behind every Jew who dares to stand up against the Zionist bullies, who wield almost absolute power over them, there are hundreds of fellow Jews out of sight on the sideline who

---

663 Writing under the pen name Josef G. Burg, he authored, for instance and most prominently: *Schuld und Schicksal: Europas Juden zwischen Henkern und Heuchlern* (Munich: Damm Verlag, 1962); *Sündenböcke: Grossangriffe des Zionismus auf Papst Pius XII. und auf die deutschen Regierungen* (Munich: G. Fischer, 1967); *NS-Verbrechen: Prozesse des schlechten Gewissens unter Zions Regie* (*ibid.*, 1968); *Majdanek in alle Ewigkeit* (Munich: Ederer, 1979); *Zionnazi-Zensur in der BRD* (*ibid.*, 1980).

664 http://holocausthandbooks.com/index.php?page_id=1004

665 The news program "60 Minutes" on March 20, 1994; and the "Phil Donahue Show" on March 21, 1994; see Mark Weber, "'60 Minutes' Takes Aim at Holocaust Revisionism," *The Journal of Historical Review*, vol. 14, no. 3, May/June 1994, 16-18; *idem*, "Smith and Cole Appear on 'Donahue' Show in Major Media Breakthrough for Revisionism," *ibid.*, 19f.

666 See the online documentation on Cole at www.codoh.com/library/categories/1103, and also his autobiography: David Cole, *Republican Party Animal: The "Bad Boy of Holocaust History" Blows the Lid off Hollywood's Secret Right-Wing Underground* (Los Angeles: Feral House, 2014).

667 www.pauleisen.blogspot.com; www.justice4germans.com

668 www.gilad.co.uk

669 His upcoming book *Tell the Truth and Shame the Devil* will tell it all.

are cheering them on. It is as if an avalanche was slowly building and could be triggered at any moment.

When will it come tumbling down to bury the mendacious Wiesel and his tall tales? Time will tell.

Tova Reich, Wife of Former Holocaust Museum Director, Lampoons Wiesel

I have argued throughout this study that many, if not most, U.S. Jews are fed up with hearing about the Holocaust, and might actually suffer from "Holocaust fatigue" more than non-Jews do. A glaring example of the validity of my assertion appeared in 2007 when Tova Reich's satirical novel, entitled *My Holocaust*, appeared. It savagely lampooned both Wiesel and his friend and fellow "survivor," Miles Lerman, for the novel's protagonist, Maurice Messer, seems to be a composite of the two men. A self-proclaimed veteran like Wiesel, the Polish-born Messer is also chairman of the board of the USHMM. Also like Wiesel, he speaks broken English and has lied outrageously about all of his supposed eyewitness experiences. Having started out selling ladies' underwear, he now hucksters the Holocaust through his company Holocaust Connections. Helped by his nebbish of a son, Norman, he has turned the Holocaust into a commodity.

The Messers organize visits, raise funds, and in many other ways enrich themselves by exploiting the Holocaust. Norman knows that his father's stories are utterly false and that his tales of derring-do in the Jewish resistance never happened. Tova Reich uses her third-person, authorial, stream-of-consciousness voice to describe Norman's dilemma:[670]

> [...] *now since his father had become such a public figure, the chairman of the premier Holocaust shop in the world, the consequences of exposure of these lies would have been not only personally catastrophic but also potentially ruinous to faith in the integrity of Holocaust history,* [and] *deniers everywhere who insisted that the entire Holocaust was a hoax would be given a field day thanks to the old man's pitiful bragging, for the life of him Norman could not understand what suicidal urge impelled his father to persist in risking everything by telling these pathetic stories.*

When, later in the novel, another character asks Norman whether his father's outlandish stories are true or not, he replies with postmodern Holocaustian panache:

> *I guess what my father is trying to say here is that the story needs to be taken as a paradigmatic or archetypal conceit rather than literally or at face value.* (*My Holocaust*, 56)

Finally, on this theme of how Holocaust mendacity fosters Holocaust denial, Reich rips another character, Bunny Bacon, who is "so new to the Holo-

[670] Tova Reich, *My Holocaust* (N.Y.: Harper Collins, 2004), 55.

caust game" that she goes around "spouting canned opinions." (85) This character's most strongly held canned opinion concerns Holocaust deniers. She states:

> *When it comes to artistic expression, I reject all forms of censorship. In my opinion, artistically speaking, nothing's off limits, even with respect to the Holocaust, except, of course, denial. Holocaust denial? That's where I draw the line, that's the only no-no. Denial has to be outlawed everywhere, across the board, universally banned as a hate crime. I personally wouldn't dignify a denier by arguing with him even for two seconds. Give a denier a platform, and you give him legitimacy, it's as simple as that. But as long as you don't deny the Holocaust happened more or less the way it happened, it's out there for everyone's creative expression.* […] *It's raw material for all humanity. The Jews don't own the Holocaust.*

Tova Reich's novel oozes with scorn for fellow Jews who con the gullible *goyim* into believing in their ridiculous folktale and, as one reads the book, one cannot help but suspect that she too may be a "denier."

Such a frank portrait, especially coming from the wife of Walter Reich, former director of the USHMM (1994–1998), hints at the degree to which many members of the Jewish elite have turned against the Holocaust fundamentalists and their imposition of the Holocaust as our state religion.

The book's truth content can be gauged by the ferocity of the review devoted to it by the Holocaust custodians at the *New York Times*. David Margolick, selected to write the review, and identified as an editor at *Vanity Fair*, condemns Reich's entire project:[671]

> *At a time when morons and bigots say the Holocaust never happened, or that it wasn't such a big deal if it did, the business of publicizing and exploiting the mass murder of European Jewry for political, financial or institutional gain is something we Jews would rather not discuss, except among ourselves. Reich has taken this taboo and built an entire novel – wickedly clever and shocking, tasteless and tedious, infuriating and maybe even marginally constructive – on it.*

Rightly, Margolick understands that Reich is targeting not only the false witnesses and other phonies who make money on the Holocaust, but also the USHMM itself, for he reminds his reader that her husband had once been the director there, but resigned in protest. The apparent reason for his departure was his basic disagreement with Miles Lerman, who chaired the museum's governing board from 1993 to 2000, about the nature of the museum's basic function. To Reich, its role was to focus on documentation of the Holocaust. It was a historical, not a political endeavor. For this reason, he opposed Lerman's attempted "universalization" of the Holocaust through various political arrangements with non-Jews.[672] Lerman, for in-

---

[671] David Margolick, "Happy Campers," *New York Times*, May 27, 2007.

[672] Avi Weiss, *Principles of Spiritual Activism* (Hoboken, N. J.: KTAV Publishing Co.,

Illustration 50: Prime Minister Benjamin Netanyahu speaks with author Elie Wiesel after speech to US Congress in Washington.
The Jerusalem Post, *March 5, 2015*

stance, had originally authorized, as a friendly gesture to Christians, that John Paul II's giant cross remain in place at Auschwitz. As a friendly gesture to Muslims, he had invited Yasser Arafat to visit the museum. But Reich opposed such moves, which he saw as inherently political and thus a betrayal of the museum's mission.

We cannot say for sure what Walter Reich's personal view of Wiesel and Lerman was, but his wife displays utter contempt for them through her portrayal of Holocaust survivors as morally impaired fakers. Margolick observes correctly that,

> [...] *apart from our righteous and very learned narrator, no one here comes off as anything but a scoundrel, fool, lecher or slob. The bile extends, inexplicably, to Holocaust survivors. Every one of them here is grotesque, obsessed with sexual organs, bodily fluids and digestion.*

Poor Margolick does not recognize satire when he sees it. Reich evidently took this approach to satirize the lowbrow cultural elements that are part and parcel of both the Holocaust story as a whole and the fictional works based on it. That is one of the things that satire does.

In a wonderful display of his own orthodox belief in the Holocaust, as contrasted to Reich's suspected apostasy, Margolick thanks her for at least including what he calls a few "Auschwitz factoids" in her book. He writes:

2002), 56.

> *Did you know, for instance, that Jews were burned in open pits when the four working crematoria, designed to process 132,000 corpses a month, could no longer handle the load?*

Ironically, Margolick does not get the irony that Reich intends with this supposed "Auschwitz factoid," for her reference to this supposed event, clearly satirical and aimed at Wiesel and his novel, should not be taken literally. After all, Reich knows as well as anybody that Wiesel's flaming pits have long been written out of the Holocaust master narrative. In reply to this cunningly thickheaded review, Reich wrote a reply to the *New York Times*. Here is a piece of it:[673]

> *I believe the review was wrongheaded and surprisingly ad hominem, reflected no understanding of either fiction or satire, was strikingly at odds with the many other very positive reviews that have appeared, and left your readers with a deeply and relentlessly distorted impression of my book.*

She was right. However, in the matter of Holocaust orthodoxy, the Holocaust fundamentalists who run the *Times* will tolerate no public display of doubt, much less ridicule, from fellow Jews.

Tova Reich's novel should be welcomed as a public manifestation of the undercurrent of discord, documented throughout this study, which exists among an unknown number of U.S. Jews about Wiesel and the Holocaust. It is a very hot topic, and it divides them. Unfortunately, the Jewish cultural instinct to maintain the *mesirah* code of silence has resulted in a tacit policy of group solidarity that has kept their discussion out of earshot of non-Jews.

Against this background, Tova Reich has courageously spoken in denunciation of both Wiesel and the false-witness veterans who exploit the gullibility of their non-Jewish fellow citizens and taxpayers. But perhaps the most welcome element in her book is her denunciation of the mendacious and utterly corrupt operation of the USHMM itself. Long after Wiesel is gone, that U.S. government-sponsored institution, which is essentially a Jewish propaganda ministry, will still be here sequestering documents, placing false or misleading captions on photographs, politically restricting access to all source materials, influencing legislation, and brainwashing future generations of American youth.

Hopefully, the present study will help to change the way that propaganda institution does business, Shoah Business. That change would consist in forcing an end to the present policy of Holocaustian Jewish censorship of its archives by opening them for the perusal of all. Once that happens, the corpse of the Holocaust scam will be able to receive a decent burial, and an unwarranted government entitlement for a subset of extremist U.S. Jews, the Holocaustians, will be cut from the federal budget. Then, finally, Holo-

---

[673] Tova Reich, "Letters to the Editor: *My Holocaust*," *New York Times*, June 10, 2007.

caust history will be rewritten, and documented, on the basis of millions of additional facts.

A Pew Research poll conducted in 2013 corroborated Rabbi Neusner's findings about the effect of Holocaust and Redemption Judaism à la Elie Wiesel on young Jews: it continues to be a factor in alienating them from their roots in unprecedented numbers. Although the Holocaust narrative has served the Zionists quite well over the years as the sword and shield of Israel, it has done a very poor job of convincing U.S. Jews to move there and, even worse, to even retain their Jewish identity. According to the *New York Times*, young Jewish men and women are abandoning their identity in growing numbers through the simple act of intermarriage with non-Jews:[674]

> *The intermarriage rate, a bellwether statistic, has reached a high of 58 percent for all Jews, and 71 percent for non-Orthodox Jews – a huge change from before 1970 when only 17 percent of Jews married outside the faith. Two-thirds of Jews do not belong to a synagogue, one-fourth do not believe in God and one-third had a Christmas tree in their home last year.*

The article goes on to quote Professor Jack Wertheimer, a specialist in American Jewish history at the Jewish Theological Seminary in New York:

> *It's a very grim portrait of the health of the American Jewish population in terms of their Jewish identification.*

Pope Pius XII: Final Considerations

I have dedicated the present study to the memory of Pius XII for several reasons.

The first is that during the war years he proved himself to be a man of probity, patience, fortitude, judgment, equanimity and calm while the fate of Europe and the world was in the balance, even as he and the Vatican were physically captive to the fascists.

The second reason is that he did everything that he possibly could, including the expenditure of his own personal funds, to help any and all threatened Jews who were within his reach.

The third reason is that, with some misgivings, he sympathized with the Allied side throughout the war, even though that made him an ally of Communism. He must have spent many a sleepless night over this decision, especially in the final months of the conflict and afterward, as all of Eastern Europe, with its tens of millions of Catholic souls, disappeared into the darkness of Communist occupation, where they were to suffer intensely for half a century.

---

674 Laurie Goodstein, "Poll Shows Major Shift in Identity of U.S. Jews," *New York Times*, October 1, 2013, A11.

Illustration 51: Pope Pius XII, March 18, 1939, 16 days after his election.

Fourth, and perhaps most important, his overall support of the Allied cause was not a blank check. Thanks to his own worldwide intelligence networks, he often had a better idea of what was happening within the German sphere of influence than the Allies did. Because of this knowledge, he was convinced – correctly – that the alleged "extermination" program of Jews was nothing but a wartime rumor. This conviction of his must also be contextualized by the fact that during the war, at every level and in all theaters, whether in the civilian or military realm, new rumors of every kind were cropping up almost every day. This is another reason why he resisted Allied blandishments to publicly refer to Jewish suffering specifically, instead of referring to it in traditional, universalist, diplomatic terms. In other words, he was convinced that the German resettlement of Europe's Jews outside of the Reich was nothing more than that, and, however brutal and unjust, it was not an "extermination" program. During his lifetime, Jewish leaders worldwide found no reason to complain about any type of "silence" on his part with regard to Jewish suffering, and this view was communicated in Israeli PM Golda Meir's press release upon his death.

When, after the 1967 war, Israel needed to justify its conquest and occupation of millions of Arabs along with the seizure of their land, it sensed a need to create an alibi and an excuse for the crimes it was committing against the Palestinians. The 1967 sneak attack had been so successful in stealing large parts of historic Palestine from its rightful owners that Israel's Jews suddenly found themselves an occupying force. They had captured the Palestinians' land but had no means of evicting them by systematic and forced transfer. Thus, they found themselves holding hundreds of thousands of Palestinians under their guns. Ironically, in this new situation the Israeli Jews were emulating the Germans who, after their successful Blitzkrieg into Poland in 1939, occupied about two thirds of that country (with the Soviet Union taking the eastern third), and enjoyed military domination over the millions of human hostages who came with that conquered land.

In 1967, this new Jewish status and image as "victors" and "conquerors" contradicted the dominant image of Jews projected in America's Zionist media: that of Jews as eternal victims. It was here, in the perceived need among powerful U.S. Jewish leaders to refocus non-Jewish attention away from Jews as land grabbers and killers and back onto Jews as eternal victims, that the seeds of "the Holocaust" as America's secular religion were planted.

To meet this goal, the Holocaust narrative was placed center stage in the media, and non-Jews were bombarded with Holocaust propaganda day and night. As in all propaganda campaigns, its originators kept the plot simple. Israel is a refuge for Jews, and everything the Jewish state does – even its crimes against humanity – must be understood in the context of the Holocaust. It was a morality tale with its "perpetrators," the Germans, and its innocent victims, the Jews. But, partly in order to settle a historic score with the Catholic Church, which had protected its people for centuries by standing in opposition to Jewish economic, media and cultural influences, a second category of guilt was established in the tale for those to be labeled as "bystanders," and that role was assigned to Catholics, with Pope Pius XII in the starring role. The fact that there was no basis in fact for this accusation did not make the slightest difference. Jewish media power would take care of it, and the success, at the time, of the propaganda operation known as *The Deputy*, is a classic example of Jewish abuse of media and academic power.

After the Catholic Church recovered from the shock of this surprise attack, Pope Paul VI, who had worked closely with Pius XII during the war years, ordered in 1964 that a team of historical experts be appointed to mount a defense of his friend. The case was to be based on evidence locked away in the Vatican Archives, and the serious expertise of trained historians would be required for this effort. It resulted in the 12-volume work entitled *Actes et documents du Saint-Siège relatifs à la seconde guerre mondiale*, which appeared from 1965 to 1982.[675] The team that conducted the work was led by four Jesuits, Pierre Blet from France, Robert A. Graham (the lead editor) from the U.S., Angelo Martini of Italy, and Burkhart Schneider of Germany. In addition to this project, each of these men also published prolifically elsewhere in defense of Pius XII during the rest of their careers. However, because the Catholic Church had suddenly, at Vatican II, become a "friend" of world Jewry and Israel, these four scholars obeyed their superiors and either suppressed or glossed over whatever

---

[675] *Actes et documents du Saint Siège relatifs à la seconde guerre mondiale*, 12 vols. (Vatican City: Libreria Editrice Vaticana, 1967-1982); available as pdf downloads at www.vatican.va/archive/actes/index_en.htm.

doubts they had about the evidence on which the Holocaust myth is largely based.

Two of these experts, Pierre Blet, and Robert H. Graham, could be considered as "deniers" today on the basis of their private relationships and correspondence with the major revisionist figures of that era, Profs. Faurisson and Butz. For instance, Faurisson's 2002 study *Le révisionnisme de Pie XII* appears to owe much to Blet, especially in the array of sources to which he had access, and this hints at the possibility that the two men engaged in a secret correspondence for many years. It must also be said that Blet, in his monumental two-volume study *Pie XII et la seconde guerre mondiale d'après les archives du Vatican* at times has difficulty in hiding what appear to be serious revisionist convictions.[676] As for Butz, he initially contacted Graham in 1977 after the publication of the first edition of his *Hoax of the Twentieth Century*. The reader will recall that Butz included a 12-page appendix in that study, entitled "The Role of the Vatican," and it presented a portrait of Pius XII and his diplomatic staff that was in conformity with the archival materials available to him. As such, it stood in opposition to the Holocaustian smear campaign then underway. Butz's first contact led to a correspondence that lasted many years until Graham's death in 1997, and during which the Jesuit scholar expressed to Butz his personal doubts about the Holocaust narrative.[677]

At present, there continue to be Catholic defenders of Pope Pius XII against the charge of silence. However, like the authors of *Actes et Documents*, they refrain from expressing their true, personal convictions, whatever they might be, about the historicity of the Holocaust. Instead, they adhere to the Vatican line on the subject and do not express doubt about the Holocaust. Nor, of course, would any of them ever think of publicly criticizing the Holocaust High Priest. They generally defend the Pontiff on the basis of his record of saving Jews and, at times, on the basis of the discovery of new documents or the reinterpretation of known sources. They also attack the work of figures like Cornwell, Carroll, Wills and similar conformist authors, whether Catholic or not, whose publications spout the traditional Holocaustian propaganda line.

William J. Doino, Jr., to whom Robert H. Graham bequeathed his personal papers, has done important work in this field. Also active have been the nun Sr. Margherita Marchione, Rabbi David Dalin and the legal scholar Ronald Rychlak.[678] Another source of support for a fair and unbiased view

[676] Pierre Blet, *Pie XII et la seconde guerre mondiale d'après les archives du Vatican* (Paris: Perrin, 1997); Engl.: *Pius XII and the Second World War: According to the Archives of the Vatican* (N.Y.: Paulist, 2000).

[677] Arthur R. Butz, "Robert Graham and Revisionism," *The Journal of Historical Review*, vol. 17, no. 2, March/April 1998, 24f.; www.codoh.com/library/document/2741.

[678] For an overview of essential works see http://popepiusxiiandthejews.blogspot.com.

of Pius XII's life and work is the Catholic League for Religious and Civil Rights.[679] Under the leadership of its director, Dr. William A. Donohue, it has sponsored and published important work in defense of the slandered pontiff. The fact that the Holocaustians have been generally successful in keeping all this work out of view in the mainstream media is surely a testament to the fact that much truth, however limited its impact, lies therein.

These defenders of Pius XII are forced to avoid reference to revisionist knowledge, and even to condemn revisionism in principle, because the people in charge of the post-conciliar Catholic Church have completely integrated the Holocaust myth into its theology of the relationship between the Old and New Testaments. The Holocaust myth is now treated as if it were some kind of divine revelation that took place in the 20th century. Through the creation of an interfaith group called The Pontifical Biblical Commission on the Jews, a number of new theological documents have been generated on this subject. They have enabled the Church to abandon its two thousand years of teaching on this subject and replace it with the new one. Two documents worthy of mention are "We Remember: A Reflection on the Shoah" (1998),[680] and *The Jewish People and Their Sacred Scriptures in the Christian Bible* (2002). These works are built on the assumption that the Holocaust myth actually tells the story of a documented historical event, which is surely not the case. The latter states, for instance:[681]

> *The horror in the wake of the extermination of the Jews (the Shoah) during the Second World War has led all the Churches to rethink their relationship with Judaism and, as a result, to reconsider their interpretation of the Jewish Bible, the Old Testament.*

One of the prime movers in the development of this new theological approach is the German theologian Johann Baptist Metz, who just happens to be a friend of the Holocaust High Priest himself. In fact, the two have actually collaborated on an interview book entitled *Hope against Hope: Johann Baptist Metz and Elie Wiesel Speak out on the Holocaust*.[682] In light of these developments, revisionist work on the Holocaust can be said to have theological as well as historical importance.

---

[679] www.catholicleague.org

[680] Commission for Religious Relations with the Jews (ed.), "We Remember: A Reflection on the Shoah," March 16, 1998; www.vatican.va/roman_curia/pontifical_councils/chrstuni/documents/rc_pc_chrstuni_doc_16031998_shoah_en.html

[681] The Pontifical Biblical Commission (ed.), *The Jewish People and their Sacred Scriptures in the Christian Bible* (Vatican City: Libreria Editrice Vaticana, 2002); www.vatican.va/roman_curia/congregations/cfaith/pcb_documents/rc_con_cfaith_doc_20020212_popolo-ebraico_en.html.

[682] Ekkehard Schuster (ed.) (N.Y.: Paulist, 1999).

Pius XII was assigned the role of villain among the "bystanders" in the Jewish Holocaust narrative in the 1960s, as that story was becoming the secular religion of the U.S. and Western Europe. But with the passing of five decades since this brutal and unjustified campaign of defamation first began against Pius XII, the playing field has been radically altered. When this assault on historical truth first began, there were, to be sure, those who doubted what was gradually coming to be called "the Holocaust," but historical revisionism as such did not exist. But ironically, as the exposures of Holocaust lies have piled up over the decades, and as the media have continued to put forth the most mendacious of all the alleged Holocaust "eye witnesses" – Elie Wiesel – as a secular saint, unimpeachable witness and ultimately the High Priest of the new religion, the revisionist backlash and resistance movement have increased in intensity. The Holocaustians, fully aware that they have lost the debate, are now circling their wagons around the Holocaust sanctuary, and are deploying the final phase of the defense of their myth: protection through the power of penal law.

I now come to my fifth reason for dedicating this study to Pius XII. As the developments mentioned above have taken place, it has become more and more clear why the first generation of revisionists like Butz and Faurisson sought to clear Pius XII's name: they saw him not only as an innocent victim of slander, they also saw him as a kind of precursor, and they are right.

As mentioned above in Chapter VII (p. 196), Pius XII did not believe the Germans had engaged in an "extermination" program against the Jews during the war. Even more startling is the fact that, in the same speech in which he expressed that view, he also condemned the moral and legal validity of the Nuremberg trials when he stated:[683]

> *Someone who is not directly involved in the disagreement gets an uneasy feeling when, after the cessation of hostilities, he sees the victor judge the vanquished for war crimes while this same victor had been guilty of doing the same thing to the vanquished.*

Let us stop for a moment and ponder this astounding statement by a head of state. Since 1946, the trials had been condemned by a few men of conscience in the U.S., but no one had done so more forcefully or eloquently as Senator Robert A. Taft of Ohio. Like Pius XII, he condemned the trial as an example of "victor's justice" based on the use of "ex post facto" laws, that is, laws that did not exist at the time the alleged crimes were committed. He saw the trials as a violation of the most basic principle of U.S. jus-

---

683 "Celui qui n'est pas impliqué dans le différend, ressent un malaise lorsqu'après la fin des hostilités, il voit le vainqueur juger le vaincu pour les crimes de guerre alors que ce même vainqueur s'est rendu coupable envers le vaincu de faits analogues." *Discours du VIe Congrès international de droit pénal* in *Documents Pontificaux*, vol. 15, 1953, 472. Again, I have used the French translation of these documents in Simon Delacroix (ed.), *Les Documents.*

tice, since the Allies played the roles of prosecutor, judge and jury, with the Germans being denied their most fundamental rights. He might have added, but did not realize, that some of them were also being tortured by Allied goons. In a word, Taft saw that the trials were a formalized exercise in neo-barbarian vengeance dressed up in juridical finery. Of course, Senator Taft was not the only American of conscience to publicly voice such an opinion, but he was probably the most important and influential one to do so. Historians agree that his principled stand cost him any chance he might have ever had to secure the Republican nomination to run for President, but he paid that price.[684] Senator John F. Kennedy later praised Taft for his principled stand in the face of criticism from across the political spectrum, and those words ring as true today as they ever did. In his Pulitzer Prize-winning *Profiles in Courage*, Kennedy chronicled the political courage of eight great American senators, and placed Taft in that elite company.[685]

But when Pius XII spoke as he did in 1953, he was making a statement of conscience that no other head of state had ever dared to make, and it is possible that it was this statement of disparagement of the Nuremberg Tribunals which is the real reason for the campaign of slander waged against him for the last half century. While we cannot be sure whether this conjecture has any basis in fact, we can be sure of the incontrovertible fact that Pius XII's position statement does indeed plant him firmly within the revisionist camp and prefigures the arguments the revisionists would make beginning in the 1960s with Paul Rassinier. It justifies completely the view shared by so many revisionists that he is indeed the precursor of their movement, and that is why this study has been dedicated to his memory.

---

[684] http://en.wikipedia.org/wiki/Robert_A._Taft

[685] John F. Kennedy, *Profiles in Courage* (N.Y.: Harper & Brothers, 1956).

Conclusion: What Is Needed to Happen Now

The major economic, social and political tempests that buffet U.S. society today threaten to shake the nation to its foundation. In the face of them, various Holocaustian groups, like the ADL, have demanded the imposition of ever-stricter limits on permitted public speech and discourse. The Holocaust, our state religion, is both their sword and their shield, for the sword of the Holocaust also shields their sacred cow, the Israeli apartheid state.

Elie Wiesel knows that the revisionists, who should actually be called something like "Holocaust liberationists," as well as untold numbers of others around the world, are increasingly aware that he is a fraud. He remains immune to well-deserved ridicule and to exposure as an imposter, because the U.S. political establishment, its academic and educational apparatus and media outlets, are all under firm Holocaustian Jewish control. These powerful individuals use their powers of censorship to silence anyone, even, and perhaps especially, those fellow Jews who know there is something wrong with both the Holocaust master narrative and Wiesel's role in its promotion. Wiesel's recent calls for the complete silencing of the revisionists, even at the expense of violating their First Amendment rights under the U.S. Constitution, offer further proof that he is a charlatan, and knows it. His excuse for censorship, to avoid causing pain to Holocaust survivors and their children, is actually a poorly concealed attempt to protect the Holocaustians' income streams and reputations.

In conclusion, I would recommend that measures be implemented to lift the censorship policies that currently protect Wiesel and his lies from public scrutiny.

First, researchers must be allowed to have access to Wiesel's complete file at *Les Éditions de Minuit*. With regard to *La Nuit*, it is imperative that all manuscripts, letters and other documents (especially those contributed by François Mauriac) relating to the novel's preparation for publication be opened to the public.

Illustration 52a-d: Whenever Elie Wiesel rolls up his sleeves, no tattoo can be seen on his lower left arm where it should be, as he himself has claimed.

Second, a diplomatic translation of *Un di velt* into both French and English should be made a top priority of the scholarly community. Such translations should be published in facing-page format to allow scholars to compare *Un di velt* and *La Nuit* line by line.

Third, Elie Wiesel must allow all the letters he exchanged with François Mauriac to be published in a scholarly edition prepared by an entity that is independent of the Holocaustian power structure.

Fourth, the video (accompanied by a printed transcript) of Wiesel's testimony at the Klaus Barbie show trial should be released to the public, as was promised by the French government decades ago.

Fifth, all personnel and health records relating to Wiesel and his family members that are currently being held in Auschwitz and Buchenwald camp files should be released.

Sixth, all documents from the International Tracing Service (ITS) relating to Elie Wiesel and his family members must be opened to public scrutiny. Those records, now held by the USHMM, are presently being censored.

Seventh, all the ITS records now in the possession of the USHMM should be transferred to the National Archives with the guarantee that inquiring scholars will have free and unfettered access to them.

And last but not least, Elie Wiesel should allow the public to see whether he has a tattoo on one of his arms showing his Auschwitz registration number, or in case it is missing, a verifiable explanation as to why it is missing, like a comprehensible reason as to why he was not tattooed at Auschwitz in the first place, or medical records and/or scars on his arm showing that the tattoo was removed.[686]

---

686 See www.eliewieseltattoo.com/the-evidence/the-tattoo/where-is-elies-tattoo/

Appendix
Elie Wiesel – the "Symbol of the Shoah"

by Carlo Mattogno

Elie Wiesel in Italy

On 27 January 2010, the tenth "Holocaust Remembrance Day," Elie Wiesel was invited into Montecitorio Hall, the seat of the Chamber of Deputies of the Italian Republic, where he gave a brief speech peppered with fatuous rhetoric and risible nonsense, such as his call to "introduce a bill defining suicide bombings as crimes against humanity," or his hope that Ahmadinejad "should be arrested and taken before the Hague Court and charged with incitement to crimes against humanity."

Elie Wiesel with Gianfranco Fini

Wiesel's most important statements, as we will see, are these:[1]

> *I, the number A-7713, am here to bring you a message about events that happened two thousand years later.* [...]
> *Just this week, seventy five years ago, my father Shlomo, son of Nissel and Eliezer Wiesel, number A-7712, died of starvation and disease in the extermination camp of Buchenwald.* (My emphasis)

This is a slightly revised English translation of Carlo Mattogno's Italian article "Elie Wiesel il 'simbolo della Shoah,'" Feb. 16, 2015; http://olodogma.com/wordpress/2015/02/16/0969

[1] See the transcript in: www.camera.it/cartellecomuni/Leg16/files/pdf/opuscolo_giorno_della_memoria.pdf

Gianfranco Fini, the president of the Chamber at that time, introduced Wiesel as follows:

> *This day today is an exceptional event, because it is the third time in the century-old history of the Italian Parliament that a guest speaks solemnly to the Assembly. It is an honor which Elie Wiesel richly deserves, because he really is an exceptional person. In fact, among the survivors of the Nazi concentration camps, he is the most authoritative living witness of the horrors of the Shoah.* (My emphasis)

Then he continued:

> *For decades, Elie Wiesel has been encouraging us in this vital effort not to forget and to advance the cause of human rights and peace in the world through his moral teachings, the energy of his intellectual and human charisma, and the strength of his commitment.* [...]
> *In addition to being an eyewitness of the Holocaust, Wiesel is also a person full of faith and love.* (My emphasis)

Is Elie Wiesel an impostor?

In 2007, Nikolaus Michael (aka Miklós) Grüner published a book in English titled *Stolen Identity. Auschwitz Number A-7713.*[2] Grüner is a Hungarian Jew who was deported from Hungary to Auschwitz in May 1944 (where he received the inmate number A-11104), then transferred to the Monowitz camp and finally evacuated to Buchenwald in January 1945 (where he received the inmate number 120762). In his book, Grüner accuses Elie Wiesel, who received the Nobel Prize for Peace in 1986, of stealing the identity of another Jewish-Hungarian inmate of Auschwitz and Buchenwald, Lazar Wiesel, and also of stealing his memoirs, which he had published in 1956 in Buenos Aires under the name of Elizier Wiesel with the Yiddish title *Un di velt hot geshvign* (*And the World Remained Silent*).

In his book, Grüner declares that at Auschwitz he had made friends with two brothers, Lazar Wiesel, born in 1913, who had the inmate number A-7713, and Abraham Wiesel, born in 1900, with the inmate number A-7712. According to Grüner, Elie Wiesel appropriated the identity of Lazar Wiesel and usurped that of Abraham for his father. Grüner adds that, during a meeting with Elie Wiesel, who had been introduced as his friend Lazar Wiesel, Wiesel refused to show the serial number allegedly tattooed on his forearm. Grüner then researched the matter and discovered that an Elie Wiesel was never interned in a concentration camp, and that he was not included on any official list of deportees.

---

2 self-published by the author; printed in Sweden, Stockholm, 2007; online at www.nazigassings.com/PDFs/StolenIdentity2.pdf.

Grüner's book contains documents of considerable importance, even if the author's interpretation of certain documents can be questioned.

Miklós Grüner's declarations have been repeated many times, but have not caused any major research effort. We will thus scrutinize them critically but soberly.

Grüner's credentials as a former deportee are impeccable. A letter from the Auschwitz Museum of July 7, 2003, addressed to Grüner states that a prisoner Miklós Grüner, a Hungarian Jew born on April 6, 1928, in Nyiregyhaza, received the inmate number A-11104 at Auschwitz. As for Buchenwald, Grüner's name and birthdate show up accurately in a "Concentration Camps Inmates Questionnaire" of the Military Government of Germany. The serial number is recorded by hand on the top left: 1207624 (see Document 1).[3]

About Elie Wiesel we only know that he claims to have been born in Sighet, Romania, on September 30, 1928, to Shlomo and Sarah Feig, daughter of Dodye Feig, and that he is said to have been deported to Birkenau on May 16, 1944.[4] As to the father Shlomo, there is no document, and we do not even know the date of his birth.

In the minutes of the trial by the State of California against Eric Hunt on July 8, 2008,[5] Elie Wiesel made under oath the following statements:

> *A. French Lanueit, L-A-N-U-E-I-T* [La Nuit], *and in English Night.*
> *Q. And was Night your first book published in English?*
> *A. Yes.*
> *Q. First book published anywhere, correct?*
> *A. First book published anywhere.*
> [...]
> *Q. And is this book Night that you wrote a true account of your experience during World War II?*
> *A. It is a true account. Every word in it is true.*
> [...]
> *Q. And what was your – what day were you born in Sighet, Romania?*
> *A. September 30th, 1928.*
> [...]
> *Q. And what* [number] *was tattooed on your left arm?*
> *A. My number was A7713. My father's number was 7712.* (emphasis added)

The key persons here are obviously Lazar Wiesel and his alleged father Abraham, who according to Grüner was actually Lazar's brother. Considering the documented age difference of just 13 years, and assuming that this

3 NARA, A 3355, RG 242.
4 *Elie Wiesel*, section on "Early life," http://en.wikipedia.org/wiki/Elie_Wiesel
5 Superior Court of California. County of San Francisco. Before the Honorable Robert Donder, Judge Presiding, Department Number 23. *People of the State of California, Plaintiff, v. Eric Hunt, Defendant*. Testimony of Elie Wiesel, July 8, 2008, pp. 7, 13; cf. https://kuruc.info/r/6/51815/.

is correct, then Abraham could indeed hardly have been Lazar's brother. Abraham's and Lazar's internment at Auschwitz and Buchenwald is well documented.

A letter dated 15 May 2002, addressed to Grüner by the Buchenwald *Gedenkstätte* (memorial), contains the following information (see Document 2):[6]

> *Lazar Wiesel, born on 4 September 1913 at Maromarossziget, arrived at Buchenwald with a transport from Auschwitz (Buchenwald archives, microfilm Auschwitz, p. 41). On this page 41, under entry number 2438, you will find the data on Lazar Wiesel: Buchenwald number 123565, born on 4 September 1913, Auschwitz number A-7713. These data are confirmed by the numerical file card at the camp office [*Schreibstube*]. Lazar Wiesel appears on the American questionnaire (NARA Washington, RG 242, microfilm 60) with the number 123165 and a different date of birth (4 October 1928); he went to Paris on 16 July 1945 with a convoy of surviving children (Buchenwald archives, 56-6-12, p. 9). Here, however, there is a disagreement with respect to the numerical file card. The* Schreibstube *file card numbered 123165 was made out for a Slovenian Jewish detainee, Pavel Kun, who died at Buchenwald on 8 March 1945.*

The above-mentioned letter from the Auschwitz Museum to Miklós Grüner dated 7 July 2003 states that detainee ID A-7713 appears in a list of the SS Hygiene Institute dated 7 December 1944-Monowitz, and that it contains the following data:

> *A-11104 Grüner Miklos, Hungarian Jew, born on 6 April 28 at Nyiregyhaza, El. Tech (electrical technician)*
> *A-7712 Viesel Abram, born on 10 October 1900 at Marmarosz*
> *A-7713 Wiesel Lazar, born on 4 September 1913 in Marmarossziget, Schlosser (locksmith)*

The above-mentioned list, which was published by Grüner,[7] is not of much help, though, because the header is illegible and the meaning of the document is unclear. It is not even clear to what the date stamp of 7 December 1944 refers, i.e., whether it was a transfer of the listed prisoners to the Monowitz camp or something else.

In a letter dated March 15, 1987, the director of the Auschwitz Museum, Kazimierz Smolen, informed Mrs. Eva Kor, founder of CANDLES (*Children of Auschwitz Nazi Deadly Lab Experiments Survivors*), as follows:[8]

> *2. In the concentration camp of Auschwitz, a Mr. Lazar Weisel* [sic] *was given A-7713. He was born 4/9/13. He was a Jew from Hungary, born in Marmarossiget. This particular prisoner arrived in Auschwitz 5/24/44. He was there until the end of 1944 in KL Auschwitz III called Monowitz. Towards the end of*

6 *Stolen Identity*, Figure 11.1.
7 *Ibid.*, Figures 19.1-3.
8 Reproduced at https://kuruc.info/r/6/51815

the evacuation he was transferred to KL Buchenwald. He was registered there on the day of 1/26/45.

The inmate file card concerning Lazar Wiesel's stay at the Buchenwald camp has in its upper left hand corner the handwritten entry "Ung. Jude" (Hungarian Jew), in the center, "Ausch. A 7713," i.e. "Auschwitz A-7713," the former Auschwitz ID number, and, on the right, "Gef.-Nr.: 123565," (Detainee number 123565, the new Buchenwald ID number). This detainee was born on 4 September 1913 (Lázár Wiesel's year of birth according to Miklós Grüner) at Maromarossziget and was the son of Szalamo Wiesel, who was at Buchenwald, and of Serena Wiesel née Feig, interned at KL Auschwitz. The stamp "26.1.45 KL. Auschwitz" indicates that Lázár Wiesel was registered at Buchenwald on 26 January 1945 coming from Auschwitz.[8]

Note: Maromarossziget [Máramarossziget in Hungarian], now Sighetu Marmatiei (in Rumanian) is the same place which Elie Wiesel calls Sighet.[9] The name "Szalamo" is the same as "Shlomo," while "Serena" is phonetically close to "Sarah."

A detainee registration card, probably stemming from the Buchenwald memorial archives, has the following data:[10]

123565
W i e s e l , Lazar *Polit.*
geb. 4.9.13 Maromarossziget *Ungar*
Schlosserlehrling *Jude*
26. Januar 1945

The list of new arrivals of January 26, 1945 (*Zugänge vom 26. Januar 1945*), prepared at Buchenwald on the same day, lists both detainees (see Documents 4f.):[11]

2438 123565 Lazar Wiesel 4. 9.13 Marmarossziget Schlol.[12] *A 7713*

And:

2372 123488 Viezel Abram 10:10:00 Marmaross Schl. A 7712

One document shows that Abraham Wiesel died at Buchenwald February 2, 1945:[13]

Database: Record of Change Buchenwald
Dataset: 9315
Inmate No.: 123488 [A 7712]
Name: Viezel, Abraham
Born: 10.10.00

---

9 *Sighetu Marmatiei*, in: http://en.wikipedia.org/wiki/Sighetu_Marma%C5%A3iei
10 *Stolen Identity*, Figure 7.1.
11 *Ibid.*, Figures 11.3 & 11.5.
12 Abbreviation for *Schlosserlehrling*, locksmith apprentice.
13 *Ibid.*, Figure 11.4.

Nationality: *Category: polit. Jew*
Admitted:
Deceased: 02.02.45 *in: Block 57*
Report of: 03.02.45

Hence, Abraham Viezel, born 10 October 1900, a Jewish political detainee with the ID numbers A-7712 for Auschwitz and 123448 for Buchenwald, died on 2 February 1945 at *Block* 57, according to the camp record of 3 February.

Concerning this detainee, we also have Document 6. In it, the date of birth and the ID number are exactly the same; "5514" is the registration number for his death.[3]

In short:

- The Auschwitz ID number A-7713 was assigned on 24 May 1944 to Lazar Wiesel, born on 4 September 1913 at Maromarossziget, who was later registered at Buchenwald under the ID number 123165.
- The Auschwitz ID number A-7712 was assigned on 24 May 1944 to Abraham Viezel (Wiesel), born on 10 October 1900 at Maromarossziget, registered at Buchenwald on 26 January 1945 under the ID number 123488, who died in this camp on 2 February.
- Elie Wiesel has stated under oath that, at Auschwitz, he was assigned the ID number A-7713, and his father the ID number A-7712.

The following table summarizes the results of the above verification:

Wiesel:	LAZAR	ELIE	ABRAHAM	SHLOMO
Registration no.	A-7713	A-7713	A-7712	A-7712
Date of birth	4 Sep. 1913	30 Sep. 1928	10 Oct. 1900	?
Place of birth	Máramarossziget = Sighet	Sighet	Máramarossziget	?
Name of father	Szalamo = Shlomo	Shlomo	/	/
Name of mother	Serena Feig	Sarah Feig	/	/
Residence, early 1945	Buchenwald	Buchenwald	Buchenwald	Buchenwald

It is therefore irrefutably ascertained that Elie Wiesel is a liar and a perjurer.

Is Elie Wiesel a Plagiarizer?

Another accusation levelled by Grüner concerns the origin of Elie Wiesel's book *La Nuit* (in English *Night*). In the Hungarian version of the internet news article on Grüner's claims,[14] it was claimed that the book was published in Hungarian in Paris in 1955 by his friend Lázár with the name of Eliezer and the title "*A világ hallgat*" (*And the World Remained Silent*).

[14] https://kuruc.info/r/6/36390/

In the English version of the article, the title was instead given in Yiddish as *Un di Velt hot Gesvigen* (*And the World Remained Silent*).[15]

A search for the title in Hungarian gave no result, whereas the Yiddish book is indeed documented. It is registered in the *Bibliography of Yiddish Books on the Catastrophe and Heroism*,[16] no. 549 on p. 81. The entry, in Yiddish, states: Eliezer Wiesel, *Un di velt hot geshvign* (*And the World Remained Silent*). Buenos Aires, 1956. Central Association of Polish Jews in Argentina. Series *Das poilische Jidntum*, vol. 117, 252 pages. There is an English translation of this book, which corresponds to chapter VII of *La Nuit*. We will discuss it further along in this article.

Michael Wiesberg provides some noteworthy details on this subject:[17]

> *Wiesel has often mentioned the story of how this book came about. Naomi Seidmann has noted that Wiesel himself, in* Alle Flüsse fließen ins Meer [*All Rivers Run to the Sea*] *has drawn attention to the fact that, in 1954, he gave the Argentinian publisher Mark Turkow the original manuscript of* "La Nuit," *written in Yiddish. According to Wiesel, he never saw it again, but Turkow strongly denies this. This manuscript was published at Buenos Aires in 1955 under the title* Und di Velt hat Geshveyn *(And the World Remained Silent). Wiesel asserts to have written it in 1954 while on a cruise in Brazil. However, in an interview he declared that it was only in May of 1955, after an encounter with François Mauriac,*[18] *that he decided to break his silence. "And in that year* [1955], *in the tenth year, begins my story. It was then translated from Yiddish into French, and I sent it to him. We were very, very good friends until his death."*
>
> *Naomi Seidmann, in her research on "La Nuit," brought to light that there are considerable differences between the Yiddish and the French versions, with respect to the length, the tone, the argumentation and the topics treated in the book. She attributes these differences to the influence of Mauriac who can be described as a very particular person*

In this respect, hence, the least that can be said is that the origin of the book is quite uncertain and misty. I will return to this question further below.

Is Elie Wiesel a False Witness?

This having been stated, we have yet to establish whether Elie Wiesel is also a false witness on the subject of Auschwitz.

---

15 www.henrymakow.com/translated_from_the_hungarian.html.

16 YIVO Institute for Jewish Research, New York, 1962.

17 Michael Wiesberg, "Unversöhnlich – Elie Wiesel zum 80," in: *Grundlagen*, Sezession 25, August 2008, p. 25; www.sezession.de/wp-content/uploads/2009/03/wiesberg_unversohnlich-elie-wiesel-zum-80.pdf

18 François Mauriac wrote the foreword to Elie Wiesel's book.

We will examine his "eye-witness account" as it is set out in his "masterpiece" (Fini), "*La notte*."[19] As early as 1986, Robert Faurisson wrote an article entitled "Un grand faux témoin: Élie Wiesel"[20] (A prominent false witness: Elie Wiesel). More recently, Thomas Kues wrote a further article entitled *Una donnola travestita da agnello*[21] (A weasel in sheep's clothing). Both authors approach the subject in general terms. Now the time has come for a more thorough analysis.

We must stress that the overall tone of the account in question is that it tells a tale rather than describing something factual. Elie Wiesel goes to great lengths to avoid any verifiable details, and what he says about Birkenau, about Auschwitz, about Monowitz or about Buchenwald is so vague that his story might have taken place just as easily somewhere in Siberia or in Canada.

Quotes are from Elie Wiesel *Night, His Record of Childhood in the Death Camps of Auschwitz and Buchenwald*, Bantam edition (Translated from the French by Stella Rodway), New York 1982.

a) Deportation

Elie Wiesel does not specify the date of his deportation to Auschwitz. His narrative starts, though, with reference to a specific date:

> *On the Saturday before Pentecost* ["Shavuòth" in the Italian edition], *in the spring sunshine, people strolled, carefree and unheeding, through the swarming streets.* (p. 10)

In 1944, this holiday fell on 28 May 1944,[22] a Sunday. The day in question was thus 27 May. The first transport of Jews left Sighet on the following day, hence, on 28 May. "Then, at last, at one o'clock in the afternoon, came the signal to leave" (p. 14). Elie Wiesel then speaks of "Monday" (p. 16), the dawn (p. 16), the day after tomorrow (pp. 15, 16) saying, at the end, "Saturday, the day of rest, was chosen for our expulsion" (p. 19) He then speaks about the traditional Friday evening meal and goes on to say: "The following morning, we marched to the station […]" (p. 20), which means that the trip to Auschwitz began on Saturday, 3 June 1944.

The duration of the trip is not given, but transports from Hungary usually took three or four days to reach Auschwitz-Birkenau. Elie Wiesel spent the night at Birkenau and was moved to Auschwitz the following day

[19] (Florence: Giuntina, 1986.

[20] In: R. Faurisson, *Écrits Révisionnistes (1974-1998)*, vol. II, De 1984 à 1989. Édition privée hors commerce, 1999, pp. 606-610. Online: www.vho.org/aaargh/fran/archFaur/1986-1990/RF861017.htm (French); www.ihr.org/leaflets/wiesel.shtml (English).

[21] Kues, Thomas, "Elie Wiesel: la donnola travestiata da agnello," January 28, 2010; http://andreacarancini.blogspot.com/2010/01/elie-wiesel-la-donnola-travestita-da.html

[22] www.hebcal.com/hebcal/?year=1944&v=1&month=5&yt=G&nh=on&nx=on&i=off&vis=on&set=on&c=off&geo=zip&zip=&m=72&.cgifields=nx&.cgifields=nh&.s=Get+Calendar

where he was given the number A-7713, which was tattooed on his arm (p. 39). Yet, according to him, "It was a beautiful April day" (p. 37).

This sequence is pure invention. If he did leave Sighet on 3 June 1944, he could not have arrived at Auschwitz in April. Moreover, the ID number A-7713 was given out on 24 May, the day on which 2,000 Hungarian Jews were assigned the numbers A-5729 through A-7728.[23] According to Randolph L. Braham, a Jewish transport left Máramarossziget on 20 May 1944.[24] Allowing four days for the journey, this was the transport of Lázár Wiesel who was assigned the ID number A-7713 precisely on 24 May 1944. But it may confidently be assumed that Elie Wiesel was unaware of all these things, as well as of the possibility that they might later be discovered.

b) Arrival at Birkenau

Elie Wiesel writes:

> *But we had reached a station. Those who were next to the windows told us its name: 'Auschwitz.' No one had ever heard that name.* (p. 24)
> *Toward eleven o'clock, the train began to move. We pressed against the windows. The convoy was moving slowly. A quarter of an hour later, it slowed down again. Through the windows we could see barbed wire; we realized that this must be the camp.* [...] *And as the train stopped, we saw this time that flames were gushing out of a tall chimney into the black sky.* (p. 25)
> *In front of us flames. In the air that smell of burning flesh. It must have been about midnight. We had arrived – at Birkenau, reception centre for Auschwitz* (p. 26)

From the spatial point of view, this tale is nonsense. The spur towards Birkenau left the main track at a station, (the so-called "old ramp") some 500 meters from the camp – as the crow flies – and then ran obliquely to the east of the camp fence. The spur was about 700 meters long.

There were four crematoria at Birkenau, named II, III, IV and V. The chimneys of the crematoria closest to the "old ramp" (II and III) were some 1,400 m away, in a straight line, and the other two (IV and V) about 1,800 meters. Over the last 400 m, the spur ran perpendicularly to the camp fence, which means that Crematoria II and III could not be seen from the windows of the train, being situated straight ahead, as they were. The others were hidden behind at least 12 rows of barracks and had, moreover, two chimneys each (see Document 7).

As far as I know, no other witness ever spoke of having seen the chimneys of the crematoria from the deportation trains, and for good reason.

---

23 Liste der Judentransporte, Museum of Auschwitz-Birkenau, microfilm no. 727/27.

24 R.L. Braham, *A Magyar Holocaust*. (Budapest/Wilmington: Gondolat/Blackburn International Inc., 1988), p. 514.

Elie Wiesel's arrival at the camp is described only vaguely in his account. He takes great care to skirt any detail that might be verifiable. Aside from the "chimney," which will be discussed later, he speaks only of "barbed wire" (p. 25), then, inside the camp, of "the square" (p. 29), a "ditch" (p. 30), "another and larger ditch" (p. 30), a "barracks" (pp. 31, 32), and "a new barracks" and "another barracks" (p. 34).

There is no mention of all the things which attracted the attention of the real deportees, as is shown in the photographs of the so-called *Auschwitz Album*[25] (which were taken a few days after the arrival of Lázár Wiesel's convoy): The entrance building (*Eingangsgebäude*) with its archway through which the trains entered the camp, the ramp (the so-called *Judenrampe* or Jewish ramp) with its three railway tracks inside the camp, the fences, the innumerable rows of barracks on either side, the long roads which split the camp lengthwise and crosswise, the drainage ditches, the watch-towers, the water basins for fire-fighting, or Crematoria II and III at the far end of the ramp.

Then the tale becomes a little more specific:

> *A barrel of petrol at the entrance. Disinfection. Everyone was soaked in it. Then a hot shower. At high speed. As we came out from the water, we were driven outside. More running. Another barracks, the store. Very long tables. Mountains of prison clothes. On we ran. As we passed, trousers, tunic, shirt, and socks were thrown to us.* (p. 34)

Again, this is pure invention: At the time, Birkenau had four disinfestation and disinfection installations (*Entwesungs- und Desinfektionsanlagen*). The main one was the so-called *Zentralsauna* (*Entwesungsanlage*, *Bauwerk* 32 (*BW*, building) in the shape of a T near the western fence of the camp with its three hot-air disinfestation chambers (*Heissluftentwesungskammern*), three steam autoclaves (*Dampf-Desinfektionsapparate*), shower hall complete with undressing room and dressing room, barbershop. There were two more such installations, designated as *BW* 5a and 5b, located in sectors BIb and BIa, similarly furnished with a shower hall, undressing room and dressing room, but one of them had a disinfestation gas chamber working with Zyklon B, the other one had two hot-air disinfestation chambers. Moreover, BIIa, the gypsy camp, had 8 electrical disinfestation devices (*elektrische Entlausungsapparate*).[26] In the first three installations, with their undressing rooms (*Auskleideraum*) and dressing rooms (*Ankleideraum*), all stages of the operation took place indoors. The disinfection procedure did not make use of petrol. But of all these things, Elie Wiesel did not have a clue.

---

25 S. Klarsfeld (ed.), *L'Album d'Auschwitz* (Paris: Éditions du Seuil, 1983).

26 These installations have been well described by Jean-Claude Pressac in: *Auschwitz: Technique and Operation of the Gas Chambers*, (New York: The Beate Klarsfeld Foundation, 1989), pp. 53-85.

We should also mention, at this point, the little tale of the "good" detainee, *en vogue* during the 1950s, who went around among the new arrivals, telling them to make themselves older or younger than their real age, in order to avoid being "gassed." Elie Wiesel, who was not yet 16, was told to say that he was 18, while his father, who was fifty, was advised to say "forty" (p. 28). This is a foolish story, because each transport was accompanied by a transport manifest which contained, *i.a.*, the last name, first name and date of birth for each of the new arrivals, which means that any such calculated deception could be discovered immediately upon registration. It is also nonsense from the point of view of the orthodox holocaust historians, because, according to a publication of the Auschwitz Museum, all children below age 14 were systematically gassed,[27] whereas there was no age limit for adults. In the Auschwitz death registers (*Sterbebücher*) for 1943 we have 4,166 entries for persons between 51 and 90 years of age (registers for 1944 have not been found or made accessible).[28]

c) "The" flaming chimney

Elie Wiesel had no idea how many crematoria there were at Birkenau, what they were like nor where they were located. Even though at one point he speaks of "six crematoria" (p. 64), he always talks about "the" chimney, as if there had been only one, without identifying the crematorium, as if there had been only one. Actually, there were six chimneys at Birkenau: *which one* was spouting flames?

He dwells on a single strange phenomenon: "Do you see that chimney over there? See it? Do you see those flames? (Yes, we did see the flames.)" (p. 28; my emphasis). Now at last we know where the chimney was: "over there"!

From the Birkenau ramp, in May 1944, the chimneys of Crematoria II and III, one for each, were perfectly visible (see Document 9), but, strangely, Elie Wiesel "saw" only one.

The tale of the flaming chimneys was very popular in the 1950s, when Elie Wiesel's *Night* was published (1958). Nowadays, nobody treats the matter seriously, not even Robert Jan van Pelt, who made an effort to prove that smoke came out of the chimneys of the crematoria… period.[29] Actually, there is no technical basis to this tale of flaming chimneys, as I have shown in a specific article.[30]

27 Franciszek Piper, Teresa Świebocka (eds.), *Auschwitz. Il campo nazista della morte* (Auschwitz: Edizioni del Museo Statale di Auschwitz-Birkenau, 1997), p. 122.

28 Thomas Grotum, Jan Parcer, "EDV-gestützte Auswertung der Sterbeeinträge," in: Staatliches Museum Auschwitz (ed.), *Sterbebücher von Auschwitz* (Munich: K.G. Saur, 1995), vol. 1, p. 248.

29 R.J.van Pelt, *The Case for Auschwitz. Evidence from the Irving Trial* (Bloomington/Indianapolis: Indiana University Press 2002), p. 504.

30 "Combustion Experiments with Flesh and Animal Fat on cremations in pits in the al-

d) The "cremation pits"

We have here the most sensational part of his "eye-witness account":

Not far from us, flames were leaping up from a ditch, gigantic flames. A lorry drew up at the pit and delivered its load – little children. Babies! Yes, I saw it – saw it with my own eyes... those children in the flames. (Is it surprising that I could not sleep after that? Sleep had fled from my eyes.)

So this was where we were going. A little farther on was another and larger ditch for adults.

I pinched my face. Was I still alive? Was I awake? I could not believe it. How could it be possible for them to burn people, children, and for the world to keep silent? No, none of this could be true. It was a nightmare...

Soon I should wake with a start, my heart pounding, and find myself back in the bedroom of my childhood, among my books...

My father's voice drew me from my thoughts:

'It's a shame... a shame that you couldn't have gone with your mother... I saw several boys of your age going with their mothers...'

His voice was terribly sad. I realized that he did not want to see what they were going to do to me. He did not want to see the burning of his only son.

My forehead was bathed in cold sweat. But I told him that I did not believe that they could burn people in our age, that humanity would never tolerate it...

'Humanity? Humanity is not concerned with us. Today anything is allowed. Anything is possible, even these crematories...'

His voice was choking.

'Father,' I said, 'if that is so, I don't want to wait here. I'm going to run to the electric wire. That would be better than slow agony in the flames.'

He did not answer. He was weeping. His body was shaken convulsively. Around us, everyone was weeping. Someone began to recite the Kaddish, the prayer for the dead. I do not know if it has ever happened before, in the long history of the Jews, that people have ever recited the prayer for the dead for themselves.

'Yitgadal veyitkadach shmé rabai... *May His Name be blessed and magnified...' Whispered my father.*

For the first time, I felt revolt rise up in me. Why should I bless His name? The Eternal, Lord of the Universe, the All-Powerful and Terrible, was silent. What had I to thank Him for?

We continued our march. We were gradually drawing closer to the ditch, from which an infernal heat was rising. Still twenty steps to go. If I wanted to bring about my own death, this was the moment. Our line had now only fifteen paces to cover. I bit my lips so that my father would not hear my teeth chattering. Ten steps still. Eight. Seven. We marched slowly on, as though following a hearse at our own funeral. Four steps more. Three steps. There it was now, right in front of us, the pit and its flames. I gathered all that was left of my strength, so that I could break from the ranks and throw myself upon the barbed wire. In

---

leged extermination camps of the Third Reich," in: *The Revisionist*, Vol. 2, Number 1, February 2004, pp. 64-72.

> *the depths of my heart, I bade farewell to my father, to the whole universe; and, in spite of myself, the words formed themselves and issued in a whisper from my lips:* Yitgadal veyitkadach shmé rabai... *May His Name be blessed and magnified... My heart was bursting. The moment had come. I was face to face with the Angel of Death...*
> *No. Two steps from the pit we were ordered to turn to the left and made to go into a barracks.* (pp. 30f.)

Where does all this take place? As always, Elie Wiesel takes care not to furnish any kind of reference point as to the location. According to the orthodox holocaust narrative, the "cremation pits" were located at two sites: one was outside the camp, across from the *Zentralsauna* at the alleged "*Bunker* 2,"[31] and another was in the yard north of Crematorium V. We must exclude the first site, because otherwise Elie Wiesel would have had to mention their leaving the camp and walking several hundred meters in open terrain.

What about the other site? In my study *Auschwitz: Open Air Incinerations*,[32] I have shown, on the basis of an analysis of all available aerial photographs of Birkenau, that the story of the "cremation pits," as far as their *number*, their *size* or their *purpose* are concerned, is not borne out by the reality on the ground. The *only* documented site of any kind of cremation that may have existed at Birkenau was a space behind Crematorium V, but it covered an area of merely some 50 square meters, as we can see from Document 10.

In contrast to this, if we follow the holocaust propaganda, the alleged extermination of the Hungarian Jews would have required "cremation ditches" with an area of about 6,000 square meters altogether.[33]

We must remember, moreover, that in order to reach this point it would have been necessary to pass Crematoria IV and V, which surely would not have escaped the eye of as acute an observer of chimneys as Elie Wiesel – there were four chimneys, after all. What is more, there were no barracks in the vicinity, there was only Crematorium V. Finally, the nearest wire fence against which our witness wanted to throw himself (on the north side) ran along the far side of a drainage ditch.

Wiesel's tale is not only historically unfounded, it is also absurd, because if Wiesel had really come within two steps of a real "cremation pit" – which would have had to be run at a temperature of about 600°C to be effective – he would have been killed by the intense heat.

The scene of the truck unloading children into a "cremation pit" is also one of the most-ludicrous propaganda arguments of the post-war era. It was

---

31 But no photograph shows the presence of smoke in this area.
32 (Chicago: Theses & Dissertations Press, 2005).
33 *Ibid.*, p. 51.

illustrated by one of David Olère's drawings in 1947 which was then to inspire a number of later "eye-witnesses" (see Documents 16a & b).[34]

Wiesel's story thus turns out to be both false and absurd, but it is also a blatant subterfuge: if he and his father had really been "selected" for work, why were they then taken anywhere near the "cremation pit"? So that they would discover the "terrible secret" of Auschwitz and spread their story to other camps?

Regarding Wiesel's route, using a criterion of charitable interpretation, the following should be noted: Inmates slated to be registered walked from the ramp along the *Hauptstrasse* (main street), passed between Crematoria II and III, then turned to the right onto the *Ringstrasse* (perimeter road) and came to the *Zentralsauna*. After disinfestation, they continued along the *Ringstrasse*, then turned right and turned onto the *Strasse B* (Avenue B), which passed between Crematoria IV and V, and separated Camp Sector BII from Sector BIII. Because the only small area where smoke can be seen on aerial photographs of the time was located in the northern courtyard of the Crematorium V, which was obscured by a pine grove, Elie Wiesel could not, under any circumstances, have gotten close to it, because there was no road leading to it. If his story were true, the SS escorts would have had to divert the column of prisoners who had left the Zentralsauna away from *Strasse B* for a sight-seeing trip in order to see the "cremation pits," and then bring them back onto *Strasse B* a little later.

It is obvious that we have here nothing but a simple subterfuge used by Wiesel to style himself as an "eye-witness" of a horrific but purely fictitious event.

e) The transfer to Auschwitz

After a night spent in a barrack of the gypsy camp, Elie Wiesel was moved to the Auschwitz main camp. Here too, the description is exceedingly vague:

> *The march had lasted half an hour. Looking around me, I noticed that the barbed wires were behind us. We had left the camp.*
> *It was a beautiful April day. The fragrance of spring was in the air. The sun was setting in the west.*
> *But we had been marching for only a few moments when we saw the barbed wire of another camp. An iron door with the inscription over it:*
> *'Work is liberty!'*
> *Auschwitz.* (pp. 37f.)

He does not even seem to have noticed passing through the archway of the Birkenau entrance building. Along the way, he notices nothing, neither the

[34] See also my study *Auschwitz – The Case for Sanity: A Historical and Technical Study of Jean-Claude Pressac's "Criminal Traces" and Robert Jan van Pelt's "Convergence of Evidence,"* (Washington, DC: The Barnes Review,, 2010), vol. 2, p. 607.

bridge across the railroad tracks, nor the long tree-lined road leading to the main camp. On the other hand, he immediately sees the inscription "*Arbeit macht frei*" (but does not render it in German), as could anyone who ever heard of Auschwitz.

Needless to say that he makes sure not to provide us with an even sketchy description of the new camp. On arrival, he was taken to *Block* 17, about which he does not tell the reader anything, for obvious reasons.

> *In the afternoon we were made to line up. Three prisoners brought a table and some medical instruments. With the left sleeve rolled up, each person passed in front of the table. The three 'veterans,' with needles in their hands, engraved a number on our left arms. I became A-7713.* (p. 39.)

Even this facet is false. I have already spoken of the fraudulent ID number. Here, Tadeusz Iwasko informs us that

> *The new arrivals (*Zugang*) were taken to the bathhouses which, at Auschwitz I, were located in Block no. 26.*[35]

Elie Wiesel keeps quiet about all the preparatory operations prior to admission, which he is obviously unfamiliar with. Iwasko writes about it:[36]

> *Registration took place immediately after the bath and the consignment of the clothes; it involved the filling-out of a form (*Häftlings-Personalbogen*) giving personal data and the address of the nearest relatives.* [...] *The detainee was then assigned a serial number which would be used instead of his name throughout his stay at the camp. Registration ended with this number being tattooed on his lower left arm.*

Wiesel goes on to speak of the evening roll call:

> *Tens of thousands of prisoners stood in rows while the SS checked their numbers.* (p. 39; my emphasis)

The Auschwitz camp strength, however, was far lower. On 12 July 1944, the camp held about 14,400 detainees.[37]

f) The transfer to Monowitz

After having spent three weeks at Auschwitz (p. 41), Elie Wiesel was transferred to the Buna camp (p. 43), also called Auschwitz III, at Monowitz. Here, again, we have no verifiable particulars.[38] What few details he gives us are all fanciful. He starts out right away with a contradiction:

> *Our convoy included a few children ten and twelve years old.* (p. 45)

Perhaps these youngsters, too, had told the Germans that they were eighteen years of age, so that they would be spared the gas chambers?

---

35 Piper, Świebocka, *Auschwitz*, p. 52.
36 *Ibid.*, p. 54.
37 D. Czech, *Kalendarium der Ereignisse im Konzentrationslager Auschwitz-Birkenau 1939-1945* (Reinbek bei Hamburg: Rowohlt Verlag, 1989), p. 821.
38 Except the mention of the barrack of the camp orchestra.

Then "[…] we were installed in two tents" (p. 45), as if Monowitz did not have the 60 barracks which Primo Levi told us about as follows:[39]

> *Our Lager is a square of about six hundred yards in length, surrounded by two fences of barbed wire, the inner one carrying a high tension current. It consists of sixty wooden huts, which are called* Blocks, *ten of which are in construction. In addition, there is the body of the kitchens, which are in brick; an experimental farm, run by a detachment of privileged* Häftlinge*; the huts with the showers and the latrines, one for each group of six or eight* Blocks. *Besides these, certain* Blocks *are reserved for specific purposes. First of all, a group of eight, at the extreme eastern end of the camp, forms the infirmary and clinic; then there is* Block *24 which is the* Krätzeblock, *reserved for infectious skin diseases;* Block *7 which no ordinary* Häftling *has ever entered, reserved for the "*Prominenz,*" that is,the aristocracy, the internees holding the highest posts;* Block *47, reserved for the* Reichsdeutsche *(the Aryan Germans, 'politicals' or criminals);* Block *49, for the* Kapos *alone;* Block *12, half of which, for use of the* Reichsdeutsche *and the* Kapos, *serves as canteen, that is, a distribution centre for tobacco, insect powder and occasionally other articles;* Block *37, which formed the Quartermaster's office and the Office for Work; and finally,* Block *29, which always has its windows closed as it is the* Frauenblock, *the camp brothel, served by Polish* Häftling *girls, and reserved for the* Reichsdeutsche.

When compared to this text, Elie Wiesel's non-description can only be characterized as pathetic.

When he spoke at Montecitorio, Elie Wiesel boasted of having known Primo Levi:[40]

> *At a certain point, both of us were assigned to the same barrack, but he was not there during the death-march towards the* [railroad] *cars which took us to Buchenwald, he stayed in the hospital.* (My emphasis)

However, Primo Levi was assigned to *Block* 30,[41] then to *Block* 45,[42] and finally to *Block* 48.[43] Which *Block* was Wiesel's? The answer is not as simple as that. Initially, Wiesel speaks of "the orchestra block"[44] which was, indeed, "near the door[!?] of the camp" (p. 47), then he mentions *Block* 36 a couple of times – "With all my might I began to run to block 36" (p. 69), "I ran to block 36" (p. 72) – without telling us whether he was actually lodged there. Finally he says clearly that he stayed in *Block* 57 (p. 80). In fact, Elie Wiesel and Primo Levi were never housed in the same barrack. A

---

39 Primo Levi, *Survival in Auschwitz. The Nazi Assault on Humanity* (re-titled edition of *If This Is a Man*) (New York: Collier, 1961), p. 27.

40 www.camera.it/cartellecomuni/Leg16/files/pdf/opuscolo_giorno_della_memoria.pdf

41 Primo Levi, *Survival in Auschwitz*, *op.cit.*, p. 33.

42 *Ibid.*, p. 51.

43 *Ibid.*, p. 116.

44 The *Block* for the orchestra was not counted with the other barracks of the camp, numbered 1 through 60.

little white lie right in the middle of Montecitorio, right smack in the face of so many listeners!

The little tale of ripping out gold teeth from the mouths of living detainees (p. 49) and the ensuing closure of the dental station (*Zahnstation*, p. 50) is unfounded. Gold teeth were removed from corpses, and the *Zahnstation*, located in *Block* 15 and run by the SS, was never closed down.

Elie Wiesel then goes on to tell us about a detainee "selected" for death in the "gas chamber":

> *When the selection came, he was condemned in advance, offering his own neck to the executioner. All he asked of us was:*
> *"In three days I shall no longer be here... Say the Kaddish for me."*
> *We promised him. In three days' time, when we saw the smoke rising from the chimney, we would think of him. Ten of us would gather together and hold a special service. All his friends would say the Kaddish.*
> *Then he went off toward the hospital, his step steadier, not looking back. An ambulance was waiting to take him to Birkenau.* (p. 73; my emphasis)

Our "eye witness" had either forgotten that he was at Monowitz where there was no crematorium or had such a keen eye that he could see the smoke from "the chimney" (one of six, the choice is yours) at Birkenau, something that would be rather improbable in view of the fact that the two camps were 5 km apart as the crow flies, and the town of Auschwitz stood between them.

Also, sending an ambulance to take *one* detainee to the gas chamber would really be an example of "*Sonderbehandlung*", a very "special treatment"!

On the subject of "selections," Elie Wiesel asserts that "the notorious Dr. Mengele" was present at one of them (p. 68). But Mengele was *Lagerarzt* of the gypsy camp (BIIe) at Birkenau, and certainly had other duties than to go to Monowitz and carry out "selections" there. Mengele, incidentally, is the only physician mentioned by Elie Wiesel, and is also the one who received him at Birkenau (p. 29). The name is very well known among those who never even came near Auschwitz.

Our eye-witness even mentions an occurrence that one can verify: an Allied air-raid. It took place "one Sunday" (p. 56). He remembers the day very well because he had decided "[…] to stay in bed late in the morning" (p. 56). "The raid lasted over an hour" (p. 57), and he comments:

> *To see the whole works* [*la fabbrica* in the Italian edition, p. 62] *go up in fire – what revenge!* (p. 57)

In reality, the raid took place on 13 September 1944, which was a Wednesday; it lasted 13 minutes, from 11:17 through 11:30 a.m., and destroyed only part of the installations. Actually, at Monowitz there was not just one factory (*la fabbrica*, singular) but quite a few.

We will not go into minor silly statements, such as the death sentence pronounced "in the name of Himmler […]" (p. 59), and move on to his stay at the camp hospital (probably inspired by Primo Levi's account). It took place "in mid-January" when his right foot swelled up because of chilblains, and he had to be operated on. He had to move into the hospital, and immediately noticed that "it was indeed true that the hospital was very small […]" (p. 75). Actually, it consisted of *only* nine *Blocks*, two for recovery (13 and 22), two for surgery (14 and 16), one for internal medicine and dentistry (15), two for internal medicine (17 and 19), one for outpatients and reception (18), and one for infectious diseases.[45]

In January 1945, 1,645 inmates were hospitalized at the Monowitz hospital (running numbers from 17,009 to 18,653). Needless to say, Elie Wiesel is not on this list, and there isn't even a single inmate with an inmate ID number starting with A.[46]

g) The transfer to Buchenwald

We do not have to go into the motivations for Wiesel's decision to leave with the Germans rather than wait for the Soviets to arrive, because, in its literary context, it is psychologically explained by the (unfounded) fear that all those remaining behind in the camp would be shot.

Leaving aside all the vicissitudes of the evacuation march itself and the ride on the train, we will only consider the details of the arrival at Buchenwald, keeping in mind only the duration of the whole trip: three days' stay at Gleiwitz (p. 91), plus one day for the march from Monowitz, and "ten days, ten nights of travelling" (p. 95) for a total of at least 14 days.

But during an interview in January 1995, Wiesel said:[47]

> *We were evacuated on January 18* [1945]. *On the 19th we were loaded on a train, that is, into open cars.*

Since the detainees boarded the train in Gleiwitz, this happened both on January 19 and 22, 1945.

On arrival at Buchenwald we have the usual fogginess – no part of the camp can be identified in any way. Wiesel speaks of showers on "the third day after our arrival at Buchenwald" (p. 102), but avoids any kind of detail regarding the registration procedure.

In the above-mentioned interview he merely repeats this:[48]

---

45 Irena Strzelecka, Piotr Setkiewicz, "Bau, Ausbau und Entwicklung des KL Auschwitz und seiner Nebenlager," in: W. Długoborski, F. Piper, *Auschwitz 1940-1945. Studien zur Geschichte des Konzentrations- und Vernichtungslager Auschwitz* (Auschwitz: Verlag des Staatlichen Museums Auschwitz-Birkenau, 1999), Bd. I, p. 128.

46 NI-10186, pp. 219-269.

47 Jorge Semprun, Elie Wiesel, "Unüberbrückbare Erinnerungen. Ein Zwiegespräch zwischen Jorge Semprun und Elie Wiesel," in: *Werkstatt Geschichte*, no. 13, 1996, p. 51.

48 *Ibid.*, p. 52

> *And we were welcomed. I remember it was already night. Finally to the shower. It was the small camp, and to me the small camp was initially almost worse than Auschwitz.*

We have already seen that Miklós Grüner and Lázár Wiesel, who really did go to Buchenwald, were assigned the ID numbers 120762 and 123565, respectively.

If Elie Wiesel had in any manner wanted to speak of the registration which he had to go through like everyone else, he obviously would have had to say something about *two* ID numbers: his own and his father's. Worse still, there is neither a record of a person by the name of Elie (or Eliezer) Wiesel nor of any Shlomo Wiesel as his father in the Buchenwald files.

In his book Elie Wiesel stated that his father was ill with dysentery (p. 102) and told about his suffering until he died:

> *Then I had to go to bed. I climbed into my bunk, above my father, who was still alive. It was January 28, 1945.*
> *I awoke on January 29 at dawn. In my father's place lay another invalid. They must have taken him away before dawn and carried him to the crematory.* (pp. 106)

In the above-mentioned interview he told a different story instead:[48]

> *It was the end of January. I remember that we were sprayed with water in front of the quarantine block with icy water. We turned into blocks of ice. I stood next to my father. And then suddenly my father was no more. My father had died.*

Let us take a look at the account of his arrival at Buchenwald to see whether it agrees with the documents.

He states that he went to take a shower "on the third day after our arrival at Buchenwald" (p. 102); then "a week went by like this" (p. 104), and that it was then "January 28, 1945" (p. 106), which means that he had arrived at Buchenwald ten days earlier, on January 18, and hence must have left Monowitz two weeks before that, on January 4, reaching Gleiwitz three days later and starting the train ride on the 8th.

This chronology is inconsistent with what Wiesel writes about his last days at Monowitz, though: "Toward the middle of January, my right foot began to swell […]. I went to have it examined. " (p. 74) "The doctor came to tell me that the operation would be the next day" (p. 75). "Two days after the operation" (p. 76) he was told that "Tomorrow […] the camp will set out" (p. 77), and so they did (p. 80). This would put the day he left the camp four days after "the middle of January", around January 19.

Actually, there were three convoys of deportees from the Auschwitz-Birkenau complex which went to Buchenwald in January of 1945:[49]

Departure	Arrival	ID numbers	Number of detainees
18 January	22 January	117195-119418	2,224
18 January	23 January	119419-120337	919
18 January	26 January	120348-124274	3,927

No convoy left on January 8 (or on the 19th or 22nd), and no convoy took longer than 8 days to arrive. The one arriving on 26 January had both Lázár Wiesel and Miklós Grüner on board, as we can see from the ID numbers assigned to them – 120762 and 123565.

The sixth chapter of *Un di velt hot geshvign*, which is entitled *Der metim-zug* (The train of the dead), is very similar to the seventh chapter of *Night* (the account of the journey from Gleiwitz to Buchenwald).[50] The two texts are very similar, except that in the first book the number of detainees loaded into Elie Wiesel's car is not 100 (pp. 92, 98) but 120.[51] Moreover, there is a mention here of the number of cars on the train: 20.[52] On the other hand, the number of detainees in Elie Wiesel's car still alive on arrival at Buchenwald is the same in both: 12 (p. 98).[51] This means that, in this car, there was a mortality of 88 or 90%, respectively. But the entire convoy would have had a similar death rate:[53]

> *The journey lasted ten interminable days and nights. Each day claimed its toll of victims and each night paid its homage to the Angel of Death.*

On the day of the arrival at Buchenwald, there were 40 deaths.[51]

Thus, initially there would have been (20 × (110 ±10) =) 2,200 ±200 detainees altogether on this train, with most of them dying on the way.

On the other hand, it is known from the train manifests that the transport which reached Buchenwald on 26 January comprised, on departure, exactly 3,987 detainees.[54] If 3,927 of them were registered at Buchenwald on arrival, then there had been 60 deaths along the way, or a mortality of 1.5%.

Taking all these aspects into account, one can see that, regarding the journey from Gleiwitz to Buchenwald, neither the description given in *Night* nor the one in *Un di velt hot geshvign* can be true.

---

49 Het Nederlandsche Roode Kruis, *Auschwitz*, Deel VI, 's-Gravenhage, 1952, p. 39.

50 This chapter has been translated into English by Moshe Spiegel under the title "The Death Train," in: Jacob Glatstein, Israel Knox, Samuel Margoshes (eds.), *Anthology of Holocaust Literature*, A Temple Book (New York: Atheneum, 1968), pp. 3-10.

51 *Un di velt hot geshvign*, p. 217.

52 *Ibid.*, p. 216; the English translation just has "infinitely long" (p. 92).

53 *Ibid.*, p. 207.

54 Andrzej Strzelecki, *Endphase des KL Auschwitz* (Auschwitz: Verlag Staatliches Museum in Oswiecim-Brzezinka, 1995), pp. 338f. Reproduction of two pages of the original transport manifest.

The story, or more exactly the non-story, of Elie Wiesel's alleged presence at Buchenwald is further proof that his story is completely invented, for in his book he jumps within half a page from events which allegedly occurred on January 29, 1945 (p. 106), to those of April 5 (p. 107)! Wiesel writes there:

> *I was transferred to the children's block, where there were six hundred of us.*

The Yiddish version reads as follows:[55]

> *I was transferred to the children's block (Kinder-Block) no. 66, where there were about 600 children.*

This block, as we shall see, is important for an accurate interpretation of the famous photograph taken on April 16, 1945.

In short, Elie Wiesel was never interned either at Birkenau, or at Auschwitz, or at Monowitz, or at Buchenwald.

Considering all this, Elie Wiesel's extreme reluctance to show his alleged serial number may be taken as a confession.

The Enigma of Lázár Wiesel

The letter by the Buchenwald Museum (*Gedenkstätte*) to Miklós Grüner of May 15, 2002, mentions a Lázár Wiesel, born on October 4, 1928, who was registered at Buchenwald with the ID number 123165. This results from a survey of the U.S. Military Government in Germany conducted in the Buchenwald camp (see Document 11).

This detainee was born at Máromarossziget on 4 October 1928, he was a student, was arrested on 16 April 1944 and interned at Auschwitz and Monowitz. According to the Buchenwald *Gedenkstätte*, he was sent to Paris on 16 July 1945 with a convoy of surviving children and is registered on the respective list. Is this Lázár Wiesel the writer Elie Wiesel?

We see right away that the dates of birth are not identical: Lázár was born on 4 October 1928, Elie on 30 September of the same year. Since Lázár Wiesel, by his own hand, signed the questionnaire mentioned above – using the last name "Wiezel" – we may exclude an error as far as the date of his birth is concerned.

The second important point is that the Auschwitz ID number of this Lázár Wiesel is not known, but it could not have been A-7713 in any case, because at the Auschwitz Museum there is only one ID number A-7713 in the men's series, assigned to Lazar Wiesel, born on 4 September 1913. What is more, on the transport manifest for the transport from Auschwitz to Buchenwald there is only one Lazar Wiesel, the one born on 4 September

[55] *Un di velt hot geshvign*, p. 239.

1913 and having the Auschwitz ID number A-7713. Where did Lázár Wiesel come from? And what connection is there between Lazar Wiesel and Lázár Wiesel or Lazar Vizel who have such similar record data (except for the dates of birth)?

At the moment, we cannot answer these questions.

To complicate matters even further, there is also a birth certificate of the "Central National Record Office" of Romania dated November 27, 1996, in the name of Lazar Vizel, born in Sighet on September 30, 1928, as a child of Solomon Vizel and Sura Feig. We will return to this record later.

The third point is the fact that the date for Lázár Wiesel's arrest – April 16, 1944 – does not agree with that of Elie Wiesel's: after May 27, 1944, as we have seen earlier.

The fourth point is the Buchenwald ID number; if Elie Wiesel is indeed Lázár Wiesel, why did he not mention the ID number 123165?

Even the name is significant. It is true that Lazar is a diminutive of Eliezer, but this name in Yiddish sounds like אליעזר (Eliezer), while Lazar is לייזער (Leizer) or לאזער (Lozer). Why did the alleged Elie Wiesel at Buchenwald sign his name as Lázár? And why did he never indicate his ID number for this camp?

Lázár Wiesel's Buchenwald ID number fits into the range of numbers assigned on 26 January 1945 to the convoy of 3,927 detainees arriving from Auschwitz: 120348 – 124274. It does not follow, however, that Lázár Wiesel was included in this list.

Actually, the question is even more complicated than that, because we have yet a third detainee, assuming that Lázár Wiesel and Lazar Vizel are the same person.

About this Lázár Wiesel, Grüner has published two important documents. The register of Block 66 contains the following annotation (see Document 12):[56] "[123]565 Wiesel Lazar U. Jun. A 4"

Grüner explained several times what he believes happened. Lazar Wiesel was assigned to Block 66:[57]

> *About a week later, I couldn't believe my own eyes to see Lazar in our Block 66. He told me that Abraham had passed away four days after our arrival at Buchenwald. He made it clear that he had received special permission to join us children in Block 66, since he was so much older than us.*

Several pages later he reaffirms Lazar Wiesel's presence in Block 66.[58] So far nothing about this is strange. But then he states cryptically and confusingly:[59]

---

56 *Stolen Identity*, Figure 2.1.
57 *Ibid.*, p. 28.
58 *Ibid.*, p. 49.
59 *Ibid.*, p. 51.

> *From the ARCHIVE'S of Buchenwald: Sabine Stein; 08.12.00 and 15:05:02. Stating that; Lazar Wiesel's identity number; 123565 according to the MILITARY GOVERNMENT OF GERMANY'S INMATES QUESTIONNAIRE (NARA Washington, RG 242, film 60) were changed to Number 123165 and the date of birth to 04.10.1928. With this new identity he (Lazar Wiesel) left Buchenwald with a HIAS convoy* [Hebrew Immigrant Aid Society] *of 675 survived children (S-414) on the 16th of July 1945 to Paris. However there is a noticeable difference of contents between Lazar Wiesel's original registration card 123565 and the new Number 123 165; which did belong to a Jewish inmate from Slovakia; Pavel Kun, who died on the 8th of March 1945 in Buchenwald.*

Later, commenting on the above-mentioned questionnaire, Grüner adds:[60]

> *Concerning Number:123165 the inmate "Wiesel Lazar" Male; Born October 4. – 1928 Dated Buchenwald: April 22– 1945 to follow.*
> *This Affidavit*[61] *was drawn up in good faith to benefit Wiesel Lazar who was originally Born 04.09.1913 in Maramorossziget; and his registered Number in Buchenwald is 123565 was changed to 123165 for reason to suit Wiesel Lazar's future and the purpose to benefit his coming future.*

In another passage he speaks of the "falsified Buchenwald ID number 123165."[62]

According to Grüner, therefore, someone (he does not clarify who) would have written "in good faith (?)" false data into the above-mentioned questionnaire. But the reasons he gives are downright silly: how could a change of the date of birth and the inmate number have benefitted Lazar Wiesel's future? And who could seriously hope to pass a man of 32 years off for a boy aged 17? And why would a man of 32 years have been included in the transport of children to Paris?

Grüner published two documents (one page of the list of new arrivals from Auschwitz to Buchenwald on 26 January 1945, and a personal card) showing that the number of 123165 Buchenwald was actually assigned to the prisoner Pavel Kun, born on July 06, 1926, in Velka Bytca, and registered at Auschwitz with the number B-14131. He died on March 8, 1945.[63] But why would the number of this inmate have been re-assigned to Lazar Wiesel, "faking" his real number 123565?

One gets the impression that this number, precisely because it had already been assigned to Pavel Kun, is the result of an error: 123***1***65 instead of 123**5**65. But how can the altered date of birth be explained: October 4, 1928?

---

60 *Ibid.*, p. 59.

61 This questionnaire can obviously not at all be considered an "affidavit," which would be a sworn statement.

62 *Ibid.*, p. 34.

63 *Ibid.*, Figures 7, 12.1 and 12.3.

The questionnaire was definitely filled out by one of three British officers listed in the document, which would certainly have been able to make such a mistake, but the person signed the document in his own hand with the last name "Wiezel," endorsing either this alleged error or this falsification with his signature, so in both cases he would be the imposter.

In this Buchenwald questionnaire, answering the question "Give names and addresses, if known, of three reliable persons living in the locality where you intend to go, who can vouch for you," Lázár Wiesel wrote:

Ur [Mr.] *Ferenc Stark, Ferenc Pollak, Sámuel Jakobovits.*

Sámuel Jakobovits was born on October 2, 1926, at Marmarossziget; his mother's maiden name was Pollak, who may have been related to the inmate Ferenc Pollak mentioned by Lázár Wiesel. Jakobovits was deported to Auschwitz and registered there on May 24, 1944, with the ID number A-5763.[64] On January 26, 1945, he was transferred to Buchenwald. His file card (Document 14) indicates that his Buchenwald ID number was 121761.

That Lázár Wiesel and Sámuel Jakobovits knew each other is confirmed by Jakobovits's questionnaire (Document 15) filled out at Buchenwald on April 22, 1945, which lists on the reverse side, as references, the names of Hersch Fischmann, Antal Meisner and, specifically, Lázár Wiesel. The front page also gives the date of Sámuel's arrest – 16 April 1944, the same date as Lázár Wiesel's.

This friendship between Lázár Wiesel and the 19-year-old Sámuel Jakobovits (or Jakubowits) and the fact that Lázár chose this Sámuel as one of his three trusted people, supports the hypothesis that this was a boy of 17 years of age choosing as a guarantor a boy of 19, rather than the theory that a 32-year-old man chose a boy of 19 as a sponsor.

It is therefore difficult to accept the explanation that Lazar Wiesel's personal information was falsified, although this would explain the disappearance of 32-year-old Lazar Wiesel and the appearance of 17-year-old Lázár Wiesel.

Conversely, if these were two different people, then why is Lázár Wiesel, born on October 4, 1928, not on the list of new arrivals from Auschwitz to Buchenwald dated January 26, 1945? And why is he not on the list of Jews deported to Auschwitz?

At this point we are confronted with the enigma of Elie Wiesel. Grüner does not explain how he would have been able to partially take over the personal data of Lazar Wiesel. Perhaps he managed to do that based on documents? Lazar Wiesel, as we have seen earlier, appears in various doc-

64 On this day 2,000 Hungarian Jews were in fact registered with the numbers A-5729 through A-7728; hence both Abram Wiesel [A-7712], and Lazar Wiesel [A-7713], born on Sept. 04, 1913, were part of this transport, although according to the questionnaire of April 22, 1945, Lázár Wiesel was born on October 4, 1928.

uments, but his parents' names are mentioned only in his Buchenwald inmate file, where, however, his date of birth is given as September 4, 1913. To impersonate Lazar Wiesel, Elie would have had to know Lázár Wiesel's documentation (especially in relation to his account on Block 66, where he joined the boys), but then why did he never mention either of the ID numbers of Buchenwald (neither 123565 nor 123165)?

The alternative is personal contact. Elie Wiesel may have known Lazar Wiesel and may have built his own history based on Lazar's stories, liberally revised. Fact is that Lazar and Abraham Wiesel lived in the same town of birth as Elie Wiesel, and it is likely that they knew each other. In 1910 this town had about 21,000 inhabitants, some 8,000 of whom were Jews; in 1930 the population had risen to about 27,000.[65] According to Braham, three transports with a total of 9,601 Jews (3,007 on May 16, 3,104 on May 20, and 3,490 on May 22) were deported from this town to Auschwitz,[66] hence virtually the entire Jewish community. It is therefore more than likely that Elie knew the two brothers Wiesel and their personal information.

The other possibility, that Elie Wiesel is actually identical with Lazar Wiesel, is already ruled out for chronological reasons, for he would be 102 years old today! On the other hand, why would he have "falsified" his date of birth 4 days backward to September 30, 1928, from the already "falsified" one on October 4, 1928?

On November 27, 1996, the "Central Services of Civil Status" of Romania provided a copy of a birth certificate in the name of a certain Lazar Vizel (see Document 13), born in Sighet to Solomon Vizel and Sura Feig. Even though it bears the date of birth of 30 September 1928,[67] this does not prove much, because it is unknown to whom it relates, by whom and why this certificate was requested, and especially, even if this refers to Elie Wiesel, it may merely be the result of Wiesel's own initiative, like the entry made by Elie Wiesel on October 8, 2004, about his father in the Central Database of Shoah Victims at Yad Vashem.[68]

Currently, the correspondences between Lázár Wiesel's data and those of the three other Wiesels don't have an unequivocal explanation:

---

65 http://en.wikipedia.org/wiki/Sighetu_Marmației.

66 R.L. Braham, *A Magyar Holocaust*, *op. cit.*, p. 514.

67 See the text at http://kuruc.info/r/6/51815, image 8.

68 www.yadvashem.org/wps/portal/IY_HON_Welcome

	LAZAR WIESEL	LÁZÁR WIESEL	LAZAR VIZEL	ELIE WIESEL
Auschwitz ID	A-7713	?	?	A-7713
Buchenwald ID	123565	123165	?	?
Date of birth	4 Sept. 1913	4 October 1928	30 Sept. 1928	30 Sept. 1928
Place of birth	Máramarossziget = *Sighet*	Máramarossziget	*Sighet*	*Sighet*
Father's name	Szalamo = *Shlomo*	?	*Solomon*	*Shlomo*
Mother's name	*Serena Feig*	?	*Sura Feig*	*Sarah Feig*
Residence, early 1945	*Buchenwald*	?	?	*Buchenwald*

It is beyond question, though, that Elie Wiesel can be neither Lazar Wiesel, nor Lázár Wiesel; the number A-7713 was not assigned to him, but to Lazar Wiesel, while the number A-7712 was not assigned to his father, but to Abram (or Abraham) Viesel (Wiesel).

The charge of identity theft raised against Elie Wiesel by Miklós Grüner does not merely concern Lazar Vizel, but Lázár Wiesel as well: from the former he took the Auschwitz ID number (A-7713), from the latter the stay at Buchenwald and the later transfer to Paris.

As far as his book *La Nuit* is concerned, what is the value of his sworn statement that "it is a true account. Every word in it is true," in the face of the analysis I presented earlier?

In this respect, it is interesting to note that the book in question does not contain any mention of the alleged "gas chambers" of Auschwitz. Elie Wiesel is perhaps the only self-styled Auschwitz witness not to speak of "gas chambers," something quite surprising, to say the least, which can – and must – be explained only by him.

Comparing *Night* and *Un di velt hot geshvign*

Grüner claims that Lazar Wiesel, with the new identity of Lázár, drafted a manuscript of 862 pages in Yiddish which the publisher Mark Turkov reduced to 253 pages.[69] The book, he wrote, was "published in Paris in 1955,"[70] but then he specifies it was only copyrighted to Eliezer Wiesel, aged 43, of Paris, and was actually published "in 1955, Buenos Aires. The copyright shall prove that he was tattooed in Birkenau with the number A-7713";[71] at another point Grüner writes "Copyright by Eliezer (in Yid-

[69] *Stolen Identity*. p. 43. To be precise, the story ends on page 245 with an explicit "Sof" (End). The following pages are advertisements (list of published works in the collection *Der poilische jidntum*, Polish Jewry).

[70] *Ibid.*, p. 44.

[71] *Ibid.*, p. 55.

dish the name means the same meaning as Lazar) Wiesel, Paris 1954."[72] Elie Wiesel, usurping the copyright of Lazar Wiesel, published a summary of *Un di velt hot geshvign* in 1958 with the title *La Nuit.*[73]

However, there is no evidence that the author of the Yiddish book is Lazar Wiesel. Grüner argues this, because on p. 87 of this book the author says he received at Auschwitz the ID number A-7713,[74] and on p. 239 that he had been housed in Block 66 while in Buchenwald,[75] but these data are not sufficient to identify with certainty Lazar Wiesel as the author.

The question of "copyright," contrary to what Grüner seems to believe, says nothing about the book's author. Indeed, it is unclear why the "copyright" was recorded in Paris, since the book was published in Buenos Aires. If Lazar Wiesel really were the author, he would have protested the blatant plagiarism allegedly perpetrated by Elie Wiesel just two years later, and the publisher, Mark Turkov, would have sued (unless he, or both, had an agreement with Elie Wiesel). But nothing happened.

Grüner seems to believe that the alleged plagiarist Elie Wiesel has somehow distorted the original text of Lazar Wiesel, inventing false stories and exposing authentic veterans to criticism by revisionists. In this regard he writes:[76]

> *The book "Night" is a masterpiece designed to defame us and our Jewish God, while spreading lies about the Holocaust without any kind of reasonable explanation. To mention the horribly twisted story making account for the huge flames coming from the ditches holding incinerated bodies of men, women and children, without mentioning of course, that they were dead, or that they were under the circumstances, already suffocated to death on arrival at the flaming ditches.*

At another point he observes:[77]

> *I had never seen or even come close to ditches burning with open fire, where people or children could be seen burning on my way to washroom in Birkenau, as written in "Night" by Elie Wiesel.*

In practice Grüner accuses Elie Wiesel of having invented at least the story of children being burned alive in "cremation pits," which I analyzed above.

In fact, the same description can be found in the Yiddish text, as is apparent from a comparison of the two related passages (left column from *Night*, right column from *Un di velt hot geshvign*):[78]

---

72 *Ibid.*, p. 46. The book's production was finished on November 10, 1955, and it was officially released in 1956; it says in its imprint "Copyright by: Eliezer Wiesel, Paris" and is undated.

73 *Ibid.*, pp. 44, 46 and Figure 17.

74 *Ibid.*, pp. 55f.

75 *Ibid.*, p. 57.

76 *Ibid.*, p. 45.

77 *Ibid.*, pp. 34f.

Not far from us, flames were leaping up from a ditch, gigantic flames. A lorry drew up at the pit and delivered its load – little children. Babies! Yes, I saw it – saw it with my own eyes... those children in the flames. [...] *A little farther on was another and larger ditch for adults.* [...] *Still twenty steps to go.* [...] *Our line had now only fifteen paces to cover.* [...] *Ten steps still. Eight. Seven. We marched slowly on, as though following a hearse at our own funeral. Four steps more. Three steps. There it was now, right in front of us, the pit and its flames.* [...] *No. Two steps from the pit we were ordered to turn to the left and made to go into a barracks.*	*A hundred feet from us, flames are rising from a pit; huge flames; they are burning something there: but what?* *A truck approaches the pit and automatically dumps its load; suddenly I see what it is transporting, what it dumps into the pit: small children! Babies! Toddlers! Yes, I saw it with my own eyes ... I saw how the children were thrown alive into the flames!* [...] *We really walk to the fireplace, in the direction of the flaming pit; evidently before* [us], *a little further, there is another and larger ditch: for adults, for us.* [...] *Twenty steps to go.* [...] *Another fifteen steps.* [...] *Ten more steps, eight, seven steps* [...] *four steps.* *Here, three steps, here, the pit, here, the flames.* *Two steps before the pit we were ordered to turn left, into a bathing barracks.*

The Yiddish book contains another passage, which is also rendered in *Night* (p. 28), which further enhances the doubt that Lazar Wiesel is its author. In this passage, an Auschwitz inmate asks the author for his age:[79]

> *I am not quite 15 years, I said.*
> *The inmate shouted, "No, 18."* [...]
> *Then he asked my father the same question.*
> *"I am 50 years old," my father replied naively.*
> *The detainee was indignant: "No! Not fifty years! Forty!"*

Why would Lazar Wiesel have claimed to have been not even 15 years old, when he was actually 31 years old at the time of his arrival at Auschwitz?

The only thing in this tangled story that is actually certain is that Elie Wiesel has lied about the Auschwitz ID numbers assigned to him and to his father, but would he have had a need to do this, if he and his father had actually been deported to Auschwitz? In this case they would have received numbers which would necessarily be different than A-7713 and A-7712. What reason could Elie Wiesel have to not declare their *real* numbers?

Regarding *Stolen Identity*, Grüner, as I pointed out, accuses Elie Wiesel of having discredited the true witnesses with his fantasies, but Grüner isn't

[78] *La Notte*, pp. 37f.; *Night*, pp. 30f.; *Un di velt hot geshvign*, pp. 67-70.
[79] *Un di velt hot geshvign*, p. 63; *La Nuit*, p. 54.

much better either. There is no need to dwell on this aspect of Grüner's book. Just one quote from it suffices:[80]

> *They had saved my skin from being turned into lampshades or from being made into a burning torch. Most of all, I was spared from being turned into a cake of soap bearing the initials R.J.F. (reine judische fett)*[[81]] *on it.*

The Buchenwald Photograph

Finally, let us go back to the Buchenwald photograph in which Elie Wiesel is said to appear:[82]

> *Photo by Harry Miller of slave laborers in the Buchenwald concentration camp after U.S. troops of the 80th Div. entered the camp. Taken on 16 April 1945. Miklos Grüner (Haft-Nr. 120762) is on the left at the bottom, while Elie Wiesel (Haft-Nr. 123565) is on the next row up, seventh along, nearest to the third pillar from the left.*

However, the claim that the face of the person depicted in the photograph was that of Elie Wiesel is based only on a statement – on his self-recognition. As for "his" serial number – 123565 – it belonged to Lázár Wiesel!

Wikipedia has this to say about this photograph:[83]

Author	*Unknown or not provided*
Title	*"These are slave laborers in the Buchenwald concentration camp near Jena; many had died from malnutrition when U.S. troops of the 80th Division entered the camp.", 04/16/1945*
Record creator	*Office for Emergency Management. Office of War Information. Overseas Operations Branch. New York Office. News and Features Bureau. (12/17/1942 - 09/15/1945)*
Date	*16 April 1945*
Current location	*National Archives and Records Administration, College Park Still Picture Records Section, Special Media Archives Services Division (NWCS-S)*
Record ID	*This media is available in the holdings of the National Archives and Records Administration, cataloged under the ARC Identifier (National Archives Identifier) 535560.* […] – *Record group: Record Group 208: Records of the Office of War Information, 1926 – 1951 (ARC identifier: 535)* […]

[80] *Stolen Identity*. unnumbered page headlined "In Gratitude".

[81] R.I.F. (rather than R.J.F.) was the acronym for *Reichsstelle für industrielle Fettversorgung*, Imperial Office of Industrial Fat Supplies. This office supplied the German army with cheap soap bearing those initials. Some of the fat used for its production may have come from slaughterhouse waste. The misinterpretation of this acronym as reines Judenfett (pure Jewish fat) is based on false rumors and propaganda lies.

[82] Christopher Hitchens, "Elie Wiesel's identitiy crisis," March 10, 2009; http://christopherhitchenswatch.blogspot.com/2009/03/elie-wiesels-identity-crisis.html

[83] http://commons.wikimedia.org; NARA 535560; see p. 166 for a reproduction in the present study.

The date of 16 April 1945 is thus confirmed officially. In his book, however, Elie Wiesel writes (pp. 108f.):

> *On April tenth, there were still about twenty thousand of us in the camp, including several hundred children.* […]
> *Three days after the liberation of Buchenwald I became very ill with food poisoning. I was transferred to the hospital and spent two weeks between life and death.*

The camp was liberated on 11 April 1945. Three days later, on 14 April, Elie Wiesel fell ill and was taken to the camp hospital where he stayed "between life and death" for two weeks, *i.e.* until 28 April.

But then, how could he have been in barrack 56 on 16 April, which was obviously a normal housing barrack for grown-up men, hence neither the children's block nor the hospital? And how could he have signed the questionnaire mentioned above on 22 April as Lázár Wiesel?

Imposture, perjury and false testimony:
Elie Wiesel is indeed the appropriate "Symbol of the Shoah"!

Editor's Caveat

Relying on the claims of yet another megalomaniac Auschwitz "survivor" – Nikolaus Grüner – to prove that Wiesel is an impostor is a risky business. To see this risk, it suffices to read Grüner's book, which is replete with bizzare accusations against his host nation Sweden for allegedly having participated in the Nazi Holocaust, even though Sweden was neutral during the war and a haven for many refugees from Nazi-dominated Europe. Grüner also seriously claims that Sweden is in the advanced process of preparing yet another Holocaust![84] Add to this that in early 2000 Grüner tried to get Wiesel's support for his initiative to establish yet another Holocaust memorial organization, appealing to him as a former fellow inmate.[85] Only after Wiesel kept ignoring him did Grüner start out on his campaign to prove that Wiesel was an impostor. Hence it looks like this could be merely a case of "hell has no fury like a 'survivor' scorned."

Thus, it is all the more important that Carlo Mattogno cross-checked Grüner's claims and separated the wheat from the chaff. Still, it is possible that Grüner and Mattogno are wrong and that Wiesel was in both Auschwitz and Buchenwald. The wrong date of birth on the Auschwitz and Buchenwald documents allegedly referring to Elie Wiesel may merely be a matter of bureaucratic bungling.

---

[84] See for instance his letters to the Swedish government, Figures 1.3 and 1.10, in his book *Stolen Identity*.

[85] *Ibid.*, Figure 14.

At any rate, the question whether Wiesel is an impostor or not may be interesting, but I think it distracts from the core issue: that Elie Wiesel's statements about so many things – his experiences during the war included – are grossly and obviously untrue, and that he therefore cannot be trusted, regardless of whether he ever was "there."

Documents

MG/PS/G/14

MILITARY GOVERNMENT OF GERMANY

FRAGEBOGEN FÜR INSASSEN DER KONZENTRATIONSLAGER
CONCENTRATION CAMP INMATES QUESTIONNAIRE

Name des Konzentrationslagers / *Name of Concentration Camp*: Buchenwald
Datum / *Date*: 6 may 1945

Ort / *Location*: Buchenwald

Name des Lagerinsassen / *Name of Inmate*: Zuname / *Last*: Grüner — *First* — Vornamen / *Initial*: Miklós

Geschlecht / *Sex*: male
Geburtsdatum / *Date of Birth*: 6 nov. 1928

Staatsangehörigkeit / *Nationality*: Hungarian
Glaubensbekenntnis / *Religion*: jew

Wohnungsanschrift / *Home Address*: Nyiregyháza [illegible] Nr. 25

[B]eruf / *Occupation*: electrical

Datum der Verhaftung / *Date of Arrest*: 26 apr. 1944
Durch Wen / *By whom*: Hungarian police

Ort der Verhaftung / *Place of Arrest*: Nyiregyháza

Grund für Verhaftung / *Reason for Arrest*: being jew

Anklage erhoben / *Charges Made*:

Erkennendes Gericht / *Court Trying Case*:

Namen der Richter / [N]*ames of Judges*:

Urteil / *Sentence*:

Wo in Haft gewesen und wie lange / *Place of Detention Giving Dates*: Birkenau 6 days, Buna 8 months, Buchenwald 3 months

Einzelheiten betreffend die Haft, im besonderen etwaige grausame Behandlung und Zeit derselben, Gründe hierfür und die Namen der Täter, falls bekannt:
Give particulars of confinement including any inhumane treatment with dates, reasons and names of perpetrators, if known:
He was beaten at several times by campleader SS [illegible]

[Ste]llungen, die Sie während der Haft hatten:
Positions held during confinement:

Haben Sie jemals der NSDAP, deren Gliederungen, angeschlossenen Verbänden oder betreuten Organisationen angehört?
Have you ever belonged to the Nazi Party or any of its affiliated or subordinate organizations?

Falls ja, geben Sie die Organisationen, die Zeit der Mitgliedschaft und die von Ihnen bekleideten Ämter an
If so, list Organizations, dates of membership and positions held:

(Bitte wenden / Please turn)

Document 1: Questionnaire concerning Miklós Grüner. Buchenwald, 6 May 1945.

Ung. Jude

Konzentrationslager Art der Haft: Gef.-Nr.:

Name und Vorname: WIESEL Lazar

geb.: 4.9.13 zu: Maramarossziget

Wohnort: Maramarossziget

Beruf: Schlosserlehrling Rel.:

Staatsangehörigkeit: Ungarn Stand:

Name der Eltern: Vater: Salomon W. in KL Bu. Rasse:

Wohnort: Mutter Sarah W. geb. Feig

Name der Ehefrau: Vater in KL Bu Rasse

Wohnort:

Kinder: Alleiniger Ernährer der Familie oder der Eltern: 26.1.45 KL. Auschwitz

Vorbildung:

Militärdienstzeit: von — bis

Kriegsdienstzeit: von — bis

Grösse: Nase: Haare: Gestalt:

Mund: Bart: Gesicht: Ohren:

Sprache: Augen: Zähne:

Document 2: Personal file card for Lázár Wiesel (KL Buchenwald).

123565

W i e s e l , Lazar Polit.
geb. 4.9.13 Maramarossziget Ungar
Schlosserlehrling Jude

26. Jan. 1945

Document 3: Buchenwald registration card for Lazar Wiesel, born Sept. 4, 1913

[illegible]	12[illegible]	[illegible]	[illegible]	3. 3.27	[illegible]	Maler	A	5887
[illegible]	12[illegible]431	[illegible]	Imre	19. 7.27	[illegible]	Schl.	A	6551
[illegible]	12[illegible]	Wiesel	Abraham	5. 1.29	Huszt	[illegible]	A	8695
[illegible]	[illegible]	[illegible]	[illegible]	[illegible]	[illegible]	[illegible]	A	[illegible]
[illegible]	123565	Wiesel	Lazar	4. 9.13	Marmarosszigef	Schl.	A	7713
[illegible]	[illegible]	[illegible]	Jozsef	14. [illegible]	Ujpest	Maler	A	[illegible]
[illegible]	12[illegible]961	Winkler	[illegible]	6.10.15	Debrecen	Glaser	A	11869
2441.	122114	Winkler	Jabor	26. 3.28	Nagy Kanizsa	Gärtn.		187105
2442.	123[illegible]	Winkler	Istvan	24. 8.25	[illegible]	Schl.	A	[illegible]
2443.	120995	Wolf	Herman	23.12.03	[illegible]	Kaufm.	A	[illegible]
2444.	123[illegible]	Wortmann	Emil	22. 1.99	Legrad	[illegible]		[illegible]
2445.	124221	Wortmann	Marton	14.10.10	[illegible]	[illegible]		[illegible]

Document 4: List of new arrivals at the Buchenwald camp on January 26, 1945 (Zugänge vom 26. Januar 1945) prepared on the same day; here with Lazar Wiesel, A 7713, born on Sept. 4, 1913.

[illegible]	121899	Weiss	Manfred	28. 7.30	Nyirlugos	Schust.	A	6622
2569.	124219	Wermes	Zoltan	9. 9.02	Budapest	El.Ing.	A	17936
2570.	122991	Widder	[illegible]	[illegible]. 6.06	[illegible]	Klempn.	A	4818
2571.	122649	Wiesel	Samuel	16.10.28	[illegible]	Klempn.	A	4062
2572.	123488	Viezel	Abram	10.10.00	Marmaroos	Schl.	A	7712
2573.	[illegible]	Winkler	Salamon	10. 1.20	[illegible]	[illegible]	A	[illegible]
2574.	123422	[illegible]	Josef	11. 2.07	Kis.Verseki	Schust.	A	8766
2575.	121935	[illegible]	Gabriel	23. 9.01	Budapest	[illegible]	A	17437
2576.	121083	[illegible]	Eugen	12.12.97	Bethlen	Arb-	A	11769
2577.	120441	[illegible]	Imre	15. 9.17	Gr.Kanizsa	Schl.		187[illegible]

Document 5: Same as Document 4, but here with Abram Viezel, A 7712, born on Oct. 10, 1900.

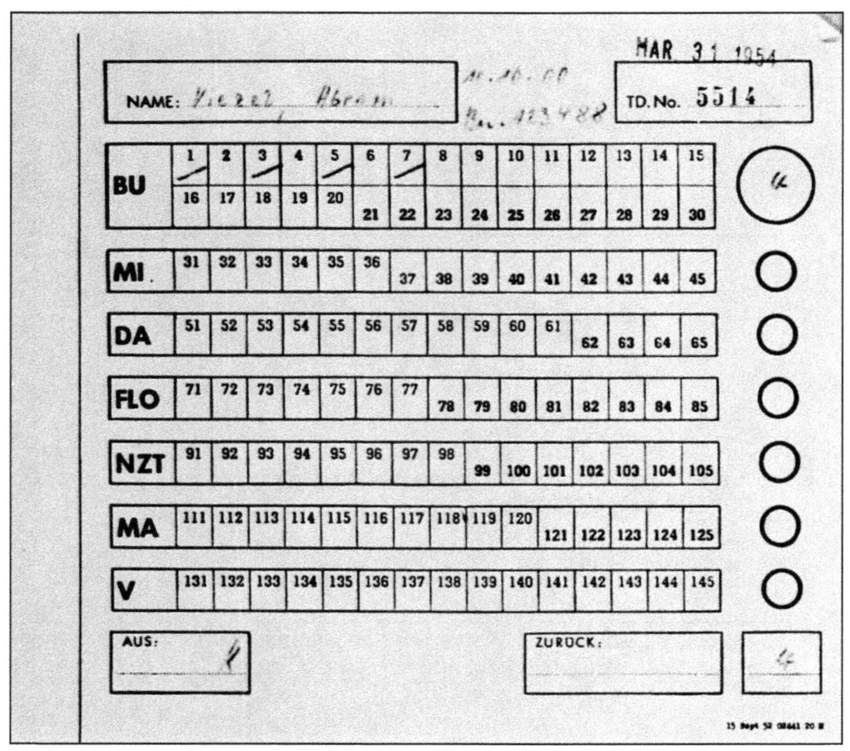
MAR 31 1954

NAME: Viezel Abram — 10.10.00 — Nr. 123488

TD.No. 5514

BU	1	2	3	4	5	6	7	8	9	10	11	12	13	14	15
	16	17	18	19	20	21	22	23	24	25	26	27	28	29	30
MI	31	32	33	34	35	36	37	38	39	40	41	42	43	44	45
DA	51	52	53	54	55	56	57	58	59	60	61	62	63	64	65
FLO	71	72	73	74	75	76	77	78	79	80	81	82	83	84	85
NZT	91	92	93	94	95	96	97	98	99	100	101	102	103	104	105
MA	111	112	113	114	115	116	117	118	119	120	121	122	123	124	125
V	131	132	133	134	135	136	137	138	139	140	141	142	143	144	145

AUS: 4

ZURUCK:

4

Document 6: Death certificate of Abram Viezel

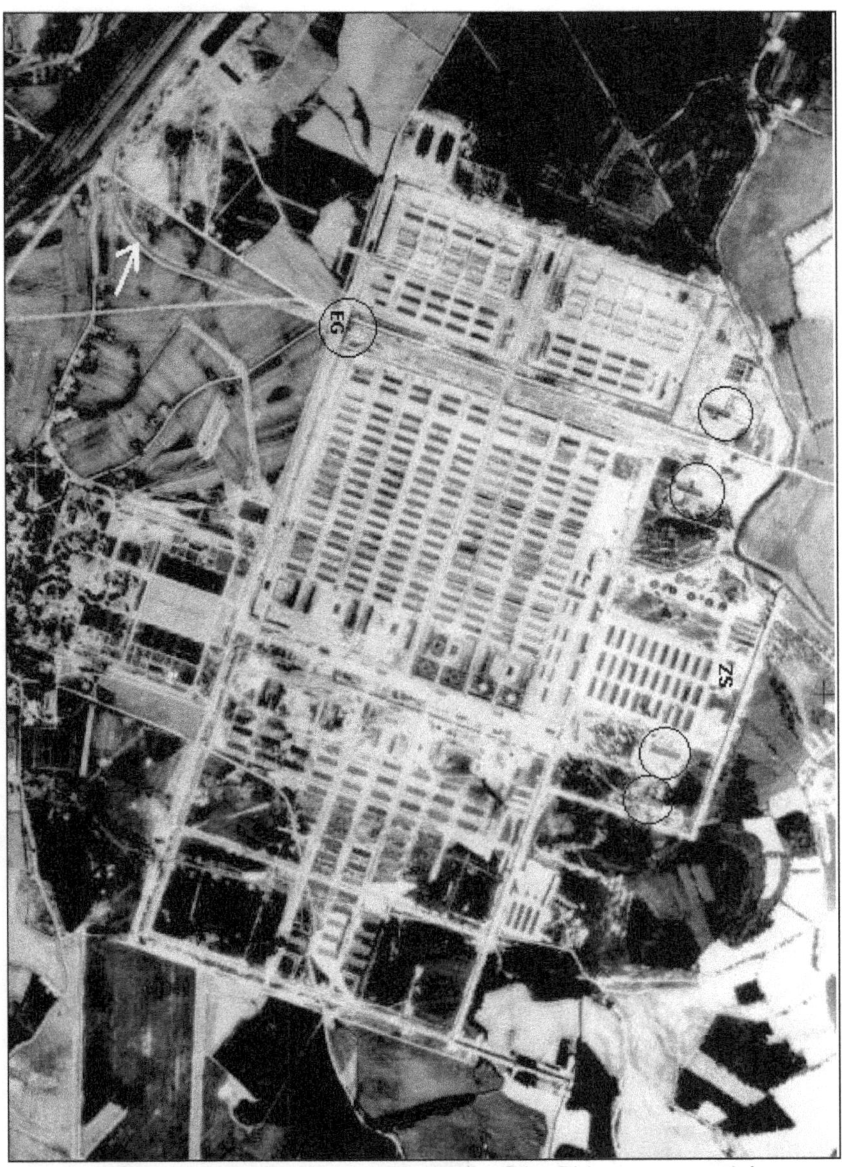

Document 7 (sideways): Aerial photograph of the Birkenau camp, taken on 31 May 1944 (NA, 60PRS/462, D 1508, Exp. 3056). The circles mark the crematoria; (left to right) II, III, IV, V. The building in the shape of a "T," marked "ZS" is the Central Sauna. "EG" is the entrance building (Eingangsgebäude). The white arrow (at bottom) marks the railway spur.

Document 8: Entrance building (Eingangsgebäude) of the Birkenau camp
© Carlo Mattogno

Document 9: A convoy of Hungarian Jews at the Birkenau camp – end of June 1944. The added arrows point to the chimneys of Crematoria II and III, without "flames" or smoke (from: L'Album d'Auschwitz*)*

Document 10: Aerial photograph of Birkenau taken on 23 August 1944 – northern yard of Crematorium V. The smoking site is very small, as can be seen from the size of crematorium V which was about 13 meters wide.

12. 1. 0 123 165   123.165

MG/PS/G/1

MILITARY GOVERNMENT OF GERMANY

FRAGEBOGEN FÜR INSASSEN DER KONZENTRATIONSLAGER

CONCENTRATION CAMP INMATES QUESTIONNAIRE

Name des Konzentrationslagers / *Name of Concentration Camp*: Buchenwald — Datum / *Date*: April 22, 1945

Ort / *Location*: Buchenwald

Name des Lagerinsassen / *Name of Inmate*: Zuname / *Last*: Wiesel — *First* — Vornamen: Lázár — *Initial*

Geschlecht / *Sex*: male — Geburtsdatum / *Date of Birth*: Oct 4 1928

Staatsangehörigkeit / *Nationality*: Roumanian — Glaubensbekenntnis / *Religion*: Jew

Wohnungsanschrift / *Home Address*: Máramarossziget Roumania

Beruf / *Occupation*: student

Datum der Verhaftung / *Date of Arrest*: April 16 1944 — Durch Wen / *By whom*: Police

Ort der Verhaftung / *Place of Arrest*: Máramarossziget

Grund für Verhaftung / *Reason for Arrest*: being a Jew

Anklage erhoben / *Charges Made*

Erkennendes Gericht / *Court Trying Case*

Namen der Richter / *Names of Judges*

Urteil / *Sentence*

Wo in Haft gewesen und wie lange / *Place of Detention Giving Dates*: Auschwitz Monowitz, Buchenwald

Einzelheiten betreffend die Haft, im besonderen etwaige grausame Behandlung und Zeit derselben, Gründe hierfür und die Namen der Täter, falls bekannt.
Give particulars of confinement including any inhumane treatment with dates, reasons and names of perpetrators, if known.

Stellungen, die Sie während der Haft hatten
Positions held during confinement:

Haben Sie jemals der NSDAP, deren Gliederungen, angeschlossenen Verbänden oder betreuten Organisationen angehört?
Have you ever belonged to the Nazi Party or any of its affiliated or subordinate organizations?

Falls ja, geben Sie die Organisationen, die Zeit der Mitgliedschaft und die von Ihnen bekleideten Ämter an
If so, list Organizations, dates of membership and positions held:

(Bitte wenden) (Please turn)

Document 11a & b (next page): Buchenwald questionnaire for Lázár Wiesel dated 22 April 1945 – front and back

594

Geben Sie Ihre Militardienstzeit unter Angabe der Organisationen, Daten und des Dienstranges an:
List periods of military service giving organizations and dates as well as ranks held:

No

Geben Sie Tatsachen an, **die Ihre etwaige Gegnerschaft gegen die Nationalsozialisten erkennen** lassen, sowie diesbezügliche Tätigkeiten:
List any facts indicating anti-Nazi attitude or activities:

Geben Sie Ihre Beschäftigung durch Regierungs- und NSDAP Behörden einschliesslich die Art der Beschäftigung und wie Sie diese Anstellung erhalten haben:
List any employment by governmental or Nazi Party agencies, giving nature of duties and method of appointment:

Waren Sie vom Militärdienst zurückgestellt?
Were you deferred from military service?

Wann? *When?* Warum? *Why?*

Sind Sie jemals wegen einer strafbaren Handlung verurteilt worden?
Were you ever convicted of any criminal offense?

Falls ja, geben Sie hier in jedem einzelnen Fall Datum, Gericht, Urteil, die strafbare Handlung und das Datum der Haftentlassung:
If so, give date, court, sentence, offense and date of release in each case:

Wohin beabsichtigen Sie zu gehen, falls Sie aus der Haft entlassen werden?
If released from detention, where do you intend to go?

Maramarossziget Roumania

Geben Sie die Namen und die Anschriften dreier vertrauenswürdiger Personen an, die in dem Orte wohnen, wohin Sie gehen wollen und die für Sie bürgen können:
Give names and addresses, if known, of three reliable persons living in the locality where you intend to go, who can vouch for you:

Ferenc Stark — Maramarossziget
Ferenc Pollak — "
Samuel Jakabovits — "

Gezeichnet *Signed* Welzel [illegible]

Entscheidung des Ausschusses *Decision of the Board*: Release

Endgültige Verfügung betreffend den Lagerinsassen
Final disposal of inmate

Gezeichnet *Signed*

Vorsitzender des Ausschusses *Presiding Officer of Board*

Rang *Rank* Waffengattung *Branch* Datum *Date*

AUSSCHUSS *BOARD*

Name	Rank	Branch
Allen B, Michell	Col.	GSC
T.A. Turacouzio	Capt.	US
Leonard M. Bessman	Capt.	Inf.(CIC)
Cyrus G. Sturgis jr.	1st Lt.	A.C.

WD 48510 sn375 1 45 250M 44 5

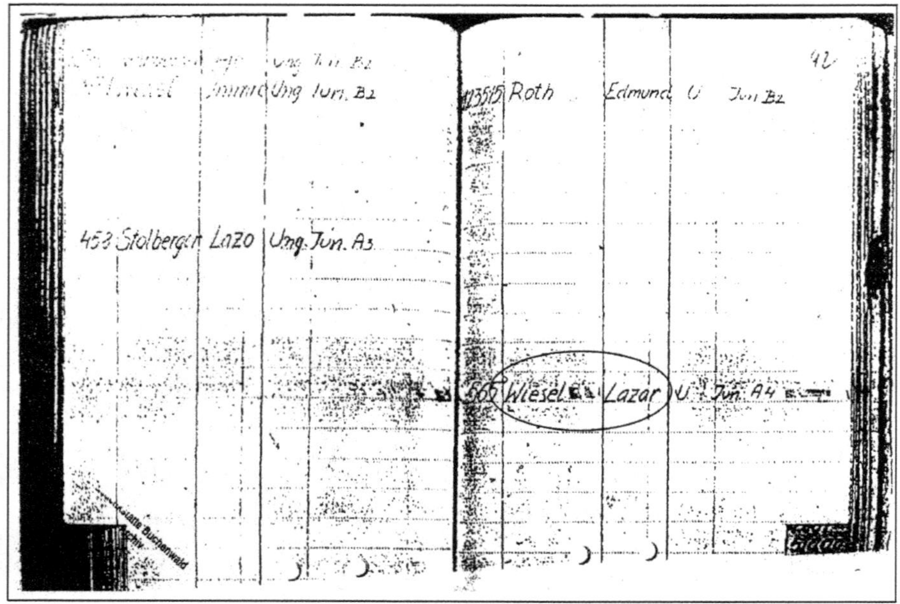

453 Stolberger Lazo Ung. Jun. A3

123515 Roth Edmund U Jun. B2

565 Wiesel Lazar U Jun. A4

Document 12: Register of Block 66 at Buchenwald:
405 Wiesel Lazar 4/10/28 Marmarossziget, " [Romanian]

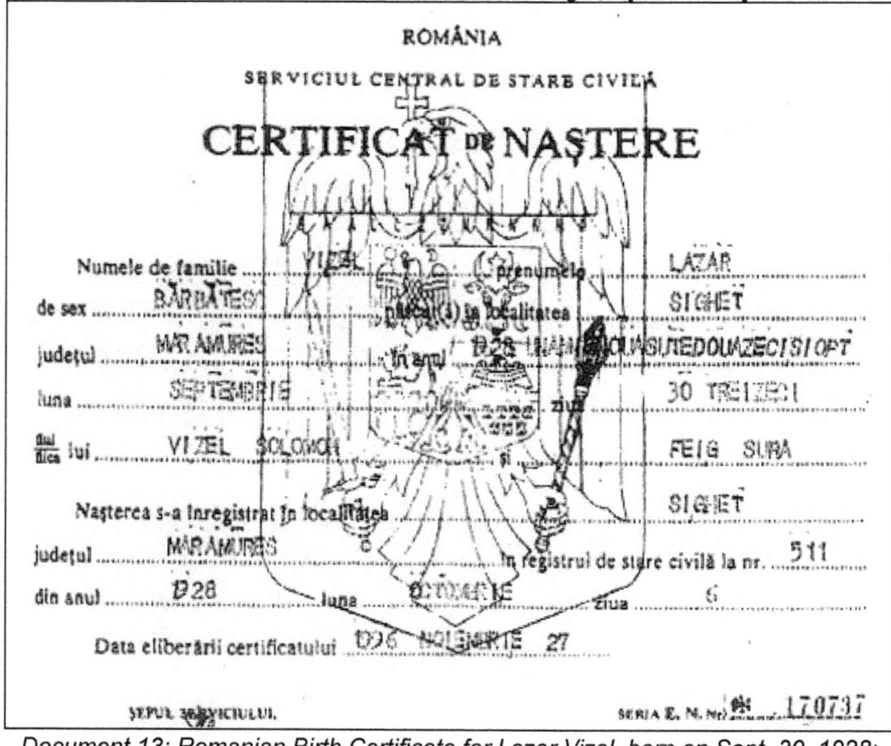

ROMÂNIA

SERVICIUL CENTRAL DE STARE CIVILĂ

CERTIFICAT DE NAŞTERE

Numele de familie VIZEL prenumele LAZĂR

de sex BĂRBĂTESC născut(ă) în localitatea SIGHET

judeţul MARAMUREŞ în anul 1928 UNAMIEDOUĂSUTEDOUĂZECIŞIOPT

luna SEPTEMBRIE ziua 30 TREIZECI

fiul/fiica lui VIZEL SOLOMON şi FEIG SURA

Naşterea s-a înregistrat în localitatea SIGHET

judeţul MARAMUREŞ în registrul de stare civilă la nr. 511

din anul 1928 luna OCTOMBRIE ziua 6

Data eliberării certificatului 1996 NOIEMBRIE 27

ŞEFUL SERVICIULUI, SERIA E. N. Nr. 170737

Document 13: Romanian Birth Certificate for Lazar Vizel, born on Sept. 30, 1928; issued on No. 27, 1996.

U. Jude

Konzentrationslager Art der Haft: A 5763 Gef.-Nr.: 121761

Name und Vorname: Jakubowits Samuel

geb.: 2.10.1926 zu Marmaros Sziget. Kom. Marmoros

Wohnort: W. o. Moric Jamo 9

Beruf: Schüler (erlernter Tischler) Rel.: mos:

Staatsangehörigkeit: Ungarn Stand: ledig

Name der Eltern: Vater: Holzhändler Ferenc Jakubowits Rasse: ...

Wohnort: Mutter: Ester geb. Pollak —"—

Name der Ehefrau: Rasse:

Wohnort:

Kinder: Alleiniger Ernährer der Familie oder der Eltern:

Vorbildung: 26/I 45 26.1.45 KL. Auschwitz

Militärdienstzeit: von — bis 4959

Kriegsdienstzeit: von — bis

Grösse: Nase: Haare: Gestalt:

Mund: Bart: Gesicht: Ohren:

Sprache: Augen: Zähne:

Document 14: Buchenwald file card of Samuel Jakobovits

12.179 121.761

MG/PS/G/14

MILITARY GOVERNMENT OF GERMANY

FRAGEBOGEN FÜR INSASSEN DER KONZENTRATIONSLAGER
CONCENTRATION CAMP INMATES QUESTIONNAIRE

Name des Konzentrationslagers / *Name of Concentration Camp*: Buchenwald — Datum / *Date*: April 22 – 1945

Ort / *Location*: Buchenwald

Name des Lagerinsassen / *Name of Inmate*: Zuname / *Last*: Jakobovits — Vornamen / *First*: Sámuel — *Initial*:

Geschlecht / *Sex*: male — Geburtsdatum / *Date of Birth*: Oct 2 – 1926

Staatsangehörigkeit / *Nationality*: Roumanian — Glaubensbekenntnis / *Religion*: Jew

Wohnungsanschrift / *Home Address*: Máramarossziget Roumania

[Be]ruf / *[O]ccupation*: student

Datum der Verhaftung / *Date of Arrest*: April 16 – 1944 — Durch Wen / *By whom*: Police

Ort der Verhaftung / *Place of Arrest*: Máramarossziget

Grund für Verhaftung / *Reason for Arrest*: being a Jew

Anklage erhoben / *Charges Made*:

Erkennendes Gericht / *Court Trying Case*:

Namen der Richter / *Names of Judges*:

Urteil / *Sentence*:

Wo in Haft gewesen und wie lange / *Place of Detention Giving Dates*: Auschwitz (2 days), Manovitz (8 months), Buchenwald (4 months)

Einzelheiten betreffend die Haft, im besonderen etwaige grausame Behandlung und Zeit derselben, Gründe hierfür und die Namen der Täter, falls bekannt:
Give particulars of confinement including any inhumane treatment with dates, reasons and names of perpetrators, if known:

Stellungen, die Sie während der Haft hatten
Positions held during confinement:

Haben Sie jemals der NSDAP, deren Gliederungen, angeschlossenen Verbänden oder betreuten Organisationen angehört?
Have you ever belonged to the Nazi Party or any of its affiliated or subordinate organizations?

Falls ja, geben Sie die Organisationen, die Zeit der Mitgliedschaft und die von Ihnen bekleideten Ämter an:
If so, list Organizations, dates of membership and positions held:

(Bitte wenden / Please turn)

Document 15a & b (next page): Buchenwald questionnaire of Sámuel Jakobovits dated 22 April 1945 – front and back

248

Geben Sie Ihre Militardienstzeit unter Angabe der Organisationen, Daten und des Dienstranges an:
List periods of military service giving organizations and dates as well as ranks held:

No

Geben Sie Tatsachen an, die Ihre etwaige Gegnerschaft gegen die Nationalsozialisten erkennen lassen, sowie diesbezügliche Tätigkeiten:
List any facts indicating anti-Nazi attitude or activities:

Geben Sie Ihre Beschäftigung durch Regierungs- und NSDAP Behörden einschliesslich die Art der Beschäftigung und wie Sie diese Anstellung erhalten haben:
List any employment by governmental or Nazi Party agencies, giving nature of duties and method of appointment:

Waren Sie vom Militärdienst zurückgestellt?
Were you deferred from military service?

Wann? *When?* Warum? *Why?*

Sind Sie jemals wegen einer strafbaren Handlung verurteilt worden?
Were you ever convicted of any criminal offense?

Falls ja, geben Sie hier in jedem einzelnen Fall Datum, Gericht, Urteil, die strafbare Handlung und das Datum der Haftentlassung:
If so, give date, court, sentence, offense and date of release in each case:

Wohin beabsichtigen Sie zu gehen, falls Sie aus der Haft entlassen werden?
If released from detention, where do you intend to go?

Maramarossziget Roumania

Geben Sie die Namen und die Anschriften dreier vertrauenswürdiger Personen an, die in dem Orte wohnen, wohin Sie gehen wollen und die für Sie bürgen können:
Give names and addresses, if known, of three reliable persons living in the locality where you intend to go, who can vouch for you:

Mr Hersch Fischmann Maramarossziget
" Antal Meisner "
" Lázár Wiesel "

Gezeichnet [signature]
Signed

Entscheidung des Ausschusses — Release
Decision of the Board

Endgültige Verfügung betreffend den Lagerinsassen
Final disposal of inmate

Gezeichnet [signature] Vorsitzender des Ausschusses
Signed *Presiding Officer of Board*

Capt [signature]

Rang / *Rank* Waffengattung / *Branch* Datum / *Date*

AUSSCHUSS
BOARD

Name	Rank	Branch
Allen B. Michell	Col.	GSC
T.A. Taracouzio	Capt.	AUS
Leonard M. Bessman	Capt.	Inf. (CIC)
Cyrus C. Sturgis jr.	1th Lt.	A,C.

W1 4851/a/e373/1 45 250m 44-5

Document 16a & b: The two 1947 drawings by David Olère showing a scene similar to the one described by Wiesel (taken from www.infocenters.co.il/).

Bibliography

- "1,000 Nazi Death Camp Survivors Meet Here; Honor British Liberator of Belsen as They Observe 20th Year of Freedom," *New York Times*, November 25, 1965, 61.
- "A Survivor's Prize," *New York Times*, January 4, 1987, XIII, 3.
- "Anti-Defamation League: Wiesel Spends Lifetime Searching for Words," *15 Minutes Magazine*, July/August 2004. http://15minutesmagazine.com/archives/issue_60/leica.htm.
- "Auschwitz Memorial Partly Opened, Water Receding," *Taiwan News*, May 20, 2010.
- "Author Defends Disputed Holocaust Memoir: Herman Rosenblat Says Love Story, Promoted by Oprah, Is Based on Vivid Childhood Memories," *CBS News*, December 26, 2008.
- "Ben-Gurion Here to Lead Zionists," *New York Times*, May 10, 1947, 4.
- "Boston Author's Book a Holocaust Hoax," *Providence Journal*, April 27, 2008, I, 1.
- "Cardinal Pio Laghi, RIP," *The Catholic World Report*, March 9, 2009, 6.
- "Flooding Causes Holocaust Site to Close," *Atlanta Journal-Constitution*, May 19, 2010, A4.
- "Jeremiah II," *Time*, December 25, 1978, 81.
- "John Paul Cites Suffering of Jews; Criticized, He Says Ordeal of All Nazis' Victims Was a 'Gift to the World,'" *New York Times*, June 26, 1988, A6.
- "Keeping Up With the Stallones: What To Remember About 1986," *Newsweek*, December 29, 1986, 66.
- "L'aide des régions pour rénover Auschwitz pourrait être de 1 à 3 M euros," *La Croix*, February 7, 2010.
- "Maya Angelou and Elie Wiesel on Love, Hate, and Humanity," *Massachusetts*, Spring 1995, 4.
- "Mission to Cambodia," *New York Times*, January 16, 1980, B2.
- "Nombre record de visites à Auschwitz," *7sur7* (Belgian TV news station), January 3, 2010.
- "Rabbi Fights Poles," *New York Times*, January 27, 1995, 5.
- "Remembering Auschwitz," *New York Times*, January 26, 1995, A20.
- "Report 'Shoah' Got Grant from Israel," *The Jewish Journal* (New York), June 27, 1986, 3.
- "Wiesel Slams Pope's Comments," *News24.com*, November 17, 2003.
- Abrahamson, Irving, *Against Silence: The Voice and Vision of Elie Wiesel* (New York: Holocaust Library, 1985).
- Agence France-Presse, "Elie Wiesel Expects Obama to Be 'Very Moved' by Visit in Buchenwald," *European Jewish News*, June 5, 2009; http://ejpress.org/index.php?option=com_content&view=article&id=14777&catid=9:germany&Itemid=5.
- Alvarez, A., "*Night*," *Commentary*, October 1964, 65.

___"The Concentration Camps," *The Atlantic Monthly*, December 1962, 69-72.

- Alvarez, Santiago, *The Gas Vans: A Critical Investigation* (Washington, D.C.: The Barnes Review, 2011).
- Arendt, Hannah, *Eichmann in Jerusalem: A Report on the Banality of Evil* (New York: Viking Press, 1963).
- Arnaud, Pierre, *Les STO: Histoire des Français requis en Allemagne nazie, 1942-1945* (Paris: Centre National de Recherche Scientifique, 2010.).
- Association Internationale de Droit Pénal, *VIe Congrès International tenu à Rome du 27 septembre au 3 octobre 1953 sous les auspices du Gouvernement de la République Italienne. Comptes rendues des discussions* (Milano: Giuffré, 1957).
- Attanasio, Paul, "Resurrecting the Horror on Film: Claude Lanzmann's Long Struggle With the Holocaust and 'Shoah,'" *The Washington Post*, November 20, 1985, B1.
- Auswärtiges Amt, *Amtliches Material zum Massenmord von Katyn* (Berlin: Franz Eher Nachf., 1943).
  ___*Amtliches Material zum Massenmord von Winniza* (Berlin: Franz Eher Nachf., 1944).
- Aynat, Enrique, "Die Sterbebücher von Auschwitz: Statistische Daten über die Sterblichkeit der 1942 aus Frankreich nach Auschwitz deportierten Juden," *Vierteljahreshefte für freie Geschichtsforschung*, vol. 2, no. 3, 1998, 188-198.
- Bacque, James, *Crimes and Mercies: The Fate of German Civilians under Allied Occupation, 1944-1950* (Vancouver: Talonbooks, 2007).
  ___*Other Losses: The Shocking Truth behind the Mass Deaths of Disarmed German Soldiers and Civilians under Gen. Eisenhower's Command* (Rocklin, Ca.: Prima Publishing, 1989).
- Badiou, Alain, "François Wahl ou la vie dans la pensée, " *Le Monde*, September 16, 2014.
- Ball, John C., *Air Photo Evidence: Auschwitz, Treblinka, Majdanek, Sobibor, Bergen Belsen, Belzec, Babi Yar, Katyn Forest* (Delta: Ball Resource Services, 1992); 3rd, corrected and expanded ed.: *Air Photo Evidence: World War Two Photos of Alleged Mass Murder Sites Analyzed* (Uckfield, UK: Castle Hill Publishers, 2015).
- Banerjee, Neela, "Conservative Rabbis to Vote on Resolution Criticizing Pope's Revision of Prayer," *New York Times*, February 9, 2008, A9.
- Banon, David *et al.*, *Présence d'Elie Wiesel* (Geneva: Labor et Fides, 1990).
- Barré, Jean-Luc, *François Mauriac, biographie intime I, 1885 – 1940*, vol. 1 (Paris: Arthème Fayard, 2009).
  ___*François Mauriac, biographie intime II, 1940 – 1970*, vol. 2 (Paris: Arthème Fayard, 2010).
- Bauer, Yehuda, *A History of the Holocaust* (New York: Benjamin Watts, 1982).
  ___*The Holocaust in Historical Perspective* (Seattle: University of Washington Press, 1978).
- Bedford, Sybille, "The Worst That Ever Happened," *The Saturday Evening Post*, October 22, 1966, 92.
- Benz, Wolfgang (ed.), *Dimension des Völkermords* (Munich: Oldenbourg, 1991).
- Berenbaum, Michael, "The Spoken Word and the Temptation of Silence," *America*, November 19, 1988, 413.
  ___"The Struggle for Civility: The Auschwitz Controversy and the Forces Behind It," in: Rittner, Roth, *Memory Offended*. .
- Berg, Friedrich P., "Poison Gas 'Über Alles'," *The Revisionist*, vol. 1, no. 1, 2003, 37-47.
- Berger, Joseph, "O'Connor Tours the Holocaust Museum," *New York Times*, January 3, 1987, A3.
  ___"O'Connor, Ending Visit to Israel, Stresses the Plight of the Palestinians," *New York Times*, January 6, 1987, A12.
  ___"Once Rarely Explored, the Holocaust Gains Momentum as a School Topic," *New York Times*, October 3, 1988, A16.
  ___"Pepi Deutsch, 101, Holocaust Survivor with Remarkable Tale," *New York Times*, November 8, 1999, A29.
  ___"The View from St. Patrick's," *New York Times*, March 28, 1989, SM38.

___"Witness to Evil," *New York Times*, October 14, 1985, I, 10.
- Bernstein, Richard, "Wiesel Testifies at Barbie's Trial," *New York Times*, June 3, 1987, A7.
- Bertram, Günter, "Panischer Schnellschuss: Die Volksverhetzungs-Novelle 2005," in: *Mitteilungen des Hamburger Richtervereins*, no. 2, 2005, 24-28.
- Black, Edwin, "Survivors Oppose the Transfer of Holocaust Archive to D. C.," *JTS Wire Service*, May 10, 2007.
- Black, Edwin, "Survivors Outraged at Holocaust Museum over Bad Arolsen," *History News Network*, May 13, 2007 ; http://historynewsnetwork.org/article/38788.
- Blet, Pierre, *Pie XII et la seconde guerre mondiale d'après les archives du Vatican* (Paris: Perrin, 1997).
  ___*Pius XII and the Second World War: According to the Archives of the Vatican* (New York: Paulist, 2000).
- Boüard, Michel de, "Où ai-je acquis la conviction qu'il y avait une chambre à gaz à Mauthausen?," *Ouest-France*, August 2/3, 1986, 3.
- Bourdieu, Pierre, *La Distinction. Critique sociale du jugement* (Paris: Minuit, 1979).
- Boxer, Sarah, "Giving Memory Its Due in an Age of License," *New York Times*, October 28, 1998, C1, C6.
- Bozonnet, Jean-Jacques, "Des évêques basques défient leur hiérarchie en honorant la mémoire de prêtres tués par des soldats de Franco," *Le Monde*, July 14, 2009.
- Braham, Randolph L., *A Magyar Holocaust* (Budapest/Wilmington: Gondolat/Blackburn International, 1988).
- Brean, Joseph, "Salman Rushdie: 'We Are in Danger of Losing the Battle for Freedom of Speech,'" *National Post*, May 31, 2010.
- Breslin S.J., John B., "Elie Wiesel, Survivor and Witness," *America*, June 19, 1976, 537ff.
- Brozan, Nadine, "Chronicle," *New York Times*, June 20, 1992, A24.
  ___"Out of Death, a Zest for Life," *New York Times*, November 15, 1982, C20.
- Brugioni, Dino A., and Robert G. Poirier, *The Holocaust Revisited: A Retrospective Analysis of the Auschwitz-Birkenau Extermination Complex* (Washington, DC: The Central Intelligence Agency, 1979).
- Burg, Josef G., *Majdanek in alle Ewigkeit* (Munich: Ederer, 1979).
  ___*NS-Verbrechen: Prozesse des schlechten Gewissens unter Zions Regie* (Munich: G. Fischer, 1968).
  ___*Schuld und Schicksal: Europas Juden zwischen Henkern und Heuchlern* (Munich: Damm Verlag, 1962). .
  ___*Sündenböcke: Grossangriffe des Zionismus auf Papst Pius XII. und auf die deutschen Regierungen* (Munich: G. Fischer, 1967).
  ___*Zionnazi-Zensur in der BRD* (Munich: Ederer, 1980).
- Butz, Arthur R., "Robert Graham and Revisionism," *The Journal of Historical Review*, vol. 17, no. 2, March/April 1998, 24f.
  ___*The Hoax of the Twentieth Century* (Brighton, UK: Historical Review Press, 1976; 4th ed.: Uckfield: Castle Hill Publishers, 2015).
- Calvet, Jean, *Le renouveau catholique dans la littérature contemporaine* (Paris: Lanore, 1927).
- Cargas, Harry James J. (ed.), *Responses to Elie Wiesel* (New York: Persea, 1978).
  ___"After Auschwitz: A Certain Script. An Interview with Elie Wiesel," *The Christian Century*, September 17, 1975, 791f.
  ___"What is a Jew? Harry James Cargas Interviews Elie Wiesel," *U.S. Catholic/Jubilee*, September 1971, 28.
  ___*Harry James Cargas in Conversation with Elie Wiesel* (New York: Paulist Press, 1976); 2nd ed.: *Conversations with Elie Wiesel* (Notre Dame, Ind.: Justice Books, 1992).
- Carroll, James, "The Pope's Big Holocaust Lie," *The Daily Beast*, December 24, 2009; www.thedailybeast.com/blogs-and-stories/2009-12-23/the-popes-big-holocaust-lie/full/.

___"Witness: For Elie Wiesel Silence Is Not an Option: *And the Sea Is Never Full, Memoirs*," *New York Times Book Review*, January 2, 2000, BR10.
___*Constantine's Sword* (Boston: Houghton-Mifflin, 2001).
- Caulfield, Brian, "Holocaust Memorial: Cardinal Asks Forgiveness for Christians Who Turned Their Backs on Jews," *Catholic New York*, September 18, 1997, 14f.
___"University Award: Cardinal Honored for Promoting Catholic Jewish Relations," *Catholic New York*, November 13, 1997, 12.
- Charlton, Angela, "Ukraine Killing Fields Not Forgotten: Elderly Provide Chilling Details," *Atlanta Journal-Constitution*, July 6, 2007, C1, C4.
- Chelain, André (=Henri Roques), *La thèse de Nantes et l'affaire Roques* (Paris: Polémiques, 1989).
___*Le procès Barbie, ou le shoah-business à Lyon* (Paris: Polémiques, 1987).
- Chmiel, Mark, *Elie Wiesel and the Politics of Moral Leadership* (Philadelphia: Temple University Press, 2001).
- Christophersen, Thies, *Auschwitz* (London: Steven Books, 2007).
___*Die Auschwitz-Lüge* (Mohrkirch: Kritik-Verlag, 1973).
- Clarity, James F., "Brandt to Visit Israel; Notes on People," *New York Times*, April 3, 1973, 39.
- Clausen, Oliver, "Auschwitz: It Still Stands," *New York Times*, October 16, 1966, B1.
- Cockburn, Alexander, "Beat the Devil," *The Nation*, November 8, 1986, 478.
___"Did Oprah Pick another Fibber? Truth and Fiction in Elie Wiesel's *Night*: Is Frey or Wiesel the Bigger Moral *Poseur*?" Counterpunch.com, April 1-2, 2006.
___"Judy Miller's War," *Counterpunch.com*, August 18, 2003.
___"Letters: Cockburn Replies," *The Nation*, December 20, 1986, 690.
- Cohen, Brigitte-Fanny, *Elie Wiesel, qui êtes-vous?* (Lyon: La Manufacture, 1987).
- Cohen, Monique-Lise, Jean-Louis Dufour, *Les Juifs dans la Résistance suivi de La Présence juive en Europe et l'écriture de l'histoire* (Paris: Tirésias, 2001).
- Cohen, Roger, "French Church Issues Apology to Jews on War," *New York Times*, October 1, 1997, A1, A8.
- Cohen, Steven M., "Half of U.S. Jews for Palestinian Homeland," *New York Times*, July 1, 1986, A22.
- Cointet, Michèle, and Rainer Riemenschneider, Philippe Bernard, Jacques Lebailly, "Histoire, déontologie, médias: à propos de l'affaire Roques," *Revue d'Histoire Moderne et Contemporaine*, vol. 34, no. 1 (Jan-Mar 1987), 174-184.Bouïeff, Boris, *Pays de rigueur* (Paris: Seuil, 1951).
- Cole, David, *David Cole in Auschwitz: David Cole Interviews Dr. Franciszek Piper, Director, Auschwitz State Museum*; http://holocausthandbooks.com/index.php?page_id=1004.
___*Republican Party Animal: The "Bad Boy of Holocaust History" Blows the Lid off Hollywood's Secret Right-Wing Underground* (Los Angeles: Feral House, 2014).
- Commission for Religious Relations with the Jews (ed.), "We Remember: A Reflection on the Shoah," March 16, 1998; www.vatican.va/roman_curia/pontifical_councils/chrstuni/documents/rc_pc_chrstuni_doc_16031998_shoah_en.html.
- Conan, Éric, "Auschwitz: la mémoire du mal," *L'Express*, January 19-25, 1995, 54-73.
- Conquest, Robert, *The Harvest of Sorrow: Soviet Collectivization and the Terror-famine* (Oxford: Oxford University Press, 1987).
- Conway, John S., "History, Hitler, and the Holocaust," *The International History Review*, vol. VII, no. 3, August 1985, 441-450.
- Cooper, Helene, "Obama Tries to Mend Fences with American Jews," *New York Times*, May 4, 2010, A6.
- Cornwell, John, *Hitler's Pope* (London: Penguin, 2002).
- Cuesta, Jose Luis de la (ed.), *Resolutions of the Congresses of the International Association of Penal Law (1926 – 2004)* (Toulouse: Érès, 2009).
- Cueva, Julio de la, "Religious Persecution, Anticlerical Tradition and Revolution: On

Atrocities against the Clergy during the Spanish Civil War," *Journal of Contemporary History*, 33 (1998), 355.
- Czech, *Danuta, Kalendarium der Ereignisse im Konzentrationslager Auschwitz-Birkenau 1939-1945* (Reinbek bei Hamburg: Rowohlt Verlag, 1989).
- Dalton, Thomas, "The Great Holocaust Mystery: Reconsidering the Evidence," *Inconvenient History*, vol. 6, no. 3, fall 2014.
  ___*Debating the Holocaust*, (New York: Theses & Dissertations Press, 2009).
- Dargis, Manohla, "Innocence Is Lost in Postwar Germany: Film Review," *New York Times*, December 10, 2008, C1.
- De Witt, Karen, "Holocaust Museum's New Chief Resigns," *New York Times*, March 4, 1995, 11.
- Defonseca, Misha, *Misha: A Memoire of the Holocaust Years* (Boston: Mt. Ivy, 1997).
- Delacroix, Simon (ed.), *Les Documents pontificaux de S.S. Pie XII*, 21 vols. (Saint-Maurice (Switzerland): Ed. Saint-Augustin, 1962/63).
- Dempsey, Judy, "Perplexity after Auschwitz Sign Theft," *New York Times*, December 24, 2009, A6.
  ___"Sign over Auschwitz Gate Is Stolen," *New York Times*, December 18, 2009, A6.
- Denny, Harold, "The World Must Not Forget," *New York Times*, May 6, 1945, 42.
- Desbois, Patrick, *Porteur de Mémoires: sur les Traces de la Shoah par Balles* (Neuilly-sur-Seine: Ed. Michel Lafon, 2007).
  ___*The Holocaust by Bullets: A Priest's Journey to Uncover the Truth Behind the Murder of 1.5 Million Jews* (New York: Palgrave Macmillan, 2009).
- Desjardins, Dan, "Critique of John S. Conway's Review," *The Journal of Historical Review*, vol. 7, no. 3, 1986, 375, 379.
- Devereaux, Elizabeth, "Elie Wiesel," *Publisher's Weekly*, April 6, 1992, 29f.
- Dionne, Jr., E. J., "O'Connor Calls for a Homeland for the Palestinians," *New York Times*, June 19, 1986, A2.
- District Court of Ontario, Her Majesty the Queen - versus - Ernst Zündel, before: The Honourable Judge H.R. Locke and a Jury; ref. AG 87 (6/76) 7540-1171; www.codoh.com/library/document/3355.
- Długoborski, Wacław, and Franciszek Piper (eds.), *Auschwitz 1940-1945. Studien zur Geschichte des Konzentrations- und Vernichtungslagers Auschwitz* (Auschwitz: Verlag des Staatlichen Museums Auschwitz-Birkenau, 1999).
- Dodd, Christopher J., with Larry Bloom, *Letters from Nuremberg: My Father's Narrative of the Quest for Justice*. (New York: Crown, 2007).
- Donadio, Rachel, "Popes Move Closer to Sainthood," *New York Times*, December 20, 2009, A13.
- Downing, Frederick L., *Elie Wiesel: A Religious Biography* (Macon, Ga., Mercer University Press, 2008).
- Dreyfus, Alfred, *Cinq Années de ma vie* (Paris: Fasquelle, 1962).
- Drieu la Rochelle, Pierre, "Journal politique: à Propos du Racisme," in: Ganier-Raymond, *Une Certaine France*, 42-47.
- Drinan, Robert F., *Honor the Promise: America's Commitment to Israel* (Garden City, New York: Doubleday, 1977).
- Droit, Michel, *Les Feux du Crépuscule, Journal 1968 -1969 -1970* (Paris: Plon, 1977).
- Dupras, Tosha L., *et al.*, *Forensic Recovery of Human Remains: Archaeological Approaches* (2nd ed., Boca Raton, Fl.: CRC Press, 2012).
- Durand, François (ed.), *Mauriac: Œuvres autobiographiques* (Paris: Pléiade, 1990).
- Ecole des Hautes Etudes en Science Sociale (ed.), *L'Allemagne nazie et le génocide juif* (Paris: Gallimard/Le Seuil, 1985).
- Ekkehard Schuster (ed.), *Hope against Hope: Johann Baptist Metz and Elie Wiesel Speak out on the Holocaust* (New York: Paulist, 1999).
- Ellis, Marc H., *Innocence and Redemption: Confronting the Holocaust and Israeli Power* (New York: Harper & Row, 1990).
  ___*Judaism Does Not Equal Israel: A Call for a Return to Prophetic Jewish Value* (N.Y.:

New Press, 2009).
- Evans, Richard J., *Lying about Hitler: History, Holocaust and the David Irving Trial* (New York: Basic Books, 2001).
- Evron, Boaz, "Holocaust, a Danger for the Jewish People," *Yiton*, no. 77, May – June 1980.
- Faurisson, Robert, "Enfants juifs: leur déportation ne signifiait pas leur extermination," February 23, 2008; http://robertfaurisson.blogspot.com/2009/03/enfants-juifs-leur-deportation-ne.html.
  ___"How many deaths at Auschwitz?", *The Revisionist*, vol. 1, no. 1, 2003, 17-23.
  ___"Les falsifications d'Auschwitz d'après un dossier de 'L'Express'," January 19, 1995; www.robertfaurisson.blogspot.com/1995/01/les-falsifications-dauschwitz-dapres-un.html.
  ___"Mémoire juive contre histoire: ou l'aversion juive pour tout examen critique de la Shoah," June 15, 2006; http://robertfaurisson.blogspot.com/2009/03/memoire-juive-contre-histoire-ou.html.
  ___"The Zündel Trials (1985 and 1988)," *The Journal of Historical Review*, vol. 8, no. 4, winter 1988/89, 417-443.
  ___*Écrits Révisionnistes (1974-1998)* (Vichy: self-published, 1999).
  ___*Le révisionnisme de Pie XII* (Genoa: Graphos Edizioni, 2002).
  ___*Mémoire en défense: contre ceux qui m'accuse de falsifier l'histore* (Paris: La Vieille Taupe, 1980).
  ___*Pope Pius XII's Revisionism* (Uckfield, UK: Historical Review Press, 2006).
- Favez, Jean-Claude, "Elie Wiesel et la Shoah," in: Banon, *Présence*, 69-75.
- Feron, James, "A Bonn Minister Visits Auschwitz; Scheel Lays Wreath during Tour of Nazi Death Camp," *New York Times*, November 9, 1970, 16.
- Fine, Ellen S., *Legacy of Night: The Literary Universe of Elie Wiesel* (Albany, N.Y.: SUNY Press, 1982).
- Finkelstein, Norman G., *The Holocaust Industry: Reflections on the Exploitation of Jewish Suffering* (London: Verso, 2000; 2nd ed., *ibid.*, 2003).
- Finkielkraut, Alain, *Remembering in Vain: The Klaus Barbie Trial and Crimes against Humanity* (New York: Columbia University Press, 1992).
- Fisher, Eugene, Leon Klenicki (eds.), *Pope John Paul II, Spiritual Pilgrimage: Texts on Jews and Judaism 1979–1995* (New York: Crossroad, 1995).
- Fisher, Ian, "A German Pope Confronts the Nazi Past at Auschwitz," *New York Times*, May 29, 2006, A7.
  ___"Pope Eases Restrictions on Wider Use of Latin Mass: Stresses Current Rite to Remain Standard," *New York Times*, July 8, 2007, A4.
  ___"Pope's Rewrite of Latin Prayer Draws Criticism from 2 Sides," *New York Times*, February 6, 2008, A8.
- Fiske, Edward B., "Elie Wiesel: Archivist with a Mission; Charisma without a Beard," *New York Times*, January 31, 1973, 43.
- Flannery, Edward H., *The Anguish of the Jews: Twenty-Three Centuries of Anti-Semitism.* (New York: Macmillan, 1965).
- Flanzbaum, Hilène (ed.), *The Americanization of the Holocaust* (Baltimore: Johns Hopkins University Press, 1999).
- Fleischner, Eva, "Mauriac's Preface to *Night*: Thirty Years Later," *America*, November 19, 1988, 419.
- Forges, Jean-François, *Eduquer contre Auschwitz* (Paris: ESF, 1997).
- Franchetti, Mark, "How the CIA Won Zhivago a Nobel," *Sunday Times* (London), January 14, 2007, 6.
- Franklin, Ruth, *A Thousand Darknesses: Lies and Truth in Holocaust Fiction* (New York: Oxford University Press, 2011).
- Freedman, Samuel G., "Bearing Witness: The Life and Work of Elie Wiesel," *New York Times*, October 23, 1983, 32-36, 40, 65-69.
- Friedlander, Albert H., *Out of the Whirlwind: A Reader of Holocaust Literature* (Garden

City, New York: Doubleday, 1968).
- Friedman, Philip, and Joseph Gar, *Bibliography of Yiddish Books on the Catastrophe and Heroism* (New York: YIVO Institute for Jewish Research, 1962).
- Friedrich, Otto, "The Kingdom of Auschwitz," *The Atlantic Monthly*, September 1981, 30-60.
- Further Glory, "Whatever happened to Ken Waltzer's proposed book about the Buchenwald orphans?," July 17, 2013; https://furtherglory.wordpress.com/2013/07/17/whatever-happened-to-ken-waltzers-proposed-book-about-the-buchenwald-orphans/.
- Ganier-Raymond, Philippe (ed.), *Une Certaine France: l'Antisémitisme 1940-1944* (Paris: Balland, 1975).
- Gauss, Ernst (ed., Germar Rudolf), *Dissecting the Holocaust*: *The Growing Critique of "Truth" and "Memory,"* (Capshaw, Al.: Theses & Dissertations Press, 2000).
  ___(ed.), *Grundlagen zur Zeitgeschichte* (Tübingen: Grabert, 1994).
  ___*Vorlesungen über Zeitgeschichte* (Tübingen: Grabert Verlag, 1993); 2nd ed.: Germar Rudolf, *Vorlesungen über den Holocaust* (Hastings, UK: Castle Hill Publishers, 2005; 3rd ed.: Uckfield, UK: Castle Hill Publishers, 2012).
- Geller, Jay, "The Wilkomirski Case: Fragments or Figments?," *American Imago* 59 (Fall 2002), 343-365.
- Gill, Brendan, "Zalmen," *The New Yorker*, November 29, 1976, 64.
- Glatstein, Jacob, and Israel Knox, Samuel Margoshes (eds.), *Anthology of Holocaust Literature* (New York: Atheneum, 1968).
- Goldberg, Jeffrey, "The Exaggerators," *New Republic*, February 8, 1993, 13f.
- Goldberg, Michael, *Why Should Jews Survive? Looking Past the Holocaust toward a Jewish Future* (New York: Oxford University Press, 1996).
- Goldman, Ari L., "A. M. Rosenthal: New York Times Editor and Advocate for Israel," *New York Times*, May 19, 2006, A1.
  ___"For Cardinal, Wiesel Visit Proved a Calm in Storm over Trip," *New York Times*, February 15, 1987, I, 67.
  ___"Jewish Groups Fault O'Connor on Mideast Trip," *New York Times*, January 11, 1987, A1.
  ___"O'Connor Is Upset by Critics of Trip," *New York Times*, January 12, 1987, A1.
  ___"Blacks and Jews Join Hands for an Even Brighter Future," *New York Times*, December 18, 1992; B1.
- Goldsmith, Samuel, "Pope Benedict Declares Pius XII 'Venerable,' Angering Jewish Groups," *New York Daily News*, December 19, 2009; www.nydailynews.com/news/world/1.433879.
- Goodman, Walter, "Elie Wiesel: A Self-Portrait," *New York Times*, November 10, 1988, A10.
- Goodstein, Laurie, "Poll Shows Major Shift in Identity of U.S. Jews," *New York Times*, October 1, 2013, A11.
- Göran Holming, "Himmlers Befehl, die Vergasung der Juden zu stoppen," *Vierteljahreshefte für freie Geschichtsforschung*, vol. 1. no. 4, 1997, 258f.
- Graf, Jürgen, "Hungarian Holocaust Debate: Otto Perge vs. Dr. Laszlo Karsai," June 2010; http://juergen-graf.vho.org/articles/hungarian-holocaust-debate.html.
  ___ and Carlo Mattogno; *Concentration Camp Majdanek: A Historical and Technical Study* (3rd ed., Washington, DC: The Barnes Review, 2012).
- Graham, Robert A., *et al.* (eds.), *Actes et documents du Saint Siège relatifs à la seconde guerre mondiale*, 12 vols. (Vatican City: Libreria Editrice Vaticana, 1967-1982).
- Gross, Tom, "Real Horrors: Phony Claims: Duping the Holocaust Experts," *WSJ*, February 6, 2002.
- Grüner, Nikolaus Michael (Miklós), *Stolen Identity: Auschwitz Number A-7713* (Stockholm: self-published by the author, 2007).
- Guttenplan, Don D., *The Holocaust on Trial: History, Justice and the David Irving Libel Case* (London: Granta Books, 2001).
- Haberman, Clyde, "Wiesel and Walesa Visit Auschwitz," *New York Times*, January 18,

1988, A3.

- Hagerty, Ryan, "Calling Holocaust a 'Failure of Humanity,' Scholar Also Targets Iranian President," *Chicago Tribune*, October 17, 2007; http://articles.chicagotribune.com/2007-10-17/news/0710160876_1_elie-wiesel-holocaust-denier-holocaust-museum.
- Halkin, Léon-Ernest, *À l'ombre de la mort* (Tournai: Casterman, 1947).
- Hall, Robert A., "The Gerstein Report: The Anatomy of a Fraud,"*The Journal of Historical Review*, vol. 7, no. 1, 1986, 115-119.
- Halperin, Irving, "From *Night* to *The Gates of the Forest*: The Novels of Elie Wiesel," in: Cargas, *Responses to Elie Wiesel*, 45-70.
- Halpérin, Jean, "Itinéraire, paysages intérieurs et message," in: Banon, *Présence.*
- Halpern, Micah, "In Defense of Pope Benedict XVI," *MicahHalpern.com*, July 18, 2007; http://archive.frontpagemag.com/readArticle.aspx?ARTID=27417.
- Handler, M. S., "Lillian Hellman Is among Nine Named to City University Chairs," *New York Times*, September 26, 1972, 38.
- Harlow, John, "Winslet Nude Scenes Trivialise Holocaust," *The Sunday Times*, December 7, 2008; http://cma.thesundaytimes.co.uk/sto/news/world_news/article136295.ece.
- Hart, Kitty, *Return to Auschwitz: The Remarkable Story of a Girl Who Survived the Holocaust* (New York: Atheneum, 1982).
- Heddesheimer, Don, *The First Holocaust*, (reprint of 2nd ed., Washington, D.C.: The Barnes Review, 2011).
- Heller, Aron, "Bush Visits Israel's Yad Vashem Holocaust Memorial," *AP Worldstream*, January 11, 2008.
- Heller, Jonathan, *War and Conflict: Selected Images from the National Archives*, (Washington, D.C., National Archives and Records Administration, 1990).
- Herman, Edward S., and Noam Chomsky, *Manufacturing Consent: The Political Economy of the Mass Media* (New York: Pantheon, 1988).
- Herzberg, Arthur, "An Open Letter to Elie Wiesel," *New York Review of Books*, August 18, 1988, 13f.
- Het Nederlandsche Roode Kruis (ed.), *Auschwitz*, Deel VI ('s-Gravenhage: Nederlandsche Roode Kruis, 1952).
- Hilberg, Raul, *The Destruction of the European Jews* (New York: Quadrangle, 1961; 2nd ed., New York: Holmes & Meyer 1985; 3rd ed.: New Haven, Conn.: Yale University Press, 2003).
- Hinsley, F. H., *et al.*, *British Intelligence in the Second World War: Its Influence on Strategy and Operations* (London: H. M. Stationary Office, 1979; 2nd ed.: London, Cambridge University Press, 1979).
- Hitchens, Christopher, "Elie Wiesel's identitiy crisis," March 10, 2009; http://christopherhitchenswatch.blogspot.com/2009/03/elie-wiesels-identity-crisis.html.
- Hoffman II, Michael A., *The Great Holocaust Trial* (Torrance, Calif.: Institute for Historical Review, 1985; 2nd ed.: Coeure d'Alene, Idaho: Independent History and Research, 2010).
- Hoffmann, Joachim, *Stalin's War of Extermination, 1941-1945: Planning, Realization and Documentation* (Capshaw: Alab.: Theses & Dissertations Press, 2001).
- Hornaday, Ann, "Documentaries and the Oscars: No Cinderellas at the Ball," *New York Times,* March 14, 1993, H13.
- Hundley, Tom, "Struggle to mark horror of Auschwitz," *Chicago Tribune*, January 27, 2005; http://articles.chicagotribune.com/2005-01-27/news/0501270319.
- Hunt, Eric, *The Majdanek Gas Chamber Myth* (20th Century Hoax, 2014); www.holocausthandbooks.com/index.php?page_id=1009.
  ___*The Treblinka Archeology Hoax* (20th Century Hoax, 2014); www.holocausthandbooks.com/index.php?page_id=1008.
- Huttenbach, Henry R., *Martyrdom and Resistance*, vol. 11, Sept.-Oct. 1984, 2, 12.
- Imatz, Arnaud, *La Guerre d'Espagne revisitée* (2nd edition, revised and expanded; Paris: Economica, 1993).
- IMT, *Trial of the Major War Criminals before the International Military Tribunal*, 42

vols. (Nuremberg, 1947).
- Institute for Historical Review, "How Jewish Terrorists Fire-Bombed the Institute for Historical Review," May 2013; www.ihr.org/other/jdl1984arson.html.
  ___"Media Coverage of the Irving-Lipstadt Trial," *The Journal of Historical Review*, vol. 19, nos. 1&2, 2000, 40-52, 47-53.
- Italie, Hillel, "Oprah's Holocaust Memoir Recommendation, *Angel at the Fence*, Defended by Author, Publisher, Following Scrutiny," *Huffington Post*, December 26, 2008.
- Jansson, Friedrich, "Jan Karski's Visit to Belzec: a Reassessment," *Inconvenient History*, vol. 6, no. 4, 2014.
- Jones, E. Michael, "Holocaust Denial and Thought Control: Deborah Lipstadt at Notre Dame University," *Culture Wars*, May 2009, 12-27.
- Judelson, Larry, "New Holocaust Museum Director Promotes the Uniqueness of the Jewish Genocide," *Jewish Telegraph Agency*, January 3, 1995.
- Kakutani, Michiko, "When History Is a Casualty: Holocaust Denial," *New York Times*, April 30, 1993, C1.
- Kamm, Henry, "Marchers with Food Aid Get No Cambodian Response," *New York Times*, February 7, 1980, A3.
  ___"Monument Unveiled for 4 Million Killed at Auschwitz Camp," *New York Times*, April 17, 1967, I, 1.
  ___"No Mention of Jews at Buchenwald," *New York Times*, March 25, 1989, A8.
- Kaplan, Edward D., *Spiritual Radical: Abraham Joshua Heschel in America* (New Haven: Yale University Press, 2007).
- Katz, Steven T., "The Holocaust as Revelation: Fackenheim and Greenberg," www.myjewishlearning.com/beliefs/Theology/Suffering_and_Evil/Responses/Modern_Solutions/Holocaust_as_Revelation.shtml.
- Kazin, Alfred, "My Debt to Elie Wiesel and Primo Levi," in: Rosenberg, *Testimony*, 115-128.
  ___*New York* Jew (New York: Alfred A Knopf, 1978).
- Keating, John, "Memories from the Living Dead," *New York Times*, April 9, 1967, B17.
- Keleny, Jeff, and Nicholas Kulish, "At a Holocaust Site, Obama Calls Denial 'Hateful,'" *New York Times*, June 5, 2009, A8.
- Kennedy, John F., *Profiles in Courage* (New York: Harper & Brothers, 1956).
- Kertész, Imre, *Fateless,* tr. Christopher C. Wilson and Katherina M. Wilson (Evanston, Ill.: Northwestern University Press, 1992).
  ___*Fatelessness*, tr. Tim Wilkinson (New York: Knopf, 2004).
- Kessler, Eve V., "The Rage That Elie Wiesel Edited Out of *Night*," *Forward*, October 4, 1996, 1.
- Khoury, Jack, *et al.*, "Survivors Angered by Pope's 'Lukewarm' Yad Vashem Speech," *Haaretz*, May 12, 2009; www.haaretz.com/news/survivors-angered-by-pope-s-lukewarm-yad-vashem-speech-1.275872.
- King, Seth S., "Professor Causes Furor by Saying Nazi Slaying of Jews Is Myth," *New York Times*, January 28, 1977, 10.
- Klarsfeld, Serge (ed.), *L'Album d'Auschwitz* (Paris: Fils et Filles des Déportés Juifs de France, 1980).
  ___(ed.), *The Auschwitz Album: Lili Jacob's Album* (New York: Beate Klarsfeld Foundation, 1980).
  ___*Les enfants d'Izieu: une tragédie juive* (Paris: Les Fils et les Filles des Déportés Juifs de France, 1984).
  ___*The Children of Izieu: A Human Tragedy* (Washington, D.C.: U.S. Holocaust Museum, 1985).
- Köchel, Heinrich, "Open Air Incineration of Corpses," *Inconvenient History*, vol. 7, no. 1, 2015.
- Kolbert, Jack, *The Worlds of Elie Wiesel* (Selinsgrove, Pa.: Susquehanna University Press, 2001).
- Kollerstrom, Nicholas, *Breaking the Spell: The Holocaust, Myth & Reality* (Uckfield,

UK: Castle Hill Publishers: 2014).
- Korolev, Anatoly, "Doctor Zhivago and the 1959 Nobel Prize: The CIA's Secret Triumph," *RIA-Novosti*, January 20, 2009.
- Kothen, R. (ed.), *Documents Pontificaux de sa sainteté Pie XII*, vol. 13, 1951; vol 15, 1953 (Paris: La Bergerie, 1952/1954).
- Krausnick, Helmut, and Hans-Heinrich Wilhelm, *Die Truppe des Weltanschauungskrieges. Die Einsatzgruppen der Sicherheitspolizei und des SD 1938-1942* (Stuttgart: Deutsche Verlags-Anstalt, 1981).
- Kues, Thomas, "Elie Wiesel: la donnola travestiata da agnello," January 28, 2010; http://andreacarancini.blogspot.com/2010/01/elie-wiesel-la-donnola-travestita-da.html.
- Kulaszka, Barbara (ed.), *Did Six Million Really Die? Report of the Evidence in the Canadian 'False News' Trial of Ernst Zündel – 1988* (Toronto: Samisdat Publishers, 1992).
- Labro, Michel, *et al.*, "Juifs-cathos: le face à face, Finkielkraut-Domenach," *L'Evénement du jeudi*, September 28 – October 4, 1989, 86-90.
- Lacouture, Jean, *François Mauriac* (Paris: Seuil, 1980).
- Lafitte, Michel, *Un engrenage fatal: L'UGIF face aux réalités de la Shoah, 1941-1944* (Paris: L. Levi, 2003).
- Lambinus, Gene, "Television Week: Poignant Pilgrimage," *New York Times*, February 1, 1981, D39.
- Landman, Beth, and Deborah Mitchell, "A Bitter Battle over Nobel Pursuit," *New York Magazine*, vol. 29, no. 3, January 1996, 9.
- Langbein, Hermann, *People in Auschwitz* (Chapel Hill, NC: The University of North Carolina Press, 2004).
- Langer, Lawrence L. "The Dominion of Death," in: Cargas, *Response to Elie Wiesels*, 29-44.
- Lask, Thomas, "The Stain That Won't Go Away," *New York Times,* December 15, 1970, 43.
- LeMénager, Grégoire, "Les Mensonges de Marek Halter," *Le Nouvel Observateur*, October 15, 2008.
- Leuchter, Fred A., and Robert Faurisson, Germar Rudolf, *The Leuchter Reports: Critical Edition* (3rd ed., Washington, D.C.: The Barnes Review, Washington, DC, 2011).
- Levi, Primo, *If This Is a Man*, Stuart Woolf, trans. (New York: Orion, 1959).
  ___*Survival in Auschwitz: The Nazi Assault on Humanity* (New York: Collier, 1961).
- Lichtenstein, Heiner, *Warum Auschwitz nicht bombardiert wurde* (Cologne: Bund-Verlag, 1980).
- Lin, Carol, "CNN Sunday Night," *CNN.com Transcripts*, May 28, 2006; http://edition.cnn.com/TRANSCRIPTS/0605/28/snn.01.html.
- Lipstadt, Deborah E., *Denying the Holocaust* (New York: Free Press/London: Penguin Books, 1993).
  ___*History on Trial: My Day in Court with a Holocaust Denier* (New York: Ecco, 2005).
- MacLennan, Nancy, "Lie Forwards Plea on Palestine Curb," *New York Times*, June 7, 1947, 5.
- Mandelbaum, Jacques, "La Shoah et ces images qui nous manquent," *Le Monde*, January 1, 2001, 17.
- Marc H. Ellis, "Exile and the prophetic: Elie Wiesel and the history of the court Jew," December 11, 2012; http://mondoweiss.net/2012/12/exile-and-the-prophetic-elie-wiesel-and-the-history-of-the-court-jew.
- Marchione, Margherita, *Crusade of Charity: Pius XII and POWs (1939-1945)* (Mahwah, NJ: Paulist Press, 2006).
- Margalit, Avishai, "The Kitsch of Israel," *NYRB*, November 24, 1988.
- Margolick, David, "Happy Campers," *New York Times*, May 27, 2007, F20.
- Mascia, Jennifer, "Surviving the Camps but Struggling in Brooklyn," *New York Times*, January 21, 2010; www.nytimes.com/2010/01/21/nyregion/21neediest.html.
- Mattogno, Carlo "'The Truth about the Gas Chambers?' Historical Considerations relating to Shlomo Venezia's 'Unique Testimony'," *Inconvenient History*, vol. 2, no. 1, 2010;

www.inconvenienthistory.com/archive/2010/volume_2/number_1.
___"'Cremation Pits' and Ground Water Levels at Birkenau," *The Revisionist*, vol. 1, no. 1, 2003, pp. 13-16.
___"Combustion Experiments with Flesh and Animal Fat on cremations in pits in the alleged extermination camps of the Third Reich," in: *The Revisionist*, vol. 2, no. 1, February 2004, pp. 64-72.
___"Dr. Mengele's 'Medical Experiments' on Twins in the Birkenau Gypsy Camp," *Inconvenient History*, vol. 5, no. 4, 2013; www.inconvenienthistory.com/archive/2013/volume_5/number_4.
___"Elie Wiesel il 'simbolo della Shoah,'" February 16, 2015; http://olodogma.com/wordpress/2015/02/16/0969.
___"Elie Wiesel, 'The Most Authoritative Living Witness' of the Shoah?," *Inconvenient History: An Independent Revisionist Blog*, February 24, 2010.
___"Elie Wiesel: New Documents," *Inconvenient History: An Independent Revisionist Blog*, March 26, 2010.
___"Obituary: Memories about Russell Granata (Aug. 22, 1923 – Aug. 14, 2004)," *The Revisionist*, vol. 2, no. 4, 2004, 442f.
___"Patrick Desbois e le 'fosse comuni' di ebrei in Ucraina," 2009; http://ita.vho.org/052_Desbois_Fucilazioni.htm.
___"The Myth of the Extermination of the Jews," *The Journal of Historical Review*, vol. 8, nos. 2f., 1988, 133-172, 261-302.
___*Auschwitz: Crematorium I and the Alleged Homicidal Gassings* (Chicago, Ill.: Theses & Dissertations Press, 2005).
___*Auschwitz: Open Air Incinerations* (Chicago, IL: Theses & Dissertations Press, 2005).
___*Auschwitz: The Case for Sanity. A Historical and Technical Study of Jean-Claude Pressac's "Criminal Traces" and Robert Jan van Pelt's "Convergence of Evidence"* (Washington, D.C.: The Barnes Review, 2010).
___*Auschwitz: The End of a Legend* (Newport Beach, Calif.: Institute for Historical Review, 1994).
___*Bełżec in Propaganda, Testimonies, Archeological Research, and History* (Chicago, IL: Theses & Dissertations Press, 2005).
___*Il rapporto Gerstein: anatomia di un falso*, (Monfalcone: Sentinella d'Italia, 1985).
___*Inside the Gas Chambers: The Extermination of Mainstream Holocaust Historiography* (Washington, D.C.: The Barnes Review, 2014).
___*My Banned Holocaust Interview: Debate, Italian Style?* (Palos Verdes, Calif.: Granata Publishing, 1996).
___*Schiffbruch: Vom Untergang der Holocaust-Orthodoxie* (Uckfield: Castle Hill Publishers, 2011).
___*The Central Construction Office of the Waffen-SS and Police Auschwitz: Organization, Responsibilities, Activities Special Treatment* (Chicago, IL: Theses & Dissertations Press, 2005).
___*The Crematories of Auschwitz: A Critique of Jean-Claude Pressac* (Palos Verdes, Calif.: Granata Publishing, 1993).
___, and Jürgen Graf, *Treblinka: Extermination Camp or Transit Camp?* (2nd ed., Chicago, IL: Theses & Dissertations Press, 2005).
___, and Thomas Kues, Jürgen Graf, *The "Extermination Camps" of "Aktion Reinhardt": An Analysis and Refutation of Factitious "Evidence," Deceptions and Flawed Argumentation of the "Holocaust Controversies" Bloggers* (Uckfield, UK: Castle Hill Publishers, 2013).
– Maurel, Micheline, *Un camp très ordinaire* (Paris: Minuit, 1957).
– Mauriac, Claude, *Ce qui était perdu* (Paris: Grasset, 1930).
___*Le temps immobile II: Les espaces imaginaires* (Paris: Grasset, 1976).
___*Le temps immobile X: L'oncle Marcel* (Paris: Grasset, 1988).
___"Le premier des nôtres," *Le Figaro*, August 25, 1945, 1.

___"Un enfant juif," *Le Figaro littéraire*, June 7, 1958, 1, 4.
___, as "Forez," *Le cahier noir* (Paris: Les Éditions de Minuit, 1943).
___*Bloc-Notes, I, 1952-1957*, ed. Jean Touzot (Paris: Seuil, 1993).
___*Bloc-Notes, III, 1961-1963*, ed. Jean Touzot (Paris: Seuil, 1993).
___*Journal du temps de l'occupation,* in *Œuvres Complètes*, vol. II, 347-351.
___*Le bâillon dénoué: Après quatre ans de silence* (Paris: Grasset, 1945).
___*Le cahier noir*, in: *Œuvres complètes*, vol. 10 (Paris: Arthème Fayard, 1952).
___*Maltaverne* (London: Eyre & Spottiswoode, 1970).
___*Mémoires politiques* (Paris: Grasset, 1967).
___*Nouvelles lettres d'une vie*, ed. Caroline Mauriac (Paris: Grasset, 1989).
___*The Black Notebook*, Robert Speaight, trans. (London, 1943).
___*Un adolescent d'autrefois* (Paris: Flammarion, 1969).

- McAfee Brown, Robert, "The Power of the Tale," *The Christian Century*, June 30, 1981, 650.
- McBee, Susanna, "These Glittering Nobel Prizes," *U.S. News and World Report*, October 27, 1986, 67.
- McLaughlin, Daniel, "Pope Bows down for the Victims of Auschwitz Killed by His Countrymen," *The Guardian*, May 29, 2006; www.theguardian.com/world/2006/may/29/secondworldwar.catholicism.
- Menuhin, Gerard, *Tell the Truth and Shame the Devil* (Washington, D.C.: The Barnes Review, in preparation (2015)).
- Merkin, Daphne, "Witness to the Holocaust: A First-Person Look at the Shy Boy Who Became the Cautious Man Who Became Elie Wiesel: *All Rivers Run to the Sea*, Memoirs," *NY Times Book Review*, December 17, 1995, BR7.
- Michael, George, "Deciphering Ahmadinejad's Holocaust Revisionism," *Middle East Quarterly*, summer 2007, 11-18; www.meforum.org/1704/deciphering-ahmadinejads-holocaust-revisionism.
- Miller, Judith, *One by One by One, Facing the Holocaust* (New York: Simon & Schuster, 1990).

  ___, and Stephen Engleberg, William Broad, *Germs: Biological Weapons and America's Secret War* (New York: Simon & Schuster, 2001).
- Mitgang, Herbert, "Wiesel to Be Honored for 3-Volume Work," *New York Times*, December 5, 1985, C17.
- Mitterrand, François, Elie Wiesel, *Mémoire à deux voix* (Paris: Odile Jacob, 1995).

  ___*Memoire in Two Voices* (New York: Arcade, 1996).
- Morgan, Ted, *An Uncertain Hour* (New York: William Morrow, 1990).
- Naumann, Bernd, *Auschwitz: A Report on the Proceedings against Robert Karl Ludwig Mulka and Others before the Court at Frankfurt* (New York: Praeger, 1967).

  ___*Auschwitz: Bericht über die Strafsache gegen Mulka u.a. vor dem Schwurgericht Frankfurt* (Frankfurt: Athanäum Verlag, 1965).
- Nelson, Andrew, "Bishop's Remarks on Holocaust Repudiated," *The Georgia Bulletin*, February 5, 2009, 3.
- Neusner, Jacob, "American Jews Embrace a Religion of Memory," *St. Petersburg Times*, April 12, 1999, A11.

  ___*Stranger at Home: "The Holocaust," Zionism and American Judaism* (Chicago: University of Chicago Press, 1981).
- Novick, Peter, *The Holocaust in American Life* (New York: Houghton-Mifflin, 1999).
- Nowak, Hans Jürgen, and Werner Rademacher, "Some Details of the Central Construction Office of Auschwitz," in: Rudolf *Dissecting*, 324-336.
- O'Brien, Conor Cruise, "A Lost Chance to Save the Jews," *New York Review of Books*, April 27, 1989, 28.
- O'Connor; John J., "America's Black Army and a Dual War Front," *New York Times*, November 11, 1992, C24.

  ___, and Elie Wiesel, *A Journey of Faith* (New York: Fine, 1991).
- O'Toole, Thomas, "44 Photos Showed Auschwitz Camp," *Washington Post*, February 23,

1979, A1, 14.
- Olsen, Arthur J., "Auschwitz Trial Enters Second Year: 20 Defendants in Frankfort Arouse Strong Emotion," *New York Times*, December 22, 1964, 11.
  ___"The Auschwitz Trial: It Holds the West Germans' Attention although They Disagree on Its Value," *New York Times*, April 3, 1964, 2.
- Orti, Vicente, *La Persecución religiosa en España durante la segunda república (1931-1939)* (Madrid: Rialp, 1990).
- Paris, Erna, *Unhealed Wounds* (New York, Grove: 1985).
- Pelt, Robert J. van, *The Case for Auschwitz: Evidence from the Irving Trial* (Bloomington: Indiana University Press, 2002).
  ___, and Deborah Dwork, *Auschwitz: 1270 to the Present* (New Haven/London: Yale University Press, 1996).
- Perlez, Jane, "Confusion Marks Polish Plan to Commemorate Auschwitz," *New York Times*, January 16, 1995, A2.
  ___"Separate Auschwitz Services Highlight Jewish-Polish Dispute," *New York Times*, January 26, 1995, A10.
  ___"Wiesel Now Agrees to Take Part in Auschwitz Rites," *New York Times*, January 20, 1995, A4.
- Peyrefitte, Roger, "Lettre ouverte à François Mauriac," *Arts*, May 6, 1964, 1.
- Piper, Franciszek, and Teresa Swiebocka (eds.), *Auschwitz: Il campo nazista della morte* (Auschwitz: State Museum Auschwitz-Birkenau, 1997).
- Poliakov, Léon, *Bréviaire de la haine* (Paris: Calmann-Lévy, 1951).
  ___*Harvest of Hate*, (Syracuse, New York: Syracuse University Press, 1954).
- Posner, Gerald L., and John Ware, *Mengele: The Complete Story* (2nd ed., New York: Cooper Square Press, 2000).
- Pressac, Jean-Claude, *Auschwitz: Technique and Operation of the Gas Chambers* (New York: Beate Klarsfeld Foundation, 1989).
  ___*Les Crématoires d'Auschwitz: la Machinerie du Meurtre de Masse* (Paris: Editions du CNRS, 1993).
- Pullella, Philip, "Elie Wiesel Attacks Pope over Holocaust Bishop," *Reuters.com*, January 28, 2009; http://in.reuters.com/article/2009/01/28/idINIndia-37701220090128.
  ___"Italy Rabbis Pull out of Dialogue, Accuse Pope," *reuters.com*, January 13, 2009; www.reuters.com/article/2009/01/13/us-pope-jews-idUSTRE50C7KF20090113.
- Rademacher, Werner, and Michael Gärtner, "Ground Water in the Area of the POW camp Birkenau," *The Revisionist*, vol. 1, no.1, 2003, pp. 3-12.
- Rajsfus, Maurice, *Des Juifs dans la collaboration: L'UGIF, 1941-1944* (Paris: ÉDI, 1980).
  ___*Des Juifs dans la collaboration: Une Terre promise?* (Paris: L'Harmattan, 1989).
- Rassinier, Paul, *Debunking the Genocide Myth: A Study of the Nazi Concentration Camps and the Alleged Extermination of European Jewry* (Los Angeles, Calif.: Noontide Press, 1978); 2nd ed.: Rassinier, Paul, *Holocaust Story and the Lies of Ulysses* (Costa Mesa: Institute for Historical Review, 1989).
  ___*L'opération vicaire* (Paris: La Table Ronde, 1965).
  ___*Le drame des juifs européens* (Paris: Les Sept Couleurs, 1964).
  ___*Le mensonge d'Ulysse* (Paris: La Librairie Française, 1950; expanded 5th ed., *ibid.*, 1961).
  ___*Le véritable procès Eichmann ou les vainqueurs incorrigibles* (Paris: Les Sept Couleurs, 1962).
  ___*The Real Eichmann Trial, or, The Incorrigible Victors* (Ladbroke, UK: Historical Review Press, 1979).
- Rees, Laurence, "Raped by their saviours: How the survivors of Auschwitz escaped one nightmare only to face another unimaginable ordeal," *Daily Mail*, Febr. 2, 2010; www.dailymail.co.uk/news/article-1247157.
- Reich, Tova, "Letters to the Editor: *My Holocaust*," *New York Times*, June 10, 2007, F6.
  ___*My Holocaust* (New York: Harper Collins, 2004).

- Reich, Walter, "Erasing the Holocaust," *New York Times*, July 11, 1993, BR1.
- Rein, Arielle, "L'historien, la mémoire et l'Etat / L'œuvre de Ben Zion Dinur pour la commémoration et la recherche sur la Shoah en Israël," *Revue d'histoire de la Shoah*, no. 182, January-June 2005, 257-278.
- Reitlinger, Gerald, *The Final Solution* (London: Mitchell, 1953).
- Reuters, "Elie Wiesel Tells Hungary to Ban Holocaust Denial," *Yahoo! India News*, December 9, 2009; http://in.reuters.com/article/2009/12/09/idINIndia-44603620091209.
- Rich, Motoko, and Joseph Berger, "False Memoir of Holocaust Is Cancelled," *New York Times*, December 28, 2008, A12.
- Rittner, Carol "An Interview with Elie Wiesel," *America*, November 19, 1988, 397-401.
  ___(ed.), *Elie Wiesel: Between Memory and Hope* (New York: New York University Press, 1990).
  ___, and John K. Roth (eds.), *Memory Offended: The Auschwitz Carmel Controversy* (New York: Praeger, 1991).
- Robin, Jean, "Elie Wiesel n'a pas le tatouage qu'il prétend avoir." *Enquête et Débat*, December 24, 2012.
- Roddy, Joseph, "How the Jews Changed Catholic Thinking," *Look*, vol. 30, no. 2, January 25, 1966, 19-23.
- Roques, Henri, "Le doyen Michel de Boüard et les chambres à gaz homicides," *Revue d'Histoire Révisionniste*, vol. 1, no. 2, August-October 1990, 46-49.
  ___*The Confessions of Kurt Gerstein* (Costa Mesa, CA: Institute for Historical Review, 1989).
- Rosenberg, David (ed.), *Testimony: Contemporary Writers Make the Holocaust Personal* (New York, Random House, 1989).
- Rosenfeld, Alvin H. (ed.), *Thinking about the Holocaust* (Bloomington: Indiana University Press, 1997).
- Rosenthal, A. M., "On My Mind: Detesting the Haters," *New York Times*, January 14, 1992, A23.
- Roudinesco, Elizabeth, "François Wahl (éditeur et philosophe), est mort," *Le Monde*, September 14, 2014.
- Rubinstein, W. D., and Walter N. Sanning, Arthur R. Butz, letters, *The Journal of Historical Review*, vol. 5, nos. 2-4, 1984, 367-373.
- Rudolf Aschenauer (ed.), *Ich, Adolf Eichmann* (Leoni, Bavaria: Druffel, 1980).
- Rudolf, Germar, "Holocaust Victims: A Statistical Analysis. W. Benz and W. N. Sanning – A Comparison", in: Rudolf, *Dissecting*, 181-213.
  ___"Statistisches über die Holocaust Opfer – W. Benz und W.N. Sanning im Vergleich," in: Gauss, *Grundlagen*, 141-168.
  ___(ed.), *Auschwitz: Plain Facts. A Response to Jean-Claude Pressac* (Chicago: Theses & Dissertations Press, 2005).
  ___(ed.), *Dissecting the Holocaust: The Growing Critique of "Truth" and "Memory,"* (2nd ed.; Chicago, IL: Theses & Dissertations Press, 2003).
  ___*Gutachten über die Bildung und Nachweisbarkeit von Cyanidverbindungen in den 'Gaskammern' von Auschwitz* (Bad Kissingen: Remker-Heipke, April 1993); 2nd, revised ed., edited by Rüdiger Kammerer and Armin Solms, *Das Rudolf Gutachten: Gutachten über die Bildung und Nachweisbarkeit von Cyanidverbindungen in den 'Gaskammern' von Auschwitz* (London: Cromwell Press, July 1993). 3rd, revised ed.: *Das Rudolf Gutachten: Gutachten über die 'Gaskammern' von Auschwitz* (Hastings, UK: Castle Hill Publishers, 2001).
  ___*Lectures on the Holocaust: Controversial Issues Cross Examined* (Chicago, Ill., Theses & Dissertations Press, 2003; 2nd ed.: Washington, D.C.: The Barnes Review, 2010).
  ___*The Rudolf Report: Expert Report on Chemical and Technical Aspects of the "Gas Chambers" of Auschwitz* (Chicago, Ill., Theses & Dissertations Press, 2003; 2nd ed., edited by Wolfgang Lambrecht, Washington, D.C.: The Barnes Review, 2011).
- Rynne, Xavier (Francis X. Murphy), *Letters from Vatican City* (New York: Farrar, Straus

and Giroux, 1963).
- Saint Cheron, Philippe-Michel de, *Elie Wiesel: Pèlerin de la Mémoire* (Paris: Plon, 1994).
- Samuels, Gertrude, "When Evil Closed In," *New York Times*, November 13, 1960, BR20.
- Sanning, Walter N., "Die europäischen Juden. Eine technische Studie zur zahlenmäßigen Entwicklung im Zweiten Weltkrieg," 4 parts, *Deutschland in Geschichte und Gegenwart*, vol. 28, nos. 1-4, 12-15, 17-21, 17-21, 25-31.
  ___*Die Auflösung des osteuropäischen Judentums* (Tübingen: Grabert 1983).
  ___*The Dissolution of Eastern European Jewry* (Torrance, Calif.: Institute for Historical Review, 1983; 2nd ed., Uckfield, UK: Castle Hill Publishers, 2015).
- Sarafian, Michael (Malachi Martin), *The Pilgrim* (New York: Farrar, Straus and Giroux, 1964).
- Schalk, Adolph, "Return to Auschwitz," *Commonweal*, July 9, 1965, 500.
- Schemo, Diana Jean, "Holocaust Museum Dedicated in Payment to Dead," *New York Times*, April 23, 1993, A1, A14.
- Schmemann, Serge, "John Paul II Meets with Waldheim Again: Arriving for Visit to Austria, Pope Avoids Mentioning Furor over President," *New York Times*, June 24, 1988, A3.
  ___"John Paul Meets with Austrian Jews; Papal Remarks at a Death Camp Are Criticized," *New York Times*, June 25, 1988, A1.
- Schult, Christoph, and Alexander Smoltczyk, "The Word Left Unspoken: For German Pope, Yad Vashem Is Everywhere," *derspiegel.de*, May 18, 2009 (translated from *Der Spiegel*, no. 21, 2009).
- Schwarz, Solomon M., *Jews in the Soviet Union* (Syracuse, New York: Syracuse University Press, 1951).
- Sciolino, Elaine, "A Priest Methodically Reveals Ukrainian Jews' Fate," *New York Times*, October 6, 2007, A1.
- Scislowska, Monika, "Germany Pledges Funds to Preserve Auschwitz," *AJC*, December 16, 2010, A18.
- Seidman, Naomi, "Elie Wiesel and the Scandal of Jewish Rage," *Jewish Social Studies*, 3 (Fall, 1996), 1-19.
- Semprun, Jorge, and Elie Wiesel, "Unüberbrückbare Erinnerungen. Ein Zwiegespräch zwischen Jorge Semprun und Elie Wiesel," in: *Werkstatt Geschichte*, no. 13, 1996.
- Serroy, Jean (ed.), *de Gaulle et les Ecrivains* (Grenoble: Presses Universitaires de Grenoble, 1991).
- Shabecoff, Philip, "17 Auschwitz Aides Get Prison Terms; 6 Must Serve Life," *New York Times*, August 20, 1965, I, 8.
- Shamir, Yoav, *Defamation*, http://wideeyecinema.com/?p=7208.
- Shenker, Israel, "The Concerns of Elie Wiesel," *New York Times*, February 10, 1970, A48.
- Shepard, Richard F., "TV: Story of Auschwitz by a Survivor," *New York Times*, February 4, 1981, C22.
- Simons, Marlise, "Chirac Affirms France's Guilt in Fate of Jews," *New York Times*, July 17, 1995, A1.
- Smith, Bradley R., "Elie Wiesel: sometimes the truth is an accident," *Smith's Report*, no. 42, April 1997, 3f.
- Smith, Mike (DenierBud), *Auschwitz: The Surprising Hidden Truth*; www.holocausthandbooks.com/index.php?page_id=1005.
- Smolar, Piotr, "Marek Halter, le bonimenteur," *La Revue XXI*, 4, autumn 2008, 142–153.
- Sparknotes, *Night*, SparkNotes Literature Guide Series (New York: SparkNotes, 2003).
- Speaight, Robert, *François Mauriac: A Study of the Man and the Writer* (London: Chatto & Windus, 1976).
- Special to the *New York Times*, "Photos of Auschwitz Extermination Unit Produced," *New York Times*, February 24, 1979, A2.
- Spiegel, Irving, "Inaction Charged to Western Jews on Soviet Issue; Dr. Heschel of the Theological Seminary Scores Americans," *New York Times*, May 17, 1966, 10.

- Springer, Markus, "The New Face of the 'Holocaust'," *The Revisionist*, vol. 2, no. 3, 2004, 297-300.
- Staatliches Museum Auschwitz (ed.), *Sterbebücher von Auschwitz* (Munich: K.G. Saur, 1995).
- Stäglich, Wilhelm, letter to the editor, *Nation Europa*, vol. 22, no. 10, October 1973, 50-52.
  ___*Der Auschwitz Mythos: Legende oder Wirklichkeit*? (Tübingen: Grabert Verlag, 1979).
  ___*The Auschwitz Myth: A Judge Looks at the Evidence*, tr. Thomas Francis (Costa Mesa, Ca.: IHR Press, 1986); 2nd ed. as *Auschwitz: A Judge Looks at the Evidence* (*ibid.*, 1990; 3rd corrected ed.: Uckfield, UK: Castle Hill Publishers, 2015).
- Sternlicht, Sanford, Student *Companion to Elie Wiesel* (Westport, CT: Greenwood Press, 2003).
- Strzelecki, Andrzej, *Endphase des KL Auschwitz* (Auschwitz: Verlag Staatliches Museum in Oswiecim-Brzezinka, 1995).
- Superior Court of California. County of San Francisco. Before the Honorable Robert Donder, Judge Presiding, Department Number 23. *People of the State of California, Plaintiff, v. Eric Hunt, Defendant*. Testimony of Elie Wiesel, July 8, 2008.
- Suskind, Martin, "A Voice from Bonn: History Cannot Be Shrugged Off," *New York Times*, November 2, 1986, D2.
- Swaim, Lawrence, "Ken Starr's Pogram: Religious Right and NeoCons Gang Up on a Progressive Jew," June 20, 2012; www.counterpunch.org/2012/06/20/ken-starrs-anti-semitism/.
- Sweet, Lynn, "Obama on Holocaust Remembrance Day: 'Contemplate the Obligations of the Living,'" *Chicago Sun-Times*, April 23, 2009; http://blogs.suntimes.com/sweet/2009/04/obama_and_holocaust_and_united.html.
- Tagliabue, John, "Elie Wiesel Back in Germany after 41 Years," *New York Times*, January 23, 1986, A4.
- Tenenbaum, Joseph, *In Search of a Lost People: The Old and the New Poland* (New York: Beechhurst Press, 1948).
- The Pontifical Biblical Commission (ed.), *The Jewish People and their Sacred Scriptures in the Christian Bible* (Vatican City: Libreria Editrice Vaticana, 2002); www.vatican.va/roman_curia/congregations/cfaith/pcb_documents/rc_con_cfaith_doc_20020212_popolo-ebraico_en.html.
- Thion, Serge (ed.), *Vérité historique ou vérité politique?* (Paris: La Vielle Taupe, 1980).
- Thomas, Jo, "'Holy Document' of Auschwitz Found: Closing the Past, Knew Her Tattoo Number," *New York Times*, August 14, 1980, A16.
- Treaster, Joseph B., "Film Halted on Blacks Freeing Jews: Movie Is Withdrawn on Unit's War Role," *New York Times*, February 12, 1993, B3.
- United Nations, General Assembly, "Resolution adopted by the General Assembly on the Holocaust Remembrance," A/RES/60/7, 1 November 2005; www.un.org/en/holocaustremembrance/docs/res607.shtml.
  ___"Ban calls on world to fight Holocaust denial, anti-Semitism and bigotry," 27 January 2009; www.un.org/apps/news/story.asp?NewsID=29679.
  ___"Resolution adopted by the UN General Assembly on Holocaust denial," A/RES/61/255, 26 January 2007; www.un.org/en/holocaustremembrance/docs/res61.shtml.
- Venezia, Shlomo, *Inside the Gas Chamber: Eight Months in the Sonderkommando of Auschwitz* (Cambridge, UK: Polity).
- Verbeke, Herbert (ed., Germar Rudolf), *Auschwitz: Nackte Fakten. Eine Erwiderung an Jean-Claude Pressac* (Berchem, Belgium: Vrij Historisch Onderzoek, 1995).
- Vidal-Naquet, Pierre, "Une entrevue avec Pierre Vidal-Naquet," *Zéro*, April 1987, 57.
  ___*Assassins of Memory: Essays on the Denial of the Holocaust* (New York: Columbia University Press, 1993).
  ___, *et al.*, "Déclaration de trente-quatre historiens," *Le Monde*, February 21, 1979, 23.

- Vinocur, John, "Pope Prays at Auschwitz: 'Only Peace,'" *New York Times*, June 8, 1979, A1.
- Waltzer, Kenneth, "Ken Waltzer on Elie Wiesel's *Night*," once at http://special.news.msu.edu/holocaust/wiesel.php?wiesel, but now removed.
- Weber, Mark, "'60 Minutes' Takes Aim at Holocaust Revisionism," *The Journal of Historical Review*, vol. 14, no. 3, May/June 1994, 16-18.
  ___"Smith and Cole Appear on 'Donahue' Show in Major Media Breakthrough for Revisionism," *The Journal of Historical Review*, vol. 14, no. 3, May/June 1994, 19f.
- Weinraub, Judith, "Holocaust Museum Chief Forced Out before Starting," *Washington Post*, March 4, 1995, 6.
- Weisberg, Jacob, "Pop Goes Elie Wiesel," *New Republic*, November 10, 1986, 12.
- Weiss, Avi, "Auschwitz is a sacred place of Jewish memory. It's no place for a Catholic church," *The Washington Post*, January 28, 2015.
  ___*Principles of Spiritual Activism* (Hoboken, N. J.: KTAV Publishing Co., 2002).
- Weissman, Gary, *Fantasies of Witnessing: Postwar Efforts to Experience the Holocaust* (Ithaca, New York: Cornell University Press, 2004).
- Wellers, Georges, and André Kaspi, Serge Klarsfeld (eds.), *La France et la question Juive, 1940-1944: actes du colloque du Centre de documentation juive contemporaine (10 au 12 mars 1979)* (Paris: S. Messinger, 1981).
- Wiesberg, Michael, "Unversöhnlich – Elie Wiesel zum 80." In: *Grundlagen*, Sezession 25, August 2008, pp. 22-25.
- Wiesel, Elezier, *Un di velt hot geshvign* (Buenos Aires: Tsentral-Farband fun poylishe yidn in Argentina, 1956), p. 217.
- Wiesel, Elie, "A Mideast Peace: Is It Impossible?," *New York Times*, June 23, 1988, A23.
  ___"An Appointment with Hate," *Commentary*, December 1962, 470-476.
  ___"Eichmann's Victims and the Unheard Testimony," *Commentary*, December 16, 1961, 510-516.
  ___"John Paul II and His Jewish Problem," *New York Post*, June 28, 1988, 27.
  ___"Le jour où Buchenwald a été libéré," *Paris-Match*, April 10-16, 2003, 116.
  ___"Learning and Respect," June 15, 1997; http://archive.humanity.org/printview.php?page=wiesel_at_depaul§ionName=voices.
  ___"*Nostra Aetate*: An Observer's Perspective," *Thought*, no. 67, December 1992, 366-370.
  ___"Pilgrimage to the Country of Night," *New York Times*, November 4, 1979, VI, 37.
  ___"Recalling Swallowed-Up Worlds, "*The Christian Century*, May 27, 1981, 609-612.
  ___"Remarks on Presenting the Congressional Gold Medal to Elie Wiesel and on Signing the Jewish Heritage Week Proclamation," April 19, 1985.
  ___"Survivors' Children Relive the Holocaust," *New York Times*, November 16, 1975, 36.
  ___"The Decision," *Parade*, August 27, 1995, 4-6.
  ___"The Last Return," *Commentary*, March 1965, 43-49.
  ___"Trivializing the Holocaust: Semi-Fact and Semi-Fiction," *New York Times*, April 16, 1978, 75.
  ___"What It Means to Be Stateless: 'How Could a People Expel and Disown Its Citizens?'" *New York Times*, July 6, 1986, E13.
  ___"When Passion Is Dangerous," *Parade Magazine*, April 19, 1992, 20f.
  ___"Wiesel Answers Green," *New York Times*, April 30, 1978, D39.
  ___"Will Soviet Jews Survive?," *Commentary*, February 1967, 47-52.
  ___*...et la mer n'est pas remplie* (Paris: Seuil, 1996).
  ___*A Beggar in Jerusalem* (New York: Random House, 1970).
  ___*A Jew Today* (New York: Random House, 1978).
  ___*All Rivers Run to the Sea* (New York: Knopf, 1995).
  ___*And the Sea Is Never Full* (New York: Knopf, 1999).
  ___*Die Nacht zu begraben, Elisha*, tr. Kurt Meyer-Clason (Berlin: Ullstein, 1962).

___*Entre deux soleils* (Paris: Seuil, 1970).
___*From the Kingdom of Memory* (New York: Summit, 1990).
___, interviewed by Werner A. Perger, "1945 und Heute: Holocaust," *Die Zeit*, April 21, 1995, 16.
___*La Notte* (Florence: Giuntina, 1986).
___*La Nuit* (Paris: Les Éditions de Minuit, 1958).
___*Le chant des morts* (Paris: Seuil, 1966).
___*Legends of Our Time* (New York: Holt Rinehart & Winston, 1968; Schocken Books, New York, 1982).
___*Night*, Stella Rodway, trans. (New York: Hill & Wang, 1960; New York: Penguin Books, 1981; New York: Bantam, 1982); new translation by Marion Wiesel (New York: Farrar, Straus & Giroux, 2006).
___*One Generation After* (New York: Random House, 1970).
___*The Jews of Silence* (N.Y.: Holt, Rinehart & Winston, 1966).
___*Tous les fleuves vont à la mer* (Paris: Seuil, 1994).
___*Un juif aujourd'hui* (Paris: Seuil, 1977).
___, *et al.*, *Dimensions of the Holocaust* (Evanston, Ill.: Northwestern University Press, 1977).

- Wilkomirski, Benyamin (Bruno Grosjean, Bruno Dössecker), *Fragments: Memories of a Wartime Childhood* (New York: Schocken Books, 1997).
  ___*Bruchstücke: Aus einer Kindheit 1939–1948* (Frankfurt: Jüdischer Verlag, 1995).
- Williams, Roger M., "Why Wasn't Auschwitz Bombed?" *Commonweal*, November 24, 1978, 746-751.
- Wills, Gary, *Papal Sin: Structures of Deceit* (New York: Doubleday, 2000).
- Winfrey, Oprah, "Elie Wiesel," *Time*, April 30, 2006, 117.
- Winston Smith, "The Most Famous Holocaust Photo a Fraud," Jan 17, 2013; http://winstonsmithministryoftruth.blogspot.com/2013/01/the-most-famous-holocaust-photo-fraud.html.
- Wisse, Ruth R., *The Modern Jewish Canon: A Journey through Language and Literature* (Chicago: University of Chicago Press, 2003).
- Wood, E. Thomas, and Stanislaw M. Jankowski, *Karski: How One Man Tried to Stop the Holocaust* (New York: John Wiley, 1994).
- Woodward, Bob, *Plan of Attack* (New York: Simon & Schuster, 2004).
- Wyatt, Edward, "It's a Matter of Timing," *New York Time*, January 19, 2006, E7.
  ___"Oprah's Book Club Turns to Elie Wiesel," *New York Times*, January 16, 2006, E1, 8.
  ___"The Translation of Wiesel's '*Night*' is New, but Old Questions Are Raised," *New York Times*, January 19, 2006, E1.
- Wyman, David S., "Why Auschwitz Was Never Bombed," *Commentary* (May 1978), 37-46.
  ___*The Abandonment of the Jews: America and the Holocaust, 1941-1945* (N.Y.: Pantheon Books, 1984).
- Yeager, Carolyn, "Gigantic Fraud Carried Out for Wiesel Nobel Prize" ; www.eliewieseltattoo.com/the-evidence/photographic-evidence/gigantic-fraud-carried-out-for-wiesel-nobel-prize/.
  ___"Is Ken Waltzer on the outs; or is he in hiding?," June 29, 2013, www.eliewieseltattoo.com/is-ken-waltzer-on-the-outs-no-longer-cited-as-a-holocaust-expert/.
  ___"Ken Waltzer inadvertantly supplies proof that Elie Wiesel was not at Buchenwald," September 8, 2013, www.eliewieseltattoo.com/ken-waltzer-inadvertantly-supplies-proof-that-elie-wiesel-was-not-at-buchenwald/.
  ___"Ken Waltzer Replies to My Question," June 30, 2011; www.eliewieseltattoo.com/ken-waltzer-replies-to-my-question.
- Zenit.org, "La Shoah par Balles: Intervention du Père Patrick Desbois," *Zenit*, April 24, 2009; www.zenit.org/fr/articles/la-shoah-par-balles-intervention-du-p-patrick-desbois.
- Zoglin, Richard, and Mitch Gelman, "Lives of Spirit and Dedication; The World Pays

Tribute to Eleven Who Stirred Emotions and Laid Foundations; Peace: Elie Wiesel," *Time*, October 27, 1986, 66f.

Other Recommeded Sources:

- Davis, Colin, *Elie Wiesel's Secretive Texts* (Gainesville: University of Florida Press, 1994).
- Estess, Ted, *Elie Wiesel* (New York: Ungar, 1980).
- Faurisson, Robert, "A Prominent False Witness: Elie Wiesel," Leaflet of the Institute for Historical Review, October 1993; http://codoh.com/library/document/858.
- Johnston, Laurie, "Feeling a Need for 'A Change of Atmosphere,'" *New York Times*, June 17, 1975, I, 25.
- Kolbert, Jack, "Elie Wiesel," in: William Thompson (ed.), *The Contemporary Novel in France* (Gainesville: University of Florida Press, 1995), 217-230.
- Lamont, Rosette C., "Elie Wiesel: In Search of a Tongue," in: Alvin H. Rosenberg and Irving Greenberg (eds.), *Confronting the Holocaust* (Bloomington: Indiana University Press, 1978), 80-98.

Image Sources

Front Cover:

Elie Wiesel UN: http://www.eliewieseltattoo.com/2013/02/
Carter: http://commons.wikimedia.org/wiki/File:JimmyCarterPortrait2.jpg
Reagan: http://commons.wikimedia.org/wiki/File:Official_Portrait_of_President_Reagan_ 1981.jpg
Clinton: http://commons.wikimedia.org/wiki/File:Bill_Clinton.jpg
Bush sen.: http://commons.wikimedia.org/wiki/File:George_H._W._Bush,_President_of_the_United_States,_official_portrait.jpg
Bush jun.: http://commons.wikimedia.org/wiki/File:GeorgeWBush.jpg
Obama: http://commons.wikimedia.org/wiki/File:Official_portrait_of_Barack_Obama.jpg
Wiesel&Clinton: http://www.nbcnews.com/video/nightly-news/51705464#51705464
Wiesel&Obama: http://www.jspacenews.com/elie-wiesel-backs-netanyahus-congress-address-iran/
Wiesel&Reagan: unknown.

Back Cover

Wiesel top 1: http://redalertpolitics.com/2013/04/30/bill-clinton-elie-wiesel-join-holocaust-survivors-to-commemorate-museums-20th-anniversary/
Wiesel top 2: http://i.huffpost.com/gen/1260883/images/o-ELIE-WIESEL-facebook.jpg
Wiesel top 3 (Merkel&Obama): http://www.badische-zeitung.de/deutschland-1/appel-von-kz-ueberlebendem-beruehrt-merkel-und-obama--15811828.html (ddp)
Wiesel bottom 1: http://www.prweb.com/releases/2014/04/prweb11738457.htm (Photo: Chapman University)
Wiesel bottom 2: http://commons.wikimedia.org/wiki/File:Elie_Wiesel.jpg
Wiesel bottom 3: unknown

Interior (where no source is given, the image was supplied by the author):

p. 52: http://www.ushmm.org/wlc/en/media_ph.php?ModuleId=10007200&MediaId=5747
p. 109: http://www.scrapbookpages.com/AuschwitzScrapbook/History/Articles/Selection2.html
p. 163: https://shirleymach.wordpress.com/2012/12/05/a-hidden-unsung-hero/
p. 167: http://www.achievement.org/autodoc/photocredit/achievers/wie0-010
p. 173 t & b: http://www.eliewieseltattoo.com/tag/buchenwald-liberation/
p. 248: http://www.ushmm.org/wlc/en/article.php?ModuleId=10007201
p. 252: http://www.bu.edu/religion/2012/02/27/professor-steven-katz-to-deliver-the-j-b-and-maurice-c-shapiro-annual-lecture-at-the-united-states-holocaust-memorial-museum/
p. 270: unkown; any info is appreciated
p. 294: http://rodoh.info/forum/viewtopic.php?f=13&t=1799&start=10

p. 321: http://www.nbcnews.com/video/nightly-news/51705464#51705464
p. 341: http://www.fpp.co.uk/Auschwitz/Lipstadt/
p. 344: http://nypost.com/2014/05/11/holocaust-scammer-to-owe-22-5m-for-bogus-memoir/ (AP)
p. 345: http://www.washingtonpost.com/national/herman-rosenblat-whose-holocaust-love-story-was-beautiful-but-false-dies/2015/02/25/1b96daec-bc39-11e4-bdfa-b8e8f594e6ee_story.html (J. Pat Carter/AP)
p. 351, Wiesel Bush jun.: http://commons.wikimedia.org/wiki/File:Dalai_Lama_and_Bush_welcome_Elie_Wiesel_(2007).jpg
p. 351, Powell: https://haitiholocaustsurvivors.wordpress.com/category/uncategorized/page/27 (Carl Cox/USHMM)
p. 355: http://www.nytimes.com/2006/05/29/world/europe/29pope.html?pagewanted=all (Pawel Kopczynski/Reuters)
p. 356: unknown, but probably as before
p. 367: http://www.judaicultures.info/histoire-6/themes-travaux-colloques/racisme-et-antisemitisme-68/Yom-Hashoah-2009-a-Geneve
p. 369: http://in.reuters.com/article/2009/01/28/idINIndia-37701220090128 (Reuters/Stefan Wermuth)
p. 371: http://www.ushmm.org/information/exhibitions/online-features/special-focus/elie-wiesel-and-oprah-winfrey-at-auschwitz
p. 372: http://www.muckety.com/Elie-Wiesel/15233.muckety
p. 374: http://www.badische-zeitung.de/deutschland-1/appel-von-kz-ueberlebendem-beruehrt-merkel-und-obama--15811828.html (ddp)
p. 375: http://www.timesofisrael.com/peres-awards-elie-wiesel-the-presidential-medal/ (photo credit: Mark Neyman/GPO/Flash90)
p. 376: https://desertpeace.wordpress.com/category/ethnic-cleansing/page/3/
p. 379: http://www.eliewieseltattoo.com/2013/02/
p. 389: http://madreigrejaemfotos.blogspot.com/2012_12_01_archive.html
p. 386: http://www.jpost.com/Opinion/No-Holds-Barred-At-Bibis-speech-with-Elie-Wiesel-393083 (photo credit: Amos Ben-Gershom/GPO)
p. 396: http://www.eliewieseltattoo.com/the-evidence/the-tattoo/where-is-elies-tattoo/
p. 399: http://www.reuters.com/article/2010/01/27/us-vatican-wiesel-idUSTRE60Q42O20100127 (Reuters/Remo Casilli)

We tried to use only illustrations that are in the public domain. Should we by accident and against our best knowledge have used images requiring a license agreement, please get in touch with the publisher (see imprint) in order to resolve this issue swiftly within the limits of license terms and conditions usually applicable for PoD books of small print runs.

Index of Names

Entries in footnotes are in italics.

HOLOCAUST HANDBOOKS

This ambitious, growing series addresses various aspects of the "Holocaust" of the WWII era. Most of them are based on decades of research from archives all over the world. They are heavily referenced. In contrast to most other works on this issue, the tomes of this series approach its topic with profound academic scrutiny and a critical attitude. Any Holocaust researcher ignoring this series will remain oblivious to some of the most important research in the field. These books are designed to both convince the common reader as well as academics. The following books have appeared so far, or are about to be released. Compare hardcopy and eBook prices at www.findbookprices.com.

SECTION ONE: General Overviews of the Holocaust

The First Holocaust. The Surprising Origin of the Six-Million Figure. By Don Heddesheimer. This compact but substantive study documents propaganda spread prior to, during and after the FIRST World War that claimed East European Jewry was on the brink of annihilation. The magic number of suffering and dying Jews was 6 million back then as well. The book details how these Jewish fundraising operations in America raised vast sums in the name of feeding suffering Polish and Russian Jews but actually funneled much of the money to Zionist and Communist groups. 5th ed., 198 pages, b&w illustrations, bibliography, index. (#6)

Lectures on the Holocaust. Controversial Issues Cross Examined. By Germar Rudolf. This book first explains why "the Holocaust" is an important topic, and that it is well to keep an open mind about it. It then tells how many mainstream scholars expressed doubts and subsequently fell from grace. Next, the physical traces and documents about the various claimed crime scenes and murder weapons are discussed. After that, the reliability of witness testimony is examined. Finally, the author lobbies for a free exchange of ideas about this topic. This book gives the most-comprehensive and up-to-date overview of the critical research into the Holocaust. With its dialog style, it is pleasant to read, and it can even be used as an encyclopedic compendium. 3rd ed., 596 pages, b&w illustrations, bibliography, index.(#15)

Breaking the Spell. The Holocaust, Myth & Reality. By Nicholas Kollerstrom. In 1941, British Intelligence analysts cracked the German "Enigma" code. Hence, in 1942 and 1943, encrypted radio communications between German concentration camps and the Berlin headquarters were decrypted. The intercepted data

Pictured above are all of the scientific studies that comprise the series *Holocaust Handbooks* published thus far or are about to be released. More volumes and new editions are constantly in the works. Check www.HolocaustHandbooks.com for updates.

refutes the orthodox "Holocaust" narrative. It reveals that the Germans were desperate to reduce the death rate in their labor camps, which was caused by catastrophic typhus epidemics. Dr. Kollerstrom, a science historian, has taken these intercepts and a wide array of mostly unchallenged corroborating evidence to show that "witness statements" supporting the human gas chamber narrative clearly clash with the available scientific data. Kollerstrom concludes that the history of the Nazi "Holocaust" has been written by the victors with ulterior motives. It is distorted, exaggerated and largely wrong. With a foreword by Prof. Dr. James Fetzer. 4th ed., 261 pages, b&w ill., bibl., index. (#31)

Debating the Holocaust. A New Look at Both Sides. By Thomas Dalton. Mainstream historians insist that there cannot be, may not be a debate about the Holocaust. But ignoring it does not make this controversy go away. Traditional scholars admit that there was neither a budget, a plan, nor an order for the Holocaust; that the key camps have all but vanished, and so have any human remains; that material and unequivocal documentary evidence is absent; and that there are serious problems with survivor testimonies. Dalton juxtaposes the traditional Holocaust narrative with revisionist challenges and then analyzes the mainstream's responses to them. He reveals the weak-

ISSN 1529-7748 · All books are 6"×9" paperbacks unless otherwise stated. Discounts are available for the whole set.

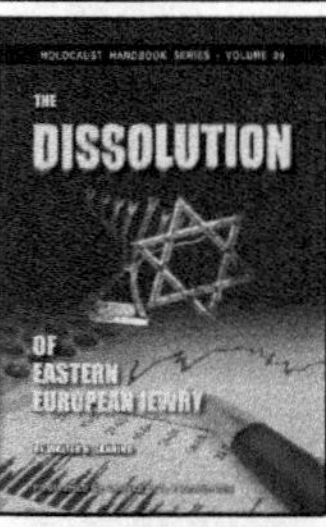

nesses of both sides, while declaring revisionism the winner of the current state of the debate. 2nd ed., 332 pages, b&w illustrations, bibliography, index. (#32)

The Hoax of the Twentieth Century. The Case against the Presumed Extermination of European Jewry. By Arthur R. Butz. The first writer to analyze the entire Holocaust complex in a precise scientific manner. This book exhibits the overwhelming force of arguments accumulated by the mid-1970s. Butz's two main arguments are: 1. All major entities hostile to Germany must have known what was happening to the Jews under German authority. They acted during the war as if no mass slaughter was occurring. 2. All the evidence adduced to proof any mass slaughter has a dual interpretation, while only the innocuous one can be proven to be correct. This book continues to be a major historical reference work, frequently cited by prominent personalities. This edition has numerous supplements with new information gathered over the last 35 years. 4th ed., 524 pages, b&w illustrations, bibliography, index. (#7)

Dissecting the Holocaust. The Growing Critique of 'Truth' and 'Memory.' Edited by Germar Rudolf. *Dissecting the Holocaust* applies state-of-the-art scientific technique and classic methods of detection to investigate the alleged murder of millions of Jews by Germans during World War II. In 22 contributions—each of some 30 pages—the 17 authors dissect generally accepted paradigms of the "Holocaust." It reads as exciting as a crime novel: so many lies, forgeries and deceptions by politicians, historians and scientists are proven. This is the intellectual adventure of the 21st century. Be part of it! 2nd ed. 620 pages, b&w illustrations, bibliography, index. (#1)

The Dissolution of Eastern European Jewry. By Walter N. Sanning. Six Million Jews died in the Holocaust. Sanning did not take that number at face value, but thoroughly explored European population developments and shifts mainly caused by emigration as well as deportations and evacuations conducted by both Nazis and the Soviets, among other things. The book is based mainly on Jewish, Zionist and mainstream sources. It concludes that a sizeable share of the Jews found missing during local censuses after the Second World War, which were so far counted as "Holocaust victims," had either emigrated (mainly to Israel or the U.S.) or had been deported by Stalin to Siberian labor camps. 2nd ed., foreword by A.R. Butz, epilogue by Germar Rudolf containing important updates; 224 pages, b&w illustrations, bibliography (#29).

Air Photo Evidence: World War Two Photos of Alleged Mass Murder Sites Analyzed. By Germar Rudolf (editor). During World War Two both German and Allied reconnaissance aircraft took countless air photos of places of tactical and strategic interest in Europe. These photos are prime evidence for the investigation of the Holocaust. Air photos of locations like Auschwitz, Majdanek, Treblinka, Babi Yar etc. permit an insight into what did or did not happen there. The author has unearthed many pertinent photos and has thoroughly analyzed them. This book is full of air photo reproductions and schematic drawings explaining them. According to the author, these images refute many of the atrocity claims made by witnesses in connection with events in the German sphere of influence. 5th edition; with a contribution by Carlo Mattogno. 168 pages, 8.5"×11", b&w illustrations, bibliography, index (#27).

The Leuchter Reports: Critical Edition. By Fred Leuchter, Robert Faurisson and Germar Rudolf. Between 1988 and 1991, U.S. expert on execution technologies Fred Leuchter wrote four detailed reports addressing whether the Third Reich operated homicidal gas chambers. The first report on Auschwitz and Majdanek became world famous. Based on chemical analyses and various technical arguments, Leuchter concluded that the locations investigated "could not have then been, or now be, utilized or seriously considered to function as execution gas chambers." The second report deals with gas-chamber claims for the camps Dachau, Mauthausen and Hartheim, while the third reviews design criteria and operation procedures of execution gas chambers in the U.S. The fourth report reviews Pressac's 1989 tome *Auschwitz.* 4th ed., 252 pages, b&w illustrations. (#16)

The Giant with Feet of Clay: Raul Hilberg and His Standard Work on the "Holocaust." By Jürgen Graf. Raul Hilberg's major work *The Destruction of European Jewry* is an orthodox standard work on the Holocaust. But what evidence does Hilberg provide to back his thesis that there was a German plan to exterminate Jews, carried out mainly in gas chambers? Jürgen Graf applies the methods of critical analysis to Hilberg's evidence and examines the results in light of modern historiography. The results of Graf's critical analysis are devastating for Hilberg. 2nd, corrected edition, 139 pages, b&w illustrations, bibliography, index. (#3)

Jewish Emigration from the Third Reich. By Ingrid Weckert. Current historical writings about the Third Reich claim state it was difficult for Jews to flee from Nazi persecution. The truth is that Jewish emigration was welcomed by the German authorities. Emigration was not some kind of wild flight, but rather a lawfully determined and regulated matter. Weckert's booklet elucidates the emigration process in law and policy. She shows that German and Jewish authorities worked closely together. Jews interested in emigrating received detailed advice and offers of help from both sides. 2nd ed., 130 pages, index. (#12)

Inside the Gas Chambers: The Extermination of Mainstream Holocaust Historiography. By Carlo Mattogno. Neither increased media propaganda or political pressure nor judicial persecution can stifle revisionism. Hence, in early 2011, the Holocaust Orthodoxy published a 400 pp. book (in German) claiming to refute "revisionist propaganda," trying again to prove "once and for all" that there were homicidal gas chambers at the camps of Dachau, Natzweiler, Sachsenhausen, Mauthausen, Ravensbrück, Neuengamme, Stutthof... you name them. Mattogno shows with his detailed analysis of this work of propaganda that mainstream Holocaust hagiography is beating around the bush rather than addressing revisionist research results. He exposes their myths, distortions and lies. 2nd ed., 280 pages, b&w illustrations, bibliography, index. (#25)

SECTION TWO:
Specific non-Auschwitz Studies

Treblinka: Extermination Camp or Transit Camp? By Carlo Mattogno and Jürgen Graf. It is alleged that at Treblinka in East Poland between 700,000 and 3,000,000 persons were murdered in 1942 and 1943. The weapons used were said to have been stationary and/or mobile gas chambers, fast-acting or slow-acting poison gas, unslaked lime, superheated steam, electricity, diesel exhaust fumes etc. Holocaust historians alleged that bodies were piled as high as multi-storied buildings and burned without a trace, using little or no fuel at all. Graf and Mattogno have now analyzed the origins, logic and technical feasibility of the official version of Treblinka. On the basis of numerous documents they reveal Treblinka's true identity as a mere transit camp. 2nd ed., 372 pages, b&w illustrations, bibliography, index. (#8)

Belzec in Propaganda, Testimonies, Archeological Research and History. By Carlo Mattogno. Witnesses report that between 600,000 and 3 million Jews were murdered in the Belzec camp, located in Poland. Various murder weapons are claimed to have been used: diesel gas; unslaked lime in trains; high voltage; vacuum chambers; etc. The corpses were incinerated on huge pyres without leaving a trace. For those who know the stories about Treblinka this sounds familiar. Thus the author has restricted this study to the aspects which are new compared to Treblinka. In contrast to Treblinka, forensic drillings and excavations were performed at Belzec, the results of which are critically reviewed. 142 pages, b&w illustrations, bibliography, index. (#9)

Sobibor: Holocaust Propaganda and Reality. By Jürgen Graf, Thomas Kues and Carlo Mattogno. Between 25,000 and 2 million Jews are said to have been killed in gas chambers in the Sobibór camp in Poland. The corpses were allegedly buried in mass graves and later incinerated on pyres. This book investigates these claims and shows that they are based on the selective use of contradictory eyewitness testimony. Archeological surveys of the camp in 2000-2001 are analyzed, with fatal results for the extermination camp hypothesis. The book also documents the general National Socialist policy toward Jews, which never included a genocidal "final solution." 442 pages, b&w illustrations, bibliography, index. (#19)

The "Extermination Camps" of "Aktion Reinhardt". By Jürgen Graf, Thomas Kues and Carlo Mattogno. In late 2011, several members of the exterminationist *Holocaust Controversies* blog posted a study online which claims to refute three of our authors' monographs on the camps Belzec, Sobibor and Treblinka (see previous three entries). This tome is their point-by-point response, which makes "mincemeat" out of the bloggers' attempt at refutation. Caution: The two volumes of this work are an intellectual overkill for most people. They are recommended only for collectors, connoisseurs and professionals. These two books require familiarity with the above-mentioned books, of which they are a comprehensive update and expansion. 2nd ed., two volumes, total of 1396 pages, illustrations, bibliography. (#28)

Chelmno: A Camp in History & Propaganda. By Carlo Mattogno. At Chelmno, huge masses of Jewish prisoners are said to have been rounded up and mercilessly gassed in "gas vans" or shot (claims vary from 10,000 to 1.3 million victims). Mattogno has examined reams of wartime documents and conducted on-site investigations at the Chelmno camp site and the neighboring countryside. The results challenge the conventional wisdom about Chelmno. Mattogno covers the subject from every angle, undermining the orthodox claims about the camp with an overwhelmingly effective body of evidence. Eyewitness statements, gas wagons as extermination weapons, forensics reports, coroners' reports, archaeological excavations, the crematoria, building plans, official U.S. reports, German documents, evacuation efforts—all come under Mattogno's scrutiny. Here are the uncensored facts about Chelmno, not the propaganda. 2nd ed., 188 pages, indexed, illustrated, bibliography. (#23)

The Gas Vans: A Critical Investigation. (A perfect companion to the Chelmno book.) By Santiago Alvarez and Pierre Marais. It is alleged that the Nazis used mobile gas chambers to exterminate 700,000 people. Up until 2011, no thorough monograph had appeared on the topic. Santiago Alvarez has remedied the situation. Are witness statements reliable? Are documents genuine? Where are the murder weapons? Could they have operated as claimed? Where are the corpses? In order to get to the truth of the matter, Alvarez has scrutinized all known wartime documents and photos about this topic; he has analyzed a huge amount of witness statements as published in the literature and as presented in more than 30 trials held over the decades in Germany, Poland and Israel; and he has examined the claims made in the pertinent mainstream literature. The result of his research is mind-boggling. Note: This book and Mattogno's book on Chelmno were edited in parallel to make sure they are consistent and not repetitive. 398 pages, b&w illustrations, bibliography, index. (#26)

The Einsatzgruppen in the Occupied Eastern Territories: Genesis, Responsibilities and Activities. By C. Mattogno. Before invading the Soviet Union, the German authorities set up special units meant to secure the area behind the German front. Orthodox historians claim that these unites called *Einsatzgruppen* primarily engaged in rounding up and mass-murdering Jews. This study tries to shed a critical light into this topic by reviewing all the pertinent sources as well as material traces. Ca. 850 pp., b&w illustrations, bibliography, index. (Scheduled for late 2018; #39)

Concentration Camp Majdanek. A Historical and Technical Study. By Carlo Mattogno and Jürgen Graf. At war's end, the Soviets claimed that up to two million Jews were murdered at the Majdanek Camp in seven gas chambers. Over the decades, however, the Majdanek Museum reduced the death toll three times to currently 78,000, and admitted that there were "only" two gas chambers. By exhaustively researching primary sources, the authors expertly dissect and repudiate the myth of homicidal gas chambers at that camp. They also critically investigated the legend of mass executions of Jews in tank trenches and prove them groundless. Again they have produced a standard work of methodical investigation which authentic historiography cannot ignore. 3rd ed., 358 pages, b&w illustrations, bibliography, index. (#5)

Concentration Camp Stutthof and Its Function in National Socialist Jewish Policy. By Carlo Mattogno and Jürgen Graf. Orthodox historians claim that the Stutthof Camp served as a "makeshift" extermination camp in 1944. Based mainly on archival resources, this study thoroughly debunks this view and shows that Stutthof was in fact a center for the organization of German forced labor toward the end of World War II. 4th ed., 170 pages, b&w illustrations, bibliography, index. (#4)

SECTION THREE: Auschwitz Studies

The Making of the Auschwitz Myth: Auschwitz in British Intercepts, Polish Underground Reports and Postwar Testimonies (1941-1947). By Carlo Mattogno. Using messages sent by the Polish underground to London, SS radio messages send to and from Auschwitz that were intercepted and decrypted by the British, and a plethora of witness statements made during the war and in the immediate postwar period, the author shows how exactly the myth of mass murder in Auschwitz gas chambers was created, and how it was turned subsequently into "history" by intellectually corrupt scholars who cherry-picked claims that fit into their agenda and ignored or actively covered up literally thousands of lies of "witnesses" to make their narrative look credible. Ca. 300

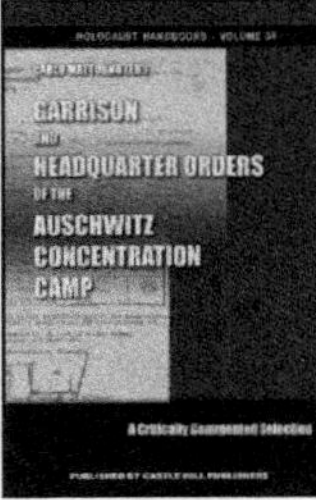

pp., b&w illustrations, bibliography, index. (Scheduled for mid-2018; #41)

The Real Case of Auschwitz: Robert van Pelt's Evidence from the Irving Trial Critically Reviewed. By Carlo Mattogno. Prof. Robert van Pelt is considered one of the best mainstream experts on Auschwitz. He became famous when appearing as an expert during the London libel trial of David Irving against Deborah Lipstadt. From it resulted a book titled *The Case for Auschwitz*, in which van Pelt laid out his case for the existence of homicidal gas chambers at that camp. This book is a scholarly response to Prof. van Pelt—and Jean-Claude Pressac, upon whose books van Pelt's study is largely based. Mattogno lists all the evidence van Pelt adduces, and shows one by one that van Pelt misrepresented and misinterpreted each single one of them. This is a book of prime political and scholarly importance to those looking for the truth about Auschwitz. 2nd ed., 758 pages, b&w illustrations, glossary, bibliography, index. (#22)

Auschwitz: Plain Facts: A Response to Jean-Claude Pressac. Edited by Germar Rudolf, with contributions by Serge Thion, Robert Faurisson and Carlo Mattogno. French pharmacist Jean-Claude Pressac tried to refute revisionist findings with the "technical" method. For this he was praised by the mainstream, and they proclaimed victory over the "revisionists." In his book, Pressac's works and claims are shown to be unscientific in nature, as he never substantiate what he claims, and historically false, because he systematically misrepresents, misinterprets and misunderstands German wartime documents. 2nd ed., 226 pages, b&w illustrations, glossary bibliography, index. (#14)

The Chemistry of Auschwitz: The Technology and Toxicology of Zyklon B and the Gas Chambers – A Crime Scene Investigation. By Germar Rudolf. While respecting the victims, whether of foul play or of circumstance, this study nonetheless tries to conduct Auschwitz research on the basis of the forensic sciences, where material traces of the crime and their interpretation reign supreme. Although it is generally agreed that no autopsy of any victim has ever been performed, most of the claimed crime scenes – the chemical slaughterhouses called gas chambers – are still accessible to forensic examination to a greater or lesser degree. This book addresses questions such as: How did these gas chambers of Auschwitz look like? How did they operate? What were they used for? In addition, the infamous Zyklon B can also be examined. What exactly hides behind this ominous name? How does it kill? And what effect has it on masonry? Does it leave traces that can be found still today? By thoroughly examining these issues, the horror of Auschwitz is meticulously dissected, and thus, for the first time, it really becomes comprehensible. 3rd ed., 442 pages, more than 120 color and almost 100 b&w illustrations, bibliography, index. (#2)

Auschwitz Lies: Legends, Lies and Prejudices on the Holocaust. By C. Mattogno and G. Rudolf. The fallacious research and alleged "refutation" of Revisionist scholars by French biochemist G. Wellers (attacking Leuchter's famous report), Polish chemist Dr. J. Markiewicz and U.S. chemist Dr. Richard Green (taking on Rudolf's chemical research), Dr. John Zimmerman (tackling Mattogno on cremation issues), Michael Shermer and Alex Grobman (trying to prove it all), as well as researchers Keren, McCarthy and Mazal (how turned cracks into architectural features), are exposed for what they are: blatant and easily exposed political lies created to ostracize dissident historians. 3rd ed., 398 pages, b&w illustrations, index. (#18)

Auschwitz: The Central Construction Office. By C. Mattogno. Based upon mostly unpublished German wartime documents, this study describes the history, organization, tasks and procedures of the one office which was responsible for the planning and construction of the Auschwitz camp complex, including the crematories which are said to have contained the "gas chambers." 2nd ed., 188 pages, b&w illustrations, glossary, index. (#13)

Garrison and Headquarters Orders of the Auschwitz Camp. By C. Mattogno. A large number of all the orders ever issued by the various commanders of the infamous Auschwitz camp have been preserved. They reveal the true nature of the camp with all its daily events. There is not a trace in these orders pointing at anything sinister going on in this camp. Quite to the contrary, many orders are in clear and insurmountable contradiction to claims that prisoners were mass murdered. This is a selection of the most pertinent of these orders together with comments putting them into their proper historical context. (Scheduled for late 2018; #34)

Special Treatment in Auschwitz: Origin and Meaning of a Term. By C. Mattogno. When appearing in German wartime documents, terms like "special treatment," "special action," and others have been interpreted as code words for mass murder. But that is not always true. This study focuses on documents about Auschwitz, showing that, while "special" had many different meanings, not a single one meant "execution." Hence the practice of deciphering an alleged "code language" by assigning homicidal meaning to harmless documents – a key component of mainstream historiography – is untenable. 2nd ed., 166 pages, b&w illustrations, bibliography, index. (#10)

Healthcare at Auschwitz. By C. Mattogno. In extension of the above study on *Special Treatment in Auschwitz*, this study proves the extent to which the German authorities at Auschwitz tried to provide appropriate health care for the inmates. In the first part of this book, the author analyzes the inmates' living conditions as well as the various sanitary and medical measures implemented to maintain or restore the inmates' health. The second part explores what happened in particular to those inmates registered at Auschwitz who were "selected" or subject to "special treatment" while disabled or sick. The comprehensive documentation presented shows clearly that everything was tried to cure these inmates, especially under the aegis of Garrison Physician Dr. Wirths. The last part of this book is dedicated to the remarkable personality of Dr. Wirths, the Auschwitz garrison physician since 1942. His reality refutes the current stereotype of SS officers. 398 pages, b&w illustrations, bibliography, index. (#33)

Debunking the Bunkers of Auschwitz: Black Propaganda vs. History. By Carlo Mattogno. The bunkers at Auschwitz, two former farmhouses just outside the camp's perimeter, are claimed to have been the first homicidal gas chambers at Auschwitz specifically equipped for this purpose. With the help of original German wartime files as well as revealing air photos taken by Allied reconnaissance aircraft in 1944, this study shows that these homicidal "bunkers" never existed, how the rumors about them evolved as black propaganda created by resistance groups in the camp, and how this propaganda was transformed into a false reality. 2nd ed., 292 pages, b&w illustrations, bibliography, index. (#11)

Auschwitz: The First Gassing. Rumor and Reality. By C. Mattogno. The first gassing in Auschwitz is claimed to have occurred on Sept. 3, 1941, in a basement room. The accounts reporting it are the archetypes for all later gassing accounts. This study analyzes all available sources about this alleged event. It shows that these sources contradict each other in location, date, victims etc, rendering it impossible to extract a consistent story. Original wartime documents inflict a final blow to this legend and prove without a shadow of a doubt that this legendary event never happened. 3rd ed., 190 pages, b&w illustrations, bibliography, index. (#20)

Auschwitz: Crematorium I and the Alleged Homicidal Gassings. By C. Mattogno. The morgue of Crematorium I in Auschwitz is said to be the first homicidal gas chamber there. This study investigates all statements by witnesses and analyzes hundreds of wartime documents to accurately write a history of that building. Where witnesses speak of gassings, they are either very vague or, if specific, contradict one another and are refuted by documented and material facts. The author also exposes the fraudulent attempts of mainstream historians to convert the witnesses' black propaganda into "truth" by means of selective quotes, omissions, and distortions. Mattogno proves that this building's morgue was never a homicidal gas chamber, nor could it have worked as such. 2nd ed., 152 pages, b&w illustrations, bibliography, index. (#21)

Auschwitz: Open Air Incinerations. By C. Mattogno. In spring and summer of 1944, 400,000 Hungarian Jews were deported to Auschwitz and allegedly murdered there in gas chambers. The Auschwitz crematoria are said to have been unable to cope with so many corpses. Therefore, every single day thousands of corpses are claimed to have been incinerated on huge pyres lit in deep trenches. The sky over Auschwitz was covered in thick smoke. This is what some witnesses want us to believe. This book examines the many testimonies regarding these incinerations and establishes whether these claims were even possible. Using air photos, physical evidence and wartime documents, the author shows that these claims are fiction. A new Appendix contains 3 papers on groundwater levels and cattle mass burnings. 2nd ed., 202 pages, b&w illustrations, bibliography, index. (#17)

The Cremation Furnaces of Auschwitz. By Carlo Mattogno & Franco Deana. An exhaustive study of the history and technology of cremation in general and of the cremation furnaces of Auschwitz in particular. On a vast base of technical literature, extant wartime documents and material traces, the authors can establish the true nature and capacity of the Auschwitz cremation furnaces. They show that these devices were inferior make-shift versions of what was usually produced, and that their capacity to cremate corpses was lower than normal, too. 3 vols., 1198 pages, b&w and color illustrations (vols 2 & 3), bibliography, index, glossary. (#24)

Curated Lies: The Auschwitz Museum's Misrepresentations, Distortions and Deceptions. By Carlo Mattogno. Revisionist research results have put the Polish Auschwitz Museum under pressure to answer this challenge. They've answered. This book analyzes their answer and reveals the appallingly mendacious attitude of the Auschwitz Museum authorities when presenting documents from their archives. 248 pages, b&w illustrations, bibliography, index. (#38)

Deliveries of Coke, Wood and Zyklon B to Auschwitz: Neither Proof Nor Trace for the Holocaust. By Carlo Mattogno. Researchers from the Auschwitz Museum tried to prove the reality of mass extermination by pointing to documents about deliveries of wood and coke as well as Zyklon B to the Auschwitz Camp. If put into the actual historical and technical context, however, these documents prove the exact opposite of what these orthodox researchers claim. Ca. 250 pages, b&w illustrations, bibliography, index. (Scheduled for early 2019; #40)

SECTION FOUR:
Witness Critique

Holocaust High Priest: Elie Wiesel, Night, the Memory Cult, and the Rise of Revisionism. By Warren B. Routledge. The first unauthorized biography of Wiesel exposes both his personal deceits and the whole myth of "the six million." It shows how Zionist control has allowed Wiesel and his fellow extremists to force leaders of many nations, the U.N. and even popes to genuflect before Wiesel as symbolic acts of subordination to World Jewry, while at the same time forcing school children to submit to Holocaust brainwashing. 468 pages, b&w illust., bibliography, index. (#30)

Auschwitz: Confessions and Testimonies. By Jürgen Graf. The traditional narrative of what transpired at the infamous Auschwitz Camp during WWII rests almost exclusively on witness testimony. This study critically scrutinizes the 40 most important of them by checking them for internal coherence, and by comparing them with one another as well as with other evidence such as wartime documents, air photos, forensic research results, and material traces. The result is devastating for the traditional narrative. (Scheduled for late-2018; #36)

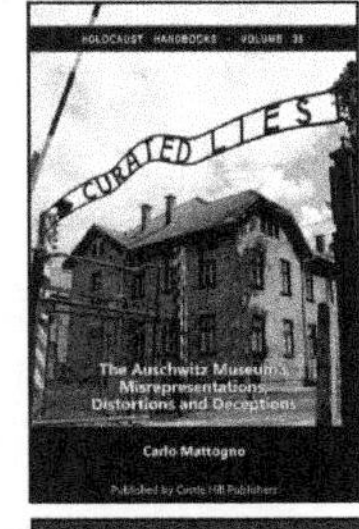

Commandant of Auschwitz: Rudolf Höss, His Torture and His Forced Confessions. By Carlo Mattogno & Rudolf Höss. From 1940 to 1943, Rudolf Höss was the commandant of the infamous Auschwitz Camp. After the war, he was captured by the British. In the following 13 months until his execution, he made 85 depositions of various kinds in which he confessed his involvement in the "Holocaust." This study first reveals how the British tortured him to extract various "confessions." Next, all of Höss's depositions are analyzed by checking his claims for internal consistency and comparing them with established historical facts. The results are eye-opening... 402 pages, b&w illust., bibliography, index. (#35)

An Auschwitz Doctor's Eyewitness Account: The Tall Tales of Dr. Mengele's Assistant Analyzed. By Miklos Nyiszli & Carlo Mattogno. Nyiszli, a Hungarian physician, ended up at Auschwitz in 1944 as Dr. Mengele's assistant. After the war he wrote a book and several other writings describing what he claimed to have experienced. To this day some traditional historians take his accounts seriously, while others reject them as grotesque lies and exaggerations. This study presents and analyzes Nyiszli's writings and skillfully separates truth from fabulous fabrication. 484 pages, b&w illust., bibliography, index. (#37)

FOR CURRENT PRICES AND AVAILABILITY SEE BOOK FINDER SITES SUCH AS BOOKFINDER.COM, ADDALL.COM, BOOKFINDER4U.COM OR FINDBOOKPRICES.COM; LEARN MORE AT WWW.HOLOCAUSTHANDBOOKS.COM
PUBLISHED BY CASTLE HILL PUBLISHERS, PO BOX 243, UCKFIELD, TN22 9AW, UK

Books by and from Castle Hill Publishers

Below please find some of the books published or distributed by Castle Hill Publishers in the United Kingdom. For our current and complete range of products visit our web store at shop.codoh.com.

Thomas Dalton, ***The Holocaust: An Introduction***

The Holocaust was perhaps the greatest crime of the 20th century. Six million Jews, we are told, died by gassing, shooting, and deprivation. But: Where did the six million figure come from? How, exactly, did the gas chambers work? Why do we have so little physical evidence from major death camps? Why haven't we found even a fraction of the six million bodies, or their ashes? Why has there been so much media suppression and governmental censorship on this topic? In a sense, the Holocaust is the greatest murder mystery in history. It is a topic of greatest importance for the present day. Let's explore the evidence, and see where it leads.

128 pp. pb, 5"×8", ill., bibl., index

Carlo Mattogno, ***Auschwitz: A Three-Quarter Century of Propaganda: Origins, Development and Decline of the "Gas Chamber" Propaganda Lie***

During the war, wild rumors were circulating about Auschwitz: that the Germans were testing new war gases; that inmates were murdered in electrocution chambers, with gas showers or pneumatic hammer systems; that living people were sent on conveyor belts directly into cremation furnaces; that oils, grease and soap were made of the mass-murder victims. Nothing of it was true. When the Soviets captured Auschwitz in early 1945, they reported that 4 million inmates were killed on electrocution conveyor belts discharging their load directly into furnaces. That wasn't true either. After the war, "witnesses" and "experts" repeated these things and added more fantasies: mass murder with gas bombs, gas chambers made of canvas; carts driving living people into furnaces; that the crematoria of Auschwitz could have cremated 400 million victims… Again, none of it was true. This book gives an overview of the many rumors, myths and lies about Auschwitz which mainstream historians today reject as untrue. It then explains by which ridiculous methods some claims about Auschwitz were accepted as true and turned into "history," although they are just as untrue.

125 pp. pb, 5"×8", ill., bibl., index, b&w ill.

Wilhelm Stäglich, ***Auschwitz: A Judge Looks at the Evidence***

Auschwitz is the epicenter of the Holocaust, where more people are said to have been murdered than anywhere else. At this detention camp the industrialized Nazi mass murder is said to have reached its demonic pinnacle. This narrative is based on a wide range of evidence, the most important of which was presented during two trials: the International Military Tribunal of 1945/46, and the German Auschwitz Trial of 1963-1965 in Frankfurt.

The late Wilhelm Stäglich, until the mid-1970s a German judge, has so far been the only *legal* expert to critically analyze this evidence. His research reveals the incredibly scandalous way in which the Allied victors and later the German judicial authorities bent and broke the law in order to come to politically foregone conclusions. Stäglich also exposes the shockingly superficial way in which historians are dealing with the many incongruities and discrepancies of the historical record.

3rd edition 2015, 422 pp., 6"×9", pb, b&w ill.

Gerard Menuhin: ***Tell the Truth & Shame the Devil***

A prominent Jew from a famous family says the "Holocaust" is a wartime propaganda myth which has turned into an extortion racket. Far from bearing the sole guilt for starting WWII as alleged at Nuremberg (for which many of the surviving German leaders were hanged) Germany is mostly innocent in this respect and made numerous attempts to avoid and later to end the confrontation. During the 1930s Germany was confronted by a powerful Jewish-dominated world plutocracy out to destroy it… Yes, a prominent Jew says all this. Accept it or reject it, but be sure to read it and judge for yourself!

The author is the son of the great American-born violinist Yehudi Menuhin, who, though from a long line of rabbinical ancestors, fiercely criticized the foreign policy of the state of Israel and its repression of the Palestinians in the Holy Land.

4th edition 2017, 432 pp. pb, 6"×9", b&w ill.

For prices and availability see www.shop.codoh.com or write to: CHP, PO Box 243, Uckfield, TN22 9AW, UK

Germar Rudolf, ***Bungled: "Denying the Holocaust" How Deborah Lipstadt Botched Her Attempt to Demonstrate the Growing Assault on Truth and Memory***

With her book *Denying the Holocaust*, Deborah Lipstadt tried to show the flawed methods and extremist motives of "Holocaust deniers." This book demonstrates that Dr. Lipstadt clearly has neither understood the principles of science and scholarship, nor has she any clue about the historical topics she is writing about. She misquotes, mistranslates, misrepresents, misinterprets, and makes a plethora of wild claims without backing them up with anything. Rather than dealing thoroughly with factual arguments, Lipstadt's book is full of *ad hominem* attacks on her opponents. It is an exercise in anti-intellectual pseudo-scientific arguments, an exhibition of ideological radicalism that rejects anything which contradicts its preset conclusions. **F for FAIL**

2nd ed., 224 pp., 5"×8", pb, bibl., index, b&w ill.

Carolus Magnus, ***Bungled: "Denying History". How Michael Shermer and Alex Grobman Botched Their Attempt to Refute Those Who Say the Holocaust Never Happened***

Skeptic Magazine editor Michael Shermer and Alex Grobman from the Simon Wiesenthal Center wrote a book in 2000 which they claim is "a thorough and thoughtful answer to all the claims of the Holocaust deniers." In 2009, a new "updated" edition appeared with the same ambitious goal. In the meantime, revisionists had published some 10,000 pages of archival and forensic research results. Would their updated edition indeed answer all the revisionist claims? In fact, Shermer and Grobman completely ignored the vast amount of recent scholarly studies and piled up a heap of falsifications, contortions, omissions, and fallacious interpretations of the evidence. Finally, what the authors claim to have demolished is not revisionism but a ridiculous parody of it. They ignored the known unreliability of their cherry-picked selection of evidence, utilizing unverified and incestuous sources, and obscuring the massive body of research and all the evidence that dooms their project to failure. **F for FAIL**

162 pp., 5"×8", pb, bibl., index, b&w ill.

Carolus Magnus, ***Bungled: "Debunking Holocaust Denial Theories". How James and Lance Morcan Botched Their Attempt to Affirm the Historicity of the Nazi Genocide***

The novelists and movie-makers James and Lance Morcan have produced a book "to end [Holocaust] denial once and for all." To do this, "no stone was left unturned" to verify historical assertions by presenting "a wide array of sources" meant "to shut down the debate deniers wish to create. One by one, the various arguments Holocaust deniers use to try to discredit wartime records are carefully scrutinized and then systematically disproven." It's a lie. First, the Morcans completely ignored the vast amount of recent scholarly studies published by revisionists; they didn't even identify them. Instead, they engaged in shadowboxing, creating some imaginary, bogus "revisionist" scarecrow which they then tore to pieces. In addition, their knowledge even of their own side's source material was dismal, and the way they backed up their misleading or false claims was pitifully inadequate. **F for FAIL.**

144 pp., 5"×8", pb, bibl., index, b&w ill.

Joachim Hoffmann, ***Stalin's War of Extermination 1941-1945***

A German government historian documents Stalin's murderous war against the German army and the German people. Based on the author's lifelong study of German and Russian military records, this book reveals the Red Army's grisly record of atrocities against soldiers and civilians, as ordered by Stalin. Since the 1920s, Stalin planned to invade Western Europe to initiate the "World Revolution." He prepared an attack which was unparalleled in history. The Germans noticed Stalin's aggressive intentions, but they underestimated the strength of the Red Army. What unfolded was the most-cruel war in history. This book shows how Stalin and his Bolshevik henchman used unimaginable violence and atrocities to break any resistance in the Red Army and to force their unwilling soldiers to fight against the Germans. The book explains how Soviet propagandists incited their soldiers to unlimited hatred against everything German, and he gives the reader a short but extremely unpleasant glimpse into what happened when these Soviet soldiers finally reached German soil in 1945: A gigantic wave of looting, arson, rape, torture, and mass murder…

428 pp. pb, 6"×9", bibl., index, b&w ill.

Udo Walendy, ***Who Started World War II:*** ***Truth for a War-Torn World***

For seven decades, mainstream historians have insisted that Germany was the main, if not the sole culprit for unleashing World War II in Europe. In the present book this myth is refuted. There is available to the public today a great number of documents on the foreign policies of the Great Powers before September 1939 as well as a wealth of literature in the form of memoirs of the persons directly involved in the decisions that led to the outbreak of World War II. Together, they made possible Walendy's present mosaic-like reconstruction of the events before the outbreak of the war in 1939. This book has been published only after an intensive study of sources, taking the greatest care to minimize speculation and inference. The present edition has been translated completely anew from the German original and has been slightly revised.

500 pp. pb, 6"×9", index, bibl., b&w ill.

Germar Rudolf: ***Resistance is Obligatory!***

In 2005 Rudolf, a peaceful dissident and publisher of revisionist literature, was kidnapped by the U.S. government and deported to Germany. There the local lackey regime staged a show trial against him for his historical writings. Rudolf was not permitted to defend his historical opinions, as the German penal law prohibits this. Yet he defended himself anyway: 7 days long Rudolf held a speech in the court room, during which he proved systematically that only the revisionists are scholarly in their attitude, whereas the Holocaust orthodoxy is merely pseudo-scientific. He then explained in detail why it is everyone's obligation to resist, without violence, a government which throws peaceful dissident into dungeons. When Rudolf tried to publish his public defence speech as a book from his prison cell, the public prosecutor initiated a new criminal investigation against him. After his probation time ended in 2011, he dared publish this speech anyway…

2nd ed. 2016, 378 pp., 6"×9", pb, b&w ill.

Germar Rudolf, ***Hunting Germar Rudolf:*** ***Essays on a Modern-Day Witch Hunt***

German-born revisionist activist, author and publisher Germar Rudolf describes which events made him convert from a Holocaust believer to a Holocaust skeptic, quickly rising to a leading personality within the revisionist movement. This in turn unleashed a tsunami of persecution against him: loss of his job, denied PhD exam, destruction of his family, driven into exile, slandered by the mass media, literally hunted, caught, put on a show trial where filing motions to introduce evidence is illegal under the threat of further proseuction, and finally locked up in prison for years for nothing else than his peaceful yet controversial scholarly writings. In several essays, Rudolf takes the reader on a journey through an absurd world of government and societal persecution which most of us could never even fathom actually exists.…

304 pp., 6"×9", pb, bibl., index, b&w ill.

Germar Rudolf, ***The Day Amazon Murdered History***

Amazon is the world's biggest book retailer. They dominate the U.S. and several foreign markets. Pursuant to the 1998 declaration of Amazon's founder Jeff Bezos to offer "the good, the bad and the ugly," customers once could buy every book that was in print and was legal to sell. However, in early 2017, a series of anonymous bomb threats against Jewish community centers occurred in the U.S., fueling a campaign by Jewish groups to coax Amazon into banning revisionist writings, false portraing them as anti-Semitic. On March 6, 2017, Amazon caved in and banned more than 100 books with dissenting viewpoints on the Holocaust. In April 2017, an Israeli Jew was arrested for having placed the fake bomb threats, a paid "service" he had offered for years. But that did not change Amazon's mind. Its stores remain closed for history books Jewish lobby groups disapprove of. This book accompanies the documentary of the same title. Both reveal how revisionist publications had become so powerfully convincing that the powers that be resorted to what looks like a dirty false-flag operation in order to get these books banned from Amazon…

128 pp. pb, 5"×8", bibl., b&w ill.

FOR CURRENT PRICES AND AVAILABILITY SEE BOOK FINDER SITES SUCH AS WWW.BOOKFINDER.COM, WWW.ADDALL.COM, WWW.BOOKFINDER4U.COM OR WWW.FINDBOOKPRICES.COM; LEARN MORE AT SHOP.CODOH.COM. PUBLISHED BY CASTLE HILL PUBLISHERS, PO BOX 243, UCKFIELD, TN22 9AW, UK